JN419150

한 권으로 끝내는

잉글리쉬앤
토익 600⁺

피터(김부로), 잉글리쉬앤 어학연구소 **지음**

LC+RC

한 권으로 끝내는

초판 1쇄 인쇄 2025년 3월 10일
초판 1쇄 발행 2025년 3월 12일

지은이 김부로(피터), 잉글리쉬앤 어학연구소
펴낸이 박성호
펴낸곳 잉글리쉬앤(주)

편　　집 박고우니, 장서원
영업마케팅 여주형, 김성윤, 방성출, 박훈효, 조민형, 이달님, 강정구, 이진희, 조병운
　　　　　　조예선, 이현정, 조광민, 노희동, 김정민, 최희성, 윤종철, 엄주아, 오지현
　　　　　　최유미, 최가연, 안혜연, 조승채, 강예빈, 김희진, 남지현

주　　소 서울 특별시 관악구 쑥고개로 67-1
대표전화 (02) 878-1945
출판등록 2002년 3월 3일 제 320-2002-00045호

ISBN 978-89-6715-225-3 13740

서문

\<한 권으로 끝내는 잉글리쉬앤 토익 600⁺\>를 내면서

독자 여러분, 안녕하세요!

우선, \<한 권으로 끝내는 잉글리쉬앤 토익 600+\>를 선택해 주신 여러분께 깊은 감사의 인사를 드립니다. 여러분의 토익 학습 여정에 함께할 수 있게 되어 매우 기쁩니다.

이 책은 토익(TOEIC) 기본서로서, 토익 시험의 전반적인 구조와 유형을 익히고 기본기를 다질 수 있도록 구성했습니다. 또한 오랜 기간 동안 영어 교육 현장에서 학생들을 지도하며 쌓아온 경험과 노하우를 바탕으로, 여러분이 효과적으로 학습할 수 있는 내용을 담았습니다.

\<한 권으로 끝내는 잉글리쉬앤 토익 600+\>은 다음과 같은 특징이 있습니다:

1. **토익 시험 소개 및 전략**: 토익 시험의 목적과 구조를 이해하고, 효과적인 학습 전략을 제시합니다.
2. **듣기**: 파트별로 출제 유형과 자주 등장하는 표현들을 분석하고, 듣기 실력을 향상시키기 위한 연습 문제를 제공합니다.
3. **문법 및 어휘**: 토익에서 자주 출제되는 문법 개념과 어휘를 정리하고, 이를 적용한 문제 풀이를 통해 실력을 다질 수 있습니다.
4. **독해**: 빈출 지문과 문제 유형을 다루며, 정확하게 지문을 읽고 지문에 근거하여 빠르게 답을 찾는 방법을 소개합니다.
5. **실전 연습 문제**: 각 장마다 실전과 유사한 연습 문제를 포함하여, 학습한 내용을 바로 적용하고 점검할 수 있습니다.
6. **해설과 팁**: 상세한 해설과 유용한 팁을 제공하여, 오답을 이해하고 점수를 향상하는 데 도움이 됩니다.
7. **추가 학습 자료**: 필요한 경우 더 많은 연습을 할 수 있도록 추가 학습 자료와 온라인 실전 모의고사(2회분)를 제공합니다.

이 책을 통해 토익 시험에 대한 자신감을 키우고, 목표 점수를 달성하기를 진심으로 바랍니다. 여러분의 노력이 결실을 맺을 수 있도록 응원하겠습니다.

감사합니다.

김부로(Peter Kim)

목차

RC

토익 소개

토익이란?

Test Of English for International Communication의 약자로, 영어가 모국어가 아닌 사람들의 일상생활이나 국제업무 등에 필요한 실용 영어 능력을 평가하는 국제 평가 시험

▶ 시험 구성

구성	Part	유형		문항 수	시간	배점
듣기(LC)	1	사진 묘사		6	45분	495점
	2	질의 응답		25		
	3	짧은 대화		39		
	4	짧은 담화		30		
읽기(RC)	5	단문 공란 채우기		30	75분	495점
	6	장문 공란 채우기		16		
	7	지문 독해	단일 지문	29		
			복수 지문	25		
TOTAL		7 Parts		200문항	120분	990점

(듣기(LC) 문항 수 합계 100, 읽기(RC) 문항 수 합계 100)

▶ 시험 내용

Part	유형	유형 내용
1	사진 묘사	제시된 사진을 알맞게 설명하는 보기 고르기
2	질의 응답	질문을 듣고 알맞은 대답 고르기
3	짧은 대화	대화를 듣고 질문에 알맞은 내용 고르기
4	짧은 담화	담화를 듣고 질문에 알맞은 내용 고르기
5	단문 공란 채우기	빈칸에 맞는 내용을 골라 문장 완성하기
6	장문 공란 채우기	빈칸에 맞는 내용을 골라 장문 완성하기
7	지문 독해	단일 지문 또는 이중 · 삼중 지문을 읽고 문제에 맞는 내용 고르기

접수 방법은?

▶ 한국 토익 위원회 사이트 혹은 앱으로 접수 ➜ www.toeic.co.kr
▶ 인터넷 접수할 때 시험일, 고사장, 개인 정보 등을 입력 (증명사진 필요)
　※ 접수 마감일 이후 추가 접수일에 접수 시 추가 비용 발생

응시 준비물은?

▶ 규정 신분증 (주민등록증, 운전면허증, 기간 만료 전의 여권, 중고등학생만 학생증 인정)
▶ 연필, 지우개 (볼펜이나 사인펜은 사용 금지)
▶ 아날로그 시계 (전자 시계 불가)

시험 진행은?

▶ 오전 9:20까지 입실 (오전 9:50 이후 입실 불가)

오전 9:30 ~ 9:45 (15분)	답안지 작성에 관한 오리엔테이션
오전 9:45 ~ 9:50 (5분)	수험자 휴식 시간
오전 9:50 ~ 10:05 (15분)	신분 확인
오전 10:05 ~ 10:10 (5분)	문제지 배부, 파본 확인
오전 10:10 ~ 10:55 (45분)	듣기 평가(LC)
오전 10:55 ~ 12:10 (75분)	읽기 평가(RC)

※ 읽기 평가(RC) 시간에 2차 신분 확인 실시

성적 확인은?

▶ 시험일로부터 약 2주 후에 토익 위원회 사이트(www.toeic.co.kr)에서 확인 가능
▶ 온라인 출력과 우편 수령은 1회 무료, 이후에는 유료 발급

파트별 유형 및 전략

PART 1

사진 묘사 6문제

파트 1은 4개의 보기 중에서 사진을 가장 잘 묘사하는 보기를 고르는 문제이다. 총 6문제가 출제되며, 인물 및 사물/풍경 사진 등 다양한 유형들이 등장한다.

| 핵심 전략 |

+ 사진 유형별로 자주 출제되는 어휘와 표현들을 익힌다.
+ 난이도가 높은 경우 주어가 사물인 보기가 자주 등장하므로 수동태, 현재완료 수동태, 수동태 진행형과 같은 문법을 완벽하게 숙지한다.
+ 오답 소거법을 통해 사진을 완벽하게 묘사한 보기가 아닌, 그 중 정답에 가장 가까운 Best Answer를 고르도록 훈련한다.
+ 유사 발음, 연상 어휘 등을 이용한 오답이나, 사람과 사물의 상태 및 동작을 잘못 묘사하는 오답들이 자주 등장한다.

| 문제 형태 |

1

Look at the picture marked number one in your test book.

(A) She is cleaning her desk.
(B) She is sharpening a pencil.
(C) She is filing some papers.
(D) She is holding a phone.

PART 2

질의 응답 `25문제`

파트 2는 3개의 보기 중에서 질문에 적절한 응답을 고르는 파트이다. 문항 수는 총 25개로, 의문사 의문문, Yes/No 의문문이 출제된다.

| 핵심 전략 |

✚ 질문의 앞부분을 집중해서 듣고 질문 유형을 파악하는 연습을 한다.

✚ 의문사 의문문은 가장 자주 출제되는 유형으로, 답변 패턴이 정해져 있다. 의문사별로 정답 유형을 숙지해 두자.

✚ 평서문은 답변 패턴이 정해져 있지 않아서 어렵게 느껴질 수 있다. 오답 소거법을 이용하여 보기 중 가장 적절한 응답을 고르면 정답을 쉽게 찾을 수 있다.

✚ 유사 발음 어휘, 질문의 단어 반복 등을 이용한 보기가 오답으로 자주 등장하므로 이를 주의하여 정답을 골라야 한다.

| 문제 형태 |

7 Mark your answer on your answer sheet.

How much longer do you need on this project?

(A) About ten pages long.
(B) Roughly half an hour.
(C) The project was successful.

PART 3

짧은 대화 **39문제**

파트 3는 2~3명이 나누는 대화를 듣고 이와 관련된 3개의 문제를 푸는 파트이다. 총 39문제가 출제되며, 3인 대화가 1~2세트 출제된다. 화자 의도 파악 문제와 시각 자료 연계 문제가 각각 2~3세트 출제된다.

| 핵심 전략 |

✦ 대화를 듣기 전에 문제를 먼저 읽고, 키워드를 파악한 후 그 부분을 집중적으로 듣는 훈련을 하자.

✦ 첫 번째 문제는 주로 주제나 장소, 신분에 관한 문제로, 정답의 단서가 대화 초반에 나오므로 처음 부분을 놓치지 않고 들어야 한다.

✦ 의도 파악 문제는 먼저 제시된 표현을 확인하고, 음성을 들으면서 해당 표현이 나올 때까지 문맥을 정확히 파악해야 한다.

✦ 표나 송장, 지도 등의 다양한 시각 자료가 출제되며, 미리 시각 자료를 읽고 지문의 내용을 예측해 본다. 또한, 시각 자료와 음성을 연계하여 정보를 파악하는 능력을 길러야 한다.

✦ 3인 대화에서 화자는 국적에 따라 발음이 구분되므로, 미국, 영국, 호주 등의 다양한 발음에 익숙해지도록 연습한다.

| 문제 형태 |

32 What does the woman imply when she says, "I got one for my friend"?

(A) She is inviting the man to meet her friend.
(B) Her friend is the same size with his wife.
(C) She is willing to pay for the product.
(D) She is emphasizing it's a good product.

Questions 32 through 34 refer to the following conversation.

M: Hi, I'm looking for a birthday present for my wife. I think she'd like one of these sweaters, but do you have any in a smaller size?

W: I'm pretty sure everything we have is out here on the display table. But I can check the stockroom in the back if you'd like.

M: Thanks, that'll be great. You know they look perfect for early spring. Light, but warm. You can wear them indoors or outdoors.

W: That's right. I got one for my friend who wears it a lot, so I'm sure your wife would love one. And we're selling them for 30% off this week.

M: That's good to know. I hope you have one in my wife's size.

PART 4

짧은 담화 [30문제]

파트 4는 담화를 듣고 이와 관련된 3개의 문제를 푸는 파트이다. 총 30문항이 출제되며, 녹음 메시지나 공지, 뉴스 등이 주로 출제된다. 파트 3와 마찬가지로, 화자 의도 파악 문제와 시각 자료 연계 문제가 등장한다.

| 핵심 전략 |

+ 담화를 듣기 전에 문제를 먼저 읽고, 키워드를 파악한 후 그 부분을 집중적으로 듣는 훈련을 하자.

+ 첫 번째 문제는 주로 주제나 장소, 신분에 관한 문제로, 정답의 단서가 담화 초반에 나오므로 처음 부분을 놓치지 않고 들어야 한다.

+ 의도 파악 문제는 파트 3와 달리 한 사람의 담화이므로 문맥의 흐름을 더 쉽게 파악할 수 있다. 따라서 담화의 전반적인 문맥 흐름을 이해하고, 해당 문장의 앞뒤 상황을 정확히 파악하도록 하자.

+ 표나 송장, 지도 등의 다양한 시각 자료가 출제되며, 미리 시각 자료를 읽고 지문의 내용을 예측해 본다. 또한, 시각 자료와 음성을 연계하여 정보를 파악하는 능력을 길러야 한다.

| 문제 형태 |

Tour Schedule	
Garden Tour	10:00 A.M.
Lunch	Noon
Museum Visit	1:30 P.M.
Theater Performance	4:00 P.M.

98 Look at the graphic. What time is this talk most likely being given?

(A) At 10:00 A.M.
(B) At noon
(C) At 1:30 P.M.
(D) At 4:00 P.M.

Questions 98 through 100 refer to the following talk and list.

Can I have everyone's attention at the front of the bus? I hope you enjoyed your lunch at Restaurant Baron. As I mentioned earlier, it first opened in 1880 and has been operating longer than any other restaurants in Charlestown. Now, if you look out the window on your right, you'll see the National Museum of History and according to our schedule, we're right on time. We'll be spending about 2 hours here. I'll pass out the brochures with the information about the permanent and temporary exhibits you'll be seeing today. We'll meet again at the main entrance at 3:30 for our next schedule. Enjoy yourselves.

단문 공란 채우기 [30문제]

파트 5는 문장 안에 있는 빈칸에 적절한 단어나 어구를 채워 넣는 파트이다. 총 30문항이 출제되며, 문법 문제와 어휘 문제가 등장한다. 문제 유형에 따라 풀이 방식이 다르므로 이를 가장 먼저 파악하는 것이 중요하다.

| 핵심 전략 |

+ 문제를 풀기 전, 보기를 통해 문제 유형을 파악하는 연습을 한다.

+ 문법 문제는 문장 구조나 빈칸 주변의 문법을 통해 문제를 풀어야 한다. 문법 문제를 단시간에 풀기 위해서 명사, 동사, 형용사 등의 기본적인 문법을 확실히 익혀 두도록 하자.

+ 어휘 문제는 해석을 통해 문맥에 가장 적절한 단어를 선택해야 한다. 가능한 한 많은 어휘를 암기하고, 예문을 통해 어휘가 어떻게 사용되는지를 이해하자.

+ 자주 함께 쓰이는 단어 및 표현들을 숙지하여 빠른 시간 내에 문제를 풀어야 한다.

| 문제 형태 |

101 Sky Motors offers a variety of training programs to help enhance ------- in the workplace.

(A) productivity
(B) produce
(C) productive
(D) productively

102 The fundraising event recorded such high ------- that the proceeds will be higher than expected.

(A) representative
(B) consultation
(C) safety
(D) attendance

PART 6

장문 공란 채우기 **16문제**

파트 6는 지문 안에 있는 4개의 빈칸에 알맞은 보기를 선택하는 파트이다. 문법, 어휘, 문장을 넣는 문제가 등장하며, 총 16문항이 출제된다. 문맥에 맞는 문장을 고르는 문제는 각 지문마다 1개씩 출제된다.

| 핵심 전략 |

- ✚ 전체 문맥을 이해해야 풀 수 있는 문법 및 어휘 문제가 나오므로 지문의 흐름을 놓치지 않는 것이 중요하다.
- ✚ 빈칸에 알맞은 문장을 넣는 문제는 빈칸 앞뒤와 전체 맥락을 파악하여 정답을 골라야 하므로 전반적인 독해력을 늘려야 한다.
- ✚ 지문을 읽으면서 흐름상 다음에 나와야 할 내용을 예측하면 정답을 쉽게 찾을 수 있다.

| 문제 형태 |

Questions 135-138 refer to the following notice.

Important Notice about Hatter Industries

Please note that the contact information for Hatter Industries changed on March 21. Due to the closure of our Dabbley office and the ------- of our operations in Buena,
135
all correspondence concerning our products and services should now be sent to the following address: Hatter Industries, 642 Mandela Lane, Buena, CA.

Our employees' e-mail addresses, as well as our Web site's address, www.hatterindustries.com, remain -------.
136
However, we are still waiting for our new telephone and fax numbers. ------- will be
137
updated on our Web site as soon as the new numbers are assigned as of March 25.

-------.
138

135 (A) decision
(B) relocation
(C) suspension
(D) result

136 (A) assigned
(B) even
(C) formal
(D) unchanged

137 (A) Yours
(B) Another
(C) These
(D) Theirs

138 (A) We apologize for any inconvenience and thank you for your understanding.
(B) Refer to the side of the packet for full details of instructions before applying.
(C) Her office location will also remain the same.
(D) For more information about the forthcoming event, visit www. lizard.org.br/events.

지문 독해 **54문제**

파트 7은 지문을 읽고 지문과 관련된 문제 2~5개를 푸는 파트이다. 총 54문항이 출제되며, 지문은 편지, 문자 메시지, 광고, 공지문 등 다양한 유형으로 나온다. 단일 지문 10개, 이중 지문 2개, 삼중 지문 3개의 세트가 등장한다.

| 핵심 전략 |

✦ 지문의 종류와 제목, 키워드를 파악하여 내용을 미리 예측하고 정답 단서를 찾는다.

✦ 지문의 단서가 보기에는 다르게 패러프레이징될 수 있으므로, 단어를 암기할 때 동의 표현을 함께 익힌다.

✦ 복수 지문에서는 2개 이상의 지문을 연계하여 풀어야 하는 문제들이 출제되므로, 지문간의 관계를 파악하는 연습을 해야 한다.

| 문제 형태 |

Questions 176-180 refer to the following Web page and e-mail.

http://www.highlightcar.ca

| Home | About Us | Reviews | Contact Us |

Highlight Car Service: Taking You Where You Want to Go

Based in Toronto, Highlight Car Service provides a wide range of transportation solutions for business travelers and individuals attending special occasions such as weddings. Our drivers are expertly trained professionals who ensure a seamless journey to your desired destination, whether it's the airport or a hotel. We also offer guided sightseeing tours and will make your travel experience enjoyable and comfortable.

Highlight Car Service operates in numerous cities worldwide from New York to Tokyo, and we are continuously expanding our presence. We are excited to announce the upcoming opening of our newest branch in Nairobi later this year.

Founded three decades ago by former taxi driver Logan Haynes, Highlight Car Service is committed to meeting the demand for top-tier transportation services. To mark our 30th anniversary this April, all new customers who make reservations during that month will enjoy a 20% discount off their total bill. Simply use the code LUX300.

From: Highlight Car Service <info@highlightcarservice.com>

To: Namiko Hideyoshi <Namiko_h@uchemical.jp>

Subject: Information

Date: April 20

Dear Ms. Hideyoshi,

We appreciate your trust in Highlight Car Service! This e-mail serves as confirmation of the reservation you made on April 18.

Customer Number: 7416
Pickup Location: Fiumicino Int'l Airport, Terminal C
Pickup Date: May 3
Pickup Time: 9:45 A.M.
Number of Passengers: 5
Destination/Route: Hilltop Hotel, Viale Europa / Piazza Benito Juarez Park
Deposit Card: *** **** 8303
Discount Code: LUX300

Should you have any inquiries or concerns or need a scheduling adjustment, please feel free to reach out to us at 1-800-904-0300 (U.S. and Canada) or internationally at (+1) 721-985-7413.

Stay connected with your driver by downloading our mobile app.

Thank you for choosing Highlight Car Service. We look forward to serving you.

Sincerely,

Highlight Car Service

176 According to the Web page, where will Highlight Car Service soon be available?

(A) In Toronto
(B) In Seoul
(C) In Tokyo
(D) In Nairobi

177 Who is Mr. Haynes?

(A) A car salesman
(B) An event planner
(C) A reservation staff
(D) A company founder

178 What does the Web page indicate about the company?

(A) It is three decades old.
(B) It has relocated its corporate offices.
(C) It focuses on budget-friendly travel.
(D) It has revised its driver training program.

179 What is the purpose of the e-mail?

(A) To book a hotel room
(B) To confirm a reservation
(C) To provide a flight itinerary
(D) To change an arrangement

180 What is suggested about Ms. Hideyoshi?

(A) She will be journeying by herself.
(B) She is employed at Fiumicino Airport.
(C) She is a first-time user of the service.
(D) She encountered an issue with the mobile app.

학습 플랜

2주 완성

		DAY 1	DAY 2	DAY 3	DAY 4	DAY 5
week 1	**LC**	PART 1_ UNIT 1-3	PART 2_ UNIT 4-5	PART 2_ UNIT 6-8	PART 3_ UNIT 9	PART 3_ UNIT 10
	RC	PART 5_ UNIT 1-2	PART 5_ UNIT 3-4	PART 5_ UNIT 5-6	PART 5_ UNIT 7-8	PART 5_ UNIT 9-10

		DAY 6	DAY 7	DAY 8	DAY 9	DAY 10
week 2	**LC**	PART 3_ UNIT 11	PART 3_ UNIT 12	PART 4_ UNIT 13	PART 4_ UNIT 14	PART 4_ UNIT 15
	RC	PART 5_ UNIT 11-12	PART 6_ UNIT 13-14	PART 5&6_ ACTUAL TEST 1~10	PART 7_ UNIT 15-16	PART 7_ UNIT 17-18

4주 완성

		DAY 1	DAY 2	DAY 3	DAY 4	DAY 5
week 1	LC	PART 1_ UNIT 1	PART 1_ UNIT 2	PART 1_ UNIT 3	PART 1 복습	PART 2_ UNIT 4
	RC	PART 5_ UNIT 1	PART 5_ UNIT 2	PART 5_ UNIT 3	PART 5_ UNIT 4	PART 5_ UNIT 5

		DAY 6	DAY 7	DAY 8	DAY 9	DAY 10
week 2	LC	PART 2_ UNIT 5	PART 2_ UNIT 6	PART 2_ UNIT 7	PART 2_ UNIT 8	PART 2 복습
	RC	PART 5_ UNIT 6	PART 5_ UNIT 7	PART 5_ UNIT 8	PART 5_ UNIT 9	PART 5_ UNIT 10

		DAY 11	DAY 12	DAY 13	DAY 14	DAY 15
week 3	LC	PART 3_ UNIT 9	PART 3_ UNIT 10	PART 3_ UNIT 11	PART 3_ UNIT 12	PART 3 복습
	RC	PART 5_ UNIT 11	PART 5_ UNIT 12	PART 6_ UNIT 13	PART 6_ UNIT 14	PART 5&6 복습 (ACTUAL TEST 1~10)

		DAY 16	DAY 17	DAY 18	DAY 19	DAY 20
week 4	LC	PART 4_ UNIT 13	PART 4_ UNIT 14	PART 4_ UNIT 15	PART 4 복습	PART 1~4 전체 복습
	RC	PART 7_ UNIT 15	PART 7_ UNIT 16	PART 7_ UNIT 17	PART 7_ UNIT 18	PART 7 복습

* 학습 플랜대로 학습하신 후 도서 인증을 통해 온라인 모의고사를 이용하실 수 있습니다. (이용 방법 p.5 참조)

PART

1

사진 묘사

LC

문제지에 인쇄된 사진을 보고, 들려주는 4개의 보기 중에서 사진 속에 등장하는 인물의 동작이나 상태, 사물의 상태나 위치를 가장 정확하게 묘사한 것을 고르는 문제로, 총 6문항이 출제된다.

구성	PART	유형	문항 수	시간	배점
Listening Comprehension	1	사진 묘사	6	45분	495점
	2	질의 응답	25		
	3	짧은 대화	39		
	4	짧은 담화	30		

문제 유형

- **1인 사진** 한 사람이 등장, 인물의 동작과 옷차림 등의 상태 묘사
- **2인 이상 사진** 두 사람 이상 등장, 인물들의 공통 동작, 상호 동작, 개별 동작 및 상태 묘사
- **사물·풍경 사진** 사물과 풍경이 중심이 되는 사진으로, 사물의 위치나 전체적 풍경 묘사

풀이 전략

대략
1분 35초

LISTENING TEST

In the Listening test, you will be asked to demonstrate how well you understand spoken English. The entire Listening test will last approximately 45 minutes. There are four parts, and directions are given for each part. You must mark your answers on the separate answer sheet. Do not write your answers in your test book.

PART 1

Directions: For each question in this part, you will hear four statements about a picture in your test book. When you hear the statements, you must select the one statement that best describes what you see in the picture. Then find the number of the question on your answer sheet and mark your answer. The statements will not be printed in your test book and will be spoken only one time.

Statement (C), "They're sitting at a table," is the best description of the picture, so you should select answer (C) and mark it on your answer sheet.

☑ **LC Directions 시간 활용하기**

옵션 1 사진 6개를 미리 살펴보면서 사람 및 사물의 동작이나 상태, 배경 등의 표현을 떠올려 본다.

옵션 2 PART 3의 질문과 보기를 미리 읽으면서 키워드를 표시해 둔다.

옵션 3 PART 5 문제를 미리 푼다.

▶ "Now Part 1 will begin."이 들리면 이때 Part 1로 돌아가서 문제를 푼다.

• **등장인물:** 여자 1명
• **동작/자세/상태:** looking, sitting, typing
• **주변 사물:** lamp, headset, laptop
• **장소/배경:** window

 Number 1. Look at the picture marked number 1 in your test book.

(A) She's typing on a laptop.
(B) She's looking at a document.
(C) She's turning on a lamp.
(D) She's wearing a headset.

☑ 오답을 소거하며 정답을 찾는다.

(A) O 노트북으로 타이핑을 하고 있는 모습이다.
(B) X 문서를 보고 있는 모습이 아니다.
(C) X 조명을 켜고 있는 모습이 아니다.
(D) X 헤드셋을 쓰고 있는 상태가 아니다.

최신 출제 경향

① 인물 중심 사진에서 인물의 동작이 아닌 상태를 묘사하는 정답도 출제되고 있다.
② 인물 중심 사진이라도 주변의 사물이나 배경을 묘사하는 정답도 출제되고 있다.
③ 사물·풍경 사진을 현재형 일반 동사로 묘사하는 정답이 출제되고 있다.

만점 전략

① PART 1에 자주 출제되는 사진의 상황별 빈출 표현들을 정리하여 암기한다.
② PART 1에 자주 출제되는 사진의 상황별 동사 형태를 익혀 둔다.
③ PART 1에 자주 출제되는 빈출 오답 유형을 익혀 둔다.
④ 각 선택지에서 정답 가능성이 높은 것은 O, 정답 가능성이 없는 것은 X 표기하면서, 오답을 소거해 최종적으로 답을 고른다.
⑤ 사람이 나오는 사진은 우선 사람의 동작을 나타내는 동사에 집중해서 듣자.
⑥ 사물의 위치가 제대로 설명되었는지 위치를 확실히 체크하면서 문제를 풀자.
⑦ 사람과 사물이 함께 나올 경우, 사람 주변의 사물이나 풍경의 상태가 정답으로 자주 출제되므로 주변 사물과 풍경 관련 빈출 어휘를 암기해 둬야 한다.

인물 등장 사진

1. 1인 사진

☰ 유형 소개 및 전략

1인 사진은 한 사람이 등장하는 사진으로, 문제 난이도가 비교적 쉬운 편이다. 1인 사진은 등장인물의 손동작이나 시선, 자세 등 동작이나 상태 묘사가 주로 정답이 된다.

녹음을 듣기 전에, 사진 속 인물의 동작을 '손동작 → 외모(옷차림) → 주변 환경' 순으로 파악하고 선택지에 나올 만한 표현을 미리 떠올려 본다. 사진에 없는 단어가 들리거나 사람의 동작, 상태 등을 잘못 묘사한 경우 X, 잘 들리지 않거나 애매모호한 경우 △, 정답인 것 같으면 O를 표시한 후 최종 답을 선택한다. 이때, 동사와 명사 중심으로 듣는다.

유형 맛보기

(A) He is removing his hat.
(B) He is speaking into a microphone.
(C) He is trimming bushes outside.
(D) He is plugging in a cord.

(A) 그는 모자를 벗고 있다. (X)
　　→ 모자를 쓰고 있지 벗고 있지 않으므로 동작 묘사 오류.

(B) 그는 마이크에 대고 말하고 있다. (O)
　　→ 사진 속 인물이 마이크에 대고 말하고 있으므로 정답.

(C) 그는 관목을 다듬고 있다. (X)
　　→ 뒤에 나무(bushes)가 보이지만 다듬고 있는 상황은 아니다.

(D) 그는 코드를 꽂고 있다. (X)
　　→ 사진에 없는 명사(cord)가 들린 오답이다.

☰ 풀이 접근법

● 사진 속 인물의 동작과 옷차림을 확인한 후, 나올 수 있는 표현들을 미리 떠올려 본다.

　▶ **인물의 주요 동작 및 외모[옷차림]**
　　speaking into a microphone / wearing a hat

　▶ **장소 및 주요 사물**
　　outside / trees / microphone / bench

● △, X, O를 표시하면서 소거법을 이용해 푼다. 사진 속 인물의 동작과 무관한 동사나 사진에 없는 명사가 들리면 바로 소거한다.

☰ 기출 포인트

1인 등장 사진은 보기 4개의 주어가 대부분 같으므로 주어의 동작에 초점을 두고 들어야 한다. 하지만 사람뿐 아니라 주변 사물에 대해서도 나올 수 있다. 두 경우 모두 동사와 명사를 집중해서 들어야 한다. **동사는 주로 현재 진행형(is + V-ing)으로 묘사된다.**

✚ 인물의 동작이나 상태를 묘사할 때는 주로 동사의 현재 진행형으로 나온다.

현재 진행형	**be동사 + 동사원형 –ing** (~하고 있다, ~하는 중이다) 주어가 3인칭 단수인 경우 is, 복수인 경우 are

✚ 1인 등장 사진의 주어 표현

남자 한 명	A man / The man / He
여자 한 명	A woman / The woman / She

✚ 인물의 상반신이 나오는 사진

① 구체적인 동작 → ② 주변의 장소나 상황에 맞는 동작 → ③ 외모, 외형과 관련된 상태 → ④ 주변 장소의 상황이나 사물

She is **typing** on a keyboard. 그녀는 키보드로 입력하고 있다.

She is **using** a laptop computer. 그녀는 노트북을 사용하는 중이다.

A woman is **working in the office**. 여자가 사무실에서 일하고 있다.

The woman is **wearing glasses**. 여자가 안경을 쓰고 있다.

There is a whiteboard beside her. 그녀 옆에는 화이트보드가 있다.

✚ 인물의 전신이 나오는 사진

① 상황에 맞는 동작 → ② 구체적인 동작 → ③ 외모, 외형과 관련된 상태 → ④ 주변 장소의 상황이나 사물

He is **using** a mobile phone. 그는 휴대폰을 사용하고 있다.

He is **carrying** a briefcase. 그는 서류 가방을 들고 있다.

The man is **wearing a jacket**. 남자가 재킷을 입고 있다.

A man is **walking down** some stairs. 한 남자가 계단을 내려가고 있다.

✚ 1인 등장 사진의 동작/상태 관련 빈출 표현

시선	looking at 보고 있다 / looking in 안을 들여다보고 있다 / checking 점검하고 있다 / examining 살펴보고 있다 / inspecting 살펴보고[검사하고] 있다 / reviewing 검토하고 있다 / concentrating 집중해서 보고 있다 / staring 응시하고 있다

자세/동작	walking 걷고 있다 / sitting 앉아 있다 / standing 서 있다 / entering 들어가고 있다 / crossing (가로질러) 건너가고 있다 / bending over 허리를 구부리고 있다 / leaning against ~에 기대어 있다 / strolling [taking a stroll] 걷고 있다, 산책하고 있다 / riding 타고 있다 / boarding 타고 있다 / talking on the phone 전화로 대화하고 있다 / waiting [standing] in line 줄을 서서 기다리고 있다

> **고득점 TIP+**
>
> | **boarding** ~을[에] 타다 | 타고 있는 '동작'을 묘사할 때 |
> |---|---|
> | **riding** ~을[에] 타다 | 타고 있는 '상태'를 묘사할 때 |
>
> | **boarding** a bus
버스에 탑승 중이다 (동작) | **riding** on a plane
비행기를 타고 있다 (상태) | **riding** in a boat
보트를 타고 있다 (상태) |
> |---|---|---|
>
> ★ getting into a car(차에 타다), getting on a boat(보트에 오르다)도 함께 알아 두자.

작업	displaying 전시하고 있다 / working 일하고 있다 / assembling 조립하고[만들고] 있다 / adjusting 조정하고 있다 / carrying 운반하고 있다 / sweeping 쓸고 있다 / mopping 닦고 있다 / wiping 닦고 있다 / dusting 먼지를 털고 있다 / cleaning 청소하고 있다 / mowing 잔디를 깎고 있다 / turning on 켜고 있다, 틀고 있다 / placing [laying] 놓고 있다, 두고 있다 / repairing [= fixing] 수리하고 있다 / opening 열고 있다 / operating 작동시키고 있다

손동작	typing 타이핑하고 있다 / using 사용하고 있다 / taking notes 메모하고 있다 / writing 쓰고 있다 / hanging up 걸고 있다 / taking an order (식당에서) 주문을 받고 있다 / reaching for ~로 손을 뻗고 있다 / picking up 집어 들고 있다 / holding [grasping/grabbing] 들고 있다 / pointing at ~을 손으로 가리키고 있다 / watering 물을 주고 있다 / rolling up 접어 올리고 있다 / pouring 붓고 있다 / lifting 들어 올리고 있다 / loading (물건을) 싣고 있다 / pushing (↔ pulling) 밀고 (↔ 당기고) 있다 / rolling up (카페트, 소매 등을) 말고 있다, 걷어 올리고 있다 / rowing [paddling] 노를 젓고 있다

> **고득점 TIP+**
>
> | **wear** ~을 입고[착용하고] 있다 | 착용 '상태'를 묘사할 때 |
> |---|---|
> | **put on / try on** ~을 입어 보다 | 착용하는 '동작'을 묘사할 때 |
>
> | **wearing** a suit
정장을 입고 있다 (상태) | **putting on** a jacket
자켓을 입고 있는 중이다 (동작) | **trying on** shoes
신발을 신는 중이다 (동작) |
> |---|---|---|
>
> (외모/착용)

2. 2인 이상 사진

유형 소개 및 전략

2인 이상 사진은 1인 사진에 비해 다양한 주어가 나올 수 있으므로 문제 난이도가 다소 높다고 느껴질 수 있다. **사진에 등장하는 2인 또는 그 이상의 인물들의 공통된 동작이나 특정 개인의 동작 및 상태 묘사가 정답으로 자주 출제된다.** 2인 이상이 등장하는 사진에서는 사진 속 인물들의 '공통된 동작 → 개별 행동 → 주변 상황이나 사물' 등의 순으로 확인한다. 사진에 없는 단어가 들리거나 사람의 동작/상태 등을 잘못 묘사한 경우에는 X, 잘 들리지 않거나 애매모호 경우에는 △, 정답인 것 같으면 O를 표시해 최종 답을 선택하되 '동사'와 '명사' 중심으로 듣는다.

유형 맛보기

(A) The man is reaching for a glass.
(B) The woman is working at a computer.
(C) They are shaking hands.
(D) They are moving chairs.

(A) 남자가 컵에 손을 뻗고 있다. (X)
→ 컵이 테이블 위에 있지만 그것에 손을 뻗는 모습은 아니다.
(B) 여자가 컴퓨터로 일하고 있다. (X)
→ 테이블 위에 컴퓨터는 있지만 그것을 이용해 일하고 있는 모습은 아니다.
(C) 그들은 악수하고 있다. (O)
→ 사진 속 인물들이 악수하고 있으므로 정답이다.
(D) 그들은 의자를 옮기고 있다. (X)
→ 사진 속에 의자가 있지만 옮기고 있는 모습은 아니다.

풀이 접근법

● 사진 속 인물들의 공통 동작 → 개별 행동 → 주변 상황이나 사물 등을 확인한 후, 나올 수 있는 표현을 미리 떠올려 본다.

▶ 공통 동작
shaking hands / facing each other / talking each other

▶ 개별 동작[외모]
wearing glasses (woman)

▶ 장소 및 주요 사물
office / glass / potted plant / a laptop computer / a tablet PC

● 주어가 복수(They, The women, The men, The people)로 나오면 공통된 동작에 초점을 맞추고, 주어가 단수 (He, She, A man, A woman)로 나오면 해당 인물의 동작에 초점을 맞춰야 한다.

≡ 기출 포인트

2인 이상이 등장하는 사진은 사진 속 인물들이 현재 하고 있는 공통적인 동작이나 부각되는 특정 인물의 동작에 초점을 맞춰 출제되기 때문에 주어가 복수(They, The women, The men)로 나오면 우선 공통된 동작을 파악한 후 눈에 띄는 인물의 동작을 함께 파악하고, 주어가 단수(He, She, A man, A woman)로 나오면 특정 인물의 동작에 초점을 맞춰 듣는다.

✚ 인물의 동작이나 상태를 묘사할 때는 주로 동사의 현재 진행형으로 나온다.

현재 진행형	**be동사 + 동사원형 –ing** (~하고 있다, ~하는 중이다) 주어가 3인칭 단수인 경우 is, 복수인 경우 are

✚ 2인 이상 사진에서 인물의 주어 표현

등장인물 전체	They / People / The people	남자 중 한 명	One of the men
전체 중 일부	Some people	여자 중 한 명	One of the women

✚ 2인 등장 사진

① 사진 속 인물들의 공통 동작 및 상태 확인 → ② 사진 속 특정 인물의 개별 동작 및 상태 확인 → ③ 주변 배경의 특이점 확인

They are drinking coffee. 그들은 커피를 마시고 있다.
They are facing each other. 그들은 마주 보고 있다.
They are resting their arms on the table.
그들은 탁자 위에 팔을 기대고 있다.
The woman has long hair. 여자는 머리가 길다.
The man is wearing glasses. 남자는 안경을 쓰고 있다.
Some napkins have been placed on the table.
테이블 위에 냅킨이 놓여 있다.

✚ 2인 이상 등장 사진

① 사진 속 인물들의 공통 동작 및 상태 확인 → ② 사진 속 특정 인물(다른 성별)의 개별 동작 및 상태 확인 → ③ 주변 배경의 특이점 확인

They are all standing. 모두 서 있다.
The women are shaking hands. 두 여자가 악수하고 있다.
The man is wearing glasses. 남자가 안경을 쓰고 있다.
The man has a beard. 남자는 턱수염이 있다.
There are **office supplies** on the desk.
테이블 위에 사무용품들이 있다.

> **고득점 TIP+** 2인 이상 사진에서 다수의 사람 중 일부의 공통 동작이나 특정 한 명을 언급하여, 그 인물의 개별 동작이나 상태 묘사를 답으로 하는 문제가 자주 출제된다.

공통 동작

heading 향하고 있다 / **waving** 손을 흔들고 있다 / **sharing** 공유하고 있다, 함께 쓰고 있다
greeting 인사하고 있다 / **shaking hands** 악수하고 있다 / **talking** 이야기하고 있다
speaking with ~와 이야기하고 있다 / **standing side by side** 나란히 서 있다 /
having a meal together 함께 음식을 먹고 있다 / **having a conversation** 대화를 나누고 있다

고득점 TIP+ 사진 속 인물들이 나란히 앉아 같은 방향을 보는지, 마주 보고 있는지를 묘사한 문제도 출제된다.

facing each other 마주 보고 있다	**sit side by side** 나란히 앉아 있다

상호 동작

paying 지불하고 있다 / **helping** 돕고 있다 / **serving** 서빙하고 있다 / **showing** 보여주고 있다
selling 팔고 있다 / **purchasing** 구매하고 있다 / **making a purchase** 구매하고 있다
examining a patient 환자를 진찰하고 있다 / **having one's hair cut** 머리를 깎고 있다

고득점 TIP+ serving은 보통ˈ음식이나 음료를 손님에게 내놓는 모습을 묘사할 때 사용된다. 주문받는 모습(taking an order)과 serving을 구분하는 문제가 출제된 바 있다.

serving 음식을 내놓고 있다	**taking an order** 주문을 받고 있다

🎧 01_1 | 정답 및 해설 p.330

■ 음원을 듣고 사진을 잘 묘사한 문장은 O에, 아닌 문장은 X에 표시하세요. 다시 들으면서 빈칸을 채우세요.

1.

(A) A man is _____ the lawn. (O / X)

(B) A man is _____ some plants. (O / X)

(C) A man is _____ outside. (O / X)

(D) A man is _____ in the garden. (O / X)

2.

(A) A woman is _____ glasses. (O / X)

(B) A woman is _____ for a book. (O / X)

(C) A woman is _____ on a laptop computer. (O / X)

(D) A woman is _____ a screen. (O / X)

3.

(A) They are _____ a meeting. (O / X)

(B) A man is _____ some paper to a woman. (O / X)

(C) One of the men is _____ at the board. (O / X)

(D) Some people are _____. (O / X)

4.

(A) A man is _____ his sunglasses. (O / X)

(B) A man is _____ a tablet PC. (O / X)

(C) A woman is _____ a suitcase to a man. (O / X)

(D) A woman is _____ with her legs crossed. (O / X)

🎧 01_2 | 정답 및 해설 p.330

1.

(A)　　(B)　　(C)　　(D)

2.

(A)　　(B)　　(C)　　(D)

3.

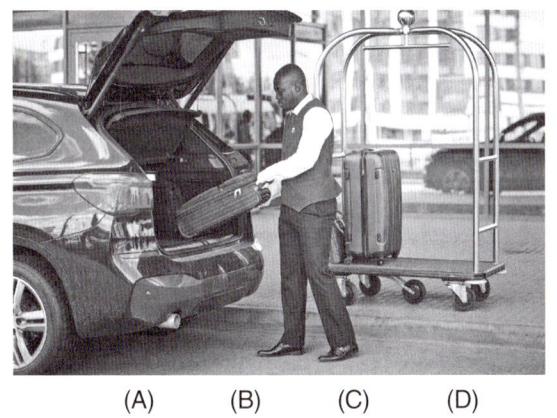

(A)　　(B)　　(C)　　(D)

4.

(A)　　(B)　　(C)　　(D)

5.

(A)　　(B)　　(C)　　(D)

6.

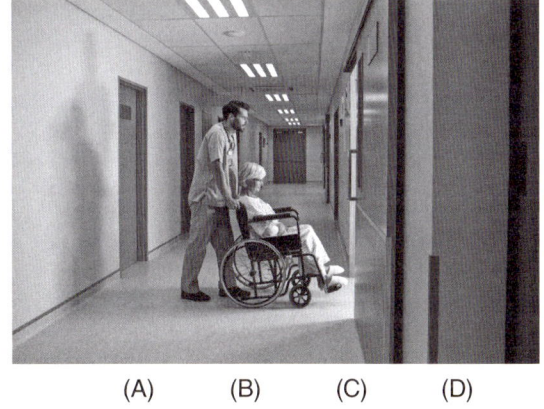

(A)　　(B)　　(C)　　(D)

LC PART 1

UNIT 02 사물·풍경 사진

≡ 유형 소개 및 전략

사물이나 풍경이 중심인 사진으로, 총 6문항 중 1~2문항 정도 출제된다. 사진 속에 등장하는 **다양한 사물의 위치나 배경을 중심으로 보기가 구성**되며, **다양한 형태의 동사**가 쓰인다. 문제를 듣기 전에 사진 중앙부터 사물의 위치를 확인한 후, 나올 수 있는 표현을 미리 떠올려 본다. 장소나 위치 전치사에 주의해서 들어야 하며, 사람이 없는 사진에 사람 명사가 보기에 나오면 바로 소거한다.

유형 맛보기

(A) A computer is being repaired.
(B) Some chairs are stacked in a corner.
(C) A potted plant has been placed on a desk.
(D) Office equipment is being unpacked.

(A) 컴퓨터가 수리되고 있다. (X)
  → 컴퓨터를 수리하고 있는 사람은 보이지 않는다. 사람이 등장하지 않는 사진에서 be being p.p.가 들리면 소거한다.
(B) 의자가 구석에 쌓여 있다. (X)
  → 사진에 의자가 한 개만 보인다.
(C) 화분이 책상 위에 놓여 있다. (O)
  → 책상에 화분이 놓여 있는 모습을 표현한 정답이다.
(D) 사무 장비를 꺼내고 있다. (X)
  → 장비를 꺼내고 있는 사람이 보이지 않는다.

≡ 풀이 접근법

● 사진에서 가장 부각되는 사물의 위치 및 상태 확인 → 주변 사물 확인 → 배경 순으로 확인한 후, 나올 수 있는 표현을 미리 떠올려 본다.

  ▶ 핵심 사물
   a desk / a computer on a desk / a potted plant / a lamp

  ▶ 주변 사물
   a vase / a chair / a bookshelf

● 사람이 없는 사진에서는 '동사'보다 '명사'에 집중해서 듣는다. be being p.p.는 '~되는 중이다'라는 의미로 그 동작을 하는 사람이 있어야 한다. 따라서 사람이 없는 사진에 be being p.p.가 들리면 일단 오답 처리한다.

기출 포인트

사물 및 풍경 사진은 사물의 명칭, 위치, 상태 등을 유심히 살펴야 한다. 사물의 상태는 주로 현재 수동태나 현재완료 수동태로 출제된다.

✚ 사물의 상태를 묘사할 때는 주로 현재 수동태나 현재완료 수동태로 표현한다.

현재 수동태	**be동사 + p.p.** (~되고 있다) 주어가 단수인 경우 is, 복수인 경우 are
현재완료 수동태	**have/has** + **been** + **p.p.** (과거분사) (~되어 있다) 주어가 단수인 경우 has, 복수인 경우 have

✚ 사물 상태 빈출 표현

주어 + be동사 + 전치사구
(주어)가 ~에 있다.

There is/are + 주어 + 전치사구
(주어)가 ~에 있다.

주어 + be placed/positioned/arranged + 전치사구
(주어)가 ~에 놓여 있다

주어 + be stacked/stocked/piled + 전치사구
(주어)가 ~에 쌓여 있다

'위치'를 나타내는 빈출 전치사

on ~의 위에
in ~의 안에
around ~주변에
along ~에 따라
over ~의 위에

under ~의 아래에
by / beside / next to ~의 옆에
in front of ~의 앞에
behind ~의 뒤에

고득점 TIP+ 장소 묘사는 <전치사+명사>의 전치사구로 나타내는데, PART 1에서는 문장 맨 끝에 위치하므로 앞에서 들리는 명사가 맞다 해도 끝까지 내용을 들어야 오답 함정을 피할 수 있다.

The building is **under construction**.
건물이 공사 중이다.

There is a lamp on the table.
탁자 위에 램프가 있다.

Potted plants **are arranged** on shelves. 화분들이 선반에 배열되어 있다.

Cushions **are stacked** on the sofa.
소파 위에 쿠션이 쌓여 있다.

A boat is floating **next to** the dock.
보트가 부두 옆에 떠 있다.

Vehicles are parked **in front of** the buildings. 차량들이 건물 앞에 주차되어 있다.

➕ 사물/풍경 사진 빈출 표현

실내 사물	closet 옷장 / cardboard box (택배 박스 같은) 판지 상자 / shelve 선반 / container 용기, 그릇 / (trash) bin (쓰레기) 통 / flowerpot[potted plant] 화분 / light bulb 전구 / rug 깔개 / toolbox 공구 상자 / utensil (특히 부엌에서 쓰는) 기구, 용구, 식기 / kitchen appliance 주방 도구 / countertop 조리대 / cutting board 도마 / counter 계산대, (식당, 도서관 등의) 카운터, 조리대 / framed picture 사진[그림] 액자 / bulletin board 게시판
실외 사물	garage 차고 / crate (물품 운송용 대형 나무) 상자 / workstation 작업장 / equipment 기기, 장비 / handrail (계단의) 난간 / railing 난간 / ladder 사다리 / wheelbarrow 손수레 / patio 옥외 테라스 / sidewalk 보도, 인도 / pavement 인도, 포장도로 / ramp 경사로, 슬로프 / umbrella 우산, 파라솔 / waterway 수로 / path 길 / fence 울타리 / lawn 잔디 / overpass 고가도로 / ferry 배 / doorway 출입구, 입구
사물 상태	be stacked [piled] 쌓여 있다 / be hanging 매달려 있다 / be suspended 매달려 있다 / be scattered 흩어져 있다 / be laid [spread] out 펼쳐져 있다, 배치되어 있다 / be turned on 켜져 있다 / be lining 줄 서 있다, 일렬로 죽 늘어서 있다 / be propped against ~에 기대어 있다 / be leaning against ~에 기대어 있다 / be pushed against (under) ~로(아래로) 밀어 붙여 있다 / be unoccupied 비어 있다 / be placed 놓여 있다 / be left open 열려 있다 / be opened 열려 있다 / be closed 닫혀 있다 / be docked (배가) 정박되어 있다 / be reflected 반사되다, 비치다 / on display 진열되어 있는
풍경 동사	overlook (건물 등) 내려다보다 / surround 둘러싸다 / reflected 비치다 / traveling 이동하고 있다 / extend 뻗다 / lead to ~로 연결되다 / shaded by ~에 의해 그늘지다 / growing 자라다, 우거지다 / floating 떠 있다 / casting a shadow 그림자를 드리우다

고득점 TIP+ 호수, 강, 바다 등 물을 배경으로 하는 사진이 자주 출제된다. 배(ferry, boat, ship 등), 다리(bridge), 수로 (waterway) 등 물가와 관련해 자주 등장하는 명사와, 떠 있는 모습을 묘사하는 표현(floating) 등은 꼭 알아 두어야 한다.

Boats are floating on the water.
배가 물에 떠 있다.

고득점 TIP+ 그림자가 드리워진 모습을 묘사하는 표현으로 'casting a shadow'가 최근에 자주 출제된다. 나무나 파라솔, 건물 기둥 등이 그림자를 드리우는 사진이 자주 나온다.

■ 음원을 듣고 사진을 잘 묘사한 문장은 O에, 아닌 문장은 X에 표시하세요. 다시 들으면서 빈칸을 채우세요.

1.

(A) Books are ＿＿＿＿＿＿ on the floor. (O / X)

(B) A lamp has been ＿＿＿＿＿＿ on a desk. (O / X)

(C) Some pictures are ＿＿＿＿＿＿ on the wall. (O / X)

(D) Some plants are ＿＿＿＿＿＿ the sofa. (O / X)

2.

(A) Some bicycles ＿＿＿＿＿＿ outside. (O / X)

(B) The bicycles are ＿＿＿＿＿＿ their sides. (O / X)

(C) People are ＿＿＿＿＿＿ on bicycles. (O / X)

(D) Bicycles are ＿＿＿＿＿＿ in front of the building. (O / X)

3.

(A) A boat is ＿＿＿＿＿＿ at the dock. (O / X)

(B) Several boats are ＿＿＿＿＿＿ on the water. (O / X)

(C) Buildings ＿＿＿＿＿＿ the water. (O / X)

(D) Some people are ＿＿＿＿＿＿ a dock. (O / X)

4.

(A) A bridge ＿＿＿＿＿＿ a river. (O / X)

(B) There are many ＿＿＿＿＿＿ on the road. (O / X)

(C) A highway is ＿＿＿＿＿＿ through the mountain. (O / X)

(D) A bridge ＿＿＿＿＿＿ a river. (O / X)

ACTUAL TEST

🎧 02_2 | 정답 및 해설 p.332

1.

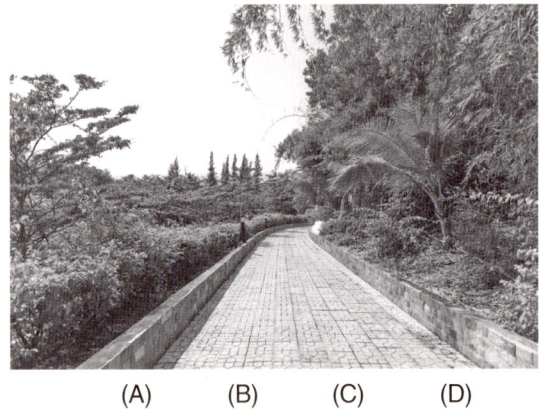

(A)   (B)   (C)   (D)

2.

(A)   (B)   (C)   (D)

3.

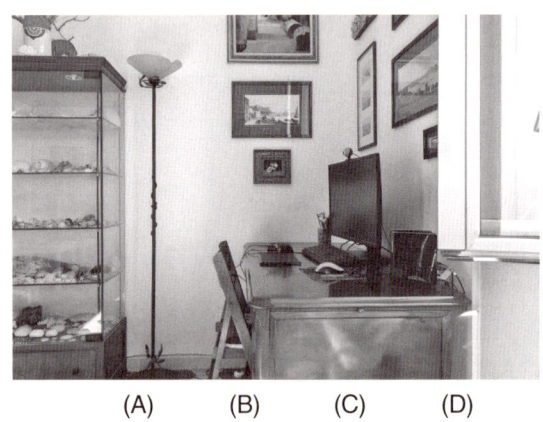

(A)   (B)   (C)   (D)

4.

(A)   (B)   (C)   (D)

5.

(A)   (B)   (C)   (D)

6.

(A)   (B)   (C)   (D)

UNIT 03 인물·풍경 혼합 사진

☰ 유형 소개 및 전략

특별히 부각되는 부분 없이 인물과 사물, 배경에 대한 묘사가 모두 다뤄지는 유형이다. 사진의 중심이 되는 인물뿐만 아니라 주변 사물 및 배경까지 놓치지 않고 파악해야 한다. **최근에는 '다수의 인물+배경'의 혼합 사진이 등장한 경우, 사람보다는 사물을 묘사한 보기가 정답으로 자주 출제되고 있다.** 2인 이상 사진과 마찬가지로, 우선 인물의 공통된 동작 및 상태를 살핀 후 사진 속 장소 및 주변 사물에 대해서도 나올 수 있는 표현을 미리 떠올려 본다. 문제를 들을 때 사람의 동작과 무관한 동사가 나온 보기와, 사진에 없는 사물을 언급한 보기에 주의한다.

유형 맛보기

(A) The road is being repaired.
(B) A lamppost is being removed.
(C) Some people are waiting for the traffic signal to change.
(D) Pedestrians are crossing the street.

(A) 도로가 수리되고 있다. (X)
→ 도로를 수리하고 있는 모습이 아니다.

(B) 가로등이 철거되고 있다. (X)
→ 사진에 가로등은 보이지 않고, 무언가를 철거하고 있는 모습도 없다.

(C) 몇몇 사람들이 신호가 바뀌기를 기다리고 있다. (X)
→ 신호를 기다리는 사람은 보이지 않는다.

(D) 보행자들이 길을 건너고 있다. (O)
→ 길을 건너고 있는 사진 속 인물들의 공통된 동작을 표현한 정답이다.

☰ 풀이 접근법

● 사진 속 인물의 공통된 동작 → 주변 장소 및 상황과 사물 등을 순차적으로 확인한 후, 나올 수 있는 표현을 미리 떠올려 본다.

▶ 공통 동작
crossing the road [street] / heading in the same direction

▶ 장소 및 주요 사물
crosswalk / street / buildings

● △, X, O를 이용한 소거법으로 접근한다. 사람의 동작과 무관한 동사나 사진에 없는 명사가 들리는 보기는 바로 오답 처리한다.

⚏ 기출 포인트

주어를 먼저 잘 듣고 인물, 사물, 배경 중 어떤 부분에 대해 언급하는지를 파악한 후, 제대로 묘사되었는지 확인한다. 사진 속 인물이 주변 사물을 어떻게 이용하는지도 집중해서 듣는다. 사물에 가해지는 동작을 나타낼 때 사물 주어와 함께 '~되고 있다, ~되는 중이다'라는 뜻의 현재 진행형 수동태 [be동사 + being + 과거분사(p.p.)]가 사용된다.

✚ 사물에 가해지는 동작 표현은 '현재 진행형 수동태'로 표현한다.

현재진행 수동태	**be동사 + being + p.p.** (~이 되고 있다, ~되는 중이다)
	주어가 단수인 경우 is, 복수인 경우 are

The wall is being painted.
벽이 칠해지는 중이다.

They are being served.
그들은 음식을 제공 받는 중이다.

The vehicle is being repaired.
자동차가 수리되고 있다.

Some plants are being watered.
식물에 물을 주고 있다.

Boxes are being unloaded.
박스가 내려지고 있다.

ⓒf Some shoes are being displayed.
신발들이 진열되어 있다.

A lawnmower is being used.
잔디 깎는 기계를 사용 중이다.

A baggage cart is being pushed.
수화물 카트를 밀고 있다.

A carpet is being vacuumed.
카펫을 진공청소기로 청소하고 있다.

Some flowers are being moved.
꽃들을 옮기고 있다.

A tree is being planted.
나무를 심고 있다.

A sign is being installed.
간판을 설치하고 있다.

고득점 TIP+ <사물 주어 + be + being + p.p.>는 '사람이 사물을 가지고 동작을 진행하고 있다'의 의미로, 사람이 없는 사진에서는 오답이다. 단, 'display (진열하다)'는 상태의 지속을 나타내어, 사람이 없더라도 진행형 수동태로 쓸 수 있다.

✚ 인물·배경 혼합 사진 관련 빈출 표현

상태	be resting 쉬고 있다 / be sitting 앉아 있다 / be standing 서 있다 / be facing ~을 마주하고 있다 / be hanging 걸려 있다 / be on display 진열되어 있다 / be decorated 장식되어 있다 / be scattered 흩어져 있다 / be located 위치해 있다 / be under construction 공사 중이다

potted plant 화분 / pottery 도자기 (그릇) / wooden structure 나무로 만든 구조물 / structure 구조물, 건물 / stairs [steps/staircase/stairway] 계단 / multiple shelves 여러 단으로 된 선반 / gardening tool 원예 도구 / rack ~걸이, 받침대 / suitcase 여행 가방 / briefcase 서류 가방 / light fixture 조명 기구 / arched roof 아치 모양 지붕 / armchair 팔걸이가 있는 의자 / stool (보통 등받이와 팔걸이가 없는) 의자 / outdoor market [open-air market] 야외 시장 / centerpiece 테이블 중앙 장식 / conveyor belt 컨베이어 벨트 / baggage claim area 수화물 수령 장소 / scaffolding (건축 공사장의) 비계 / overhead compartment (기차·비행기 등의) 짐칸 / baggage cart 수화물 카트 / awning (= canopy) (창이나 문 위) 차양, 가리개

> **고득점 TIP+** 카페 등 실내 배경을 묘사할 때, 의자를 단순히 chair로 묘사하기도 하지만 armchair나, stool로 표현하기도 한다.

armchair
팔걸이가 있는 의자

stool
등받이나 팔걸이가 없는 의자

> **고득점 TIP+** 공항에서 승객들이 탑승하는 사진이나 건물 외부의 경사로를 묘사할 때 등장하는 단어로 ramp가 있다.

사물 명사

ramp
항공기 탑승 등을 위한 경사 계단

ramp
경사로(짐이나 휠체어 이동을 위해 만든 경사면 또는 계단)

> **고득점 TIP+** 난이도 높은 문제의 경우 공사장이나 건설 현장을 묘사할 때 나올 수 있는 단어로 scaffolding이 있다. 평소에 자주 접하는 단어가 아니라 어렵게 느껴질 수 있지만 사진과 함께 익혀 두어 해당 단어가 나왔을 때 당황하지 않도록 한다. 또한 야외 카페나 테라스가 등장하는 사진에 자주 나오는 단어로 awning이 있다.

scaffolding
(건축 공사장의) 비계

awning (= canopy)
(창이나 문 위) 차양, 가리개

■ 음원을 듣고 사진을 잘 묘사한 문장은 O에, 아닌 문장은 X에 표시하세요. 다시 들으면서 빈칸을 채우세요.

1.

(A) There is _____ at a construction site. (O / X)

(B) There is a building _____ the river. (O / X)

(C) Some workers are standing on a _____. (O / X)

(D) Some cars are stopped at a _____. (O / X)

2.

(A) A bicycle is _____ against the wall. (O / X)

(B) A sign is _____ on the road. (O / X)

(C) A woman is _____. (O / X)

(D) A woman is _____ in front of a building. (O / X)

3.

(A) A _____ people has gathered in the open market. (O / X)

(B) _____ the open market. (O / X)

(C) Some people are standing near a _____. (O / X)

(D) The street is _____. (O / X)

4.

(A) The passengers are riding _____. (O / X)

(B) There are some _____ compartments open. (O / X)

(C) A plane is taking off _____. (O / X)

(D) Some passengers _____ from a plane. (O / X)

ACTUAL TEST

1.

(A)   (B)   (C)   (D)

2.

(A)   (B)   (C)   (D)

3.

(A)   (B)   (C)   (D)

4.

(A)   (B)   (C)   (D)

5.

(A)   (B)   (C)   (D)

6.

(A)   (B)   (C)   (D)

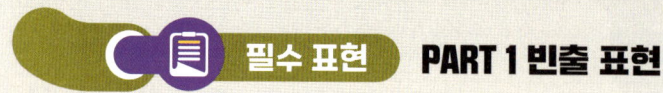

PART 1 빈출 표현

■ 전치사구

in front of ~	~ 위에	in clusters	무리지어
next to ~	~ 옆에	in piles/stacks	겹겹이
across from ~	~ 건너편에	from a ceiling	천장에
between A and B	A와 B 사이	against the wall	벽에 기대어
both sides of ~	~의 양쪽에	along the street	길을 따라
in the corner of ~	~ 구석에	near the river	강 가까이에
in the center/middle of ~	~의 중앙에	on the platform	승강장에
on top of ~	~의 맨 위에	under the counter	조리대[계산대] 아래
in a row/line	한 줄로	behind the counter	조리대[계산대] 뒤에

■ 손동작

filling a glass with water	유리잔에 물을 채우고 있다	packing some merchandise	상품을 포장하고 있다
adjusting a camera	카메라를 조정하고 있다	paying for a purchase	계산을 하고 있다
loading a cart	카트에 짐을 싣고 있다	putting away some tools	도구를 치우고 있다
unloading a truck	트럭에서 짐을 내리고 있다	pouring a beverage	음료수를 따르고 있다
taking an order	(식당에서) 주문을 받고 있다	taking notes	메모하고 있다
reaching into a cabinet	캐비닛 안으로 손을 뻗고 있다	tying a shoe	신발 끈을 매고 있다
reaching for an item	물건에 손을 뻗고 있다	typing on a keyboard	키보드를 치고 있다
rowing a boat	노를 젓고 있다	grasping the handle	손잡이를 잡고 있다
opening a drawer	서랍을 열고 있다	unzipping a backpack	배낭을 열고 있다
operating a machine	기계를 조작하고 있다	mopping the floor	바닥을 닦고 있다
holding a piece of paper	종이를 한 장 들고 있다	sweeping a walkway	보도를 쓸고 있다
hanging up a painting	그림을 걸고 있다	stacking some boxes	상자들을 쌓고 있다
handing out papers	서류를 전달하고 있다	wiping a counter	카운터를 닦고 있다
folding a newspaper	신문을 접고 있다	weighing some merchandise	상품 무게를 달고 있다
unpacking a suitcase	여행가방의 짐을 풀고 있다	writing a letter	편지를 쓰고 있다
pointing at a screen	스크린을 가리키고 있다	fixing a car	차를 수리하고 있다

■ 발동작

crossing a road	길을 건너고 있다	stepping onto a bus	버스에 타다
entering the building	건물 안으로 들어가고 있다	stepping off a bus	버스에서 내리다
going up the stairs	계단을 오르고 있다	stepping onto a ladder	사다리를 오르고 있다
going down the stairs	계단을 내려오고 있다	boarding [getting onto] a bus	버스에 올라타고 있다
ascending a staircase	계단을 오르고 있다	walking toward a doorway	출구를 향해 걷고 있다
climbing up some steps	계단을 오르고 있다	strolling along a beach	해안을 따라 걷고 있다
climbing down the steps	계단을 내려오고 있다	exiting a vehicle	차에서 내리고 있다

■ 시선

looking at a notebook	노트를 보고 있다	viewing some documents	서류를 보고 있다
checking some merchandise	상품을 살펴보고 있다	reviewing the contents	내용을 살펴보고 있다
staring out a window	창밖을 응시하고 있다	studying the menu	메뉴를 살펴보고 있다
gazing at the scenery	풍경을 바라보고 있다	examining a document	문서를 검토하고 있다
glancing at the computer screen	컴퓨터 화면을 보고 있다	appreciating some artwork	예술품을 감상하고 있다
concentrating on a monitor	모니터를 집중해서 보고 있다	facing each other	서로 마주보고 있다
watching a presentation	발표를 관람하고 있다	searching a bookshelf	책장을 살펴보고 있다
browsing some books	몇몇 책들을 훑어보고 있다	inspecting some machinery	기계를 살펴보고 있다

■ 착용 동작/상태

putting on sunglasses	선글라스를 착용해 보고 있다	wearing a helmet	헬멧을 착용하고 있다
trying on a scarf	스카프를 착용해 보고 있다	wearing a backpack	가방을 메고 있다
removing a coat	코트를 벗고 있다	wearing a jacket	재킷을 입고 있다
taking off a hat	모자를 벗고 있다	wearing glasses	안경을 쓰고 있다

PART

2

질의 응답

LC

의문사로 시작되는 의문문 또는 비의문사 의문문을 듣고, 이어서 들려주는 3개의 보기 중에서 가장 적절한 답변을 고르는 유형으로, 7~31번까지 구성되며 총 25문항이 출제된다.

구성	PART	유형	문항 수	시간	배점
Listening Comprehension	1	사진 묘사	6	45분	495점
	2	**질의 응답**	**25**		
	3	짧은 대화	39		
	4	짧은 담화	30		

🔊 문제 유형

- **의문사 의문문**　Who, When, Where, What, Which, How, Why
- **비의문사 의문문**　① 일반 의문문(Yes/No 응답 가능): be동사 의문문, 조동사 의문문(Have, Can, Will 등), Do동사 의문문
　　　　　　　　　　② 특수 의문문: 부정 의문문, 부가 의문문, 선택 의문문, 제안/요청 의문문, 평서문

🔊 풀이 전략

대략 30초

PART 2

Directions: You will hear a question or statement and three responses spoken in English. They will not be printed in your text book and will be spoken only one time. Select the best response to the question or statement and mark the letter (A), (B), or (C) on your answer sheet.

☑ **LC Directions 시간 활용하기**

- PART 3 의도 파악 문제를 찾아 미리 읽어 읽어 둔다.
- "Now let us begin with question number 7."이 들리면 PART 2로 돌아와 문제를 푼다.

◎ PART 1 디렉션 시간은 대략 1분 30초이기 때문에, 이때 사진들을 미리 훑어보거나 PART 5문제를 몇 문제라도 푸는 것을 추천하지만, PART 2 디렉션은 30초 정도기 때문에 PART 5 문제를 푸는 것은 집중력을 떨어뜨릴 수 있으므로 추천하지 않는다. PART 3의 의도 파악 문제를 읽어 두고 키워드를 표시해 두는 것이 좋다.

PART 2

Directions: You will hear a question or statement and three responses spoken in English. They will not be printed in your test book and will be spoken only one time. Select the best response to the question or statement and mark the letter (A), (B), or (C) on your answer sheet.

7. Mark your answer on your answer sheet.
8. Mark your answer on your answer sheet.
9. Mark your answer on your answer sheet.
10. Mark your answer on your answer sheet.
20. Mark your answer on your answer sheet.
21. Mark your answer on your answer sheet.
22. Mark your answer on your answer sheet.
23. Mark your answer on your answer sheet.

☑ 질문과 보기가 문제지에 표시되지 않으므로 고도의 집중력을 요한다.

Number 7.
Q **Who's in charge of** this campaign?
　　(PAUSE: 1.5초)
(A) Yes, that's really large.
(B) I think so, too.
(C) Mr. Gibbons is.

(다음 문제까지의 여유 시간: 약 4~5초)

☑ 질문과 키워드를 파악한다.

질문 유형: 의문사 의문문 Vs. 비의문사 의문문
키워드: 의문사, 주어, 동사에 집중

☑ 오답을 소거하며 정답을 찾는다.

(A) X 의문사 의문문에서는 Yes/No로 답할 수 없다.
(B) X 상대방의 의견에 동의하는 응답이다.
(C) O Who 의문문에, 구체적인 이름을 언급한 정답이다.

✍️ 최신 출제 경향

① 의문사 의문문

가장 큰 특징은 Yes/No로 답할 수 없고, 의문사에 해당하는 구체적인 내용을 포함한 답변을 찾아야 한다는 것이다. 다른 의문문에 비해 난이도가 쉬운 편이다.

과거에는 의문사 의문문이 평균 절반 이상을 차지했으나, 최근에는 총 25문제 중 9~10문제 정도로 출제 비율이 줄었다.

② 비의문사 의문문

제안/요청 의문문, 부정/부가 의문문, 그리고 평서문의 출제 비중이 높아지고 있다. 이 중에서도 응답을 예측하기 어려운 평서문이 예전보다 많이 출제되고 있고 난이도도 높아지고 있다.

③ 다양해진 응답 패턴

질문에 직접적인 답변을 주지 않고 우회/간접적으로 답하는 경우가 늘고 있다. 따라서 다양한 응답 패턴을 미리 익혀두는 것이 좋다. 잘 모른다거나 알아보겠다는 답변, 또는 아무 얘기를 못 들었으니 다른 사람에게 물어보라는 답변, 아직 결정되지 않았다는 답변 등이 정답으로 자주 출제된다. 최근에는 반문 형태의 정답 보기도 늘고 있다.

UNIT 04 Who/When/Where 의문문

1. Who 의문문

유형 소개 및 전략

Who 의문문은 매회 평균 1~2문제씩 출제된다. 주로 행위의 주체를 물어보기 때문에 답변에서 주어에 해당하는 부분을 잘 들어야 하며, 사람 이름, 인칭대명사, 직위, 부서명, 회사 이름이 들리는 선택지가 주로 정답이다. who 의문문은 Yes/No로 답할 수 없다. 정답 답변으로는 주로 사람 이름, 직책, 부서명, 회사명 등이 등장하지만, '잘 모르겠다, 확인해 보겠다, ~해봐라'는 식의 답변도 자주 출제된다. 또한, 최근에는 '책임자는 누구인가요?'라는 뜻의 Who's in charge of ~?, Who's responsible for ~? 표현이 자주 출제되고 있다.

유형 맛보기

Q **Who's** interviewing the job candidate? 누가 구직자를 면접할 건가요?
  → Who 의문문으로, 답변에서 인칭대명사가 들리면 정답일 확률이 높다.

(A) In my office. 제 사무실이에요.
  → Where 의문문에 적합한 오답

(B) I am planning to. 제가 할 거예요.
  → 인칭대명사 I를 이용한 정답

(C) He can't do that. 그는 그것을 할 수 없어요.
  → 그가 구체적으로 누군지 알 수 없으므로 오답

Q **Who's** sponsoring this event? 누가 이 행사를 후원하나요?
  → Who 의문문으로, 사람이나 회사 이름이 정답이 될 수 있다.

(A) Near the restaurant. 레스토랑 근처에서요.
  → Where 의문문에 적합한 오답

(B) Yes, it took about three days. 네, 3일 정도 걸립니다.
  → 의문사 의문문에 Yes/No로 응답 불가

(C) The PK Corporation is. PK 사요.
  → 후원 주체로 회사 이름을 언급한 정답

풀이 접근법

● 질문의 의도는 의문사를 포함해 첫 3~4 단어에서 결정되는 경우가 많다. 따라서 앞부분을 집중해서 듣자. 특히 의문사는 놓치지 않고 꼭 들어야 한다.

● Who 의문문은 사람 이름이나 직업, 직책, 부서, 회사 이름이 정답 보기로 자주 등장한다.

● '모른다, 결정된 바 없다, ~에게 물어봐라' 등의 반문 유형의 답변은 99% 정답이다.

☰ 기출 질문 & 답변 패턴

인명/직책으로 답하는 유형

Q Who is visiting our headquarters today?
오늘 누가 본사를 방문하나요?

A Mr. Frost.
Frost 씨요.

Q Who is in charge of the promotional campaign?
홍보 캠페인은 누가 담당하나요?

A The director of public relations.
홍보 담당 이사님이요.

Q Who is responsible for his schedule?
그의 일정은 누가 책임지고 있나요?

A The vice president's secretary.
부사장님의 비서가요.

인칭대명사로 답하는 유형

Q Who was the man I saw with Mr. Jackson?
Jackson 씨와 함께 있던 그 남자는 누구인가요?

A He is our new supervisor.
우리의 신임 상사입니다.

Q Who will attend the meeting?
누가 회의에 참석할 예정인가요?

A Everyone except Barney.
Barney를 제외하고 모두 다요.

Q Who will help him move the desk?
누가 그를 도와 책상을 옮길 건가요?

A I can help him.
제가 도울게요.

부서/회사/조직명으로 답하는 유형

Q Who will inform the staff about the new policy?
누가 직원들에게 새로운 정책을 알려줄 건가요?

A The Human Resources Department.
인사부서가요.

Q Who is repairing the air conditioner?
누가 에어컨을 수리하나요?

A The Maintenance Department.
유지보수 부서가요.

Q Who is organizing this advertising campaign?
누가 이번 광고 캠페인을 준비하나요?

A The ENC Company.
ENC 사입니다.

모른다거나 반문으로 답하는 유형

Q Who is going to the training session?
누가 교육에 가나요?

A I don't know.
모르겠습니다.

Q Who should I talk to about the program?
프로그램에 대해 누구와 이야기해야 하나요?

A Which program is it?
어떤 프로그램이죠?

Q Who is in the conference room now?
지금 누가 회의실에 있나요?

A You'd better ask your manager.
매니저에게 물어보세요.

LC PART 2

2. When 의문문

유형 소개 및 전략

When 의문문은 매회 평균 1~2문제씩 출제된다. 행위나 사건이 일어난 시점을 묻는 문제로, 시간부사(절) 등의 특정 시간 표현이 나오면 정답이다. when 의문문은 Yes/No로 답할 수 없다. 주로 출발/도착 시점, 물건의 배송/수령 시점, 업무 나 공사의 시작/종료 시점, 상점의 개점/폐점 시점, 회의나 발표의 시작/종료 시점, 각종 서류의 마감/제출 시점, 서비스나 보상의 이용/만료 시점 등을 묻는 질문이 나온다.

유형 맛보기

Q When do employees usually go to lunch? 직원들은 보통 언제 점심을 먹으러 가나요?
→ 점심을 먹으러 가는 시점을 묻고 있다.

(A) Yes, I know her. 네, 그녀를 알아요.
→ 의문사 의문문에 Yes/No가 들리면 오답

(B) Around noon. 정오쯤에요.
→ '전치사 + 특정 시점, 정확한 시간, 날짜, 요일'로 응답한 정답

(C) They will leave at 10 o'clock. 그들은 10시에 출발할 거예요.
→ 연상되는 단어(go-leave)로 혼동을 유도한 오답

Q When does the art exhibit open? 미술 전시회가 언제 열리나요?
→ 미술 전시회가 시작되는 시점을 묻고 있다.

(A) Hasn't it been canceled? 취소되지 않았나요?
→ 열리는 시점을 말하는 대신, 취소되지 않았냐고 반문하는 형태의 정답

(B) I can't find the exits. 출구를 찾을 수 없어요.
→ 유사 단어(exhibit-exits)를 사용해 혼동을 유도한 오답

(C) No, it never closes. 아뇨, 그곳은 절대 닫지 않습니다.
→ 의문사 의문문에 Yes/No가 들리면 오답

풀이 접근법

- When 의문문은 <전치사+시간 명사>, 시간 부사(구/절)' 등이 나오면 정답이다.

- '잘 모르겠다'나 '다른 사람에게 물어보라'는 등의 우회적인 답변 유형도 파악해 두어야 한다.

- When이 나오면 시점이나 시간 표현에 주목해야 한다.

- 최근에는 단순 시간 부사(구)보다 시간 부사절의 정답을 선호하는 경향이 있다.

☰ 기출 질문 & 답변 패턴

'전치사+시간 명사'로 답하는 유형

Q **When** will the event be held?
행사는 언제 개최되나요?

A On Sunday.
일요일이에요.

Q **When** is your vacation?
휴가가 언제예요?

A In October.
10월에요.

Q **When** do you finish your work?
일은 언제 마치나요?

A Around 6 o'clock.
6시쯤에요.

Q **When** are you planning to visit her?
언제 그녀를 방문할 예정인가요?

A Before dinner.
저녁식사 전에요.

시간 부사(구)나 시간 부사절로 답하는 유형

Q **When** is the flight departing?
비행기가 언제 출발하나요?

A As soon as everyone has boarded.
전부 탑승하면 바로요.

Q **When** will you leave the office?
언제 퇴근하나요?

A Later.
이따가요.

Q **When** do you do a volunteer activity?
언제 봉사활동을 하나요?

A Every month.
매달요.

모른다거나 반문으로 답하는 유형

Q **When** can we get together for a meeting?
언제 회의를 위해 만날 수 있을까요?

A How about on Monday?
월요일은 어떠세요?

Q **When** should I submit the report?
언제 보고서를 제출하면 되나요?

A Can I see it now?
지금 봐도 될까요?

Q **When** are you going to leave for vacation?
언제 휴가를 떠날 예정인가요?

A I don't know yet.
아직 모르겠어요.

Q **When** is the training seminar scheduled for?
교육 세미나는 언제로 예정되어 있죠?

A It's been canceled, actually.
실은 취소됐어요.

3. Where 의문문

📘 유형 소개 및 전략

Where 의문문은 매회 평균 1~2문제씩 출제된다. Where 의문문은 행위가 일어난 장소를 묻는 문제로, 특정 장소 표현이 나오면 정답이다. where 의문문은 Yes/No로 답할 수 없다. 최근에는 Where 의문문에 출처(사람, 부서, 회사, 신문)로 답변하는 경우도 출제되고 있다.

유형 맛보기

Q Where do you keep the files? 파일을 어디에 보관하세요?
→ 파일 보관 장소를 묻고 있다.

(A) In my cabinet. 제 캐비닛에요.
→ '전치사+장소'로 보관 장소를 언급한 정답

(B) Every day at 6:00. 매일 6시에요.
→ When 의문문에 적합한 오답

(C) Thanks, but I asked her already. 고맙지만, 이미 그녀에게 물어봤어요.
→ 권유/제안 의문문에 적합한 오답

Q Where are the instructions for the new computers? 새 컴퓨터의 설명서가 어디에 있나요?
→ 컴퓨터의 설명서가 어디 있는지 묻고 있다.

(A) It's a new computer system. 새로운 컴퓨터 시스템입니다.
→ 같은 단어(computer)를 사용해 혼동을 유도한 오답

(B) They're still in the boxes. 아직 상자 안에 있습니다.
→ 전치사를 이용해 보관 장소를 언급한 정답

(C) No, I won't attend it. 아뇨, 참석하지 않을 겁니다.
→ 의문사 의문문에 Yes/No로 응답 불가

📘 풀이 접근법

● Where 의문문은 장소 부사(구)가 나오면 정답이다.

● '잘 모르겠다'나 '다른 사람에게 물어보라'는 등의 우회적인 답변 유형도 파악해 두어야 한다.

● Where이 나오면 장소나 위치를 나타내는 표현에 주목해야 한다.

● 최근에는 사람 이름이나, 신문, 광고 등의 출처가 답이 되는 경우가 자주 출제되고 있다.

☰ 기출 질문 & 답변 패턴

'전치사+장소 명사'로 답하는 유형

Q **Where** can I find the department store?
백화점을 어디에서 찾을 수 있나요?

A Near the bank.
은행 근처에서요.

Q **Where** is the bus station?
버스 정류장이 어디에 있나요?

A In front of the park.
공원 앞에요.

Q **Where** is the entrance to the museum?
박물관 입구가 어디에 있나요?

A Around the corner.
모퉁이를 돌면요.

'장소 명사나 장소 부사(구)'로 답하는 유형

Q **Where** will the meeting be held?
회의는 어디에서 열리나요?

A The registration office will help you.
등록처에서 도와드릴 겁니다.

Q **Where** is the user manual?
사용자 매뉴얼이 어디에 있나요?

A Right here.
바로 여기에 있어요.

출처(사람, 부서, 회사, 신문)로 답하는 유형

Q **Where** did you get this coupon?
이 쿠폰을 어디에서 구했나요?

A I got it from a magazine.
잡지에서요.

Q **Where** did you learn about it?
그것에 대해 어디에서 알았나요?

A I asked James.
James에게 물어봤어요.

Q **Where** can I buy it?
그것을 어디에서 살 수 있나요?

A I bought it at the department store.
저는 백화점에서 구입했어요.

모른다거나 반문으로 답하는 유형

Q **Where** is the supermarket?
슈퍼마켓이 어디에 있나요?

A I am a stranger here.
저는 이곳이 처음이에요.

Q **Where** should I submit this application?
이 지원서를 어디에 제출해야 하나요?

A You should ask the manager.
매니저에게 물어보세요.

Q **Where** do you plan to go this weekend?
이번 주말에 어디로 갈 계획인가요?

A I have no idea yet.
아직 모르겠어요.

■ 다음을 듣고 적절한 응답을 고른 후, 빈칸을 채우세요.

1. Mark your answer.
(A)　(B)　(C)

_____ the director's new secretary?

(A) It's Betty Rodman.

(B) _____ an e-mail.

(C) _____ .

2. Mark your answer.
(A)　(B)　(C)

Who's coming to the _____ tomorrow?

(A) In the museum.

(B) The _____ .

(C) Yes, _____ .

3. Mark your answer.
(A)　(B)　(C)

_____ the restaurant?

(A) The _____ .

(B) No, she didn't.

(C) In red.

4. Mark your answer.
(A)　(B)　(C)

Who should I call _____ a meeting room?

(A) It's in the cinema.

(B) _____ Andy _____ it.

(C) _____ .

5. Mark your answer.
(A)　(B)　(C)

When will the office supplies _____ ?

(A) _____ days.

(B) The professor _____ .

(C) To my _____ .

6. Mark your answer.
(A)   (B)   (C)

When was Mr. Erickson _____ arrive?

(A) _____.

(B) Yes, _____.

(C) _____ o'clock.

7. Mark your answer.
(A)   (B)   (C)

_____ submit the travel expense report?

(A) Yes, _____ do it as soon as possible.

(B) _____ the office today.

(C) I'm going on a _____ next Monday.

8. Mark your answer.
(A)   (B)   (C)

_____ find our office supplies?

(A) We _____ 6 o'clock.

(B) In that cabinet _____.

(C) No, I haven't _____.

9. Mark your answer.
(A)   (B)   (C)

Where should I _____?

(A) By _____.

(B) After 5:00 P.M.

(C) _____.

10. Mark your answer.
(A)   (B)   (C)

Where should I _____?

(A) _____ you leave.

(B) On the second bookshelf.

(C) I _____ him.

ACTUAL TEST

🎧 04_2 | 정답 및 해설 p.338

1. Mark your answer on your answer sheet.
   (A)   (B)   (C)

2. Mark your answer on your answer sheet.
   (A)   (B)   (C)

3. Mark your answer on your answer sheet.
   (A)   (B)   (C)

4. Mark your answer on your answer sheet.
   (A)   (B)   (C)

5. Mark your answer on your answer sheet.
   (A)   (B)   (C)

6. Mark your answer on your answer sheet.
   (A)   (B)   (C)

7. Mark your answer on your answer sheet.
   (A)   (B)   (C)

8. Mark your answer on your answer sheet.
   (A)   (B)   (C)

9. Mark your answer on your answer sheet.
   (A)   (B)   (C)

10. Mark your answer on your answer sheet.
    (A)   (B)   (C)

UNIT 05

What·Which/How/Why 의문문

1. What·Which 의문문

☰ 유형 소개 및 전략

What 의문문은 매회 2문제 정도 출제되며 What 뒤의 명사나 동사가 답을 결정하므로 명사, 동사를 정확히 듣는 연습을 해야 한다. Which 의문문도 매회 2문제 정도 출제되며, 'Which+명사' 형태의 선택의문문이 많이 나오므로 Which 뒤에 나오는 명사를 잘 들어야 한다. What·Which 의문문은 Yes/No로 답할 수 없다. What 의문문의 경우, 무엇을 원하는지 묻거나 의견을 묻는 'What would you like ~?' 또는 'What do you think of ~?'와 같은 표현도 종종 출제된다.

유형 맛보기

Q **What** will the parking fee be? 주차 요금은 얼마가 될까요?
→ What 뒤의 명사와 동사를 정확히 들어야 한다.

(A) He is five feet two inches tall. 그는 키가 5피트 2인치입니다.
→ 유사 단어(fee-feet)를 이용한 오답

(B) No, he can't drive. 아니요, 그는 운전을 못 해요.
→ 의문사 의문문에 Yes/No로 응답 불가

(C) Twenty-five dollars a day. 하루에 25달러입니다.
→ 주차 요금을 묻는 질문에, 구체적인 금액으로 답한 정답

Q **Which** color do you prefer to paint the new house? 새집을 페인트 칠하기에 어떤 색을 선호하세요?
→ Which 뒤 명사(color)를 정확히 듣고 그것을 지칭하는 답변을 선택한다.

(A) The caller left a message. 전화를 건 사람이 메시지를 남겼어요.
→ 유사 단어(color-caller)를 이용한 오답

(B) Blue looks good. 파란색이 좋아 보이네요.
→ 구체적인 색깔을 언급한 정답

(C) It is not the one that I like. 이건 제가 좋아하는 게 아니에요.
→ 연상 어휘(prefer-like)로 혼동을 준 오답

☰ 풀이 접근법

● What 의문문은 What 뒤에 나오는 명사나 동사가 결정적인 단서다.

● 'Which + 명사' 의문문은 Which 뒤에 나오는 명사를 잘 듣는다. 구체적인 명사를 언급한 후 부가 설명을 하는 선택지가 정답일 확률이 높다.

● 'Which + 명사' 의문문에서 'The one ~'이 포함된 정답이 자주 등장한다.

기출 질문 & 답변 패턴

What 뒤의 명사가 답을 결정하는 유형

Q **What** color did you paint your office?
무슨 색으로 당신의 사무실을 칠했나요?

A I chose yellow.
노란색을 골랐어요.

Q **What** time does the meeting start?
회의는 몇 시에 시작하나요?

A At 9 o'clock.
9시에요.

Q **What** type of business are you in?
무슨 업종에 종사하고 계시나요?

A I work at a design company.
저는 디자인 회사에서 일합니다.

What 뒤의 동사가 답을 결정하는 유형

Q **What** will we bring to the seminar?
세미나에 우리는 무엇을 가져가야 하나요?

A Some documents.
몇 가지 서류요.

Q **What** did Tommy give you as a housewarming gift?
Tommy가 집들이 선물로 무엇을 줬나요?

A He gave me a flowerpot.
그는 화분을 줬어요.

Q **What** happened to you yesterday?
어제 당신에게 무슨 일이 있었나요?

A I lost my bag.
가방을 잃어버렸어요.

Which 뒤의 명사가 답을 결정하는 유형

Q **Which** car do you want?
어떤 차를 원하세요?

A I want the compact one.
소형차를 원해요.

Q **Which** department does he work in?
그는 어느 부서에서 일하나요?

A He works in the Marketing Department.
마케팅 부서에서 일합니다.

Q **Which** employee will be going to the meeting tomorrow?
어떤 직원이 내일 회의에 갈 건가요?

A Jeffrey will go.
Jeffrey가 갈 거예요.

'The one ~'이 답이 되는 유형

Q **Which** hotel are you staying at?
어느 호텔에서 지낼 건가요?

A The one in front of the sea.
바다 앞에 위치한 호텔이요.

Q **Which** office has a problem with its photocopier?
어느 사무실이 복사기에 문제가 있나요?

A The one next to the restroom.
화장실 옆에 있는 거요.

2. How 의문문

═ 유형 소개 및 전략

How 의문문은 매회 1~2문제가 출제된다. <How + 형용사/부사 ~?> 유형이 자주 출제되며, 이때 How 뒤에 나오는 형용사/부사가 정답을 결정하므로 How 뒤에 나오는 형용사/부사를 놓치지 않고 잘 들어야 한다. How 의문문은 Yes/No로 답할 수 없다. 그러나 권유나 제안할 때 쓰이는 'How about ~?' 같은 표현에는 That's good 등으로 승낙하거나 거절의 답변을 할 수 있다.

유형 맛보기

Q **How** long did your job interview take? 면접이 얼마나 걸렸나요?
→ How 뒤에 나오는 형용사가 답을 결정한다. 'How long ~?' 의문문은 기간과 소요 시간을 나타내는 선택지가 답이다.

(A) About the position of branch manager. 지점장 직책에 관해서요.
→ 연상 어휘(job-position)를 이용한 오답

(B) A new employee. 신입사원이요.
→ 연상 어휘(job interview-employee)를 이용한 오답

(C) Only half an hour. 겨우 30분요.
→ 면접에 걸린 시간을 묻는 질문에, 구체적인 소요 시간을 언급한 정답

Q **How** may I help you? 어떻게 도와드릴까요?
→ 권유나 제안을 하는 의문문이다.

(A) I'm looking for the mailroom. 우편물실을 찾고 있습니다.
→ 우편물실을 찾고 있는 것을 도와달라는 표현의 정답

(B) It's my pleasure. 천만에요.
→ Thank you에 적합한 응답

(C) It will be helpful for you. 당신에게 도움이 될 거예요.
→ 유사 어휘 (help-helpful)를 이용한 오답

═ 풀이 접근법

● How 의문문은 How 뒤에 나오는 형용사나 부사가 정답을 결정하는 중요 단서다.

● How 뒤에 나오는 다양한 형용사/부사와 대표적인 빈출 표현들을 숙지해 둬야 한다.

● 'How about ~?'이나 'How + 동사 + ~?'의 형태도 익혀 둬야 한다.

☰ 기출 질문 & 답변 패턴

How 뒤 형용사나 부사가 답을 결정하는 유형

Q How long have you worked for this company?
이 회사에서 얼마나 오래 일하셨나요?

A About five years.
5년 정도요.

Q How far is the bus station from here?
버스 정류장이 여기서 얼마나 멀어요?

A Only five minutes away on foot.
걸어서 5분밖에 안 걸려요.

Q How much is it for a one-way ticket?
편도 티켓은 얼마인가요?

A It's 50 dollars.
50달러입니다.

Q How often does your department hold meetings?
당신 부서는 얼마나 자주 회의를 하나요?

A Once a week.
일주일에 한 번이요.

Q How soon will you be able to deliver it?
언제쯤 배송해 주실 수 있나요?

A Before next week.
다음 주 전에요.

수단이나 방법으로 답하는 유형(by, through 이용)

Q How can I get to the airport from here?
여기에서 공항까지 어떻게 가면 되나요?

A By taxi.
택시로요.

Q How can I reach him?
그에게 어떻게 연락하죠?

A Through e-mail.
이메일로요.

권유나 출처로 답하는 유형

Q How about this desk for my new office?
저의 새 사무실에 두기에 이 책상은 어떤가요?

A Why don't you look at the other design?
다른 디자인을 보는 게 어때요?

Q How did you know about the exhibition?
전시회에 대해 어떻게 아셨나요?

A I saw an ad for it on TV.
TV에서 광고를 봤어요.

상태나 의견의 형용사로 답하는 유형

Q How was my presentation yesterday?
어제 제 연설이 어땠나요?

A It was interesting.
흥미로웠어요.

Q How do you like the new vice president?
새 부사장님은 어때요?

A He is very friendly.
그는 매우 친절해요.

3. Why 의문문

유형 소개 및 전략

Why 의문문은 매회 2~3문제가 출제된다. Why 의문문은 이유 접속사(because). 이유 전치사구(because of, due to, in order to)나 to부정사 등으로 연결된 문장이 나오면 대부분 정답이다. Why 의문문은 Yes/No로 답할 수 없다. 워크숍, 연수, 회의, 발표와 같은 회사 행사를 연기/취소하는 이유, 행사 불참 이유, 교통수단의 출발/도착 시간이 지연되는 이유, 상점이 빨리 개점/폐점하는 이유 등을 묻는 문제들이 출제된다.

유형 맛보기

Q **Why** is the office closed today? 사무실이 오늘 왜 문을 닫았나요?
→ 이유를 묻는 문제로, 이유 접속사나 to부정사가 나오는 문장을 잘 들어야 한다.

(A) It's close to the park. 그곳은 공원과 가까워요.
→ 유사 어휘(closed-close)를 이용한 오답

(B) Because it's a holiday. 휴일이거든요.
→ because를 이용해 사무실이 문을 닫은 이유를 언급한 정답

(C) Turn left and then go straight. 왼쪽으로 돌아서 직진하세요.
→ How 의문문에 적합한 오답

Q **Why** is Mr. Bell being transferred to another branch office? Bell 씨가 왜 다른 지점으로 전근 가나요?
→ 다른 지점으로 전근을 가는 이유를 묻고 있다.

(A) In Barcelona. 바르셀로나에요.
→ Where 의문문에 적합한 오답

(B) Why don't you ask the personnel director? 인사부장에게 물어보는 게 어때요?
→ 본인은 모르니 다른 사람에게 물어보라는 식의 회피형 정답

(C) Because we're understaffed. 우리의 인력이 부족하기 때문이에요.
→ Because만 보고 정답으로 혼동할 수 있으나 뒤의 내용이 맞지 않는 오답

풀이 접근법

● Why 의문문은 이유 접속사, 이유 전치사 또는 (in order) to부정사 등이 정답 보기에 등장할 가능성이 높다.

● Why 의문문 외에 'For what ~?', 'How come ~?', 'What's the reason for ~?' 등도 이유를 묻는 질문으로 나올 수 있다.

● 최근에는 because, for, so that 등이 생략된 형태가 정답으로 나오기도 한다.

🔆 기출 질문 & 답변 패턴

이유 접속사나 목적으로 답하는 유형

Q **Why** were you late?
왜 늦었어요?

A Because of a traffic jam.
교통 체증 때문에요.

Q **Why** was Mr. Hill here?
왜 Hill 씨가 여기에 있나요?

A Due to a special seminar.
특별 세미나 때문에요.

Q **Why** did you leave the office early?
왜 일찍 퇴근했어요?

A In order to go to the dentist.
치과에 가기 위해서요.

Q **Why** has the marketing director called a meeting?
왜 마케팅 부장이 회의를 소집했나요?

A Because the survey results were disappointing.
설문 조사 결과가 실망스러워서요.

변명을 하거나 우회적인 표현으로 답하는 유형

Q **Why** didn't you call me yesterday?
왜 어제 전화하지 않았나요?

A I was too busy with my project.
프로젝트로 너무 바빴어요.

Q **Why** isn't he in the office?
왜 그는 사무실에 없나요?

A He is taking a short break now.
지금 잠깐 쉬는 중이에요.

승낙이나 거절로 답하는 유형

Q **Why don't you** ask the manager?
매니저에게 물어보는 게 어때요?

A That's a good idea.
좋아요.

Q **Why don't you** take a break?
휴식을 취하는 게 어때요?

A I have to finish this work by today.
오늘까지 이 일을 끝내야 해요.

🎧 05_1 | 정답 및 해설 p.339

■ 다음을 듣고 적절한 응답을 고른 후, 빈칸을 채우세요.

1. Mark your answer.
   (A) (B) (C)

   _____ the registration _____?

   (A) It's a _____.

   (B) One of the staff members finished it.

   (C) _____ of Bull Street.

2. Mark your answer.
   (A) (B) (C)

   _____ should I use?

   (A) Only a _____.

   (B) The manager has arrived.

   (C) _____ the door.

3. Mark your answer.
   (A) (B) (C)

   What are the papers in the _____?

   (A) _____ hall beside the stairs.

   (B) A report I'm writing.

   (C) I will _____.

4. Mark your answer.
   (A) (B) (C)

   How long will it take us to _____?

   (A) I'm leaving town soon.

   (B) It _____ 7:00 P.M.

   (C) _____.

5. Mark your answer.
   (A) (B) (C)

   How can I _____ Bruce gets this form?

   (A) I will _____.

   (B) _____ his mailbox.

   (C) He is in New York now.

6. Mark your answer.
(A)   (B)   (C)

_____ to process my order?

(A) _____.

(B) No, it _____.

(C) Yes, _____ I expected.

7. Mark your answer.
(A)   (B)   (C)

_____ the office early yesterday?

(A) I had _____.

(B) I lost it this morning.

(C) _____.

8. Mark your answer.
(A)   (B)   (C)

Why is there a _____?

(A) The computer system _____.

(B) I just saw it today.

(C) Yes, _____.

9. Mark your answer.
(A)   (B)   (C)

Why _____ that calendar?

(A) Yes, I'm _____ to the meeting.

(B) It was _____.

(C) _____, I think.

10. Mark your answer.
(A)   (B)   (C)

Why is the J&J _____?

(A) Because the company _____.

(B) The restaurant is open.

(C) _____.

ACTUAL TEST

1. Mark your answer on your answer sheet.
   (A)   (B)   (C)

2. Mark your answer on your answer sheet.
   (A)   (B)   (C)

3. Mark your answer on your answer sheet.
   (A)   (B)   (C)

4. Mark your answer on your answer sheet.
   (A)   (B)   (C)

5. Mark your answer on your answer sheet.
   (A)   (B)   (C)

6. Mark your answer on your answer sheet.
   (A)   (B)   (C)

7. Mark your answer on your answer sheet.
   (A)   (B)   (C)

8. Mark your answer on your answer sheet.
   (A)   (B)   (C)

9. Mark your answer on your answer sheet.
   (A)   (B)   (C)

10. Mark your answer on your answer sheet.
    (A)   (B)   (C)

LC
PART 2

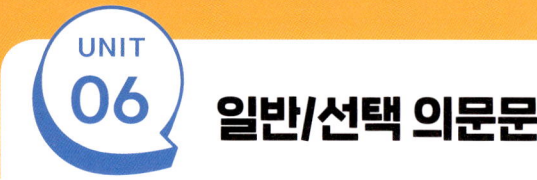

UNIT 06 일반/선택 의문문

1. 일반 의문문

유형 소개 및 전략

일반 의문문은 be동사 의문문, 조동사 의문문, Do 동사 의문문으로 나누며, 매회 7~8문제가 출제된다. 질문자와 답변자의 주어 일치 여부, 질문자의 동사와 답변자의 동사 시제 일치 여부를 확인해야 한다. 일반 의문문은 Yes/No로 응답이 가능하지만, Yes/No를 생략해서 답하는 경우도 있다. 질문에서 들렸던 유사한 발음이 들리는 선택지는 대부분 오답이다. 'I think ~, I believe ~, I suppose ~, I hope ~(내가 알기로는)'과 'Actually(사실), Certainly(확실히)' 등이 포함된 선택지가 정답으로 자주 등장한다.

유형 맛보기

Q Has the air conditioner been fixed yet? 아직 에어컨 수리되지 않았나요?
→ 일반 의문문은 주어와 동사의 시제를 잘 듣는다. 에어컨이 수리되었는지 완료 시제로 묻고 있다.

(A) The fax machine is on the desk. 팩스기는 책상 위에 있습니다.
→ 유사 어휘(fixed-fax)로 혼동을 노린 오답

(B) No, but someone's coming tomorrow. 아니요, 하지만 내일 (고치러) 사람이 올 거예요.
→ No로 답한 후, 내일 할 거라고 부가 설명한 정답

(C) They already fixed the computer. 그들이 이미 컴퓨터를 수리했어요.
→ 같은 단어(fixed)가 들리는 선택지는 거의 오답

Q Do you have a table for three? 3명이 앉을 자리가 있나요?
→ 일반 의문문은 주어와 동사의 시제를 잘 듣는다. 현재 자리가 있는지 묻고 있다.

(A) Yes, certainly. 네, 물론이죠.
→ 긍정으로 답한 정답

(B) On a label. 상표로요.
→ 유사 어휘(table-label)를 이용한 오답 함정

(C) So do I. 저도 그래요.
→ 의견에 동의하는 표현의 오답

풀이 접근법

● 질문자와 답변자의 주어가 일치되어야 한다. 선택지에 나온 인칭대명사가 어색하지 않은지 확인한다.

● 질문의 동사와 선택지에 나온 동사의 시제가 일치되었는지 확인해야 한다.

● 질문에서 들렸던 단어와 유사한 발음이 들리는 선택지는 대부분 혼동을 유도한 오답 함정이다.

≡ 기출 질문 & 답변 패턴

Yes/No로 답한 후 부가 설명하는 유형

Q Have you seen Anna today?
오늘 Anna 만났어요?

A Yes, she just left the office.
네, 방금 퇴근했어요.

Q Are you planning to go to the annual party?
연례 파티에 갈 거예요?

A No, I haven't finished my project yet.
아니요, 아직 프로젝트를 못 끝냈어요.

Yes/No를 생략하고 부가 설명만으로 답하는 유형

Q Have you heard about the new office?
새로운 사무실에 대해 들은 게 있나요?

A It must be perfect.
틀림없이 완벽할 거예요.

Q Didn't she ask you about the meeting?
그녀가 미팅에 대해 물어보지 않았나요?

A I haven't even met her.
그녀를 만나지도 못했어요.

권유, 제안, 요청 의문문에 답하는 유형

Q Would you please call the manager?
매니저에게 전화해 주시겠어요?

A Of course.
당연하죠.

Q Can you attend the meeting instead of me?
저 대신 회의에 참석해 주시겠어요?

A Sure, I would be happy to help you.
물론이죠, 기꺼이 도와드릴게요.

'그렇다/그렇지 않다'로 답하는 유형

Q Do we have to submit this report by today?
우리 오늘까지 이 보고서를 제출해야 하나요?

A I think so.
그런 것 같아요.

Q Is he the new manager of our department?
그가 우리 부서의 새로운 매니저인가요?

A That's what I believe.
제가 알기로는 그래요.

'모른다, 확인해 보겠다'로 답하는 유형

Q Have you ever visited our headquarters?
저희 본사를 방문해 본 적이 있나요?

A I haven't had a chance to yet.
아직 그럴 기회가 없었어요.

Q Is Mr. Garcia still in the meeting now?
Garcia 씨는 아직도 미팅 중인가요?

A Let me check on that for you.
확인해 볼게요.

Actually, Certainly로 답하는 유형

Q Is he the best employee at our company?
그가 우리 회사에서 가장 훌륭한 직원이에요?

A Actually, he will leave the company soon.
실은 그는 곧 우리 회사를 떠날 거예요.

Q Do you think our project will succeed?
우리 프로젝트가 성공할 거라고 생각해요?

A Certainly.
물론이죠.

LC
PART 2

2. 선택 의문문

유형 소개 및 전략

선택 의문문은 둘 중 하나를 선택하라는 질문으로, 매회 2문제 이상 출제된다. Yes나 No로 답한 선택지는 오답이다. 둘 중 하나를 선택해서 답하거나, 둘 다 좋거나 싫다고 답하거나, 둘 중 어느 쪽이든 상관없다고 답할 수 있다. 최근에는 선택 의문문에 'The one'을 이용해 답변하는 경우가 늘었다. 선택 의문문은 원칙적으로 Yes/No로 답할 수 없지만, 권유하는 문장은 예외이다. (Q: Would you care for some coffee or tea? 차나 커피 좀 드실래요? / A: Yes, please. 네, 주세요.)

유형 맛보기

Q Is it faster to go to the airport by bus **or** by train?
공항까지 버스로 가는 게 더 빠를까요, 기차로 가는 것이 더 빠를까요?
→ 선택 의문문이므로 or 앞뒤를 집중해서 듣는다.

(A) Probably by train. 아마 기차일 거예요.
→ 둘 중 하나를 선택한 정답

(B) No, I have no idea. 아니요, 모르겠어요.
→ 선택 의문문에 No로 응답 불가

(C) Yes, I think so. 맞아요, 저도 그렇게 생각해요.
→ 선택 의문문에 Yes로 응답 불가

Q Should we arrange a lunch **or** a dinner for our annual party?
우리 연례 파티를 위해 점심을 준비해야 할까요, 저녁을 준비해야 할까요?
→ 선택 의문문이므로 or 앞뒤를 집중해서 듣는다.

(A) Dinner would be better. 저녁이 좋겠네요.
→ 둘 중 하나를 선택한 정답

(B) All the employees will come. 모든 직원이 올 거예요.
→ 질문과 관련 없는 오답. All이 들어간 선택지는 오답일 확률이 높다.

(C) Yes, I will be there. 네, 제가 거기에 있을 거예요.
→ 선택 의문문에 Yes로 응답 불가

풀이 접근법

● 선택 의문문에 Yes/No로 응답할 수 없다. (권유하는 문장은 제외)

● A, B 둘 중 하나를 선택하여 답하거나, 둘 다 좋다/싫다고 답하거나, 어느 쪽이든 상관없다고 답할 수 있다.

기출 질문 & 답변 패턴

둘 중 하나를 선택해서 답하는 유형

Q Which do you prefer, black **or** white?
검정과 흰색 중 어느 것이 더 좋아요?

A Black will be good.
검정이 좋겠네요.

Q Did you meet the president **or** his secretary?
사장님을 만났나요, 아니면 그의 비서를 만났나요?

A I met his secretary.
그의 비서를 만났어요.

Q Should we meet **or** talk on the phone?
우리 만날까요, 아니면 전화로 이야기할까요?

A Let's meet up tomorrow.
내일 만나죠.

'둘 다 좋다' 또는 '둘 다 싫다'고 답하는 유형

Q Do you prefer the bigger **or** smaller furniture?
큰 가구와 작은 가구 중 어떤 게 좋아요?

A Either one will be fine.
어떤 거든 좋습니다.

Q Which would you prefer, coffee **or** tea?
커피와 차 중 어떤 게 좋아요?

A Neither, thanks.
둘 다 괜찮아요. 고마워요.

Q Where would be better to have the promotion, at the restaurant **or** at the department store?
식당이랑 백화점 중 어디에서 홍보하는 것이 나을까요?

A It doesn't matter.
어느 곳이든 상관없습니다.

제3의 제안으로 답하는 유형

Q Do you want me to send you an e-mail today **or** tomorrow?
오늘 이메일을 보내드릴까요, 아니면 내일 보내드릴까요?

A I want you to send it now.
지금 보내주셨으면 합니다.

Q Can I see Dr. Mane tomorrow **or** later this week?
Mane 씨를 내일 볼 수 있을까요, 아니면 이번 주 중으로 만날 수 있을까요?

A He is free on Thursday.
그는 목요일에 한가합니다.

모른다거나 반문으로 답하는 유형

Q Is Laurie going to the training session today **or** tomorrow?
Laurie는 오늘 교육에 가요, 아니면 내일 가요?

A She hasn't told me.
저한테 말해주지 않았어요.

Q Do you know **whether** our company will move to the new building **or not**?
우리 회사가 새로운 건물로 이전할 건지 아닌지 알아요?

A I'm not sure.
잘 모르겠습니다.

Q Which do you prefer, the traveling **or** hiking club?
여행 동호회와 등산 동호회 둘 중 뭐가 좋아요?

A Which one is better?
어떤 게 더 낫나요?

LC PART 2

■ 다음을 듣고 적절한 응답을 고른 후, 빈칸을 채우세요.

1. Mark your answer.
  (A)   (B)   (C)

_____ an apartment to rent?

(A) Yes, I just _____.

(B) It's in the _____.

(C) He asked me yesterday.

2. Mark your answer.
  (A)   (B)   (C)

_____ Paul going to the train station?

(A) No, it's not raining.

(B) Attend the _____.

(C) He was _____.

3. Mark your answer.
  (A)   (B)   (C)

_____ Mr. Smith send the papers to us yesterday?

(A) _____ here.

(B) From a newspaper article.

(C) Yes, they're _____.

4. Mark your answer.
  (A)   (B)   (C)

Will the _____ today?

(A) _____.

(B) _____.

(C) I'm sorry.

5. Mark your answer.
   (A)   (B)   (C)

_____ my home _____ work address?

(A) Yes, I will be there.

(B) He will _____ soon.

(C) Could I _____?

6. Mark your answer.
   (A)   (B)   (C)

_____ a house or renting?

(A) 110 Main Street.

(B) We're renting _____.

(C) No, it isn't.

7. Mark your answer.
   (A)   (B)   (C)

_____ dessert or coffee?

(A) He _____ yesterday.

(B) She _____.

(C) _____ coffee.

8. Mark your answer.
   (A)   (B)   (C)

Are the best seats _____ in the balcony?

(A) At the _____.

(B) I'll _____ later.

(C) You can _____ the balcony.

ACTUAL TEST

1. Mark your answer on your answer sheet.
    (A)   (B)   (C)

2. Mark your answer on your answer sheet.
    (A)   (B)   (C)

3. Mark your answer on your answer sheet.
    (A)   (B)   (C)

4. Mark your answer on your answer sheet.
    (A)   (B)   (C)

5. Mark your answer on your answer sheet.
    (A)   (B)   (C)

6. Mark your answer on your answer sheet.
    (A)   (B)   (C)

7. Mark your answer on your answer sheet.
    (A)   (B)   (C)

8. Mark your answer on your answer sheet.
    (A)   (B)   (C)

9. Mark your answer on your answer sheet.
    (A)   (B)   (C)

10. Mark your answer on your answer sheet.
    (A)   (B)   (C)

UNIT 07 제안·요청 의문문/평서문

1. 제안·요청 의문문

유형 소개 및 전략

제안·요청 의문문은 매회 2~3문제가 출제된다. 제안·요청 의문문은 승낙할 경우에는 Sure ~, Okay ~, Let's ~, That's good, That sounds great 등으로, 거절할 경우 I'm sorry ~, No thanks ~, I'm afraid ~, Thanks but ~ 등으로 답한다. 최근에는 반문하거나 기다리라는 답변이 자주 출제되고 있으며, 모른다는 답변 역시 계속 출제되고 있다.

유형 맛보기

Q **Would you like to** join our club? 저희 동호회에 가입하시겠어요?
→ 첫 3~4단어를 듣고 제안문인지 파악한다.

(A) Thanks. I'd like that. 고마워요. 그거 좋겠네요.
→ Thanks라고 한 후, 그렇게 하겠다고 한 정답

(B) No, he's not a member. 아니요, 그는 회원이 아니에요.
→ 연상 어휘(club-member)로 혼동을 노린 오답

(C) I enjoyed your meal. 맛있게 먹었습니다.
→ 질문 속 join의 유사 발음(enjoyed)을 이용한 오답

Q **Can you** call a taxi for me? 택시 좀 불러주시겠어요?
→ 첫 3~4단어를 듣고 제안문인지 파악한다.

(A) He called me last night. 그가 어젯밤 저한테 전화했어요.
→ 유사 어휘(call-called)를 이용한 오답

(B) The tax will be paid. 세금은 납부될 거예요.
→ 유사 어휘(taxi-tax)를 이용한 오답

(C) I'd be glad to. 기꺼이 그러죠.
→ 제안/요청 의문문에 동의하는 표현이 들리면 정답

풀이 접근법

- 동의/수락의 표현인 Yes, Okay, Sure, Thanks, Certainly, Absolutely 등이 포함된 선택지는 정답이다.

- 거절의 표현인 Thanks, but ~, Unfortunately, I don't think so 등의 선택지는 정답이다.

- '기꺼이 하겠다'는 뜻의 I'd be happy [glad, love, like] to ~는 정답 보기에 자주 등장한다.

- 반문하거나 '기다리라'는 뜻의 정답 보기가 자주 등장한다.

기출 질문 & 답변 패턴

'승낙'으로 답하는 유형

Q Could I read your magazine?
당신의 잡지를 볼 수 있을까요?

A Yes, it's on the table.
네, 탁자 위에 있어요.

Q Would you like to join us for dinner?
저희와 함께 저녁 식사하러 가시겠어요?

A Okay, please wait for a while.
좋아요, 잠시만 기다려 주세요.

Q Can I borrow your mobile phone for a while?
휴대전화를 잠시 빌릴 수 있을까요?

A Sure.
물론이죠.

Q Can you tell our manager that I will be late?
저희 매니저에게 제가 늦을 거라고 말씀해 주시겠어요?

A I'd be glad to tell him.
기꺼이 말해 드리죠.

Q Could you attend the meeting instead of me?
저 대신 미팅에 참석해 주시겠어요?

A I'd be happy to do it.
기꺼이 그렇게 하죠.

Q Can you help me send this e-mail?
이메일 보내는 것 좀 도와주시겠어요?

A I'd love [like] to help you.
기꺼이 도와드리겠습니다.

Q How about finishing this project?
이 프로젝트를 끝내는 게 어때요?

A That's a good idea.
좋은 생각인 것 같아요.

Q Why don't you go to the café after lunch?
점심 식사 후에 카페에 가는 게 어때요?

A That would be nice.
그게 좋겠네요.

'거절'로 답하는 유형

Q Could you tell me about the meeting?
미팅에 대해 말씀해 주시겠어요?

A Sorry, but I have to meet my client now.
죄송하지만 지금 고객을 만나야 해서요.

Q Would you like to go to the concert tomorrow?
내일 연주회에 가실래요?

A I would, but I have a previous engagement.
그러고 싶지만, 선약이 있어요.

Q Can I see Natalia?
Natalia를 만날 수 있을까요?

A Unfortunately, she just left.
안타깝게도 방금 나갔어요.

Q Are you going to attend the speech today?
오늘 연설에 참석하실 건가요?

A I don't think so.
안될 것 같네요.

'모른다, 확인해 보라, 기다리라'로 답하는 유형

Q Can we start our new project now?
지금 새로운 프로젝트를 시작해도 될까요?

A Let me check.
확인해 보겠습니다.

2. 평서문

유형 소개 및 전략

평서문은 매회 3~4문제가 출제되고 있으며, 난이도 높은 유형에 해당한다. 평서문은 동의나 맞장구칠 때, 그리고 다음에 할 일을 제시할 때 사용되는 표현들을 꼭 암기해 두어야 하고, 특히 'I will ~' 답변이 많이 출제된다. 평서문에 대해 제안이나 요청을 하는 대답도 가능하다. 평서문은 Yes/No보다는 간접적으로 답하며, 보기 중에 유사 발음이 들리면 오답일 확률이 높다.

유형 맛보기

Q I sent you the latest sales proposal. 최신 판매 제안서를 보내드렸습니다.
→ 평서문은 전체 문장을 듣고 키워드를 잘 기억해야 한다.

(A) I'll mail a letter to you. 당신에게 편지를 보낼게요.
→ Who 의문문에 적합한 오답

(B) Sorry, but we will leave soon. 죄송합니다만, 우리는 곧 떠날 거예요.
→ 질문과 맞지 않는 오답

(C) All right. I'll review it this afternoon. 알겠습니다. 오늘 오후에 검토해 보겠습니다.
→ 'I'll ~'은 평서문에서 정답 보기로 자주 등장하는 표현

Q Our call must have been disconnected. 아무래도 전화 연결이 끊어진 것 같습니다.
→ 평서문은 전체 문장을 듣고 키워드를 잘 기억해야 한다.

(A) I think you're right. 당신 말이 맞는 것 같아요.
→ Yes를 대신하는 긍정 표현으로 답한 정답

(B) Callum is having dinner with him. Callum이 그와 저녁을 할 예정이에요.
→ Who 의문문에 적합한 오답

(C) Nobody received a call. 아무도 전화를 받지 않았어요.
→ 단어 반복(call)으로 혼동을 유도한 오답

풀이 접근법

● 동의하거나 맞장구치는 의미의 선택지는 정답일 확률이 높다.

● 'I will (I'm going to) ~' 표현이 포함된 선택지는 정답일 확률이 높다.

● '잘 모르겠다'거나, 반문하는 선택지는 정답일 확률이 높다.

● 상대방에게 제안(요청)하는 선택지는 정답일 확률이 높다.

기출 질문 & 답변 패턴

반문으로 답하는 유형

Q I lost my file this morning.
오늘 아침 서류철을 잃어버렸어요.

A Is that yours?
이것이 당신 건가요?

Q I want you to send the documents to Caroline.
당신이 Caroline에게 서류들을 보내줬으면 합니다.

A Where can I find them?
서류가 어디에 있는데요?

제안·요청으로 답하는 유형

Q We should finish this project by this week.
이번 주 안으로 이 프로젝트를 끝내야 합니다.

A Okay, let's start tomorrow.
좋습니다, 내일 시작하죠.

Q Please tell Gloria about the meeting.
Gloria에게 미팅에 대해서 말해 주세요.

A Sure, what's her extension number?
물론이죠, 그녀의 내선번호가 뭐죠?

'모르겠다'로 답하는 유형

Q I'm curious why the meeting has been delayed.
회의가 왜 지연됐는지 궁금합니다.

A I don't know either.
저도 모르겠습니다.

Q I think the seminar will be held next week.
세미나가 다음 주에 열릴 것 같아요.

A Let me check for you.
제가 확인해 볼게요.

Q I wonder why Mr. Barber will change departments.
Barber 씨가 왜 부서를 옮기는지 궁금합니다.

A He didn't tell me anything.
그는 저에게 알려주지 않았어요.

Q The president will announce the new policy.
사장님이 새로운 정책을 발표할 거예요.

A Actually, that hasn't been decided yet.
사실, 아직 결정되지 않았습니다.

사실이나 의견으로 답하는 유형

Q The meeting was very boring today.
오늘 회의는 매우 따분했어요.

A Yes, but at least it finished early.
네, 하지만 어쨌든 일찍 끝났잖아요.

Q Dora will leave the company soon.
Dora는 곧 회사를 떠날 거예요.

A I'll miss her a lot.
그녀가 많이 그리울 거예요.

■ 다음을 듣고 적절한 응답을 고른 후, 빈칸을 채우세요.

1. Mark your answer.
   (A)   (B)   (C)

_____ see our latest catalog?

(A) I'll _____.

(B) In five categories.

(C) Do you _____?

2. Mark your answer.
   (A)   (B)   (C)

_____ an idea for a new product?

(A) _____.

(B) I _____ for you.

(C) I'd be glad to _____.

3. Mark your answer.
   (A)   (B)   (C)

_____ travel together?

(A) At the _____.

(B) When _____?

(C) I don't want to _____.

4. Mark your answer.
   (A)   (B)   (C)

Can you _____ with this project?

(A) Sure, I'll be _____.

(B) We _____ a document.

(C) I _____.

PART 2

LC

5. Mark your answer.
(A)　(B)　(C)

Today's meeting shouldn't _____.

(A) I _____.

(B) What will we _____?

(C) This is _____.

6. Mark your answer.
(A)　(B)　(C)

The copy machine is making _____.

(A) I waited for you.

(B) You _____.

(C) I think _____.

7. Mark your answer.
(A)　(B)　(C)

Maybe we should _____.

(A) It's _____.

(B) Okay, let's do that.

(C) No. I don't _____.

8. Mark your answer.
(A)　(B)　(C)

I _____ this window latch.

(A) It _____ 7:00 P.M.

(B) I _____ an attachment.

(C) Let me _____.

ACTUAL TEST

1. Mark your answer on your answer sheet.
   (A)   (B)   (C)

2. Mark your answer on your answer sheet.
   (A)   (B)   (C)

3. Mark your answer on your answer sheet.
   (A)   (B)   (C)

4. Mark your answer on your answer sheet.
   (A)   (B)   (C)

5. Mark your answer on your answer sheet.
   (A)   (B)   (C)

6. Mark your answer on your answer sheet.
   (A)   (B)   (C)

7. Mark your answer on your answer sheet.
   (A)   (B)   (C)

8. Mark your answer on your answer sheet.
   (A)   (B)   (C)

9. Mark your answer on your answer sheet.
   (A)   (B)   (C)

10. Mark your answer on your answer sheet.
    (A)   (B)   (C)

LC PART 2

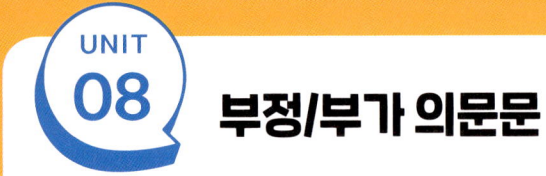

부정/부가 의문문

1. 부정 의문문

☰ 유형 소개 및 전략

부정 의문문은 매회 1~2문제가 출제되며, not을 포함한 be동사 혹은 조동사로 시작하는 의문문이다. 상대방의 동의를 구하거나 사실 여부를 확인하는 유형으로, 답변으로는 주로 <Yes/No + 부연 설명> 또는 Yes/No를 함축한 내용으로 나온다. 질문의 not을 제외한 내용에 대해 일반 의문문과 같은 방식으로 답하면 된다.

유형 맛보기

Q Aren't you going to work out at the gym tonight? 오늘 밤 헬스클럽에 운동하러 안 가요?
→ 부정어 Not을 제외한 키워드인 going to work out tonight에 집중한다.

(A) He doesn't fit in with that group. 그는 그 그룹과 어울리지 않아요.
→ 연상 어휘(work out-fit)로 혼동을 유도한 오답

(B) You should be able to walk there. 거기까지 걸어갈 수 있을 거예요.
→ 유사 발음(work-walk)을 이용한 오답

(C) No, I won't have time. 아니요, 시간이 없을 것 같아요.
→ 오늘 밤 운동하러 안 가냐는 질문에, 시간이 없다며 부정적으로 답변한 정답

Q Didn't you get Mr. Miller's e-mail this morning? 오늘 아침에 Miller 씨의 이메일을 받지 않았나요?
→ 부정어 Not을 제외한 키워드인 did you get e-mail에 집중한다.

(A) I'll mail it to him. 제가 그에게 메일을 보낼게요.
→ 유사 어휘(e-mail-mail)을 이용한 오답

(B) No, I never received it. 아니요, 못 받았어요.
→ 메일을 받았냐는 질문에, 부정적으로 답변한 정답

(C) By phone. 전화로요.
→ How 의문문에 대한 답변으로 어울리는 오답

☰ 풀이 접근법

● 질문이 부정형으로 시작하는지 확인한다.

● Not을 제외한 내용에 대해, 긍정이면 Yes, 부정이면 No로 답한다.

● Yes 또는 No가 함축되어 질문과 내용이 어울리는 보기를 고른다.

● '모른다'는 응답을 비롯해, 질문의 의도에 따라 다양한 반응이 답이 될 수 있음에 유의한다.

기출 질문 & 답변 패턴

Yes/No를 포함해 답하는 유형

Q Isn't it supposed to rain tonight?
오늘 밤에 비가 오기로 되어 있지 않나요?

A Yes, so you should take your umbrella.
맞아요, 그래서 우산을 챙겨야 해요.

Q Isn't the seminar scheduled for next week?
세미나가 다음 주로 예정되어 있지 않나요?

A No, it's this Friday.
아니요, 이번 금요일이에요.

Q Aren't you coming to the party?
파티에 안 올 거예요?

A Yes, are you going, too?
갈 거예요, 당신도 갈 거죠?

Q Don't you supervise the warehouse in Boston?
보스턴에 있는 창고를 관리하지 않나요?

A No, I quit last month.
아뇨, 지난달에 그만뒀어요.

Yes/No를 생략해서 답하는 유형

Q Haven't you made a reservation yet?
아직 예약 안 했어요?

A Actually, I just did.
실은, 지금 막 했어요.

Q Didn't you sign the contract?
계약서에 서명하지 않았어요?

A Well, it will be finalized tomorrow.
음, 내일 마무리될 거예요.

Q Shouldn't we buy tickets in advance?
표를 미리 사야 하지 않나요?

A I don't think we need to.
그럴 필요 없을 것 같아요.

제3의 답변으로 답하는 경우

Q Aren't you supposed to be at work now?
지금 일하고 계셔야 하지 않나요?

A Actually, I'm off today.
사실, 오늘 쉬는 날이에요.

Q Aren't we meeting with the client tomorrow?
우리 내일 고객과 만나지 않나요?

A I'm not sure. I'll need to check the schedule.
잘 모르겠어요. 일정을 확인해야 해요.

Q Didn't he file the tax return last month?
그가 지난달에 세금 신고를 하지 않았나요?

A I'll ask him later.
제가 나중에 물어볼게요.

Q Didn't you receive the memo from headquarters?
본사에서 온 회람 못 받았어요?

A When did they send it?
그들이 언제 보냈는데요?

2. 부가 의문문

유형 소개 및 전략

부가 의문문은 매회 1~2문제가 출제된다. 평서문 끝에 did[didn't] you?/ is[isn't] she?/ have[haven't] you? 등의 꼬리 질문이 붙는 형태로, 사실을 확인하거나 상대방의 동의를 구하는 의문문이다. 주로 <Yse/No + 부연 설명> 또는 Yes/No를 우회적으로 표현하는 응답이 나온다. 일반적인 형태의 정답뿐 아니라, '확인해 보겠다'며 모른다는 답변도 자주 등장한다.

유형 맛보기

Q Dinner yesterday was delicious, **wasn't it**? 어제 저녁식사는 정말 맛있었어요, 그렇죠?

→ 꼬리 질문의 형태와 상관없이 평서문의 내용이 긍정이면 Yes, 부정이면 No로 대답한다.

(A) No, he's the new manager. 아니요, 그는 새로운 매니저입니다.

→ 인칭 대명사(it-he) 오류 오답

(B) On Monday, I think. 월요일인 것 같아요.

→ When 의문문의 응답으로 적절한 오답

(C) Yes, the pizza was great. 네, 피자가 훌륭했죠.

→ 긍정의 Yes 이후 특정 메뉴가 맛있었다고 부연 설명한 정답

Q The clothing sale lasts until Friday, **doesn't it**? 의류 세일이 금요일까지죠?

→ 꼬리 질문의 형태와 상관없이 평서문의 내용이 긍정이면 Yes, 부정이면 No로 대답한다.

(A) It needs the original receipt. 영수증 원본이 필요합니다.

→ 연상 어휘(sale-receipt)로 혼동을 유도한 오답

(B) I'll try them on. 제가 한번 입어 볼게요.

→ 연상 어휘(clothing-try on)로 혼동을 유도한 오답

(C) No, it ends on Thursday. 아니요, 목요일에 끝나요.

→ 부정의 No 이후 부연 설명한 정답

풀이 접근법

● 부정 의문문과 마찬가지로, 긍정/부정과 상관 없이 답변의 내용이 긍정이면 Yes, 부정이면 No로 답한다.

● Yes/No로 응답한 후, 이어지는 부연 설명이 질문의 내용과 일치하지 않는 오답 함정에 유의한다.

☰ 기출 질문 & 답변 패턴

Yes/No를 포함해 답하는 유형

Q That meeting was boring, **isn't it**?
회의가 지루했어요, 그렇지 않나요?

A Yes, it was longer than I thought.
네, 제가 생각했던 것보다 더 길었어요.

Q You've finished the project, **haven't you**?
프로젝트를 끝냈죠, 그렇죠?

A Yes, I completed it this morning.
네, 오늘 아침에 마쳤어요.

Q She hasn't submitted the report yet, **has she**?
그녀는 아직 보고서를 제출하지 않았죠, 그렇죠?

A No, she's still working on it.
아니요, 아직 작업 중이에요.

Q They haven't released the new product, **have they**?
그들이 아직 신제품을 출시하지 않았죠, 그렇죠?

A No, it's still in development.
아니요, 아직 개발 중이에요.

Yes/No를 생략해서 답하는 유형

Q You've read the proposal, **haven't you**?
제안서 읽었죠, 그렇죠?

A It was very thorough.
매우 완벽했어요.

Q You've already booked the flights, **haven't you**?
이미 항공편을 예약했죠, 그렇죠?

A Everything is confirmed.
모든 것이 확정됐어요.

Q You haven't found someone to replace Mr. Kim yet, **have you**? Kim 씨를 대체할 누군가를 아직 못 찾았죠, 그렇죠?

A We finally hired someone last week.
우리는 마침내 지난주에 누군가를 고용했어요.

우회적으로 답하는 유형

Q You haven't seen the latest update, **have you**?
최신 업데이트를 못 봤죠, 그렇죠?

A I haven't had the chance yet.
아직 그럴 기회가 없었어요.

Q We're receiving our bonuses this month, **right**?
우리 이번 달에 보너스 받죠, 그렇죠?

A I haven't heard that.
그런 얘기 못 들었는데요.

Q You heard about Paul's promotion to supervisor, **didn't you**?
Paul이 매니저로 승진한다는 소식 들었죠, 그렇죠?

A He really deserves it.
그는 그럴만한 자격이 있죠.

■ 다음을 듣고 적절한 응답을 고른 후, 빈칸을 채우세요.

1. Mark your answer.
   (A)   (B)   (C)

_____ Rosa Sanchez the most experienced candidate?

(A) _____ interviews.

(B) No, she just _____ university.

(C) In the _____.

2. Mark your answer.
   (A)   (B)   (C)

_____ Emma usually leave at 6:00?

(A) Yes, but she's working _____.

(B) Actually, I think she does _____.

(C) It shouldn't _____.

3. Mark your answer.
   (A)   (B)   (C)

_____ new copier become a bestseller?

(A) _____ the start button.

(B) Thanks for the _____.

(C) No, but it's gaining _____.

4. Mark your answer.
   (A)   (B)   (C)

Isn't the budget report _____?

(A) You've been a _____.

(B) The budget committee has _____.

(C) I'm _____ that.

5. Mark your answer.
(A)   (B)   (C)

The packaging machine was repaired yesterday,
_____?

(A) No, _____ tomorrow.

(B) Several large packages.

(C) Yes, I have _____.

6. Mark your answer.
(A)   (B)   (C)

I really liked the job candidate we _____.
Didn't you?

(A) _____ tomorrow.

(B) Yes, I think _____ her the position.

(C) I _____ of my résumé.

7. Mark your answer.
(A)   (B)   (C)

The prototype will _____ next Monday,
right?

(A) Yes, I can type.

(B) No, we need _____.

(C) I read that book _____.

8. Mark your answer.
(A)   (B)   (C)

You get your bank statements online, _____?

(A) No, a _____.

(B) It's a _____.

(C) I do, but they are _____.

ACTUAL TEST

08_2 | 정답 및 해설 p.349

1. Mark your answer on your answer sheet.
   (A)   (B)   (C)

2. Mark your answer on your answer sheet.
   (A)   (B)   (C)

3. Mark your answer on your answer sheet.
   (A)   (B)   (C)

4. Mark your answer on your answer sheet.
   (A)   (B)   (C)

5. Mark your answer on your answer sheet.
   (A)   (B)   (C)

6. Mark your answer on your answer sheet.
   (A)   (B)   (C)

7. Mark your answer on your answer sheet.
   (A)   (B)   (C)

8. Mark your answer on your answer sheet.
   (A)   (B)   (C)

9. Mark your answer on your answer sheet.
   (A)   (B)   (C)

10. Mark your answer on your answer sheet.
    (A)   (B)   (C)

필수 표현 **PART 2 빈출 오답 유형**

① Yes/No로 응답한 오답

의문사 의문문은 Yes, Sure, Okay와 같은 긍정적 응답이나, No, Not at all과 같은 부정적 응답을 할 수 없다.

> **질문** **Who**'s retiring next month? 내년에 누가 은퇴하죠?
>
> **오답** **No**, we're not tired. 아니요, 우리는 피곤하지 않아요.
>
> **정답** I believe Rachel is. Rachel이라고 생각해요.

② 다른 의문사에 대해 응답한 오답

질문에 사용된 의문사가 아닌 다른 의문사에 대한 응답이 오답 보기로 나오기도 한다. 질문의 의문사와 키워드를 명확히 기억해야 이러한 오답을 피할 수 있다.

> **질문** **Where** is the nearest bank around here? 근처에 가장 가까운 은행이 어디에 있죠?
>
> **오답** **Three years ago.** 3년 전에요. (의문사 When에 대한 응답)
>
> **정답** On the next corner. 다음 모퉁이에요.

③ 유사 발음, 단어 반복, 파생어를 이용한 오답

질문에서 들린 어휘와 발음이 동일하거나 유사한 단어, 혹은 파생어를 이용한 오답이 등장한다. 하지만 이러한 보기가 간혹 정답이 될 수도 있으니 무조건 소거하면 안 된다.

> **질문** Can we **walk** to the bus station, or should we drive?
> 버스 역에 걸어서 갈 수 있나요, 아니면 운전해서 가야 하나요?
>
> **오답** We **work** at the bank. 저희는 은행에서 일합니다.
>
> **정답** I think we should **drive**. 운전해야 할 것 같습니다.

▶ **토익 함정으로 자주 나오는 유사 발음 어휘**

coffee 커피	—	copy 복사(하다)
closing 폐쇄	—	clothing 옷
work 일하다	—	walk 걷다
arrive 도착하다	—	drive 운전하다
(the) apartment 아파트	—	department 부서
contact 연락하다	—	contract 계약
(to) rain 비가 내리다	—	train 기차
movie 영화	—	move 움직이다

질문	Could you **give** me a ride to the airport? 저 좀 공항까지 태워 주실 수 있나요?
오답	No, I didn't **give** him any. 아니요, 저는 그에게 아무것도 주지 않았어요.
정답	Sure, what time is your flight? 물론이죠, 몇 시 비행기죠?

질문	Which **printer** should we order? 어떤 프린터를 주문해야 하죠?
오답	**Print** your name here. 여기에 이름을 써주세요.
정답	Let's get the latest model. 최신 모델로 합시다.

④ 다의어를 이용한 오답

질문의 특정 단어가 서로 다른 의미로 쓰여 오답 보기에 나오기도 한다.

질문	Who's in **charge** of designing the item? 이 물건은 디자인을 누가 담당하나요?
오답	There's no **charge** for that. 그것에 대한 수수료는 없습니다.
정답	Our production department. 저희 생산 부서요.
	(질문의 charge는 '책임'을, 오답 보기의 charge는 '요금, 수수료'를 뜻한다.)

▶ **토익 함정으로 자주 나오는 다의어**

charge	담당; 비용; 청구(하다)	order	순서; 주문하다
park	공원; 주차하다	last	지난; 지속되다
hand	손, 도움; 건네주다	light	전등; 가벼운
book	책; 예약하다	review	비평; 검토하다
store	상점; 보관하다	leave	휴가; 떠나다
board	이사회; 탑승하다	change	잔돈; 바꾸다
carry	나르다; 취급하다	watch	시계; 보다
face	얼굴; 직면하다	train	기차; 교육하다
check	수표; 점검하다	break	휴식; 고장 나다
work	작품; 작동하다	address	주소; 다루다
meet	만나다; 충족시키다	close	닫다; 가까운
free	자유로운; 무료의	firm	회사; 확실한

⑤ 연상 어휘를 이용한 오답

질문에 쓰인 특정 단어에서 연상되는 어휘가 오답 보기에 나오기도 한다. 다만, 응답 패턴이 다양해진 만큼 정답에도 나올 가능성이 있으므로 보기를 듣기 전에 질문을 정확히 파악하는 데 중점을 두도록 한다.

> **질문** What are we ordering for **lunch**? 점심으로 뭘 주문할까요?
>
> **오답** Near the **café** on Main Street. 메인 가에 있는 카페 근처에요.
>
> **정답** How about Italian food? 이탈리아 음식 어때요?

⑥ 주어 불일치 오답

질문의 주어와 일치하지 않는 주어가 언급된 오답이 나오기도 한다.

> **질문** Can **you** tell me when **the meeting** starts? 회의가 언제 시작하는지 말씀해 주시겠어요?
>
> **오답** **She** started at a young age. 그녀는 젊은 나이에 시작했어요.
>
> **정답** It begins at eight. 8시에 시작해요.
>
> (질문의 주어는 you와 the meeting, 오답 보기는 She가 주어로, 서로 일치하지 않는다.)

⑦ 대명사/시제 불일치 오답

의문사 의문문에서는 질문과 답변의 시제가 일치하는 것이 원칙이다. 다만, 일반 의문문에서 부연 설명의 시제는 질문의 시제와 일치하지 않는 경우도 있다.

> **질문** When **can we schedule** an appointment? 우리가 약속을 언제 정할 수 있나요?
>
> **오답** **It was** last week. 그것은 지난주였습니다.
>
> **정답** I'm available after 6. 저는 6시 이후가 괜찮습니다.
>
> (질문의 시제는 현재 혹은 미래이므로 답변의 시제는 과거 시제가 될 수 없다.)

PART

3

짧은 대화

LC

두 사람, 혹은 세 사람이 나누는 대화를 듣고 이와 관련된 세 개의 문제를 푸는 유형으로, 32~70번까지 총 13세트 39문항이 출제된다.

구성	PART	유형	문항 수	시간	배점
Listening Comprehension	1	사진 묘사	6	45분	495점
	2	질의 응답	25		
	3	**짧은 대화**	**39**		
	4	짧은 담화	30		

 문제 유형

- **전체 내용을 묻는 문제** 주제/목적, 대화가 이루어지는 장소, 화자들의 직업/업종, 근무지
- **세부 내용을 묻는 문제** 세부사항, 문제점/걱정거리, 화자의 요청/제안/추천 사항, 화자의 의도 파악, 앞으로 할 일/다음에 일어날 일, 시각 정보 연계

 대화 패턴 및 질문 유형

빈출 대화 유형	질문 순서별 빈출 유형	
· 문의, 정보 요구 · 약속 잡기 및 일정 변경 · 예약, 주문, 취소, 변경 · 뉴스, 정보 · 영업, 판매, 거래 · 사람에 대한 정보 · 매뉴얼, 사용법 · 길 안내, 위치 안내 · 지연, 교통체증, 공사	① 첫 번째 문제	주제(subject)나 목적(purpose), 남자(the man)/여자(the woman)의 신분/직업, 장소 등 해당 대화에 대한 기본적인 사항을 묻는다. 보통 대화의 도입부에서 정답 단서가 제시된다.
	② 두 번째 문제	구체적인 행위나 장소, 시간, 이유, 수단, 방법 등을 묻는다. 대화에서 언급되고 있는 구체적인 내용과 관련된 정보를 묻는다. 보통 대화의 중반부에 정답 단서가 제시된다.
	③ 세 번째 문제	앞으로의 행동 또는 제안, 요청 등에 관한 문제가 나온다. 남자와 여자의 미래 행동과 관련된 내용을 묻거나 상대방에게 제안, 요청하는 사항들이 질문으로 등장한다. 대화 후반부에서 정답 단서를 찾아야 한다.

 최신 출제 경향

① 문제 유형별

세부사항 유형의 출제 비율이 가장 높고, 주제/목적 및 장소/직업을 묻는 문제가 30% 내외로 출제된다. 매회 의도 파악 문제가 2문항, 시각 정보 연계 문제(62-70번 사이)가 3문항씩 나온다.

② 대화 내용별

업무 관련 대화가 주를 이루며, 쇼핑, 교통, 부동산 등 일상생활과 관련하여 다양한 내용이 등장한다.

풀이 전략

PART 3는 듣기와 읽기 능력을 모두 요하는 영역이다. 듣기와 읽기를 동시에 하는 것은 쉽지 않기 때문에, 반드시 대화를 듣기 전에 질문 및 보기를 읽어 두어야 한다. 보통 문제 순서에 맞춰 대화 속 정답 단서가 차례대로 주어지므로, 질문을 보고 대화의 흐름을 예상해 보는 것도 도움이 된다.

STEP 1 질문과 키워드를 파악한다.

문제를 읽으면서 키워드에 표시해 둔다.

키워드 1: man/woman/speaker(s)
키워드 2: 질문에 제시된 핵심 단어(고유명사, 특정 명사 및 동사, 시간, 날짜, 요일 등)

STEP 2 대화를 듣기 전에 핵심 내용을 추측한다.

문제와 보기의 키워드를 표시하면서 미리 읽어 두면 어떤 내용이 나올지 추측할 수 있다.

STEP 3 문제 순서와 문제에 대한 힌트가 나오는 순서는 대부분 일치한다.

대화 전반부 대화의 화두를 던지고 대화가 펼쳐지는 장소, 화자들의 신분에 대한 정보 등이 제시	**첫 번째 문제 힌트** (보기를 보고 있다가 힌트가 들리면 바로 정답 체크)
↓	↓
대화 중반부 화제에 대한 구체적인 정보, 즉 문제 상황, 요청 내용, 기타 세부사항 등이 제시	**두 번째 문제 힌트** (보기를 보고 있다가 힌트가 들리면 바로 정답 체크)
↓	↓
대화 후반부 대화를 마무리하며 앞으로의 계획이나 요청 사항 등을 언급	**마지막 문제 힌트** (보기를 보고 있다가 힌트가 들리면 바로 정답 체크)
3문제를 읽어주고 정답을 선택할 시간을 준다. (문제 간 간격 8초)	대화가 끝남과 동시에 정답 체크를 끝내고, 남은 시간 약 24초 동안 다음 문제를 미리 읽는다.

STEP 4 대화가 끝난 후, 성우가 세 개의 문제를 읽는 동안 다음 문제 파악으로 넘어간다.

UNIT 09 주제·목적/대화 장소 문제

1. 주제·목적 문제

유형 소개 및 전략

주제나 목적을 찾는 문제는 매회 4문제 정도 출제된다. 첫 번째 화자가 화두를 꺼내면서 그와 관련된 내용의 대화가 이어지므로 90% 이상 대화 초반부에서 정답 단서가 언급된다.

유형 맛보기

W Have you heard that **Mr. Scott wants to change the packaging materials for our new laptop samples?**
→ 첫 번째 대화문에서 현재 논의 중인 것은 '포장'에 관한 것임을 알 수 있다.

여 Scott 씨가 우리의 새로운 노트북 샘플의 포장 재질을 바꾸고 싶어 한다는 거 들었어요?

M No, I haven't heard about that yet. When do we need to finish the work?

남 아니요, 아직 못 들었어요. 그 작업을 언제까지 끝내야 하나요?

W Well, the laptop will be officially launched on June 1, so all of them will have to be ready by then.

여 글쎄요, 노트북은 공식적으로 6월 1일에 출시될 예정이라 그때까지 준비되어야 해요.

M Okay, I'll contact our supplier.

남 알겠어요. 제가 공급처에 연락해 볼게요.

Q. What are the speakers discussing?

(A) A new store opening
(B) The price of a new product
(C) Packaging some samples
(D) Changing suppliers

화자들은 무엇을 논의하고 있는가?

(A) 새로운 점포 개업
(B) 신제품의 가격
(C) 샘플 포장
(D) 업체 교체

풀이 접근법

● 대화 시작 전에 문제와 보기의 키워드를 빨리 파악하고 대화를 들어야 한다.

● 주제와 목적을 묻는 문제의 단서는 보통 대화 첫 부분에 언급된다. 대화의 도입부를 듣고 파악하기 어려운 난이도 높은 문제의 경우, 대화의 전체 내용을 듣고 적절한 답을 선택해야 한다.

☰ 기출 질문 & 답변 패턴

주제/목적을 묻는 질문 유형

- Why is the man calling? 남자는 왜 전화하는가?
- What are the speakers talking about? 화자들은 무엇을 이야기하고 있는가?
- What is the topic[subject] of the report? 보고서의 주제는 무엇인가?
- What is the purpose[topic] of the conversation? 대화의 목적[주제]는 무엇인가?
- What are the speakers discussing? 화자들은 무엇을 논의하고 있는가?
- What is the conversation mainly about? 대화는 주로 무엇에 대한 것인가?
- What is the purpose of the event? 행사의 목적은 무엇인가?
- What is the purpose of the woman's call? 여자가 전화를 건 목적은 무엇인가?

주제/목적을 나타내는 단서 표현

LC PART 3

바람/희망	• **I'd like to ~. / I want to ~. / I hope to ~.** **I'd like to** talk to her about the orientation for our new salespeople. 그녀와 영업직 신입사원 오리엔테이션에 관해 이야기하고 싶은데요.
용건	• **I need to ~. / We should[have to] ~.** **I need to** cancel my appointment for an eye exam on Wednesday. 수요일의 눈 검사 예약을 취소하려고요.
전화한 목적	• **I'm calling about ~. / I'm calling to ~. / I'm calling because ~.** **I'm calling to** check on your baggage policy. 귀사의 수하물 정책을 확인하려고 전화했어요.
질문	• **Did you hear ~? / Have you heard ~?** **Did you hear** the news about our company's merger with Cello Electronics? 우리 회사가 Cello Electronics 사와 합병할 거라는 소식 들으셨나요?

2. 대화 장소 문제

유형 소개 및 전략

대화 장소를 묻는 문제는 매회 6문제 정도 출제되며, 대화문의 도입부에서 대부분 정답을 유추할 수 있으므로 첫 부분에 주목해야 한다.

유형 맛보기

M I can't believe I'm here on time! My car wouldn't start this morning, so I had to take the bus, which usually takes about fifteen minutes longer.

남 늦지 않게 도착했다니 믿을 수 없네요! 오늘 아침에 차에 시동이 안 걸려서 버스를 타야 했는데, 버스는 보통 15분 정도 더 걸리거든요.

W It's a good thing you made it in. The meeting is in half an hour. **I'm just wondering if we should use the meeting room instead of this office.** → 여자가 회의 시작 시각을 알려 주며 사무실 대신 회의실을 사용하는 게 좋겠다고 제안하는 것으로 보아, 두 사람은 현재 사무실에 있음을 알 수 있다.

여 제시간에 도착해서 다행이에요. 회의는 30분 후에 시작해요. 여기 사무실 대신 회의실을 사용해야 하지 않을까요?

M You're right. Let's take some refreshments and all the handouts over there.

남 맞아요. 다과와 유인물을 모두 거기로 가져가죠.

Q. Where does this conversation most likely take place?

(A) At an office
(B) At a bakery
(C) At a newsstand
(D) At a café

이 대화는 어디에서 이루어지는 것 같은가?

(A) 사무실에서
(B) 빵집에서
(C) 신문 가판대에서
(D) 카페에서

풀이 접근법

- 대화 시작 전에 문제와 키워드를 빨리 파악하고 들어야 한다. 대화 장소를 찾는 문제는 대화 중에 현재 장소를 유추할 수 있는 단서가 제시된다. 따라서 평소에 특정 장소 관련 키워드에 대한 정리가 필요하다.

- 대화 장소를 묻는 문제는 대화의 초반부에 직접적인 단서가 등장한다.

- 전반부에서 단서를 놓쳤다면 대화 전체에서 들리는 장소 관련 어휘를 종합해서 답을 유추한다.

☰ 기출 질문 & 답변 패턴

장소를 묻는 질문 유형

- Where are the speakers? 화자들은 어디에 있는가?
- Where do the speakers work? 화자들은 어디서 일하는가?
- Where does this conversation take place? 대화는 어디에서 이루어지고 있는가?
- Where does this conversation most likely take place? 대화는 어디에서 이루어지는 것 같은가?
- Where do the speakers most likely work? 화자들은 어디에서 근무할 것 같은가?
- Where does the woman most likely work? 여자는 어디에서 근무할 것 같은가?
- Where is the technical services office located? 기술 지원부는 어디에 있는가?
- What type of company do the speakers most likely work for? 화자들은 어떤 회사에서 일하겠는가?

장소 관련 어휘

museum 박물관	exhibit 전시물 painting 그림 pottery 도자기 curator 관장
airport 공항	departure 출발 landing 착륙 boarding 탑승 gate 탑승 게이트 check-in counter 짐 부치는 곳 customs 세관 cabin 기내 cart 카트 boarding pass 탑승권 carry-on baggage 기내용 짐
post office 우체국	mail 우편물 package 소포 parcel 소포 express mail 속달 우편 courier 배달원 courier service 택배 서비스 fragile 깨지기 쉬운
restaurant 식당	special 특선요리 menu 메뉴 dish 접시 chef 요리사 cafeteria 구내식당 plate 접시
hotel 호텔	room 객실 single 1인실 double 2인실 suite 특실 check in 체크인하다 check out 체크아웃하다
library 도서관	librarian 사서 check out 대출하다 overdue 마감이 지난 late fee 연체료
bookstore 서점	aisle 통로, 복도 section 구간 writer/author 작가 book signing 책 사인회
hospital 병원 **/ pharmacy** 약국	physician 의사 examine 진찰하다 prescribe 처방하다 dentist 치과의사 fill 조제하다 pick up 약을 찾다 take pills 약을 먹다 dose 복용량
real estate agency 부동산	apartment 아파트 property 부동산 real estate 부동산 landlord 집주인 tenant 세입자 deposit 보증금
bank 은행	account 계좌 balance 잔고 teller 창구직원 loan 대출 deposit 입금하다 transfer money 송금하다 ATM 현금인출기
house 집	plumber 배관공 electrician 전기공 toilet 변기 faucet 수도꼭지 sink 세면대 leak 새다 install 설치하다 electricity 전기 light bulb 전구 wire 전선 power 전기
travel agency 여행사	itinerary 일정 accommodations 숙박 book 예약하다 cancel 취소하다 reserve 예약하다

■ 음원을 듣고 답을 고르세요. 다시 들으면서 빈칸을 채우세요.

1. What is the conversation about?
(A) Using a computer program
(B) Purchasing a new computer
(C) Inviting customers
(D) Hiring requirements

M　How are you doing with the computer program
_____ customer data?

W　I'm quite _____ it. I did the same kind of
data entry _____.

M　_____ really great! If you have any
problems, don't _____ call me.

2. What is the purpose of the woman's call?
(A) To place an order
(B) To ask for repairs
(C) To buy a new refrigerator
(D) To confirm a delivery

W　Hello. I bought a refrigerator _____
this morning, and I heard from the store that
_____ my new refrigerator today.

M　Yes, we will. You are Ms. Jackson, right?

W　Yes, I am. Can you _____ my old
refrigerator as well?

M　Sure. There will be _____ for that service
though.

3. What type of company do the speakers most likely work for?
(A) An advertising company
(B) An office supply store
(C) A printing company
(D) A sporting-goods manufacturer

W　I can't believe the trouble we had _____
the design for our new logo. It seemed to _____.

M:　Yes, but the _____. It sums up exactly
what our _____: It looks both sporty and
dependable.

W　Yes, and it _____ both small on our
letterhead and large on our products. Look at these
badminton rackets and our new treadmills. They
_____!

ACTUAL TEST

1. Why is the man calling?

   (A) To make a reservation
   (B) To change his seat
   (C) To confirm a reservation
   (D) To make a payment

2. What does the man ask for?

   (A) A discount
   (B) A window seat
   (C) An aisle seat
   (D) A vegetarian meal

3. According to the conversation, what will the man probably do next?

   (A) Provide his personal information
   (B) Pay for his plane ticket
   (C) Go to the airport
   (D) Call another airline

4. What are the speakers discussing?

   (A) The retirement of a staff member
   (B) The hiring of a new manager
   (C) The financial difficulties of the company
   (D) The inauguration of the new president

5. What position does Victor have at the company?

   (A) Director
   (B) Manager
   (C) Supervisor
   (D) President

6. What does the man ask the woman to do?

   (A) Take Victor's position
   (B) Find a new employee
   (C) Train the new staff member
   (D) Interview a job applicant

7. Where is this conversation most likely taking place?

   (A) At an office
   (B) At a healthcare seminar
   (C) At a fitness center
   (D) At a sporting goods store

8. What do the men say about the new facility?

   (A) It has some secondhand sports equipment.
   (B) It was more crowded on the first floor.
   (C) It has been upgraded in many ways.
   (D) It has more expensive machines than before.

9. What does the woman say she will do?

   (A) Visit the first floor
   (B) Go to a facility
   (C) Work out at the park
   (D) Call a fitness center

10. Where most likely are the speakers?

    (A) At a bank
    (B) At a clothing shop
    (C) At a restaurant
    (D) At a shoe store

11. What does the woman ask for?

    (A) Different patterns
    (B) Something longer
    (C) A unique design
    (D) Some other colors

12. What is the man going to do next?

    (A) Offer a reduced rate
    (B) Call other stores
    (C) Refund a purchase
    (D) Get some more items

LC PART 3

UNIT 10 세부사항/다음에 할 일 문제

1. 세부사항 문제

≡ 유형 소개 및 전략

다양한 의문사로 '누가, 언제, 어디서, 무엇을, 어떻게, 왜'에 해당하는 세부 정보를 묻는 문제로, 매회 12문제 정도 출제된다. 문제 및 보기의 키워드가 대화에 그대로 또는 패러프레이징되어 등장하므로, 문제를 먼저 읽어 키워드를 파악한 후 듣는 것이 유리하다. 특히, 화자가 언급한 내용을 묻는 질문의 경우, say/mention 뒤에 나오는 단어나 구문이 키워드이므로 집중해서 들어야 한다.

유형 맛보기

W Hi, Philip. I found a really nice office space for our new startup. It's in the old iFAST Global Bank. It has been turned into an office **building**. → 여자가 '빌딩'을 언급

M **I've always admired the architecture of that bank, but the building is almost a hundred years old.** → 남자가 빌딩에 대해 언급하며, 그 건물의 구조는 멋지지만 너무 오래됐다고 말하고 있다.

W Don't worry. The building has been completely renovated. Do you want to look at it with me this afternoon?

M I'd like to, but I have to meet the investors this afternoon. Could we go tomorrow morning?

Q. What does the man say about the building?

(A) He likes how it was renovated.
(B) **He likes how it was designed.**
(C) He likes the size of its offices.
(D) He likes its conference room.

여 안녕하세요, Philip. 시내에서 우리 새로운 회사를 위한 정말 멋진 사무 공간을 찾았어요. 그것은 예전 iFAST Global Bank 안에 있어요. 그곳이 사무 빌딩으로 바뀌었네요.

남 전 항상 그 은행의 건축 양식에 대해 감탄했어요. 하지만 건물은 거의 100년이 됐어요.

여 걱정하지 마세요. 그 건물은 완전히 개조되었어요. 오늘 오후에 저와 같이 가서 보실래요?

남 그러고 싶지만, 오늘 오후에 투자자들을 만나야 해요. 내일 아침에 가도 될까요?

남자는 빌딩에 대해 뭐라고 말하는가?

(A) 그는 건물이 개조된 방식이 맘에 든다.
(B) **그는 건물의 설계가 맘에 든다.**
(C) 그는 사무실 크기가 맘에 든다.
(D) 그는 회의실이 맘에 든다.

≡ 풀이 접근법

● 세부사항 문제는 대화의 순서가 중요하다. 첫 번째 문제로 나오면 대화의 초반부, 두 번째 문제로 나오면 중반부, 세 번째 문제로 나오면 후반부에 정답 단서가 나올 가능성이 크다.

● 질문의 키워드에 표시해 놓고 대화에서 키워드에 대한 언급이 나올 때 집중한다.

● 질문에 성별이 지정될 경우 해당 성별의 대화에 특히 집중해서 듣는다.

● 정답 단서는 패러프레이징되어 나오는 경우가 많다. 단, 숫자 요일, 지명 등은 그대로 나온다.

≡ 기출 질문 & 답변 패턴

세부사항을 묻는 질문 유형

1. 시간, 장소 관련 문제

질문의 키워드에 표시하고 대화를 들을 때 시간, 장소 표현(6:00 P.M., Friday, in front of the center, Richmond Street 등)을 집중해서 듣는다. 단, 시간이나 장소가 여러 번 언급될 수 있는데, 그중 질문과 맞는 것을 고르는 게 중요하다.

- When is the woman's appointment? 여자의 약속은 언제인가?
- What will begin at 6:00 P.M.? 오후 6시에 무엇이 시작될 것인가?
- Where can the woman catch the bus? 여자는 어디서 버스를 탈 수 있는가?
- Where does the man anticipate a traffic jam? 남자는 어디의 교통체증을 예상하는가?

2. 특정 인물 관련 문제

질문의 키워드에 표시하고 대화를 들을 때 사람 이름이 언급되는 곳에 집중한다.

- Who are the workers waiting for? 작업자들이 기다리는 사람은 누구인가?
- Who is the man going to meet? 남자는 누구를 만날 것인가?
- What does the man mention about Peter? 남자는 Peter에 대해 뭐라고 언급하는가?
- How does David feel about the new rule? David는 새로운 규칙을 어떻게 느끼는가?

3. 방법, 이유, 문제점을 묻는 문제

대화의 내용이 선택지에 패러프레이징되어 나오는 경우가 많으므로 빈출 패러프레이징 표현을 숙지한다.

- How can a visitor get a discount? 방문자들은 어떻게 할인을 받을 수 있는가?
- What problem does the man have? 남자가 가진 문제점은 무엇인가?
- What is the woman concerned about? 여자가 걱정하는 것은 무엇인가?
- Why is the man unable to find Donna? 왜 남자는 Donna를 찾을 수 없는가?
- What solution does the woman offer? 여자가 제안하는 해결책은 무엇인가?

4. 행위, 언급, 진술 내용을 묻는 문제

키워드를 잘 기억하고 듣는다. 마찬가지로, 패러프레이징 표현에 유의해 정답을 고른다.

- What does the woman mention about the agency? 여자는 대리점에 대해 뭐라고 언급하는가?
- What does the man tell the woman to do? 남자는 여자에게 무엇을 하라고 말하는가?
- What does the man say about the computer? 남자는 컴퓨터에 대해 뭐라고 말하는가?

☰ 기출 패러프레이징 표현

stuck in traffic 교통체증에 걸린	→ caught in traffic 교통체증에 걸린
a list of similar buildings 비슷한 건물의 목록	→ a list of properties 부동산 목록
get an estimate 견적을 뽑다	→ obtain a cost estimate 비용 견적을 받다
work overtime 초과 근무하다	→ work extended[extra] hours 연장 근무하다
reschedule a doctor's appointment 진료 예약을 변경하다	→ change an appointment 약속을 변경하다
take a survey 설문조사에 응하다	→ complete a form 양식을 작성하다
airport limousine bus 공항버스	→ transportation 이동수단
hired some new staff members 신입 직원을 몇 명 고용했다	→ recruited several new people 새로운 사람들을 채용했다
the founder of the company 회사의 설립자	→ a company's owner 회사 소유자
corporate meeting 회사 미팅	→ company gathering 회사 모임
go to see the head of the project 프로젝트의 책임자를 만나러 가다	→ visit an organizer 주최자를 방문하다
a large screen 큰 화면	→ a big monitor 큰 모니터
The machine is not working properly. 기계가 제대로 작동하지 않는다.	→ A product is faulty. 제품에 결함이 있다.
Use the back door. 뒷문을 사용하세요.	→ Exit through the rear door. 뒷문을 통해 나가세요.
plane tickets and passport 비행기 표와 여권	→ travel documents 여행 서류
attracting new people 새로운 사람들을 끌어들이는 것	→ finding new customers 새로운 고객을 찾는 것
flyers 전단지	→ a publicity campaign 홍보물
personal fitness equipment in my house 집에 있는 개인적인 운동 장비	→ a home exercise machine 가정용 운동기기
Get in touch with a courier company. 택배회사에 연락하세요.	→ Call a delivery company. 배달업체에 전화하세요.
A Web site is going to be redesigned. 웹사이트가 새로 디자인된다.	→ updating a Web site 웹사이트 업데이트하기

2. 다음에 할 일 문제

유형 소개 및 전략

화자가 다음에 할 일을 묻는 문제로 매회 2~5문제가 출제된다. 주로 마지막 순서로 출제되며, 대화 후반부에서 정답 단서가 제시된다.

유형 맛보기

W Welcome to Twining's Gift Shop! May I help you, sir?	여 Twining's 선물 가게에 오신 것을 환영합니다! 무엇을 도와드릴까요?
M Yes, please. I just dropped by here to look for a birthday gift for my colleague. Oh, this would be nice.	남 네, 제 동료의 생일 선물을 사러 들렀습니다. 아, 이게 좋겠네요.
W Good choice! **If you just fill out this application form, you'll receive 20% off any purchase.**	여 제대로 고르셨네요! 이 신청서를 작성하시면, 어떤 구매에도 20퍼센트 할인을 받으실 수 있습니다.
M Okay. That sounds like a great deal. → 여자가 앞에서 '신청서를 작성하면, 어떤 구매에도 20% 할인을 받을 수 있습니다.'라고 한 말에, 남자가 Okay라고 했으므로 남자가 신청서를 작성할 것임을 유추할 수 있다.	남 알겠습니다. 좋은 거래 같네요.

Q. What will the man probably do next?

(A) Go to another shop
(B) Pay for a gift
(C) **Fill out a form**
(D) Call his colleague

남자는 다음에 무엇을 할 것 같은가?

(A) 다른 가게에 간다
(B) 선물값을 지불한다
(C) **신청서를 작성한다**
(D) 동료에게 전화한다

풀이 접근법

● 다음에 할 일을 묻는 문제는 대화 마지막 부분에 정답 단서가 나오므로 끝까지 집중해서 들어야 한다.

● 요청하거나 제안하는 내용에서 정답 단서가 나올 가능성이 크다.

● 미래를 나타내는 다양한 시제뿐만 아니라 화자의 의지/결심이 드러나는 표현이나 제안/청유 표현에 주목해야 한다.

☰ 기출 질문 & 답변 패턴

다음에 할 일을 묻는 질문 유형

- What will the man do next? 남자는 다음에 무엇을 할 것인가?

- What will the woman probably do next? 여자는 다음에 무엇을 할 것 같은가?

- What will the speakers most likely do next? 화자들은 다음에 무엇을 할 것 같은가?

- Where will the speakers go next? 화자들은 다음에 어디로 갈 것인가?

다음에 할 일을 나타내는 단서 표현

미래 시제	① 미래/계획: will / be going to / be planning to **I'll** make a copy of it for you. 일정표를 복사해 드릴게요. **I'm going to** e-mail you a voucher for thirty percent off a night at any of our locations. 저희 호텔 전 지점에서 사용 가능한 1박 30% 할인 쿠폰을 이메일로 보내 드리겠습니다. ② 예정된 가까운 미래: 단순 현재형, be + V-ing **I'm placing an order** for supplies this afternoon. 오늘 오후에 용품을 주문할 예정입니다.
제안	Let me ~ / I can[could] **Let me** ask my manager if I can leave early tomorrow. 내일 일찍 퇴근할 수 있는지 제 상사에게 물어볼게요. **I can** send you the link so that you can download it. 귀하께서 설명서를 내려받으실 수 있도록 링크를 보내 드리겠습니다.

■ 음원을 듣고 답을 고르세요. 다시 들으면서 빈칸을 채우세요.

1. What does the man receive from the woman?

(A) A signed lease

(B) A registration form

(C) Schedule information

(D) A utility bill

M Hello there. I _____ the apartment complex last month. I'd like to _____ the fitness center.

W No problem. I'll _____ your lease, a utility bill, or anything that proves you are currently living in your apartment.

M Unfortunately, I didn't _____. Can I come back after work?

W Of course. We _____ Wednesdays though, so try to _____ 7 o'clock. This information brochure lists our gym hours and the _____.

2. Why was the woman late for the meeting?

(A) She was using public transportation.

(B) She just came back from vacation.

(C) She was stuck in traffic.

(D) She lives far from the company.

W Hi, Mr. Anderson. I'm sorry. I was _____ this morning because of a traffic jam. What _____?

M Oh, on Thursday, we are going to _____ on all of the computers in the Sales Department.

W So is there anything we have to do _____?

M No, but I suggest that you come _____. We will have a lot of _____.

3. What will the woman most likely do next?

(A) Report to a manager

(B) Give a speech

(C) Make a phone call

(D) Have a meeting

M Hi, Rhonda. I _____ Jordan Mitts, one of the speakers. He said that he cannot _____ the training session for our new employees.

W Oh, that's really _____. We only have ten days left before the training session. What _____?

M Well, why don't we ask Andrew Ling in the Marketing Department? He _____ about time management last year. The audience response was very positive. I also _____ a very good speech.

W That's a great idea. I'll _____ right now.

ACTUAL TEST

1. Who does the woman want to have stay at the Manchester Hotel?

   (A) Her coworkers
   (B) Her family
   (C) Her friends
   (D) Her clients

2. What does the man want to know about the hotel?

   (A) Its location
   (B) Its profits
   (C) Its facilities
   (D) Its prices

3. Why does the woman suggest going to her office?

   (A) To check a Web site
   (B) To meet with clients
   (C) To make a reservation
   (D) To prepare for a meeting

4. Where did the woman get the coupon?

   (A) From a book
   (B) From a magazine
   (C) From a newspaper
   (D) From a Web site

5. What problem does the man mention about the coupon?

   (A) It can only be used at lunch.
   (B) It can only be used on the weekend.
   (C) It has already expired.
   (D) It's for another restaurant.

6. What does the man say is happening now?

   (A) A grand opening sale
   (B) A clearance sale
   (C) Happy hour
   (D) A special offer

7. What does the man ask about?

   (A) A meeting with an employee
   (B) A new secretary
   (C) A repair problem
   (D) An international meeting

8. What does the man say he has to delay?

   (A) A reservation
   (B) A training session
   (C) A business trip
   (D) A meeting

9. What will the woman probably do next?

   (A) Submit a report
   (B) Call a maintenance man
   (C) Prepare for a meeting
   (D) Open a window

10. What are the speakers discussing?

    (A) Making a dinner reservation
    (B) Reducing the cost of dinner
    (C) Rescheduling dinner
    (D) Renovating a restaurant

11. What does the man suggest?

    (A) Booking another restaurant
    (B) Redoing an estimate
    (C) Asking for a donation
    (D) Changing the menu

12. What will the woman probably do next?

    (A) Contact a restaurant
    (B) Inform all of the employees
    (C) Visit another department
    (D) Cancel a reservation

요청·제안/화자 문제

1. 요청·제안 문제

유형 소개 및 전략

요청, 제안한 것이 무엇인지 묻는 문제로, 주로 세 번째 문제로 출제되며, 매회 5문제 정도 나온다. 제안 표현 'Why don't ~?, Could you ~?' 뒤에 정답 단서가 제시될 확률이 높으므로 이 부분을 잘 들어야 한다.

유형 맛보기

M Hi. This is the first time for me to visit the gallery, so can I learn more about the paintings on this floor?

W **Well, why don't you take a tour?** It goes to all of our exhibits. The next one begins in 20 minutes. → 'Why don't ~?' 표현을 써서 '미술 투어'를 제안하고 있다.

M Unfortunately, I don't have enough time today.

Q. What does the woman suggest that the man do?

    (A) Buy a membership
    (B) Return another day
    (C) Take a tour
    (D) Join an art class

남 안녕하세요. 미술관을 방문하는 것은 처음인데 이 층에 있는 그림들에 대해 조금 더 알아볼 수 있을까요?

여 그러시면, 투어를 하시는 건 어떠세요? 모든 전시품을 살펴보실 수 있어요. 다음 투어가 20분 후에 시작해요.

남 안타깝지만, 오늘은 시간이 충분치 않네요.

여자는 남자에게 무엇을 하라고 제안하는가?

    (A) 회원권을 구입하라고
    (B) 다른 날 다시 오라고
    (C) 미술 투어를 하라고
    (D) 미술 수업에 등록하라고

LC PART 3

풀이 접근법

● 대화 시작 전에 문제와 키워드를 빨리 파악하고 대화를 들어야 한다.

● 제안 사항을 묻는 문제는 'Why don't ~?, Would you ~?, Could you ~?, Would you like me to ~?, I suggest ~, I can ~' 뒤에 이어지는 문장에 정답 단서가 나온다.

● 요청과 제안은 상대방(you)에게 하는 것이므로 '~해라' 식의 표현이 정답으로 자주 등장한다.

☰ 기출 질문 & 답변 패턴

제안 사항을 묻는 질문 유형

- What does the man[woman] suggest[recommend]? 남자[여자]는 무엇을 제안하는가?

- What does the man offer to do? 남자는 무엇을 하겠다고 하는가?

- What does the man ask[encourage] the woman to do? 남자는 여자에게 무엇을 하라고 요청하는가?

- What does the man ask for? 남자는 무엇을 요청하는가?

정답 단서 표현

- Why don't you ~? ~하는 게 어때요?

- What[How] about ~? ~하는 게 어때요?

- Would[Could/Should] you ~? ~하는 게 어때요?

- Shall[Can/May] I[we] ~? 제가[우리가] ~해도 될까요?

- You would[should/could/must/have to] ~. 당신은 ~해야 합니다.

- You want[need/hope] to ~. 당신은 ~을 원할(필요할) 겁니다.

- I[We] can ~. 제가[우리가] ~할 수 있습니다.

- I[We] suggest[recommend] ~. 저는[우리는] ~를 제안합니다.

- Please + 동사원형 ~. ~ 하세요.

2. 화자 문제

유형 소개 및 전략

화자의 직업이나 신분을 묻는 문제는 매회 4문제 정도가 출제된다. 대부분 대화 도입부에서 직접적인 힌트가 제시되지만 그렇지 않은 경우에는 다른 문제를 풀고 나서 마지막에 정답을 선택해야 한다.

유형 맛보기

W **Mr. Collins, I just contacted the owner of the apartment. I'm pleased to tell you that the owner wants to sign a contract with you.** → 대화 도입부에서
'아파트 주인과 통화한 후 집주인이 계약하겠다는 사실을 알리고 있으므로 여자는 '부동산 중개인'임을 유추할 수 있다.

여 Collins 씨, 방금 막 아파트 주인과 통화했어요. 집주인이 계약하겠다는 사실을 전하게 되어 너무 기쁘네요.

M That's great news. However, we are concerned about the electrical wiring in the living room.

남 정말 좋은 소식이군요. 하지만 저희는 거실 전기 배선이 걱정입니다.

W You don't have to worry about that. The owner will renovate every single part of the apartment.

여 그건 걱정 안 하셔도 됩니다. 집주인이 아파트의 모든 곳을 보수해 줄 겁니다.

Q. What most likely is the woman's job?

(A) Real estate agent
(B) Building inspector
(C) Lawyer
(D) Interior designer

여자의 직업은 무엇인 것 같은가?

(A) 부동산 중개인
(B) 건축 감리사
(C) 변호사
(D) 실내 장식가

풀이 접근법

- 직업 및 신분을 묻는 문제는 대부분 대화 도입부에 정답 단서가 등장한다.

- 도입부에서 단서를 놓쳤다면 대화 전체에서 들리는 직업 및 신분 관련 어휘를 종합해 답을 추론한다.

- 특정 직업 및 신분과 관련된 어휘를 알아둬야 한다.

LC
PART 3

☰ 기출 질문 & 답변 패턴

직업이나 신분을 묻는 질문 유형

- Who most likely is the man? 남자는 누구인 것 같은가?
- Who most likely are the speakers? 화자들은 누구인 것 같은가?
- Who is the man speaking[talking] to? 남자는 누구에게 얘기하고 있는가?
- What do the speakers probably do? 화자들은 무엇을 하겠는가?
- What is the woman's job[occupation]? 여자의 직업은 무엇인가?

직업, 신분 관련 빈출 어휘

caterer 출장 요리사	consultant 컨설턴트, 고문
staff member 직원	architect 건축가
CEO 최고경영자	representative 직원, 대표
director 이사	president 사장
manager 부장, 과장	chief (부서)장
accountant 회계사	supervisor 관리자
technician 기술자	plumber 배관공
landscaper 조경업자	mechanic 정비공
boss 상사	agent 직원
head (부서)장	vice president 부사장
executive officer 중역, 임원	assistant 비서, 부하직원
receptionist 접수직원	department manager 부서장

■ 음원을 듣고 답을 고르세요. 다시 들으면서 빈칸을 채우세요.

1. What does the man offer to do?

(A) Help the woman the next day
(B) Call another support team
(C) Find her password
(D) Find a telephone number

W David, I've been _____ my e-mail, but when I enter my password, I _____ that it's invalid.

M Did you ask the technician about that?

W I already tried calling _____, but it appears that no one is working there now.

M There is a 24-hour technical service line you can call. I _____ the phone number for you.

2. What does the man suggest that the woman do?

(A) Buy a car
(B) Take the subway
(C) Speak with her colleagues
(D) Commute to work by walking

W I was _____ this morning. I _____ a terrible traffic jam.

M Really? Driving is _____ taking the subway.

W _____ take the subway, too, but my house is quite far from the subway station.

M Maybe _____ near you would like to carpool to the station. _____ talk with some of our colleagues?

3. What are the speakers working on?

(A) Clothing design
(B) Creating a brochure
(C) An advertising budget
(D) A safety manual

W Hi, Tom. How's the design work for our _____?

M I've completed most of it. I can e-mail you the final design _____.

W Sounds good. Then we can send it to the printing office tomorrow _____. Come to think of it, we should put some _____ on the last page.

M _____. I'll add some testimonials from our satisfied customers on the back page.

W Great. And please contact B&M Printers and _____ the printing will take and how much _____. I have always been happy with its high-quality work.

M Okay, I'll call the store _____.

ACTUAL TEST

1. Where most likely is the conversation taking place?

   (A) At a supermarket
   (B) At a furniture store
   (C) At an electronics store
   (D) At a clothes store

2. What does the man say is going on at the store?

   (A) Maintenance work
   (B) A grand opening sale
   (C) A clearance sale
   (D) A special promotion

3. What does the woman request?

   (A) The newest item
   (B) The cheapest item
   (C) The lightest item
   (D) The smallest item

4. What does the man say he has requested?

   (A) Information about remodeling
   (B) The contact number of the owner
   (C) The location of the restaurant
   (D) The price of the property

5. What does the woman suggest that the man do?

   (A) Change his business hours
   (B) Make an invitation card
   (C) Contact a real estate agent
   (D) Visit the agent by tomorrow

6. What is the woman worried about?

   (A) Finding an interior designer
   (B) Purchasing a restaurant
   (C) Removing some old furniture
   (D) Hiring a new staff member

7. What type of business is the woman calling?

   (A) An office machine store
   (B) A bookstore
   (C) A restaurant
   (D) A print shop

8. What problem does the woman mention?

   (A) A bill has an unexpected fee.
   (B) The wrong photocopiers were delivered.
   (C) Some photocopiers were delivered late.
   (D) There are some broken parts.

9. What does the man say about Ms. Park?

   (A) She made an order.
   (B) She signed a contract.
   (C) She will receive a new bill.
   (D) She will make photocopies of the contract.

10. Who most likely is the man?

    (A) An accountant
    (B) An architect
    (C) A bank clerk
    (D) A technician

11. What is the woman's problem?

    (A) She cannot install a program.
    (B) Her computer broke down.
    (C) She cannot finish her project on time.
    (D) She lost some documents.

12. What does the woman request that the man do?

    (A) Extend the deadline of the report
    (B) Invite her to an international seminar
    (C) Attend a meeting instead of her
    (D) Repair her computer by tomorrow

UNIT 12 의도 파악/시각 자료 문제

1. 의도 파악 문제

유형 소개 및 전략

대화 중에 나올 문장 하나를 질문에서 보여주고 그 말을 하는 화자의 숨은 의도를 묻는 문제로, 매회 2~3문제 출제된다. 제시문의 앞뒤 문장과의 흐름을 파악해 문맥상 의미를 이해하는 것이 중요하다.

유형 맛보기

W Hi, Gerald. I have to enter some sales figures in our network database, but I'm having trouble signing in. My password keeps being rejected. Can you come over here and help me?

M **I'm really busy with the presentation for tomorrow.** If you can't sign in, it's probably a problem with the server. Why don't you ask one of the IT technicians to take a look at it? → 와달라는 여자의 부탁에 남자가 내일 발표로 정말 바쁘다고 말한 것으로 보아, 여자의 부탁을 거절하는 의미가 포함되어 있다고 볼 수 있다.

W Oh, yes, I should do that. Do you know who our contact in the IT Department is?

M Umm... I don't know. You should just call and ask for someone who's available right now.

Q. Why does the man say, "I'm really busy with the presentation for tomorrow"?
(A) To ask for assistance
(B) To postpone a presentation
(C) **To make an excuse**
(D) To make some changes

여 안녕하세요. Gerald. 네트워크 데이터베이스에 판매 수치를 입력해야 하는데, 로그인하는 데 문제가 있어요. 비밀번호가 자꾸만 틀렸다고 나오네요. 와서 좀 도와주실 수 있나요?

남 내일 발표 때문에 지금 정말 바빠요. 로그인이 안 되면 아마 서버 문제일 거예요. 기술자 중 한 명한테 봐달라고 하는 게 어때요?

여 아, 네. 그래야겠어요. IT 부서에서 우리랑 연락하는 직원이 누군지 아시나요?

남 음… 모르겠어요. 그냥 전화해서 지금 시간 되는 사람을 요청하세요.

남자가 "내일 발표 때문에 지금 정말 바빠요"라고 말한 이유는 무엇인가?
(A) 도움을 요청하기 위해
(B) 발표를 미루기 위해
(C) **변명을 하기 위해**
(D) 변화를 주기 위해

풀이 접근법

● 반드시 문제에 제시된 인용문의 뜻을 파악한 후 대화를 들어야 한다.

● 해당 문장만이 아닌 앞뒤 문장과의 전체적인 문맥을 파악한다.

● 연결어로 앞사람의 의견에 긍정하는지 부정하는지를 판단할 수 있다. But, I'm sorry, Actually, I'm afraid, Unfortunately, However가 나오면 상대방의 의견에 반박하는 내용이, Okay, Therefore, So, Sure, Right, Certainly 등이 나오면 상대방의 의견에 동조하는 내용이 이어진다.

LC PART 3

의도 파악 관련 기출 표현

상대방 의견에 긍정 vs. 반대할 때

- I can't agree with you more.
  당신 말에 전적으로 동의해요
- I think so. 저도 그렇게 생각합니다.
- It sounds proper. 타당한 것 같습니다.
- I agree with you on that point.
  그 점에 대해 동의합니다.
- It's quite a good idea. 좋은 생각입니다.
- I'm of the same opinion. 전적으로 같은 생각입니다.
- That's exactly what I'm saying. 제 말이 바로 그거예요.
- You're making sense. 당신 말에 일리가 있군요.
- Just as you say. 당신이 말한 대로예요.

- I can't agree with you. 당신 말에 동의할 수 없습니다.
- I'm sorry, but I have a different opinion.
  죄송합니다만, 이견이 있습니다.
- That's not my idea of ~. ~에 대한 제 생각과는 다릅니다.
- I don't think so. 저는 그렇게 생각하지 않습니다.
- Certainly not. [Absolutely not. Surely not.]
  확실히 아닙니다.
- Nothing at all. 절대 그렇지 않습니다.
- I'm against ~. / I object to ~. / I am opposed to ~.
  ~에 대해 반대합니다.
- I have a different opinion about it. 제 생각은 다릅니다.

상대의 의견을 공감/이해할 때 vs. 공감/이해하지 못할 때

- I see. 이해합니다.
- I see what you mean. 당신이 하는 말을 이해합니다.
- I see your point. 이해합니다.
- I understand what you mean.
  당신이 말하는 바를 이해합니다.
- I get the point of what you're saying.
  당신이 말하는 요지를 이해합니다.

- I don't know what you mean. 무슨 말인지 모르겠어요.
- What do you mean? 무슨 말씀이시죠?
- Would you come again, please?
  좀 더 자세히 말씀해 주시겠습니까?
- I have no idea about what he is saying.
  그가 무슨 말을 하는지 모르겠어요.

알고 있는 사실을 상기시킬 때

- Please think ~ over again.
  다시 한번 생각해 ~을 보시기 바랍니다.
- As you see [know], 아시다시피,
- I think you are well aware of ~.
  당신이 ~을 잘 알고 계실 거라고 생각합니다.

잘못된 점을 사과할 때

- I'm not sure, but I think ~ is a ridiculous mistake.
  잘은 모르겠지만, ~은 터무니없는 실수였다고 생각해요.
- I apologize for my mistake.
  제 잘못에 대해 사과드립니다.
- It's my fault [mistake]. 제 잘못입니다.

요구나 제안을 정중하게 거절할 때

- I'm afraid I can't accept ~. ~을 받아들이기 힘든데요.
- That's absolutely unacceptable.
  그건 정말 받아들일 수 없네요.
- It would be difficult. 어렵겠네요.

책임을 물을 때

- You have to be responsible for ~.
  당신은 ~에 대해 책임져야 해요.
- You are to blame. 당신 책임이에요.
- That's your fault. 당신 책임이에요.

뜻밖의 상황에 놀랄 때

- You surprise me. 놀랍네요.
- I didn't expect to ~. ~할 거라고 기대 안 했어요.
- I'm really surprised to hear ~. ~을 듣고 정말 놀랐어요.

요점에서 벗어났음을 지적할 때

- I think your statement misses the point.
  당신 말은 요지에서 벗어났습니다.
- Would you give it to me straight?
  요점을 말씀해 주실래요?
- So what's your point? 그래서 요점이 뭔가요?

2. 시각 자료 문제

유형 소개 및 전략

'Look at the graphic.'으로 시작하는 문제로, 대화 내용과 시각 자료를 연계해서 푸는 유형이다. Part 3 후반부에 3문제가 출제되며, 시각 자료로는 표, 그래프, 일정표, 지도 등이 다양하게 나온다. 시각 자료 문제를 풀 때 중요한 점은 시각 자료 유형에 따라 대화 내용을 미리 예상해 보는 것이다. 또한, 시각 자료에서 중요한 내용을 미리 파악하여 표시해 두고 대화를 들으면서 연결시켜 가며 풀어야 한다.

유형 맛보기

M Hello, Martha. I'm just calling to remind you about the presentation schedule for this morning's meeting. You know you're scheduled for 11:00, right?

W About that... **I need to change my presentation time because a client is coming to see me for an urgent meeting at 10:30, and I think it will take a little longer than 30 minutes to deal with her.**

M Okay... Well, Georgia **is scheduled for right before you while** Jeffrey **is speaking as soon as you're done. Do you want to change sessions with one of them?**

W Yes. **I think I'll take the later time** since I'll need some time to get prepared.

M Okay, I'll revise the timetable right away.

→ 원래 11시에 발표 예정인 Martha(여자)가 10시 30분에 손님이 오기로 해서 시간을 바꾸고 싶다고 했고, 남자가 앞뒤 시간 중 바꾸길 권하고 있다. 여자는 후자를 택했으므로 Jeffrey와 시간을 바꿀 것임을 예상할 수 있다.

Presenter	Time
Pauline	9:00
Georgia	10:00
Martha	11:00
Jeffrey	12:00

Q. Look at the graphic. When will Jeffrey make his presentation?

(A) At 9:00
(B) At 10:00
(C) At 11:00
(D) At 12:00

남 안녕하세요, Martha. 오늘 아침 회의 발표 일정에 대해 상기시키려고 전화드립니다. 11시로 예정된 거 아시죠?

여 그거에 대해서요... 제 발표 시간을 바꿔야 할 것 같아요. 10시 30분에 고객이 급하게 저를 만나러 오기로 했는데, 그녀와 상담하는 데 30분이 조금 넘게 걸릴 것 같아서요.

남 알겠어요. Georgia랑 Jeffrey가 각각 당신 전후로 잡혀 있으니까 그들 중 한 명과 바꾸시겠어요?

여 네, 준비할 시간이 필요하니까 나중 것으로 할게요.

남 알았어요. 시간표를 바로 수정할게요.

발표 시간	
Pauline	9시
Georgia	10시
Martha	11시
Jeffrey	12시

도표를 보시오. Jeffrey는 언제 발표할 것인가?

(A) 9시에
(B) 10시에
(C) 11시에
(D) 12시에

풀이 접근법

● 대화를 듣기 전에 도표 내용을 파악해 중요 부분에 표시해 둔다.

● 시각 자료에서 질문의 보기와 상응하는 정보나 질문의 일부가 단서로 등장할 가능성이 높다.

● 지도나 평면도에서는 위치 관련 표현에 주목해야 한다.

☰ 기출 유형 패턴

가격 목록을 보고 해당 제품을 고르는 문제

Look at the graphic. Which storage capacity will the man probably order?

도표를 보시오. 남자는 어느 저장 용량을 주문할 것인가?

(A) 16GB
(B) 32GB
(C) 64GB
(D) 128GB

Storage Capacity Price	
16GB	$199.00
32GB	$249.00
64GB	$299.00
128GB	$399.00

M PC prices greatly vary according to their storage capacity. I'm not sure which ones I should order.

W Well, the more storage space, the better. But let's not exceed 300 dollars per PC.

남 PC 가격대가 저장 용량에 따라 크게 달라지네요. 어떤 것을 주문해야 할지 잘 모르겠어요.

여 음, 용량은 클수록 좋지만 한 대당 300달러는 넘지 않는 것으로 합시다.

→ 300달러를 넘지 않으면서 용량이 가장 큰 PC는 표에서 64G임을 알 수 있다. 이처럼 조건과 딱 맞는 사항을 갖춘 물품이 무엇인지를 찾는 유형이 나온다.

지도를 보고 해당 위치를 찾는 문제

Look at the graphic. Which booth will the woman reserve?

도표를 보시오. 어느 부스를 여자가 예약할 것인가?

(A) Booth 5
(B) Booth 6
(C) Booth 8
(D) Booth 9

Booth 9	Stage	Booth 8
Booth 5	Booth 6	████	Booth 7
	Entrance	

W We want to reserve the two booths next to the entrance, but booth 6 has already been taken. So I signed up for booth 7, and now we have to choose one more spot.

M Okay. Let's just go with the one close to booth 7. It's also right next to the stage, so I think it'll get plenty of attention as well.

여 출입구 옆에 있는 두 부스를 잡고 싶은데, 6번 부스는 이미 차 있더라고요. 그래서 7번 부스를 신청했고 이제 한 군데 더 골라야 해요.

남 네, 그냥 7번 부스랑 가까운 곳으로 하죠. 무대 바로 옆에 있기도 하니까 충분히 주목도 받을 수 있을 거예요

→ 7번 부스와 가깝고 무대 옆에 있는 부스는 8번 부스다. 이처럼 도면이나 지도를 보고 해당 위치를 찾는 문제가 출제된다.

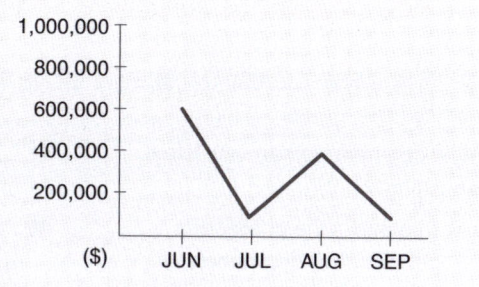
그래프에서 최고점/최저점의 정보를 묻는 문제

Look at the graphic. What was the sales figure
when the company held a discount event?

도표를 보시오. 회사가 할인 행사를 했을 때 판매 수치는 무엇인가?

(A) $200,000

(B) $400,000

(C) $600,000

(D) $1,000,000

M Did you see our sales figures for the last few months? Our most successful month was June, but
after that, the figures dropped dramatically and are still maintaining a downward tendency.

W Yes, I saw that. The figures rose a bit when we had that discount event in August, but it wasn't
enough to set a record. So we need to come up with some new and innovative ideas.

남 지난 몇 달간의 우리 판매 수치를 보았나요? 가장 성공적인 달은 6월이었는데, 그 이후로는 판매 수치가 급격히 줄어들었고, 아직까지
하향세가 계속되고 있어요.

여 네, 봤어요. 우리가 8월에 할인 이벤트를 했을 때 수치가 약간 오르는 듯 했지만, 기록을 세우기에는 충분하지 않았나 봐요. 그래서 우
리는 새롭고 혁신적인 아이디어를 생각해야 해요.

→ 8월에 할인 행사를 했고, 그때 조금 판매 수치가 올랐다고 했다. 따라서 할인 행사를 한 8월의 판매 수치는 40만 달러로 정답은 (B)이다. 이처럼
판매 비교, 제품 점유율, 수량 증감률을 나타낸 그래프 연계 문제가 출제된다.

양식, 영수증, 티켓, 쿠폰과 연계된 정보를 묻는 문제

Look at the graphic. Which discount will the man
most likely receive?

도표를 보시오. 남자는 어떤 할인 금액을 받을 것인가?

(A) $3

(B) $20

(C) $25

(D) $50

Discount Coupon	
Monitor Sizes	
20-24 inch	$30 Value
25 inch and above	$50 Value
Gilbut Tech	
Expiration Date 10/30	

M Excuse me. I'm looking for a 27-inch computer monitor, but I can only see 21- and 24-inch monitors.
Do you have any larger monitors in stock? And I have this discount coupon. Is it valid for your store?

W Yes, you can get a discount. The monitors used to be all together, but we recently moved the larger
displays to a separate aisle. I'll show you where they are.

남 실례합니다. 27인치 컴퓨터 모니터를 찾고 있는데요, 21인치와 24인치 모니터만 보여요. 더 큰 모니터 있나요? 그리고 제가 이 쿠폰이
있는데 이 매장에서 사용 가능한가요?

여 네, 할인을 받을 수 있겠네요. 모니터들이 함께 있었는데, 최근 큰 제품들을 다른 통로로 옮겼어요. 어디에 있는지 보여드릴게요.

→ 남자는 27인치 모니터를 찾고 있는데, 도표(할인 쿠폰)를 보면 25인치보다 큰 모니터는 50달러 할인을 받을 수 있다고 명시되어 있다. 이처럼 양식,
영수증, 쿠폰, 티켓을 보고 정보를 연계시켜 푸는 유형이 자주 나온다.

■ 음원을 듣고 답을 고르세요. 다시 들으면서 빈칸을 채우세요.

1. Why does the woman say, "How shocking"?

(A) She thinks the quality of a performance was poor.

(B) She heard that a show was overbooked.

(C) She found out about a low turnout.

(D) She found out a concert was canceled.

M _____ the radio announcement about the blue jazz concert yesterday?

W Yes, I did. I thought the show would _____. How shocking!

M I know. Everyone was _____ the concert. Who would've _____ so few people would attend?

W _____ the reason was?

M Well, critics are saying that the tickets were _____. The venue, the Golden Lion Theater, does have _____.

2. Why does the woman say, "I can't believe it"?

(A) She is surprised that an employee left the company.

(B) She does not trust the man.

(C) She has received some false information.

(D) She is happy to hear some news.

W Hello. _____ a mortgage application. Could I speak to Marianne Lemoute, please?

M I'm sorry, but Ms. Lemoute _____ here.

W Really? I can't believe it! I have always gotten excellent advice and service from her _____.

M She doesn't work in the banking industry anymore from _____.

W Oh, that's too bad. Well, then who can I talk to _____?

M It's best if _____ Mr. Flooder. He is the new regional manager.

1
Front Desk

2	
Secretary's Office	4
3	Conference Room
Personnel Office	

3. Look at the graphic. What location is the man told to go to?

(A) Room 1

(B) Room 2

(C) Room 3

(D) Room 4

M Excuse me, Amanda. I _____ my ID. It doesn't open the doors to the building, so I have to get someone on the _____ to let me in. Could you add my information to the _____?

W Well, the staff in Human Resources is only _____ IDs for our building. Why don't you go to the _____? Someone there should be able to put you _____.

M Okay. I'll try. Thanks.

ACTUAL TEST

1. What does the woman like about her album?

(A) It can interest people in all age groups.
(B) It is her best-selling album yet.
(C) It features classical music.
(D) It is her first album.

2. What is the woman planning to do?

(A) Release her next album
(B) Give a performance
(C) Visit her hometown
(D) Take a break from music

3. What does the woman mean when she says, "Thanks for asking"?

(A) She wants to ask the same question again.
(B) She wants to talk about a new topic.
(C) She has heard a question many times.
(D) She cannot give an answer now.

4. Where are the speakers?

(A) At a restaurant
(B) At a hotel
(C) At an office
(D) At an electronics store

5. What does the man mean when he says, "I can't put up with it"?

(A) He hopes that the fridge will be fixed immediately.
(B) He cannot speak with the woman for long.
(C) He is not satisfied with the room service.
(D) He will cancel his reservation.

6. What will the woman most likely do next?

(A) Serve a dessert
(B) Process a refund
(C) Bring some water
(D) Check a schedule

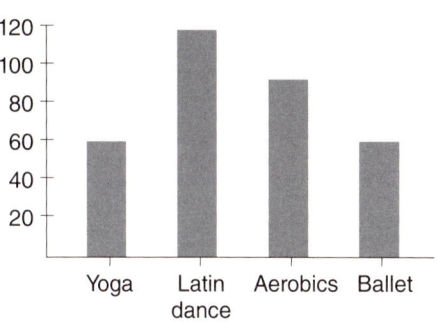

Employee Turnout

7. What event did the woman just attend?

(A) A seminar
(B) A trade fair
(C) A meeting
(D) An awards ceremony

8. Look at the graphic. Which class will be discontinued?

(A) Yoga
(B) Latin dance
(C) Aerobics
(D) Ballet

9. Why is the man concerned?

(A) The survey is way behind schedule.
(B) He is going to be late for an upcoming meeting.
(C) He is not ready for a presentation.
(D) A recent decision will let down some employees.

PART
4

짧은 담화

LC

한 사람이 하는 짧은 담화를 듣고 이와 관련된 세 개의 문제를 푸는 유형으로, 71~100번까지 총 10세트 30문항이 출제된다.

구성	PART	유형	문항 수	시간	배점
Listening Comprehension	1	사진 묘사	6	45분	495점
	2	질의 응답	25		
	3	짧은 대화	39		
	4	**짧은 담화**	**30**		

✍ 문제 유형

- **전체 내용을 묻는 문제**   주제/목적, 담화가 이루어지는 장소, 화자/청자의 직업/업종, 근무지
- **세부 내용을 묻는 문제**   세부사항, 문제점/걱정거리, 화자의 요청/제안/추천 사항, 화자의 의도 파악, 앞으로 할 일/다음에 일어날 일, 시각 정보 연계

✍ 담화 패턴 및 질문 유형

빈출 담화 유형	질문 순서별 빈출 유형	
· Telephone message (전화 메시지) · Advertisement (광고) · Announcement (공지, 안내) · Talk (담화) · News report (교통정보/일기예보) · Broadcast (방송) · Excerpt from a meeting (회의 발췌) · Introduction (소개)	① 첫 번째 문제	주제, 목적, 장소, 인물(직업/신분), 문제점을 묻는 문제 등, 담화의 전체 내용과 관련된 문제는 대개 첫 번째 문제로 출제되며 도입부에서 정답 단서가 언급된다.
	② 두 번째 문제	원인, 수단, 수량, 일정, 시간 등의 세부사항을 묻는 문제는 두 번째 문제로 출제되며 정답 단서는 중반부에 주로 언급된다.
	③ 세 번째 문제	앞으로의 계획이나 할 일, 제안/요청 사항을 묻는 문제는 주로 마지막 순서로 출제된다. 정답 단서는 담화 후반부에 언급된다.

✍ 최신 출제 경향

① 문제 유형별

세부사항 문제의 비율이 가장 높고, 주제/목적 및 화자나 청자의 장소/직업을 묻는 문제가 30% 내외로 꾸준히 출제된다. 매회 화자 의도 파악 문제가 3문항, 시각 정보 연계 문제(95-100번 사이)가 2문항씩 나온다.

② 지문 내용별

회의 및 업무 관련 공지, 전화 메시지가 가장 많이 출제되며, 방송/광고, 발표/소개, 관광/견학 지문도 나온다. PART 3보다 내용 전개 패턴이 비교적 명확한 편이다.

풀이 전략

PART 4 역시 듣기와 읽기 능력을 모두 요하는 영역이다. 듣기와 읽기를 동시에 하는 것은 쉽지 않기 때문에, 반드시 담화를 듣기 전에 질문 및 보기를 읽어 두어야 한다. 보통은 문제 순서에 맞춰 정답 단서가 차례대로 주어지므로, 질문을 보고 담화의 흐름을 예상해 보는 것도 도움이 된다.

STEP 1 담화를 듣기 전에 문제를 먼저 읽어 둔다.
문제를 읽으면서 키워드에 표시해 둔다.

키워드 1: 질문의 키워드 (고유명사, 특정 명사, 특정 동사, 시간, 날짜, 요일)
키워드 2: 화자와 청자 확실히 구분하기

STEP 2 담화를 듣기 전에 핵심 내용을 추측한다.
① 담화의 종류에 따른 내용 전개 패턴 예측
② 문제의 유형에 따른 단서의 위치 예측
③ 화자의 의도 파악 문제로 나온 표현의 일차적 의미 확인
④ 시각 자료의 주요 정보 확인 및 담화에서 언급될 내용 예측

STEP 3 문제 순서와 문제에 대한 힌트가 나오는 순서는 대부분 일치한다.

담화 전반부 화두를 던지고 담화가 펼쳐지는 장소, 화자들의 신분에 대한 정보 등이 제시 ↓ **담화 중반부** 화제에 대한 구체적 정보, 문제 상황, 기타 세부사항 등이 제시 ↓ **담화 후반부** 담화를 마무리하며 앞으로의 계획이나 요청 사항 등을 언급 3문제를 읽어주고 정답을 선택할 시간을 준다. (문제 간 간격 8초)	**첫 번째 문제 힌트** (보기를 보고 있다가 힌트가 들리면 바로 정답 체크) ↓ **두 번째 문제 힌트** (보기를 보고 있다가 힌트가 들리면 바로 정답 체크) ↓ **마지막 문제 힌트** (보기를 보고 있다가 힌트가 들리면 바로 정답 체크) 담화가 끝남과 동시에 정답 체크를 끝내고, 남은 시간 약 24초 동안 다음 문제를 미리 읽는다.

STEP 4 담화가 끝난 후, 성우가 세 개의 문제를 읽는 동안 다음 문제 파악으로 넘어간다.

UNIT 13 공지&소개

1. 공지

유형 소개 및 전략

회사 관련 소식을 전하는 사내 공지, 공항, 마트, 백화점 등 공공장소에서 하는 안내 방송이 주로 나온다. 공지의 주제나 목적, 안내가 나오는 장소, 청자에게 요청/당부하는 내용을 묻는 문제가 주로 출제된다. 담화 후반부에는 주의 사항이 자주 언급된다.

유형 맛보기

Good afternoon. **I just want to let you know that the new customer reporting system will be installed** on the Customer Service Department's computers next week. (→ 지문 초반에 공지 목적 등장) This system will help us by making it easier to enter customers' information. **There will be a training session for two hours next Monday starting at 9:00 A.M.** (→ 키워드인 'next Monday' 부분에서 교육 일정 공지) The technical support team will train us to use the software. **Please make sure all of you attend the training session. If you have any questions, please let me know.** (→ 요청 문제의 단서는 주로 후반부에 등장)

안녕하십니까. 다음 주에 우리 고객 서비스의 컴퓨터에 새로운 고객 보고 시스템이 설치될 예정임을 알려드립니다. 이 시스템은 우리가 고객 정보를 쉽게 입력할 수 있도록 해줄 것입니다. 다음 주 월요일 오전 9시부터 2시간 동안 교육이 있을 것입니다. 기술지원팀이 소프트웨어 사용법에 대해 우리에게 교육할 것입니다. 반드시 모두 교육에 참석해 주시기 바랍니다. 질문이 있으면 말씀해 주십시오.

1. What is the announcement about?
  (A) A new system
  (B) A new policy
  (C) A promotional campaign
  (D) An employee benefit

무엇에 관한 공지인가?
(A) 새로운 시스템
(B) 새로운 정책
(C) 홍보 캠페인
(D) 직원 복지

2. What will happen next Monday?
  (A) An international seminar
  (B) A trade show
  (C) A staff workshop
  (D) The launching of a new product

다음 주 월요일에는 무슨 일이 일어날 것인가?
(A) 국제 세미나
(B) 무역 박람회
(C) 직원 워크숍
(D) 신제품 출시

3. What are the listeners asked to do?
  (A) Be present at the training session
  (B) Bring some documents
  (C) Prepare for a presentation
  (D) Forward an e-mail

청자들은 무엇을 하도록 요청받는가?
(A) 교육에 참석한다
(B) 서류를 가져온다
(C) 프레젠테이션을 준비한다
(D) 이메일을 전달한다

풀이 접근법

● 구체적인 사항을 묻는 'What will happen + 시점?' 문제는 지문에서 시점 앞뒤로 나오는 문장을 집중해서 듣는다.
● 지문 내용이 선택지에 패러프레이징되어 나오는 경우가 많다.
  ex) training session 교육 일정 → staff workshop 직원 워크숍

기출 패턴 및 표현

담화의 흐름 및 관련 표현

공지의 목적 및 장소
⇩

- I'd like to let everyone know ~.
  모두에게 ~을 알려드리고자 합니다.

- I'm happy to announce that ~.
  ~을 알려드리게 되어 기쁩니다.

- Thank you all again for ~.
  ~에 대해 다시 한번 감사드립니다.

- Welcome to ~.
  ~에 오신 것을 환영합니다.

일정 및 변경사항
⇩

- next Friday morning
  다음 주 금요일 오전에

- It will take several hours to ~.
  ~하는 데 몇 시간이 걸릴 겁니다.

- We're going to ~.
  우리는 ~할 예정입니다.

- They will repair ~.
  ~을 수리할 겁니다.

당부 및 요청 사항
⇩

- Please make sure that ~.
  ~해 주시기 바랍니다.

- You should ~.
  ~하셔야 합니다.

- You're required to ~.
  ~하셔야 합니다.

- Can I ask you for ~?
  ~을 요청해도 되겠습니까?

문의 및 연락처

- If you have any questions, ~.
  질문이 있으시면 ~,

- Please let me know ~.
  ~을 알려 주세요.

사내 공지 관련 빈출 어휘

expense 비용, 경비
reimbursement 상환
receipt 영수증
timecard 근무카드
time sheet 근무시간표
survey 설문조사
office equipment 사무기기
office supplies 사무용품
application 지원서
replacement 후임
payroll division 월급 관리부
Accounting Department 회계부
Marketing Department 마케팅부
Human Resources Department 인사부
sales figure 판매 수치
install 설치하다
customer information 고객 정보
workstation 작업 장소, 작업 공간
employee training 직원 교육
workshop 워크숍
annual 연례의
upcoming 다가오는, 곧 있을

gallery 화랑
move 이동하다, 움직이다
convenience 편의, 편리
refreshment 다과
feedback 의견
advice 조언
pleasant environment 쾌적한 환경
opportunity 기회
mover 물건을 옮기는 사람
make an announcement 발표하다, 공표하다
reservation 예약
direction 방향
sales figure 판매 수치
audit 회계 감사
statistics 통계
income 소득
profit 수입
revenue 수익
loss 손실
reduce costs 비용을 절감하다
increase sales 판매를 늘리다
boost sales 판매를 늘리다

2. 소개

유형 소개 및 전략

회사에 새로 들어온 직원이나 승진/은퇴하는 직원의 업적을 소개하는 내용이 주를 이룬다. 소개 대상에 관한 정보를 묻는 문제와 다음에 할 일/일어날 일을 묻는 문제가 자주 출제된다.

유형 맛보기

I'm very pleased to introduce Steve Hilton, the new manager of the Housekeeping Department. (→ 초반부 'I'm pleased to introduce ~.'로 시작되는 부분에 소개 대상과 소개 이유 제시) **Steve will manage all of the housekeeping operations at our hotel.** (→ 장소, 직업, 업종 등은 초반부에 등장) Since we recently changed our housekeeping system, he will assign tasks to employees in several different sections. **So if you want to be in a particular section, you should tell Steve** by the end of the day. (→ 다음에 할 일을 묻는 문제의 정답 단서는 후반부에 등장)

우리 객실 관리 부서의 새로운 매니저 Steve Hilton 씨를 소개하게 되어 기쁩니다. Steve 씨는 우리 호텔에서 모든 객실 관리 서비스의 운영을 관리할 것입니다. 우리는 최근에 객실 관리 시스템을 교체했으므로 그는 직원들에게 여러 다른 구역으로 각각의 업무를 할당할 것입니다. 따라서 희망하는 구역이 있으시다면, 오늘까지 Steve 씨에게 말해 주십시오.

---

1. What is the purpose of the speech?

(A) To introduce a new staff member
(B) To announce a new policy
(C) To explain a new training program
(D) To notify employees of a meeting

연설의 목적은 무엇인가?

(A) 새로운 직원을 소개하려고
(B) 새로운 정책을 발표하려고
(C) 새로운 훈련 프로그램을 설명하려고
(D) 직원 미팅을 통보하려고

2. Where is this speech probably taking place?

(A) At a museum
(B) At a hotel
(C) At a hospital
(D) At a library

이 연설은 어디에서 이루어지고 있는가?

(A) 박물관에서
(B) 호텔에서
(C) 병원에서
(D) 도서관에서

3. What will the listeners do next?

(A) They will tell Steve about sections.
(B) They will ask Steve for an off day.
(C) They will print out some résumés.
(D) They will speak to customers.

청자들은 다음에 무엇을 할 것인가?

(A) Steve에게 구역에 대해 말할 것이다.
(B) Steve에게 휴무일을 요청할 것이다.
(C) 이력서를 출력할 것이다.
(D) 고객들과 대화할 것이다.

풀이 접근법

● 연설의 목적, 소개 대상 등은 초반부에 단서가 제시된다.

● 장소, 업종, 직업을 묻는 문제는 초반부에 단서가 제시된다.

● 앞으로 해야 할 일을 묻는 문제의 단서는 담화 후반부에 제시된다.

🗐 기출 패턴 및 표현

담화의 흐름 및 관련 표현

인사, 프로그램 및 사람 소개 ⇩

- Hi, everyone. Welcome to ~. 안녕하세요, 여러분. ~에 오신 것을 환영합니다.
- I'm Jim, your instructor. 저는 여러분의 강사 Jim입니다.
- Thank you for coming ~. ~에 와주셔서 감사합니다.
- Good evening. You're listening to ~. 안녕하세요. 여러분은 ~을 청취하고 계십니다.

오늘의 게스트 및 주인공 소개 ⇩

- Our special guest is ~. 우리의 특별 게스트는 ~입니다.
- I proudly present ~. ~을 자랑스럽게 소개합니다.
- I'm pleased to introduce ~. ~을 소개하게 되어 기쁩니다.
- We welcome journalist Paul. 저널리스트 Paul을 환영합니다.

게스트의 정보 (직위, 과거 경력) ⇩

- Mr. Rubin was our executive director. Rubin 씨는 우리 회사의 임원이었습니다.
- After he retired, Mr. O'Brien started ~. O'Brien 씨는 은퇴한 후 ~를 시작했습니다.
- Ms. Maddow has worked in the financial sector.
  Maddow 씨는 재무 분야에서 근무했습니다.

시상 및 연설, 당부 및 요청

- Tonight, 오늘 밤,
- On today's show, 오늘 이 시간에는,
- Please come forward. 앞으로 나와 주세요.
- And now let's welcome Mr. Crowe. 이제 Crowe 씨를 환영합시다.

소개 관련 빈출 어휘

awards ceremony 시상식
founder 창립자, 설립자
insightful 통찰력 있는
contribute 공헌하다
dedicated to ~에 전념하는, 헌신하는
hold 개최하다
landmark 주요 지형 기물
guided tour 안내원이 딸린 여행[견학]
excursion 소풍, (단체) 여행
admission fee 입장료
conference 대회, 회의
job fair 취업 박람회
convention 박람회

function 행사
activity 활동
leading expert 뛰어난 전문가
do an outstanding job 뛰어난 업적을 이루다
begin one's career as ~로서 경력을 쌓기 시작하다
as a token of our appreciation 감사의 표시로
sign up 신청하다
schedule/itinerary (여행) 일정
enroll 등록하다
go over 검토하다
take place 일어나다
fill out a form 양식을 작성하다
organization 조직

LC PART 4

■ 음원을 듣고 답을 고르세요. 다시 들으면서 빈칸을 채우세요.

1. Where are the listeners?

(A) At an office

(B) At an airport

(C) At a supermarket

(D) At a museum

2. Who is the announcement for?

(A) Technicians

(B) Customers

(C) Office workers

(D) Store managers

3. According to the announcement, what will begin this afternoon?

(A) Office renovations

(B) The replacement of some equipment

(C) A work site inspection

(D) A board meeting

Attention, all employees. _____ you that some of the printers in our department _____ new ones this afternoon. A maintenance man will come _____ this afternoon. All employees should _____ the office while the replacement work _____. If you have any further questions, please call the _____.

4. What is the main purpose of the speech?

(A) To propose a project

(B) To notify employees of a meeting

(C) To recognize an employee

(D) To give a bonus

5. How long has Jinny been working in the Sales Department?

(A) Half a year

(B) 1 year

(C) 2 years

(D) 3 years

6. According to the speaker, what did Jinny do?

(A) She visited many countries.

(B) She completed many projects.

(C) She developed a lot of products.

(D) She signed a contract.

Thank you for coming to our annual _____. I'm pleased to announce this year's _____ is Jinny. She joined the Sales Department nearly three years ago. She _____ many projects, and they were all very successful. Our sales have also _____. And now I would like to invite Jinny to _____ to receive her award. Let's _____ for Jinny, who has worked tirelessly to _____ our company.

1. According to the speaker, what is the new office like?

   (A) It has a fully equipped meeting space.
   (B) It has a pleasant environment.
   (C) It has a beautiful view.
   (D) It has a spacious parking area.

2. When will the company move to the new building?

   (A) On Monday
   (B) On Thursday
   (C) On Friday
   (D) On Saturday

3. What are the listeners asked to do?

   (A) Order some office supplies
   (B) Remove their old furniture
   (C) Arrange their office supplies
   (D) Move their own documents

4. Where does this announcement most likely take place?

   (A) On a plane
   (B) At a bus station
   (C) On a cruise ship
   (D) At an airport

5. What is the cause of the problem?

   (A) Inclement weather conditions
   (B) Mechanical problems
   (C) The delay of a previous flight
   (D) The repairing of the runway

6. According to the announcement, what has been changed?

   (A) The departure date
   (B) The departure time
   (C) The schedule for a trip
   (D) The meal time

7. Where is the talk taking place?

   (A) At a conference
   (B) At an awards ceremony
   (C) At an employee training session
   (D) At a local broadcasting station

8. What is the purpose of the talk?

   (A) To notify the staff of a meeting
   (B) To advertise a new book
   (C) To introduce a guest speaker
   (D) To select a new manager

9. Who is Michael Rupin?

   (A) A salesperson
   (B) A conference planner
   (C) The general manager of a hotel
   (D) An accountant

10. Who most likely is the speaker?

    (A) A photographer
    (B) A technician
    (C) An architect
    (D) A tour guide

11. According to the talk, how does the B.P. Mosque differ from other mosques?

    (A) It has a different color than other mosques.
    (B) It looks older than other mosques.
    (C) It is larger than other mosques.
    (D) Its design is different than those of other mosques.

12. What will the listeners do next?

    (A) Take photographs of artworks
    (B) Look at another of Mr. Peter's structures
    (C) Take a short break at the mosque
    (D) Return to their hotel on their tour bus

LC PART 4

1. 음성 메시지

유형 소개 및 전략

음성 메시지는 전화를 건 사람이 남기는 것으로, 예약 확인, 변경 사항, 업무 협조 요청, 업무 진행 상황 등에 대한 내용이 주로 나온다.

유형 맛보기

Hi, Charlene. This is Jordan Cooper from World Journeys. **I'm calling to schedule an interview with you.** We received your application last week. (→ 'I'm calling ~.'으로 시작되는 부분에 전화 건 목적이 제시) You are someone who has the work experience that we are looking for. **You're going to interview with our supervisor Alex.** (→ 전화 건 목적 다음에는 구체적인 정보 등장) I will explain our staff policy to you after your interview. **Please let me know if you are available next Monday from 3:00 to 4:00 P.M.** You can reach me at 333-1928. (→ 명령문으로 요청 사항 언급) I look forward to hearing from you soon. Thank you.

안녕하세요. Charlene 씨, 저는 World Journeys 사의 Jordan Cooper입니다. 면접 일정을 잡으려고 전화드렸습니다. 지난주에 당신의 지원서를 받았습니다. 당신이 바로 우리가 찾던 경력을 갖춘 사람입니다. 당신은 저희 관리자인 Alex 씨와 면접을 보게 될 것입니다. 면접이 끝난 후 제가 직원 정책에 관해 설명해 드릴 겁니다. 다음 주 월요일 오후 3~4시에 면접 가능하신지 알려주시기 바랍니다. 333-1928로 저한테 연락하시기 바랍니다. 연락 기다리겠습니다. 감사합니다.

1. What is the purpose of the message?
(A) To reserve a meeting room
(B) To schedule an appointment
(C) To confirm an appointment
(D) To change a schedule

메시지의 목적은 무엇인가?
(A) 회의실을 예약하기 위해
(B) 약속을 잡기 위해
(C) 약속을 확인하기 위해
(D) 일정을 변경하기 위해

2. Who will be interviewing Charlene?
(A) A manager
(B) A supervisor
(C) A director
(D) A president

누가 Charlene을 인터뷰할 것인가?
(A) 지배인
(B) 관리자
(C) 감독
(D) 사장

3. What does the speaker ask the listener to do?
(A) Apply for a position
(B) Call him to confirm an interview
(C) Send him more details
(D) Contact a reference

3. 화자는 청자에게 무엇을 하라고 요청하는가?
(A) 자리에 지원한다
(B) 면접을 확정하기 위해 그에게 전화한다
(C) 그에게 더 많은 세부사항을 보낸다
(D) 추천인에게 연락한다

풀이 접근법

● 메시지의 목적은 주로 초반부에 발신인과 수신인이 나온 후 I'm calling to ~로 시작되는 부분에 제시된다.

● 요청 사항을 묻는 문제는 후반부에 나오는 관련 표현(명령문)을 잘 듣는다.

≡ 기출 패턴 및 표현

담화의 흐름 및 관련 표현

인사말, 발신자, 수신자 정보, 직업, 업종, 회사
⇩

- Hi, Mr. Decker ~. 안녕하세요, Decker 씨.
- This is (이름) from (회사) ~. 저는 ~ 회사의 ~입니다.
- This is George Santos, the sales manager at Star Boutique.
  저는 Star Boutique의 영업 관리자 George Santos입니다.

목적, 문제점
⇩

- I'm calling about ~. ~에 대해 전화 드렸습니다.
- I'm calling to ~. ~하기 위해 전화 드렸습니다.
- I'd like to inform ~. ~을 알려 드리려고 합니다.
- You sent us a message with your concerns about ~.
  ~에 관한 우려의 메시지를 저희에게 보내셨습니다.

시점과 관련된 구체적인 정보
⇩

- On Friday 금요일에
- On August 15 8월 15일에

요구 및 제안
⇩

- Please call me back at + (연락처). ~로 연락해 주세요.
- We ask that ~. ~을 요청합니다.
- I want you to ~. ~해주시기 바랍니다.

추후 일정
⇩

- We'll be posting answers. 답변을 공지할 겁니다.

연락 정보 문의처 및 연락처

- You can visit our Web site. 저희 웹사이트를 방문해 주세요.
- I can be reached at (연락처). ~로 연락해 주세요.

음성 메시지 관련 빈출 어휘

reach 연락이 닿다	connect 연결하다
contact 연락하다	voicemail box 음성 사서함
extension (number) 내선번호	leave a message 메시지를 남기다
respond to ~에 회신하다	take a message 메시지를 받아 적다
beep 삐 하는 소리	return one's call ~에게 회신 전화하다

LC PART 4

2. ARS

유형 소개 및 전략

ARS는 수신자가 부재중임을 알리는 녹음된 메시지로, 회사의 자동 안내 메시지가 자주 등장한다. 주로 업체 소개나, 영업 시간, 내선번호 등을 안내하는 내용이 나온다. 지문의 구조나 흐름이 대부분 비슷하므로 미리 숙지해 두면 좋다.

유형 맛보기

Hello. **You have reached Chancy Bank.** (→ 초반부에 '은행'이라고 언급) **We are currently closed because of the public holiday.** (→ 지문 초반부는 회사, 수신자 소개 또는 부재중 이유 언급) Our regular working hours are from 9:00 A.M. to 4:00 P.M. from Monday to Friday, and we are closed on all public holidays. For instructions in Chinese, press 2. **To check on information regarding new accounts, press 3.** (→ 서비스 번호 안내는 주로 후반부에 등장) If you need to speak with a customer service representative, please call back during our regular business hours. Thank you for calling and have a nice day.

안녕하십니까. Chancy 은행입니다. 공휴일이므로 현재는 영업하고 있지 않습니다. 저희 정규 근무 시간은 월요일부터 금요일까지 오전 9시부터 오후 4시까지이며, 모든 공휴일에는 영업하지 않습니다. 중국어 안내는 2번을 누르십시오. 신규 계좌에 대한 안내 확인은 3번을 누르십시오. 저희 고객 서비스 상담원과 통화를 원하신다면 정규 영업 시간에 다시 전화 주십시오. 전화 주셔서 감사드리며, 좋은 하루 보내십시오.

---

1. Who is the message intended for?
- (A) Hospital patients
- (B) Tourists
- **(C) Bank customers**
- (D) Chinese workers

누구를 위한 메시지인가?
- (A) 병원 환자
- (B) 관광객
- **(C) 은행 고객**
- (D) 중국인 노동자

2. What does the speaker say about the customer service representatives?
- (A) They work in another office.
- **(B) They are not currently working.**
- (C) They are on other lines.
- (D) They haven't arrived yet.

화자는 고객 서비스 직원에 대해 뭐라고 말하는가?
- (A) 다른 사무실에서 일하고 있다.
- **(B) 현재 근무하고 있지 않다.**
- (C) 다른 전화를 받고 있다.
- (D) 아직 도착하지 않았다.

3. What will the listener hear by pressing 3?
- (A) Instructions in Chinese
- **(B) Information about an account**
- (C) The bank's working hours
- (D) The bank's location

3번을 누르면 청자는 어떤 정보를 듣게 되는가?
- (A) 중국어 안내
- **(B) 계좌 정보**
- (C) 은행 영업 시간
- (D) 은행 위치

풀이 접근법

- 메시지를 남기는 주체는 담화 초반 인사말 뒤 'Thank you for calling ~, You have reached ~'에 제시된다.
- 서비스 번호 안내는 담화 중후반부 'Please press + 번호 (to find ~). Press + 번호 (to check ~)'가 언급된 곳에서 등장한다.

☰ 기출 패턴 및 표현

인사말(회사 또는 수신자 소개) ⇩	• Hello. You've reached + (회사/부서). 안녕하세요. ~입니다. • Thanks for calling ~. ~에 전화 주셔서 감사합니다.
회사 소개, 부재 이유, 영업 시간 안내 ⇩	• Our company is known for ~. 저희 회사는 ~로 유명합니다. • The office is currently closed ~. ~로 인해 현재 문을 닫았습니다. • Our business hours are ~. 저희 영업 시간은 ~입니다.
서비스 번호 및 연락처 안내 ⇩	• Please press 3 to find ~. ~을 찾으시려면 3번을 누르세요. • Press 1 to check ~. ~을 확인하시려면 1번을 누르세요. • Please call back ~. ~로 다시 전화해 주세요.
제안&요청 및 당부 사항	• For more information, 더 자세한 사항은, • Please call again. 다시 전화해 주세요.

ARS 관련 빈출 어휘

pound key 우물 정자(#)
star key 별표(*)
page 호출하다
stay on the line 전화를 끊지 않고 기다리다
hold the line 끊지 않고 기다리다
operator 전화 상담원
business hours 영업시간

talk on the phone 통화하다
Press number + 번호. ~번을 누르세요.
Thank you for calling ~. ~에 전화 주셔서 감사합니다.
Our store is at ~. 저희 매장은 ~에 있습니다.
We are open from ~. 저희 영업 시간은 ~입니다.
automated message 자동 응답 메시지
after the tone 신호음이 나온 후

■ 음원을 듣고 답을 고르세요. 다시 들으면서 빈칸을 채우세요.

1. Where does the speaker work?

(A) At a recruiting agency

(B) At a paper supply company

(C) At a hospital

(D) At a university

2. Why does the speaker say, "We already have many volunteers signed up for this event"?

(A) To make a request

(B) To extend an invitation

(C) To reassure an event planner

(D) To decline an offer

3. What does the speaker ask the listener to do?

(A) Pay a registration fee

(B) Attend a meeting

(C) Complete an online form

(D) Pick a date and a time

4. According to the message, what is the Victory Zoo known for?

(A) Its delicious food

(B) A diverse number of animals

(C) A wide range of insects

(D) Its unusual plants

5. Why should the listeners press 1?

(A) To book a ticket

(B) To speak to a representative

(C) To cancel a reservation

(D) To ask for information

6. How can the listeners get more information?

(A) By pressing the number 1

(B) By visiting a Web site

(C) By calling the given number

(D) By reading a brochure

Hello, Sam Taylor. This is Emily from the Meadowlands _____. Thank you so much for _____ helping out at our medical center's fundraising banquet next week. We already have many volunteers _____ this event, but I'd love to add you to our list for future _____. Could you please visit our Web site and complete a short volunteer _____? This way, we'll have your information on file, and _____ as soon as there's a chance to get involved _____. Thanks again and have a fantastic day!

_____ the Victory Zoo. Our zoo is internationally famous for our _____ animals. We're open every day from 10:00 A.M. to 5:00 P.M. Entrance tickets can only _____. If you want to make a reservation now, _____. Cash and credit cards are accepted, and you can pay at the ticket booth _____. For more information, please call one of our customer _____ at 999-6738.

ACTUAL TEST

1. Who most likely is the caller?

   (A) An office tenant
   (B) A maintenance man
   (C) A real estate agent
   (D) A landlord

2. What is the purpose of the message?

   (A) To give the location of an office
   (B) To notify the man that an office is available to rent
   (C) To announce some construction work
   (D) To advertise a new building

3. What will the listener do next?

   (A) Sign a contract
   (B) Move to a new office
   (C) Contact Linda Rey
   (D) Call the owner of a building

4. What is the man waiting for?

   (A) His boarding pass to be printed
   (B) His hotel room to be cleaned
   (C) His clients to arrive
   (D) His luggage to be returned

5. What is scheduled for Friday?

   (A) A job interview
   (B) A product presentation
   (C) A factory inspection
   (D) A press release

6. Why does the man say, "I know it's a long trip"?

   (A) To advise the listener to get some rest
   (B) To suggest that a trip is unnecessary
   (C) To apologize for an inconvenience
   (D) To remind the listener to plan carefully

Isabella's Afternoon Schedule	
10:00 A.M.	Client Lunch
11:00 A.M.	Board Meeting
3:00 P.M.	Personal Conference
4:00 P.M.	Board Meeting
5:00 P.M.	Performance Review

7. What does the speaker want to discuss with the listener?

   (A) Traveling to North America
   (B) Revising a customer survey
   (C) Adding subtitles to a video
   (D) Reducing departmental spending

8. What does the speaker say she will lead tomorrow?

   (A) An international conference
   (B) An advertising workshop
   (C) A final interview
   (D) A quarterly review

9. Look at the graphic. When will the speaker and the listener most likely meet?

   (A) At 10:00 A.M.
   (B) At 11:00 A.M.
   (C) At 4:00 P.M.
   (D) At 5:00 P.M.

UNIT 15 방송&광고

1. 방송

≡ 유형 소개 및 전략

방송은 크게 일기예보와 교통방송으로 나뉜다. 일기예보는 날씨와 관련된 표현들을 꼭 암기해 두고 반전(however, but), 결론(so) 등의 표현 다음에 이어지는 문장은 반드시 정답 단서가 등장하므로 놓치지 말고 들어야 한다. 교통방송의 경우, 도로 공사, 악천후 등의 원인으로 생기는 교통체증을 안내하는 내용이 주로 나온다. 이때 '우회하라', '대중교통을 이용하라'는 등의 조언이 이어지는 흐름이 일반적이다. 방송 시간, 청자가 해야 할 일, 권유 사항 등이 문제로 자주 출제된다.

유형 맛보기

This is Stacy Howard with your weather update.
(→ 초반에 방송 종류 소개) Today's weather is going to be rainy. If you are going to leave your house today, **don't forget to bring your umbrella with you**. (→ 프로그램 종류를 언급한 후 바로 뒤이어 날씨에 대한 조언이 나온다.) Tomorrow will be sunny, and the weather will be nice. **However, on the weekend, we will see some unseasonably hot and humid weather throughout the country.** (→ 후반부는 향후 날씨에 관한 내용이 나온다. 특히 However 뒤에 이어지는 문장에 정답 단서가 자주 등장) The temperature is expected to continue rising during the weekend. That is all for the morning weather report.

저는 여러분께 날씨 정보를 알려드릴 Stacy Howard 입니다. 오늘은 비가 오겠습니다. 오늘 집을 나가신다면, 우산 챙기시는 거 잊지 마세요. 내일은 화창하고 맑은 날이 되겠습니다. 그러나 주말은 전국에 걸쳐 때아닌 덥고 습한 날씨가 예상됩니다. 기온은 주말 동안 계속해서 오를 것으로 예상합니다. 지금까지 아침 날씨 소식이었습니다.

1. What is the purpose of the report?

   (A) To advertise public transportation
   (B) To report on the weather conditions
   (C) To interview some politicians
   (D) To announce some construction work

이 보도의 목적은 무엇인가?

   (A) 대중교통을 광고하기 위해
   (B) 우비 상태를 보도하기 위해
   (C) 정치인을 인터뷰하기 위해
   (D) 건설 작업을 공지하기 위해

2. What does the speaker suggest the listeners do today?

   (A) Take their umbrellas
   (B) Wear raincoats
   (C) Use public transportation
   (D) Drink a lot of water

화자는 청자들에게 오늘 무엇을 하라고 제안하는가?

   (A) 우산 챙기기
   (B) 우비 입기
   (C) 대중교통 이용하기
   (D) 물 많이 마시기

3. How will the weather be on the weekend?

   (A) Partly cloudy
   (B) Rainy
   (C) Hot and humid
   (D) Sunny

주말 날씨는 어떻겠는가?

   (A) 부분적으로 흐린
   (B) 비가 오는
   (C) 덥고 습한
   (D) 화창한

풀이 접근법

- 일기예보의 경우, 프로그램 소개 → 오늘 날씨 소개 → 날씨에 따른 조언 순으로 나온다.
- 향후 날씨는 후반부에 구체적 시점(tomorrow, on the weekend)과 함께 등장한다.
- 교통방송의 경우, 정체 이유를 묻는 문제가 자주 출제된다. 초반부에 인사 후 정체 이유가 언급되므로 잘 들어야 한다.
- 반전의 표현(however, but) 뒤에 정답 단서가 등장할 확률이 높다.

기출 패턴 및 표현

일기예보의 흐름 및 관련 표현

인사, 프로그램 소개 ⇩	• Good evening. You're listening to ~. 안녕하세요. 여러분은 ~을 청취하고 있습니다. • This is the morning weather forecast. 아침 일기예보입니다.
현재 날씨, 조언 ⇩	• The current temperature is ~. 현재 기온은 ~입니다. • Don't forget to take ~. ~을 가져가는 것을 잊지 마세요.
앞으로의 날씨 ⇩	• However, the sky ~. 그러나 하늘은 ~. • Tomorrow will ~. 내일은 ~할 겁니다.
다음 방송 안내	• I'll have the next weather report in + 시간. ~에 다음 날씨 정보를 알려드리겠습니다.

교통방송의 흐름 및 관련 표현

인사 ⇩	• Good morning, commuters. 안녕하세요, 통근자 여러분. • This is the 7:00 A.M. traffic report. 오전 7시 교통정보입니다.
교통 상황 및 정체 이유 ⇩	• Because of the ongoing thunderstorm, 계속되는 폭풍우 때문에, • There was repair work. 수리 작업이 있었습니다.
대안 제시 ⇩	• We recommend avoiding ~. ~을 피할 것을 권합니다. • Drivers should consider using ~. 운전자들은 ~을 이용할 것을 고려하시기 바랍니다. • We advise you to take Route 15. 15번 도로를 이용하세요.
다음 방송 시간 안내	• Coming up at 7:00. 7시에 다시 뵙겠습니다.

일기예보 관련 빈출 어휘

weather report 일기예보

inclement weather 악천후

high pressure 고기압

low pressure 저기압

temperature 온도

humidity 습도

degree (온도 단위) 도

precipitation 강수량

Celsius 섭씨

Fahrenheit 화씨

rain check 우천 교환권

drought 가뭄

rain shower 소나기

drizzle 이슬비

gusty windy 돌풍

flood 홍수

downpour 폭우

foggy/misty 안개 낀

cloudy/overcast 구름 낀

humid 습한

dry 건조한

sunny/clear 맑은

교통방송 관련 빈출 어휘

road/route 도로

traffic report 교통방송

commuter 통근자

motorist 운전자

driver 운전자

stall 오도가도 못하다

lane 차선

expressway 고속도로

accident 사고

construction 공사

renovation 보수 공사

time-consuming 시간이 걸리는

avenue/street/path 길

take an alternate route 다른 길로 가다, 우회하다

be closed down 폐쇄되다

traffic jam [congestion] 교통체증

be stuck in traffic 교통체증에 걸리다

be held up 막히다

destination 목적지

detour 우회하다, 둘러 가다

2. 광고

≡ 유형 소개 및 전략

제품, 서비스, 업체 광고가 주를 이루며, 광고 대상, 특징 및 장점, 혜택, 추가 정보와 관련하여 묻는 문제가 자주 출제된다. 특히, 제품 광고는 제품의 특징을 설명하는 different, special, 최상급 같은 표현을 잘 들어야 한다. 특히 후반부에 나오는 '명령문 + 주어 + 동사 ~ / please ~'은 문제와 직결되는 정답 단서 표현이다.

유형 맛보기

Why don't you subscribe to the *Milan Times*? (→ 광고 제품이나 서비스 종류는 초반부에 등장) We are a nationally popular newspaper that provides our readers with plenty of information. You don't have to waste your precious time buying the paper anymore. Now, you can conveniently receive the paper at your home and get it at an affordable price. **If you subscribe to the *Milan Times*, you'll get a free copy of our weekend fashion magazine.** (→ 구매 혜택과 같은 세부 정보는 중후반부에 제시) **For more information or to subscribe now, please call 3451-5359.** (→ 구매 방법, 구매처, 연락 방법 등은 후반부에 등장)

저희 <Milan Times>를 구독해 보시는 것은 어떠세요? 저희는 독자들에게 풍부한 정보를 제공하는 신문으로 전국적으로 유명합니다. 귀하는 신문을 구매하느라 더 이상 소중한 시간을 낭비할 필요가 없습니다. 이제 귀하의 집에서 저렴한 가격으로 편리하게 신문을 받아보세요. <Milan Times>를 구독하실 경우, 주간 패션잡지를 무료로 받아보시게 될 것입니다. 더 자세한 사항이나 바로 구독을 원하시면, 3451-5359로 연락 주십시오.

1. What is being advertised?
(A) Office supplies
(B) A medical journal
(C) A fashion magazine
(D) A newspaper

광고되고 있는 것은 무엇인가?
(A) 사무용품
(B) 의학저널
(C) 패션잡지
(D) 신문

2. What advantage does the company offer?
(A) Discount coupons
(B) Promotional gifts
(C) Free magazines
(D) Free download services

회사는 어떤 혜택을 제공하는가?
(A) 할인 쿠폰
(B) 사은품
(C) 무료 잡지
(D) 무료 다운로드 서비스

3. How can customers subscribe?
(A) By visiting a Web site
(B) By sending an e-mail
(C) By going to the office
(D) By calling a phone number

고객들은 어떻게 구독할 수 있는가?
(A) 홈페이지에 방문함으로써
(B) 이메일을 보냄으로써
(C) 사무실을 방문함으로써
(D) 전화를 함으로써

≡ 풀이 접근법

● 광고 대상은 초반부에서 Are you looking for ~?, Are you interested in ~? 다음에 등장한다.

● 구매 혜택 관련 내용은 주로 중후반에 등장한다.

● 구매 방법, 구매처, 연락 방법 등은 주로 후반부에서 명령문(please ~) 형태로 나온다.

기출 패턴 및 표현

담화의 흐름 및 관련 표현

광고하는 물건이나 서비스 광고 대상, 제품에 대한 문제점 ⇩	• We have a good reputation for having ~. 저희는 ~으로 평판이 좋습니다. • Are you looking for ~? ~을 찾고 계십니까? • Are you having trouble ~? ~에 어려움을 겪고 계십니까? • If you have a problem ~. ~에 문제가 있으면 ~.
제품의 특징과 장점 회사에 대한 소개 ⇩	• One of the features is ~ 한 가지 특징은 ~ • Our firm has ~. 저희 회사는 ~을 갖고 있습니다.
구매/할인 혜택 ⇩	• We offer the best prices. 저희는 최저 가격으로 제공합니다. • You'll also receive ~ for free. 무료로 ~도 받으실 수 있습니다. • You'll get a free gift. 무료 선물을 받으실 겁니다. • Winter clothing is half price. 겨울옷은 반값입니다. • Members will receive a complimentary gift. 회원들은 무료 선물을 받으실 수 있습니다. • Apparel is 30 percent off. 의류는 30% 할인됩니다. • ~ is only available until the end of the month. ~은 이달 말까지만 이용 가능합니다.
영업시간 ⇩	• We open for business at 8:00 A.M. 오전 8시에 문을 엽니다. • We open at 9:00 A.M. every day. 저희는 매일 오전 9시에 개장합니다.
구매처 및 연락 방법	• Give us a call at ~. ~로 전화해 주세요. • Please call ~. ~로 전화해 주세요. • Visit our Web site at www.aka.ms.com. 저희 웹사이트 www.aka.ms.com을 방문하세요. • Order your new mobile phone today. 오늘 새 휴대전화를 주문하세요.

feature ~을 특징으로 하다

reliable 믿을만한

excellent service 훌륭한 서비스

promotion 홍보, 판촉 행사

complimentary 무료로 제공되는

at no extra charge 무료로

free shipping 무료 배송

trial period 무료 체험 기간

clearance sale 재고정리 세일

opening sale 개점 세일

anniversary sale 기념 세일

holiday sale 휴일 세일

today only 오늘만

half off 50% 할인

for a limited time only 제한된 기간에만, 한시적으로

guarantee 보장하다

helpful employee 도움이 되는 직원

durable/strong 튼튼한

good quality 좋은 품질

best deal 최상의 거래

material 재료

ingredient 재료

reasonable [affordable/low] price 저렴한 가격

expired 기간이 지난

effective 유효한

valid 유효한

special offer 특가 상품

discount 할인

off 할인되어

mark down 할인하다, 가격을 내리다

souvenir 기념품

demonstration 시연, 설명

patron 후원자, 고객

remarkable 주목할 만한

prestigious 명성 있는, 유명한

world-renowned 세계적으로 유명한

nutritious 영양가 있는

comfortable 편안한

innovative 혁신적인

adjustable 조절 가능한

easy to assemble 조립하기 쉬운

handy 유용한, 편리한

word-of-mouth 구두의, 입소문의

durability 내구성

emerging 부상하는, 최근 생겨난

water-resistant 방수의

one-of-a-kind 특별한

top-of-the-line 최고급의, 최신식의

LC PART 4

■ 음원을 듣고 답을 고르세요. 다시 들으면서 빈칸을 채우세요.

1. How will the weather change today?

(A) It will snow.

(B) It will be colder.

(C) It will get hotter.

(D) It will become foggy.

2. What will happen on Sunday?

(A) The temperature will increase.

(B) Fierce winds will blow.

(C) Snow is expected.

(D) The temperature will remain the same.

3. What will the listeners probably hear next?

(A) A traffic report

(B) An advertisement

(C) A sports report

(D) Business news

Good morning. There will be no rain _____.
Through the morning, the temperature will
_____, and there will be scorching
hot weather _____. However,
I have some good news for you. The wind will blow
on Saturday, and it will be a _____
surfing. But it looks like a big typhoon is coming
our way on Sunday. We'll _____.
Now, let's go to Jane Watson for an update on
today's _____.

4. What is the advertisement for?

(A) A network system

(B) Office furniture

(C) Electronic devices

(D) Kitchen supplies

5. What advantage of the item is mentioned?

(A) It is very easy to use.

(B) It is cheaper than last year's model.

(C) It is the smallest one in the world.

(D) It comes in a variety of colors.

6. How can the listeners get more information?

(A) By visiting a store

(B) By sending an e-mail

(C) By calling a specific number

(D) By visiting a Web site

The UCA Company's new digital camera looks very
cute, and it _____. First, it's easy
to use. It has an auto-system, so you only
have to set up the camera _____
once. It uses Wi-Fi as well, and it can be connected
to a personal computer _____.
This adorable camera is easy for _____.
For more information, _____
www.ucaelectronics.com.

1. What is the main purpose of the report?

   (A) To provide a weather report
   (B) To announce a city festival
   (C) To provide construction information
   (D) To advertise a new car

2. What does the speaker recommend?

   (A) Listening for news updates
   (B) Driving carefully
   (C) Taking public transportation
   (D) Taking another route

3. How can the listeners get updated information?

   (A) By listening to the radio
   (B) By watching TV
   (C) By visiting a Web site
   (D) By calling a number

4. What is being advertised?

   (A) Real estate
   (B) A sporting goods store
   (C) A furniture factory
   (D) A paint store

5. When will the apartments be available to rent?

   (A) The following month
   (B) Next year
   (C) Next Friday
   (D) At the end of the year

6. What is free for all residents of LX Apartments?

   (A) The supermarket
   (B) The fitness facilities
   (C) The playground
   (D) The parking lot

Room Type	Rate
Superior Room	190 Euros
Executive Standard	215 Euros
Executive Suite	245 Euros
Luxury Suite	270 Euros

7. Who most likely is this advertisement intended for?

   (A) Company executives
   (B) Renovation workers
   (C) Travelers
   (D) Hotel staff

8. Why is the business offering a special deal?

   (A) To celebrate its anniversary
   (B) To promote its opening
   (C) To raise money for renovations
   (D) To commemorate its remodeling

9. Look at the graphic. For what price will the luxury suite be available this month?

   (A) 190 euros
   (B) 215 euros
   (C) 245 euros
   (D) 270 euros

◆ **패러프레이징 (PARAPHRASING)**

패러프레이징이란 '다른 말로 바꾸어 표현하는 것'을 뜻한다. 대화 내의 단서가 보기에 그대로 나오는 경우도 있지만, 바뀌어 제시되는 경우가 많으므로 대표적인 표현을 미리 알아두면 도움이 된다.

① **동의어, 유의어 활용**

W As soon as I've finished **handing out these department memos**, I'll take care of it for you. 이 부서 회람을 다 나눠드리는 대로 처리해 드릴게요.	Q What will the woman do next? A **Distribute some documents** **질문** 여자는 다음에 무엇을 할 것인가? **정답** 문서 배포하기

② **포괄적 개념을 지닌 상위어 활용**

M Hello. This Nic Gill from Office Max. We received **three boxes of stationery** from your store today. 안녕하세요. Office Max의 Nic Gill입니다. 귀하로부터 오늘 문구 3박스를 받았습니다.	Q Where does the man work? A At an **office supply** company **질문** 남자는 어디서 일하는가? **정답** 사무용품 회사에서

③ **품사 변경**

W I submitted my **application** for the sales position last week. 제가 지난주에 영업직에 지원서를 제출했어요.	Q What did the woman do last week? A She **applied for** a job. **질문** 여자가 지난주에 한 일은 무엇인가? **정답** 일자리에 지원했다.

④ **내용 축약**

M Do you think we should start doing something to **cut down on our electricity bill**? 우리가 전기요금을 줄이기 위해 조치를 취해야 한다고 생각해요?	Q What is the conversation mainly about? A **Energy conservation** **질문** 대화의 주제는 무엇인가? **정답** 에너지 절약

⑤ 어휘들을 종합한 정답 유추 (대화 장소/직업/근무 분야)

menu, main dish, server, dining area, reserve a table	→	restaurant 식당
room, suite, front desk, housekeeping, check in [out]	→	hotel 호텔
washing machine, clothes, dryer	→	laundromat 빨래방
open account, withdrawal, deposit, account number	→	bank teller 은행 창구 직원
house, condo, apartment, property, rent, tenant, landlord, move in [out]	→	real estate agent 부동산 중개인

⑥ 페러프레이징 예시 1

| I'd like to welcome everyone to TFL Healthcare's annual **shareholders'** meeting.
TFL Healthcare 사의 연례 주주 총회에 참석하신 모든 분들을 환영합니다. | **Q** Who are the listeners?
A **People who own stock** in a company
질문 청자들은 누구인가?
정답 회사 주식 보유자들 |

⑦ 페러프레이징 예시 2

| All employees are reminded that they must **attach the bill from the moving company** to the correct form in order to be eligible for reimbursement.
모든 직원들은 환급 받기 위해 이사업체로부터 받은 청구서를 알맞은 양식에 꼭 첨부해야 합니다. | **Q** What do employees need to get reimbursed?
A **Certain documents**
질문 직원들은 환급을 받으려면 무엇이 필요한가?
정답 특정 서류 |

⑧ 페러프레이징 예시 3

| I would also like to ask everyone to **turn off your cell phones and laptops during takeoff and landing**.
또한 이륙과 착륙 시에는 휴대폰과 노트북 전원을 꺼 주실 것을 부탁드립니다. | **Q** What are the passengers asked to do during takeoff and landing?
A **Turn off electrical devices**
질문 승객들은 이착륙시 무엇을 하도록 요청받는가?
정답 전자기기 끄기 |

PART

5

단문 빈칸
채우기

RC

단문의 빈칸을 채우는 유형으로, 101번에서 130번까지 총 30문항이 출제된다. 문제 유형은 크게 문법 문제와 어휘 문제 두 가지로 나눌 수 있다. 어휘 문제의 비중이 더 높으며, 문법과 어휘가 혼합된 유형이 등장하기도 한다.

구성	PART	유형		문항 수	시간	배점
Reading Comprehension	5	단문 빈칸 채우기 (문법/어휘)		30	75분	495점
	6	장문 빈칸 채우기		16		
	7	독해	단일 지문	29		
			이중 지문	10		
			삼중 지문	15		

📢 문제 유형

● **문법 문제** 문장 구조에 맞는 명사, 동사, 형용사, 부사, 전치사, 접속사를 고르는 품사 자리 판단 문제, 인칭대명사의 격, 재귀대명사, 동사의 태, 시제, 수 일치, 비교급 및 최상급, 관계대명사의 용법 문제 등이 출제된다.
● **어휘 문제** 의미상 알맞은 명사, 동사, 형용사, 부사, 전치사, 접속사 선택 문제 등이 출제된다.

📢 풀이 전략 1 [문법편]

101. Consumers can ------- enroll online in our marketing course.
    (A) ease
    (B) easy
    (C) **easily**
    (D) easing

해석 소비자들은 온라인으로 저희의 마케팅 과정을 쉽게 등록할 수 있습니다.

① 빈칸의 앞뒤와 보기를 확인한다.
② 보기가 각기 다른 품사가 나열되면, 빈칸이 어떤 품사의 자리인지 판단한다.
➡ 빈칸 앞에는 조동사, 뒤에는 동사원형이 있으므로 동사를 수식하는 부사 자리이다.

102. The requirements for the position will ------- on the Web site.
    (A) post
    (B) posting
    (C) posts
    (D) **be posted**

해석 직책에 대한 요구 사항은 웹 사이트에 게시됩니다.

① 빈칸의 앞뒤와 보기를 확인한다.
② 보기에 같은 동사의 여러 형태가 나열되면, 시제, 수, 태를 고려해 어떤 동사의 형태가 와야 하는지를 판단한다.
➡ 빈칸 앞 조동사의 뒤에는 동사원형이 와야 하며 빈칸 뒤에 목적어가 아닌 부사구가 나오므로 수동태가 와야 한다.

풀이 전략 2 [어휘편]

103. He responded ------- to the questions from the customers.
(A) highly
(B) centrally
(C) significantly
(D) swiftly

해석 그는 고객들의 질문에 신속하게 답했다.

① 빈칸의 앞뒤와 보기를 확인한다.

② 빈칸은 동사를 수식하는 부사 자리로, 보기가 모두 부사 어휘이므로 해석이 필요하다.

➲ 빈칸을 제외한 문장을 해석한 후, 동사 responded(응답했다)와 호응하는 부사 swiftly(신속히)를 선택하고 전체 해석을 검토한다.

104. The director will ------- a speech before tonight's benefit dinner.
(A) accept
(B) notify
(C) deliver
(D) damage

해석 이사님이 오늘밤 자선 만찬 전에 연설을 하실 겁니다.

① 빈칸의 앞뒤와 보기를 확인한다.

② 빈칸은 동사 자리로, 보기가 모두 동사 어휘이므로 해석이 필요하다.

➲ 목적어 speech와 짝을 이루는 동사 deliver를 선택한다. speech와 짝을 이루는 동사에는 give, make, deliver 등이 있다. 이와 같이 빈출 collocation을 암기해 두면 어휘 문제를 빠르게 풀 수 있다.

최신 출제 경향

① 문법적 지식과 어휘력을 동시에 묻는 문제들이 출제된다.
➲ 명사 자리인데 보기에 형태가 비슷한 명사(가산명사와 불가산 명사, 사람 명사와 사물 명사)가 두 개 이상 나오는 문제가 출제된다.

② 두 가지 이상의 문법 포인트를 묻는 문제들이 출제된다.
➲ 동사의 문장 형식을 이해하고 수 일치, 태(수동태와 능동태), 시제를 결정하는 복합적인 문제가 출제된다.

③ 다양한 품사의 보기로 구성된 문제들이 출제된다.
➲ 부사 문제이지만 전치사, 접속사, 관용표현 등으로 선택지가 구성된다.

만점 전략

- 무조건 해석부터 하지 말고 보기를 보고 어휘 문제와 문법/어형 문제 중 어떤 유형인지부터 확인한다. 어형 문제는 해석 없이도 빈칸의 자리만 확인하면 답을 고를 수 있는 문제가 대부분이므로 최대한 시간을 절약할 수 있는 방법으로 풀어가야 한다.
- 고득점을 얻기 위해서는 한 단어를 외우더라도 품사, 파생어, 용법을 함께 암기해야 한다. 예를 들어, ask를 외울 때 <ask 목적어[사람] to do>와 같은 형식으로 암기하면, ask 다음 목적어 자리에 사람 명사와 사물 명사의 구별 문제, to do 자리에 to부정사와 동명사의 구별 문제를 동시에 대비할 수 있다. 뿐만 아니라 수동태 형태 [be asked to V]와 같은 패턴도 함께 알아두면 PART 5 문제를 빠르게 해결할 수 있다.

UNIT 01 명사

기출 패턴 1 **명사 자리 문제가 출제된다.**

① 명사는 문장에서 주어, 목적어, 보어 자리에 올 수 있다.

주어 자리
The **renovation** of the hotel's main lobby is scheduled to begin in May.
호텔 메인 로비의 보수공사는 5월에 시작될 예정이다.

동사의 목적어 자리
Metro Transportation does not offer **refunds** for lost tickets.
메트로 교통은 분실된 티켓에 대한 환불을 제공하지 않습니다.

전치사의 목적어 자리
All of the attendees must present valid tickets at the **entrance**.
모든 참가자는 입구에서 유효한 티켓을 제시해야 합니다.

보어 자리
It will be Ms. Cox's **responsibility** to review all corporate contracts.
모든 기업의 계약들을 검토하는 것은 Cox 씨의 책무가 될 것이다.

② 명사는 관사, 소유격, 형용사 뒤에 올 수 있다.

관사 뒤
Mr. Hewson has arranged a **tour** of the building for all new employees.
Hewson 씨는 신입사원들을 위해 건물 견학을 마련했다.

소유격 뒤
Ms. Gadon announced her **intent** to open a new retail clothing outlet.
Gadon 씨는 새로운 의류 소매점을 열겠다는 뜻을 밝혔다.

형용사 뒤
The fragile **package** should be handled with care during shipping.
파손되기 쉬운 패키지는 배송 중 주의해서 취급해야 한다.

③ 명사 자리에 동사, 형용사 등이 오답 보기로 제시된다.

Mr. Jackson has performed an [~~invent~~, **inventory**] of the electronic equipment.
Jackson 씨는 전자 장비에 대한 재고 조사를 했다.

CHECK-UP
☑ 다음 문장의 빈칸에 들어갈 알맞은 말을 고르세요.   정답 및 해설 p.376

1. Ms. Blackwell received an impressive recommendation from her previous -------.

(A) employ   (B) employer

2. Our team is currently working on the ------- of a new marketing strategy.

(A) develop   (B) development

3. G-Motors has demonstrated extraordinary ------- in the design of electric vehicles.

(A) creative   (B) creativity

가산 명사(셀 수 있는 명사)와 불가산 명사(셀 수 없는 명사)의 구별 문제가 출제된다.

① 관사 a/an은 단수 가산 명사 앞에만 오며, 복수 가산 명사나 불가산 명사 앞에는 올 수 없다.

빈출 가산 명사		빈출 불가산 명사	
certificate 증명서	interest 이익, 이자	interest 관심, 흥미	advice 조언
survey (설문) 조사	profit 이익	merchandise 상품	satisfaction 만족
detail 세부사항	permit 허가증	knowledge 지식	participation 참가
discount 할인	request 요청	information 정보	construction 건설
refund 환불	requirement 요구사항	access 접근, 출입	luggage/baggage 짐

A more detailed [~~descriptions~~, **description**] will be available on the company Web site.
더 상세한 설명은 회사 홈페이지에서 볼 수 있다.

[~~Accesses~~, **Access**] to the laboratory is restricted to authorized researchers.
실험실 출입은 권한을 부여 받은 연구자들로 제한된다. → 불가산 명사는 복수형으로 쓸 수 없으며, 앞에 a/an이 올 수 없다. 단, 정관사 the는 올 수 있다.

▶ 주의해야 할 가산/불가산 명사

가산 명사	불가산 명사	가산 명사	불가산 명사
a plan 계획	planning 계획	a permit 허가증	permission 허가
a ticket 티켓/표	ticketing 발권	a seat 좌석	seating 좌석 배치
an account 계좌	accounting 회계	a fund 자금	funding 자금 조달

The director believes the project will receive [~~fund~~, **funding**].
책임자는 그 프로젝트가 자금을 받을 것이라고 믿는다.

② 가산 명사와 불가산 명사 앞에 올 수 있는 수량 표현이 따로 있다.

가산 명사 앞		불가산 명사 앞	가산/불가산 명사 앞
단수 명사 앞	복수 명사 앞		
one 하나의	(a) few 약간의	(a) little 적은	all 모든
each 각각의	many 많은	less 더 적은	most 대부분의
every 모든	both 둘 다의	much 많은	some 몇몇의

The company received <u>many</u> [~~applicant~~, **applications**] from qualified candidates.
회사는 자격을 갖춘 후보자들로부터 많은 지원을 받았다.

[~~A few~~, **Each**] <u>business transaction</u> will be recorded in writing.
각각의 사업 거래 내용이 서면으로 기록될 것이다.

CHECK-UP
✅ 다음 문장의 빈칸에 들어갈 알맞은 말을 고르세요. 정답 및 해설 p.376

4. After three days of talks, Elite Decor signed a ------- with Max Marketing.
   (A) construction   (B) contract

5. Employees should ask for ------- before using company resources.
   (A) permit   (B) permission

6. Review ------- page of the contract carefully before signing on the final page.
   (A) little   (B) each

사람 명사와 사물/추상 명사의 구별 문제가 출제된다.

① 명사 자리에 사람 명사와 사물/추상 명사를 문맥에 맞게 구별해야 한다.

사람 명사	의미	사물/추상 명사	의미
analyst	분석가	analysis	분석
assistant	조수, 비서	assistance	보조, 도움
attendant – attendee	종업원 – 참석자	attendance	출석, 참석
applicant	지원자, 신청자	application	지원, 신청서
consultant	상담가	consultation	상담, 상담업
competitor	경쟁자[사]	competition	경쟁, 경연
correspondent	특파원, 기자	correspondence	서신, 통신문
delegate	대표자	delegation	대표 파견, 대표단
employee – employer	직원 – 고용주	employment	고용, 취업
manufacturer	제조업자[체], 제조사	manufacture	제조, 생산
participant	참가자, 참여자	participation	참가, 참여
recipient	수취(수령)인	receipt – reception	영수증 – 환영회
resident	지역주민, 거주자	residence	거주지, 주거
subscriber	구독자	subscription	구독
replacement	후임자, 대신할 사람	replacement	교체[물], 대체[물]

[Participants, **Participation**] in the company's seminar is required for all staff members.
회사 세미나 참여는 모든 직원에게 요구된다.

[Applicants, **Applications**] for jobs at Trica, Inc. will remain on file for a year.
Trica 사의 입사 지원서는 1년 동안 파일로 보관될 것이다.

We hired additional [accounting, **accountants**] to keep up with increasing client demands.
늘어나는 고객 수요에 대응하기 위해 회계사를 추가로 고용했다.

CHECK-UP   ✓ 다음 문장의 빈칸에 들어갈 알맞은 말을 고르세요.   정답 및 해설 p.376

7. Blue Café is highly regarded by area ------- for its delicious seafood dishes.

  (A) residents (B) residence

8. If your parking permit is damaged, bring it to the entrance station for -------.

  (A) recipients (B) replacement

9. The certificate should be submitted along with your -------.

  (A) applicants (B) applications

복합 명사를 이루는 어휘 문제가 출제된다.

① 빈출 복합 명사

application fee 신청비, 지원비	employment rates 고용률	pay raise [increase] 봉급 인상
attendance records 출근 기록	expiration date 만기일[유효기간]	registration form 등록서
submission deadline 제출 마감일	furniture delivery 가구 배달	retirement party 은퇴식
customer satisfaction 고객 만족	health benefits 의료보장 혜택	return policy 반환 정책
employee participation 직원 참여	job appraisal 업무 평가	safety precautions 안전 수칙
employee productivity 직원 생산성	job openings 일자리	office supplies 사무용품

[Safe, **Safety**] precautions are posted on the wall above each machine.
각 기계 위쪽 벽면에 안전 수칙이 게시되어 있다.

Please contact Ms. Theron to arrange the time for your furniture [deliver, **delivery**].
Theron 씨에게 연락하여 가구 배달 시간을 정하십시오.

② 주의해야 할 복합 명사

명사(e)s + 명사	현재분사 + 명사	
awards ceremony 시상식	advertising strategy 광고 전략	ordering process 주문 절차
benefits package 봉급 외 수당	marketing strategy 시장[마케팅] 전략	operating manual 작동 설명서
customs regulations 세관 규정	working conditions 근무환경	opening remarks 개회사
sales figures 판매 수치[실적]	writing experience 집필 경험	recycling plan 재활용 계획
overseas investment 해외 투자	shipping charge 운송비	parking facilities 주차시설
earnings growth 수익 성장	housing loan 주택 자금 대출	closing remarks 폐회사

The company decided to revise its [marketed, **marketing**] strategy for better results.
회사는 더 나은 결과를 위해 마케팅 전략을 수정하기로 했다.

CHECK-UP ✓ 다음 문장의 빈칸에 들어갈 알맞은 말을 고르세요. 정답 및 해설 p.376

10. Our customer service department addresses all customer ------- within 24 hours.

　(A) inquires　　(B) inquiries

11. Our quarterly ------- figures indicate a steady increase in revenue.

　(A) sells　　(B) sales

12. Please designate a ------- to attend the upcoming meeting.

　(A) represent
　(B) representative

RC PART 5

정답 및 해설 p.377

기출 포인트 1 명사 자리

명사는 문장 안에서 주어, 목적어, 보어 역할을 한다. '주어, 동사와 전치사의 목적어, 동명사와 to부정사의 목적어, 동사의 보어, 한정사 뒤' 자리가 빈칸으로 제시되면 명사 형태가 정답이다. 한정사의 종류에는 부정관사(a/an), 정관사(the), 소유격(my/her/his), 지시형용사 (this, that), 수량 표현(many) 등이 있다.

1. Fortunately, the cost of the construction project was covered by your generous -------.

(A) donate   (B) donation   (C) donated   (D) donating

2. The sales manager is seeking ------- from his team for effective ways to boost sales.

(A) suggest   (B) suggested   (C) suggestions   (D) suggesting

3. The managers of the staff training office reviewed the ------- of every new employee.

(A) to perform   (B) performing   (C) performed   (D) performance

기출 포인트 2 가산 명사 Vs. 불가산 명사

가산 명사는 관사가 붙거나 복수형으로 쓰이고, 불가산 명사는 복수형으로 쓸 수 없으며, 앞에 부정관사 a/an이 올 수 없다. 단, 정관사 the 는 불가산 명사 앞에 올 수 있다.

4. Employees who want to use a designated parking space must obtain a -------.

(A) permission   (B) permits   (C) permitted   (D) permit

기출 포인트 3 복합 명사

[명사 + ----] 또는 [---- + 명사] 형태가 출제되면 명사를 수식하는 형용사가 정답이 될 수도 있지만, 복합 명사일 수도 있으므로 정확한 해석이 필요하다.

5. The company's sales ------- will meet with clients at a workshop this weekend.

(A) represent   (B) represents   (C) representatives   (D) representation

6. Until the renovation of its ------- facility is complete, H&K expects its domestic sales to worsen temporarily.

(A) produced   (B) productive   (C) production   (D) produces

기출 포인트 4 사람 명사 Vs. 사물/추상 명사

같은 어근에서 파생된 명사가 둘 이상 보기로 제시되면 우선 해석을 하되, 사람 명사는 한정사 없이 단수 형태로 쓸 수 없다는 것을 기억하자.

7. Mr. Ryan will be available for brief ------- from 10:00 A.M. to 12:00 P.M. tomorrow.

(A) consultant   (B) consultations   (C) consulted   (D) consultants

8. ------- to TX Chemicals must pick up a security pass from the receptionist at the main entrance.

(A) Visit   (B) Visitation   (C) Visitors   (D) Visits

대명사

기출 패턴 1 인칭대명사의 격 문제가 출제된다.

① 인칭대명사의 종류

격		주격 (~은, ~는, ~이, ~가)	소유격 (~의)	목적격 (~을, ~를)	소유대명사 (~의 것)
인칭	수				
1인칭	단수	I	my	me	mine
	복수	we	our	us	ours
2인칭	단수	you	your	you	yours
	복수	you	your	you	yours
3인칭	단수	he	his	him	his
		she	her	her	hers
		it	its	it	-
	복수	they	their	them	theirs

- **주격 인칭대명사:** 동사 앞 주어 자리에 온다.

As one of our best customers, **you** are invited to a special event.
우리의 최고의 고객 중 한 명으로서, 귀하를 특별 행사에 초대합니다.

- **소유격 인칭대명사:** 명사 앞에서 명사를 수식하는 한정사로 쓰인다.

The Egerton House Hotel offers complimentary breakfast to **its** guests.
Egerton House 호텔은 투숙객에게 무료 아침 식사를 제공한다.

- **목적격 인칭대명사:** 동사나 전치사 뒤에 온다.

Rather than archiving routine e-mails, please delete **them** instead.
일상적인 이메일은 보관하지 말고 삭제해 주세요.

- **소유대명사:** <소유격+명사>의 역할을 하는 소유대명사는 '~의 것'이라고 해석하며, 명사처럼 주어, 목적어, 보어 자리에 모두 쓸 수 있다.

You will be given a courtesy car while [you, **yours**] is being repaired.
당신의 자동차가 수리되는 동안 서비스 차량을 받게 될 것이다.

CHECK-UP
☑ 다음 문장의 빈칸에 들어갈 알맞은 말을 고르세요. 정답 및 해설 p.378

1. Managers have been asked to update ------- contact information.

(A) their　　(B) them

2. Ms. Shaw asked for volunteers to help ------- with the employee fitness program.

(A) hers　　(B) her

3. Ms. Dian turned in her vacation request form, but Mr. Boden has yet to submit -------.

(A) his　　(B) him

재귀대명사의 용법을 묻는 문제가 출제된다.

① 목적어가 주어와 같은 사람이나 사물을 지칭할 때, 목적어 자리에 재귀대명사가 온다.

• 재귀 용법 (생략 불가)

The CEO introduced **himself** to the new employees during the orientation.

CEO는 오리엔테이션 동안 새 직원들에게 자신을 소개했다.

② 주어나 목적어를 강조할 때, 강조하고자 하는 말 바로 뒤나 문장 맨 뒤에 재귀대명사가 올 수 있다.

• 강조 용법 (생략 가능)

<u>Ms. Wong</u> **herself** delivered the contract to the managers after work.

Wong 씨는 퇴근 후 그녀가 직접 매니저들에게 계약서를 전달했다.

<u>Noel Woodward</u> analyzed the results of the customer survey **himself**.

Noel Woodward 씨는 그가 직접 고객 설문 조사 결과를 분석했다.

③ 재귀대명사가 포함된 관용 표현

by oneself (= on one's own) 혼자서, 스스로	for oneself 혼자 힘으로
of itself 저절로	in itself 그 자체로, 본질적으로
establish oneself as ~로서 자리를 잡다	familiarize oneself with ~을 익숙하게 하다, ~에 정통하다
dedicate oneself to ~하는 데 노력/시간을 기울이다	devote oneself to ~에 몰두하다

Ms. Rampling completed the monthly sales report **by herself**.

Rampling 씨는 혼자서 월간 판매 보고서를 작성했다.

She worked hard to establish **herself** as a leading expert in the field.

그녀는 그 분야에서 선도적인 전문가로 자리 잡기 위해 열심히 일했다.

CHECK-UP ✔ 다음 문장의 빈칸에 들어갈 알맞은 말을 고르세요. 정답 및 해설 p.378

4. Mr. Kim began the project by ------- but later was assisted by two colleagues.

(A) him   (B) himself

5. Mary prepared ------- for the speech by looking at the notes she had made.

(A) ourselves   (B) herself

6. V-Lands established ------- as a leading company in agriculture.

(A) its   (B) itself

지시대명사와 지시형용사 용법을 묻는 출제된다.

① 지시대명사 that은 앞에서 언급된 단수 명사를, those는 복수 명사를 대신한다.

Our customer service is much better than [it, **that**] of other airlines.
저희 고객 서비스는 다른 항공사들의 고객 서비스보다 훨씬 좋습니다.

Our service fees are lower than [that, **those**] of other consulting firms.
저희 서비스 수수료는 다른 컨설팅 회사의 수수료보다 저렴합니다.

② 지시대명사 those는 '~한 사람들'이라는 의미로도 쓰일 수 있다. 이때 those 뒤에 관계절, 분사구, 전치사구 등이 온다.

↱분사구
[That, **Those**] (who are) interested in attending the seminar should register in advance.
세미나에 참가하고자 하는 사람들은 사전에 등록해야 한다.

↱전치사구
The government program provides legal services to [them, **those**] in need.
정부 프로그램은 도움이 필요한 사람들에게 법률 서비스를 제공한다.

③ 지시형용사 this/that은 단수 명사를, these/those는 복수 명사를 수식하며, 각각 '이 ~', '저 ~'를 의미한다.

[These, **This**] service is available 24 hours a day, 7 days a week.
이 서비스는 일주일 내내 하루 24시간 이용할 수 있다.

[That, **Those**] materials may be obtained through the Internet.
저 자료들은 인터넷을 통해 얻을 수 있다.

RC
PART 5

CHECK-UP ☑ 다음 문장의 빈칸에 들어갈 알맞은 말을 고르세요. 정답 및 해설 p.378

7. If the hiking trip is canceled, ------- who prepaid the registration fee will receive a full refund.

  (A) those   (B) them

8. Because they are fragile, ------- items must be packed with great care.

  (A) these   (B) this

9. The report clearly shows that this year's overhead expenses are comparable to ------- of the preceding year.

  (A) that   (B) those

단어	의미	품사		수	
		명사	형용사	명사로 쓰일 때	형용사로 쓰일 때
one	하나	o	o	단수 취급	단수 가산 명사 수식
another	또 다른 하나	o	o	단수 취급	단수 가산 명사 수식
the other	나머지 하나	o	o	단수 취급	단(복)수 가산 명사/불가산 명사 수식
others	다른 몇몇	o	x	복수 취급	-
the others	나머지 전부	o	x	복수 취급	-
other	다른 몇몇	x	o	-	복수 가산 명사/불가산 명사 수식
each other one another	서로	• 주어 자리에 올 수 없음 • 동사와 전치사의 목적어가 될 수 있음 • 명사를 수식할 수 없음			

① **another**는 '(이미 언급된 것 이외의) 또 다른 하나'라는 의미로, 단수 가산 명사를 대신하거나 수식한다.

Toria Bank's customers can easily transfer funds from one account to **another**.
Toria 은행의 고객들은 한 계좌에서 다른 계좌로 쉽게 자금을 이체할 수 있다.

② **other/others**는 '(이미 언급된 것 이외의) 다른 몇몇'이라는 의미로, **the other(s)**는 '나머지 하나 또는 전부'라는 의미로 쓰인다.

T-5 printer is expensive and prints a bit more slowly than **others**.
T-5 프린터는 가격이 비싸고 다른 프린터들보다 인쇄 속도가 조금 느리다.

③ 부분이나 전체를 나타내는 부정대명사 다음에는 [of + the/소유격]이 나온다. 단 all과 both는 예외적으로 of를 생략할 수 있다.

수		양		수/양	
each 각각 several 몇몇	(a) few 적은 many 많은 both 둘 다	(a) little 적은 less 더 적은 much 많은		some 일부 most 대부분 all 모두 none 아무[하나]도 any 누구든/어느 것이든	

Most of the employees are satisfied with the new benefits package.
대부분의 직원들이 새로운 복지 혜택에 만족하고 있다.

CHECK-UP
☑ 다음 문장의 빈칸에 들어갈 알맞은 말을 고르세요.   정답 및 해설 p.378

10. If there is a problem with one of our products, we will replace it with -------.

   (A) another   (B) other

11. ------- people do not think the decision will benefit the city.

   (A) Most   (B) Most of

12. ------- the local farmers sell their produce at Borough Greenmarket.

   (A) Most   (B) All

PRACTICE

정답 및 해설 p.379

기출 포인트 1 인칭대명사의 격

빈칸에 알맞은 인칭대명사를 고르는 문제는 해당 명사의 인칭과 수를 확인한 후 주격, 소유격, 목적격에 맞는 대명사를 선택한다.

1. Enjoy a complimentary breakfast during ------- stay at our hotel.

(A) you   (B) yours   (C) your   (D) yourself

2. Ms. Green will review the applicants' résumés before ------- meets with them on Wednesday.

(A) she   (B) her   (C) hers   (D) herself

기출 포인트 2 재귀대명사

재귀대명사의 재귀 용법과 강조 용법이 출제된다. 명사(특히 주어)를 강조하여 재귀대명사가 명사 바로 뒤 또는 문장 끝에 위치하는 형태의 강조 용법이 자주 출제된다.

3. Ms. Parisse will give the presentation to the Schindler Electronics' representatives -------.

(A) she   (B) her   (C) hers   (D) herself

기출 포인트 3 지시대명사 those

those는 '저것들'이라는 의미 외에 '사람들(= people)'이라는 뜻이 있으며, 이때 관계대명사가 이끄는 관계사절, 분사구, 전치사구 등의 수식어가 뒤따른다.

4. The company will conduct a survey of ------- who purchase its products.

(A) them   (B) those   (C) this   (D) that

5. For ------- interested in our new product, a lot of information will be provided at the seminar.

(A) that   (B) they   (C) those   (D) them

기출 포인트 4 부정대명사와 부정형용사

부정대명사와 부정형용사 one/another/the other/others/the others/each other(= one another)는 각각의 의미와 수를 중심으로 암기한다. 또한, 전체 중 일부를 나타내는 대명사 표현은 [of + the/소유격] 뒤에 오는 명사의 단/복수 형태가 정해져 있다. 대명사에 따라 결합하는 동사의 단/복수도 달라지므로 정확히 숙지해야 한다. (UNIT 3 참고)

6. Some of the books are out of print, but ------- are available at bookstores.

(A) the other   (B) others   (C) other   (D) another

7. If you lose your parking card, the parking garage manager will deactivate it and issue -------.

(A) other   (B) other one   (C) one another   (D) another

8. ------- of the employees are going to participate in the conference next week.

(A) Every   (B) Much   (C) Some   (D) Each

형용사

기출 패턴 1 형용사 자리[어휘] 문제가 출제된다.

① 형용사는 명사 앞 또는 뒤, 보어 자리에 올 수 있다.

명사 앞 Each quarter, Colorado Exports sets **realistic** sales goals for its staff.
Colorado Exports 사는 매 분기 직원들을 위해 현실적인 매출 목표를 정한다.

명사 뒤 Customers will receive a coupon **good** for one medium-sized coffee.
고객들은 중간 사이즈의 커피 한 잔에 대한 쿠폰을 받게 됩니다.

주격 보어 The conference rooms in Blue Hall are **available** only for morning meetings.
Blue Hall에 있는 회의실은 오전 회의용으로만 이용 가능합니다.

목적격 보어 Including customer reviews makes online advertisements more **effective.**
고객 후기를 포함하는 것은 온라인 광고를 더욱 효과적으로 만든다.

② 형용사 자리에 부사, 명사가 오답 보기로 제시된다.

Goldman Financial offers a [~~widely~~, **wide**] range of banking services.
Goldman 금융사는 광범위한 은행 서비스를 제공한다.

Our staff has [~~extension~~, **extensive**] knowledge of current hardware systems.
우리 직원들은 현재 하드웨어 시스템에 대한 폭넓은 지식을 가지고 있다.

③ [전치사+명사]가 형용사 역할을 하여 be동사의 보어 자리에 올 수 있다.

- Mr. Adams is currently **in charge of** the sales division. ▶ ~을 맡은, 담당인
  Adams 씨는 현재 영업부를 담당하고 있다.

- The copier is currently **out of service**. ▶ 고장 난, 작동을 멈춘
  복사기는 현재 고장 나 있다.

- The item is temporarily **out of stock**. ▶ 재고가 없는
  그 물건은 일시적으로 재고가 떨어졌다.

CHECK-UP ✓ 다음 문장의 빈칸에 들어갈 알맞은 말을 고르세요. 정답 및 해설 p.379

1. Dr. Miller provides patients with exceptional dental care at ------- prices.

   (A) affordable (B) affordably

2. The network is expected to be ------- for more than two hours.

   (A) availability (B) unavailable

3. Most of the residents have found the new recycling program -------.

   (A) convenient (B) conveniently

① 가산 명사와 불가산 명사 앞에 올 수 있는 수량[부정] 형용사가 따로 있다.

단수 가산 명사와 어울리는 형용사	each applicant (O) 단수 가산 명사	each applicants (X) 복수 가산 명사	each information (X) 불가산 명사
a(an) 하나의　another 또 다른 each 각각의　every 모든			

'every + 숫자 + 복수 명사'는 '~마다'라는 뜻이다. ex every two months 두 달마다
'another + 숫자 + 복수 명사'는 '추가적인'이라는 뜻이다. ex another two months 두 달 더

복수 가산 명사와 어울리는 형용사	many products (O) 복수 가산 명사	many product (X) 단수 가산 명사	many furniture (X) 불가산 명사
a few 몇몇의　few 거의 없는　many 많은 both 둘 다의　several 몇몇의 numerous 수많은			

불가산 명사와 어울리는 형용사	little information (O) 불가산 명사	little product (X) 단수 가산 명사	little products (X) 복수 가산 명사
much 많은　a little 약간의　less 더 적은 little 거의 없는			

불가산 명사, 복수 가산 명사와 어울리는 형용사	all equipment (O) 불가산 명사	some employees (O) 복수 가산 명사	some employee (X) 단수 가산 명사
all 모든　more 더 많은　most 대부분의 some 몇몇의　other 다른 몇몇			

[Many, **Every**] employee is required to attend the training workshop once a year.
모든 직원은 1년에 한 번 교육 워크숍에 참석해야 한다.

Weil, Inc. had [much, **many**] applicants for the position, but few were qualified.
Weil 사는 지원자는 많았지만, 적임자는 거의 없었다.

The company lowered its prices to compete with [another, **other**] suppliers.
회사는 다른 납품업체들과 경쟁하기 위해 가격을 낮췄다.

CHECK-UP
✅ 다음 문장의 빈칸에 들어갈 알맞은 말을 고르세요. 　　　정답 및 해설 p.379

4. The attached document contains too ------- confidential information.

   (A) many　　(B) much

5. Editors must submit ------- revisions to the books to the authors by Friday.

   (A) all　　(B) every

6. This product is not in stock here but may be available in ------- place.

   (A) other　　(B) another

RC　PART 5

① 토익에 자주 출제되는 [be + 형용사 + 전치사] 표현

be subject to	~에 영향받기 쉽다	be aware of	~을 알다, 인지하다
be attached to	~에 첨부되다	be notable (= famous) for	~로 저명하다
be available to	~에게 이용 가능한	be eligible for	~의 자격이 있다
be comparable to	~에 필적하다	be suitable for	~에 적합하다
be used (= accustomed) to	~에 익숙하다	be responsible for	~을 책임지다
be related to	~와 관련되다	be familiar with	~에 익숙하다
be based on	~에 기초하다, 근거하다	be compatible with	~와 호환되다
be reliant on	~에 의존하다	be absent from	~에 불참하다
be dependent on	~에 의존하다	be exempt from	~이 면제되다

The schedule **is subject to** change without prior notice.
일정은 사전 통보 없이 변경될 수 있습니다.

Candlewood Suites **is famous for** its high standard of service.
Candlewood Suites는 높은 수준의 서비스로 유명하다.

You will **be responsible for** the coordination of the Marketing and Accounting departments.
당신은 마케팅 및 회계 부서의 조정을 담당하게 될 것입니다.

CHECK-UP   ☑ 다음 문장의 빈칸에 들어갈 알맞은 말을 고르세요.   정답 및 해설 p.379

7. The novel is ------- on a documentary which was produced in the 1910s.

  (A) based   (B) checked

8. Those attending the seminar are ------- from turning in their travel expense receipts.

  (A) obliged   (B) exempt

9. The job is complex and requires various skills, and Mr. Lee is suitable ------- those conditions.

  (A) to   (B) for

혼동하기 쉬운 형용사 자리[어휘] 문제가 출제된다.

① 형태가 비슷해 혼동하기 쉬운 형용사

informative meeting 유익한 회의	**informed** decision 신중한(정보에 입각한) 결정
confident manner 자신 있는 태도	**confidential** document 기밀문서
favorite color 가장 좋아하는 색상	**favorable** circumstance 우호적인 환경
successful campaign 성공적인 캠페인	**successive** failure 연속적인 실패
competent manager 유능한 매니저	**competitive** price 경쟁력 있는 가격
beneficial result 유익한 결과	**beneficent** employer 인정 많은 고용주
complete trust 완전한 신뢰	**completed** application form 작성 완료된 신청서
impressive résumé 인상적인 이력서	**impressed** audience 감명받은 청중

Of all the business plans, Mr. Kim's idea is the most [~~impressed~~, **impressive**]
모든 사업 계획서 중에서 Kim 씨의 안이 가장 인상적이다.

② -ly로 끝나는 형용사

daily routine 일상 업무	**friendly** working environment 우호적인 근무 환경
weekly schedule 주간 스케줄	**costly** product 값비싼 제품
monthly report 월례 보고서	in a **timely** manner 적시에, 시기적절하게
yearly income 연간 소득	in an **orderly** fashion 질서정연하게
quarterly meeting 분기별 회의	**lovely** weather 매우 좋은 날씨

고득점 TIP+ 횟수를 나타내는 daily, weekly, monthly, yearly, quarterly는 형용사와 부사로 둘 다 쓰인다.

Some of the clothing at the fashion show is very [~~cost~~, **costly**].
패션쇼 옷 중 일부는 매우 비싸다.

After the performance, the audience left the concert hall in an [~~ordered~~, **orderly**] fashion.
공연이 끝난 후 관객들은 질서정연하게 콘서트홀을 떠났다.

CHECK-UP ✅ 다음 문장의 빈칸에 들어갈 알맞은 말을 고르세요. 정답 및 해설 p.379

10. The guests were ------- with the table decorations at the company banquet.

(A) impressive (B) impressed

11. Please note that we aim to respond to all correspondence in a ------- manner.

(A) timing (B) timely

12. Effective planning is essential for the ------- completion of projects.

(A) successful (B) successive

RC PART 5

PRACTICE

정답 및 해설 p.380

기출 포인트 1   형용사 자리[어휘]

빈칸이 명사를 수식하는 경우 형용사가 정답이다. 이때 보기로 형용사가 2개 이상 제시되면 해석해서 답을 골라야 한다. be, become, stay, remain, look, appear와 같은 2형식 동사의 보어 자리가 빈칸이면 주로 형용사 자리이고, 주어와 보어가 동격인 경우 명사가 정답이다. 보기에 형용사가 둘 이상이면 해석해서 답을 골라야 한다.

1. Finding a ------- venue for the marketing meeting would be difficult at this late date.

(A) suitably   (B) suitable   (C) suitability   (D) suiting

2. Our new president is very ------- about the necessity of increasing our market share.

(A) emphatic   (B) emphasized   (C) emphasize   (D) emphatically

기출 포인트 2   수량 형용사

결합하는 명사의 수가 정해져 있는 형용사들이 보기로 제시되면, 빈칸 뒤 명사의 수에 알맞은 형용사를 선택해야 한다.

3. There are ------- reference books on the market that can help you start a business.

(A) a little   (B) much   (C) a few   (D) each

4. ------- administrative policies are outdated and are being reviewed by the executive officers.

(A) Several   (B) Much   (C) Every   (D) Another

기출 포인트 3   [형용사 + 전치사/to 부정사] 어구

형용사 어휘 문제는 해석이 필요하지만, 빈칸 뒤에 전치사나 to부정사로 이어지면 숙어 문제로 보면 된다. 보통 [be + 형용사 + 전치사] 또는 [be + 형용사 + to부정사] 패턴 중 하나가 출제된다.

5. To be ------- to apply for the program, you must submit your application by the deadline.

(A) systematic   (B) eligible   (C) familiar   (D) successful

기출 포인트 4   형태가 유사해 헷갈리는 형용사

impressed/impressive, favorable/favorite, successful/successive, dependable/dependent 등과 같이 형태는 비슷하지만 의미가 다른 형용사들이 보기로 제시된다.

6. The company invested a ------- sum of money to upgrade its infrastructure.

(A) considerate   (B) considerably   (C) consideration   (D) considerable

7. A.T. Analysis Group, Inc. recommended a ------- way to balance the annual budget.

(A) succeeded   (B) success   (C) successful   (D) successive

UNIT 04 부사

RC PART 5

기출 패턴 1 **동사, 형용사, 부사를 수식하는 부사 자리[어휘] 문제가 출제된다.**

① 부사는 동사 앞이나 뒤에 올 수 있다.

Yesterday's storm **temporarily** interrupted the services of our communications system.
어제 폭풍으로 인해 통신 서비스가 일시적으로 중단되었다.

We reviewed the budget report **thoroughly** before submitting it.
우리는 예산 보고서를 제출하기 전에 꼼꼼히 검토했다.

② 부사는 형용사나 부사 앞에 올 수 있다.

Mr. Ryan was **largely** responsible for the failure of the marketing campaign.
Ryan 씨에게 마케팅 캠페인 실패의 주된 책임이 있었다.

Your efforts to help our customers feel welcome are **always** truly appreciated.
저희 고객들이 환영받을 수 있도록 도와주신 귀하의 노고에 항상 진심으로 감사드립니다.

③ 부사는 [be동사 + -ing/p.p.], [조동사 + 동사원형], [have + (been) p.p.] 사이나 뒤에 올 수 있다.

We are **actively** seeking qualified correspondents to join our team.
우리는 팀에 합류할 자격 있는 기자를 적극적으로 찾고 있다.

This issue is **closely** related to the current economic downturn.
이 사안은 현재의 경제 침체와 밀접하게 연관되어 있다.

All laboratory personnel must **annually** complete a course in safety practices.
모든 실험실 직원은 매년 안전 실습 과정을 이수해야 한다.

The technology has advanced **markedly** over the past decade.
기술은 지난 10년 동안 현저하게 발전했다.

Diageo PLC has **officially** announced the appointment of its new president.
Diageo PLC 사는 새 사장의 임명을 공식적으로 발표했다.

CHECK-UP
✓ 다음 문장의 빈칸에 들어갈 알맞은 말을 고르세요.   정답 및 해설 p.381

1. The customer service representative responded ------- to my inquiries.

(A) prompt   (B) promptly

2. These inexpensive cleaning products from Nellie's are ------- strong.

(A) unbelievably (B) unbelievable

3. Our housekeepers ------- fold the bath towels in the shapes of flowers.

(A) creative   (B) creatively

to부정사, 동명사, 분사를 수식하는 부사 자리[어휘] 문제가 출제된다.

① **부사는 [준동사 + (목적어)] 앞이나 뒤에 올 수 있다.**

↳ 준동사인 to부정사, 동명사, 분사는 동사적 성질을 가지고 있어 목적어와 보어를 가질 수 있고, 부사의 수식을 받는다.

to부정사 수식 It's important to store **perishable items properly** to maintain freshness.
신선도를 유지하기 위해서는 부패하기 쉬운 품목을 적절하게 보관하는 것이 중요하다.

동명사 수식 After **carefully** reviewing **your job application**, we have decided to hire you.
입사 지원서를 주의 깊게 검토한 후, 우리는 당신을 채용하기로 결정했습니다.

분사 수식 Goldman Bank's **newly** launched **online banking services** are reliable.
Goldman 은행이 새로 출시한 온라인 뱅킹 서비스는 신뢰할 수 있습니다.

기출 패턴 3 **구, 절, 문장 전체를 수식하는 부사 자리[어휘] 문제가 출제된다.**

구 수식 The video conference will start **exactly** at 8:00 P.M. on Monday.
화상 회의는 정확히 월요일 오후 8시에 시작할 것이다.

→ 시각 앞에서 '~에'를 뜻하는 전치사 at은 [promptly/exactly/precisely at+시각] 또는 [at+시각 sharp] 등으로 쓰이며 '~정각에'라는 뜻이다.

절 수식 All materials will be distributed at the venue **shortly** before the seminar begins.
세미나 시작 직전에 행사장에서 모든 자료가 배포될 예정이다.

→ 부사 right, just, soon, promptly, shortly, immediately는 접속사 before, after나 전치사 prior to, following 앞에 쓰여 '~직전에, ~직후에'라는 뜻을 의미한다.

문장 전체 수식 **Unfortunately**, the data on Mr. Cole's laptop computer could not be retrieved.
유감스럽게도, Cole 씨의 노트북 컴퓨터에 있는 데이터는 복구되지 못했다.

→ 문장 전체를 수식하는 부사는 문장 맨 앞에 콤마(,)로 분리되어 쓰이며, 'regrettably(유감스럽게도), fortunately(다행히), presumably(아마도), apparently/obviously(명백히)' 등이 출제된다.

CHECK-UP ☑ 다음 문장의 빈칸에 들어갈 알맞은 말을 고르세요. 정답 및 해설 p.381

4. ------- after graduating from Aston University, Paul Rudd founded a consulting firm.

　(A) Short　　(B) Shortly

5. Tom Seaver is responsible for ------- checking the heating system at the company.

　(A) regular　　(B) regularly

6. -------, the business decided to lay off a third of its workforce.

　(A) Unfortunate (B) Unfortunately

숫자, 수량을 수식하는 부사 자리[어휘] 문제가 출제된다.

대략	거의	~이상	최소한 / 딱 / 겨우 / 기껏해야
about, around approximately, roughly	nearly, almost	over, more than	at least / just / only / at most

Applicants must have **at least** three years of experience in marketing.
지원자들은 마케팅 분야에서 최소 3년의 경력을 보유하고 있어야 한다.

We've achieved **nearly** 30% cost reduction through efficient resource management.
효율적인 자원 관리를 통해 거의 30%의 비용을 절감했다.

증감 동사를 수식하는 부사 자리[어휘] 문제가 출제된다.

증감 동사	increase 증가하다 rise 증가하다 raise 인상하다 hike 인상하다 expand 확대하다 decrease 감소하다 decline 감소하다 drop/fall 떨어지다 reduce 줄이다 wane 줄어들다 improve 개선하다 grow 성장하다
부사	rapidly, quickly 빠르게 sharply, drastically 급격히 dramatically 극적으로 constantly, continuously 끊임없이 steadily 꾸준히 gradually 서서히 considerably, significantly, substantially 상당히 sharply, drastically 급격히 noticeably, remarkably 현저히 slightly 약간, 조금 greatly 크게, 매우

Earnings for this quarter have increased **significantly**.
이번 분기의 수입은 상당히 증가했다.

Guard Insurance grew **quickly** from a small business to a mid-sized company.
Guard 보험사는 중소기업에서 중견기업으로 빠르게 성장했다.

The company's revenues **dramatically** decreased due to the economic downturn.
경기 침체로 인해 그 회사의 수익이 극적으로 감소했다.

CHECK-UP

✔ 다음 문장의 빈칸에 들어갈 알맞은 말을 고르세요.   정답 및 해설 p.381

7. Ms. Lynskey has given ------- a dozen presentations in only three months.

(A) nearly　　(B) near

8. During the past two months, Fine Theater's attendance has increased -------.

(A) dramatic　　(B) dramatically

9. Our profits have ------- increased since we launched the new product line.

(A) greatly　　(B) proudly

시간 부사   CM Financial is [~~shortly~~, **currently**] looking for highly qualified accountants.
CM Financial 사는 현재 매우 자격을 갖춘 회계사들을 찾고 있다.

▶ 특정 시제와 함께 쓰이는 시간 부사

현재 시제	regularly 정기적으로 usually, normally 보통, 대개 periodically 주기적으로 frequently 자주
미래 시제	soon, shortly 곧
과거 시제	previously 이전에 once 한때 recently 최근에
현재완료 시제	just 막 since ~이래로 recently 최근에 yet 아직 (부정문일 때만 사용)
현재진행 시제	currently, presently 현재

접속부사   We have received your order; **however**, the items you ordered are currently out of stock.
우리는 당신의 주문을 받았습니다. 하지만, 주문하신 상품은 현재 품절입니다.

* 접속부사란 두 문장을 의미적인 관계에 따라 연결하는 부사로, therefore(따라서), however(그러나), moreover(게다가), otherwise(그렇지 않으면) 등이 있다. 접속사와 달리 독립적으로 절을 연결할 수 없으므로 세미콜론(;) 뒤에 오며 이후에 콤마(,)를 사용해 문장을 연결한다.

late lately	⟨형⟩ 늦은 ⟨부⟩ 늦게 ⟨부⟩ 최근에(= recently)	will stay **late** 늦게까지 남아있을 것이다 received many complaints **lately** 최근에 많은 불만 사항을 받았다 *cf.* latest 최신의 / at the latest 아무리 늦어도
hard hardly	⟨형⟩ 어려운 ⟨부⟩ 열심히, 힘들게 ⟨부⟩ 거의 ~하지 않다	work very **hard** 매우 열심히 일하다 **hardly** make any mistakes 실수를 거의 하지 않다
high highly	⟨형⟩ 높은 ⟨부⟩ 높이, 높게 ⟨부⟩ 매우(= very, much)	be piled **high** 높이 쌓여 있다 be **highly** profitable 매우 수익성이 있다
most mostly	⟨형⟩ 대부분 ⟨부⟩ 가장 ⟨부⟩ 대체로, 주로(= largely)	the **most** visited city 가장 많은 사람들이 방문하는 도시 be **mostly** due to~ 주로 ~때문이다
close closely	⟨형⟩ 가까운 ⟨부⟩ (거리상) 가까이에 ⟨부⟩ 면밀하게, 친밀하게, 밀접하게	stay **close** to the meeting location 회의 장소와 가까운 곳에 머무르다 work **closely** with ~ ~와 밀접하게 일하다
near nearly	⟨형⟩ 가까운 ⟨부⟩ 가까이 ⟨부⟩ 거의	be located **near** the airport 공항 근처에 위치하다 be **nearly** complete 거의 완료되다

CHECK-UP

✅ 다음 문장의 빈칸에 들어갈 알맞은 말을 고르세요.   정답 및 해설 p.381

10. All of our employees ------- participate in professional development seminars.

   (A) soon   (B) regularly

11. The CEO has ------- expressed concerns about the quarterly profits.

   (A) previously   (B) recently

12. The ------- anticipated new play *Homecoming* opened in Louis Auditorium last night.

   (A) high   (B) highly

PRACTICE

정답 및 해설 p.382

기출 포인트 1 동사, 형용사, 부사 등을 수식하는 부사

빈칸을 제외했을 때 필요한 문장 성분이 모두 갖춰져 있다면, 빈칸은 부사가 들어갈 확률이 높다. 부사는 동사의 앞이나 뒤에서 동사를 수식하며 형용사, 부사, 준동사, 구, 절, 문장 전체를 꾸며 주기도 한다. 이때 부사의 위치는 비교적 자유로운 편이나, 앞에서 수식하는 부사 자리 문제가 많이 출제된다.

1. After postponing his studies for many years, Mr. Baker ------- earned a degree in biology.

   (A) eventual   (B) eventualize   (C) eventually   (D) eventuality

2. Jo Maer, the marketing director, will examine our current sales strategies more -------.

   (A) closely   (B) closer   (C) closest   (D) close

3. Unlike other hotels in the E-bay area, the Waverly Inn is ------- close to the waterfront.

   (A) relative   (B) relatives   (C) related   (D) relatively

4. With the rise of online sales, consumers leave home to shop much less -------.

   (A) frequency   (B) frequent   (C) frequently   (D) frequence

5. Mr. Kern submitted the financial aid application to the Dulwich School ------- before the deadline.

   (A) immediate   (B) immediacy   (C) immediately   (D) immedicable

기출 포인트 2 시간 부사

시간 부사는 문장에서 동작이나 상태가 발생한 시점을 나타내므로 특정 시제와 어울려 사용된다. 현재, 과거, 미래, 완료 시제 등의 특정 시제와 자주 쓰이는 부사를 알아두자.

6. Customers ------- return to Garret Savings because of its excellent customer service.

   (A) frequently   (B) soon   (C) previously   (D) yet

기출 포인트 3 접속부사

접속부사는 문장과 문장을 이어주는 역할을 한다. 접속부사 문제를 풀 때는 앞뒤 문맥을 잘 파악한 후 자연스럽게 이어지는 것으로 선택해야 한다.

7. Mr. Smith had manipulated transaction records; -------, we made the decision to fire him.

   (A) therefore   (B) however   (C) otherwise   (D) meanwhile

기출 포인트 4 -ly가 붙어서 의미가 달라지는 부사

late/lately, short/shortly 등 혼동하기 쉬운 형태의 부사가 보기에 함께 제시되면 빈칸이 형용사 자리인지 부사 자리인지 판단한 후, 부사 자리일 경우 해석을 통해 정답을 찾는다.

8. Mr. McCallan's flight arrived too ------- for him to attend the special welcoming reception.

   (A) late   (B) latest   (C) lately   (D) lateness

RC PART 5

UNIT 05 전치사

시간과 장소를 나타내는 전치사 문제가 출제된다.

① 시간 전치사

at	시각, 시점 등 매우 짧은 시간 (시, 분, 초)	at 8:00 8시에 at noon 정오에 at midnight 자정에
in	비교적 긴 시간이나 기간 (연, 월, 계절, 하루 중 오전, 오후, 저녁)	in the morning 아침에 in October 10월에 in winter 겨울에 in 2002 2002년에
on	특정 시간 (요일, 날짜)	on Monday 월요일에 on May 5 5월 5일에

② 장소 전치사

at	비교적 좁은 장소나 특정 지점	at the station 역에서 at the café 카페에서
in	비교적 넓은 장소나 내부 공간	in London 런던에서 in Europe 유럽에서 in the meeting room 회의실에서
on	표면이 접촉되어 있는 경우	on the table 테이블 위에 on the second floor 2층에서

Passengers normally start lining up for buses [on, **at**] six in the morning.
승객들은 보통 아침 6시에 버스 줄을 서기 시작한다.

시점과 기간을 나타내는 전치사 문제가 출제된다.

① 시점을 나타내는 전치사

after the vacation 방학 후에	**before** noon 정오 전에	**since** last year 작년부터
prior to lunch 점심 전에	**by** next month 다음 달까지	**until** further notice 추후 통지가 있을 때까지

* by, until은 시점 명사와 쓰여 '~까지'라고 해석되지만, 함께 쓰이는 동사가 다르다. 특정 시점까지 완료를 나타내는 by는 arrive, submit, complete와, 특정 시점까지 유지됨을 나타내는 until은 last, postpone, stay 등과 함께 쓰인다.

② 기간을 나타내는 전치사

for ten years 10년 동안	**during** the meeting 회의 동안	**over** the weekend 주말 동안
within 7 days 일주일 이내에	**in** a week 일주일 이후에	**throughout** the year 일 년 내내

* for는 숫자 기간 명사와, during은 숫자가 아닌 기간 명사와 짝을 이룬다.

The construction project will be completed [~~within~~, **before**] December 23. 공사는 12월 23일 이전에 완료될 예정이다.

CHECK-UP ✓ 다음 문장의 빈칸에 들어갈 알맞은 말을 고르세요. 정답 및 해설 p.383

1. ------ May 6, the Aron Company announced the appointment of its new president.

　(A) In　　　(B) On

2. The presentation about the new software will be postponed ------ next Monday.

　(A) by　　　(B) until

3. We need to finalize the strategy ------ two weeks to meet the deadline.

　(A) within　　　(B) during

① 위치를 나타내는 전치사

over ~위에	near ~가까이에	below/under ~아래에	between/among ~사이에
behind ~뒤에	beside/next to ~옆에	within ~내에	throughout ~도처에, 전역에

* between은 둘 사이, among은 셋 이상 사이를 나타내므로 among 뒤에는 주로 복수 가산 명사가 온다.

The company exports its products to markets **throughout** the world.
회사는 제품을 전 세계 시장에 수출한다.

② 방향을 나타내는 전치사

to ~에게, ~쪽으로	from ~로부터	through ~을 통하여	across ~을 가로질러	along ~을 따라

Starting next month, we will be providing free lunches **to** our employees.
다음 달부터 직원들에게 무상급식을 제공할 예정이다.

이유	because of, due to, owing to, on account of, for ~ 때문에 thanks to ~덕분에
양보	despite, in spite of, notwithstanding ~에도 불구하고
목적	for ~을 위해서
제외	without ~없이 except (for) ~을 제외하고
부가	in addition to ~에 더하여 besides ~이외에도

Dr. Shaw could not continue his project **because of** a shortage of research funds.
Shaw 박사는 연구 자금 부족으로 인해 프로젝트를 계속할 수 없었다.

Workers were able to complete the work **despite** the shortage of equipment.
인부들은 장비의 부족에도 불구하고 작업을 마칠 수 있었다.

The city council plans to adopt new policies **for** waste management.
시의회는 폐기물 관리를 위한 새로운 정책을 채택할 계획이다.

CHECK-UP
☑ 다음 문장의 빈칸에 들어갈 알맞은 말을 고르세요. 　　　　　정답 및 해설 p.383

4. Croy Station, located ------- the conference center, was recently renovated.

   (A) next to　　(B) from

5. ------- the impending snowstorm, all city government offices will be closed tomorrow.

   (A) Despite　　(B) Due to

6. Most of the employees refused to work overtime ------- proper compensation.

   (A) thanks to　　(B) without

RC PART 5

① 기타 전치사

with ~와 함께, ~을 가지고	by ~함으로써, ~에 의해	of ~의
unlike ~과 달리	as ~로서	on(upon) ~하자마자
beyond ~을 넘어	against ~에 반대하여	toward ~을 향해, ~쯤(경)

Mr. Kim is scheduled to visit a branch in Boston **toward** the end of this month.
Kim 씨는 이달 말쯤 보스턴에 있는 지점을 방문할 예정이다.

② 구 전치사

as to ~에 대하여	in front of ~앞에	instead of ~대신에
as of ~부로,~부터	according to ~에 따라	by means of ~에 의해서
along with ~와 함께	aside from ~외에도	close to ~가까이에
on behalf of ~을 대신하여	regardless of ~에 상관없이	in favor of ~에 찬성하여

At E-Gord, standard shipping is always free **regardless of** the customer's address.
E-Gord 사에서는 고객의 주소지와 관계없이 기본 배송은 항상 무료다.

③ 분사형 전치사

following ~이후에	barring ~이 없으면	excluding ~을 제외하고
including ~을 포함하여	pending ~을 기다리는 동안	depending on ~에 따라
regarding, concerning ~에 관한	based on ~에 근거해서	considering, given ~을 고려하면

All e-mail messages **regarding** legal issues should be stored in a separate folder.
법적 문제에 관한 모든 이메일 메시지는 별도의 폴더에 저장되어야 한다.

Following the economic downturn, many people lost their jobs.
경제 침체 이후에 많은 사람이 직장을 잃었다.

CHECK-UP

✓ 다음 문장의 빈칸에 들어갈 알맞은 말을 고르세요.   정답 및 해설 p.383

7. ------- the building contractor, the office renovations will cost just under $10,000.

  (A) According to   (B) Instead of

8. Onsite parking passes are issued ------- the availability of spaces in the garage.

  (A) such as   (B) depending on

9. ------- the team meeting, we will distribute the meeting minutes to all participants.

  (A) Barring   (B) Following

다양한 품사와 함께 쓰이는 전치사 문제가 출제된다.

① 자동사 + 전치사

apply for ~에 신청[지원]하다	deal with ~을 다루다, 대처하다	focus on ~에 중점을 두다
comply with ~을 준수하다	benefit from ~으로부터 혜택을 얻다	contribute to ~에 공헌하다
depend [rely] on ~에 의존하다	reply [respond] to ~에 응답하다	specialize in ~을 전문으로 하다

② 타동사 + 목적어 + 전치사

exchange A for B A를 B로 교환하다	substitute A with B A를 B로 교체하다	substitute A for B B를 A로 교체하다
replace A with B A를 B로 바꾸다	expand A into B A를 B로 확장하다	attribute A to B A를 B탓으로 돌리다
share A with B A를 B와 나누다	provide A with B A에게 B를 제공하다	notify [inform] A of B A에게 B를 알리다
reimburse A for B A에게 B에 대해 상환[보상]하다		

③ 전치사 + 명사

in detail 상세히	in advance 미리	at all times 항상
with ease 쉽게	with care 조심해서, 신중하게	under consideration 고려중인
on sale (할인) 판매 중인	in writing 서면으로	on [upon] request 요청하면

④ 전치사 + 명사 + 전치사

in accordance with ~과 일치하여	in honor of ~을 기념하여	in case of ~의 경우에
in charge of ~을 책임지는	in excess of ~을 초과하여	in the event of ~의 경우에
in response to ~에 대한 응답으로	as a result of ~의 결과로서	in terms of ~라는 점에서

⑤ 명사 + 전치사 + 전치사의 목적어

rise [increase] in sales 매출의 증가	decline [decrease] in sales 매출의 감소	investment in stock 주식에 투자
contribution to the project 프로젝트에 대한 공헌	solution to the problem 문제에 대한 해결책	access to the facility 시설에 접근
demand for a pay raise 임금 인상에 대한 요구	interest in medicine 의학에 대한 관심	influence on environment 환경에 대한 영향

CHECK-UP ☑ 다음 문장의 빈칸에 들어갈 알맞은 말을 고르세요. 정답 및 해설 p.383

10. We intend to focus ------- developing a new material with greater flexibility.

(A) to (B) on

11. In ------- to your request, we have sent your account password by e-mail.

(A) response (B) responds

12. The company will reimburse you ------- your travel expenses this year.

(A) with (B) for

기출 포인트 1 시간/장소 전치사

각각의 시간 표현과 장소 표현에 어울리는 전치사가 따로 있다. 시간과 장소 관련 전치사의 정확한 의미와 예시를 숙지하여 풀어야 한다.

1. All company files in the current system will be transferred to the new system ------- September 1.

    (A) on   (B) at   (C) in   (D) of

기출 포인트 2 다양한 품사와 함께 쓰이는 전치사

의미가 다른 전치사들이 보기로 제시될 경우, 빈칸 앞뒤로 바로 연결되는 숙어나 동사와 연결되는 전치사가 있는지 살펴보고, 그에 해당하는 전치사를 선택한다.

2. Mr. Chappelle provided me ------- a great deal of information regarding the regulations.

    (A) in   (B) for   (C) with   (C) about

기출 포인트 3 해석으로 푸는 전치사

의미가 다른 전치사들이 보기로 제시되고 빈칸 앞뒤로 짝을 이루는 표현이 없을 경우, 해석을 통해 적절한 전치사 어휘를 골라야 한다. 특히 구 전치사와 분사형 전치사가 보기로 자주 출제되므로 암기해 두어야 한다.

3. To ensure the freshness of every menu item, we use ingredients only ------- local farms.

    (A) with   (B) during   (C) along   (D) from

4. On Thursday, the CEO held a press conference ------- plans to merge with Adecco Financials.

    (A) except   (B) versus   (C) along   (D) concerning

기출 포인트 4 혼동되는 전치사

의미는 비슷하지만 쓰임이 다른 전치사를 구별해야 한다. 대표적인 예로는 by Vs. until / for Vs. during / before Vs. within / between Vs. among 등이 있다.

5. When your application is approved, you will receive your new credit card by mail ------- one week.

    (A) during   (B) while   (C) before   (D) within

기출 포인트 5 기타 전치사

보기에 부사절 접속사, 등위접속사, 전치사, (접속)부사가 제시될 때는 빈칸 앞뒤 구조를 살펴본다. 빈칸이 문장을 연결하는 경우에는 접속사가 정답이 되고, 빈칸 뒤에 명사(구) 있는 경우에는 전치사가 정답이 된다.

6. ------- the success of his restaurant, chef Peter Carr wrote a bestselling cookbook.

    (A) Therefore   (B) Because   (C) Following   (D) Already

7. ------- signing the contract, we need to review all the terms and conditions carefully.

    (A) Since   (B) Either   (C) Before   (D) Although

06 동사의 형태와 종류

기출 패턴 1   동사원형 자리 문제가 출제된다.

① 조동사 뒤에는 동사원형이 온다.

→ 조동사는 동사에 '가능, 의무' 등 보조적 의미를 첨가하는 말로, can, must, will 등이 있다.

Roxy Footwear will [to relocate, **relocate**] its main factory to London next year.
Roxy Footwear 사는 내년에 주 공장을 런던으로 이전할 예정이다.

The main entrance of building will [closed, **be closed**] for 30 minutes starting at 8:00 A.M.
오전 8시부터 30분간 건물 정문이 폐쇄될 것이다.

② 조동사처럼 쓰이는 표현 뒤에는 동사원형이 온다.

had better ~하는 게 좋다	have to ~해야 한다	be able to ~할 수 있다
would like to ~하고 싶다	used to ~하곤 했다	be going to ~할 것이다

cf. be used to -ing ~하는 데 익숙하다

If anyone would like to [worked, **work**] additional hours, let me know as soon as possible.
만약 추가 근무를 하고 싶은 분이 계시면, 저에게 가능한 한 빨리 알려주세요.

We won't be able to [attending, **attend**] the Snowbound Festival 2025 this winter.
올겨울 우리는 Snowbound Festival 2025에 참석할 수 없을 것이다.

③ 주어가 없는 명령문은 동사원형으로 시작한다.

Please [to call, **call**] me back, and let me know when you're available to meet.
언제 당신을 만날 수 있는지 전화해서 알려 주세요.

→ 명령문은 주어 you가 생략된 문장으로, 공손함을 나타내는 표현인 please를 동사 앞에 자주 쓴다.

When assembling this device, [following, **follow**] the instruction manual carefully.
이 장치를 조립할 때는 사용 설명서를 주의 깊게 따르십시오.

→ if절이나 when절 뒤에 나오는 명령문의 동사 형태를 묻는 문제도 자주 출제된다.

CHECK-UP   ☑ 다음 문장의 빈칸에 들어갈 알맞은 말을 고르세요.   정답 및 해설 p.384

1. Departing employees must ------- their employee cards to the human resources office.

  (A) returned   (B) return

2. Let us know how many additional tickets you would like to -------.

  (A) purchasing   (B) purchase

3. During my absence, please ------- any important e-mails to my colleague, Jane.

  (A) forward   (B) forwards

자동사와 타동사를 구별하는 문제가 출제된다.

① 자동사는 목적어를 취할 때 반드시 전치사가 필요하지만, 타동사는 전치사 없이 목적어를 바로 취한다.

> **자동사** Please [follow, **comply**] with all safety regulations when using our facilities.
>
> 저희 시설을 사용할 때는 모든 안전 규정을 준수하십시오.
>
> → 자동사는 목적어가 필요 없는 동사로, 자동사 뒤에는 명사가 오지 않고 주로 전치사구나 부사가 온다.

> **타동사** All factory workers should [comply, **follow**] the safety procedures.
>
> 모든 공장 근로자들은 안전 절차를 따라야 한다.
>
> → 타동사 뒤에는 목적어(명사)가 반드시 있어야 하고, 전치사구나 부사는 목적어 역할을 대신할 수 없다.

② 혼동하기 쉬운 자동사와 타동사를 구별해야 한다.

의미	자동사 + 전치사 + 목적어	타동사 + 목적어
말하다	speak to the staff 직원에게 말하다 talk to the customers 고객과 이야기하다 refer to the matter 문제를 언급하다 account for the accident 사고를 설명하다 converse with the manager 매니저와 대화하다	tell the truth 사실을 말하다 discuss the plan 계획을 논의하다 mention the problem 문제를 언급하다 explain the process 과정을 설명하다
답하다	respond to a call 요청에 응하다 reply to a query 질문에 답하다	answer the question 질문에 답하다
찬성하다	agree with/to/on the idea 의견에 동의하다 consent to the contract 계약에 동의하다	approve the proposal 제안에 찬성하다
반대하다	object to the offer 제안에 반대하다	oppose the plan 계획에 반대하다
기타	wait for news 소식을 기다리다 participate in the conference 회의에 참석하다 arrive at the venue 장소에 도착하다	await the decision 결정을 기다리다 attend the meeting 회의에 참석하다 reach the airport 공항에 도착하다

We need to set up a meeting to [**discuss,** talk] the project's progress.
프로젝트 진행 상황에 대해 논의하기 위해 회의를 준비해야 한다.

고득점 TIP+ 자동사는 목적어가 필요 없고, 타동사는 목적어가 필요하다. <자동사+전치사>, <타동사+목적어> 패턴을 암기하자. 결합하는 목적어나 전치사를 이용해서 동사 어휘 문제를 해결할 수 있다.

CHECK-UP

✓ 다음 문장의 빈칸에 들어갈 알맞은 말을 고르세요. 정답 및 해설 p.384

4. Plant managers must ------- calmly to delays caused by equipment malfunctions.

(A) answer (B) react

5. Over 100 people are expected to ------- in our annual conference.

(A) attend (B) participate

6. Many residents in the community ------- to the construction of the new highway.

(A) object (B) oppose

① **be동사와 have동사는 현재분사(-ing)나 과거분사(p.p.)와 결합하여 진행형, 수동형, 완료형이 된다.**

진행형: be + -ing Fargo Holdings in London **is offering** a range of financial services.

런던에 있는 Fargo Holdings 사는 다양한 금융 서비스를 제공하고 있다.

→ 타동사의 진행형은 뒤에 목적어가 필요하다.

수동형: be + p.p. The flight **was delayed** for more than ten hours due to bad weather.

악천후로 인해 비행기가 10시간 이상 지연되었다.

→ 대부분의 수동태 동사 뒤에는 목적어가 없고, 전치사 등의 수식어를 동반한다.

완료형: have + p.p Company revenues **have grown** quickly in the last 10 years.

회사 수익이 지난 10년 동안 빠르게 증가했다.

→ 타동사의 완료형은 뒤에 목적어가 필요하다. have동사 뒤에 빈칸을 두고 p.p. 형태를 채우는 문제가 자주 출제된다.

② **be동사와 have동사 뒤에 동사원형이 올 수 없다.**

The new assembly-line machinery was [~~design~~, **designed**] with the safety of users in mind.

새 조립라인 기계는 사용자들의 안전을 염두에 두고 설계되었다.

Please ensure that you save changes you have [~~make~~, **made**] to the file.

수정한 변경 사항은 파일에 반드시 저장하십시오.

CHECK-UP ☑ 다음 문장의 빈칸에 들어갈 알맞은 말을 고르세요. 정답 및 해설 p.384

7. Ms. Martin's application was not completely ------- until November 15.

 (A) reviews (B) reviewed

8. The steadily growing economy has ------- to a decline in unemployment.

 (A) lead (B) led

9. Sam Derek is ------- to New York for a business trip next week.

 (A) flying (B) flew

단수 동사와 복수 동사를 구별하는 문제가 출제된다.

The library [~~charge~~, **charges**] a small fee for overdue books.
도서관은 연체된 책에 대해 약간의 수수료를 부과한다.

↪ 사람 이름, 회사명 등의 고유명사는 복수형일지라도 단수 취급한다.

Ms. Fields [~~are received~~, **has received**] several awards for her innovative ideas.
Fields 씨는 혁신적인 아이디어로 여러 상을 받았다.

고득점 TIP+ 주어와 동사 사이에 수식어가 있으면, 주어와 동사의 사이가 멀어져 수 일치 여부를 판단하기가 쉽지 않다. 이런 경우에는 전체 문장 구조를 파악해서 문장 전체의 주어와 동사를 찾은 후에 수 일치를 판단해야 한다.

<u>Restaurants</u> in Redbridge [~~follows~~, **follow**] all of the local health guidelines.
Redbridge 지역의 식당들은 모든 지역 보건 지침을 따른다.

<u>Every customer</u> who submits payments after May 10 [~~charge~~, **is charged**] a late fee.
5월 10일 이후에 결제하는 모든 고객에게는 연체료가 부과됩니다.

수량 표현의 수 일치 문제가 출제된다.

▶ **결합하는 명사에 관계없이 단수/복수 취급하는 수량 표현**

단수 취급 수량 표현	단수 동사	복수 취급 수량 표현	복수 동사
Each (각각의) + 단수 명사 Every (모든) + 단수 명사 Each of the (각각의) + 복수 명사 The number of (~의 수) + 복수 명사	is / was has / had does / did 동사원형 (e)s	a number of (많은) + 복수 명사 a variety of (다양한) + 복수 명사 a range of (다양한) + 복수 명사 an array of (다양한) + 복수 명사	are / were have / had do / did 동사원형

▶ **결합하는 명사에 수 일치하는 수량 표현**

all(~의 전부), most (~의 대부분), some (~의 일부, 몇몇) half(~의 절반), any(~의 어느 것이든), the rest(~의 나머지)	+ of the/소유격 +	단수 명사 + 단수 동사 복수 명사 + 복수 동사

A variety of <u>online courses</u> covering safety [~~is offered~~, **are offered**] to employees.
안전을 다루는 다양한 온라인 강좌가 직원들에게 제공된다.

[~~Each~~, **Some**] of the <u>information</u> about the artwork <u>is</u> available at the front desk.
미술품에 대한 일부 정보는 프런트에서 확인할 수 있다.

CHECK-UP ☑ 다음 문장의 빈칸에 들어갈 알맞은 말을 고르세요. 정답 및 해설 p.384

10. Buses leaving the city terminal ------- delayed due to icy conditions on the roads.

    (A) was   (B) were

11. All of the employees at Berkshire, Inc. ------- 36.5 hours a week.

    (A) work   (B) works

12. The number of applicants for our marketing manager position -------.

    (A) is increasing (B) have increased

PRACTICE

정답 및 해설 p.385

기출 포인트 1 　동사원형 자리

명령문은 주어 없이 동사원형으로 시작하고, 조동사 뒤에는 동사원형이 온다.

1. Please ------- the rear entrance while workers install a sign on the front of the building.

　(A) using 　　　　　(B) to use 　　　　　(C) use 　　　　　(D) usage

2. Residents visited City Hall to ask whether developers will ------- the historic properties.

　(A) preserve 　　　　(B) preserved 　　　　(C) preservation 　　　　(D) preserving

기출 포인트 2 　자동사와 타동사의 구별

빈칸이 동사 자리이고, 보기에 여러 동사 어휘가 제시되면, 어휘 문제 또는 자/타동사 구별 문제이다. 타동사는 목적어를 취하고, 자동사는 짝을 이루는 전치사와 함께 출제되므로 시험에 자주 나오는 [자동사 + 전치사] 표현을 암기해 두면 쉽게 해결할 수 있다. (UNIT 05 전치사 참고)

3. Hotel management promptly ------- to all guest inquiries and complaints.

　(A) answers 　　　　(B) addresses 　　　　(C) responds 　　　　(D) suggests

4. To deal with the current financial crisis, TD Bank should ------- with another financial institution.

　(A) recall 　　　　(B) collaborate 　　　　(C) comply 　　　　(D) employ

기출 포인트 3 　주어와 동사의 수 일치

빈칸이 동사 자리로 확인되면 문장의 주어를 정확히 찾아 동사의 수를 일치시킨다.

5. During working hours, the managers ------- the staff from making personal phone calls.

　(A) restricting 　　　　(B) restrict 　　　　(C) has restricted 　　　　(D) to restrict

6. Motivating employees to work more efficiently ------- a crucial part of being an effective manager.

　(A) being 　　　　(B) are 　　　　(C) is 　　　　(D) were

기출 포인트 4 　수량 표현의 수 일치

전체 중 일부를 나타내는 특정 수량 표현은 뒤에 [of + the(소유격) + 명사]를 동반한다. 이때 특정 수량 표현의 단/복수는 결합하는 명사와 관계 없이 정해져 있다. 결합하는 명사에 수 일치하는 [all, most, some, half, any, the rest + of + the(소유격)] 패턴과 구분하여 알아 두어야 한다.

7. All of the agreements in the contract ------- thoroughly checked and reviewed by the board.

　(A) has 　　　　(B) having had 　　　　(C) to have 　　　　(D) have been

8. The survey shows that almost half of our employees ------- more stressed at work than they did a year ago.

　(A) feel 　　　　(B) is feeling 　　　　(C) has felt 　　　　(D) was felt

RC PART 5

UNIT 07 태와 시제

1. 태

능동태와 수동태의 개념

① 능동태는 주어가 어떤 일을 스스로 한다는 의미이고, 수동태는 주어가 어떤 일을 당한다는 의미이다.

능동태 The company **achieved** its sales target this quarter. 회사는 이번 분기에 판매 목표를 달성했다.
수동태 Taxes **are deducted** from your salary each month. 세금은 매월 급여에서 공제된다.

수동태의 형태

② 수동태의 기본 형태는 <주어 + be동사 + p.p.(과거분사) + by + 행위자>이다. 여기서 주어의 수와 시제에 따라 be동사의 형태가 달라진다. 수동태 형태에서 <by + 행위자>는 굳이 언급할 필요가 없는 경우 생략 가능하다.

현재	am/is/are + p.p.	A new item **is released** by the company. 신제품이 회사에 의해 출시된다.
과거	was/were + p.p.	A new item **was released** by the company. 신제품이 회사에 의해 출시되었다.
미래	will be + p.p.	A new item **will be released** by the company. 신제품이 회사에 의해 출시될 것이다.
현재진행	am/is/are + being + p.p.	The sales report **is being written** by him. 영업 보고서가 그에 의해서 작성되고 있는 중이다.
과거진행	was/were + being + p.p.	The sales report **was being written** by him. 영업 보고서가 그에 의해서 작성되고 있었다.
미래진행	will be + being + p.p.	The sales report **will be being written** by him. 영업 보고서가 그에 의해서 작성되고 있는 중일 것이다.
현재완료	have/has + been + p.p.	Our schedule **has been changed** by the manager. 일정이 관리자에 의해 변경되었다.
과거완료	had + been + p.p.	Our schedule **had been changed** by the manager. 일정이 관리자에 의해 변경되어 있었다.
미래완료	will have + been + p.p.	Our schedule **will have been changed** by the manager. 일정이 관리자에 의해 변경되어 있을 것이다.

CHECK-UP
✓ 다음 문장의 빈칸에 들어갈 알맞은 말을 고르세요. 정답 및 해설 p.386

1. The company will ------- its headquarters to a larger city next year.

  (A) relocate (B) be relocated

2. Ms. Cafferky requested a full refund because the photocopier -------.

  (A) was damaged (B) damaged

3. After years of hard work, he was finally ------- to the position of senior analyst.

  (A) promoting (B) promoted

기출 패턴 3 · 능동태와 수동태를 구별하는 문제가 출제된다.

⤷ '주어가 ~하다'라는 의미로, 주어가 행위의 주체

① 타동사 뒤에 목적어가 있으면 **능동태**를, 목적어가 없으면 **수동태**를 선택한다.

⤷ '주어가 ~되다'라는 의미로, 주어가 행위의 대상

능동태 After much discussion, we [~~were canceled~~, **canceled**] the plan to build a new highway.
많은 논의 끝에 우리는 새 고속도로 건설 계획을 취소했다.

수동태 The festival [~~canceled~~, **was canceled**] because of the recent rain.
최근 내린 비로 축제가 취소되었다.

② 감정을 나타내는 타동사는 주어가 감정의 원인이면 능동태, 주어가 감정을 느끼면 수동태를 쓴다.

interest 흥미를 일으키다	excite 흥분시키다	please 기쁘게 하다	exhaust 지치게 하다
disappoint 실망시키다	delight 즐겁게 하다	surprise 놀라게 하다	satisfy 만족시키다

능동태 The low profits [~~were disappointed~~, **disappointed**] both the CEO and the investors.
낮은 수익은 최고 경영자와 투자자들 모두를 실망시켰다.

수동태 The client [~~disappointed~~, **was disappointed**] that the item he ordered was out of stock.
고객은 요청한 상품의 재고가 떨어져서 실망했다.

기출 패턴 4 · 수동태가 될 수 없는 자동사 문제가 출제된다.

▶ 수동태로 쓰지 않는 자동사

happen / occur / take place 발생하다	emerge 출현하다	arrive 도착하다	expire 만기가 되다
exist 존재하다	remain ~로 남다	rise 오르다	last 지속되다	work 효과가 있다

고득점 TIP+ 목적어를 취하지 않는 자동사는 수동태(be + p.p)가 될 수 없다.

The cost of fuel [~~has been risen~~, **has risen**] quickly over the past five years.
지난 5년간 연료비가 급격히 올랐다.

AGU's insurance rates [~~are remained~~, **have remained**] steady for the last three years.
AGU 사의 보험료는 지난 3년간 보합세를 유지하고 있다.

CHECK-UP ✓ 다음 문장의 빈칸에 들어갈 알맞은 말을 고르세요.

정답 및 해설 p.386

4. Mr. Page ------- all questions about the new payroll policy in a company e-mail.

(A) was answered (B) answered

5. The equipment-use guidelines can ------- on our internal corporate Web site.

(A) find (B) be found

6. All factory visitors must ------- at the front desk before entering the production area.

(A) arrive (B) be arrived

4형식/5형식 동사의 수동태 관련 문제가 출제된다.

① 목적어가 2개인 4형식 동사가 수동태가 될 때는, 목적어 중 하나가 동사 뒤에 남는다.

고득점 TIP+ 4형식 동사는 목적어가 2개이므로, 간접 목적어가 주어로 바뀌어도 동사 뒤에 여전히 목적어가 남는다.

be offered N N을 제공받다	be given N N을 받다	be sent N N을 받다
be issued N N을 발급받다	be granted N N을 받다	be awarded N N을 수여받다

┌→ 간접 목적어   ┌→ 직접 목적어

능동태 We will [be sent, **send**] Mr. Belle his tickets and coupon by e-mail tomorrow.
우리는 내일 Belle 씨에게 항공권과 쿠폰을 이메일로 보낼 것이다.

수동태 Mr. Belle will [send, **be sent**] his tickets and coupon by e-mail tomorrow.
Belle 씨는 내일 항공권과 쿠폰을 이메일로 받을 것이다.

→ 간접 목적어(Mr. Belle)가 주어 자리로 가서 수동태가 될 경우에는 직접 목적어(his tickets and coupon)가 동사(will be sent) 뒤에 그대로 남아 수동태 동사가 목적어를 가진 것처럼 보이므로 주의한다.

② 목적격 보어를 취하는 5형식 동사가 수동태가 될 때, 목적격 보어가 수동태 동사 뒤에 남는 경우가 있다.

고득점 TIP+ 5형식 문장은 목적어와 목적격 보어를 가지며, 목적격 보어 자리에는 명사, 형용사, to부정사 등 다양한 형태가 올 수 있다.

┌→ 목적어   ┌→ 목적격 보어

능동태 The CEO of Glaxo [was named, **named**] Mr. Cohen his successor at yesterday's meeting.
Glaxo 사의 CEO는 어제 회의에서 Cohen 씨를 후임자로 지명했다.

수동태 Mr. Cohen **was named** his successor at yesterday's meeting (by the CEO of Glaxo).
Cohen 씨는 어제 회의에서 Glaxo 사의 CEO의 후임자로 임명되었다.

→ 능동태의 목적어(Mr. Cohen)가 주어 자리로 가서 수동태가 될 때, 명사구 목적격 보어(his successor)가 수동태 동사(was named) 뒤에 그대로 온다. 이것은 수동태 동사의 목적어가 아니므로 주의한다.

▶ 명사구를 목적격 보어로 취하는 5형식 동사

be considered N	be elected N	be called N	be named N
N로 여겨지다	N로 선출되다	N로 불리다	N로 명명(선정)되다

CHECK-UP   ☑ 다음 문장의 빈칸에 들어갈 알맞은 말을 고르세요.   정답 및 해설 p.386

7. Workers ------- training to transition to other roles within the company.

　(A) offered　　(B) were offered

8. Ms. Griffin ------- the most professional person in the marketing field.

　(A) considered　(B) is considered

9. Allergan, Inc. ------- the Best Emerging Company in a recent survey.

　(A) named　　(B) was named

① 수동태 + 전치사

be satisfied with ~에 만족하다	be pleased with ~에 기뻐하다	be equipped with ~을 갖추다
be interested in ~에 관심을 가지다	be involved in ~에 관련되다	be limited to ~로 제한되다
be related to ~와 관련되다	be exposed to ~에 노출되다	be concerned about ~을 걱정하다
be confused at ~에 혼란스럽다	be composed of ~로 구성되다	be known for ~으로 유명하다

The Yorkshire Kitchen is [~~knowing~~, **known**] for its frequent special offers.
Yorkshire Kitchen은 특가를 자주 제공하는 것으로 유명하다.

Mr. Topher [~~interests~~, **is interested**] in medical and health-related careers.
Topher 씨는 의료와 건강 관련 직업에 관심이 많다.

② 수동태 + to부정사

be asked to V ~하라고 요청받다	be required to V ~하라고 요구받다	be requested to V ~하라고 요구받다
be forced to V ~하도록 강요받다	be expected to V ~하리라 기대되다	be instructed to V ~하도록 지시받다
be urged to V ~하라고 요구받다	be allowed to V ~하도록 허가받다	be permitted to V ~하도록 허용되다
be scheduled to V ~할 예정이다	be advised to V ~하라는 충고를 듣다	be encouraged to V ~하라고 권고받다
be projected to V ~할 것으로 예상되다	be invited to V ~하도록 초대받다	be reminded to V ~하라는 말을 듣다

All passengers [~~required~~, **are required**] to stay seated while the bus is in motion.
모든 승객은 버스가 운행되는 동안 자리에 앉아 있도록 요구받았다.

No one is [~~allowing~~, **allowed**] to enter the lab without an identification badge.
신분증 없이는 어느 누구도 실험실에 들어가는 것이 허용되지 않는다.

RC PART 5

CHECK-UP   ☑ 다음 문장의 빈칸에 들어갈 알맞은 말을 고르세요.   정답 및 해설 p.386

10. The audience is ------ to be seated ten minutes before the performance begins.

   (A) asking   (B) asked

11. Mr. Scott ------ with the fabric samples; as a result, he placed an order for a variety of styles.

   (A) pleased   (B) was pleased

12. Employees ------ to shut down their computers before leaving for the day.

   (A) are reminded
   (B) are reminding

2. 시제

단순 시제(현재, 과거, 미래) 문제가 출제된다.

① 현재 시제[동사원형 또는 동사원형 + (e)s]는 현재 상황, 반복되는 사건이나 습관, 일반적인 사실을 표현할 때 사용한다.

현재 시제와 어울리는 시간 표현	always 항상 routinely 일상적으로	often/frequently 자주 every week [month] 매주[달]	usually 보통 regularly/periodically 정기적으로

New entrepreneurs <u>often</u> **seek** advice from experienced business owners.
새로 시작하는 기업가들은 종종 경험이 풍부한 사업주들로부터 조언을 구한다.

② 과거 시제[동사원형 + (e)d/불규칙 동사]는 특정 과거 시점에 일어난 일이나 상태를 표현할 때 사용한다.

과거 시제와 어울리는 시간 표현	yesterday 어제 previously 이전에	시간 표현 + ago ~전에 in + (과거) 연도 ~년에	recently 최근에 last week [month] 지난주[달]

* 부사 ago(~ 전에)는 단독으로 사용되지 않고, 항상 기간을 나타내는 단어와 함께 사용된다.

The company <u>recently</u> **decided** to open a new branch in Hanoi.
그 회사는 하노이에 신규 지점을 열기로 최근에 결정했다.

③ 미래 시제[will + 동사원형]는 미래의 일에 대한 추측이나 의지를 표현할 때 사용한다.

미래 시제와 어울리는 시간 표현	tomorrow 내일 soon/shortly 곧	next week [month] 다음 주[달]에 in the near future 가까운 미래에	this coming Friday 다가오는 금요일에 as of/effective + 미래 시점 ~부터

Mr. Roberts **will complete** his internship at Gold Coast Bank <u>next week</u>.
Roberts 씨는 다음 주에 Gold Coast 은행에서의 실습을 마칠 예정이다.

CHECK-UP
✅ 다음 문장의 빈칸에 들어갈 알맞은 말을 고르세요. 정답 및 해설 p.386

13. Our management team periodically ------- incentives to stimulate employee productivity.

(A) offers (B) are offering

14. Last year, the city ------- 500 building permits to small business owners.

(A) issues (B) issued

15. Over the next few months, Alfa Vehicles ------- more features to its sedans.

(A) added (B) will add

완료 시제(현재완료, 과거완료, 미래완료) 문제가 출제된다.

① 현재완료 시제[have/has + p.p.]는 과거에 발생한 일이나 상태가 현재까지 계속되거나 영향을 미치고 있음을 나타낸다.

현재완료 시제와 어울리는 시간 표현	recently/lately 최근에 for + 기간 ~동안 since + 과거 시점 ~이래로 over[for/in] the last[past] + 기간 지난 ~에 걸쳐[동안] so far 지금까지

The Knife Restaurant **has offered** a special menu <u>for the past decade</u>.
Knife 레스토랑은 지난 10년간 특별한 메뉴를 제공해 왔다.

고득점 TIP+ 현재완료 시제는 명확한 과거 시점을 나타내는 yesterday, ago, 'last+시점' 등과 함께 쓸 수 없다.

He [~~has retired~~, **retired**] as plant manager <u>three years ago</u>.
그는 3년 전에 공장 관리자직에서 은퇴했다.

② 과거완료 시제[had + p.p]는 과거의 어떤 시점을 기준으로 그보다 이전에 일어난 일을 나타낸다.

과거완료 시제와 어울리는 시간 표현	before + 주어 + 과거 시제 동사 ~하기 전에 by the time + 주어 + 과거 시제 동사 ~했을 즈음에

<u>Before I reached</u> the station, the train **had** already **left**.
내가 정거장에 도착하기 전에, 기차는 이미 떠나버렸다.

<u>By the time she arrived</u> at the office, the meeting **had** already **started**.
그녀가 사무실에 도착했을 때쯤, 회의는 이미 시작되었다.

③ 미래완료 시제[will have + p.p.]는 과거나 현재에 시작된 일이 미래까지 계속되거나 미래의 특정 시점에 완료될 것임을 나타내며, 보통 접속사 by the time(~할 즈음에)과 함께 쓰인다.

미래완료 시제와 어울리는 시간 표현	By the time 주어 + 현재 시제 동사 ~, 주어 + 동사(will have p.p.) ~ ~할 무렵이면 ~했을 것이다

<u>By the time the product goes</u> on the market, we **will have corrected** its remaining flaws.
제품이 시장에 출시될 때쯤이면, 남아 있는 결함이 해결된 상태일 것이다.

CHECK-UP
✓ 다음 문장의 빈칸에 들어갈 알맞은 말을 고르세요.   정답 및 해설 p.386

16. Ms. Kelly enjoys sharing with new colleagues the knowledge she ------- over the years.

(A) has gained   (B) gains

17. By the time we launch the product, our competitors ------- theirs.

(A) had released
(B) will have released

18. The manager was pleased to find that the team ------- the task before the deadline.

(A) will be completed
(B) had completed

특정 시제와 함께 쓰이는 표현을 구별하는 문제가 출제된다.

과거	시점 + ago ~전에	last + 시점 지난 ~에	yesterday 어제	in + 과거년도 ~년에	previously 이전에
현재	usually 보통	often 종종	every + 시점 매 ~마다	frequently 자주	generally 일반적으로
미래	tomorrow 내일	next + 시점 다음 ~에	shortly 곧	soon 곧	later this + 시점 이번 ~ 후반에
현재 완료	since + 과거 시점 ~이래로		over[for, in] the last[past] 지난 ~동안		
	lately/recently 최근에		consistently 지속적으로		

The planning board [~~approves~~, **approved**] the park renovation project <u>yesterday</u>.
어제 기획 위원회에서 공원 보수 공사를 승인했다.

<u>Over the past three years</u>, Mr. Lee [~~implements~~, **has implemented**] four new programs.
지난 3년 동안, Lee 씨는 4개의 새로운 프로그램을 시행했다.

Mr. Chapman [~~previously~~, **usually**] <u>attends</u> trade shows by himself.
Chapman 씨는 주로 혼자 무역 박람회에 참석한다.

고득점 TIP+

① 특정 시제와 사용되는 표현 및 부사들이 자주 출제되므로, 시제별로 어울리는 표현을 암기해야 한다. (UNIT 4 부사 참고)

② 현재 시점에 진행 중인 일을 나타내는 '~하는 중이다'로 해석되는 현재진행[am/is/are + V-ing] 시제와 어울리는 시간 부사 currently/presently/now 등을 묻는 문제가 자주 출제된다.

We <u>are</u> [~~once~~, **currently**] <u>seeking</u> volunteers to participate in an upcoming event.
우리는 현재 다가오는 행사에 참여할 자원봉사자를 찾고 있습니다.

CHECK-UP
☑ 다음 문장의 빈칸에 들어갈 알맞은 말을 고르세요. 정답 및 해설 p.386

19. Every Thursday, our team members ------- to discuss novels written by local authors.

(A) will have met   (B) meet

20. The Portney Company has ------- donated to local charities each year.

(A) consistently   (B) shortly

21. The CEO has ------- expressed concerns about the quarterly profits.

(A) soon   (B) recently

시제 일치 예외 문제가 출제된다.

① 시간이나 조건을 나타내는 부사절에서는 현재 시제가 미래 시제를 대신한다.

If it **rains** tomorrow, we will not participate in the workshop.
내일 비가 온다면, 우리는 워크숍에 참석하지 않을 것이다.

As soon as we **receive** all the relevant information, the problem will be discussed.
모든 관련 정보를 받는 대로 그 문제가 논의될 것이다.

고득점 TIP+ 시간, 조건 부사절을 이끄는 접속사에는 when, before, as soon as, once, if, unless 등이 있다.

② 주절에 주장, 제안, 요청, 의무를 나타내는 동사가 나오면, that절에는 동사원형이 와야 한다.

주어	insist / urge / order / suggest / ask recommend / require / request	+ that + 주어 + (should) + 동사원형

Mr. Kim requested that this month's sales report [is completed, **be completed**] by tomorrow.
Kim 씨는 이번 달 매출 보고서를 내일까지 완성해 달라고 요청했다.

③ 'It is + 보어(형용사) + that + 주어 + 동사' 구문의 보어 자리에 형용사가 '필수, 의무' 의미를 나타낼 때 **that 절**의 동사는 동사원형이 와야 한다.

It is [was]	important / essential / crucial imperative / necessary	+ that + S + (should) + 동사원형

It is necessary that the project [will be completed, **be completed**] by next week.
프로젝트는 다음 주까지 완료되어야 한다.

고득점 TIP+ 보어 자리에 빈칸을 두어 알맞은 형용사(important, necessary, essential 등)를 묻는 문제도 자주 출제된다.

RC PART 5

CHECK-UP

✓ 다음 문장의 빈칸에 들어갈 알맞은 말을 고르세요.
정답 및 해설 p.386

22. Mr. Jones will receive his voicemail messages when he ------- to the office on Monday.

(A) will return (B) returns

23. The Pot Bistro has requested that we ------- the number of dinner guests by Monday.

(A) specify (B) specified

24. It is imperative that every safety precaution ------- on the factory floor.

(A) is taken (B) be taken

정답 및 해설 p.388

기출 포인트 1　　**능동태 Vs. 수동태**

동사 자리에 빈칸이 제시되는 문제에서 타동사인 경우, 빈칸 뒤에 목적어가 있으면 능동태, 없으면 수동태를 쓴다.

1. In an effort to meet the needs of customers, we will ------- a Web site for our new products.

(A) launching　　　　　(B) launch　　　　　(C) be launched　　　　　(D) launches

2. If we receive the author's final approval, the manuscript will ------- to the printer.

(A) be sending　　　　　(B) send　　　　　(C) be sent　　　　　(D) sending

기출 포인트 2　　**4형식/5형식 동사의 수동태**

4형식/5형식 동사가 보기로 제시되면 빈칸 뒤에 명사가 있더라도 수동태가 정답이 될 수 있으므로 해석을 통해 문제를 풀어야 한다.

3. The salesperson with the best sales record will ------- a one-week vacation at a seaside hotel.

(A) awarding　　　　　(B) award　　　　　(C) awarded　　　　　(D) be awarded

4. Milton House, which served as Luton's first schoolhouse, has been ------- a historical landmark.

(A) designation　　　　　(B) designating　　　　　(C) designate　　　　　(D) designated

기출 포인트 3　　**수동태가 불가능한 자동사**

보통 빈칸 뒤에 목적어가 없으면 수동태가 정답이 되지만, 보기가 자동사로 제시되면 자동사는 수동태로 쓸 수 없기 때문에 능동태가 정답이다.

5. Dr. Elliott ------- for 30 years at BPA Volks Pharmaceuticals by the time she retires.

(A) serve　　　　　(B) had been served　　　　　(C) serving　　　　　(D) will have served

6. The keynote speaker was not able to ------- in time as the road construction was not completed.

(A) arriving　　　　　(B) arrive　　　　　(C) be arrived　　　　　(D) being arrived

기출 포인트 4　　**수동태 숙어 표현**

현재분사(V-ing)와 과거분사(V-ed)를 구별하는 문제와, 수동태 뒤 전치사 자리가 빈칸으로 제시되는 문제가 출제된다. 수동태 숙어 표현들은 묶어서 암기한다.

7. If you are not ------- with our new dishwasher, you may return it for a full refund.

(A) satisfaction　　　　　(B) satisfying　　　　　(C) satisfied　　　　　(D) satisfy

8. City residents are extremely concerned ------- the closing of the Vic Theater due to its financial difficulties.

(A) in　　　　　(B) about　　　　　(C) by　　　　　(D) to

시제 문제는 각 시제에 어울리는 단서를 익히고 그에 맞는 시제를 선택한다.

9. At yesterday's meeting, Mr. Franco ------- the need to hire enough workers during the peak season.

(A) emphasizing   (B) emphasized   (C) will emphasize   (D) emphasizes

10. Next month, AT Motors ------- its employees at the head office to work at the new branch in Iran.

(A) sent   (B) had sent   (C) send   (D) will send

11. Mr. Bush ------- overtime to meet the proposal submission deadline since last week.

(A) work   (B) will work   (C) has been working   (D) worked

기출 포인트 6   **수/시제 일치의 예외**

'주장/제안/요청/의무'의 의미를 나타내는 동사나 가주어/진주어 구문에서 형용사가 '필수, 의무'를 나타내는 경우에 that절의 동사는 주어의 수와 시제와 관계 없이 [(should)+동사원형]의 형태로 쓴다.

12. Ms. Redgrave requests that this month's sales totals ------- by the end of the month.

(A) submitted   (B) would submit   (C) be submitted   (D) submits

13. It is important that a manager ------- how to prevent potential problems occurring at the workplace.

(A) to learn   (B) learn   (C) is learned   (D) learning

14. It is very ------- that all aspects of the contract be examined in as much detail as possible.

(A) useful   (B) important   (C) available   (D) sensitive

기출 포인트 7   **시간이나 조건 부사절에서의 시제**

주절의 시제가 미래이면 종속절의 시제도 미래 시제를 사용하지만, 시간이나 조건 부사절에서는 미래 시제 대신에 현재 시제를 쓴다.

15. Mr. Highmore will supervise the construction of the new factory when it ------- next December.

(A) open   (B) will open   (C) opened   (D) opens

기출 포인트 8   **특정 시제와 어울리는 부사 어휘 문제**

usually(보통)/regularly(정기적으로)는 현재 시제, currently(현재)는 현재진행 시제, recently/lately(최근)는 현재완료/과거 시제와 어울린다. 각 시제마다 어울리는 부사를 암기해 두자.

16. Cimic Ltd. has ------- hired a consultant to search for qualified candidates to join its management team.

(A) currently   (B) regularly   (C) recently   (D) highly

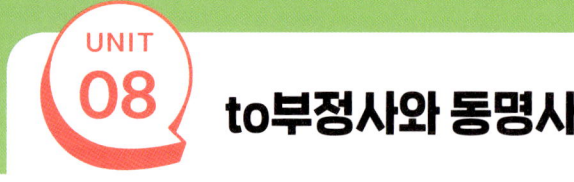

UNIT 08 to부정사와 동명사

1. to부정사

기출 패턴 1 **to부정사 자리 문제가 출제된다.**

① to부정사는 문장에서 명사, 형용사, 부사 역할을 한다.

• **명사 (~하는 것)**: 문장의 주어, 동사의 목적어, 보어 자리에 온다.

주어 **To boost** sales volume is the goal this quarter.
판매량을 늘리는 것이 이번 분기 목표다.

동사의 목적어 The sales manager decided **to change** the current supplier.
영업 관리자는 현재의 공급업체를 바꾸기로 결정했다.

주격 보어 One of your new tasks is **to update** our Web site regularly.
귀하의 새로운 직무 중 하나는 웹 사이트를 정기적으로 업데이트하는 것입니다.

목적격 보어 The manager encouraged all the employees **to attend** the seminar.
매니저는 모든 직원이 세미나에 참석하도록 독려했다.

• **형용사 (~할, ~하기 위한)**: 명사 뒤에서 명사를 수식한다.

명사 수식 The manager devised a plan **to maximize** profits.
매니저는 수익을 최대화할 계획을 고안했다.

• **부사 (~하기 위해서, ~해서)**: 목적, 이유 등을 나타낸다. '목적'의 의미일 때 to부정사 대신 in order to를 쓸 수 있다.

목적 **To discuss** the issues, the board of directors will have a meeting.
= **In order to discuss the issues**, ~
사안들을 토론하기 위해 이사회는 회의를 할 것이다.

이유 UCL is pleased **to announce** the expansion of its east campus facilities.
UCL은 동쪽 캠퍼스 시설의 확장을 발표하게 되어 기쁩니다.

고득점 TIP+ '~하기 위해서'의 의미로 목적을 나타내는 부사 역할의 to부정사가 가장 많이 출제되며, in order to + 동사원형, so as to + 동사원형으로 표현할 수 있다.

CHECK-UP ☑ 다음 문장의 빈칸에 들어갈 알맞은 말을 고르세요. 정답 및 해설 p.389

1. Our company policy is ------- the workplace environment clean at all times.

   (A) to keep (B) to keeping

2. New computer technology will enable people ------- more efficient at work.

   (A) to be (B) being

3. In order to ------- its employees' hard work, the company held a banquet.

   (A) honoring (B) honor

to부정사를 목적어로 취하는 동사, 명사, 형용사 관련 문제가 출제된다.

① to부정사를 목적어로 취하는 동사 [타동사 + 목적어(to부정사)]

afford to V	~할 경제적 여유가 있다	intend to V	~할 작정이다
decide to V	~하려고 결심[결정]하다	strive to V	~하기 위해서 노력하다, 애쓰다
expect to V	~할 것을 기대[예상]하다	plan to V	~하려고 계획하다
fail to V	~하려던 것을 하지 못하다	refuse to V	~를 거절하다

Tespo, Inc. strives [~~ensure~~, **to ensure**] the safety of everyone in the workplace.
Tespo 사는 직장 내 모든 사람의 안전을 보장하기 위해 노력한다.

The company agreed to [~~revising~~, **revise**] the contract terms after lengthy negotiations.
긴 협상 끝에 회사는 계약 조건을 수정하기로 동의했다.

② to부정사를 취하는 명사 [명사 + to부정사]

plan to V	~할 계획	ability to V	~할 수 있는 능력
right [authority] to V	~할 권리	chance to V	~할 기회
decision to V	~하려는 결정	opportunity to V	~할 기회
effort to V	~하려는 노력	attempt to V	~하려는 시도

The position requires the ability [~~developing~~, **to develop**] a wide variety of policies.
그 직책은 다양한 정책을 개발할 수 있는 능력이 요구된다.

③ to부정사를 취하는 형용사 [be + 형용사 + to부정사]

be (un)able to V	~할 수 있다[없다]	be easy to V	~하기 쉽다/쉽게 ~하다
be eager to V	간절히 ~하고 싶어 하다	be likely to V	~할 것 같다
be willing to V	기꺼이 ~하다	be scheduled to V	~하기로 예정되어 있다
be reluctant to V	~하기를 꺼려하다	be hesitant to V	~하는 것을 망설이다

I am sorry to say that our company is unable [~~acceptance~~, **to accept**] your offer.
당신의 제안을 수락할 수 없다는 것을 전하게 되어 유감입니다.

CHECK-UP

✓ 다음 문장의 빈칸에 들어갈 알맞은 말을 고르세요. 정답 및 해설 p.389

4. Management decided ------ a new performance evaluation system.

  (A) to implement   (B) implemented

5. Mr. Foley's ability ------ well with others is his most admirable quality.

  (A) work   (B) to work

6. A series of workshops is scheduled ------ employees' skills.

  (A) enhancement   (B) to enhance

RC PART 5

to부정사와 원형 부정사를 목적격 보어로 취하는 동사 관련 문제가 출제된다.

① **to부정사를 목적격 보어로 취하는 동사 [타동사 + 목적어 + 목적격 보어(to부정사)]**

allow A to V	A가 ~하는 것을 허락하다	enable A to V	A에게 ~할 수 있게 하다
permit A to V	A가 ~하는 것을 허락하다	expect A to V	A가 ~하기를 기대하다
ask A to V	A에게 ~하는 것을 부탁하다	advise A to V	A에게 ~하도록 조언하다
require A to V	A에게 ~하도록 요구하다	encourage A to V	A에게 ~하도록 장려하다

We asked employees [~~limit~~, **to limit**] personal conversations during the meeting.
우리는 직원들에게 회의 중에 개인적인 대화를 자제해 달라고 부탁했다.

→ Employees <u>were asked</u> **to limit** personal conversations during the meeting.
  ↳ 수동태로 쓰이면 뒤에 목적격 보어가 남는다.

② **사역동사(make, let, have)는 원형 부정사를 목적격 보어로 취한다.**
  ↳ 목적어가 ~하도록 만들다/시키다

The director made all department employees [~~to submit~~, **submit**] annual sales report.
이사는 모든 부서 직원들에게 연간 매출보고서를 제출하도록 시켰다.

③ **준사역동사 help는 원형 부정사와 to부정사 모두 목적어 또는 목적격 보어로 취할 수 있다.**
  ↳ 목적어가 ~하는 것을 돕다

The new marketing strategies will <u>help</u> **(to) generate** high annual profits.
새로운 마케팅 전략은 높은 연간 수익을 내는 데 도움을 줄 것이다.

The training program <u>helps</u> employees **(to) enhance** their skills.
교육 프로그램은 직원들이 그들의 능력을 향상하도록 돕는다.

to부정사의 의미상 주어를 묻는 문제가 출제된다.

to부정사의 의미상 주어가 필요한 경우, to 앞에 'for + 명사' 또는 'for + 대명사의 목적격'을 쓴다.

It is mandatory <u>for factory workers</u> **to wear** protective clothing.
공장 근로자들은 의무적으로 보호 의복을 착용해야 한다.

CHECK-UP

☑ 다음 문장의 빈칸에 들어갈 알맞은 말을 고르세요. 　　정답 및 해설 p.389

7. Sarah's persistence allowed her ------ numerous challenges and achieve her sales targets.

　(A) to overcome　(B) overcoming

8. Our new system lets managers ------ with technicians in real time.

　(A) communicate
　(B) to communicate

9. Your feedback will help us ------ our products and services.

　(A) improve　(B) improving

전치사 to와 to부정사를 구별하는 문제가 출제된다.

① [명사 + 전치사 to + 명사]

access to N ~로의 접근(이용)	transfer to N ~로의 전근	contribution to N ~에 대한 기여
change to N ~에 대한 변경	transition to N ~로의 전환	commitment to N ~에 대한 헌신
solution to N ~에 대한 해결책	exposure to N ~로의 노출	key to N ~에 대한 열쇠/방법

During the street construction project, **access to** the library will be difficult.
도로 건설 프로젝트 동안 도서관 이용은 어려울 것이다.

② [be + 형용사 + 전치사 to + 명사]

be accessible to N	~에 접근 가능하다	be adjacent to N	~에 인접하다
be beneficial to N	~에 이득이 되다	be payable to N	~에 지불하다
be equivalent to N	~에 상응하다	be subject to N	~의 대상이다, ~의 영향을 받다
be vulnerable to N	~에 취약하다	be transferable to N	~로 이동할 수 있다, ~에게 양도 가능하다

The newly built community center **is adjacent to** the post office.
새롭게 지어진 시민 문화 회관은 우체국과 인접해 있다.

고득점 TIP+

① 전치사 to 뒤에는 명사, 동명사가 오고 동사원형은 올 수 없다. to부정사는 '~하는 것', '~해야 할' 등으로 해석되고, 전치사 to는 '~에게, ~로' 라는 의미로 '방향'을 나타낸다.

② to부정사의 부정은 to부정사 앞에 not이나 never를 사용한다.

It's important not **to disregard** warning signs for safety.
안전을 위해 경고 표시를 무시하지 않는 것이 중요하다.

③ have yet to V (아직 ~하지 않았다)

The contract has yet **to be** finalized by the legal team at the Globex Corporation.
Globex Corporation의 법률팀은 아직 계약을 최종적으로 승인하지 않았다.

CHECK-UP

✓ 다음 문장의 빈칸에 들어갈 알맞은 말을 고르세요.   정답 및 해설 p.389

10. Please thank the team at the Detroit office for their continued ------- to this merger project.

   (A) authority   (B) contributions

11. Early departures are considered cancelations and are subject to ------- fees.

   (A) cancel   (B) cancelation

12. The research team has ------- to conduct market analysis for the upcoming quarter.

   (A) still   (B) yet

RC
PART 5

2. 동명사

동명사 자리 문제가 출제된다.

① 동명사는 문장에서 명사 역할을 하며 주어, 목적어, 보어 자리에 온다.

> **주어**   **Wearing** a seatbelt is a legal obligation when driving.
> 안전벨트 착용은 운전할 때 법적 의무이다.

고득점 TIP+ 동명사가 문장의 주어로 쓰일 때는 동사는 단수 취급한다.

Following traffic rules is imperative for the smooth flow of vehicles.
교통 규칙을 지키는 것은 원활한 차량 흐름을 위해서 필수다.

> **동사의 목적어**   Mr. Scott suggested **recruiting** additional new employees.
> Scott 씨는 신입 사원을 추가로 채용하자고 제안했다.

> **전치사의 목적어**   All of our items will be shipped within a day of **receiving** an order.
> 모든 저희 물품들은 주문을 받은 후 하루 안에 배송될 것입니다.

> **보어**   One of her main jobs is **maximizing** the promotion effects.
> 그녀의 주된 업무 중 하나는 홍보 효과를 극대화하는 것이다.

② 동명사와 to부정사는 동사의 성질은 가지고 있지만, 동사가 될 수 없다.

The new tenant [~~to complain~~, **complained**] about the lack of parking spaces.
새로운 세입자는 주차 공간 부족에 대해 불평했다.

The tour guide [~~explaining~~, **explained**] the day's itinerary before starting the excursion.
여행 가이드는 여행을 시작하기 전에 그날의 여행 일정을 설명했다.

③ 동명사의 수동형은 'being p.p.'이다.

The product will undergo quality control before [~~releasing~~, **being released**].
제품이 출시되기 전에 품질 관리를 거치게 된다.

→ 제품이 '출시하는' 것이 아니라 '출시되는' 것이라는 의미를 나타내기 위해서 동명사의 수동형(being released)을 쓴다.

CHECK-UP
✓ 다음 문장의 빈칸에 들어갈 알맞은 말을 고르세요.   정답 및 해설 p.389

13. ------- new strategies requires careful planning and execution.

   (A) Implementation
   (B) Implementing

14. Using a reusable water bottle ------- to reduce plastic waste.

   (A) helps   (B) helping

15. Mr. Hardy is in charge of ------- office supplies for the entire company.

   (A) orders   (B) ordering

동명사를 목적어로 취하는 동사 관련 문제가 출제된다.

① 동명사를 목적어로 취하는 동사 [타동사 + 동명사]

include -ing ~하는 것을 포함하다	suggest -ing ~하는 것을 제안하다	finish -ing ~하는 것을 끝내다
enjoy -ing ~하는 것을 즐기다	consider -ing ~하는 것을 고려하다	avoid -ing ~하는 것을 피하다
recommend -ing ~하는 것을 추천하다	mind -ing ~하는 것을 꺼리다	postpone -ing ~하는 것을 연기하다

I highly recommend **checking** the report for errors.
보고서에 오류가 없는지 확인할 것을 강력히 추천합니다.

② 동명사와 to부정사 모두 목적어로 취하는 동사 [타동사 + 동명사/to 부정사]

▶ **의미가 같은 경우**

begin -ing/to V	~하기 시작하다	continue -ing/to V	~하는 것을 계속하다
attempt -ing/to V	~하려고 시도하다	intend -ing/to V	~하려고 의도하다
like -ing/to V	~하는 것을 좋아하다	prefer -ing/to V	~하는 것을 선호하다

Ely City continues (experienced, **experiencing/to experience**) a 4 percent annual population increase.
Ely 시는 매년 4%의 인구 증가를 계속해서 겪고 있다.

▶ **의미가 다른 경우**

stop -ing ~하는 것을 멈추다, 중단하다	stop to V ~하기 위해서 멈추다
remember -ing ~한 것을 기억하다	remember to V ~할 것을 기억하다
forget -ing ~한 것을 잊다	forget to V ~할 것을 잊다
regret -ing ~한 것을 후회하다	regret to V ~하게 되어 유감이다

We regret **to inform** you that your visa could not be approved at this time.
귀하의 비자가 이번에는 승인되지 않았다는 것을 알리게 되어 유감입니다.

Stephen Graham regrets **not going** to attend a yesterday's meeting.
Stephen Graham 씨는 어제 회의에 참석하지 않은 것을 후회한다.

CHECK-UP ☑ 다음 문장의 빈칸에 들어갈 알맞은 말을 고르세요. 정답 및 해설 p.389

16. Our company consultants suggested ------- unnecessary expenses.

(A) to reduce　(B) reducing

17. To avoid ------- a late fee, you have to return the books by the due date.

(A) to pay　(B) paying

18. We regret ------- you that your job application was not successful.

(A) informing　(B) to inform

RC PART 5

동명사 숙어 표현 문제가 출제된다.

① 동명사 숙어 표현

be capable of -ing	~할 수 있다	have a problem -ing	~하는 데 어려움을 겪다
be busy -ing	~하느라 바쁘다	have difficulty[trouble] -ing	~하는 데 어려움을 겪다
be worth -ing	~할 만한 가치가 있다	keep (on) -ing	계속해서 ~하다
succeed in -ing	~하는 데 성공하다	spend time[money] -ing	~하는 데 시간[돈]을 쓰다

I spend so much time [to look, **looking**] for creative ways to market products.
나는 제품을 시장에 내놓기 위한 창의적인 방법을 찾는 데 많은 시간을 쓴다.

② [전치사 + 동명사] 숙어 표현

by -ing	~함으로써	instead of -ing	~대신에
in -ing	~하는 데 있어서	before -ing	~하기 전에
on -ing	~하자마자	without -ing	~하는 것 없이

Voda, Inc. is planning to grow by [expansion, to expand, **expanding**] its operations to Europe.
Voda 사는 유럽으로 사업을 확장해 성장할 계획이다. → 전치사 다음에 to부정사는 쓸 수 없다.

③ [전치사 to + 동명사] 숙어 표현

look forward to V-ing	~하는 것을 기대하다, 고대하다	be devoted to V-ing	~하는 데 헌신하다, 바치다
be used[accustomed] to V-ing	~하는 데 익숙하다	be dedicated to V-ing	~하는 데 헌신하다, 전념하다
contribute to V-ing	~하는 데 기여(공헌)하다	be committed to V-ing	~하는 데 몰두하다, 전념하다

Funded Co. is committed to [help, **helping**] its employees develop their careers.
Funded 사는 직원들의 경력 개발을 돕는 데 최선을 다하고 있다.

고득점 TIP+ 전치사 to 다음에는 명사나 동명사가 온다.

We are looking forward **to** your prompt response. 귀하의 즉각적인 회신을 기다리겠습니다.

We are looking forward **to** meeting you soon. 우리는 곧 당신을 만나는 것을 기대하고 있습니다.

CHECK-UP
☑ 다음 문장의 빈칸에 들어갈 알맞은 말을 고르세요.   정답 및 해설 p.389

19. Ms. Kaplan worked hard and eventually succeeded in ------- her own business.

   (A) launching   (B) launches

20. Written permission must be obtained before ------- the Obget Company's logo.

   (A) to use   (B) using

21. I look forward to ------- from you when you make your final hiring decision.

   (A) hear   (B) hearing

① 동사의 성질을 가지고 있는 동명사는 목적어를 가질 수 있지만, 명사는 목적어를 가질 수 없다.

[~~Disclosure~~, **Disclosing**] personal information without permission is strictly prohibited.
허락 없이 개인 정보를 공개하는 것은 엄격하게 금지된다.

② 동명사 앞에는 관사(a, an, the)가 올 수 없지만, 명사 앞에는 올 수 있다.

Moran, Inc. has signed an [~~agreeing~~, **agreement**] to purchase a new headquarters building.
Moran 사는 새로운 본사 건물을 인수하는 계약에 서명했다.

③ '-ing형' 명사를 주의해야 한다.

The director will oversee the [~~open~~, **opening**] of a new branch in the region.
관리자는 그 지역 내 새로운 지점을 여는 것을 감독할 것이다.

고득점 TIP+   -ing형 명사를 동명사로 혼동하지 않도록 주의해야 한다. -ing형 명사에는 meeting(회의), gathering(모임), shipping(선박, 선적), training(훈련), opening(개장, 공석), funding(자금 조달), seating(좌석), findings(연구 결과) 등이 있다.

④ 동사의 성질을 가지고 있는 동명사는 형용사가 아닌 부사의 수식을 받는다.

After [~~careful~~, **carefully**] reviewing your application, we will contact you as soon as possible.
신청서를 꼼꼼히 검토한 후, 빠른 시일 내에 연락드리겠습니다.

고득점 TIP+   review(검토하다)와 함께 자주 쓰이는 부사로 carefully(신중히), closely(면밀히), thoroughly(철저히)가 자주 출제된다.

기출 패턴 10   **동명사의 의미상 주어 문제가 출제된다.**

① 동명사의 의미상 주어가 필요한 경우, 동명사 앞에 명사나 대명사의 소유격을 쓴다.

We look forward to the mayor's **attending** the management seminar.
우리는 시장님이 시카고에서 있을 경영 세미나에 참석하길 기대한다.

I appreciate your **offering** me a position as a personnel manager.
인사부장 자리를 제안해 주셔서 감사합니다.

RC PART 5

CHECK-UP   ✓ 다음 문장의 빈칸에 들어갈 알맞은 말을 고르세요.   정답 및 해설 p.389

22. Mr. Redmayne is responsible for ------- the company's Web sites.

   (A) development   (B) developing

23. The company awarded bonuses in ----- of the exceptional team performance this quarter.

   (A) appreciation   (B) appreciating

24. The project was successfully completed thanks to careful -------.

   (A) plan   (B) planning

PRACTICE

정답 및 해설 p.392

기출 포인트 1 **to부정사의 명사적 용법**

빈칸이 명사 자리이거나 동사의 목적어 자리이고, '~하는 것'으로 해석되면 to부정사가 정답이다. 또한 to부정사를 목적어로 취하는 동사 어휘 문제로도 출제된다.

1. The company decided ------- the number of employees to save labor costs.

   (A) reducing   (B) reduced   (C) reduce   (D) to reduce

2. CB & I, Inc. ------- to build three more centers in eastern Spain within the next two years.

   (A) refers   (B) delivers   (C) intends   (D) indicates

기출 포인트 2 **to부정사의 부사적 용법**

to V가 '~하기 위해서'라고 해석되면 to부정사는 so as to V 또는 in order to V로 바꿔 쓸 수 있다.

3. Larsen & Toubro Ltd. employees must have a valid ID badge ------- enter the building.

   (A) in order to   (B) as long as   (C) regarding   (D) always

기출 포인트 3 **to부정사의 형용사적 용법**

명사 뒤에 빈칸을 두어 '~할', '~하는'이라는 의미로 사용되는 to부정사의 형용사적 용법을 묻는 문제가 출제된다.

4. We should discuss the ways ------- operation costs by the end of this month.

   (A) reducing   (B) to reduce   (C) reduced   (D) reduction

기출 포인트 4 **to부정사를 목적격 보어로 취하는 동사**

동사의 목적어 다음 빈칸을 두어, 목적격 보어 자리에 to부정사를 취하는 특정 동사를 묻는 문제가 출제된다.

5. The company asked an event planner ------- the staff dinner.

   (A) organizing   (B) organize   (C) to organize   (D) organized

기출 포인트 5 **to부정사의 관용 표현**

일부 형용사와 어울리는 to부정사가 포함된 관용 표현이 출제된다. 시험에 자주 출제되는 [be동사 + 형용사 + to부정사] 형태의 관용 표현들을 암기해 놓으면 쉽게 해결할 수 있다.

6. GK Motors is eager ------- its business into the European market.

   (A) to expand   (B) will expand   (C) be expanded   (D) expanding

7. The Butcher's Tale has ------- to find a replacement for the chef who left last month.

   (A) finally   (B) once   (C) yet   (D) soon

동명사 Vs. to부정사

타동사 뒤에 빈칸을 두어 목적어 자리에서 to부정사와 동명사를 구별하는 문제가 출제된다. 시험에 자주 출제되는 to부정사와 동명사를 목적어로 취하는 특정 동사들을 분류해서 암기해 놓으면 쉽게 해결할 수 있다.

8. If sales do not improve, it would be wise to consider ------- different strategies to increase consumer interest.

(A) use   (B) to use   (C) using   (D) used

9. GE Power ------- using authentic parts to avoid any damage to your device.

(A) strives   (B) decides   (C) recommends   (D) hopes

전치사 + 동명사

전치사 뒤에 빈칸이 있는 경우, 빈칸 뒤 관사(a/an/the/소유격)와 명사가 이어지면 목적어를 취할 수 있는 동명사가 정답이다. 단, 관사나 소유격 없이 명사가 오면 ① 동명사 ② 명사를 수식하는 형용사 ③ 복합명사 세 가지 모두 정답이 될 수 있으므로 해석을 통해 문제를 풀어야 한다.

10. We sincerely apologize for the delay in ------- your order.

(A) deliver   (B) delivering   (C) delivered   (D) delivery

11. Fluor Corp. has reduced expenses by ------- travel and encouraging the use of Internet conferencing.

(A) limitation   (B) limiting   (C) limited   (D) limit

동명사를 수식하는 품사

동명사는 명사와 달리 동사의 성질이 있기 때문에 형용사가 아닌 부사의 수식을 받는다. 따라서 동명사 앞에 빈칸을 두어 형용사와 부사를 구별하는 문제가 출제된다.

12. Mr. Gates is well known for ------- donating to many charities.

(A) generous   (B) generously   (C) generosity   (D) generousness

13. After ------- inspecting the quality of our products, we start selling them.

(A) thoroughness   (B) thorough   (C) thoroughly   (D) most thorough

동명사의 관용 표현

to부정사 또는 전치사 to를 포함한 동명사 숙어 표현을 구별하여 암기해 두어야 한다.

14. Calaca Global Industries is committed to ------- its clients achieve their financial goals.

(A) helped   (B) helps   (C) helping   (D) help

15. To track the location of your package, be sure to ------- the order number to the Shipping Department.

(A) provide   (B) provided   (C) provision   (D) providing

RC PART 5

UNIT 09 분사

분사의 자리 문제가 출제된다.

① 분사는 문장에서 형용사 역할을 한다.

• 형용사처럼 명사 앞이나 뒤에서 명사를 수식한다.

명사 앞 수식 The Trust Group gained a reputation as a **leading** marketing company.
Trust Group 사는 선도적인 마케팅 회사로서 명성을 얻었다.

명사 뒤 수식 We thoroughly reviewed the annual report **submitted** by Mr. Wyatt.
우리는 Wyatt 씨가 제출한 연례 보고서를 철저히 검토했다.

• 형용사처럼 주격 보어나 목적격 보어로 쓰인다.

주격 보어 The team was **disappointed** with the project's outcome. 팀은 프로젝트 결과에 실망했다.
↳ 주어(the team)와 수동 관계

목적격 보어 All of the employees found Mr. Kim's presentation **boring**.
전 직원이 Kim 씨의 발표가 지루하다고 생각했다. ↳ 목적어(Mr. kim's presentation)와 능동 관계

고득점 TIP+ 분사는 동사에 -ing, -ed가 붙는 형태로, 형용사 역할을 하는 준동사이다. 수식 및 보충하는 명사와 능동 관계일 때는 현재분사
(-ing), 수동 관계일 때는 과거분사(-ed)를 쓴다.

② 분사 자리에는 동사가 올 수 없다.

Further details on the event are explained in the [attach, **attached**] documents.
행사에 대한 더 상세한 내용은 첨부된 문서에 설명되어 있다.

③ 분사와 복합 명사를 구별해야 한다.

Jessica's [retiring, **retirement**] party will take place on December 30. (복합 명사)
Jessica의 은퇴 파티는 12월 30일에 열릴 예정이다.

The meeting room has a [designation, **designated**] area for presentations. (분사)
회의실에는 프레젠테이션을 위한 지정된 공간이 있다.

CHECK-UP ✓ 다음 문장의 빈칸에 들어갈 알맞은 말을 고르세요. 정답 및 해설 p.393

1. An ------- problem occurred while
Bob was installing the program.

　(A) unexpectedly (B) unexpected

2. Unfortunately, the second
quarter performance this year
was very -------.

　(A) disappoint (B) disappointing

3. Tom wishes to modify the
terms of his ------- contract
before signing it.

　(A) employed (B) employment

① 분사 구문은 부사절(부사절 접속사 + 주어 + 동사)이 축약된 구문으로, [(접속사) + 분사]의 형태를 가진다.

While she reviewed the draft of the contract, Emma found some errors in it.
Emma 씨는 계약서 초안을 살펴보다가 잘못된 부분을 몇 군데 발견했다.

⬇ 부사절 접속사 while 생략

~~While~~ she reviewed the draft of the contract, Emma found some errors in it.

⬇ 부사절의 주어 she 생략 (부사절의 주어와 주절의 주어와 같은 경우에 생략된다. she = Emma)

~~While she~~ reviewed the draft of the contract, Emma found some errors in it.

⬇ 부사절의 동사를 분사 형태로 변경

Reviewing the draft of the contract, Emma found some errors in it.

고득점 TIP+ 정확한 의미를 전달하기 위해 접속사를 생략하지 않는 경우가 있다.

While reviewing the draft of the contract, Emma found some errors in it.

② 분사 구문은 문장에서 부사절 역할을 하여 시간, 조건, 이유 등을 나타낸다.

시간   **(When) assembling** the new bookcase, please follow the set-up instructions.
= When you assemble the new bookcase, ~.
새 책장을 조립할 때는 설치 지침을 따라 주세요.

조건   **Hiring** a renowned chef, the restaurant will make a bigger profit.
= Once it hires a renowned chef, ~.
유명한 주방장을 고용하면, 그 식당은 더 많은 수익을 낼 것이다.

이유   **(Being) approved** by management, the project will be announced.
= Once it is approved by management, ~.
경영진의 승인을 받으면 프로젝트는 발표될 것이다.

→ 수동태 분사 구문에서 be동사는 being으로 바뀌는데, being은 생략 가능하므로 p.p. 형태만 남을 수 있다.

고득점 TIP+ 분사 구문의 시제가 주절의 시제보다 앞설 때 완료 분사구문으로 쓸 수 있다.

After she had reviewed all the relevant data, she submitted the report.
= [**Having reviewed,** ~~Reviewed~~] all the relevant data, she submitted the report.
그녀는 모든 관련 데이터를 검토한 후 보고서를 제출했다.

CHECK-UP   ✅ 다음 문장의 빈칸에 들어갈 알맞은 말을 고르세요.   정답 및 해설 p.393

4. ----- market research, the company decided to launch a new product line.
   (A) Conduction   (B) Conducting

5. ------- recently, the office computers were much faster.
   (A) Upgraded   (B) Upgrade

6. When ------- for travel costs, managers should review the company policy.
   (A) budgets   (B) budgeting

RC PART 5

① 분사가 명사를 수식하는 경우, 수식을 받는 명사와 분사의 관계가 능동이면 현재분사, 수동이면 과거분사를 쓴다.

We are looking for an agency [~~specialized~~, **specializing**] in online marketing.
우리는 온라인 마케팅을 전문으로 하는 대행사를 찾고 있다.

Coyne Air [~~basing~~, **based**] in Hong Kong is offering budget flights to Jakarta.
홍콩에 본사를 둔 Coyne 항공은 자카르타로 가는 저가 항공편을 제공하고 있다.

② 분사가 보어로 쓰이는 경우, 주어와 주격 보어 또는 목적어와 목적격 보어의 관계가 능동이면 현재분사, 수동이면 과거분사를 쓴다.

The team members were [~~impressing~~, **impressed**] by the new director's enthusiasm.
팀원들은 새로운 부장의 열정에 깊은 인상을 받았다.

Please have all packages [~~delivering~~, **delivered**] to the reception desk.
모든 소포를 접수처로 보내주시기 바랍니다.

③ 주절의 주어와 분사 구문의 동사의 관계가 능동이면 현재분사, 수동이면 과거분사를 쓴다.

All personnel are required to wear safety glasses when [~~operated~~, **operating**] machinery.
기계를 조작할 때는 모든 직원이 보안경을 착용해야 한다.

Once [~~registering~~, **registered**], you will be able to start or cancel your service.
일단 등록이 되면, 귀하의 서비스를 시작하거나 취소할 수 있습니다.

CHECK-UP ☑ 다음 문장의 빈칸에 들어갈 알맞은 말을 고르세요.   정답 및 해설 p.393

7. The ------- meeting with the client has been postponed until next week.

　(A) scheduled　(B) scheduling

8. We apologize for the error in the amount ------- for your window repairs.

　(A) charging　(B) charged

9. When ------- accomplishments on a résumé, be sure to include specific dates.

　(A) listed　(B) listing

기출 패턴 4 혼동하기 쉬운 분사 문제가 출제된다.

① 과거분사 + 명사

revised procedures	개정된 절차	**unlimited** guarantee	무제한 보장
preferred means	선호되는 수단	**detailed** information	자세한 정보
written consent	서면 동의	**damaged** luggage/baggage	파손된 수하물
guided tour	가이드 투어	**discounted** price	할인된 가격
reduced hours	단축 근무시간	**distinguished** member	뛰어난 직원
qualified candidate	자격을 갖춘 후보자	**devoted/motivated** worker	헌신적인 직원
completed application	작성된 신청서	**designated** area	지정된 구역
updated manual	개정된 설명서	**renovated** building	개조된 건물
informed decision	신중한(충분한 정보를 바탕으로 한) 결정	**recognized** organization	인정받는 기관
enclosed brochure	동봉된 소책자	**attached** documents	첨부된 서류
experienced mechanic	능숙한 기계공	**talented** employee	재능이 있는 직원

We will provide you with a [~~writing~~, **written**] estimate within 7 days of the visit.
방문 일주일 이내에 서면으로 견적서를 제공해 드립니다.

② 현재분사 + 명사

existing equipment	기존 장비	**missing** luggage/baggage	없어진(분실된) 짐
lasting impression	오래가는(지속적인) 인상	**increasing** demand	증가하는 수요
demanding supervisor	까다로운 상사	**mounting** pressure	증가하는 압력
remaining inventory	남아있는 재고	**deteriorating** economy	악화되는 경제
leading company	선도/일류 기업	**overwhelming** demand	압도적인 수요

The [~~remained~~, **remaining**] candidates for the sales position will be interviewed tomorrow.
나머지 영업직 지원자들은 내일 면접을 볼 예정이다.

고득점 TIP+ 자동사(exist, rise, last, remain, miss 등)는 목적어가 필요 없는 동사로, 목적어가 없으므로 수동태(be p.p.)나 과거분사 (p.p.) 형태로 쓰지 않는다.

③ 숙어처럼 사용하는 분사 표현

as expected 예상했던 대로	as mentioned 언급된 대로	as discussed 논의된 대로
as requested 요청한 대로	as scheduled [planned] 일정[계획]대로	than anticipated 예상했던 것보다

The construction project will begin in July as [planning, **planned**]. 공사가 계획대로 7월부터 시작할 것이다.

The costs are rising faster than originally [~~anticipation~~, **anticipated**]. 원래 예상했던 것보다 비용이 빠르게 상승하고 있다.

CHECK-UP ☑ 다음 문장의 빈칸에 들어갈 알맞은 말을 고르세요.   정답 및 해설 p.393

10. The ------- safety manual includes guidelines for the entire factory.

(A) updating   (B) updated

11. Our new Galaxy store will be much bigger than our ------- commercial space.

(A) existed   (B) existing

12. As -------, one of my team members will contact you to arrange the schedule.

(A) requested   (B) requesting

기출 포인트 1 **현재분사 Vs. 과거분사**

명사 앞뒤에 빈칸을 두어 현재분사(V-ing)와 과거분사(p.p.)를 구별하는 문제인 경우, 수식 받는 명사와의 관계가 능동일 때는 현재분사를, 수동일 때는 과거분사를 선택한다. 참고로 자동사는 수동태나 과거분사 형태로 쓸 수 없다.

1. Please notify our office if you cannot open the ------- workshop schedule.

   (A) attach   (B) attached   (C) attaching   (D) attachment

2. Employees ------- in the office facilities after 9:00 P.M. are asked to turn off the lights when leaving.

   (A) remained   (B) will be remained   (C) remaining   (D) remain

기출 포인트 2 **감정을 나타내는 분사**

사람의 감정을 나타낼 때는 과거분사를, 감정을 일으키는 원인이나 대상을 나타낼 때는 현재분사를 쓴다.

3. Residents ------- in joining the fitness program should complete an enrollment form.

   (A) interest   (B) interests   (C) interesting   (D) interested

4. The ------- news about the project delay left everyone feeling frustrated.

   (A) disappoint   (B) disappointing   (C) disappointed   (D) disappointment

기출 포인트 3 **분사 형태의 형용사**

동사에서 파생된 분사 중에 일부는 일반 형용사처럼 사용하므로 [현재분사+명사], [과거분사+명사], [2형식 동사+분사 형용사] 형태로 묶어서 암기해 두면 쉽게 해결할 수 있다.

5. Chevron Motors, based in New York is one of the ------- companies in the rental vehicle industry.

   (A) expected   (B) leading   (C) dependent   (D) complicated

6. Any ------- parts will be replaced free of charge within a year of purchase.

   (A) damage   (B) damaging   (C) damages   (D) damaged

기출 포인트 4 **분사 구문**

분사 구문의 형태는 목적어의 유무, 주어와의 관계가 능동인지 수동인지에 따라 결정한다. 이때, 분사 구문에서 명확한 의미를 위해 접속사를 생략하지 않는 경우도 있다.

7. ------- by the board, the new policy will be implemented next month.

   (A) Approve   (B) Approving   (C) Approved   (D) Have approved

8. When ------- the quarterly report, he highlighted the company's achievements.

   (A) present   (B) presenter   (C) presenting   (D) was presented

UNIT 10 등위/상관/형용사절 접속사

RC PART 5

기출 패턴 1 등위 접속사 문제가 출제된다.

① 등위 접속사 종류

and	그리고 (추가)	or	혹은, 그렇지 않으면(= or else) (선택)
but (yet)	그러나 (반대)	so	그래서 (결과) * 완전한 문장만 연결

Previous publishing experience is desirable **but** not required.
이전 출판 경험은 우대되지만 필수는 아니다.

Residents have access to an outdoor pool **and** a playground on the property.
거주민들은 그 부지 내에 있는 야외 수영장과 놀이터를 이용할 수 있다.

② 문맥에 맞는 등위 접속사를 선택하는 문제가 출제된다.

The project requires a significant amount of time [but, **and**] dedication.
그 프로젝트는 상당한 양의 시간과 헌신을 요구한다.

Admission to the concert is free, [or, **but**] seating is limited to 300 people.
콘서트 입장료는 무료이지만, 좌석은 300명으로 제한되어 있다.

If you have any problems, simply call us on [so, **or**] before March 13.
문제가 있으시면 3월 13일 당일 또는 전에 저희에게 전화주시면 됩니다.

③ 등위 접속사는 앞뒤에 오는 동일한 품사를 연결한다.

Mr. Rice's duties include identifying and [resolved, **resolving**] problems on the factory floor.
Rice 씨의 임무는 공장 현장의 문제를 확인하고 해결하는 것을 포함한다.

Our new laptop model, the Taggers 7, is [economically, **economical**] and easily portable.
저희의 새로운 노트북 모델인 The Tagger 7은 경제적이고 휴대가 용이합니다.

고득점 TIP+ 등위 접속사는 단독으로 단어와 단어, 구와 구, 절과 절을 연결한다. 단, so는 완전한 절과 절만 연결할 수 있다.

CHECK-UP ☑ 다음 문장의 빈칸에 들어갈 알맞은 말을 고르세요. 정답 및 해설 p.395

1. A new computer server has been installed in the office, ------- it is not yet operational.

(A) and (B) but

2. Employees have the option of attending a training class or ------- an online tutorial.

(A) complete (B) completing

3. The newly released product is lightweight, portable and ------.

(A) durable (B) breakable

① 상관 접속사의 종류

both A and B	A와 B 모두, A와 B 양쪽 다
either A or B	A 혹은 B, A 이거나 B
neither A nor B	A도 B도 아닌
not only A but (also) B	A뿐만 아니라 B도 (= B as well as A) * 예외적으로 짝을 이루지 않는다.
not A but B	A가 아니라 B

Registration may be done **either** over the phone **or** on the Internet.
등록은 전화 또는 인터넷으로 가능합니다.

② 상관 접속사의 짝을 묻는 문제가 출제된다.

Adventure Hogs toys are **both** educational [nor, **and**] fun to play with.
Adventure Hogs 사의 장난감은 교육적이면서도 가지고 놀기에 재미있다.

You can [neither, **either**] e-mail **or** phone to request a copy.
이메일이나 전화로 사본을 요청하실 수 있습니다.

The Graham Show was **not only** funny [although, **but**] **(also)** very informative.
Graham Show는 재미있었을 뿐만 아니라 매우 유익했다.

고득점 TIP+ 상관 접속사는 단어들이 짝을 이루어 단어와 단어, 구와 구, 절과 절을 연결한다. 상관 접속사가 주어 자리에 사용된 경우 주어와 동사의 수 일치에 유의한다.

Neither the manager **nor** the employees [is, **are**] available. 관리자도 직원들도 여유가 없다.

1. Either A or B / Neither A nor B: B에 수 일치한다.
Neither the CEO **nor** the directors have announced the decision. CEO나 이사들도 결정을 발표하지 않았다.

2. Both A and B: 항상 복수형 동사를 사용한다.
Both the manager **and** the employees are responsible for the project.
관리자와 직원들 모두 그 프로젝트에 책임이 있다.

3. Not only A but also B: B에 수 일치한다.
Not only the employees **but also** the manager is attending the meeting.
직원들뿐만 아니라 관리자도 회의에 참석하고 있다.

CHECK-UP
✅ 다음 문장의 빈칸에 들어갈 알맞은 말을 고르세요.　　　정답 및 해설 p.395

4. ------ the marketing team and the sales team contributed to the successful launch of the product.
　(A) Both　　(B) Either

5. The manager has suggested that ------ Mr. Harris or Ms. Haynes attend the conference next month.
　(A) either　　(B) neither

6. Mr. Davis must finish the report today ------ cancel tomorrow's meeting.
　(A) not only　　(B) as well as

선행사의 종류와 격에 맞는 관계대명사 선택 문제가 출제된다.

① 관계대명사는 형용사절 접속사로, 주격, 소유격, 목적격이 있다.

선행사	주격 : 바로 뒤에 동사가 옴	소유격 : 바로 뒤에 명사가 옴	목적격 : 뒤에 <주어+동사>가 옴
사람	who, that	whose	who(m), that
사물	which, that	whose, of which	which, that

* 선행사와 관계없이 who, which 자리에 that을 쓸 수 있으나 콤마(,) 뒤에는 사용할 수 없다.

Ella is a competent employee [~~whom~~, **who**] can handle various tasks effectively.
Ella는 다양한 업무를 효과적으로 처리할 수 있는 유능한 직원입니다.

We are looking for a person [~~who~~, **whose**] primary role will be expanding business.
우리는 사업 확장에 주된 역할을 할 사람을 찾고 있습니다.

The item, [~~that~~, **which**] Mr. Hill ordered from our catalog, is unavailable until May 10.
Hill 씨가 카탈로그에서 주문한 제품은 5월 10일까지 사용할 수 없다.

② **<주격 관계대명사 + be동사>와 목적격 관계대명사는 생략할 수 있다.**

Every purchase **(which is)** [~~pricing~~, **priced**] over $100 comes with a coupon.
100달러 이상이 넘어가는 물건을 구매하면 쿠폰을 준다.

→ <주격 관계대명사 + be동사>가 생략된 문장에서 명사 뒤에 들어갈 분사 형태를 묻는 문제가 출제된다.

The coupon code **(that)** [**you** / ~~your~~ / ~~yours~~] entered is not valid.
입력하신 쿠폰 코드가 유효하지 않습니다.

→ 목적격 관계대명사가 생략된 문장에서 관계사절의 주어 자리에 들어갈 대명사의 격을 묻는 문제가 출제된다.

고득점 TIP+ 전치사가 관계대명사를 목적어로 취하는 문제가 출제된다. 목적격 관계대명사가 이끄는 절의 전치사는 관계대명사 앞으로 올 수 있다.

This seminar covers various issues **which** investors are interested **in**.
= This seminar covers various issues [~~about~~, **in**] **which** investors are interested.
이 세미나는 투자가들이 관심 있어 하는 다양한 이슈들을 다룬다.

CHECK-UP ☑ 다음 문장의 빈칸에 들어갈 알맞은 말을 고르세요. 정답 및 해설 p.395

7. Employees ------ have not used their vacation time should take it by the end of the year.

  (A) whom (B) who

8. Media World, ------ is located in Maryland, has over 100 employees.

  (A) that (B) which

9. New products ------ in the show window are sold at discounted prices.

  (A) displaying (B) displayed

① 관계절은 형용사 역할을 하는 수식어 절이며, 수식하는 명사(선행사) 뒤에 온다.

We hired <u>the candidate</u> **who** was recommended by the director. 우리는 이사에 의해 추천된 후보자를 고용했다.

선행사

② 관계절을 이끄는 관계대명사 자리에 대명사는 올 수 없다.

Chef Michael prepares meals for <u>200 sailors</u> [~~they~~, **who**] live on the ship.
요리사 Michael은 배에 사는 200명의 선원들을 위해 식사를 준비한다.

③ 관계절을 이끄는 관계대명사와 명사절과 부사절을 이끄는 접속사를 구분해야 한다.
→ UNIT 11. 부사절/명사절 접속사 참조

Applicants [~~because~~, **whose**] qualifications meet our requirements will be invited to an interview.
우리의 필요조건을 충족시키는 자격을 가진 지원자들은 면접에 초대될 것이다.

→ 관계절(형용사절)을 이끄는 관계대명사 whose

The prototype shows [~~what~~, **how**] the machine will work.
그 견본은 그 기계가 어떻게 작동할지를 보여준다.

→ 명사절을 이끄는 명사절 접속사 how

[~~That~~, **Although**] Mr. Murray retired last year, he still visits the office each week.
Murray 씨는 작년에 퇴직했지만, 여전히 매주 사무실을 방문한다.

→ 부사절을 이끄는 부사절 접속사 although

CHECK-UP   ✅ 다음 문장의 빈칸에 들어갈 알맞은 말을 고르세요.   정답 및 해설 p.395

10. Tommy's kitchen tools come with a warranty ------- is valid for three years.

(A) it   (B) that

11. Refunds will be given to all customers ------- orders are damaged during shipping.

(A) whose   (B) that

12. Each security camera ------- was installed in the laboratories operates 24 hours a day.

(A) which   (B) because

PRACTICE

정답 및 해설 p.396

기출 포인트 1   등위 접속사

대등한 단위를 연결할 수 있는 등위 접속사는 and, but (= yet), or가 있으며, 앞뒤 문장에서 반복되는 부분을 생략할 수 있다. 등위 접속사 문제는 빈칸 앞뒤를 해석하여 알맞은 접속사를 선택한다.

1. We would like to thank all employees for their hard work ------- commitment to excellence.

    (A) so   (B) and   (C) but   (D) yet

2. Angie's Online now offers overnight shipping, ------- this option does involve an additional charge.

    (A) nor   (B) still   (C) or   (D) but

기출 포인트 2   상관 접속사

보기가 상관 접속사와 짝을 이루는 단어일 경우, 문장에서 짝을 찾아 정답을 선택한다.

3. ------- Mr. Graham or Ms. Krause will be in the office to answer the phone.

    (A) Neither   (B) Both   (C) Either   (D) Not only

4. Mr. Bruno's shop is known not only for its fine products ------- its friendly and knowledgeable staff.

    (A) and   (B) or   (C) even   (D) but

기출 포인트 3   관계대명사 who(m), which, that

[명사 + ---- + 문장(절)]의 형태로 빈칸 뒤의 문장이 앞의 명사를 수식하는 경우, 수식을 받는 명사가 사람인지 사물인지 확인한다. 그리고 빈칸 뒤 문장의 형태를 확인한 후, 관계대명사 who, which, that 중 하나를 선택한다.

5. The company trains all of its employees ------- are responsible for handling confidential information.

    (A) who   (B) whom   (C) which   (D) whose

6. We provide members with benefits ------- include discount coupons and free movie tickets.

    (A) whom   (B) that   (C) who   (D) when

기출 포인트 4   소유격 관계대명사

빈칸 뒤에 완전한 문장이 오고, [선행사 + ---- + 명사]의 형태로 의미가 '선행사의 명사'가 되는 경우에는 소유격 관계대명사 whose를 선택한다.

7. We are currently seeking a distributor ------- track record is excellent in the field.

    (A) who   (B) their   (C) them   (D) whose

8. Lou Dorfman's Houses has a good reputation for architects ------- designs are original.

    (A) that   (B) whom   (C) whose   (D) who

RC PART 5

UNIT 11 부사절/명사절 접속사

1. 부사절 접속사

기출 패턴 1 **부사절 접속사의 자리 문제가 출제된다.**

① 부사절은 문장에서 부사 역할을 하는 수식어절이며, 주절의 앞이나 뒤에 온다.

If you cancel your reservation late, you may incur a cancelation fee.
예약을 늦게 취소하시면 취소 수수료가 발생할 수 있습니다.

We may need to postpone the project deadline since we are short-staffed.
직원이 부족하므로 프로젝트 기한을 연기해야 할 수도 있다.

② 부사절 접속사 자리에 전치사는 올 수 없다.

[~~Because of~~, **Since**] the budget was reduced, we have had to cut back on marketing expenses.
예산이 줄어들었기 때문에 마케팅 비용을 줄여야 했다.

The evaluation report will be completed only [~~following~~, **after**] auditors inspect the laboratory.
평가 보고서는 감사관들이 실험실을 살피고 나서 완료될 것이다.

고득점 TIP+

① before / after / since / until / as 등은 전치사와 접속사 둘 다 가능하다.
- [전치사] Sophia arrived **before** me. Sophia는 나보다 먼저 도착했다.
- [접속사] We should make a reservation **before** we go there. 우리는 거기에 가기 전에 예약해야 한다.

② 두 가지 이상의 품사를 가지는 since
- [전치사] ~이후로
  I have been working here **since** 2024. 2024년 이후로 나는 여기에서 일하고 있다.

- [접속사1] ~이기 때문에
  Since the budget is reduced, we should reduce expenses. 예산이 줄었기 때문에 비용을 줄여야 한다.

- [접속사2] ~이후로
  Since I joined this company, I have worked here for 5 years. 입사 후 여기서 5년째 근무하고 있다.

- [부사] 그 이후로
  Tom lost his job two years ago, but he has **since** found other job.
  Tom은 2년 전에 직업을 잃었지만, 그 이후로 다른 직업을 찾았다.

CHECK-UP

✓ 다음 문장의 빈칸에 들어갈 알맞은 말을 고르세요. 정답 및 해설 p.397

1. Sales are expected to increase ------- Mr. Barry has taken over the department.

  (A) because   (B) despite

2. ------- registering for online banking is not required, we strongly recommend it.

  (A) If   (B) Although

3. Mr. Elgar did not purchase the product ------- it was extremely expensive.

  (A) since   (B) due to

시간 부사절 접속사 문제가 출제된다.

① 시간을 나타내는 부사절 접속사

when, as ~할 때	since ~이후로	while ~하는 동안에	as soon as ~하자마자, ~하자 곧
after ~한 후에	before ~전에	until ~할 때까지	by the time ~할 즈음에

Before he came to Perth, Mr. Lowe had worked as a researcher at the York Museum.
Lowe 씨는 Perth에 오기 전에 York 박물관에서 연구원으로 일했다.

As soon as Sarah Hicks finds a full-time job, she will open a savings account.
Sarah Hicks 씨는 정규직 일자리를 구하면 바로 저축계좌를 개설할 예정이다.

조건, 양보 부사절 접속사 문제가 출제된다.

① 조건을 나타내는 부사절 접속사

if[provided] (that) 만약 ~라면	once 일단 ~하면
unless, if not 만약 ~이 아니라면	as long as ~하는 한
in case (that) ~하는 경우에 (대비해서)	in the event (that) ~하는 경우에

Unless you have a parking permit, you are not allowed to park here.
주차 허가증이 없으면 여기에 주차하실 수 없습니다.

The office will be renovated next year **provided that** the budget proposal is approved.
예산안이 승인되면 내년에 사무실을 새롭게 단장할 예정이다.

② 양보를 나타내는 부사절 접속사

though, although, even though, even if　~에도 불구하고

Although Catherine works overtime, she is still behind schedule.
Catherine은 야근하고 있지만 아직도 일정보다 뒤처져 있다.

Even if it does not rain tomorrow, tents will be set up for any scheduled outdoor events.
내일 비가 오지 않더라도 예정된 야외 행사를 위해 텐트가 설치될 것이다.

CHECK-UP

☑ 다음 문장의 빈칸에 들어갈 알맞은 말을 고르세요.　　　　정답 및 해설 p.397

4. All tickets will be refunded ------- the soccer game is canceled because of bad weather.

  (A) if　　　(B) although

5. ------- the ventilation system is being repaired, conference room 3 will be inaccessible.

  (A) Unless　　　(B) While

6. ------- the project was challenging, we completed it on time.

  (A) Although　　　(B) In case

RC PART 5

이유, 목적, 결과 등의 부사절 접속사 문제가 출제된다.

① 이유를 나타내는 부사절 접속사

because, since, as, now that ~ 때문에

Mr. Coon is unable to attend the lunch meeting **as** his flight has been delayed.
Coon 씨는 비행기가 연착되어 점심 회의에 참석할 수 없다.

② 목적을 나타내는 부사절 접속사

so that ... may/can/might/could …가 ~할 수 있도록	in order that ~하기 위해서

Ms. Rigg agreed to work on the holiday **so that** Mr. Foy **could** attend the conference.
Rigg 씨는 Foy 씨가 회의에 참석할 수 있도록 휴일에 일하는 것에 동의했다.

③ 결과를 나타내는 부사절 접속사

so/such ~ that ... 매우 ~해서 …하다

The movie was **so** successful **that** it was in the theater for five months.
It was **such** a successful movie **that** it was in the theater for five months.
그 영화는 매우 흥행해서 극장에서 5개월 동안 상영되었다.

고득점 TIP+ 결과를 나타내는 부사절 접속사 so ~ that 사이에는 형용사나 부사가 오고, such ~ that 사이에는 명사가 온다.

기출 패턴 5 **기타 다양한 뜻의 부사절 접속사가 출제된다.**

고려	considering (that), given that ~을 고려할 때	비유	as if, as though 마치 ~인 것처럼
제외	except that ~라는 점을 제외하고	대조	whereas, while ~인 반면에

Their acting is superb, particularly **considering (that)** the performers are amateurs.
특히 출연자들이 아마추어라는 점을 고려하면 그들의 연기는 일품이다.

Our sales increased this quarter, **whereas** last quarter they were lower than normal.
이번 분기에는 매출이 증가한 반면, 지난 분기에는 매출이 평소보다 낮았다.

CHECK-UP ✓ 다음 문장의 빈칸에 들어갈 알맞은 말을 고르세요. 정답 및 해설 p.397

7. The product is ------- expensive that most shoppers are reluctant to buy it.

   (A) so   (B) very

8. Ritzy Boutique expanded its store hours ------- it could remain competitive.

   (A) as though   (B) so that

9. Our competitors lowered prices, ------- we maintained our rates.

   (A) although   (B) whereas

기출 패턴 6 · 부사절 접속사와 전치사의 구별 문제가 출제된다.

① 부사절 접속사는 절 앞에 오고, 전치사는 명사(구) 앞에 온다.

[~~In spite of~~, **Although**] its sales increased, the company's profits declined. <부사절 접속사>
매출은 늘었지만 회사의 이익은 감소했다.

[~~Although~~, **In spite of**] an increase in sales, the company's profits declined. <전치사>
매출이 증가했음에도 불구하고 회사의 이익은 감소했다.

② 유사한 의미의 부사절 접속사와 전치사

의미	접속사	전치사
~때문에	because, since, as, now that	because of, due to, owing to
~에도 불구하고	although, even though, even if	in spite of, despite
~하는 동안에	while	during
~한 경우에	in case (that), in the event (that)	in case of, in the event of
~까지	until	by, until
~이전에	before	before, prior to
~이후에	after	after, following
~하자마자	as soon as, once	on, upon
~이 아닌 한	unless	but for

E-Union will be closed for 2 days [~~during~~, **while**] a new electrical device is installed. <부사절 접속사>
E-Union은 새로운 전기 장치가 설치되는 동안 이틀간 문을 닫는다.

Gallow Real Estate's revenue typically declines [~~while~~, **during**] the winter months. <전치사>
Gallow 부동산의 수익은 일반적으로 겨울철에는 감소한다.

고득점 TIP+ 부사절 접속사는 절과 절을 연결하는 역할을 하며 '접속사+주어+동사'의 절을 만든다. 전치사는 '전치사+명사(구)'의 수식어구를 만들며, 뒤에 '주어+동사'가 올 수 없다. PART 5에서는 접속사와 전치사 중 적절한 품사를 선택하는 문제가 특히 자주 출제된다.

CHECK-UP ☑ 다음 문장의 빈칸에 들어갈 알맞은 말을 고르세요. 정답 및 해설 p.397

10. ------- Ms. Hart met her targets, her boss was still not satisfied.

    (A) Although (B) Despite

11. The Garden Bridge has been preserved ------- its historical significance.

    (A) because (B) because of

12. ------- analyzing the global market trends we decided to launch a new advertising strategy.

    (A) Upon (B) As soon as

2. 명사절 접속사

기출 패턴 7 **명사절의 자리 문제가 출제된다.**

① 명사절은 문장에서 명사 역할을 하며 주어, 목적어, 보어 자리에 온다.

주어   **That** Tim is a competent manager is obvious to those who know him.
팀이 유능한 매니저라는 것은 그를 아는 사람들에게는 분명하다.

동사의 목적어   Rollie doesn't understand **why** the package has not arrived.
Rollie는 왜 소포가 도착하지 않았는지 이해하지 못한다.

전치사의 목적어   He wants more information on **what** caused the delay of his order.
그는 무엇이 그의 주문을 지연시켰는지 더 많은 정보를 원한다.

보어   My problem is **how** I can write two reports in a week.
문제는 어떻게 일주일에 두 개의 보고서를 쓸 수 있느냐 하는 것이다.

② 명사절 접속사와 관계대명사를 구별할 수 있어야 한다.

명사절 접속사 that '~라는 것'	수식을 받는 명사 필요없음, that + 완전한 절
관계대명사 that '~하는'	수식을 받는 명사[선행사] 필요, that + 불완전한 절

We ensure **that** customers only receive fresh and safe food.
   ↳ 동사   ↳ 완전한 절 [주어+동사+목적어]
저희는 고객들이 신선하고 안전한 식품만 받도록 보장합니다.
→ that 명사절이 ensure의 목적어 역할을 하고 있다.

The first customer **that** visits the restaurant will receive the discount coupon.
   ↳ 명사[선행사]   ↳ 불완전한 절 [동사+목적어]
레스토랑을 방문하는 첫 고객은 할인 쿠폰을 받을 것이다.
→ that 관계사절이 선행사(The first customer)를 수식하고 있다.

고득점 TIP+   that 절이 주어, 목적어, 보어 역할을 하면 명사절이고, 앞 명사를 수식하면 관계사절이다.

CHECK-UP
✅ 다음 문장의 빈칸에 들어갈 알맞은 말을 고르세요.   정답 및 해설 p.397

13. Please note ------- any expenses incurred during the business trip will be reimbursed.
   (A) which   (B) that

14. The problem with the current logo is ------- it has too many different colors.
   (A) that   (B) about

15. Sales representatives know ------- they should reach their quarterly sales targets.
   (A) what   (B) that

명사절 접속사 that과 어울리는 어휘 문제가 출제된다.

① 명사절 접속사 that절을 목적어로 자주 취하는 동사

indicate that ~을 알리다, 나타내다	state that ~라고 진술하다	ensure that ~을 보증하다, 확실하게 해주다
announce that ~를 발표하다	note that ~에 유념하다	reveal that ~을 밝히다

Customer surveys <u>indicate</u> **that** our newest product is too expensive.
고객 설문 조사 결과, 우리 신제품이 너무 비싼 것으로 나타났다.

② 명사절 접속사 that절을 직접 목적어 자리에 쓰는 4형식 동사

tell A that A에게 ~을 말하다	inform/notify A that A에게 ~을 알리다	convince A that A에게 ~을 확신시키다
remind A that A에게 ~을 상기시키다	advise A that A에게 ~을 충고하다	assure A that A에게 ~을 보증하다

↱ 직접 목적어(~을/를)

Mr. Durant <u>assured his staff</u> **that** the company's merger would benefit them.
Durant 씨는 직원들에게 회사의 합병이 그들에게 이익이 될 것이라고 확신시켰다.

③ 명사절 접속사 that절을 자주 취하는 [be + 형용사 + that] 숙어 표현

be aware that ~을 알다	be sure[certain] that ~을 확신하다	be likely[probable] that ~일 것 같다
be afraid that ~을 걱정하다	be confident that ~에 자신 있다	be optimistic that ~라고 낙관하다

It **is likely that** our competitor will launch a similar product soon.
우리의 경쟁사가 곧 유사한 제품을 출시할 것 같다.

We **are confident that** we will exceed last year's production targets.
우리는 지난해 생산 목표액을 초과할 것으로 확신한다.

RC PART 5

CHECK-UP ☑ 다음 문장의 빈칸에 들어갈 알맞은 말을 고르세요. 정답 및 해설 p.397

16. Please notify the team ------- the project deadline has been extended by one week.

  (A) because　　(B) that

17. The inspection revealed ------- the building was deficient in safety features.

  (A) that　　(B) unless

18. Mr. Andrews is confident ------- the new marketing campaign will be a great success.

  (A) that　　(B) whether

① 명사절 접속사 whether는 '~인지 (아닌지)'를 의미하며 문장에서 주어, 목적어, 보어로 쓰인다.

주어 Whether he will attend the meeting is uncertain. 그가 회의에 참석할지는 불확실하다.

목적어 I would like to know whether[if] I can get a pay raise next year.
나는 내년에 급여가 인상되는지 알고 싶다.

보어 The problem is whether customers are willing to buy the product at this high price.
문제는 고객들이 이렇게 높은 가격에 제품을 살 것인지다.

② 명사절 접속사 if는 주어, 보어, 전치사의 목적어 자리에 올 수 없다.

[If, Whether] she is participating in the meeting or not isn't certain yet.
그녀가 회의에 참석할지는 안 할지는 아직 확실하지 않다.

고득점 TIP+ whether와 같은 의미로 사용되는 명사절 접속사 if는 동사 뒤에서 목적어절을 이끌 때만 쓴다.

The manager hasn't yet decided [if, whether] to attend the seminar.
부장은 세미나에 참석할지를 아직 결정하지 않았다.

고득점 TIP+ 명사절 접속사 whether 뒤에 to부정사가 오는 경우, 동사의 목적어절을 이끌 때라도 if로 바꾸어 쓸 수 없다.

③ 명사절 접속사 if, whether는 부사절 접속사로도 쓰일 수 있다.

If you want to buy a new chair, select one that matches your desk.
새 의자를 구매하고 싶다면, 당신의 책상과 어울리는 것을 선택하세요.

Whether he likes it or not, he has to attend the meeting. 그는 좋든 싫든 회의에 참석해야 한다.

Whether you travel for business or for pleasure, we will make your stay enjoyable.
출장이든 여행이든 상관없이, 저희는 여러분의 숙박을 즐겁게 만들어드릴 것입니다.

고득점 TIP+ 접속사 whether는 명사절과 부사절 둘 다 이끌 수 있다. whether가 명사절 접속사로 사용될 때는 뒤에 or not이 생략될 수 있으며, 주어가 생략되고 to부정사가 whether 뒤에 올 수 있다. 그러나 부사절 접속사로 사용될 때는 뒤에 반드시 or 또는 or not이 와야 한다.

CHECK-UP

✓ 다음 문장의 빈칸에 들어갈 알맞은 말을 고르세요. 정답 및 해설 p.397

19. Mr. Taylor e-mailed the clients to ask ------- there is a train station near their office.

(A) if   (B) though

20. The president of Berks is considering ------- to renew the contract with Xenon.

(A) whether   (B) if

21. ------- we receive additional funding or not, we will proceed with the project.

(A) Whether   (B) Because

명사절 접속사 that과 관계대명사 what을 구별하는 문제가 출제된다.

① 명사절 접속사 that 뒤에는 완전한 절이, 관계대명사 what 뒤에는 불완전한 절이 온다.

The CEO suggested [~~what~~, **that**] employees receive a $1,000 bonus this year.
CEO는 직원들에게 올해 1,000달러의 보너스를 받을 것을 제안했다.

[~~That~~, **What**] is mistakenly reported should be corrected immediately.
잘못 보고된 것은 즉시 수정되어야 한다.

명사절을 이끄는 의문사

① 의문대명사(what, which, who, whom) + 불완전한 문장

• 의문대명사는 명사절에서 주어나 목적어 역할을 한다.

Who will preside over the meeting tonight has yet to be decided. → 주어 자리
오늘 밤 회의를 누가 주재할지는 아직 결정되지 않았다.

② 의문형용사(what, which, whose) + 완전한 문장

• 의문형용사는 명사절에서 '의문사+명사'의 형태로 형용사 역할을 한다.

Which marketing strategies best suit your company is not clear. → 주어 자리
어떤 마케팅 전략이 귀사에 가장 적합한지 명확하지 않다.

③ 의문부사(when, where, how, why) + 완전한 문장

• 의문부사는 명사절에서 부사 역할을 한다.

The planning committee disagreed about **where the fair should be held**. → 전치사의 목적어 자리
박람회 개최 장소를 놓고 기획 위원회가 이견을 보였다.

고득점 TIP+ 의문사가 이끄는 명사절은 문장 내에서 명사 역할을 하므로 주어, 목적어, 보어 자리에 올 수 있다. 의문사별로 의미뿐만 아니라 뒤에 이어지는 문장 구조가 다르므로 잘 정리해 두자.

CHECK-UP

✓ 다음 문장의 빈칸에 들어갈 알맞은 말을 고르세요. 정답 및 해설 p.397

22. Most of the conference attendees do not understand ------- the presenter is saying now.

  (A) what   (B) since

23. Management has not yet decided ------- they will launch their new product.

  (A) when   (B) who

24. The manager will decide ------ team will handle the new project.

  (A) where   (B) which

RC PART 5

PRACTICE

정답 및 해설 p.399

기출 포인트 1 접속사 Vs. 전치사

보기에 부사절 접속사, 전치사, (접속)부사 등이 제시될 때는 빈칸 앞뒤 구조를 살펴본다. 빈칸이 문장을 연결하는 경우에는 접속사가 정답이고, 빈칸 뒤에 명사구가 있는 경우에는 전치사가 정답이다. 이때 같은 의미의 전치사와 접속사가 나열되는 경우가 많으므로 품사를 확실히 구분해야 한다.

1. Ms. Kravitz will assist Mr. Casey ------- he is on a business trip in Venezuela.

    (A) during   (B) for   (C) while   (D) meanwhile

2. The manager postponed the meeting ------- a scheduling conflict.

    (A) otherwise   (B) since   (C) because of   (D) In case

기출 포인트 2 여러 의미를 나타내는 부사절 접속사

보기에 부사절 접속사, 전치사, (접속)부사 등이 제시될 때는 빈칸 앞뒤 구조를 살펴본다. 어법상 문제가 없는 보기가 둘 이상인 경우에는 해석을 통해 정답을 선택한다.

3. Monthly sales at Glam Uniforms doubled ------- the Luxe Medical Center opened nearby.

    (A) as soon as   (B) due to   (C) even though   (D) during

4. ------- space is limited, we need a quick response in order to reserve enough seats.

    (A) In order that   (B) Meanwhile   (C) Instead   (D) Because

5. ------- the seminar is free, attendees must register by phone at least two weeks in advance.

    (A) Although   (B) Before   (C) Nonetheless   (D) Until

6. Nobody has the right to see medical records ------- they has written authorization from the appropriate doctor.

    (A) though   (B) in order   (C) unless   (D) despite

7. Sales representatives are asked to make use of online data storage ------- they can access files remotely.

    (A) due to   (B) whereas   (C) so that   (D) despite

8. Enrollment at private universities is declining, ------- public universities are enjoying steady growth.

    (A) until   (B) unless   (C) whereas   (D) whenever

9. ------- he has extensive experience, Edward Smith is the best candidate for the job.

    (A) Given that   (B) Whereas   (C) Currently   (D) According to

기출 포인트 3 **명사절 접속사 자리**

명사절 접속사는 문장에서 명사 역할을 하는 절을 이끌며 주어, 목적어, 보어 자리에 온다. 명사절 접속사로는 that, whether, if, what, 의문사가 있다.

10. It is imperative ------- each employee be at their desk precisely at 8:00 each morning.

(A) for   (B) whose   (C) that   (D) to

11. Our office manager will decide ------- to purchase the new filing cabinets from Ryman Supply or WHSmith.

(A) whether   (B) neither   (C) even if   (D) what

기출 포인트 4 **명사절 접속사 if Vs. whether**

whether과 if는 '~인지 아니지'라는 의미로 명사절을 이끈다. 단, 명사절 접속사 if는 타동사의 목적어 자리에만 쓸 수 있다.

12. ------- we should invest in the new construction project is uncertain.

(A) If   (B) Because   (C) Neither   (D) Whether

13. The decision on ------- to merge with the competitor will impact our market position.

(A) that   (B) whether   (C) if   (D) yet

기출 포인트 5 **명사절 접속사 that Vs. 관계대명사 what**

빈칸이 명사절 접속사 자리이고 보기에 명사절 접속사가 두 개 이상일 경우, 해석과 빈칸 뒤의 문장이 완전한지 불완전한지에 따라 정답을 선택한다.

14. Job descriptions enable current employees to know ------- is expected of them.

(A) that   (B) whether   (C) if   (D) what

15. Ms. Keough has confirmed ------- she will present the advertising campaign to the clients.

(A) that   (B) what   (C) though   (C) unless

기출 포인트 6 **명사절 접속사 that과 어울리는 특정 동사와 형용사**

특정 동사나 형용사와 자주 함께 쓰이는 명사절 접속사 that을 묻는 문제가 출제된다. 명사절 접속사 that이 특정 동사 또는 형용사 어휘 문제에 대한 단서가 되기도 한다.

16. Our customer surveys indicate ------- we should enhance our customer support services.

(A) what   (B) which   (C) that   (D) those

17. The doctors were ------- that Mr. Ibrahim could be ready to work within a month.

(A) confidential   (B) responsible   (C) strict   (D) confident

UNIT 12 비교/도치

1. 비교

기출 패턴 1 원급 비교 표현 문제가 출제된다.

① 원급 비교는 '~만큼 ...한[하게]'라는 의미로, 두 대상의 동등함을 나타낼 때 쓴다.

Our new dishwasher is **as** <u>reliable</u> **as** the previous model.
우리의 새로운 식기 세척기는 이전 모델만큼 믿을 만하다.

We resolve consumer complaints **as** <u>efficiently</u> **as** possible.
우리는 소비자 불만 사항들을 가능한 한 효율적으로 해결한다.

② **as와 as 사이에는 형용사 또는 부사가 올 수 있다.**

The new product <u>was</u> not **as** [**attractive**, ~~attractively~~] **as** customers expected.
신제품은 고객들이 기대했던 것만큼 매력적이지 않았다.

Mr. Patel will thoroughly <u>examine</u> your report **as** [**quickly**, ~~quick~~] **as possible**.
Patel 씨는 가능한 한 빠른 시일 내에 당신의 보고서를 철저히 검토할 것이다.

고득점 TIP+ 시험에는 'as + 형용사/부사 + as' 구문의 짝 찾기나 원급 비교 as와 as 사이에 형용사, 부사의 품사를 판단하는 문제가 자주 출제된다. 이때 원급의 품사를 판단하려면 as ~ as를 빼고 문장 구조를 살펴야 한다. 문장이 완전하면 부사, be동사나 일반동사의 보어 자리면 형용사가 알맞다.

CHECK-UP
☑ 다음 문장의 빈칸에 들어갈 알맞은 말을 고르세요.   정답 및 해설 p.400

1. The Natale Group is now ------ famous as its competitor, Super Supreme Protection.

   (A) as   (B) very

2. The renovated breakroom is as ------- as the cafeteria on the seventh floor.

   (A) spacious   (B) spaciously

3. We need to work as ------- as possible to meet the deadline.

   (A) efficient   (B) efficiently

① **비교급은 '~보다 더[덜] 한[하게]'라는 의미로, 두 대상 간의 차이를 나타낸다.**

With the new system, our efficiency is **higher than** ever.
새로운 시스템으로, 우리의 효율성은 그 어느 때보다 더 높아졌다.

The quality of this product is **less** satisfactory **than** we anticipated.
이 제품의 품질은 우리가 예상한 것보다 만족스럽지 않다.

② **more과 than 사이에는 형용사 또는 부사가 올 수 있다.**

This system is **more** [**efficient**, ~~efficiently~~] **than** the existing one.
이 시스템은 기존 시스템보다 더 효율적이다.

Organizing your kitchen will help you cook **more** [**efficiently**, ~~efficient~~] **than** before.
주방을 정리하면 이전보다 더 효율적으로 요리할 수 있다.

③ **비교급 강조 부사(much, even, still, far, a lot)는 비교급 앞에 사용되어 '훨씬 더[덜] ~한[하게]'라는 의미를 나타낸다.**

Wembley Arena is [~~very~~, **much**] **larger** than the Georgia Convention Center.
Wembley Arena는 Georgia Convention Center보다 규모가 훨씬 크다.

④ **토익에 자주 출제되는 비교급 표현**

no later than 늦어도 ~까지	no longer = not any longer 더 이상 ~않다
rather than ~보다는, ~대신에	more and more 더욱더[갈수록 더]
more than ~이상의	less than ~미만의

More and more manufacturers are transporting their products by train **rather than** by road.
점점 더 많은 제조업체들이 도로가 아닌 기차로 제품을 운송하고 있다.

CHECK-UP ☑ 다음 문장의 빈칸에 들어갈 알맞은 말을 고르세요. 정답 및 해설 p.400

4. The project progressed less smoothly ------- we initially expected.

(A) with   (B) than

5. Investors believe that the BMC Group's growth will be ------- stronger than expected.

(A) since   (B) much

6. Ms. Perri most recent analysis of market conditions was significantly ------- than her previous ones.

(A) more positive   (B) positive

RC PART 5

최상급 관련 표현 문제가 출제된다.

① **최상급은 '...중에 가장 ~한[하게]' 이라는 의미로, 셋 이상 중에서 가장 뛰어난(혹은 낮은) 대상을 나타낸다.**

최상급을 나타내는 단서 표현	의미
the 또는 소유격 + 최상급 + of all (the) + 복수 명사(대상)	…중에 가장 ~한
the 또는 소유격 + 최상급 + in (the) + 단수 명사(단체, 기관, 장소)	…중에서 가장 ~한
the 또는 소유격 + 최상급 + among/of + 복수 명사	…중에서 가장 ~한
the 또는 소유격 + 최상급 + 명사 of any + 단수 명사	다른 어떤 …보다 가장 ~한
the 또는 소유격 + 최상급 + ever	이제껏 중에서 가장 ~한
the 또는 소유격 + 최상급 + (that) + 주어 + have (ever) p.p.	'주어'가 …했던 중에서 가장 ~한
the 또는 소유격 + 최상급 + 명사 + possible/available	가능한 한 가장 ~한

Daunt Books is **the oldest** continuously operating bookstore <u>in London</u>.
Daunt Books는 런던에서 지속적으로 운영 중인 가장 오래된 서점이다.

Ms. Sly is **the most qualified** <u>of all the applicants</u> who applied for the sales position.
Sly 씨는 영업직에 지원한 모든 지원자 중에서 가장 적임이다.

② **최상급 표현은 the 뒤에 위치하며, 명사를 수식할 수 있다.**

Nature is **the most popular** <u>television show</u> among men ages 40 to 55.
Nature는 40세에서 55세 사이의 남성들에게 가장 인기 있는 텔레비전 쇼이다.

③ **최상급 강조 부사(much, easily, by far, quite)는 최상급 앞에 사용되어 '단연코 가장 ~한[하게]'라는 의미를 나타낸다.**

This year's festival is being considered [~~extremely~~, **by far**] **the most successful**.
올해 축제는 단연코 가장 성공적이었다고 평가받고 있다.

고득점 TIP+ 최상급 앞에는 주로 the가 오기 때문에 the 뒤에 빈칸이 있으면 형용사나 부사의 최상급이 올 수 있다.

CHECK-UP ☑ 다음 문장의 빈칸에 들어갈 알맞은 말을 고르세요. 정답 및 해설 p.400

7. Steel is the ------- among all the materials used in the auto industry.

  (A) strong　　(B) strongest

8. Mr. Hill is regarded as ------- outstanding of all sales personnel.

  (A) the most　　(B) more

9. Our company just closed the largest deal ------- in our history.

  (A) ever　　(B) still

2. 도치

도치 구문 문제가 출제된다.

① 부정어의 도치: 부정어가 맨 앞으로 오면서 주어와 동사의 위치가 바뀐다.

▶ **부정어의 종류**

never 결코 ~아니다	**hardly** 거의 ~아니다	**seldom** 거의 ~하지 않다	**few** 거의 없는
rarely 드물게	**little** 극히 적게	**neither** 또한 ~아니다	**nor** 또한 ~아니다

▶ **부정어의 도치 어순**

부정어 + be동사 + 주어	부정어 + do/does/did + 주어 + 동사원형
부정어 + 조동사 + 주어 + 동사원형	부정어 + have/has/had + 주어 + p.p.

I never spend time at the office after 9:00 P.M.
➡ **Never** [**do**, ~~does~~] I spend time at the office after 9:00 P.M.
나는 9시 이후에는 절대 사무실에서 시간을 보내지 않는다.

He had seldom seen an employee with so much talent.
➡ [**Seldom**, ~~Openly~~] had he seen an employee with so much talent.
그는 그렇게 많은 재능을 가진 직원을 본 적이 거의 없었다.

② 보어의 도치: 보어를 강조할 때는 '보어 + 동사 + 주어' 어순을 취한다.

Enclosed is/are ~ + 주어 ~이 동봉되다	**Attached is/are** ~ + 주어 ~이 첨부되다	**Included is/are** ~ + 주어 ~이 포함되다

A copy of my purchase receipt is enclosed.
➡ [**Enclosed**, ~~Enclosure~~] is a copy of my purchase receipt. 구매 영수증 사본을 동봉합니다.

③ 가정법 도치: if가 생략되면서 가정법 과거완료에서는 **had**가, 가정법 미래에서는 **should**가 맨 앞에 온다.

가정법 과거완료 도치	Had + 주어 + p.p. ~, 주어 + would[could, might, should] + have p.p.

Had you come earlier, you might have met the newly appointed vice president.
당신이 좀 더 일찍 왔더라면 새로 임명된 부사장을 만났을지도 모릅니다.

가정법 미래 도치	Should + 주어 + 동사원형, 주어 + will[can, may, should] + 동사원형 * 또는 주절에 명령문이 올 수 있다.

Should you require additional information, please call me at your convenience.
추가적인 정보가 필요하시면, 편하실 때 저에게 전화를 주십시오.

CHECK-UP

☑ 다음 문장의 빈칸에 들어갈 알맞은 말을 고르세요. 정답 및 해설 p.400

10. ------ did Mr. Overton speak in public, particularly in meetings.

    (A) Moreover   (B) Seldom

11. ------ is the tentative itinerary for your trip to New York.

    (A) Enclosed   (B) Enclosure

12. ------ the campaign been more effective, the company would have gained a larger market share.

    (A) Had   (B) Should

PRACTICE

정답 및 해설 p.401

기출 포인트 1 　원급 비교

[as + ------- + as] 형태가 출제되면 형용사나 부사의 원급을 정답으로 선택한다. 이때 빈칸 앞의 as를 생략한 후 빈칸에 들어갈 품사를 따져보고 형용사와 부사 중 하나를 선택한다.

1. Eric Corp. is confident that its newly launched photocopier this year is just as ------- as its old one.

(A) rely　　　　　(B) reliable　　　　　(C) relied　　　　　(D) reliably

2. All session participants were asked to fill out an evaluation form as ------- as possible.

(A) compete　　　　(B) competitive　　　　(C) completely　　　　(D) competitiveness

기출 포인트 2 　비교급

빈칸 뒤에 than이 제시되거나 빈칸 앞에 비교급 강조 부사가 제시된 경우에는 비교급이 정답이다. 비교급 강조 부사에는 much, even, still, far, a lot 등이 있으며 '훨씬'이라는 의미를 나타낸다.

3. The new tool allows scientists to get a ------- measurement than before.

(A) precise　　　　(B) precisely　　　　(C) more precise　　　　(D) most precisely

4. My career as a biologist had been ------- more rewarding than I had expected.

(A) soon　　　　(B) alone　　　　(C) about　　　　(D) even

기출 포인트 3 　최상급

최상급은 셋 이상을 비교할 때 쓰며, 최상급 표현 앞에는 반드시 the나 소유격이 있어야 한다.

5. An increase in consumer spending in the retail sector is typically the ------- in autumn.

(A) greatness　　　　(B) greatest　　　　(C) greatly　　　　(D) great

6. The construction of the ------- building ever built near Tewkesbury is now in the final stage.

(A) big　　　　(B) bigger　　　　(C) bigness　　　　(D) biggest

기출 포인트 4 　도치

가정법 if절이나 주절의 동사 자리가 빈칸으로 제시되고 동사의 알맞은 형태나 시제를 묻는 문제나, 주어와 동사가 도치된 문장에서 맨 앞부분을 빈칸으로 제시하는 문제가 출제된다.

7. Had we ------- that the company was suffering from a money shortage, we would not have given it the contract.

(A) known　　　　(B) knew　　　　(C) be known　　　　(D) been known

8. ------- is a customer survey which will help us meet your future needs.

(A) To attach　　　　(B) Attachment　　　　(C) Attaching　　　　(D) Attached

■ 타동사

close overseas branch	해외지점을 폐쇄하다	**prevent** traffic congestion	교통 체증을 막다
generate substantial interest	상당한 관심을 자아내다	**build** lasting relationships	지속적인 관계를 구축하다
reduce operating costs	운영비를 줄이다	**express** one's appreciation	감사를 표하다
address customers' complaints	고객들의 불만사항을 처리하다	**offer** overnight shipping	익일 배송 서비스를 제공하다
order office supplies	사무용품을 주문하다	**emphasize** the importance	중요성을 강조하다
obtain up-to-date information	최신 정보를 얻다	**increase** one's customer base	고객 기반을 늘리다

■ 자동사

respond to all inquiries	모든 문의에 답하다	**specialize** in software development	소프트웨어 개발을 전문으로 하다
work as an interior designer	인테리어 디자이너로 일하다	**contribute** to the success of the project	프로젝트 성공에 기여하다
apply for a loan	대출을 신청하다	**participate** in the meeting	회의에 참석하다
interfere with daily business	일상 업무에 방해가 되다	**depend** on the year-end results	연말 실적에 달려있다
proceed to the reception desk	접수처로 가다	**conform** to company standards	회사 기준을 따르다
focus on developing new products	신제품 개발에 집중하다	**dispose** of confidential documents	기밀 서류를 처분하다

■ 명사

top **priority**	최우선 사항	prevent **corrosion**	부식을 방지하다
provide **assistance** to the staff	직원들에게 도움을 제공하다	maintain high safety **standards**	높은 안전 기준을 유지하다
without written **consent**	서면 동의 없이	get a cost **estimate**	비용 견적을 받다
meet the **requirements**	필수조건을 충족시키다	in spite of the **recession**	경기 침체에도 불구하고
reach a **consensus** on	~에 합의를 보다	have no **obligation** to pay	지불할 의무가 없다
look for a new **supplier**	새로운 공급업체를 찾다	go through an economic **depression**	경제 불황을 겪다
demand for organic food	유기농 식품에 대한 수요	a sensible **solution**	합리적인 해결책
a **contribution** to the company	회사에 대한 기여	extensive training and **expertise**	폭넓은 교육과 전문 지식
pass a safety **inspection**	안전 검사를 통과하다	a probable **outcome**	있을 법한 결과

RC PART 5

223

an ambitious **expansion** plan	야심찬 확장 계획	make an **appointment**	약속을 잡다
solicit **nominations** for	후보 지명을 간청하다	seek an **alternative**	대안을 찾다
meet the rigorous **criteria**	엄격한 기준을 충족하다	an initial **investment**	초기 투자
a detailed **description**	상세한 묘사	due to traffic **congestion**	교통 혼잡 때문에
build a **reputation**	명성을 쌓다	a (wide) **variety** of dishes	각양각색의 요리
host a **reception**	연회를 개최하다	without **authorization**	허가 없이
on the **agenda**	의제[안건]에 올라가 있는	despite a few **flaws**	몇 가지 결점에도 불구하고
primary **responsibilities**	주요 책무	meet the **quota**	할당량[목표량]을 충족하다
a food [meal] **preference**	음식 선호도	receive an immediate **dismissal**	즉각 해고되다

■ 형용사

until **further** notice	추후 통지가 있을 때까지	**hold** a **brief** meeting	간략한 회의를 하다
it is **customary** to do	~하는 것이 관례다	**spacious** and well lit	공간이 넓고 빛이 잘 드는
take **additional** action	추가 조치를 취하다	**valuable** reference material	매우 귀중한 참고자료
ensure **adequate** space	충분한 공간을 확보하다	in the **foreseeable** future	가까운 장래에
be **valid** until June 30	6월 30일까지 유효하다	improve **overall** productivity	전반적인 생산성을 개선하다
a **temporary** employee	임시 직원	only in **designated** areas	지정된 구역에서만
reliable service	믿을 만한 서비스	provide **convincing** explanations	설득력 있는 설명을 하다
give **constructive** feedback	건설적인 피드백을 제공하다	a **sophisticated** system	정교한 시스템
at an **affordable** price	합리적인 가격으로	seek **qualified** applicants	자격을 갖춘 지원자를 찾다
submit a **competitive** offer	경쟁력 있는 제안을 하다	under **mounting** pressure	점점 더 압박을 받는
receive **positive** comments	긍정적인 의견을 받다	take longer than **anticipated**	예상했던 것보다 오래 걸리다
set **realistic** sales goals	현실적인 판매 목표를 세우다	have a **lasting** effect	지속적인 효과를 지니다
a **feasible** alternative	실현 가능한 대안	create **compelling** videos	주목할 만한 비디오를 제작하다
hold a **dominant** position	우위를 차지하다	**overwhelming** demand	압도적인 수요
crucial evidence	결정적인 증거	a **limited** number of parking spaces	제한된 수의 주차 공간

the office **adjacent** to the lobby	로비에 인접한 사무실	the **remaining** paperwork	남아있는 서류 업무
an **inevitable** consequence	필연적인 결과	an **unexpected** delay in production	예상치 못한 생산 지연
an **appropriate** advertising strategy	적절한 광고 전략	receive **unanimous** approval	만장일치로 승인을 얻다

■ 부사

be **properly** installed	올바르게 설치되어 있다	be **strictly** prohibited	엄격히 제한되다
a **recently** upgraded building	최근에 개조된 건물	**officially** assume the position	공식적으로 직책을 맡다
differ **significantly** from	~와 상당히 다르다	**barely** noticeable	거의 알아볼 수 없는
donate **generously** to	~에 후하게 기부하다	**voluntarily** recall defective items	자발적으로 불량품을 회수하다
last **nearly** two hours	거의 두 시간 동안 지속하다	be **solely** responsible for	~에 전적으로 책임지다
completely free of charge	완전히 무료로	decline the invitation **respectfully**	정중하게 초대를 거절하다
a **densely** populated area	빽빽이 인구가 들어선 지역	**strongly** recommend	강력히 추천하다
at a **relatively** low price	상대적으로 낮은 가격으로	be **partly** responsible for	부분적으로 ~에 대한 책임이 있다
be **slightly** modified	약간 수정되다	speak most **eloquently**	가장 설득력 있게 말하다
than we **originally** predicted	우리가 원래 예상했던 것보다	unless **otherwise** indicated	별도의 표시가 없다면
dramatically increase [decrease]	극적으로 증가[감소]하다	**separately** from a paycheck	급여와는 별도로
adversely affect	부정적인 영향을 끼치다	**quickly** alter the sales strategy	영업 전략을 빠르게 바꾸다
extremely hot weather	극도로 더운 날씨	**immediately** after purchase	구매 직후에
primarily due to its low cost	특히 저렴한 가격 때문에	be **prominently** displayed	눈에 띄게 전시되다
be **frequently** delayed	자주 지연되다	as **previously** scheduled	이전에 정해진 대로
work **collaboratively** to develop	개발을 위해 협업하다	be **mutually** beneficial	상호 이득이 되다
be **agreeably** located	알맞은 곳에 위치하다	be **perfectly** suited for	~에 최적화되어 있다
pay the fee **electronically**	온라인으로 수수료를 지불하다	take place **simultaneously**	동시에 일어나다

RC PART 5

225

PART

6

장문 빈칸
채우기

PART 6는 총 4개의 지문이 출제되고 각 지문당 4개의 문제가 나온다. 4개의 문제는 문법/어휘 문제 3문항과 문장 고르기 문제 1문항으로 구성된다. PART 5와 비슷한 유형의 문법/어휘 문제가 주를 이루며, 앞뒤 문장을 의미상 자연스럽게 연결하는 접속부사(연결어)를 선택하는 문제도 종종 출제된다.

구성	PART	유형		문항 수	시간	배점
Reading Comprehension	5	단문 빈칸 채우기 (문법/어휘)		30	75분	495점
	6	**장문 빈칸 채우기**		**16**		
	7	독해	단일 지문	29		
			이중 지문	10		
			삼중 지문	15		

 지문 유형 편지·이메일, 기사, 공지, 지시문, 광고, 회람, 설명서, 발표문, 정보문 등

 문제 유형

- **문법 문제** 문장 구조를 파악하며 빈칸의 자리로 알맞은 품사나 형태를 고르는 문제
- **어휘 문제** 같은 품사인 네 개의 어휘 중 정확한 용례를 파악하여 알맞은 단어를 고르는 문제
- **문장 고르기** 지문의 흐름을 파악하여 네 개의 문장 중에 빈칸 앞뒤 문맥과 어울리는 문장을 고르는 문제

 최신 출제 경향

① 빈칸 앞뒤 문맥을 통해 시제를 결정하는 문제의 출제 비중이 높다. 시제를 묻는 문제는 PART 5에서는 시간 부사나 시간 부사구를 단서로 활용하지만, PART 6에서는 맥락을 함께 파악해야 풀 수 있다.

② 두 문장을 자연스럽게 이어주는 접속부사[연결어]를 선택하는 문제가 평균 1~2문제가 출제된다.

③ 맥락으로 파악해야 하는 대명사의 인칭 일치 문제가 자주 출제된다.

④ 어휘 문제는 빈칸을 포함한 문장만 보고는 해결되지 않고 앞뒤 문맥을 파악하여 고르는 문제가 출제된다.

 만점 전략

① 지문을 처음부터 읽는다.

PART 6는 문맥을 파악해야 풀 수 있는 문제가 대부분이므로, 지문을 처음부터 읽어야 한다. 시간을 절약하려고 빈칸이 있는 문장만 읽는 것은 위험할 수 있다.

② 순서대로 한 문제씩 해결해 나간다.

문법 문제는 해당 문장만 보고 풀 수 있는 경우가 간혹 있지만, 시제/지시어/대명사 등의 일부 문제는 내용의 흐름을 파악하고 풀어야 한다. 따라서 문제 유형과 상관없이, 반드시 순서대로 한 문제씩 해결해 나가도록 한다.

To: Camada Hotel staff
From: Maya Yellen
Date: August 7
Subject: Conserving resources

To All Housekeeping Staff,

Hotel management has decided to implement a new policy ------- the daily laundering of towels.
131.

Going forward, all towels left on the floor by guests will be collected and washed each day, but any used towels hung up on hooks or racks will be left in the room for guests to reuse. This policy will ------- our daily laundry load. -------, our electricity and water use will be reduced.
132.   **133.**

Notices will be posted in each room informing our guests of this policy. -------. Management is
134.

deeply committed to conservation.

Thanks,

---

131. (A) regards
(B) regardless
(C) regarding
(D) regarded

문법 문제 ○ 주변 문장 또는 어구에서 정답 단서가 제공된다.
빈칸 뒤 the daily laundering of towels를 목적어로 갖는 전치사 자리이다. 문맥상 '수건 세탁과 관련된 새로운 정책'이라는 의미가 적절하다.

132. (A) minimize
(B) double
(C) require
(D) eliminate

어휘 문제 ○ 글의 주제와 앞뒤 문맥이 정답을 결정한다.
빈칸 앞은 객실의 수건 일부는 고객이 재사용하도록 하자는 새로운 정책에 관한 내용이다. 따라서 빈칸에 들어갈 동사는 세탁물을 '최소화할 것이다'라는 의미가 적절하다.

133. (A) Despite this
(B) However
(C) As a result
(D) Evidently

접속부사 문제 ○ 빈칸 앞뒤 논리적 관계를 따져서 정답을 고른다.
빈칸 앞은 세탁물을 최소화할 수 있는 정책을 제시하고 빈칸 뒤는 이 정책이 전기와 물 사용을 감소시킬 것이라고 했으므로 '결과'를 의미하는 접속부사를 고른다.

134. (A) We would greatly appreciate your cooperation with this effort.
(B) Please inform us if you identify any maintenance needs.
(C) During this time, please limit showers to 10 minutes.
(D) You will be asked to share all kinds of ideas at the staff meeting.

문장 고르기 문제 ○ 주제, 문맥, 문법적 요소(대명사, 지시어)를 따져서 정답을 고른다.
빈칸 앞에서 전기와 물 사용을 감소시킬 새로운 정책을 소개하고 빈칸 뒤에서는 경영진이 절약에 심혈을 기울이고 있다고 했으므로 직원들에게 협조를 바란다는 (A)가 문맥상 가장 적합하다.

1. 시제 문제

≡ 유형 소개 및 전략

PART 6의 최대 빈출 유형으로, 시제 문제는 빈칸 문장만으로는 답을 찾을 수 없는 경우가 대부분이다. 정답의 근거는 이메일이 작성된 날짜, 주변 문장에 쓰인 시제, 글의 종류 등이 될 수 있다. 이메일의 발신 날짜와 지문에 나타난 날짜를 비교하면 풀 수 있는 쉬운 유형에서, 특정 단서 없이 지문의 전체 흐름을 파악해야 하는 고난도 유형까지 고루 출제된다.

≡ 풀이 접근법

지문의 종류에 따라 자주 사용되는 시제들이 있다. 공지(Notice), 회람(Memo), 발표(Announcement)의 경우, 주로 앞으로 일어날 일에 대한 내용을 다루므로 미래 시제가 정답일 확률이 매우 높다. 광고(Advertisement)의 경우, 보통 현재/현재완료/미래 시제 중 하나가 정답이다. 현재 시제는 일반적인 사실이나 반복되는 습관 등을 나타내므로 어떤 회사가 특정 서비스나 제품을 제공한다는 내용에 주로 사용되고, 현재완료 시제는 과거부터 오랫동안 일해 왔거나 서비스 등을 제공해 오고 있다는 내용에 쓰일 수 있다. 또한, 신제품 출시 등의 일정을 설명하는 경우에는 미래 시제가 정답이 되는 경우가 대부분이다.

유형 맛보기

To: Hugo Monye <monye@oceansky.co.uk>
From: Toby Ojo <ojo@victoriamuseum.org.uk>
Subject: Membership
Date: July 7

Dear Mr. Monye,

I hope you are enjoying your Tane Museum membership. Please note that your membership ------- on August 10. By renewing your membership now, you can take advantage of a special 10-percent discount.

(A) to be expiring   (B) must have expired
(C) has expired   **(D) will expire**

수신: Hugo Monye <monye@oceansky.co.uk>
발신: Toby Ojo <ojo@victoriamuseum.org.uk>
제목: 회원 자격
날짜: 7월 7일 → 이메일 작성일

Monye 씨에게,

저희는 여러분이 Tane 미술관 회원 자격을 즐기시고 있기를 바랍니다. 귀하의 회원 자격은 8월 10일에 만료(→ 미래에 일어날 일)됩니다. 회원 자격을 갱신하면 특별한 10% 할인 혜택을 누릴 수 있습니다.

→ 이메일을 보낸 날짜는 7월 7일이며 8월 10일에 회원 자격이 만기가 된다는 내용이므로 미래 시제인 (D) will expire가 정답이다.

주의해야 할 시제 표현

현재진행 시제 [be -ing]	① ~하고 있는 중이다 We **are offering** a 20% discount on these items. 이 제품들은 20퍼센트 할인 중입니다. (현재 상황) ② ~할 것이다 I'm **starting** my new job next week. 나는 다음 주에 새 일을 시작할 것이다. (계획된 미래) She's **leaving** for London in three weeks. 그녀는 3주 뒤에 런던으로 떠날 것이다. (확정된 미래)
미래진행 시제 [will be v-ing]	We **will be offering** special discounts during the holidays. 저희는 연말연시 기간에 특별 할인을 할 것이다. (미래에 진행될 일)
be to 용법	The festival **is to** take place on Sunday. 축제는 일요일에 개최될 예정이다. (예정)

1.

Attention, employees:

We are going to introduce a new electronic timecard system next week. Replacement identification badges ------- to all of you by this Friday. These ID badges will also function as your timecards. The timecard machine will be set up at the entrance closest to your office.

(A) distribute
(B) were distributed
(C) will be distributed
(D) have distributed

2.

To All eMachines Store Managers:

Please be informed that, starting on June 1, new refund rules will go into effect at all eMachines stores. From this date, eMachines ------- a policy guaranteeing that customers can receive refunds under certain conditions. Under this policy, all items that have been purchased in the last three months may be returned for a full refund if they are still in good condition and show no signs of extensive wear.

(A) implemented
(B) implements
(C) has implemented
(D) will implement

3.

Management is pleased to announce that our staff member of the year is Ms. Neeta Joshi, who has been working at Rina Boutique for seven years. Ms. Joshi ------- as an office assistant on a part-time basis during her sophomore year of college. Then, after graduating from the prestigious Fashion School of Drexel University, she was employed as a junior fashion designer here.

(A) serves
(B) will serve
(C) served
(D) is serving

RC PART 6

2. 대명사/지시어 문제

☰ 유형 소개 및 전략

PART 6 대명사/지시어 문제는 대부분 문맥을 파악하면 간단히 풀 수 있다. 한 문장 안에서 빈칸에 알맞은 대명사의 격을 고르는 PART 5 문제와 달리 PART 6는 빈칸을 포함한 문장의 앞부분에서 대명사가 가리키는 대상이 무엇인지를 찾아야 한다.

☰ 풀이 접근법

빈칸에 들어갈 내용이 가리키는 대상이 무엇인지 지문 내에서 파악하여, 알맞은 대명사(he, she, it, they 등)와 지시어 (this, that, these, those 등)를 선택하는 유형이다. 이때 지칭하는 대상과의 수 일치와 격을 꼼꼼히 살펴야 한다.

유형 맛보기

To: Human Resources Team
From: Ben Brown

Hello, everyone, I just want to remind you of the annual convention which will be held on Wednesday in Convention Hall C. This is a crucial meeting, so I recommend that everyone be in attendance. All staff members must be well prepared to discuss various topics during the meeting. In addition, Frank and Daniel will be introduced as new staff members. Please welcome ------- and prepare a short self-introduction about yourself.

(A) it
(B) them
(C) that
(D) theirs

수신: 인사팀
발신: Ben Brown

안녕하세요, 여러분, 저는 여러분에게 컨벤션 홀 C에서 수요일에 열릴 예정인 연례 회의에 대해 상기시키고자 합니다. 이 미팅은 매우 중요하므로, 모두 참석하는 것을 권장합니다. 전 직원들은 회의 동안 다룰 다양한 주제를 논의할 수 있게끔 잘 준비해야 합니다. 또한, Frank와 Daniel이 신입 사원으로 소개될 겁니다. (→ 빈칸 앞: 소개될 구체적인 인물) 그들(→ 앞서 언급된 신입사원 2명을 가리킴)을 환영해 주시고 짧은 자기소개도 준비해 놓으세요.

→ 빈칸은 타동사 welcome(환영하다)의 목적어 자리로, 목적격 대명사가 들어갈 수 있다. 빈칸에 들어갈 내용은 앞 문장의 Frank and Daniel이 적절하므로 복수인 사람을 대신할 수 있는 (B) them이 정답이다.

1.

Dear Mr. Houston,

Thank you for your message on December 3. Our records indicate that you ordered four Chemex snow tires (model DW04 145R13) through our Web site on November 28 and that they were scheduled to arrive on December 2. I am sorry to hear that you have not yet received -------. Deliveries usually take no more than two or three days.

(A) one
(B) it
(C) some
(D) them

2.

To: Martin Branson
From: Ella Moore
Date: March 9
Re: Job posting

Hello, Mr. Branson,

I'm sorry for not being able to answer your call. I was so busy leading a group discussion on the construction of the new branch in Miami.
Anyway, as I told you a few days ago, the former accounting manager, Jerry Page, has unexpectedly left the company, and it is very difficult to find a suitable replacement. I'd like you to place the job posting on ------- company's Web site. We need a manager who can perform Mr. Page's duties, and we also have several open positions at the Hong Kong branch.

(A) his
(B) your
(C) our
(D) their

3.

Dear Mr. Ellison,

Welcome to the Workipedia network, the leading online career matching service. Your e-mail address, work experience, and preferences have been recorded in our database. This information will be used to identify employers who are seeking job candidates just like -------. In the future, you will receive periodic notifications about open positions in your area.

(A) me
(B) you
(C) us
(D) ours

3. 접속부사[연결어] 문제

유형 소개 및 전략

접속부사 문제는 PART 6에서 매회 1~2문제 정도 출제된다. 지문의 내용 흐름과 글의 맥락을 이해해야 문제를 풀 수 있다.

풀이 접근법

접속부사는 문장과 문장을 논리적으로 연결하는 부사이다. 따라서 빈칸 앞뒤 문장의 논리적 관계에 따라 역접, 인과, 첨가, 대조 등 알맞은 접속부사를 선택해야 한다. 빈칸의 앞뒤 내용을 모두 이해해야 하기 때문에 풀이 시간이 많이 소요될 수 있으므로 최소의 단어로 문맥을 파악하는 연습이 필요하다.

유형 맛보기

To Whom It May Concern;

I received one of your G4-Portable wind protection kits for my mattress and took it on my 3-day camping trip with my friends. Thank you for the prompt delivery. When I opened the box, it included all the necessary parts for assembly, and every item seemed perfect. -------, on the first night of my trip, I noticed it didn't provide good protection against the wind.

(A) Therefore
(B) Consequently
(C) In addition
(D) **However**

관련자 분께;

저는 귀하의 매트리스용 G4 휴대용 방풍 키트 중 하나를 받아 3일간의 친구들과의 캠핑 여행에 가져갔습니다. 신속한 배송에 감사드립니다. 박스를 열었을 때, 조립에 필요한 모든 부품들이 있었고, **모든 물품은 외관상으로는 완벽해 보였습니다. 그러나,** 캠핑 첫날 저는 이 제품이 방풍이 잘 되지 않는다는 것을 알게 되었습니다.

→ 앞 문장(물건이 완벽해 보였다)과 뒤 문장(하자를 발견했다)이 상반된 내용이므로 대조[역접] 관계를 나타내는 (D) However가 정답이다.

접속부사의 종류

역접	앞 문장에서 언급한 내용과 상반되는 내용을 연결한다.
	however 그러나 even so 그렇다 해도 nevertheless 그럼에도 불구하고 to the contrary 그와는 반대로 in contrast 그에 반해서
추가	앞 문장에 내용을 덧붙이거나 예시를 들 때 쓴다.
	in addition 추가로 additionally 추가로 furthermore 게다가 moreover 게다가 besides 게다가, 뿐만 아니라 likewise 마찬가지로
인과	앞 문장의 내용을 근거로 발생하게 될 결과를 연결한다.
	therefore 그러므로 as a result 결과적으로 hence 그런 이유로 thus 따라서 consequently 결과적으로, 그 결과
시간	앞 문장의 발생 시점과 다음 문장의 발생한 시점의 차이 또는 순서를 나타낸다.
	afterward(s) 그 후에 finally 마침내 then 그 다음에, 그때 in the meantime 그동안 meanwhile 그동안

1.

Dear Ms. Keller:

I am responding to your inquiry about our security camera installation service. We are definitely able to work around your regular business hours to minimize any inconvenience to you. -------, members of our staff with expertise in security cameras can show you a wide variety of affordable and simple options like our SimpliCam and Wyze Cam.

(A) However
(B) As a result
(C) In fact
(D) In addition

2.

Hello, Ms. Goldberg,

At the meeting this morning, it was decided that we cannot afford to build a new logistics center for the east coast. -------, we must move into a larger facility if we want to satisfy the increasing demand for our products. So what I need you to do is to locate some existing logistics facilities in the area that fit the following specifications:

(A) Therefore
(B) However
(C) Besides
(D) Similarly

3.

To All Employees:

I am writing this memo to give you advance notice of a change that will be introduced next month. It is a new and more refined system for handling employees' annual raises.

It is important that employees understand this system and have a chance to ask questions about it. -------, there will be a series of meetings on the topic next week led by me and other human resources managers.

(A) For this reason
(B) Nevertheless
(C) In short
(D) For instance

RC PART 6

4. 어휘 문제

☰ 유형 소개 및 전략

PART 6에서 어휘 문제는 글을 읽고 주제와 흐름을 파악해야 풀 수 있는 문제가 대부분이다. 따라서 빈칸을 포함하고 있는 문장뿐만 아니라 주변 문장에서 단서를 찾아 정답을 결정해야 한다. 또한, 지시어나 접속부사 같은 단서를 활용하거나, 첫 문장 또는 빈칸 뒤의 문장을 통해 빈칸에 들어갈 알맞은 어휘를 고르는 유형으로 출제된다.

☰ 풀이 접근법

● 어휘 문제를 풀 때 활용할 수 있는 정답 단서

지문 첫 문장	첫 문장은 글의 주제나 종류, 그리고 전체 흐름을 파악할 수 있는 단서이기 때문에 주의 깊게 읽어야 한다.
지시어/접속부사	빈칸이 포함된 문장에 지시어(this/that/such), 대명사, 정관사, 소유격 등이 있는 경우, 앞 문장의 문맥을 살펴 해당 대상을 찾아야 하고, 접속부사가 있는 경우에는 빈칸 앞뒤 문장과의 의미 관계를 확인해야 한다.
빈칸 뒤 문장	빈칸이 포함된 문장에 지시어나 접속부사 같은 정답의 단서가 없는 경우, 보통 빈칸 뒤 문장에 단서가 나온다. 특히, 첫 문제가 어휘 문제인 경우, 대부분 바로 다음 문장에 단서가 주어진다.
전체 맥락	고난도 문제는 지문을 읽고 그 내용을 종합적으로 이해해야 답을 고를 수 있다. 따라서 어휘 문제의 정답 단서를 바로 찾을 수 없는 경우, 다른 문제들을 먼저 풀고 전체 맥락을 파악한 후 마지막에 푸는 것이 좋다.

유형 맛보기

Dear Mr. Harris,

I'm writing to inform you that your request for a ------- has been approved. Your final day at the Regina branch will be May 15, and your first day at the Lloyds branch will be May 19. The manager at the new branch completely understands that it will take you some time to get used to the new environment.

(A) permit
(B) vacation
(C) meeting
(D) transfer

Harris 씨에게,

귀하의 전근 요청이 승인되었음을 알리고자 이 글을 씁니다. Regina 지점에서의 마지막 날은 5월 15일이 될 것이고, Lloyds 지점에서의 첫날은 5월 19일이 될 것입니다. 새 지점의 관리자는 귀하가 새로운 환경에 익숙해지는 데 시간이 다소 필요할 것임을 충분히 이해합니다.

→ '-------에 대한 요청'이라는 문맥에서 무엇에 대한 요청이 승인되었는지 파악해야 한다. 뒤 문장에서 Regina 지점에서의 마지막 날(final day)과 the Lloyds branch에서의 첫날(first day)을 명시한 것, 그리고 바로 이어서 '새 지점(new branch)', '새 환경(new environment)' 등이 언급된 것으로 보아 Harris 씨가 다른 지점으로의 근무지 변경을 요청했음을 알 수 있다. 따라서 '전근, 이전'이라는 뜻의 명사 (D) transfer가 정답이다.

PRACTICE 4

정답 및 해설 p.405

1.

Hello, Mr. Taylor.

I am Stephen Miller from Magnolia Journal. This e-mail is to let you know that your subscription to our magazine will end in November. If you renew your subscription this month, we will give you a 20% discount. This special offer is to express our ------- for your loyal patronage over the past 5 years.

(A) dedication
(B) sympathy
(C) enthusiasm
(D) gratitude

2.

Dear Mr. Reyes,

Thank you for your ------- to be a guest speaker at the upcoming annual Sales Success Conference. It is an honor to be found worthy of consideration. Unfortunately, I am currently engaged in writing the final draft of my latest book and simply cannot take any time away from that.

(A) proposal
(B) temptation
(C) acceptance
(D) approval

3.

The classic mystery film *Perfect Blue* starring Nick Frost and Halle Parker will be returning to theaters next week. Because of the huge success of its reboot, which came out in theaters last year, many fans have expressed a desire to see the original in theaters once again. Many fans who were too young to see the original in theaters are also ------- to get a chance to see it on the big screen.

(A) decisive
(B) fearful
(C) hesitant
(D) eager

RC PART 6

문장 삽입

1. 대명사/지시어 활용

≡ 유형 소개 및 전략

문장 삽입 문제는 매회 4문제씩 출제된다. 보기 문장이나 빈칸의 앞뒤 문장에서 지시어가 보인다면 가리키는 대상을 먼저 확인하는 것이 유리하다.

≡ 풀이 접근법

주어진 보기 문장 중에 대명사(it, they, he, she 등)나 지시어(this, that, these, those 등)가 있으면 빈칸 앞 문장에 나온 명사와 수가 일치하는지 확인해야 한다. 또한, 빈칸 뒤 문장에 대명사나 지시어가 있다면 보기 문장에 나온 명사와 연결되는지 확인해야 한다. 이때 대명사/지시어와 명사의 연결이 적합하지 않으면 오답으로 소거한다.

유형 맛보기

Fauna Kitchen is pleased to announce that it will change its hours of operation. We've had a lot of comments from our patrons requesting this change, and we hope this demonstrates to you that we are listening. From May 15, Fauna Kitchen will be open until 11:00 P.M. on weekdays and until midnight on weekends. Please note that diners on the outdoor patio should keep their conversations to a minimum after 10:00 P.M. -------. This is one reason we were reluctant to stay open later.

(A) The full menu will be served both indoors and outdoors during the summer.

(B) We do not want to disturb tenants living in the surrounding apartments.

(C) It is located at the rear of the store and connects to the main dining area.

(D) The opening time of, 11:00 A.M. daily, will remain the same.

Fauna Kitchen이 영업시간 변경을 알리게 되어 기쁩니다. 저희는 고객들로부터 이 변화를 요청하는 많은 의견을 받아 왔고, 이 결정이 저희가 귀 기울이고 있음을 여러분께 보여드리길 바랍니다. 5월 15일부터 Fauna Kitchen은 평일에는 오후 11시까지 그리고 주말에는 자정까지 문을 열 것입니다. 야외 테라스에서 식사하시는 손님들은 오후 10시 이후에는 대화를 최소한으로 하셔야 함을 유념해 주세요. **저희는 주변 아파트에 사는 세입자들을 방해하고 싶지 않습니다.** 이것이 저희가 늦게까지 문을 열기를 꺼려했던 한 가지 이유입니다.

(A) 전체 메뉴는 여름 동안 실내와 야외에서 제공될 것입니다.

(B) 저희는 주변 아파트에 사는 세입자들을 방해하고 싶지 않습니다.

(C) 그것은 주 식사 구역과 연결된 식당 뒤쪽에 위치해 있습니다.

(D) 개점 시간인 매일 오전 11시는 동일하게 유지될 것입니다.

→ 빈칸 앞에서 Fauna Kitchen이 영업시간을 연장했고 야외 테라스 손님들은 오후 10시 이후에는 대화를 최소한으로 해달라고 당부한다. 빈칸 뒤에서 지시어 This는 빈칸 문장 전체를 가리키며, 이것이 늦게까지 문을 열기 꺼려했던 한 가지 이유라고 언급한다. 따라서 주변 아파트에 사는 세입자들을 방해하고 싶지 않다는 내용의 (B)가 정답이다.

1.

February 8—This morning, software engineer Lucas Ellison launched a new company. The new firm, L-Ellison Tech, will specialize in enhancing the look and functionality of online stores. Mr. Ellison's team of technicians is engaged in gathering data from clients' sites and reorganizing the sites based on users' preferences. -------. Mr. Ellison expects his firm's services to be in demand, saying, "We will upgrade a client's Web interface to provide improved user experience on all screen sizes from mobile phones to tablets."

(A) Meanwhile, it will help most online stores reach a wider audience.

(B) Market studies show an increase in online stores that sell home goods.

(C) This can be done with the help of new software that examines visitors' behavior.

(D) Customers often prefer shopping online rather than visiting stores.

2.

Dear Mr. Green,

Our records show that your last dental checkup was on December 8. --------. The reason for this is that research has shown that getting a checkup every three months will help keep your teeth and gums healthy. To book a time slot, simply contact us at 7928-4474 any weekday between 9:00 A.M. and 6:00 P.M.

(A) Please take a moment to give us some feedback about your experience.

(B) We suggest that you make another appointment soon.

(C) This service still has an outstanding charge of $39.99.

(D) You should know that we have moved our clinic to 7th Street.

3.

Next Friday, December 23, the office Christmas party is scheduled to take place. Many employees look forward to this event each year, and this year is no different. As the event date approaches, decorations will be put up around the office. -------. To join in any or all of them, just put your name on the appropriate sign-up sheets located in HR.

(A) The party committee is currently recruiting new members.

(B) This celebration will be a great way to kick off the holiday weekend.

(C) Several activities have been planned to take place throughout the day.

(D) Employees who are interested in exchanging gifts may bring presents.

RC

PART 6

2. 정관사 활용

☰ 유형 소개 및 전략

앞에서 언급된 사람이나 사물, 장소, 상황 등을 뒤에서 재차 지칭할 때 명사 앞에 정관사 the를 붙인다. 이러한 정관사의 특징을 이해하고 활용하면 문장 삽입 문제의 답을 쉽게 고를 수 있다.

☰ 풀이 접근법

문장에 처음 등장한 대상을 지칭할 때는 단수 명사 앞에 a나 an을 사용하고, 복수 명사는 관사 없이 사용할 수 있다. 따라서 보기나 빈칸 뒤에 '정관사+(복수)명사'가 있으면 앞 문장에서 해당 명사와 관련된 상황이 언급되어야 한다. 보기 문장 중 관련 없는 명사에 the가 붙어 있다면 오답으로 소거하는 것도 정관사를 활용하는 방법이다.

유형 맛보기

Norfolk Airport Shut Down

Norfolk International Airport handled almost 2,000 domestic flights in May alone, making it the second busiest airport in the country. -------. The decision has been made due to the dangerous condition of the airport's sole runway, which has ruptured in several places.

(A) Norfolk International Airport is well known for its clean facilities.
(B) But it will shut down for 2 weeks starting on Friday, August 9.
(C) Several flights were delayed due to the bad weather.
(D) Passengers will be updated on the construction at the airport.

Norfolk 공항 폐쇄

Norfolk 국제공항은 5월에만 거의 2천 건의 국내 비행편을 운행하면서 국내에서 두 번째로 많은 승객을 보유한 공항으로 자리매김했다. **하지만 이 공항은 8월 9일 금요일을 시작으로 2주일간 폐쇄될 예정이다.** 그 결정은 여러 군데에 균열이 생긴 공항 내의 유일한 활주로가 위험한 상태라는 이유에서 내려졌다.

(A) Norfolk 국제공항은 깨끗한 시설로 잘 알려져 있다.
(B) 하지만 이 공항은 8월 9일 금요일을 시작으로 2주일간 폐쇄될 예정이다.
(C) 몇몇 비행 편이 악천후로 인해 지연되었다.
(D) 승객들은 공항의 공사 관련 최신 정보를 안내받을 것이다.

→ 빈칸 앞은 Norfolk 공항이 많은 승객을 보유한 공항으로 자리매김했다는 내용이고, 빈칸 뒤는 Norfolk 공항이 어떠한 결정을 한 이유로, 활주로의 균열이 언급되었다. 따라서 접속사 But으로 시작하며 공항이 2주일간 폐쇄될 거라는 내용의 (B)가 문맥상 가장 적절하다. 접속사 But은 앞 내용과 상반되는 내용을 연결한다.

1.

Due to unforeseen problems, the completion date for the renovation of Starfall's main lobby is now May 13 instead of May 6. This delay means that you should continue to enter the building through the south entrance. In addition, offices adjacent to the lobby will experience occasional noise disruptions through next week. We apologize for the inconvenience, but the end result will be an attractive, modern space that impresses customers. -------.

(A) We have experienced disruptions ourselves.

(B) We are confident that you will all agree once the work is finished.

(C) The main problem is the issue with the floor.

(D) The south entrance is open 24 hours a day.

2.

Good afternoon, everyone,

Our annual job satisfaction survey (JSS) is your opportunity to share your opinions about working at Bridgerock. Your opinions will help shape the future of our company. We invite you to fill out the online survey no later than November 30. In the coming days, you will receive an e-mail containing a link to the survey. -------. Contributing in this way helps our company improve.

(A) All employees replied promptly to the message.

(B) The deadline for the project is the 30th of this month.

(C) The final deadline for the work is 6:00 P.M. tomorrow.

(D) Please take the time to provide some feedback.

3.

Newfoundland (April 3)—Construction of a new hydroelectric power plant is scheduled to begin next month. The Churchill Falls Generating Station (CFGS) estimates that the plant will generate enough power to handle the entire Newfoundland power grid. -------. To cover the initial costs, residents of Newfoundland have been told to expect an increase of about 15% for utilities.

(A) Initial estimates put the cost of the power plant at nearly 50 million dollars.

(B) Construction of the new power plant will likely take several years.

(C) The government is expected to issue grants to pay the initial costs.

(D) Environmental protection groups support the renewable energy source.

RC PART 6

3.접속부사[연결어] 활용

유형 소개 및 전략

문장 삽입 문제의 보기나 빈칸 앞뒤 문장에 접속부사가 포함될 때가 있다. 접속부사는 앞뒤 문장의 논리적 관계를 설정해 주는 연결어이므로 정답을 결정하는 중요한 단서가 된다. 접속부사가 있는 경우 연결되는 두 문장이 자연스럽게 연결되는지 확인하자.

풀이 접근법

접속부사는 앞 문장과 뒤 문장이 어떤 관계로 연결되었는지를 보여주는 실마리가 된다. 접속부사를 기준으로 두 문장의 관계가 원인과 결과인지, 추가적인 내용을 덧붙이는지, 앞에서 언급한 내용과 상반되는 내용이 이어지는지, 시간이나 순서를 나타내는지 확인하고 답을 골라야 한다.

유형 맛보기

The Utopia Library no longer accepts donations of books from the public. Evaluating, sorting, and processing donations of books take a tremendous amount of resources. It is better use of our resources to purchase new books and media. -------. Cash donations will help us buy new books and media for our library.

(A) However, we still accept monetary contributions.
(B) Please return your books to the library.
(C) We sell donated books in our store and online.
(D) Find one of our drop boxes at a location near you.

Utopia 도서관은 더 이상 대중으로부터 책을 기부받지 않습니다. 기부받은 책을 감정하고, 분류하고, 처리하는 작업에는 엄청난 양의 자원이 듭니다. 새로운 도서와 미디어를 구입하는 것이 저희 자원을 더 잘 활용하는 방법입니다. **하지만 저희 도서관은 여전히 금전적인 기부는 받습니다.** 현금 기부는 저희 도서관이 새로운 도서와 미디어를 구입하도록 도울 것입니다.

(A) 하지만 저희 도서관은 여전히 금전적 기부는 받습니다.
(B) 책을 도서관에 반납해 주십시오.
(C) 저희는 매장과 온라인에서 기증된 책을 판매합니다.
(D) 집 근처에 있는 반납함 중 하나를 찾으십시오.

→ 빈칸 앞은 도서관이 자원을 더 잘 활용하기 위해 더 이상 대중으로부터 책을 기부받지 않는다는 내용이고, 빈칸 뒤에 현금 기부는 도서관에 도움이 될 것이라는 내용이 이어지고 있다. 따라서 빈칸에 상반되는 흐름을 자연스럽게 연결해주는 내용이 들어가야 하므로 '하지만 여전히 현금 기부는 받는다'는 내용의 (A)가 문맥상 적절하다. 접속부사 However(하지만, 그러나)는 역접 관계인 문장을 연결한다.

1.

The big day for the Eton Marathon in London is coming soon. We have fourteen people in our running group attending, and you should have already received the information about the hotel I've booked. -------. We will be sharing double rooms, each with two people.

(A) Please wear our group T-shirt during the race.

(B) We'll carpool together on Saturday morning.

(C) The race requires an entrance fee of $30.

(D) If not, let me know, and I can send it again.

2.

Weather experts in our area expect a severe snowstorm tomorrow, so I think it's good idea for us to cancel our city band practice. That way, you won't have to travel in cold and icy conditions. -------. Therefore, please take some time this week to work on the music on your own. Our concert to commemorate the city's founding day is fast approaching, so we want everyone to be prepared.

(A) We don't want to get behind on the practice schedule.

(B) Everyone sounded fantastic at last week's practice.

(C) It would be best to recruit a few more members to our band.

(D) Fortunately, all of our rehearsals are held indoors.

3.

The renovations are scheduled to be completed by May 7, and we decided to shut down our office temporarily. The office will be closed this Friday and Saturday and on Monday morning. -------. I hope that everyone finds the office a much more comfortable place to work.

(A) We will be e-mailing you a questionnaire concerning the office relocation.

(B) And the recent renovation work may have caused inconvenience to you.

(C) During the renovations, employees in Office Building B worked in Office Building A.

(D) Therefore, employees should return to work by 12:00 P.M. on Monday.

RC PART 6

1. Please ------- inquiries about your salary to Mr. Turner in the accounting office.

   (A) directing
   (B) direct
   (C) directly
   (D) directed

2. ------- account will be credited after we receive the returned merchandise.

   (A) You
   (B) Yours
   (C) Your
   (D) Yourself

3. Mr. Cameron displayed a ------- talent for the piano from his early childhood.

   (A) remarks
   (B) remarkable
   (C) remarkably
   (D) remarked

4. Home Grown charges customers' credit cards only ------- the merchandise has left the warehouse.

   (A) from
   (B) should
   (C) up
   (D) when

5. Elemental Ads is looking for managers who can ------- understand clients' needs.

   (A) intuit
   (B) intuition
   (C) intuitive
   (D) intuitively

6. Emma Decor appeals to customers ------- tastes in home furnishings are simple yet sophisticated.

   (A) that
   (B) each
   (C) whose
   (D) who

7. ------- the safety standards is a requirement for all construction projects.

   (A) Meeting
   (B) Meet
   (C) To meeting
   (D) Meets

8. After ------- closed for 2 months, the Darnell Grocery Store in Preston will finally reopen on Saturday.

   (A) has been
   (B) having been
   (C) had been
   (D) having

9. Mr. Watt has ------- as mechanical engineer in Kempten Tech for over ten years.

   (A) come
   (B) served
   (C) hired
   (D) provided

10. Company policy requires ------- all employees attend the quarterly meetings.

    (A) what
    (B) because
    (C) that
    (D) those

11. The company is looking for prospective candidates who are eager ------- and grow.

    (A) learn
    (B) to learn
    (C) learning
    (D) learned

12. The departments store's promotion will allow shoppers to ------- obtain a 10% discount or get a voucher.

    (A) unless
    (B) both
    (C) either
    (D) neither

13. This year's annual meeting was the ------- ever, with over two thousand attendees.

(A) lager
(B) largely
(C) large
(D) largest

14. ------- to the memo is a copy of the revised agenda for tomorrow's seminar.

(A) Attaching
(B) Attach
(C) Attached
(D) Attachable

Questions 15-18 refer to the following notice.

Updates on the Construction of Belgrave Road

The construction of Belgrave Road ------- to be done by October 31. However, the annual Notting Hill
15.

Carnival, which was held from last Friday to Sunday, inevitably caused a 3-day ------- in the construction
16.

schedule. -------. Local access to business and residences will be permitted throughout the construction
17.

period. -------, Kensington Park Road will continue to be directed to Westbourne Grove while the
18.

eastbound lanes on Stanley Avenue will be permanently closed to all traffic between 5th Street and 6th

Street. Other updates on the project schedule are available on the town's Web site at www.cityinfo.org.

and are kept current.

Thank you for your patience and understanding during the construction period.

---

15. (A) will be scheduled
(B) had scheduled
(C) was scheduled
(D) are being scheduled

16. (A) revision
(B) notice
(C) delay
(D) advance

17. (A) Therefore, Belgrave Road will be permanently closed from this point.
(B) As a result, Belgrave Road will be open on November 3, when the construction will be done.
(C) Local residents are not allowed to attend the festival until further notice.
(D) Please drive slowly while you pass the construction site.

18. (A) Meanwhile
(B) Regrettably
(C) At last
(D) Alternatively

풀이 시간: 7분 30초

1. Our new marketing campaign was ------- in increasing brand awareness.

   (A) success
   (B) succeed
   (C) successfully
   (D) successful

2. Ms. Lopez organized the company event from planning to execution by -------.

   (A) her
   (B) she
   (C) herself
   (D) hers

3. ------- of the team members have suggested new strategies for our marketing campaign.

   (A) Every
   (B) Some
   (C) Each
   (D) Much

4. In 2021, we ------- our operations to Europe by opening offices in Paris and Madrid.

   (A) expands
   (B) expansion
   (C) expanded
   (D) have expanded

5. Sales have increased dramatically since the new marketing strategy was -------.

   (A) implement
   (B) implemented
   (C) implementing
   (D) implements

6. The number of subscribers has risen ------- since the launch of the new service.

   (A) considering
   (B) consideration
   (C) considerable
   (D) considerably

7. ------- budget cuts, the department's expenses will decrease by 10%.

   (A) Due to
   (B) Because
   (C) Since
   (D) Unless

8. When the second quarter performance -------, we will hold a press conference.

   (A) announcement
   (B) had announced
   (C) is announced
   (D) will be announced

9. ------- have expressed their satisfaction with the company's efforts to reduce noise pollution.

   (A) Reside
   (B) Residences
   (C) Residential
   (D) Residents

10. We are dedicated to ------- customer satisfaction through quality services.

    (A) improve
    (B) improvement
    (C) improving
    (D) improved

11. The sales team exceeded their targets ------- they implemented a new marketing strategy.

    (A) since
    (B) provided
    (C) in case of
    (D) whereas

12. Due to the ------- nature of this topic, it's important to approach it with care.

    (A) appropriate
    (B) effective
    (C) careful
    (D) sensitive

13. The price of yearly subscription to *Morning Journal* will increase ----- $5.00 next month.

(A) across
(B) except
(C) onto
(D) by

14. The project manager is ------- praised for her leadership and organizational skills.

(A) widely
(B) unhappily
(C) closely
(D) separately

Questions 15-18 refer to the following e-mail.

To: Donovan Blake <d.blake@quickmail.net>
From: Customer Service
Subject: Re: Answer to your inquiry
Date: February 4

Dear Mr. Blake,

Thank you for your ------- in our program. We at Kurtosys Systems always try hard to offer the best **15.** programs to our customers. You mentioned that you would like to sign up for our new ------- program for **16.** your budget. However, we are sorry to let you know that program is not available anymore. -------. And **17.** we cannot offer the program to more than 100 customers.

Instead, we have another program in which ------- can receive a 10-percent discount for all orders over **18.** $50. If you are interested, please let me know. Then, we will send you the details of this program.

We look forward to hearing from you soon.
Thank you.

---

15. (A) interest
(B) interesting
(C) interestingly
(D) interested

16. (A) saving
(B) cooking
(C) exercise
(D) supply

17. (A) I was unable to attend the program due to a family emergency.
(B) So, there are not any alternatives that can make it up for you.
(C) You know that we tried our best to resolve this issue.
(D) 100 customers have already signed up for the program.

18. (A) you
(B) he
(C) we
(D) they

ACTUAL TEST 3

풀이 시간: 7분 30초

1. If you plan to attend the luncheon, please indicate your meal ------- on the enclosed card.

    (A) prefer
    (B) preference
    (C) preferred
    (D) preferring

2. The sunny weather last month enabled farmers in rural Cheshire to complete ------- corn planting.

    (A) they
    (B) their
    (C) them
    (D) theirs

3. Please be ------- that the terms and conditions of the contract are subject to change annually.

    (A) aware
    (B) informal
    (C) present
    (D) recognized

4. Customers ------- return to Middleton Market because of its excellent customer service.

    (A) frequence
    (B) frequently
    (C) frequent
    (D) frequency

5. At the EMI Group, we are always careful to ------- strictly to safety rules.

    (A) observe
    (B) conform
    (C) comply
    (D) follow

6. The city is ------- its public transportation system in preparation for two international trade fairs.

    (A) improves
    (B) improved
    (C) improving
    (D) improvement

7. Excel Softworks, Inc. ------- with another software company early next year.

    (A) merged
    (B) merging
    (C) to merge
    (D) will merge

8. We are sorry to let you know that we are not able ------- your order.

    (A) complete
    (B) to complete
    (C) will complete
    (D) completing

9. ------- the project has been complete, we will schedule a team meeting.

    (A) Unless
    (B) In case of
    (C) On account of
    (D) As soon as

10. The managerial position you applied for is open only to an ------- sales worker.

    (A) experience
    (B) experiencing
    (C) experienced
    (D) experiences

11. Blue National Park is a popular tourist location, ------ its mild climate can be enjoyed year round.

    (A) but
    (B) due to
    (C) and
    (D) as if

12. ------- the train arrived on time, we would have participated in the meeting.

    (A) Whether
    (B) If
    (C) Had
    (D) Regarding

13. All warehouse workers are advised that fragile items be packed ------- for shipment.

(A) slightly
(B) relatively
(C) powerlessly
(D) carefully

14. We will ------- on the charity event to raise funds for the local hospital.

(A) collaborate
(B) compete
(C) ignore
(D) oppose

Questions 15-18 refer to the following notice.

Attention, all customers:

Recently, we discovered some ------- problems with the Web site for our online store.
　　　　　　　　　　　　　　　　15.

Some customers complained about not being able to access our Web site, and after analyzing the problem, we determined that the Web site was automatically blocking ------- access by visitors. -------.
　　　　　　　　　　　　　　　　　　　　　　　　　　　　　　　　16.　　　　　　　　　**17.**

We are currently doing our best to find out the cause of this. -------, the Web site has allowed all visitors
　　　　　　　　　　　　　　　　　　　　　　　　　　　18.
access if they use the browser Wavebox. So, if you are having trouble accessing our Web site, please use a Wavebox-based browser.

Thank you for your cooperation.

15. (A) multiple
(B) financial
(C) technical
(D) social

16. (A) any
(B) some
(C) other
(D) all

17. (A) None of the visitors had a hard time accessing our online store.
(B) We have placed new ads on our Web site.
(C) Online purchases are not available in your area.
(D) We apologize for any inconvenience this problem has caused.

18. (A) In advance
(B) Accordingly
(C) Nevertheless
(D) Once

풀이 시간: 7분 30초

1. The director asked ------- assistant to book a conference room for the team meeting.

   (A) hers
   (B) she
   (C) herself
   (D) her

2. The recycling bin is located ------- the microwave for your convenience.

   (A) from
   (B) up
   (C) among
   (D) beside

3. The gym will be ------- closed for equipment upgrades this weekend.

   (A) briefly
   (B) briefest
   (C) brief
   (D) briefer

4. Next month, the new marketing campaign ------- to attract more customers.

   (A) to start
   (B) starting
   (C) will start
   (D) had started

5. ------- employees are encouraged to apply for internal promotion opportunities.

   (A) Qualification
   (B) Qualifies
   (C) Qualified
   (D) Qualify

6. We offer loyalty programs to reward our ------- customers for their continued support.

   (A) satisfied
   (B) satisfying
   (C) satisfies
   (D) satisfaction

7. The marketing team decided to delay the product ------- of the new line until the next quarter.

   (A) to launch
   (B) launchable
   (C) launch
   (D) launched

8. The CEO decided to handle the negotiations ------- to secure the best deal.

   (A) she
   (B) her
   (C) herself
   (D) hers

9. The company improved customer satisfaction ------- providing 24/7 support services.

   (A) onto
   (B) under
   (C) behind
   (D) by

10. Providing ------- feedback can lead to better team performance and morale.

    (A) constructive
    (B) constructor
    (C) construction
    (D) construct

11. ------- there were unexpected technical issues, the meeting started on time at 10:00 A.M.

    (A) Because
    (B) Even though
    (C) Unless
    (D) Until

12. To celebrate the end of the project, the team held a ------- game night for all members.

    (A) beautiful
    (B) lively
    (C) current
    (D) erasable

13. The newly updated software is ------- more user friendly than the previous version.

(A) highly
(B) much
(C) very
(D) overly

14. The study on food preferences conducted by W-Labs yields results ------- were contrary to what we expected.

(A) that
(B) who
(C) whom
(D) when

Questions 15-18 refer to the following e-mail.

To: All Council Members
From: Maurice Richard, General Manager
Date: November 18
Subject: Annual World Investment Conference

The annual world investment conference ------- this Friday in the same place where the last conference
      15.

was held: the 3rd floor of the Sibelius Center, South Wharf. ------- year, however, since the forum will be
      16.

held for a full four hours from noon to 4:00 P.M., a free lunch will be provided to every attendee during a

short break. -------, we ask all council members to reply to this e-mail indicating whether you will attend
    17.

the forum or not no later than this Wednesday so that the meals can be prepared beforehand according

to the number of attendees. -------.
    18.

Thank you in advance for your prompt reply. We look forward to seeing you on Friday.

15. (A) was held
(B) has held
(C) will be held
(D) being held

16. (A) Once
(B) This
(C) First
(D) Each

17. (A) Accordingly
(B) Otherwise
(C) Ultimately
(D) Nonetheless

18. (A) We also recommend that all members try the new dish at our restaurant.
(B) Therefore, we will prepare extra meals in case you do not give us your reply.
(C) Last year's conference lasted for three hours and did not have a lunch break.
(D) Please also indicate in your reply if a vegetarian meal is required.

1. The ------- of funds for Cowall's development project was approved by the city council at last week's meeting.

    (A) allocating
    (B) allocate
    (C) allocates
    (D) allocation

2. Luxe Interior's fees reflect the value our ------- team provides to clients.

    (A) create
    (B) creates
    (C) creatively
    (D) creative

3. Economists predict that consumer spending will increase ----- 5 and 10 percent over the next six months.

    (A) between
    (B) versus
    (C) in
    (D) about

4. Unfortunately, the data on Mr. Hopper's computer could not be -------.

    (A) retrieved
    (B) retrieve
    (C) retrieving
    (D) retrieves

5. The Tribute Museum in Philadelphia averages ------- 3,000 visitors per month.

    (A) nearer
    (B) nearly
    (C) nearest
    (D) nearing

6. Please note that the item ------- ordered from our summer catalog is no longer available.

    (A) your
    (B) yours
    (C) you
    (D) yourself

7. Because you are a valued member, we are ------- an invitation to you to join our special rewards program.

    (A) extends
    (B) extension
    (C) extending
    (D) extended

8. BizAid is an organization ------- mission is to support local communities by partnering with nonprofit organizations.

    (A) that
    (B) what
    (C) which
    (D) whose

9. ----- the building contractor, the office renovation will cost just under $10,000.

    (A) According to
    (B) Next to
    (C) Instead of
    (D) Out of

10. During the next strategy meeting, we will examine the ------- benefits of expanding into the European market.

    (A) capable
    (B) motivated
    (C) dependent
    (D) potential

11. ------- unpredictable weather conditions, flights may be canceled without prior notice.

    (A) As for
    (B) Due to
    (C) Now that
    (D) Despite

12. Ms. Keller ------ her staff members that the company's merger would benefit them.

    (A) observed
    (B) assured
    (C) denied
    (D) inspired

13. ------- the budget proposal is approved, the office will be renovated next year.

(A) Alongside of
(B) Provided that
(C) In addition to
(D) As a result of

14. ------- over 50 years ago, Apsley House is the oldest continuously operating museum in Barnet.

(A) Appeared
(B) Settled
(C) Established
(D) Originated

Questions 15-18 refer to the following notice.

Attention, all employees:

We learned that some employees have not gotten their ------- employee ID cards yet. If you have not
        15.

picked yours up yet but need to it ------- next week, please visit the Human Resources office during
        16.

business hours to pick it up. -------, all the remaining cards will be sent to each department next Monday,
        17.

so you can get yours then.

Please also note that the reissuance of an ID card is provided for free upon first request only, and it will

cost $10 the next time you request one. You will need to complete a brief request form before being

reissued an ID card as well. -------.
        18.

15. (A) extra
(B) printed
(C) online
(D) reissued

16. (A) before
(B) during
(C) after
(D) while

17. (A) Consequently
(B) Therefore
(C) Otherwise
(D) In addition

18. (A) Again, the end of next week is the earliest you can receive your ID card.
(B) We hope this will help you find your missing ID card.
(C) Therefore, it is always advisable that you be careful not to lose your ID card.
(D) Thank you for your cooperation in returning ID cards to their respective owners.

ACTUAL TEST 6

🕐 풀이 시간: 7분 30초

1. Please ------- through the entire contract before consulting Mr. Christie.

   (A) to read
   (B) read
   (C) had read
   (D) reading

2. The CEO of Nice Service ----- explained the strict standards he set for the employees.

   (A) comprehend
   (B) comprehensively
   (C) comprehensive
   (D) comprehension

3. ------- who demonstrate exceptional leadership skills will be considered for a promotion.

   (A) Those
   (B) That
   (C) These
   (D) Them

4. Electro Ltd. promises to respond to all customer complaints within 24 hours of receiving -------.

   (A) it
   (B) that
   (C) them
   (D) those

5. ------- Mr. Gurus, Mr. Cook voted against the board's proposed expansion strategy.

   (A) Unless
   (B) Moreover
   (C) Unlike
   (D) Opposed

6. Dr. Smith could not continue his project because of a ------- of research funds.

   (A) supply
   (B) direction
   (C) program
   (D) shortage

7. Until the paving work on River Road is completed, drivers ------- to use Mary Street to go downtown.

   (A) direct
   (B) directs
   (C) are directed
   (D) directed

8. With its architectural and scenic beauty, the region ------- more than half a million visitors annually.

   (A) attract
   (B) attracting
   (C) attracts
   (D) has attracted

9. Prior to ------- her financial consulting company, Ms. Moore spent more than ten years in the banking industry.

   (A) launch
   (B) to launch
   (C) launching
   (D) launched

10. Please wait to post job openings until the ----- budget has been approved.

    (A) revised
    (B) revise
    (C) revises
    (D) revision

11. Mr. Kelly said he would be ------- to give a presentation at this year's medical technology conference.

    (A) delight
    (B) delightful
    (C) delighted
    (D) delighting

12. ------- the restaurant did not offer a spectacular view of the beach, the superb food was well worth the visit.

    (A) Although
    (B) Within
    (C) Therefore
    (D) However

13. Technical support personnel are available 24 hours a day to ------- you if you have a problem with your computer.

(A) assist
(B) tell
(C) lend
(D) explain

14. Fab Café is looking for an assistant manager to oversee the evening ------- on weekdays.

(A) chance
(B) shift
(C) practice
(D) effect

Questions 15-18 refer to the following memo.

From: Howard Lee, Production Supervisor
To: All Plant Employees
Date: March 25
Subject: Reminder about the Executive's Visit

As you already know, Mr. Barrett, an executive at Rian Automotive, will make his ------- visit to the
15.
manufacturing plant to boost our morale next Friday.

Accordingly, all employees ------- to gather in the seminar room by 6:00 P.M. on Friday. -------.
16. **17.**

After the executive's brief speech of -------, a banquet will be held in the cafeteria. Please also note that
18.
this year's visit has been delayed by 5 days, and the next visit is scheduled for March 20 next year.

See you all in the seminar room next Friday.

15. (A) informal
(B) abrupt
(C) annual
(D) allowed

16. (A) advises
(B) are advised
(C) has been advised
(D) be advising

17. (A) The room can't accommodate all the participants.
(B) You are supposed to discuss the problems in the room.
(C) Those who are assigned the night shift are to participate as well.
(D) A lecture about self-development will be delivered.

18. (A) farewell
(B) encouragement
(C) apology
(D) gratitude

ACTUAL TEST 7

풀이 시간: 7분 30초

1. Many analysts are confident that our new products will ------- in the market.
   - (A) success
   - (B) successor
   - (C) successive
   - (D) succeed

2. Our warehouses across the country are stocked with a ------- of new products.
   - (A) varies
   - (B) variety
   - (C) various
   - (D) vary

3. You are entitled to a full refund within 7 days from the day of ------- purchase.
   - (A) you
   - (B) yours
   - (C) your
   - (D) yourself

4. ------- customer who purchases over $100 of goods is eligible to receive a free gift.
   - (A) All
   - (B) Every
   - (C) A few
   - (D) Little

5. Social Media 33 is well known as a ------- firm in the marketing industry.
   - (A) promised
   - (B) promise
   - (C) promises
   - (D) promising

6. If you have another opinion, do not ------- to leave a comment.
   - (A) hesitant
   - (B) hesitating
   - (C) hesitate
   - (D) hesitated

7. Ms. Mary Somerville ------- the new president of Smart Media in 2020.
   - (A) appointing
   - (B) has appointed
   - (C) was appointed
   - (D) will be appointing

8. We are looking for someone ------- has extensive knowledge of marketing strategies.
   - (A) whom
   - (B) who
   - (C) which
   - (D) whose

9. Due to the unpredictable weather, flights may be canceled ------- prior notice.
   - (A) besides
   - (B) over
   - (C) without
   - (D) unless

10. All employees are required to ------- in at least one of the training programs.
    - (A) attend
    - (B) register
    - (C) sign
    - (D) enroll

11. We help clients remain within their budgets while ------- the right apartment.
    - (A) choose
    - (B) choice
    - (C) chosen
    - (D) choosing

12. The managing director at Giant Food Stores remains ------- to any changes to the company logo.
    - (A) opposed
    - (B) anxious
    - (C) eager
    - (D) interfered

13. Applications for jobs at Global Partners will remain on file for a ------- of one year.

(A) calendar
(B) period
(C) capacity
(D) section

14. ------- your luggage remain missing for more than three days, please visit our Web site for further instructions.

(A) Had
(B) Should
(C) After
(D) During

Questions 15-18 refer to the following e-mail.

To: h.wilson@connect.net
From: cusomerservice@bellsavageinn.com
Date: December 3
Subject: Free Room Upgrade

Dear Mr. Wilson,

Thank you for being a regular guest at the Bell Savage Inn. This letter is to inform you that you are ------- to get a room upgrade at no cost on your next visit. -------.
15. **16.**

The free room upgrade is available if you get a deluxe room or something bigger. If you ------- a deluxe room, your room will be upgraded to a suite or business room.
17.

If you ------- in this offer, please fill out the attached form and send it to us by the end of the month.
18.

We look forward to seeing you soon and hope you have a great time with the upgraded room.

15. (A) likely
(B) acceptable
(C) suitable
(D) eligible

17. (A) find
(B) keep
(C) reserve
(D) browse

16. (A) Please be aware that our rates will increase next month.
(B) The dining area has been renovated and will reopen soon.
(C) Our hotel is well known for its spectacular view of the East Lyn River.
(D) Please don't miss out on this great chance by checking the detailed information below.

18. (A) will be interested
(B) are interesting
(C) interests
(D) are interested

ACTUAL TEST 8

풀이 시간: 7분 30초

1. Simply complete the enrollment form on our Web site or call our customer service line at 708-555-0115 for -------.

   (A) assistants
   (B) assists
   (C) assisting
   (D) assistance

2. After examining several competitive products on the market, Mr. Crates decided to purchase one of -------.

   (A) us
   (B) our
   (C) ours
   (D) ourselves

3. Maintenance of the walks in Sarek Park is made ------- thanks to substantial donations from several organizations.

   (A) clear
   (B) possible
   (C) generous
   (D) honorary

4. According to PCL Electronics' policy, employees must ------- request vacation time at least one month in advance.

   (A) formal
   (B) formality
   (C) formalize
   (D) formally

5. More than 500 people ------- over 20 nations participated in the 3rd International Environment Forum.

   (A) toward
   (B) beside
   (C) from
   (D) off

6. The Arizona Tourism Authority reported that opening the convention center will ------- hundreds of jobs in the city.

   (A) agree
   (B) create
   (C) arrive
   (D) refer

7. The National Olive Theater is one of Redwood's most treasured historic landmarks and needs -------.

   (A) preserve
   (B) to preserve
   (C) to being preserved
   (D) to be preserved

8. As soon as the Sales Department received approval, the team ------- recruiting additional sales clerks.

   (A) has begun
   (B) began
   (C) were beginning
   (D) begin

9. After the impressive performance, audience members were ------- to stay for a brief survey.

   (A) asked
   (B) continued
   (C) depended
   (D) accomplished

10. The government has made a more ------- effort to find ways to solve the continuing unemployment problem.

    (A) last
    (B) lastly
    (C) lasted
    (D) lasting

11. Products with any problems will be replaced, ------- you will be fully refunded for the original purchase.

    (A) nor
    (B) but
    (C) instead of
    (D) or

12. ------- Mr. Wang has transferred to the Paris headquarters, a new manager is responsible for our Hong Kong office.

    (A) Now that
    (B) In case of
    (C) Considering that
    (D) Furthermore

13. The CEO stated ------- addressing customer concerns consistently was one crucial element for the company's success.

(A) that
(B) what
(C) who
(D) which

14. The laboratory manual details our procedures for handling materials as ------- as possible.

(A) safety
(B) safely
(C) safe
(D) safest

Questions 15-18 refer to the following memo.

To: All employees
From: Tom Clift, Executive
Date: August 7
Subject: Comments on the Retirement Party

Dear employees,

Thank you all for great preparations you did at the ------- retirement party for Mr. Garcia on his last day at
15.
Catalyst Pharmaceuticals. He ------- enjoyed the party and thanks each of you for making the day filled
16.
with unforgettable moments.

Mr. Garcia was a very passionate and diligent man, and without his dedication, the company would not
have been able to get to where it is now. -------. Catalyst Pharmaceuticals will always remember his
17.
service and contributions.

Although Mr. Garcia ------- the company, his spirit will remain here. Let us encourage him to continue
18.
supporting Catalyst Pharmaceuticals as we strive for excellence.

15. (A) upcoming
(B) approaching
(C) past
(D) ultimate

16. (A) probably
(B) preferably
(C) gradually
(D) truly

17. (A) Thanks to his cooperation, we may be able to extend our partnership.
(B) Therefore, we would like everyone to attend the retirement party to say farewell.
(C) He will be done for long periods of time until he resumes his work here.
(D) He sincerely served the company as a senior sales manager for 30 years.

18. (A) has left
(B) will leave
(C) is leaving
(D) was leaving

풀이 시간: 7분 30초

1. To cut production -------, KG Electronics has purchased state-of-the-art assembly machines that will reduce the need for human labor.

   (A) values
   (B) profits
   (C) costs
   (D) outcomes

2. The president of Oak Office Furniture hires salespeople who enjoy helping ------- with their office design needs.

   (A) ones
   (B) others
   (C) any
   (D) that

3. Before our manufacturing team creates a product, we need to be certain that the prototype is ------- to the client.

   (A) accepts
   (B) accepting
   (C) acceptable
   (D) acceptance

4. Better Furniture's annual meeting went ------- thanks to the collaboration of the various departments involved.

   (A) smoothly
   (B) entirely
   (C) justly
   (D) tightly

5. ------- the recent survey, the price of property in the area rose by 15 percent last year.

   (A) Instead of
   (B) Whether
   (C) According to
   (D) Upon

6. Excessive waste of raw materials during production ------- profits to decline at Pepsico Industries Ltd.

   (A) were caused
   (B) has caused
   (C) have been caused
   (D) to have caused

7. Please be ------- that the book you ordered from our summer catalog is no longer in print.

   (A) advise
   (B) advising
   (C) advised
   (D) advice

8. The president requested that Mr. Gruber ------- all available options for reducing operating costs of his office.

   (A) to investigate
   (B) has investigated
   (C) investigate
   (D) is investigating

9. Ms. Haselton is highly qualified, so I have no problem ------- her for the position with DHL Chemicals.

   (A) recommend
   (B) to recommend
   (C) recommending
   (D) recommended

10. The ------- initiative aims to provide public transportation for commuters living in the outer suburbs.

    (A) proposed
    (B) proposing
    (C) proposal
    (D) propose

11. Toray Group Holdings announced in a press release ------- it is planning to expand into South America.

    (A) which
    (B) that
    (C) whom
    (D) what

12. ------- purchases of over 1,000 dollars are exempt from shipping charges, value added taxes still apply.

    (A) However
    (B) Because
    (C) Although
    (D) Nonetheless

13. ------- the two companies will merge to become the largest food manufacturer or not remains to be seen.

(A) How
(B) Either
(C) Unless
(D) Whether

14. Gottlieb Steen Industries will expand its production floor ------- buy a new facility.

(A) at first
(B) rather than
(C) with reference to
(D) for instance

Questions 15-18 refer to the following notice.

At Technova Solutions, we take employee ------- seriously. When severe weather is expected, we monitor
15.
the event closely. If conditions are expected to become potentially hazardous, an office closure may be

necessary.

Shift supervisors are responsible for communicating closures to team members. -------. Employees
16.
------- their regular pay for any hours they were scheduled to work during a closure. When the company
17.
reopens, they must return ------- for their next scheduled shift. Please contact supervisors if you have
18.
any questions about company closures.

15. (A) safety
(B) satisfaction
(C) compensation
(D) recommendation

16. (A) Severe weather cannot always be predicted.
(B) Fortunately, there were no closures at all last year.
(C) This policy is under review and is subject to change.
(D) Every effort will be made to ensure all employees get the message.

17. (A) received
(B) will receive
(C) have received
(D) had been receiving

18. (A) to work
(B) working
(C) the work
(D) workable

🕐 풀이 시간: 7분 30초

1. On the ------- of a financial consultant, we reorganized our accounting system.

   (A) adviser
   (B) advice
   (C) advisory
   (D) advised

2. Mr. Curtis has provided ------- guidelines on how to implement the new policy measures.

   (A) specify
   (B) specific
   (C) specifics
   (D) specifically

3. All new hires will receive a copy of the employee ------- at the orientation session.

   (A) authority
   (B) handbook
   (C) locker
   (D) lunchroom

4. The renovation of the Greenbrier Hotel's main lobby ------- to begin later this month.

   (A) schedule
   (B) schedules
   (C) has scheduled
   (D) is scheduled

5. Some new software has been installed in our office, ------- it is not yet operational.

   (A) which
   (B) but
   (C) whether
   (D) than

6. It is a company ------- for employees to wear their ID badges while at the company.

   (A) require
   (B) requires
   (C) requiring
   (D) requirement

7. Employees are ------- to use the copier on the second floor until our machine is repaired.

   (A) adjusted
   (B) instructed
   (C) responded
   (D) respected

8. The enclosed brochure details the company's progress in boosting -------.

   (A) secure
   (B) secures
   (C) security
   (D) securely

9. All incoming packages requiring a signature must be ------- to the reception desk in the Ritz Tower.

   (A) handled
   (B) responded
   (C) delivered
   (D) checked

10. The Fairfield Clinic is being redesigned to -------- capacity while improving patient care.

    (A) maximize
    (B) specialize
    (C) summarize
    (D) visualize

11. Reducing operating expenses is a top ------- for Chief Financial Officer Jamie Brooks.

    (A) incident
    (B) excellence
    (C) priority
    (D) imagination

12. TVC News Channel reported incorrectly that Mayfair's new parking signs had ------- been installed.

    (A) highly
    (B) hourly
    (C) already
    (D) every

13. The high efficiency fridges from Atlantic Electrics use 25 percent less energy than ------- refrigerators.

(A) reasonable
(B) individual
(C) responsible
(D) conventional

14. The executive board responded ------- to Mr. Webb's proposal than to any of the others.

(A) as positively
(B) positively
(C) more positively
(D) most positively

Questions 15-18 refer to the following information.

The East Camphill Civil Center is ------- located within easy walking distance of East Camphill's historic
15.
downtown district. East Camphill residents play an active role in ------- the quality of life of everyone in
16.
the community through various volunteer programs provided by the civil center. Volunteers can be seen
in every aspect of community life, including the arts, education, and city government. East Camphill
benefits from the ------- of those who are willing to share their time and talents. -------. If you would like to
17. **18.**
become a volunteer, please call us at 7739-8066.

15. (A) conveniently
(B) exactly
(C) approximately
(D) almost

16. (A) maintain
(B) to maintain
(C) maintaining
(D) maintenance

17. (A) privilege
(B) responsibility
(C) obligation
(D) generosity

18. (A) Various classes and programs were previously provided.
(B) Please consider joining our volunteer programs.
(C) We currently have a vacancy in the sales division.
(D) You'll find lots of entertainment events to add to your calendar.

PART

7

독해

단일·이중·삼중 지문을 읽고 그에 따른 2~5개의 문제를 푸는 유형으로, 총 15개 지문, 54문제가 출제된다.

구성	PART	유형		문항 수	시간	배점
Reading Comprehension	5	단문 빈칸 채우기 (문법/어휘)		30	75분	495점
	6	장문 빈칸 채우기		16		
	7	독해	단일 지문	29		
			이중 지문	10		
			삼중 지문	15		

문제 유형

- **주제/목적**   주제 또는 목적과 같이 지문의 핵심적인 내용을 파악해야 한다.
- **세부사항**   의문사로 시작해 특정 정보를 묻는 유형으로, 지문에서 질문의 키워드와 관련된 부분을 찾아 정답을 고른다.
- **NOT/TRUE (사실 확인)**   지문 내용 중 보기와 일치하는 것과 아닌 것을 확인하는 유형으로, 오답 보기를 소거하며 푸는 것이 좋다.
- **추론**   지문의 내용을 바탕으로 전체 흐름을 이해하며 지문에 직접 언급되지 않은 사항을 추론해야 한다.
- **화자 의도 파악**   특정 표현에 숨겨진 화자의 의도를 묻는 유형으로, 문자 메시지나 2인 이상의 온라인 채팅 지문에서 출제된다.
- **동의어**   주어진 단어의 사전적 의미가 아니라 문맥상 의미를 파악하여 대체될 수 있는 동의어를 골라야 한다.
- **문장 삽입**   지문의 흐름상 주어진 문장이 들어갈 적절한 위치를 고르는 유형으로, 세부적인 정보보다 전체적인 문맥 파악이 중요하다.

최신 출제 경향

① 지문에서 보기의 정답 근거를 일일이 확인할 필요가 있는 사실 확인 유형의 비중이 늘고 있다.
② 지문에 나와 있는 정보를 토대로 추론해야 풀 수 있는 유형의 비중이 증가하고 있다.
③ 동의어 찾기 유형은 매회 1~4 문제의 출제 비율을 유지하고 있다.

만점 전략

① 지문의 앞부분을 훑어보며 기본적인 정보를 확인한다.
② 질문을 먼저 읽고, 키워드를 표시하며 지문에서 어느 부분을 신경 써서 읽어야 할지 대략적으로 파악해 둔다.
③ 지문을 읽으며 글의 제목이나 본문에 언급된 특정 자격이나 조건 또는 사람 이름이나 회사/제품명 같은 고유명사를 키워드로 표시해 둔다.
④ 지문에서 파악한 내용과 보기 (A)~(D)를 대조하여 정답을 찾는다.

 **풀이 전략**

To: Robert Graham <george@grahamgym.com>
From: Grace Lewis <glewis@linkedmail.net>
Date: March 26
Subject: Fitness Center Membership

Dear Mr. Graham,

This e-mail is in response to your letter of March 14, which stated that my membership at your fitness center will expire on March 31. I wish to let you know that I have chosen not to renew it.

When I first became a member, the cost was $30 per month. Now, the cost is $55 per month. Aside from this significant increase in cost, I have been dissatisfied with some of the services at the fitness center. There never seems to be enough equipment available for use at peak hours during the day. In addition, many of the new aerobics classes that I registered for were canceled due to low attendance.

Sincerely,

Grace Lewis

147. Why did Ms. Lewis send the e-mail?
  (A) To explain why she will not renew her membership
  (B) To recommend an increase in the staff
  (C) To ask for information about the center
  (D) To report that a machine is not working

148. What is NOT one of Ms. Lewis's concerns?
  (A) Fitness equipment is sometimes unavailable.
  (B) Some aerobics classes were canceled.
  (C) The membership fees are too high.
  (D) The fitness trainers are inexperienced.

주제/목적 문제 ◑ 주제와 목적은 지문의 첫 단락에 등장하는 경우가 대부분이다. 따라서 지문의 첫 부분에 특히 집중하여 읽어야 한다.

첫 번째 단락의 마지막 문장 "I wish to let you know that I have chosen not to renew it"에서 회원권을 갱신하지 않겠다고 밝히고, 두 번째 단락에서 그 이유를 상세히 설명하고 있으므로 (A)가 정답이다.

NOT/TRUE 문제 ◑ 모든 보기의 내용을 지문과 대조하여 오답 보기를 하나씩 소거해 가며 정답을 찾는다.

두 번째 단락 "There never seems to be enough equipment available for use at peak hours during the day"를 통해 (A)를, "In addition, many of the new aerobics classes that I registered for were canceled due to low attendance"를 통해 (B)를, "When I first became a member, ~ $55 per month."를 통해 (C)를 확인할 수 있지만, 헬스 트레이너에 대한 언급은 없으므로 (D)가 정답이다.

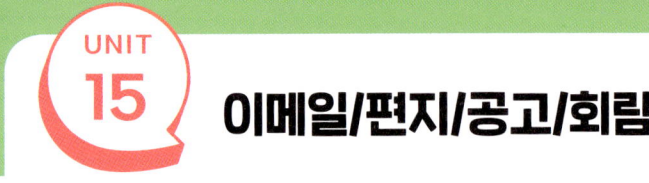

UNIT 15 이메일/편지/공고/회람

1. 이메일/편지

유형 소개 및 전략

이메일/편지는 PART 7에서 가장 많이 출제되는 지문 유형으로, 매회 평균 3~4개 이상 출제된다. 주로 격식을 갖춘 서신이나 회사의 행사 및 업무, 시설이나 설비에 관한 내용, 서비스에 대한 불만 또는 사과, 칭찬/감사 그리고 서비스에 대한 문의/답변 혹은 합격 통보 같은 내용이 자주 나온다. 글의 흐름은 일반적으로 주제/목적 → 세부사항 → 추가 안내/요청사항 순서로 전개된다.

기출 질문

1) 목적

What is the purpose of this letter? 편지의 목적은 무엇인가?
Why was the e-mail written? 왜 이메일이 쓰였는가?

2) 동봉

What is enclosed [included] with this letter? 편지와 함께 동봉된 것은 무엇인가?

3) 요청 및 부탁

What is Mr. Bell asked to do? Bell 씨는 무엇을 하도록 요청 받는가?

4) 세부사항

Why does Ms. Shelley request a refund? Shelley 씨는 왜 환불을 요구하는가?
When is the deadline for this application? 신청 마감일은 언제인가?

풀이 접근법

● 이메일/편지의 일반적인 전개 순서를 알아둔다. 특히, **수신인과 발신인의 정보를 정확히 파악한다.**

● 목적을 묻는 문제는 보통 초반부에 단서가 등장한다.

● 당부 및 요청 사항을 묻는 문제의 단서는 대부분 지문 후반부에 있으며, 특정 표현이 자주 사용되므로 알아 두자.

● 시간이나 날짜와 같은 세부사항을 묻는 문제의 단서는 보통 지문 속에서 시간을 나타내는 부사구와 함께 언급되므로 다른 문제보다 수월하게 정답을 고를 수 있다. 단, 지문에서 두 개 이상의 시간이나 날짜가 언급되는 경우가 있으므로 조심해야 한다.

🟰 빈출 표현 및 어휘

이메일/편지 단서 표현

I'm writing to V ~하기 위해 편지를 씁니다.

This letter is to V 이 편지는 ~하기 위한 것입니다.

We are please to announce ~ ~을 알리게 되어 기쁩니다.

This is to inform you that ~
이 편지는 ~을 알리기 위한 것입니다.

I would appreciate it if you ~
당신이 ~한다면 감사하겠습니다.

Please let me know if you ~
당신이 ~한다면 알려주세요.

Enclosed [Attached] is/are ~
~가 동봉[첨부]되어 있습니다.

사무

accurate 정확한
administrative 관리의
appointment 임명
assignment 할당, 업무
assume 떠맡다, 가정하다
colleague (= coworker) 동료
complete 완성하다; 완전한
meet a deadline 마감일을 맞추다
prepare 준비하다
representative 직원, 대표
request 요청하다
revise 수정하다
submit 제출하다
task 업무

불만/문제

apology 사과
breakage 파손
cancel 취소하다
complaint 불평
concern 걱정, 염려; 관련시키다
damaged 손상된
defective (= faulty) 결함 있는
exchange 교환; 교환하다
explain 설명하다
inconvenience 불편
postpone (= delay) 미루다
refund 환불; 환불하다
repair 수리; 수리하다
sincere 진심의

감사/축하

accomplished 뛰어난
achieve 달성하다
appreciate 감사히 여기다
award 수여하다
celebrate 축하하다
commitment 헌신, 약속
contribute 공헌하다
donation 기부
hold 열다, 개최하다
impressed 감명받은
pleased (= delighted, glad) 즐거운
reason 이유
recognize 인정하다
retirement 은퇴

출장/여행

accommodations 숙소
belongings 소지품
destination 목적지
book 예약하다
board 탑승하다
departure 출발
expense 비용
itinerary 여행 일정표
passport 여권
reservation 예약
round trip 왕복 여행
take off 이륙하다
tourist attraction 관광 명소
travel agent 여행사 직원

구매/주문

account 계정, 계좌
brochure (= booklet) 소책자
bulk 대량
clarify 명확히 하다
confirm 확인하다
include 포함하다
method 방법
parcel 소포
purchase 구매; 구매하다
receipt 영수증, 수령
respond 응답하다
status 상태, 지위
warehouse 창고
valued (= valuable) 소중한

추천

beneficial 유익한
compliment 칭찬하다
confident 자신감 있는
effective 효과적인
encourage 격려하다
experienced (= skilled) 노련한
expertise 전문 지식
highly 매우
prefer 선호하다
qualified 자격이 있는
recommend 추천하다
a record + N 기록적인 ~
reliable 믿을 만한
reputation 명성, 평판

RC PART 7

To: Marley Shelton 받는 사람: Marley Shelton
From: Adam Peaty 보내는 사람: Adam Peaty
Date: June 25 날짜: 6월 25일
Subject: Apology 주제: 사과

Dear Ms. Shelton,
Shelton 씨께,

Thank you for taking the time to call our customer service line.
저희 고객센터에 시간을 내어 전화 주셔서 감사합니다.

First, I would like to apologize for the horrible experience you had when you visited the Fiola's Restaurant at the Hampton Hotel on June 18.
먼저 6월 18일에 저희 Hampton 호텔의 Fiola's 레스토랑을 방문하여 불쾌한 경험을 하셨다니 사과의 말씀을 드립니다.

I want you to know that I personally have handled this situation and there will be no further issues. While I cannot change what happened to you and your family on that day, I can offer you a free meal for three when you come again. We have been servicing the Washington area for more than 20 years.
이번 일은 제가 별도로 처리하였으며, 다시는 이런 일이 일어나지 않을 것입니다. 하지만 그날 고객님과 가족분들에게 일어났던 일을 되돌릴 수 없기에, 다시 방문하실 때 무료 식사 3인분을 제공하겠습니다. 저희는 워싱턴 지역에서 20년 넘게 식당을 운영해 오고 있습니다.

I hope that you will receive better service in the future. If there should be any more problems, please don't hesitate to call me directly.
앞으로 더 나은 서비스를 받으실 수 있을 것이며, 혹시 어떠한 추가적인 문제가 생기거든 주저하지 말고 바로 전화 주십시오.

Sincerely,

Adam Peaty
F&B Manager, Fiola's Restaurant
안녕히 계세요,
Adam Peaty
F&B 매니저 Fiola's 레스토랑

목적
'I would like to ~' 표현을 통해 이메일의 목적을 표현하고 있다.

세부사항
'offer A B(A에게 B를 제공하다)' 표현으로 고객에게 제공할 보상을 설명하고 있다.

요청사항
Please가 쓰이면 보통 수신자에게 요청하는 내용이 나온다.

발신자 정보
이메일 하단에 이름, 직책, 회사명 등의 정보가 언급된다.

이메일 도입부에 수신자(받는 사람), 발신자(보내는 사람), 발신 날짜, 제목(이메일의 주제, 목적)이 제시된다.

Questions 1-2 refer to the following e-mail.

To: Marley Shelton
From: Adam Peaty
Date: June 25
Subject: Apology

Dear Ms. Shelton,

Thank you for taking the time to call our customer service line.

First, I would like to apologize for the horrible experience you had when you visited Fiola's Restaurant at the Hampton Hotel on June 18.

I want you to know that I personally have handled this situation and that there will be no further issues. While I cannot change what happened to you and your family on that day, I can offer you a free meal for three when you come again. We have been servicing the Washington area for more than 20 years.

I hope that you receive better service in the future. If there should be any more problems, please don't hesitate to call me directly.

Sincerely,

Adam Peaty
F&B Manager, Fiola's Restaurant

---

1. What is the main purpose of the e-mail?

   (A) To offer a free meal
   (B) To apologize to a customer
   (C) To describe a restaurant's recent business
   (D) To thank a customer for providing feedback

2. What does Mr. Peaty say he will do?

   (A) Give a voucher for a free gift to Ms. Shelton
   (B) Give a free meal to Ms. Shelton's family
   (C) Provide his workers with adequate training
   (D) Give a discount on any food that Ms. Shelton orders

2. 공고/회람

☰ 유형 소개 및 전략

공고는 회사, 공공장소, 공공기관 등에서의 행사나 정책에 대한 세부사항이나 변경사항을 알리는 내용이 다뤄지며 매회 1~2개 이상 출제된다. 회람은 업무 관련 정보를 직원들에게 전달하기 위해 보내는 짧은 메시지로, 이메일과 형식이 비슷하고, 매회 1개 이상 출제된다.

☰ 기출 질문

1) 주제/목적

What is the purpose of this notice/memo? 공고/회람의 목적은 무엇인가?

What is being announced? 무엇이 안내되고 있는가?

What is mainly discussed in the memo? 회람에서 주로 논의되는 것은 무엇인가?

For whom is the notice intended? 공고는 누구를 대상으로 하는가?

Where would the notice most likely be found? 공고는 어디서 볼 수 있을 것 같은가?

2) 세부사항/요청사항

According to the memo, what will be held on weekends? 회람에 따르면, 주말에 무엇이 열릴 것인가?

What are the employees asked to do? 직원들은 무엇을 하도록 요청받는가?

☰ 풀이 접근법

● 공고와 회람에서 반복적으로 등장하는 어휘와 표현을 익혀둔다.

● 공고는 주제, 목적, 대상을 묻는 문제가 주로 출제된다. 공고의 주제나 목적은 대부분 첫 문장이나 첫 단락에 나온다. 공고 대상을 묻는 문제는 전반적인 내용을 알아야 풀 수 있는 경우가 대부분이므로 다른 문제를 먼저 푼 후 마지막에 푸는 것이 좋다.

● 회람은 주제, 목적을 묻는 문제가 기본적으로 출제된다. 주제, 목적은 이메일처럼 Subject(주제), RE(= regarding ~에 관하여) 부분에 나와 있는 경우가 많으므로 이 부분을 통해서 정답을 찾을 수 있다.

☰ 빈출 표현/어휘

공고	회람
pay raise (= salary increase) 급여 인상	make arrangements for ~을 계획하다, 준비하다
benefits 수당, 복지 혜택	defer (= delay, postpone, put off) 연기하다
be on probation 수습[견습] 기간 중이다	reschedule 일정을 변경하다
probational period 수습 기간	tentative schedule 잠정적인 계획
be on duty 근무 중이다	cancelation 취소
work from home 재택근무하다	leave a message 메시지를 남기다
keynote address (= keynote speech) 기조연설	take a message 메시지를 받다
reduce the workforce 인력을 감축하다	voice mail 음성 메일
lay off 해고하다	extension (number) (전화의) 내선, 구내번호
off-limits 출입 금지의	be under warranty 보증기간 중이다
repository 저장실, 창고	directly report to 바로 ~로 보고하다

패러프레이징 표현

지문 reusable tableware 재사용 가능한 식탁 용품
보기 reusable plates and untensils 재사용 가능한 접시와 식기

지문 launching its tenth branch 10번째 지점의 개점
보기 An additional store will be opened. 추가 매장이 오픈합니다.

지문 He has worked for almost 30 years. 그는 거의 30년 동안 일했다.
보기 He has worked for the company for decades. 그는 수십 년 동안 근무했다.

지문 close to the warehouse 창고와 가까운
보기 near the storage facility 저장 시설과 가까운

지문 sophisticated equipment 정교한 장비
보기 modern equipment 현대적 장비

지문 a variety of light refreshments 다양한 가벼운 다과
보기 a selection of appetizers 다양한 전채 (애피타이저)

지문 her regular Monday meeting 그녀의 월요일 정기 모임
보기 She participates in a meeting every Monday. 그녀는 매주 월요일마다 회의에 참석한다.

지문 one of the state's leading companies 주 최고의 기업 중 하나
보기 It has a major presence in the state. 그곳은 주에서 주요 입지를 구축하고 있다.

지문 It drew a sizable crowd. 상당한 군중을 끌어들였다.
보기 The event was well attended. 그 행사는 참석자가 많았다.

지문 portable items 휴대용 품목
보기 They are packable. 수납이 가능하다.

지문 stick around for many years 몇 년 동안 머무르다
보기 stay with the company over the long term 장기적으로 회사에 머무르다

지문 The coupon can be redeemed. 쿠폰을 사용할 수 있다.
보기 The coupon is valid [good] for use. 쿠폰은 유효하다.

지문 customer referral 고객 추천
보기 customers invite others to shop with us 고객들이 다른 사람들에게 우리 매장에서 쇼핑하도록 하다

RC PART 7

NOTICE 공지

The annual sales meeting of Starlight Metal Industrials will be held in Richmond, Virginia, on September 6.

9월 6일 버지니아의 리치몬드에서 Starlight Metal Industrials 사의 연례 영업 회의가 열릴 것입니다.

All major shareholders and company representatives are invited to attend.

모든 대주주님과 회사 임원들은 참석해 주시길 바랍니다.

We will be celebrating the achievements of the sales team. Those who cannot attend can participate by video conferencing through the company's Web site. A transcript of the meeting will be available to the general public within forty-eight hours of the meeting.

우리는 영업팀의 실적을 축하할 것입니다. 참석할 수 없으신 분들은 회사의 웹사이트를 통해 화상 회의로 참여할 수 있습니다. 회의가 열리고 48시간 이내에 일반인들도 회의록을 볼 수 있을 겁니다.

Please **call** 585-493-4848 for further information.

추가 정보가 필요하신 분은 585-493-4848로 전화 주십시오.

주제
공고의 주제는 첫 문장이나 첫 단락에서 제시된다.

공고 대상
회의에 참석해야 하는 대상을 언급하고 있다.

세부사항
회의 주제를 알리고, 회의에 참석할 수 없는 사람들에게 대안을 제시하고 있다.

call, contact 등의 단어 앞뒤에 연락 가능한 시간 또는 문의 방법이 언급된다.

Questions 3-4 refer to the following notice.

NOTICE

The annual sales meeting of Starlight Metal Industrials will be held in Richmond, Virginia, on September 6. All major shareholders and company representatives are invited to attend.

We will be celebrating the achievements of the sales team. Those who cannot attend can participate by video conferencing through the company's Web site. A transcript of the meeting will be available to the general public within forty-eight hours of the meeting.

Please call 585-493-4848 for further information.

---

3. Who is NOT invited to the meeting?

(A) The board of directors

(B) People who own a lot of shares

(C) Starlight Metal Industrials' business partner

(D) Sales team members

4. How can people who do not attend the meeting participate in it?

(A) By watching it through the Internet

(B) By calling the meeting organizers

(C) By canceling their reservations

(D) By going to the Richmond

ACTUAL TEST

Questions 1-2 refer to the following e-mail.

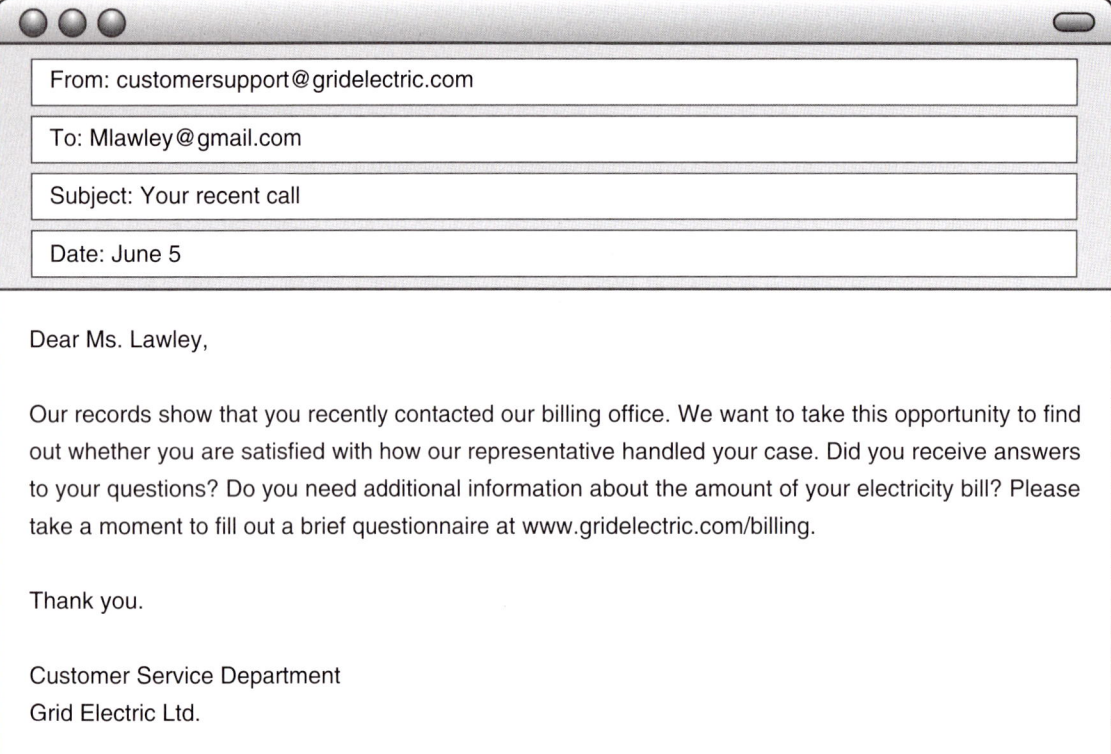

From: customersupport@gridelectric.com

To: Mlawley@gmail.com

Subject: Your recent call

Date: June 5

Dear Ms. Lawley,

Our records show that you recently contacted our billing office. We want to take this opportunity to find out whether you are satisfied with how our representative handled your case. Did you receive answers to your questions? Do you need additional information about the amount of your electricity bill? Please take a moment to fill out a brief questionnaire at www.gridelectric.com/billing.

Thank you.

Customer Service Department
Grid Electric Ltd.

1. What is the purpose of the e-mail?

(A) To suggest ways to save money
(B) To advertise a new service
(C) To confirm a repair date
(D) To request an opinion

2. What did Ms. Lawley probably inquire about?

(A) Opportunities for employment
(B) Payments for electrical service
(C) The cause of a recent power failure
(D) Directions to Grid Electric Ltd.

Questions 3-4 refer to the following letter.

Metro National Bank

12 Queens St, GLA

1-322-221-2860

Charline Turner
17 Oxford Road
GLA city

October 15

Dear Mr. Turner,

Thank you for activating your Metro National Bank credit card. One of the most popular benefits enjoyed by Metro National Bank customers is our online account management system. This system gives account holders access to up-to-date account information 24 hours a day from any computer, tablet, or smartphone. If you haven't already done so, be sure to go to www.metronationalbank.ca to sign up today.

We've enclosed a convenient summary guide to help you get started.

Sincerely,

Jessica Bailey
Customer Service Representative

Enclosure

---

3. Why was the letter sent?

   (A) To explain how to activate an account
   (B) To gather customer opinions
   (C) To promote an available service
   (D) To announce a new Web site

4. What was sent with the letter?

   (A) Instructions
   (B) Forms to fill out
   (C) A credit card
   (D) A billing statement

Questions 5-6 refer to the following e-mail.

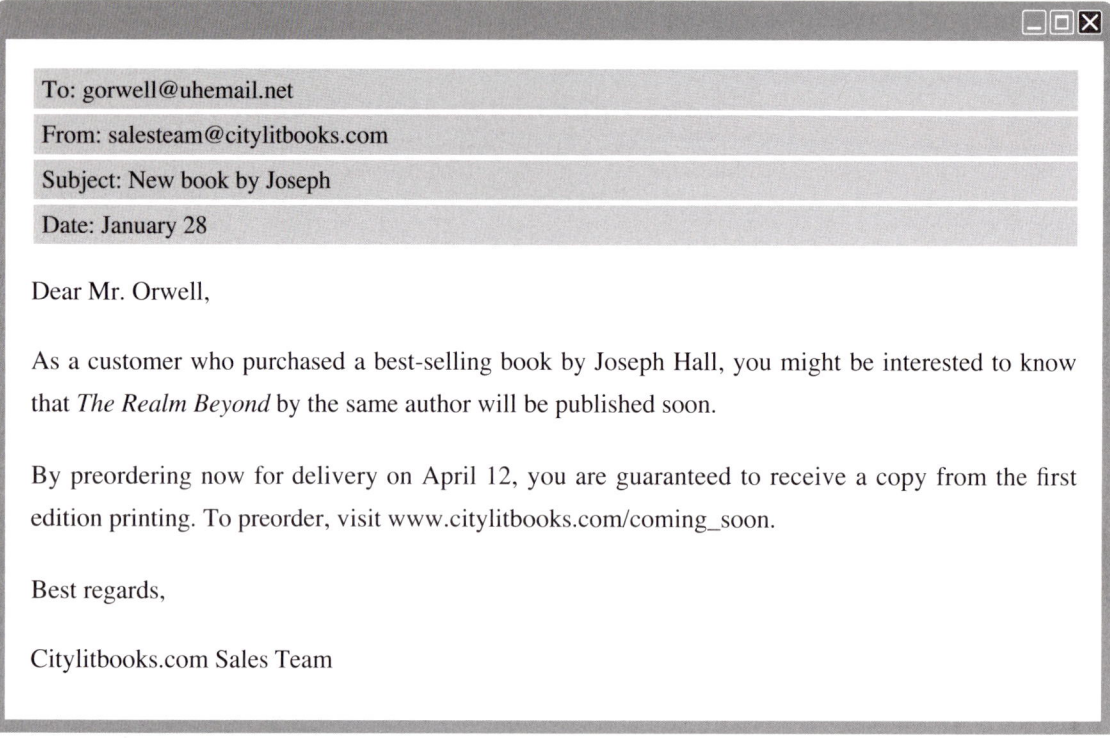

To: gorwell@uhemail.net

From: salesteam@citylitbooks.com

Subject: New book by Joseph

Date: January 28

Dear Mr. Orwell,

As a customer who purchased a best-selling book by Joseph Hall, you might be interested to know that *The Realm Beyond* by the same author will be published soon.

By preordering now for delivery on April 12, you are guaranteed to receive a copy from the first edition printing. To preorder, visit www.citylitbooks.com/coming_soon.

Best regards,

Citylitbooks.com Sales Team

5. Why was the e-mail sent?

(A) To confirm a purchase
(B) To advertise a product
(C) To announce a book tour
(D) To request a customer review

6. What is indicated about *The Realm Beyond*?

(A) It is not yet available.
(B) It has already sold out.
(C) It is a best-selling title.
(D) It has been reviewed on a Web site.

Questions 7-8 refer to the following notice.

Sixth Annual Dinos Book Convention

Main Plaza

September 23-24, 9:00 A.M. to 5:00 P.M.

We welcome all of you to the Sixth Annual Dinos Book Convention sponsored by the Dinos Public Library. Booklovers of all ages may join this event and spend a good time with family or friends. There will be various events such as poetry readings, author interviews, book introduction, and signings. This year, we have invited the following guests:

• Elena Hutts, author of *Mommy Tells the Best Fairy Tales*

• James Castellano, author of *The Greatness of the Renaissance Era*

• Cindy Houston, screenwriter and author of *Time Is Up*

• Elise Pierna, musical director of *Within Me, Outside You*

The Dinos Book Convention is a free event for anyone to join. For more information about this year's events, please visit www.dinosconvention.com/eventlist.

7. What is indicated about the book convention?

(A) It is offered six times a year.
(B) It is held at the Dinos Public Library.
(C) It is available by invitation only.
(D) It is intended for children and adults.

8. Who most likely will discuss a historical topic?

(A) Elena Hutts
(B) James Castellano
(C) Cindy Houston
(D) Elise Pierna

Questions 9-11 refer to the following memo.

Memo

From: Cole McQueen, President

To: Allbirds Holdings Employees

Date: September 27

Re: Meeting in November

You are invited to attend an exploratory meeting to discuss plans for our company's new space on the fifth floor. Micro Research, which was formerly on the fifth floor, has relocated, and our company has decided to lease the newly available space.

We are planning for the space to include a new multimedia conference room and a fitness center for employees. Before hiring a contractor, we would like to hear from you about what you would like to see in the fitness center.

For example, would you prefer state-of-the-art exercise equipment or more open space?

To contribute your ideas to the project, join us in the cafeteria on November 7 at 2:00 P.M.

If you are unable to attend, you may e-mail your suggestions to Simon in the Human Resources Department by tomorrow.

9. What is the purpose of the memo?

(A) To get suggestions from employees
(B) To review new attendance policy
(C) To recruit volunteers for an upcoming event
(D) To select a contractor for the renovation of a building

10. What is Allbirds Holdings planning to do?

(A) Change its name
(B) Relocate to a new city
(C) Hire several employees
(D) Lease more office space

11. Where will the meeting be held?

(A) In the conference room
(B) In the cafeteria
(C) In the Human Resources office
(D) In the fitness center

Questions 12-13 refer to the following notice.

Road Enhancements Near MidFirst Bank

Road enhancements on Scottsdale Street are scheduled to begin next Tuesday. The repair job will include traffic signal installation, sewer replacement, stairway repair, and concrete work on curbs and sidewalks.

Because of safety concerns, the main entrance to MidFirst Bank will not be accessible for two days from May 23. We suggest that MidFirst Bank employees and customers use the back entrance on Van Buren Street.

In addition, the renovation project might cause noise and dust which will bother you. We would appreciate your understanding.

12. Why was the notice written?
(A) To report the replacement of an old door
(B) To describe some changes to a company's policies
(C) To announce the temporary closure of a door
(D) To update employees on a new business project

13. What can be inferred about MidFirst Bank?
(A) It is going to relocate on Tuesday.
(B) Its main door is on Scottsdale Street.
(C) It has retained many regular customers.
(D) The repair work on it will take more than a week.

Questions 14-16 refer to the following notice.

Havertys Furniture Exchange Policy

— [1] —. If you're not totally satisfied with your purchase, you can exchange any item within 30 days. — [2] —. But don't forget that exchanges must be accompanied by the original receipt. Return your merchandise with your receipt to the store and select new furniture. You will also be required to present a valid photo ID. — [3] —. Information from your ID will be retained in a company-wide database to be used only for authorizing exchanges. — [4] —.

If you would like to have your merchandise picked up, please contact the Havertys Furniture customer service center at 888-428-3789. Our operating hours are from 8:00 A.M. to 7:00 P.M. In all cases, exchange delivery fees will apply.

---

14. What is true about the company's exchange policy?

(A) Products purchased online are ineligible.
(B) It doesn't apply to sold-out merchandise.
(C) Customers need proof of purchase for an exchange.
(D) Customers can return items at any branch.

15. What is NOT mentioned as an exchange procedure?

(A) Requesting a pickup truck
(B) Paying a delivery charge
(C) Showing photo identification
(D) Sending pictures of a damaged item

16. In which of the positions marked [1], [2], [3], and [4] does the following sentence best belong?

"We're unable to exchange your merchandise if it is found to be dirty, stained, or damaged."

(A) [1]
(B) [2]
(C) [3]
(D) [4]

Questions 17-19 refer to the following letter.

Bround Coffee Machines Corporation

577 Farmer Street
Lubbock Texas
October 3

Jim Freeman
449 Orange Grove
Dallas Texas

Dear Mr. Freeman,

We appreciate your contacting us regarding the defect in your espresso machine. — [1] —.

We at Bround Coffee Machines would like to ensure the satisfaction of every customer. We have received a number of letters about the espresso machine that you bought. — [2] —.

We will be taking back all of these machines and repairing them at no cost to customers. We will also pay for shipping and handling. — [3] —. Or if it is more convenient for you, just take it into any of our nearest outlets, where we will have a technician on hand specifically to repair these machines. — [4] —. For a list of outlets with a repair person in your area, please call 1800-888-7000.

Sincerely,

Jerry Spangler

Jerry Spangler
Customer Service Team

---

17. Why did Mr. Spangler write this letter?

(A) To respond to a customer's letter
(B) To request replacement parts
(C) To advertise the latest coffee makers
(D) To confirm a purchase order

18. What is Mr. Freeman advised to do?

(A) Purchase a new espresso machine
(B) Go into an outlet for repairs
(C) Add a missing part to his espresso machine
(D) Contact Mr. Spangler as soon as possible

19. In which of the positions marked [1], [2], [3], and [4] does the following sentence best belong?

"Therefore, we will be having a recall for these machines as there appears to be a problem with them."

(A) [1]
(B) [2]
(C) [3]
(D) [4]

UNIT 16 기사/안내문/광고

1. 기사/정보

유형 소개 및 전략

기사는 대부분 지문의 길이가 길고 경제, 건강, 에너지 등 다양한 주제를 다루므로 높은 수준의 독해력을 요구한다. 매회 3~4개의 지문이 출제되며, 대부분 주제는 첫 단락에 나오고, 나머지 단락에서는 세부사항을 다룬다. 난이도가 높은 문제들과 다양한 세부사항을 묻는 문제들이 출제되므로 문제의 키워드에 해당하는 내용을 지문에서 빨리 찾는 것이 관건이다.

안내문은 서비스 신청 방법, 제품 사용 방법, 시설물 소개 및 이용 안내 등을 주로 다룬다. 안내문이 게시되는 장소나 안내문이 흥미를 끄는 대상, 세부사항을 묻는 문제가 자주 출제된다.

빈출 질문

1) 기사

What is the purpose of the article? 기사의 목적은 무엇인가?

What is the article mainly about? 기사에서 주로 다루는 내용은 무엇인가?

What is NOT mentioned in this article? 이 기사에서 언급되지 않은 것은?

What is NOT true in this article? 이 기사에서 사실이 아닌 것은?

2) 안내문

What is the purpose of the information? 정보의 목적은 무엇인가?

For whom is this information intended? 이 정보는 누구를 대상으로 한 것인가?

What is the information about? 안내문은 무엇에 관한 것인가?

Where would this information most likely be found? 이 정보는 어디서 볼 수 있겠는가?

풀이 접근법

● 먼저 문제에서 키워드를 확인한 후, 지문에 키워드가 나오면 표시하며 읽는다.

● 기사나 안내문의 제목에서 지문의 대략적인 내용을 확인할 수 있으므로 꼭 읽어둔다.

● 기사나 안내문은 대부분 첫 번째 단락에서 목적을 찾을 수 있다는 것을 기억한다.

● 안내문이 누구를 대상으로 하는 것인지 묻는 문제는 마지막에 푸는 것이 좋다.

● 기사는 문제를 푸는 데 많은 시간이 소요되므로 가급적 마지막에 푸는 것이 좋다.

☰ 빈출 표현 및 어휘

경제

adverse effect 역효과, 부작용
analyze 분석하다
debt 빚
commerce 상업, 무역
expenditure 지출, 경비
figures 수치
investment 투자
lack 부족; 부족하다
market share 시장 점유율
quarter 분기
recession (= downturn) 불황
spokesperson 대변인
stable 안정적인
statistics 통계

경영

aid 원조, 지원; 돕다
aspiring 장차 ~이 되려는
associate 제휴하다, 결합시키다
boost 북돋우다
competitor 경쟁자
corporation 기업, 법인
entrepreneur 기업가
executive 임원; 행정의
expand 확장하다
founder 설립자
morale 의욕, 사기
motivate 동기를 부여하다
revenue (= profit) 수익
strategy 전략

부동산

commercial 상업적인; 광고
flat 아파트
floor plan 평면도
fully furnished 가구가 완비된
landlord 집주인
lease 임대하다
realtor 부동산 중개인
rent 임대료; 임대[임차]하다
residential 거주용의
separate 분리된
located (= situated) ~에 위치한
studio 원룸 (아파트)
tenant 세입자
utilities (= utility bills) 공공요금

공사/건축

aim 목표; 겨냥하다
annex 부속 건물, 별관
contractor 도급업자
interrupt 방해하다, 중단시키다
launch 시작하다
plumbing 배관 (작업)
procedure 절차
put into action 실행에 옮기다
refurbish 재단장하다
repave 재포장하다
restoration 복원, 복구
resume 재개하다
transport 수송하다, 옮기다
upon completion 완료(완공) 시에

교통

closed 폐쇄된
complimentary shuttle bus
무료 셔틀버스
commuter 통근자
renovation 보수
traffic congestion 교통 혼잡
transportation network 교통망
time-consuming 시간이 걸리는
take a detour 우회도로를 이용하다
take an alternative route
다른 길로 가다, 우회하다
expect delays on
~에서의 정체가 예상되다
rush hour (출퇴근) 혼잡 시간대

정책 변경

activate 작동시키다, 활성화시키다
alternative entrance 대체 출입구
appraisal 평가
compensation 보상
comply with ~를 준수하다
immediate supervisor 직속 상관
install 설치하다
implement 시행하다
mandatory 의무적인, 필수적인
penalty 처벌, 벌금
sign up (= enroll) 등록하다
tutorial (개별) 교육 자료
violation 위반
revised 개정된, 수정된

Lewis Grand Hotel in Guam Opens on July 10 •

곰에서 Lewis Grand 호텔이 7월 10일에 개장하다

The Lewis Grand Hotel opens its third overseas hotel in Guam on July 10.

Lewis Grand 호텔이 7월 10일 곰에서 세 번째 해외 호텔을 개장한다.

The hotel company renovated the former Rockwood Resort to open the new branch in the hot vacation spot. The 15-story building has 200 guest rooms, three food and beverage outlets, and five banquet halls as well as a swimming pool, a spa, a tennis court, and a fitness club.

호텔은 기존에 있던 Rockwood 리조트를 개조하여 활기 넘치는 휴가지에 새로운 지점을 냈다. 15층 건물에는 수영장, 스파, 테니스장, 피트니스 센터뿐만 아니라 200개의 객실, 3개의 식음료 매장, 5개의 연회장을 갖추고 있다.

The hotel, which overlooks popular Tumon Bay, is 10 minutes from Guam International Airport by car. It's also located close to entertainment venues such as Cocos Island, Matapang Beach, and other famous tourist attractions. The hotel is currently offering some special promotions on its Web site to celebrate its opening.

유명한 Tumon 만을 내려다보는 이 호텔은, 곰 국제공항에서 차로 10분 거리이다. 호텔은 Cocos 섬, Matapang 해변, 다른 유명한 관광지 같은 즐길거리가 많은 장소와도 가깝다. 현재 웹사이트에서 호텔 개장을 기념하기 위해 몇 가지 특별 행사가 진행 중이다.

기사 제목

기사의 제목을 통해 주제나 글의 목적을 알 수 있다.

세부사항

새롭게 개장하는 호텔의 특징들을 언급하고 있다.

세부사항

호텔의 위치와 행사 내용을 언급하고 있다.

Questions 1-3 refer to the following article.

Lewis Grand Hotel in Guam Opens on July 10

The Lewis Grand Hotel opens its third overseas hotel in Guam on July 10. The hotel company renovated the former Rockwood Resort to open the new branch in the vacation hot spot. The 15-story building has 200 guest rooms, three food and beverage outlets, and five banquet halls as well as a swimming pool, a spa, a tennis court, and a fitness club.

The hotel, which overlooks popular Tumon Bay, is 10 minutes from Guam International Airport by car. It's also located close to entertainment venues such as Cocos Island, Matapang Beach, and other famous tourist attractions. The hotel is currently offering some special promotions on its Web site to celebrate its opening.

---

1. What is the main purpose of the article?

(A) To announce the opening of a new branch of a hotel chain

(B) To attract investors for a new hotel in Guam

(C) To notify employees about some hotel renovations

(D) To give information about the location of a hotel

2. The word "overlooks" in paragraph 2, line 1, is closest in meaning to

(A) ignores

(B) forgives

(C) looks down

(D) monitors

3. What is suggested about the Lewis Grand Hotel in the article?

(A) It is located beside Guam International Airport.

(B) It has other branches in other countries.

(C) It has more than 200 guest rooms.

(D) It is also called the Rockwood Resort.

2. 광고

유형 소개 및 전략

광고는 매회 2~3개의 지문이 출제되며, 크게 일반 광고와 구인 광고로 나뉜다. 일반 광고는 상품이나 서비스 또는 시설이나 행사를 홍보한다. 상품·서비스 광고에서는 상품의 특징 및 할인과 관련된 세부사항을 묻는 문제가 출제된다. 시설이나 행사를 광고할 때 홍보 대상 및 광고가 게재된 장소, 광고에서 언급한 특정 사항을 묻는 문제가 출제된다. 구인 광고에서는 직책, 자격요건, 업무, 지원 방법과 관련된 내용을 주로 다룬다.

기출 질문

1) 일반 광고

What is the purpose of the advertisement? 광고의 목적은 무엇인가?

For whom is the advertisement intended? 광고는 누구를 대상으로 하는가?

Where would this advertisement most likely be seen? 이 광고는 주로 어디서 볼 수 있겠는가?

What is being advertised? 무엇이 광고되고 있는가?

What is offered to customers free of charge? 무엇이 고객들에게 무료로 제공되는가?

2) 구인 광고

What position is being advertised? 어떤 직책이 광고되고 있는가?

What is NOT mentioned as a job requirement? 자격요건으로 언급되지 않은 것은?

How can candidates apply for the position? 지원자들이 그 직책에 어떻게 지원할 수 있는가?

풀이 접근법

● 일반 광고는 할인, 구매자가 얻을 수 있는 혜택, 무언가를 받거나 신청할 수 있는 자격에 관한 내용이 많으므로 관련 표현을 알아두자.

● 구인 광고나 상품 광고에서 광고되는 직책과 상품이 무엇인지는 지문의 앞부분에서 찾을 수 있다. 보통 지문의 맨 위에 언급되는 것이 특징이다.

● 구인 광고는 보통 직책/업무 개요 → 자격요건 및 혜택 → 지원 방법 순으로 구성되므로, 이 순서를 알아두면 빠르게 정답을 찾을 수 있다.

빈출 표현 및 어휘

일반 광고

special offer 특별 할인 (제품)

exclusive deal 독점 혜택

additional discount 추가 할인

clearance sale 재고 정리 세일

loyalty program 고객 우대 프로그램

free delivery service 무료 배송 서비스

affordable price 적당한 가격

appliance 가전제품

line 제품군, 제품의 종류

feature ~을 특징으로 하다

authentic 정품의, 진짜의

state-ot-the-art 최신식의

fuel-efficient 연료 효율이 좋은

trial period 무료 체험 기간

used 중고의

reasonable (가격이) 합리적인

half off 50% 할인

in a row 연속해서

storage container 보관함

large order 대량 주문

professionally 전문적으로

warranty (품질) 보증

durable 내구성이 좋은

campaign 캠페인

kitchenware 주방용품

arts and crafts 공예

emporium 큰 상점, 백화점

supplies 용품

decorative 장식용의

expert 전문가

material 재료

picture frame 액자

individualized 맞춤식의

enrollment 등록

limited 제한적인

grand opening 개장

reduced rate 할인 요금

catering 출장 뷔페

within walking distance
걸어서 갈 수 있는 거리에 있는

city center 도심지

facilities (편의) 시설

luxury 호화로운

suite 스위트룸

early bird special 조기 예약 특가

complimentary 무료의

book 예약하다

in business 사업을 하는

specification 설명서, 사양

구인 광고

We are currently looking for ~
저희는 현재 ~을 찾고 있습니다

successful candidate 합격자

possess communication skills
의사소통 기술을 보유하다

be preferred 선호되다

responsibilities (= duties)
업무 사항(직무)

competitive salary 경쟁력 있는 급여

prior experience 경력

applicant 지원자

benefits 복지 혜택

bilingual 두 개 언어를 구사하는

candidate 후보자

certified 공인된

cover letter 자기소개서

desirable 바람직한

deadline (= due date) 마감일

degree 학위

fluent 능숙한

assistant 비서

hire (= employ) 고용하다

Human Resources 인사부서

job opening 공석

perform tasks 업무를 수행하다

permanent 정규직의

primary duty 주요 업무

proficiency 능숙함

qualified 자격을 갖춘

reference 추천서

relevant (= related) 관련된

replacement 교체, 후임자

required 필수적인

résumé 이력서

salary requirement 희망 연봉

shift 교대 근무조

temporary 임시의, 임시직의

willingness 기꺼이 하는 마음

attach 첨부하다

based in ~에 근거지를 둔

corporate 기업의

requirement 자격조건

managerial 경영의, 관리의

working knowledge 실무 지식

party 당사자, 관계자

post 게시하다

forward 보내다

immediate 즉각적인

minimum 최소한의

have responsibility for ~을 책임지다

preference 우대 사항

experienced 능숙한, 경험이 많은

Do Not Miss This Special Chance!
특별한 기회를 잡으세요!

Premium self-drive cars are available at reasonable rates at Budget Motors.
Budget Motors에서 프리미엄 렌터카를 합리적인 가격으로 제공합니다.

Whether your rental needs are for leisure, business, or special events, we provide the best vehicles available. We also offer personalized special customer service, competitive rates, and the opportunity to rent the latest models from any manufacturer you want.
렌탈이 여가, 사업, 특별 행사 중 무엇에 필요하든지 저희는 최고 품질의 차량을 제공합니다. 저희는 또한 개인 맞춤 특별 고객 서비스와 경쟁력 있는 비용, 그리고 원하시는 모든 제조사의 최신 모델을 렌트할 수 있는 기회를 제공합니다.

Now start to enjoy your exciting life with Budget Motors! We are open 24 hours a day, 365 days a year.
이제 Budget Motors와 함께 신나는 생활을 즐겨 보십시오! 저희는 연중무휴 하루 24시간 운영합니다.

Our services include:
- Every day low rates plus weekend and holiday discounts
- Free local pickup and return
- Long-term rentals
- An easy online booking system
저희 서비스는 다음을 포함합니다.
- 언제나 낮은 요금과 주말 및 공휴일 할인
- 지역 내 픽업과 반납 무료
- 장기 렌트
- 쉬운 온라인 예약 시스템

Please contact:
Mark Johnson, 212-853-4268
Mark Johnson에게 212-853-4268로 연락 주십시오.

광고하는 상품 소개
합리적인 가격의 렌터카

혜택 및 장점
provide, offer, present 등의 동사를 사용해 광고하는 상품이나 서비스의 장점과 고객들이 받을 혜택을 언급한다.

서비스의 특징
include 뒤에는 예시가 나열되므로 어떤 서비스를 특징으로 제공하는지를 파악할 수 있다.

연락 방법
웹사이트 주소, 전화번호, 이메일 주소 등의 연락 방법이 대부분 광고 마지막에 언급된다.

Questions 4-5 refer to the following advertisement.

Do Not Miss This Special Chance!

Premium self-drive cars are available at reasonable rates at Budget Motors. Whether your rental needs are for leisure, business, or special events, we provide the best vehicles available. We also offer personalized special customer service, competitive rates, and the opportunity to rent the latest models from any manufacturer you want.

Now start to enjoy your exciting life with Budget Motors! We are open 24 hours a day, 365 days a year.

Our services include:
- Everyday low rates plus weekend and holiday discounts
- Free local pickup and return
- Long-term rentals
- An easy online booking system

Please contact:
Mark Johnson, 212-853-4268

---

4. What is being advertised?

(A) A car rental agency

(B) A pick-up service

(C) A travel package

(D) New cars

5. What is mentioned in the advertisement?

(A) A complicated booking system

(B) The excellent quality of the cars

(C) Daily discounts

(D) Free gifts for all customers

RC PART 7

ACTUAL TEST

Questions 1-3 refer to the following article.

Flexport Automotive Pay Cut

Chicago, 3 October—In light of the recent economic downturn, Flexport Automotive has announced that it is doing all that it can not to lay off any of its workers yet save money and maintain a profit margin. All of the company executives worked over the weekend brainstorming and trying to find a solution to their problem. On Monday morning, Chief Executive Officer Henry Petersen, announced that in order to meet their goals they would have to ask their workers to accept a 15-percent pay cut and that they will place a hold on all planned raises and bonuses until the economy picks back up again. The workers at Flexport Automotive said that they are, of course, disappointed with the executive decision, but the employees would rather have a pay cut than not have jobs at all in today's difficult market. So beginning on November 1, all staff, including executives, will see a reduction in their take-home pay.

---

1. What kind of company policy does the article discuss?
   (A) Advertising
   (B) Budgetary
   (C) Educational
   (D) Hiring

2. When will Flexport Automotive put its new plolicy in place?
   (A) In January
   (B) In October
   (C) In November
   (D) In December

3. What is mentioned about the company's new policy?
   (A) It was devised by an international team of experts.
   (B) It is expected to help the company save jobs and money.
   (C) It was decided on by the staff and management.
   (D) It was modeled after the policy of another company.

Questions 4-5 refer to the following information.

New Discounts!

Z-Mobile is currently offering a 30% discount on mobile phones and data plans to all employees of Dole Electronics. If you do not want to miss out on this wonderful deal, head over to the Human Resources Department and pick up a Z-Mobile discount coupon there. The coupons can be used at any authorized retailer for a new Z-Mobile phone with a 12-month data plan.

You are expected to present your employee identification card upon purchase. If you have any questions, call the Z-Mobile Customer Service Department at 917-488-4884 and consult with a representative.

---

4. Where most likely would this information be found?
   (A) In a local newspaper
   (B) In a mobile phone catalog
   (C) In a technology magazine
   (D) In a company newsletter

5. How can a discount coupon be used?
   (A) By consulting a customer service representative
   (B) By presenting a staff ID card
   (C) By visiting the Human Resources Department
   (D) By telephoning an authorized retailer

Questions 6-7 refer to the following advertisement.

Product of the Week: Kirk's Coconut Soap

Kirk's Coconut Soap is handmade by Mapleton resident, Kirk Walmsley. Mr. Walmsley sells the soap locally through a contract with Bubble & Body Works. The organic coconut oil hand soap is long lasting with a shelf life of one year when properly stored in a cool, dry location. It has been available since January and remains a popular item for Bubble & Body Works customers. Currently on sale for $6.50 for a pack of two bars, it boasts many benefits for its users.

- Cleans hands thoroughly
- Keeps hands soft
- Features a delicate scent
- Consists of purely organic materials
- Contains no artificial chemicals

To receive 15% off your purchase of Kirk's Coconut Soap, simply mention discount code KCS466 to a cashier at the Bubble & Body Works on New Oxford Street in London.

6. What is the purpose of the advertisement?

(A) To explain a cleaning procedure
(B) To demonstrate how soap is made
(C) To advertise the opening of a new store
(D) To market a local resident's merchandise

7. What is mentioned about the soap?

(A) It is made from natural ingredient.
(B) It is sold at major department stores.
(C) It can be purchased only in single-bar packs.
(D) It will be manufactured in several locations.

Questions 8-10 refer to the following article.

Los Angeles (15 June) — Party Fight 3, the new version of a popular computer game by Japan-based Fujio Games, Inc., was released yesterday. —[1]—. Hundreds of people eager to be among the first to purchase the updated game waited for hours outside retail stores across the region. —[2]—.

The marketing strategy planned by Fujio turned out successfully by spreading the news of the release of its most popular action game. Game critics believed that Party Fight 3 would receive less of a spotlight than its previous series. —[3]—. Instead, Fujio invested in its own marketing divisions, and their strategy was to reflect suggestions from gaming fans. In addition, using professional fighters to capture their fighting motions has brought this game to a higher level of intense gaming experience. —[4]—. To further popularize the game, some high-profile fighters even made guest appearances at stores, where they did live interviews and took photographs with fans.

8. According to the article, why were people waiting for hours?

   (A) To order a new computer model
   (B) To meet celebrities
   (C) To attend a party after a big event
   (D) To buy a computer game

9. What is suggested about Fujio Games, Inc?

   (A) Its headquarters is located in Los Angeles.
   (B) It recently merged with another company.
   (C) Its products are more expensive than those of its competitors.
   (D) It pays attention to comments from its customers.

10. In which of the positions marked [1], [2], [3], and [4] does the following sentence best belong?

   "The reason is that Fujio did not rely on any marketing companies."

   (A) [1]
   (B) [2]
   (C) [3]
   (D) [4]

Questions 11-12 refer to the following advertisement.

Job Opening

Michael's Clothing Store is currently looking for a full-time manager for our branch on the corner of Newbury Street and Sunset Boulevard. The ideal candidate should have at least one year of managerial experience and at least five years in retail. Interested parties should send a cover letter with salary requirements, a résumé, and a reference from your previous employer to Rebecca Clarke at rclarke@michaels.com.

---

11. What position is being advertised?

(A) Retail sales associate
(B) Administrator assistant
(C) Store supervisor
(D) Community center director

12. What is mentioned as a requirement for the job?

(A) A university degree
(B) Willingness to travel
(C) Management experience
(D) Organizational skills

Questions 13-14 refer to the following advertisement.

Archer Travel Services

Ready for a fantastic holiday? Archer Travel Services is here to help!

Save up to €100 on companion fares from June 1 to August 31.

- Applies only to flights within continental Europe
- Good for one companion fare only
- Offer valid when you book by May 15

Go to www.atservices.com to book your hotel and car as well. And join our loyalty club to stay informed of all future discounts and last-minute sales.

13. What is being discounted?

(A) Car rentals
(B) Airplane tickets
(C) Cruise package
(D) Hotel accommodations

14. What is indicated about discounts?

(A) They are available for a limited time.
(B) They are limited to online purchases.
(C) They are valid for travel anywhere.
(D) They are available only to Archer Travel Services loyalty club members.

Questions 15-17 refer to the following information.

Welcome to Sydney's Shangri-La Hotel!

Whether you are visiting Sydney for work or pleasure, we hope that you will take the time to enjoy our world-class amenities. We are pleased to provide the highest-quality services to enhance your stay.

Do you need to work on a document or conduct some Internet research? Our business center on the first floor, the Enterprise Hub, is open 24 hours a day and has state-of-the art equipment, including a fax machine, computers, and printers. Located next to the Enterprise Hub is the Horizon Lounge, which offers a variety of reasonably priced beverage and snacks.

Do you wish to stay in shape while on business or holiday? Then visit the F-Zone, our newly renovated fitness center, located on the second floor. It has the latest exercise equipment.

Are you hungry? For the hotel's room service menu, see the dining section, beginning on page 37 of the directory. Or dine at our award-winning bistro. The bistro offers contemporary and traditional French cuisine and is open for breakfast, lunch, and dinner.

Thank you for choosing the Shangri-La Hotel during your visit to Sydney.

Please enjoy your stay.

---

15. What is stated about the hotel?

(A) It is located near a tourist attraction.
(B) It offers a variety of services for guests.
(C) It is popular with business professionals.
(D) It provides discounts to frequent guests.

16. What is indicated about the Horizon Lounge?

(A) It requires a reservation.
(B) It was recently renovated.
(C) It offers free tea and coffee.
(D) It is located on the first floor.

17. What is NOT mentioned as a feature of the hotel?

(A) An exercise center
(B) A restaurant
(C) A swimming pool
(D) A business center

Questions 18-21 refer to the following article.

Bruen carmaker merges with Headley carmaker

Bruen, the foremost car manufacturer in North America, and a renowned global brand, yesterday held a press conference to say that it had indeed merged with Britain's Headley automaker. —[1]—. Lately, Bruen has been facing many financial difficulties due to the recent slowdown in the economy.

Headley, the biggest British car manufacturer, says that it is happy with the result of the merger. Headley CEO Jonathon Green will be heading the new company. He said that he plans on reshaping the Bruen image. —[2]—. He said that he will go ahead and produce more electric cars as this is the wave of the future.

This merger has upset a number of Americans, who were hoping that Bruen would merge with a national company within its borders. —[3]—.

Many people at Bruen are concerned about losing their jobs, but Headley has promised that no jobs will be cut. —[4]—. However, it plans to discontinue the poor-selling sports car made by Bruen.

---

18. According to the article, why has the merger of Bruen been disappointing to some people?

(A) Many people will now lose their jobs.
(B) It chose to merge with a foreign company.
(C) Americans will have to relocate to England.
(D) There is little interest in electric cars.

19. What is Headley's plan for Bruen?

(A) To cut the number of employees by half
(B) To improve the sports car model
(C) To make more electric cars
(D) To move Bruen's headquarters to England

20. What is NOT mentioned as a result of the merger?

(A) Making more electric cars
(B) Reshaping Bruen's image
(C) Discontinuing some models
(D) Staff downsizing

21. In which of the positions marked [1], [2], [3], and [4] does the following sentence best belong?

"Both parties agreed that the merger will be mutually beneficial."

(A) [1]
(B) [2]
(C) [3]
(D) [4]

UNIT 17 기타 지문

1. 문자 메시지/온라인 채팅

유형 소개 및 전략

비즈니스 또는 일상생활과 관련된 여러 정보를 모바일이나 온라인 메신저로 2인 또는 그 이상이 주고받는 지문으로, 매회 총 2지문이 출제된다. 회의, 일정, 업무 등에 대해 사내 또는 회사 간 직원들이 주고받는 내용과 행사 초대, 도움 요청 등의 내용이 나온다.

빈출 질문

1) 의도 파악 문제

At 4:16 P.M., what does Mr. Dale most likely mean when he writes, "That's a relief"?
4시 16분에, Dale 씨가 "다행이네요"라고 쓴 의도는?

2) 주제/목적 문제

What's Mr. Haney's problem? Haney 씨의 문제는 무엇인가?

Why did Mr. Riko send the message to his colleagues? Riko 씨는 왜 그의 직장동료들에게 메시지를 보냈는가?

3) 세부사항 문제

What did Ms. Carrera ask Mr. Lang? Carrera 씨는 Lang 씨에게 무엇을 부탁했는가?

4) 추론 문제

What will Mr. Perez most likely do next? Perez 씨가 다음에 할 행동은 무엇일 것 같은가?

풀이 접근법

● **의도 파악 문제**

1. 해당 표현이 쓰인 문장을 빠르게 확인한다.
   → 대화문 각 문장 옆에 메시지를 보낸 시간이 표시되어 있다. 메시지 시간을 기준으로 지문에서 메시지의 위치를 빠르게 확인한다.
   → 문장 그 자체의 의미가 아니라 맥락 안에서 어떤 의미를 갖는지 파악해야 한다.

2. 문맥상 가장 적절한 의미로 바꾸어 표현한 보기를 선택한다.
   → 다른 독해 지문과 달리 구어체 표현이 상당수 등장한다. 구어체 표현이 등장할 때 대화의 흐름이 전환되므로 주의 깊게 봐야 한다.

● **빈출 구어체 표현**

Not at all. 괜찮다.	Sure thing. 물론이지.
It seems fine. 괜찮을 것 같다.	I'm on my way. 가는 중이야.
That won't work. 안될 거야.	It makes sense. 말이 된다.
I don't see why not. 안될 이유가 없다.	Let's wait and see. 일단 두고 보자.
Let's give it a try. 시도해 보자.	Do you follow me? 이해되니?
I'll get to it right away. 즉시 할게.	It's been a while. 오랜만이네.
I can't make it. 갈 수 없다.	I'd be happy to. 기꺼이 그렇게 할게.

빈출 표현 및 어휘

지문 a sale, a discount 판매, 할인
보기 a special promotion 특별 프로모션

지문 complimentary coffee 무료 커피
보기 provide coffee at no charge 커피를 무료로 제공하다

지문 gather data 데이터를 모으다
보기 collect information 정보를 수집하다

지문 programs and applications 프로그램 및 응용 프로그램
보기 computer software 컴퓨터 소프트웨어

지문 moved last month 지난달에 이사했다
보기 recently relocated to a new location 최근에 새로운 장소로 이전했다

지문 thoroughly and with care 철저하고 조심스럽게
보기 paying attention to detail 세부사항에 주의를 기울이며

지문 easy mobility 간편한 이동성
보기 It can be moved around. 이리저리 이동할 수 있다.

지문 The item is fragile. 물품이 깨지기 쉽다.
보기 It may break easily. 쉽게 깨질 수 있다.

지문 a historic landmark structure 역사적인 랜드마크 건축물
보기 an old building 오래된 건물

지문 present a brief training session 간단한 교육과정을 발표하다
보기 give a short presentation 짧은 프레젠테이션을 하다

지문 increased ridership 승객 수 증가
보기 increased use of public transportation 대중교통 이용 증가

지문 items with slight blemishes 약간의 흠집이 있는 품목
보기 tiles with minor defects 사소한 결함이 있는 타일

지문 do preliminary research 사전 조사를 수행하다
보기 review information in advance 사전에 정보를 검토하다

Amanda Perry [10:30 A.M.]

David, where are you now? The job applicants are here.

Daivd, 지금 어디예요? 지원자들이 여기에 와있어요.

연락 목적
보통 첫 번째 메시지에 상대방의 위치를 물어보고 바로 이어서 연락한 목적을 말한다.

David Garcia [10:31 A.M.]

Sorry! The bridge is under construction. My bus had to take a detour. I should be there in about an hour. Please start without me.

죄송해요. 다리가 공사 중이라 버스가 우회해야만 했어요. 대략 1시간 후에 도착할 것 같아요. 일단 저 없이 시작해 주세요.

세부사항
제 시간에 갈 수 없는 이유를 설명하고 있다.

Amanda Perry [10:34 A.M.]

Okay. I am going to interview Raymond Fleer first.

알겠습니다. 제가 먼저 Raymond Fleer 씨를 면접 볼게요.

세부사항
새로운 인물(Raymond Fleer)이 등장했고, 그가 면접 지원자라는 정보를 확인한다.

David Garcia [10:35 A.M.]

Good. He is the one with experience at another T-shirt company.

좋아요. 그는 다른 T-shirt 회사에서 경험이 있는 사람 중 한 명이에요.

세부사항
Raymond Fleer의 추가 정보를 제시하고 있다.

Amanda Perry [10:36 A.M.]

Yes. Can you believe our company has grown so much that we need to hire someone just to process orders?

알겠어요. 우리 회사가 너무도 빨리 성장해서 주문을 처리하기 위해 누군가를 고용한다는 것이 믿어지세요?

추론
회사가 빠른 시간 내에 성공을 이루었음을 알 수 있다.

David Garcia [10:37 A.M.]

I know! I will see you soon.

그러게요! 곧 봐요.

Questions 1-2 refer to the following text-message chain.

Amanda Perry [10:30 A.M.]

David, where are you now? The job applicants are here.

David Garcia [10:31 A.M.]

Sorry! The bridge is under construction. My bus had to take a detour.

I should be there in about an hour. Please start without me.

Amanda Perry [10:34 A.M.]

Okay. I am going to interview Raymond Fleer first.

David Garcia [10:35 A.M.]

Good. He is the one with experience at another T-shirt company.

Amanda Perry [10:36 A.M.]

Yes. Can you believe our company has grown so much that we need to hire someone just to process orders?

David Garcia [10:37 A.M.]

I know! I will see you soon.

---

1. What does Mr. Garcia want Ms. Perry to do?

   (A) Process some orders

   (B) Make a hiring decision

   (C) Reschedule a meeting

   (D) Talk to a job applicant

2. At 10:37 A.M., what does Mr. Garcia mean when he writes, "I know"?

   (A) He is also surprised by the company's growth.

   (B) He thinks salaries should be higher.

   (C) He has met Mr. Fleer before.

   (D) He is sure his bus will arrive in an hour.

2. 양식

유형 소개 및 전략

특정한 형태를 갖춘 다양한 양식이 매회 2~3개 이상 출제된다. 대표적인 양식으로는 초대장(invitation), 송장(invoice), 일정표(schedule), 쿠폰(coupon), 전단지(flyer), 설문지(survey), 영수증(receipt) 등이 있다. 양식은 독해력과 함께 표를 이해하는 능력이 요구되는데, 양식의 각 항목을 하나하나 읽을 필요 없이 문제에서 묻는 특정 부분에서 답을 찾으면 되는 비교적 쉬운 난이도의 유형이다.

빈출 질문

What is the purpose of this event? 행사의 목적은 무엇인가?
What will take place on November 17? 11월 17일에 무슨 일이 일어나는가?
When will the event begin? 언제 행사가 시작될 것인가?
What is NOT stated in the invoice? 송장에 언급되지 않은 것은?
To whom is the invitation most likely directed? 초대장은 누구를 위한 것이겠는가?
For whom is the schedule probably intended? 일정표는 누구를 대상으로 하는 것 같은가?
How much did Ms. McBride pay in shipping charges? McBride 씨는 얼마의 배송비를 부담했는가?

풀이 접근법

● 보통 **표로 주어지는 경우**는 지문 전체를 다 읽을 필요가 없다. **문제를 먼저 읽고 관련된 정보를 빠르게 찾아가는 방식**으로 푸는 것이 효율적이다.
● 양식에 따라 자주 출제되는 내용이 정해져 있다. **초대장의 경우 행사의 종류와 주체, 송장에서는 물품의 수량과 가격, 일정표에서는 각 시간별 행사 내용과 주체**에 대해 질문하므로 자주 출제되는 양식의 빈출 표현을 알아두는 것이 좋다.

빈출 표현 및 어휘

일정

excursion/tour/voyage 짧은 여행/견학/항해	hospitality industry 숙박업
itinerary 여행 일정(표)	accommodations 숙박(시설)
tourist attraction 관광명소	accommodate 숙박을 제공하다, 수용하다
tour guide 여행 안내자, 안내서	lodge 숙소
landmark 표지물, 역사적인 건물	toll-free phone 무료 전화
scenery 경치	amenity 편의 시설
reserve 예약하다	public transportation 대중교통
confirm reservation 예약을 확인하다	commute 통근하다; 통근
embarkation/departure/destination 출국/출발/목적지	detour 우회로; 우회하다
carry-on baggage 기내에 들고 탈 수 있는 짐	highway/sidewalk 고속도로/인도
boarding pass 탑승권	on time 정시에
customs declaration 세관 신고서	round-trip 왕복

송장

cost 비용
quantity 양
regular price 정가
deposit paid 선급금
total balance 총계
invoiced to ~로 송장이 발송된
shipped to ~로 물건이 보내진
method of payment 지불 방법
shipping charge 배송비

초대장

You are cordially invited to attend ~
당신을 ~로 정중히 초대합니다
a celebration in honor of ~ ~을 기념하는 행사
Refreshments will be served. 다과가 제공될 것입니다.
The event will be held at the Grand Ballroom of
Siesta Hotel. 그 행사는 Siesta 호텔의 대연회장에서 열릴
것입니다.
Please present this invitation at ~
~에서 이 초대장을 제시해 주시기 바랍니다.

패러프레이징 표현

동사	폐업하다	go out of business, shut down, close down, halt operations
	조사하다, 검사하다	investigate, examine, inspect, check out, diagnose, review
	보상하다	reimburse, compensate, pay back, repay
	준수하다	follow, obey, observe, adhere to, abide by, conform to, comply with
	시작하다	commence, begin, start, initiate, launch, be effective
	제출하다	file, submit, hand in, give in, turn in
	임명하다	name, appoint, nominate
명사	부하 직원	subordinate, assistant, associate
	회사 임원	company officer, president, director, executive, CEO
	요금	rate, charge, price, fee
	사업가	entrepreneur, businessman, owner
	인사과	personnel department, human resources department
	안내서	handbook, manual, instructions
형용사	정가	regular price, original price, net price, usual price, sticker price
	무료로	for free, complimentary, at no charge, as no cost, free of charge
	해외	overseas, international, abroad, worldwide, in other countries
	시간외 근무	overtime, additional hours, extra hours
	질긴, 오래가는	durable, outlast, lasting
	최신의	state-of-the-art, modern, contemporary
	맞춤형의	customized, personalized, tailored

RC PART 7

Join Us for the 10th Annual IWMA Banquet

제10회 IWMA 연례 회의에 참여하세요

All of the members of the International Working Men's Association (IWMA) are cordially invited to its 10th annual banquet to promote mutual friendly relationships among members and to facilitate the activities of the association.

회원들 상호간의 친근한 관계를 도모하고 협회의 활동을 촉진하기 위해서 International Working Men's Association (IWMA)의 모든 회원들을 제10회 연례 연회에 정중히 초대합니다.

초대 대상
'A is invited to B'에서 누가, 어디에 초대되는지 확인한다.

Wednesday, December 17
6:00 P.M. to 8:00 P.M.

12월 17일 수요일
오후 6시부터 오후 8시까지

행사 일정

Banquet Hall
Laughlin Harrah's Hotel
Blue Hill Avenue, Maryland

연회장
Laughlin Harrah's 호텔
Blue Hill 가, 메릴랜드

행사 장소

Formal dress is required.
Please bring your IWMA membership card.

격식을 차린 복장이 요구됩니다.
IWMA 회원 카드를 가져오시기 바랍니다.

요청사항
Please 이후에 요청사항이 언급된다.

Please reply to James McGough, the event coordinator, to indicate whether you will participate in the dinner by fax 662-24457-7535 or call 240-301-4103.

행사 준비자인 James McGough에게 저녁 만찬 참석 여부를 662-24457-7535로 팩스를 보내거나 240-301-4103에 전화하여 알려주시기 바랍니다.

요청사항과 연락 방법

Questions 3-4 refer to the following invitation.

Join Us for the 10th Annual IWMA Banquet

All of the members of the International Working Men's Association (IWMA) are cordially invited to
its 10th annual banquet to promote mutual friendly relationships among members
and to facilitate the activities of the association.

Wednesday, December 17
6:00 P.M. to 8:00 P.M.

Banquet Hall
Laughlin Harrah's Hotel
Blue Hill Avenue, Maryland

Formal dress is required.
Please bring your IWMA membership card.

Please reply to James McGough, the event coordinator,
to indicate whether you will participate in the dinner
by fax 662-24457-7535 or call 240-301-4103.

---

3. To whom was this invitation most likely sent?

(A) Banquet planners

(B) Hotel managers

(C) Event coordinators

(D) Members of the association

4. What are recipients asked to do?

(A) Attend a luncheon

(B) Bring a copy of the invitation

(C) State their availability for an event

(D) E-mail the event coordinator

ACTUAL TEST

Questions 1-2 refer to the following text-message chain.

Eleanor Jones (10:22 A.M.)

Hi, Anastasia. Have you sent me those contracts?

Anastasia Phillips (10:30 A.M.)

No, I haven't had a chance yet. We've been extremely busy trying to catch up after the long holiday weekend.

Eleanor Jones (10:32 A.M.)

I know what you mean! Everyone here in the Legal Affairs Department is going to work late this evening.

Anastasia Phillips (10:33 A.M.)

I can have a messenger bring them to the downtown office after lunch. Would that work?

Eleanor Jones (10:35 A.M.)

Yes, that should be fine as long as they are all signed and ready to go.

Anastasia Phillips (10:36 A.M.)

They are. They should be there by about 1:00 P.M.

1. At 10:32 A.M., what does Ms. Jones most likely mean when she writes, "I know what you mean"?

   (A) She forgot about the contracts.
   (B) She will fix an error in the contracts.
   (C) She also enjoyed her holiday.
   (D) She also has a lot to do.

2. What is suggested about the writers?

   (A) They will meet for lunch.
   (B) They often work late.
   (C) They work in different buildings.
   (D) They are messengers.

Questions 3-4 refer to the following text-message chain.

Alice Stone [8:45 A.M.]

Hi, Cory. Human Resources has asked that we schedule your annual review. What day works for you?

Cory Glover [8:50 A.M.]

I'll be traveling to Interlaken for the conference next week. How about Wednesday, December 19?

Alice Stone [8:52 A.M.]

That won't work. All of the annual reviews need to be completed before then so that we can process the paperwork. Can you clear a couple hours on Monday or Tuesday?

Cory Glover [9:10 A.M.]

I've just rescheduled my morning meeting on the 18th, so I can be in your office at 9:00 A.M. How does that sound?

Alice Stone [9:12 A.M.]

Perfect. I'll send you an e-mail reminder next week. Enjoy the conference and safe travels.

---

3. Why did Ms. Stone contact Mr. Glover?

(A) To review plans for a conference
(B) To inform him of a late report
(C) To request a meeting with him
(D) To help with a flight schedule

4. At 8:52 A.M., what does Ms. Stone most likely mean when she writes, "That won't work"?

(A) She will not be able to travel to Interlaken.
(B) Mr. Glover needs to choose a different time.
(C) Mr. Glover made an error on some paperwork.
(D) She will not be available to help with a project.

Questions 5-7 refer to the following invoice.

Abraxas Cookshop

Order Invoice

Serving our valued customers for more than 10 years
42 St Giles Street
Northampton, NN1 1JW, England

Customer name: Melinda Paraie
billing address: 44 St James Mill Road, Northampton, NN5 5RA, England
Shipping address: 268 Wellingborough Road, Northampton, NN1 4EJ, England
Shipping date: February 8

Item Code	Description	Quantity
34GU	Measuring Cups	1
*657UH	Roasting Pan	2
*466GT	Decorative Napkins	20
54RD	Professional Knife Set	1

*Items 466GT and 657UH will be delivered on a later date because they are currently out of stock.

---

5. What kind of business does Ms. Paraie most likely own?

   (A) A laundry
   (B) A restaurant
   (C) A pharmacy
   (D) A grocery store

6. According to the invoice, what will happen on February 8?

   (A) An additional order will be placed.
   (B) A payment will be made.
   (C) An item will be returned.
   (D) A shipment will be sent.

7. What is indicated about the Abraxas Cookshop?

   (A) It has been doing business for over two decades.
   (B) Some items are currently not in its warehouse.
   (C) It imports products from other countries.
   (D) It has many locations around the world.

Questions 8-9 refer to the following receipt.

Metro Outfitters

1520 N Milwaukee Ave
Chicago, IL 60622
(215) 454-5500

Cashier: Frank Conforti
Cash Register: No.3
Date/Time: December 19 / 6:15 P.M.

Item Number	Description	Quantity	Amount
854387	Extra Large Vintage Tommy Puffer Jacket (Black)	1	$125.00
543978	Extra Large Sweater (Red)	2	$120.00

Subtotal: $245.00
Metro Outfitters Member Discount: $49.00
Tax: $19.60

Total: $215.60
Paid: Cash $216.00
Change: $0.40

Metro Outfitters Member Personal Information:
Name: Kate Spencer   Phone: (215) 457-7685
Points Earned Today: 216   Remaining Points: 3,233

Visit our Web site at www.metrooutfitters.com/event before December 31 to participate in a drawing for fantastic prizes, including a $3,000 gift certificate!
Enter the following promotion code: FLASH504395800

8. What is suggested about Ms. Spencer?

(A) She is employed at Metro Outfitters.
(B) She purchased some new pants.
(C) She met Mr. Conforti in person on December 19.
(D) She paid with her credit card.

9. What will Ms. Spencer most likely do with the promotion code?

(A) Get an additional discount
(B) Subscribe to a newsletter
(C) Get a shipping fee waived
(D) Enter a raffle

Questions 10-11 refer to the following invitation.

To: Pablo McHenry

The MedStar Medical Center cordially invites you to its
Summer Dreamland Dinner on Saturday, August 15,
at 7:00 P.M. in the Venetian Room at the Plaza Hotel.

This event is hosted annually to thank our donors for their
generous financial support. The dinner will include a five-
course meal and entertainment provided by select members
of the Philharmonic Symphony.

Please respond no later than August 1 by sending an e-mail
to Ashley Hinson at a.hinson@medstarmc.com.
You are welcome to bring up to two guests with you.
Please present this invitation at the entrance for entry.
We hope you will be able to join us!

10. Why was Mr. McHenry most likely invited to the event?

(A) He was nominated for an award.
(B) He worked as a volunteer.
(C) He is a member of the staff.
(D) He made a monetary donation.

11. What is NOT true about the event?

(A) It will be held on the weekend.
(B) It will include a speech by Ashley Hinson.
(C) Its invitees may bring their guests.
(D) It will include a musical performance.

Questions 12-13 refer to the following text-message chain.

Landon Hemsworth [9:12 A.M.]

Are you in the office?

Dakota Malone [9:12 A.M.]

Yes, I've been here since 9:00.

Landon Hemsworth [9:13 A.M.]

My printer is broken. I called the repair service center, but a technician cannot come until this afternoon. I need some questionnaires to be printed before my meeting with a client at 10:00.

Dakota Malone [9:14 A.M.]

I can print them for you. Where can I find the questionnaires?

Landon Hemsworth [9:15 A.M.]

I've uploaded them on our internal Web site. You can find them in the Client Survey folder.

Dakota Malone [9:16 A.M.]

Okay. I will get to it right away.

Landon Hemsworth [9:17 A.M.]

Thanks a lot! I will stop by your office to pick them up in 5 minutes.

---

12. What problem does Mr. Hemsworth mention?

(A) His assistant is late for work.
(B) A technician is not immediately available.
(C) A meeting will take place earlier than expected.
(D) Some questionnaires have not been approved.

13. At 9:16 A.M., what does Ms. Malone most likely mean when she writes, "I'll get to it right away"?

(A) She will print some documents.
(B) She will copy some questionnaires.
(C) She will call a repair service.
(D) She will delete the Client Survey folder.

Questions 14-17 refer to the following online chat discussion.

Mia Thompson (2:15 P.M.)

Hi, Ellie and Fatima. How are things coming along with those weblogs I asked you to start?

Fatima Rashad (2:17 P.M.)

I'm thinking of profiling our investment advisors.

Mia Thompson (2:19 P.M.)

Could you give me some more details on that?

Fatima Rashad (2:21 P.M.)

Well, I want to feature an interview with a different team member every month. I could get a little personal and professional background information and inquire about the member's views on investment strategies—that sort of thing.

Mia Thompson (2:22 P.M.)

Nice. Our customers would really like that. What about you, Ellie?

Ellie Friedman (2:24 P.M.)

I'm thinking of reporting on emerging stock market trends. I've already collected a lot of material about this topic.

Mia Thompson (2:25 P.M.)

Sounds interesting. Do you need assistance with the research?

Ellie Friedman (2:26 P.M.)

Thanks, but I think I've got it covered.

Mia Thompson (2:27 P.M.)

Okay. I'd like both of you to get back to me about your progress on these ideas by Monday.

14. In what industry do the participants most likely work?

(A) Finance
(B) Health care
(C) Technology
(D) Real estate

15. What is suggested about Ms. Thompson?

(A) She will help Ms. Friedman with her research.
(B) She supervises Ms. Rashad's work.
(C) She will be out of the office on Monday.
(D) She needs information about a job applicant.

16. What is indicated about Ms. Rashad's weblogs?

(A) They will be ready by the end of the day.
(B) They will be written by several team members.
(C) They will be published once a month.
(D) They will be designed for internal company use.

17. At 2:25 P.M., what does Ms. Thompson mean when she writes, "Sounds interesting"?

(A) She wants to know more about Ms. Rashad's team members.
(B) She likes the subject matter of Ms. Friedman's weblog.
(C) She is pleased with recent stock market trends.
(D) She likes to receive positive customer feedback.

UNIT 18 복수 지문

유형 소개 및 전략

복수 지문은 두 개 또는 세 개의 지문을 읽고 5문제를 푸는 유형이다. 편지/이메일이 포함된 구성이 가장 일반적이며 주제나 목적 등 전체적으로 지문을 파악하는 문제, 요청사항이나 변동 사항 등 세부내용을 찾는 문제, 두 지문의 연결 고리를 파악하는 연계 문제 등이 주로 출제된다. 문제를 풀기 전에 복수 지문의 종류, 제목, 수신인/발신인 등을 빠르게 훑고 각 지문 간의 관계를 파악하면 전체 흐름과 내용을 이해하는 데 유리하다.

빈출 질문

1) 주제/목적 문제

What is the purpose of the first e-mail? 첫 번째 이메일의 목적은 무엇인가?

What is the purpose of the advertisement? 광고의 목적은 무엇인가?

Why did Ms. Pinkman write an e-mail? Pinkman 씨가 이메일을 쓴 이유는 무엇인가?

For whom is the notice intended? 누구를 대상으로 하는 공지인가?

2) 세부사항 문제

What are Ms. Levy and Mr. Bank planning to do? Levy 씨와 Bank 씨는 무엇을 할 계획인가?

What is suggested about Mr. Johanson? Johanson 씨에 대해서 암시된 내용은?

What is NOT mentioned about West Incorporated? West 사에 대해 언급되지 않은 것은?

How can an interview be arranged? 면접 일정은 어떻게 잡을 수 있는가?

According to the announcement, what comes with the price of the tour?
공고에 따르면, 여행 비용은 무엇을 포함하는가?

3) 동의어 문제

In the letter, the word "cover" in paragraph 3, line 4, is closest in meaning to
편지에서 세 번째 단락, 네 번째 줄의 "cover"와 의미가 가장 가까운 단어는 무엇인가?

풀이 접근법

1) 편지 또는 이메일이 포함된 복수 지문의 경우, 이름이 언급되어 있는 문제가 많다. 따라서 문제에 나온 이름이 발신자인지 수신자인지를 반드시 확인하고 문제를 풀어야 오답을 피할 수 있다.

2) 5문제 중 첫 번째, 두 번째 문제는 첫 번째 지문에 단서가 있는 경우가 대부분이므로, 단일 지문을 풀 때와 같은 방법으로 문제를 먼저 읽고, 첫 번째 지문에서 단서를 찾는다.

3) 나머지 3문제는 두 지문 또는 세 지문을 모두 읽어야만 풀 수 있는 문제(연계 문제)로 구성되며, 연계 문제는 보통 1문제, 많게는 2문제까지 출제된다. 두 번째 또는 세 번째 지문에서 반복되는 키워드가 있거나, 첫 번째 지문에서 언급된 내용에 대한 예외적인 상황이나 변경된 내용이 두세 번째 지문에 있을 경우 단서가 되므로 집중적으로 살펴본다.

🟰 빈출 표현 및 어휘

동사	방문하다, 들르다	come in person, visit, drop by, come by, stop by
	거절하다	decline, turn down, reject
	사직하다, 은퇴하다	step down, quit, resign, leave
	연락하다	be in touch with, reach, contact
	처리하다	deal with, take care of, handle, work out, manage, address, resolve
	취소하다	cancel, call off, withdraw
	환불하다	get money back, refund, rebate
	연기하다	postpone, put off, reschedule, delay
	시행하다	implement, put into action, practice, perform, carry out, conduct
명사	회담, 연설	discussion, speech, address
	광고, 홍보	publicity, advertisement, ads, promotion
	회사	establishment, company, firm, corporate, enterprise
	휴가	time off, vacation, leave, day off
	건축물	premises, building, structure, property, facility, landmark
	봉급	salary, payment for employees, pay, wage, compensation
	자금	fund, budget, finance, investment, resources, grant
	암호	code, encryption, password
	장소	venue, place, location, spot
	상품(재고)	inventory, item, goods, merchandise, stock
형용사	추가적인	additional, extra, more
	실종된	lost, missing, misplaced
	편안한	cozy, comfortable, comfy
	협상 가능한	negotiable, changeable
	불결한, 비위생적인	unsanitary, unclean
	품질이 좋은	superior, top of the line, outstanding, noticeable
	선호하는	favorite, preferred, ideal, desirable
	값이 적당한	affordable, reasonably priced
	지속적인	sustainable, continuous

To: Technical Support <techsupport@bsb.com> 수신: 기술지원팀
From: Ofir Graizer <Orgraizer@bsb.com> 발신: Ofir Graizer
Date: March 15, 11:10 A.M. 날짜: 3월 15일 오전 11시 10분
Subject: Problem with the Online Account Information System
제목: 온라인 계정 정보 시스템 오류

I am writing to you because I have been unable to get into the online account system this morning. I accessed the system on Friday afternoon with no problem, but every time I have entered my password today, I have received an "access denied" message. I don't know whether this is a company-wide problem or just a problem with my computer. At any rate, it's imperative that I enter account information for six new loan applicants by 5:00 P.M. today. Can you help me resolve this?

오늘 아침 온라인 계정 시스템에 접속할 수 없었기 때문에 편지를 드립니다. 금요일 오후에는 문제없이 시스템에 접속했지만 오늘 암호를 입력할 때마다 "액세스가 거부되었습니다."라는 메시지가 나타납니다. 이것이 회사 차원의 문제인지 제 컴퓨터의 문제인지는 알 수 없습니다. 어쨌든, 오늘 저는 오늘 오후 5시까지 6명의 신규 대출 신청자에 대한 계좌 정보를 입력해야 합니다. 이 문제를 해결하도록 도와주시겠습니까?

복수 지문에 이메일이 나올 경우 수신자와 발신자를 구분하여 지문을 읽어야 한다.

이메일 제목에서 주제와 관련된 키워드를 확인한다.

세부사항
금요일 오후에 시스템이 정상 운영됐으나 월요일 오전에 오류가 발견됐다.

세부사항
발신자(Ofir)는 오후 5시까지 대출 신청자 계좌 정보를 입력해야 한다.

To: Ofir Graizer <Orgraizer@bsb.com> 수신: Ofir Graizer
From: Technical Support <techsupport@bsb.com> 발신: 기술지원팀
Date: March 15, 11:40 A.M. 날짜: 3월 15일 오전 11시 40분
Subject: Re: Problem with the Online Account Information System
제목: 답장: 온라인 계정 정보 시스템 오류

Hi, Ofir, 안녕하세요, Ofir 씨

I am sorry you've been inconvenienced. The online account system was updated over the weekend, and the work was completed at 6:00 this morning. We did the update over the weekend with the hope that full access would be available by the start of the workday today. Unfortunately, there have been scattered problems with these "access denied" messages this morning. We have already looked into the issue and expect to have the system fully operational within the next couple of hours, which will be in time for you to submit your clients' loan applications.

불편을 끼쳐 드려 죄송합니다. 온라인 계정 시스템은 주말에 업데이트되었으며, 이 작업은 오늘 아침 6시에 완료되었습니다. 저희는 주말에 오늘 근무 시작일까지 모든 접속이 가능할 것이라는 기대로 업데이트를 수행했습니다. 유감스럽게도, 오늘 아침에 간간이 "액세스가 거부되었습니다"라는 메시지가 나타나는 문제가 있었습니다. 우리는 이미 이 문제를 조사 중이며 몇 시간 내에 시스템이 정상 작동될 것으로 예상합니다. 그리고 귀하의 고객의 대출 신청서를 제시간에 제출할 수 있을 것입니다.

Thank you for your patience. 양해해 주셔서 감사합니다.

Stephanie Shaw
Technical Support Manager 기술 지원팀 매니저

세부사항
기술지원팀에서 주말 동안 업데이트를 시작하여 월요일 오전 6시에 완료했다.

PRACTICE

정답 및 해설 p.442

Question 1 refers to the following e-mails.

To: Technical Support <techsupport@bsb.com>

From: Ofir Graizer <Orgraizer@bsb.com>

Date: March 15, 11:10 A.M.

Re: Problem with the Online Account Information System

I am writing to you because I have been unable to get into the online account system this morning. I accessed the system on Friday afternoon with no problem, but every time I have entered my password today, I have received an "access denied" message. I don't know whether this is a company-wide problem or just a problem with my computer. At any rate, it's imperative that I enter account information for six new loan applicants by 5:00 P.M. today. Can you help me resolve this?

To: Ofir Graizer <Orgraizer@bsb.com>

From: Technical Support <techsupport@bsb.com>

Date: March 15, 11:40 A.M.

Subject: Re: Problem with the Online Account Information System

Hi, Ofir,

I am sorry you've been inconvenienced. The online account system was updated over the weekend, and the work was completed at 6:00 this morning. We did the update over the weekend with the hope that full access would be available by the start of the workday today. Unfortunately, there have been scattered problems with these "access denied" messages this morning. We have already looked into the issue and expect to have the system fully operational within the next couple of hours, which will be in time for you to submit your clients' loan applications.

Thank you for your patience.

Stephanie Shaw

Technical Support Manager

---

1. According to Ms. Shaw, when should Mr. Graizer be able to access the online account system again?

   (A) By 6:00 Monday morning

   (B) Before 5:00 Monday evening

   (C) By Friday morning

   (D) Over the weekend

ACTUAL TEST

Questions 1-5 refer to the following advertisement and e-mail.

Equinox Health Clubs

Come and visit our brand-new club in Dakota. As patrons of the Equinox Health Club, you will soon have access to this amazing facility in Fargo and Williston as a part of your membership. This exclusive free preview event allows you to experience it before anyone else.

Date: Saturday, September 15
Time: 1:00 P.M. ~ 5:00 P.M.
Activities: Take tours, try samples of our café items, and meet our skilled instructors

Why Try the Dakota Club?
- The Clean Eats Café serves nutritious sandwiches, salads and fruit juice.
- The indoor pool has different areas for exercise and relaxation.
- Gold's Gym offers activities for children from 5 to 12 years of age.
- The Spinning Hub Room has state-of-the-art exercise bicycles with advanced monitors and controls, the first of their kind in the area.

Our grand opening to the general public will be held on Saturday, September 22.
Come back for trial classes and more free treats. Some guests will even win Equinox T-shirts and hats.

To: ajames@equinox.com
From: jhernandez@freemayle.net
Date: September 23
Subject: Employment Opportunities

Dear Mr. James,

I enjoyed talking with you yesterday afternoon. Thank you for the tour of your health club. The employees showed a lot of enthusiasm, and it was great to learn that so many families are interested in joining Equinox. I would like to continue our discussion about becoming a part of your team at Equinox Health Club in Dakota. I have attached my résumé for your consideration, as per our conversation.

You will see from my professional experience that I thrive in environments that promote good health. Most importantly, I enjoy working with young people and have always sought out opportunities for coaching and counseling children. I think it is important to encourage daily physical activity for our youth. Please call me at (607) 555-0118 to discuss any possible positions.

Sincerely,

Jennifer Hernandez

---

1. For whom is the advertisement most likely intended?

   (A) New residents in the Dakota area
   (B) People training to become exercise instructors
   (C) Current members of the Equinox Health Club
   (D) Commercial real estate investors

2. What will attendees receive for free on September 15?

   (A) Food and drinks
   (B) Private instruction
   (C) A one-week guest pass
   (D) An article of clothing

3. According to the advertisement, what is available only at the club in Dakota?

   (A) Swimming lessons
   (B) Nutrition counselling
   (C) Discounted membership rates
   (D) Specialized exercise bicycles

4. When did Ms. Hernandez most likely meet Mr. James?

   (A) During a scheduled job interview
   (B) During a hiring conference
   (C) During the club's preview event
   (D) During the club's grand opening

5. Where in the club would Ms. Hernandez most likely wish to work?

   (A) In the Clean Eats Café
   (B) In the swimming areas
   (C) In Gold's Gym
   (D) In the Spinning Hub Room

Questions 6-10 refer to the following advertisement and letter.

Position: Manager, Hip Kitchen, Inc., retail store

Store Location (opening mid-June): 4528 Hornet Avenue, Memphis

Tasks: Managing the sales staff, ensuring that all customers receive high-quality service, and meeting monthly sales goals. Should be able to work a minimum of six closing shifts per month.

Qualifications: Basic knowledge of the retail industry and good organizational skills. Must have the ability to train and lead employees. Recommend an individual who is familiar with cooking equipment and the culinary industry. A bachelor's degree in marketing and at least 4 years of experience as a manager both required. The selected candidate must be available for training on June 5.

Company Introduction: Hip Kitchen, Inc. is the leading retailer of culinary equipment. Operates 30 stores which provide kitchen tools from the best suppliers in the mid-southern region.

How to Apply: Send a copy of your résumé, a cover letter, and a completed employment application to:
Gina Webb, Director of Personnel Department
Hip Kitchen, Inc., 595 Arby Road, Nashville TN, 37458
or to ginawebb@hipkitchen.com by March 3.

You may download an employment application form at www.hipkitchen.com/jobs.

Brian Somerset · 1870 Trump Street · Memphis, TN 37514

February 21

Gina Webb
Director of Personnel Department
Hip Kitchen Inc.
595 Arby Road
Nashville TN, 37458

Dear Ms. Webb,

I would like to apply for the manager's position advertised in Tennessee Job Search. As you can see from my résumé, I graduated from Crown University with a degree in marketing. I have worked for five years as a sales manager for County Attire, which will be closing its Memphis branch this year. While I was at County Attire, I have trained 15 new staff members and was awarded for exemplary customer service by my sales staff several times.

Despite my lack of experience with the type of merchandise Hip Kitchen, Inc. handles, I have some basic knowledge of this particular industry as I spent three years as a manager at Savory Caterers. In addition, my employment with County Attire ends roughly a month before the opening of your new store on Hornet Avenue. Therefore, I should have no problem participating in the training session on June 5, the date mentioned in your advertisement. Thank you for your consideration.

Sincerely,

Brian Somerset
Brian Somerset

6. What is NOT a stated duty of the advertised position?

   (A) Finding new suppliers of merchandise to be sold
   (B) Maintaining a high level of customer service
   (C) Making sure that sales goals are reached
   (D) Working some closing shifts

7. By what date should applications be sent?

   (A) February 21
   (B) March 3
   (C) May 31
   (D) June 5

8. Where is Mr. Somerset currently employed?

   (A) Hip Kitchen, Inc.
   (B) Crown University
   (C) County Attire
   (D) Savory Caterers

9. Why might Ms. Webb NOT consider Mr. Somerset an ideal candidate for the position?

   (A) He has not yet obtained the required academic degree.
   (B) He has too few years of managerial experience.
   (C) He is unfamiliar with cooking equipment.
   (D) He has never been responsible for training employees.

10. What does Mr. Somerset expect to happen in May?

   (A) His sales staff will be expanded by fifteen people.
   (B) He will relocate to Nashville.
   (C) He will receive an award for customer service.
   (D) His contract with his current employer will end.

Questions 11-15 refer to the following memo, Web page, and text message.

To: Fortress Holdings Staff
From: Daniel Bass, HR Director

October 16

We are pleased to announce that Andrew McKnight has been promoted to the position of branch manager of the Marana branch. He has done an amazing job as the assistant manager here at the Phoenix branch, and we're sure that his leadership skills will be an excellent asset to his new team.

We will hold a party for Mr. McKnight on Wednesday, October 31, in the conference room at 4:00 P.M. Fortress Holdings' vice president will give a speech, and then refreshments will be served. The company will prepare a gift for Mr. McKnight. We will also have a card for him. Please stop by Julia Hartz's office to sign it and to write a personal message.

Mr. McKnight's last day of work here will be Friday, November 2, and he will start work at his new place on Monday, November 5. For those of you who have worked closely with Mr. McKnight, I'm sure you will not be surprised that he's not taking any time off before jumping into his new role. We wish him all the best.

---

https://www.fortresshols.com/staffforum

To post a message, you must be logged in to your Fortress Holdings employee account.

Update! / Posted October 23 by Daniel Bass

The party for Mr. McKnight has been moved to Friday, October 26.
Unfortunately, he is needed at the Marana branch one week earlier than expected. A major client from Singapore will come to the branch, and Mr. McKnight needs more time to prepare for that. Luckily, he has already done a good job of handing off his responsibilities to others to make a smooth transition. I hope you are all still able to make it to the farewell party despite the change.

To: Andrew McKnight (602) 555-0295
From: Vera Simmons (602) 555-3081

October 26, 17:33:37

I tried to reach you on your office line, but there was no answer. I'm sorry I was unable to be at your farewell party today. I hope you had a great time! I heard that Mr. Cole's speech was quite moving.
If you have time before you leave, I'd love to take you to lunch. Just let me know if you are free.

11. Why are people asked to go to Ms. Hartz's office?

(A) To contribute money for a gift
(B) To express food preferences
(C) To write a note on a card
(D) To confirm attendance at an event

12. When will Mr. McKnight's first day at the Marana branch be?

(A) October 29
(B) October 16
(C) November 2
(D) November 5

13. According to the Web page, what is the reason for the change?

(A) A visitor is coming.
(B) A large order came in.
(C) A job offer was rejected.
(D) A travel ticket was unavailable.

14. In the text message, the word "reach" in paragraph 1, line 1, is closest in meaning to

(A) accomplish
(B) grasp
(C) extend
(D) contact

15. Who most likely is Mr. Cole?

(A) The HR director
(B) The vice president
(C) The assistant manager
(D) The branch manager

Questions 16-20 refer to the following e-mails and report.

To: Cox Network <inquiries@coxnetwork.ca>

From: Eddie Garcia <egarcia@garcediting.ca>

Date: August 3

Subject: Account No. 120805

Dear Cox Network Representative,

I have been a Cox Network customer for the past few months, and I was surprised by the charge on my July invoice. I made the payment in full this morning so as to avoid any possible late fees, but there is an issue that needs to be resolved.

I was charged for the entire month of July—$49.95—despite having some downtime on my connection in July. While I understand that this can happen as your system is being upgraded, I don't think I should have to pay for the service on days when I did not use it. Therefore, I ask that you issue a refund for those days. If possible, I would like it returned to the credit card I used to pay the bill. If not, I would prefer a check sent to my residence. I would prefer not to have my Cox account credited.

Sincerely,

Eddie Garcia

Cox Network

Downtime Report for July

Submitted by Matthew Haymond

Service Area	Rating	Total Down Time	Notes
Aurora	Fair	1 day	Damaged cables
Naperville	Fair	2 days	Damaged cables
Bloomington	Good	12 hours	None
Springfield	Unrated	N/A	Launched July 20

To: Eddie Garcia <egarcia@garcediting.ca>

From: Cox Network <inquiries@coxnetwork.ca>

Date: August 4

Subject: Re: Account No.120805

Dear Mr. Garcia,

I'm sorry that you recently had a disappointing experience with Cox Network. We do our best to have the service running continuously, but this is not always possible. Normally, we do not give refunds for downtime, but in your case, it seems reasonable to do so.

Therefore, you will receive a refund based on the days of downtime you experienced. We cannot issue refund checks, but we can accommodate your other requested method for issuing the refund. This may take a few days to process. I will e-mail you again when everything is done.

Sincerely,

Katherine Lee
Customer Service Agent, Cox Network

16. What is the purpose of the first e-mail?

(A) To add an Internet line
(B) To dispute a bill
(C) To make a payment
(D) To upgrade a service

17. How will Mr. Garcia be issued a refund?

(A) By check
(B) By bank transfer
(C) By credit card
(D) By Cox account credit

18. In which area does Mr. Garcia most likely live?

(A) Aurora
(B) Naperville
(C) Bloomington
(D) Springfield

19. In the second e-mail, the word "case" in paragraph 1, line 3, is closest in meaning to

(A) task
(B) container
(C) argument
(D) situation

20. What does Ms. Lee say she will do?

(A) Get in touch when a task is complete
(B) E-mail information about a policy
(C) Report a problem to her supervisor
(D) Send a technician to Mr. Garcia's home

정답과
해설

PART 01 사진 묘사

UNIT 01 인물 등장 사진

PRACTICE
본문 p.28

1. mowing, moving, sweeping, working
   (A) 남자가 잔디를 깎고 있다. (O)
   (B) 남자가 화분을 옮기고 있다. (X)
   (C) 남자가 밖에서 빗자루로 쓸고 있다. (X)
   (D) 남자가 정원에서 일하고 있다. (O)

2. putting on, reaching, working, looking at
   (A) 여자가 안경을 쓰고 있다. (동작) (X)
   (B) 여자가 책을 향해 손을 뻗고 있다. (X)
   (C) 여자가 노트북 컴퓨터로 일하고 있다. (O)
   (D) 여자가 화면을 보고 있다. (O)

3. attending, handing, pointing, clapping
   (A) 사람들이 회의에 참석하고 있다. (O)
   (B) 남자가 여자에게 종이를 건네고 있다. (X)
   (C) 남자 중 한 명이 보드를 가리키고 있다. (O)
   (D) 몇몇 사람들이 박수를 치고 있다. (X)

4. adjusting, holding, handing, sitting
   (A) 남자가 선글라스를 고쳐 쓰고 있다. (X)
   (B) 남자가 태블릿 PC를 들고 있다. (O)
   (C) 여자가 여행가방을 남자에게 건네고 있다. (X)
   (D) 여자가 다리를 꼬고 앉아 있다. (O)

ACTUAL TEST
본문 p.29

1. (A) 2. (C) 3. (C) 4. (B) 5. (B) 6. (D)

1.

(A) She is reaching for a book.
(B) She is assembling some shelves.
(C) She is sticking labels on the boxes.
(D) She is filing some papers.

(A) 여자가 책을 향해 손을 뻗고 있다.
(B) 여자가 선반을 조립하는 중이다.
(C) 여자가 박스에 상표를 붙이는 중이다.
(D) 여자가 서류를 철하고 있다.

해설 (A) 여자가 책을 향해 손을 뻗고 있는(reaching for) 모습을 묘사한 정답이다.
(B) 여자가 선반을 조립하고 있는(assembling) 모습이 아니므로 오답이다.
(C) 여자가 상표를 붙이고 있는(sticking) 모습이 아니므로 오답이다.
(D) 여자가 서류를 철하고 있는(filing) 모습이 아니므로 오답이다.

어휘 reach for ~을 향해 손을 뻗다 assemble 조립하다 shelve 선반, 책꽂이 stick 붙이다, 부착하다 file (문서 등을 정리하여) 보관하다[철하다]

2.

(A) The man is wiping off a counter.
(B) The man is filling a cup with coffee.
(C) The man is typing on a laptop computer.
(D) The man is writing in a notebook.

(A) 남자가 카운터를 닦고 있다.
(B) 남자가 컵에 커피를 채우고 있다.
(C) 남자가 노트북으로 타자를 치고 있다.
(D) 남자가 공책에 쓰고 있다.

해설 (A) 남자가 카운터를 닦고 있는(wiping) 모습이 아니므로 오답이다.
(B) 남자가 컵에 커피를 채우고 있는(filling) 모습이 아니므로 오답이다.
(C) 남자가 노트북으로 타자를 치고 있는(typing) 모습을 묘사한 정답이다.
(D) 남자가 공책에 무언가를 쓰고 있는(writing) 모습이 아니므로 오답이다.

어휘 wipe off 정리하다, 닦다 fill 채우다 type (타자기나 컴퓨터로) 타자 치다 notebook 노트, 공책

3.

(A) He is driving a car down the street.

(B) He is carrying a suitcase up some stairs.

(C) He is putting luggage into a vehicle.

(D) He is adjusting his seat.

(A) 그는 길 아래로 차를 몰고 있다.

(B) 그는 여행 가방을 들고 계단을 오르고 있다.

(C) 그는 자동차에 짐을 넣고 있다.

(D) 그는 좌석을 조정하고 있다.

해설 (A) 남자가 차를 몰고 있는(driving) 모습이 아니므로 오답이다.
(B) 남자가 가방을 들고 계단을 오르고 있는(carrying a suitcase up some stairs) 모습이 아니므로 오답이다.
(C) 남자가 자동차 트렁크에 짐을 넣고 있는(putting luggage) 모습을 묘사한 정답이다.
(D) 남자가 좌석을 조정하고 있는(adjusting) 모습이 아니므로 오답이다.

어휘 drive a car 차를 운전하다 suitcase 여행 가방 stair 계단 adjust 조정[조절]하다

4.

(A) They are paying for a purchase.

(B) They are shopping for clothing.

(C) They are loading some shirts into a cart.

(D) They are seated across from each other.

(A) 그들은 구매 비용을 지불하고 있다.

(B) 그들은 옷을 사기 위해 쇼핑하고 있다.

(C) 그들은 셔츠 몇 장을 카트에 싣고 있다.

(D) 그들은 서로 마주 보고 앉아 있다.

해설 (A) 구매 비용을 지불하고 있는(paying) 모습이 아니므로 오답이다.
(B) 쇼핑을 하고 있는(shopping) 모습을 묘사한 정답이다.
(C) 카트에 셔츠를 싣고 있는(loading into a cart) 모습이 아니므로 오답이다.
(D) 앉아 있는(seated) 모습이 아니므로 오답이다.

어휘 pay 지불하다 purchase 구매하다; 구매한 것 shop 쇼핑을 하다 clothing 옷 load 싣다 across from ~의 바로 맞은편에

5.

(A) Some food is being carried on a tray.

(B) A server is handing a customer a menu.

(C) A worker is serving some beverages.

(D) Some customers are paying at a register.

(A) 음식이 쟁반에 담겨 운반되고 있다.

(B) 종업원이 고객에게 메뉴판을 건네고 있다.

(C) 직원이 음료수를 제공하고 있다.

(D) 고객들이 계산대에서 계산하고 있다.

해설 (A) 음식이 운반되고 있는(is being carried) 모습이 아니므로 오답이다.
(B) 종업원이 고객에게 메뉴판을 건네고 있는(handing a menu) 모습을 묘사한 정답이다.
(C) 직원이 음료수를 제공하고 있는(serving some beverages) 모습이 아니므로 오답이다.
(D) 고객들이 계산하고 있는(paying) 모습은 아니므로 오답이다.

어휘 carry 나르다, 운반하다 tray 쟁반 hand 건네다 beverage 마실 것, 음료 register 계산대

6.

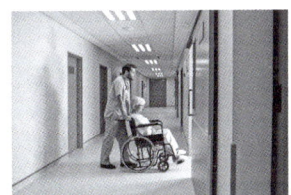

(A) A man is pulling a suitcase.

(B) They are walking side by side.

(C) The chairs are stacked in the corner.

(D) A wheelchair is being pushed.

(A) 남자가 여행 가방을 끌고 있다.

(B) 그들이 나란히 걷고 있다.

(C) 의자들이 구석에 쌓여 있다.

(D) 휠체어를 밀고 있다.

해설 (A) 사진에 없는 명사(suitcase)를 이용한 오답이다.
(B) 나란히 걷고 있는(walking side by side) 모습이 아니므로 오답이다.
(C) 코너에 쌓여 있는(are stacked in the corner) 의자는 보이지 않으므로 오답이다.
(D) 남자가 휠체어를 밀고 있는 모습을 묘사한 정답이다.

어휘 pull 끌다 side by side 나란히 stack 쌓다, 쌓이다 corner 모서리, 구석 push 밀다

UNIT 02 사물·풍경 사진

PRACTICE
본문 p.33

1. piled up, placed, hanging, behind
   (A) 책들이 바닥에 쌓여 있다. (X)
   (B) 램프가 책상 위에 놓여 있다. (O)
   (C) 벽에 그림이 걸려 있다. (X)
   (D) 식물이 소파 뒤에 있다. (X)

2. have been left, lying on, riding, lined up
   (A) 자전거가 밖에 놓여 있다. (O)
   (B) 자전거가 옆으로 눕혀 있다. (X)
   (C) 사람들이 자전거를 타고 있다. (X)
   (D) 자전거가 건물 앞에 줄지어 있다. (O)

3. being tied, floating, overlook, fishing from
   (A) 배가 부두에 정박되고 있다. (X)
   (B) 배 몇 척이 물 위에 떠 있다. (O)
   (C) 건물이 물을 내려다보고 있다. (O)
   (D) 사람들이 부두에서 낚시하고 있다. (X)

4. crosses over, vehicles, being built, extends over
   (A) 강 위로 다리가 가로질러 놓여 있다. (O)
   (B) 도로에 차량이 많다. (X)
   (C) 고속도로가 산을 관통해 건설되고 있다. (X)
   (D) 다리가 강 위를 가로질러 뻗어 있다. (O)

ACTUAL TEST
본문 p.34

1. (A) 2. (B) 3. (A) 4. (B) 5. (B) 6. (C)

1.

(A) The trail is paved with bricks.
(B) The path is crowded with visitors.
(C) Some trees are being cut down.
(D) Some pillars are being painted.

(A) 산책로가 벽돌로 포장되어 있다.
(B) 방문객들로 길이 붐비고 있다.
(C) 나무가 베어지는 중이다.
(D) 기둥이 칠해지고 있다.

해설 (A) 오솔길(trail)이 벽돌로 포장되어 있는(paved with bricks) 모습을 묘사한 정답이다.
(B) 사진에 길(path)은 보이지만 사람은 보이지 않으므로 오답이다.
(C) 사물을 주어로 하는 수동태 진행형(are being cut down)은 그 동작을 행하는 인물이 있어야 하는데 사진 속에서 나무를 자르고 있는 사람은 없으므로 오답이다.
(D) 보기 (C)와 마찬가지로 수동태 진행형으로, 페인트를 칠하고 있는 사람은 보이지 않으므로 오답이다.

어휘 trail 산책로 pave (벽돌 등으로) 포장하다 path 길 pillar 기둥

2.

(A) A server is handing out some menus.
(B) Some light fixtures are suspended from the ceiling.
(C) Some of the tables are occupied.
(D) Some artwork is hanging on the walls.

(A) 종업원이 메뉴판을 건네고 있다.
(B) 조명이 천장에 매달려 있다.
(C) 몇몇 테이블이 차 있다.
(D) 예술 작품이 벽에 걸려 있다.

해설 (A) 종업원이 메뉴판을 건네는 모습(handing out some menus)은 보이지 않는다.
(B) 조명이 천장에 매달려 있는(are suspended from the ceiling) 모습을 묘사한 정답이다.
(C) 테이블이 차 있다는(are occupied) 표현으로, 사진에 사람들이 보이지 않으므로 오답이다.
(D) 예술 작품이 벽에 걸려 있는(is hanging on the walls) 모습은 보이지 않으므로 오답이다.

어휘 server (식당에서) 서빙하는 사람 light fixture 조명 기구 suspend 매달다 ceiling 천장 occupied 사용(되는) 중인, 채워져 있는 artwork 미술[예술]품

3.

(A) A chair is pushed under a desk.

(B) A potted plant is placed at the corner of the desk.

(C) Some papers are scattered on the desk.

(D) A lamp is turned on next to the computer.

(A) 의자가 책상 밑으로 들어가 있다.
(B) 책상 구석에 화분이 놓여 있다.
(C) 서류가 책상 위에 흩어져 있다.
(D) 컴퓨터 옆에 전등이 켜져 있다.

> **해설** (A) 의자가 책상 밑으로 들어가 있는(is pushed under a desk) 모습을 묘사한 정답이다.
> (B) 사진에 화분(potted plant)은 보이지 않으므로 오답이다.
> (C) 책상 위에 흩어져 있는(are scattered) 서류가 보이지 않으므로 오답이다.
> (D) 사진에 전등(lamp)은 보이지만 컴퓨터 옆에 있지 않으므로 오답이다.

> **어휘** be pushed under ~아래로 들어가 있다 potted plant 화분
> be scattered 흩어져 있다 lamp 램프, 등

4.

(A) Some flowers are being planted near the water.

(B) Water is flowing from the fountain.

(C) Some workers are trimming bushes.

(D) A fence is being repaired.

(A) 물가 주변에 꽃을 심고 있다.
(B) 분수대에서 물이 흐르고 있다.
(C) 작업자들이 덤불을 다듬고 있다.
(D) 울타리가 수리 중이다.

> **해설** (A) 사진에 꽃은 보이지만 심고 있는(are being planted) 사람은 보이지 않으므로 오답이다.
> (B) 물이 분수대에서 흘러내리는 모습을 묘사한 정답이다.
> (C) 사진에 덤불은 보이지만, 다듬는 사람은 보이지 않으므로 오답이다.
> (D) 울타리를 고치고 있는(is being repaired) 사람은 보이지 않으므로 오답이다.

> **어휘** plant (나무를) 심다 flow 흐르다 fountain 분수 trim 다듬다, 손질하다 bush 관목, 덤불 fence 울타리 repair 수리하다

5.

(A) The worker is climbing up the ladder.

(B) Airplanes are lined up in a row at the airport.

(C) Most of the passengers are seated on the airplane.

(D) A lane is being painted on the runway.

(A) 인부가 사다리를 올라가고 있다.
(B) 비행기들은 공항에 일렬로 줄지어 서 있다.
(C) 탑승객들은 대부분 기내에 앉아 있다.
(D) 활주로에 차선이 도색되고 있다.

> **해설** (A) 사진 속에 사다리를 올라가고 있는(climbing up the ladder) 사람의 모습은 보이지 않으므로 오답이다.
> (B) 비행기들이 일렬로 줄지어 있는(lined up) 모습을 묘사한 정답이다.
> (C) 기내에 사람들이 앉아 있는(are seated) 모습은 아니므로 오답이다.
> (D) 활주로에 차선을 칠하고 있는(is being painted) 사람의 모습은 보이지 않으므로 오답이다.

> **어휘** climb up ~에 오르다 ladder 사다리 in a row 일렬로 airport 공항 passenger 승객 lane 차선 runway 활주로

6.

(A) The road is being paved.

(B) The buildings overlook the fountain.

(C) The buildings are reflected in the water.

(D) Some people are crossing a bridge.

(A) 도로가 포장되고 있다.
(B) 건물에서 분수가 내려다보인다.
(C) 건물들이 물 위에 비치고 있다.
(D) 몇몇 사람들이 다리를 건너고 있다.

> **해설** (A) 도로가 포장되고 있는(is being paved) 모습은 아니므로 오답이다.
> (B) 사진에 없는 명사(fountain)를 이용한 오답이다.
> (C) 건물들이 물 위로 비추어 있는(are reflected in the water) 모습을 묘사한 정답이다.
> (D) 다리를 건너고 있는(crossing a bridge) 사람들은 보이지 않으므로 오답이다.

정답과 해설

UNIT 03 인물·풍경 혼합 사진

PRACTICE 본문 p.38

1. heavy machinery, overlooking, scaffolding, traffic light

(A) 공사 현장에 중장비들이 있다. (O)
(B) 건물이 강을 내려다보고 있다. (X)
(C) 일부 작업자들이 비계 위에 서 있다. (X)
(D) 몇몇 자동차들이 신호등에 멈춰 있다. (X)

2. propped, being installed, talking on the phone, parking a vehicle

(A) 자전거가 벽에 기대어 있다. (O)
(B) 표지판이 도로에 설치되는 중이다. (X)
(C) 여자가 통화 중이다. (O)
(D) 여자가 건물 앞에 주차 중이다. (X)

3. crowd of, Buildings overlook, lamppost, under construction

(A) 많은 사람이 노천 시장에 모여 있다. (O)
(B) 건물들이 노천 시장을 내려다보고 있다. (O)
(C) 몇몇 사람들이 가로등 옆에 서 있다. (X)
(D) 거리가 공사 중이다. (X)

4. on an airplane, overhead, from the runway, are disembarking

(A) 승객들이 비행기에 탑승해 있다. (O)
(B) 머리 위 짐칸이 열려 있다. (X)
(C) 비행기가 활주로에서 이륙하고 있다. (X)
(D) 일부 승객들이 비행기에서 내리고 있다. (X)

ACTUAL TEST 본문 p.39

1. (A) **2.** (C) **3.** (C) **4.** (D) **5.** (A) **6.** (B)

1.

(A) A man is pushing a baggage cart.
(B) Suitcases are being loaded onto an aircraft.
(C) Fitness equipment has been lined up.
(D) The floor is being mopped.

(A) 남자가 수화물 카트를 밀고 있다.
(B) 여행 가방이 비행기에 실리고 있다.
(C) 운동 기구가 일렬로 세워져 있다.
(D) 바닥이 대걸레로 닦이고 있다.

해설 (A) 한 남자가 수화물 카트(baggage cart)를 밀고 있는 모습을 묘사한 정답이다.
(B) 사물을 주어로 하는 수동태 진행형(are being loaded)은 해당 동작을 행하는 사람이 있어야 한다. 사진에서 짐을 싣는 사람은 없으므로 오답이다.
(C) 일렬로 세워져 있는(has been lined up) 운동 기구(fitness equipment)는 보이지 않는다.
(D) 사물을 주어로 하는 수동태 진행형(is being mopped)은 해당 동작을 행하는 사람이 있어야 한다. 사진에서 걸레질을 하는 사람은 보이지 않으므로 오답이다.

어휘 baggage cart 수화물 카트 suitcase 여행 가방 load 싣다 be lined up 일렬로 줄을 서다 mop 걸레질하다

2.

(A) People are gathered in front of the box office.
(B) Some musicians are walking onto a stage.
(C) Some people are watching a performance.
(D) Some chairs are being set up in an auditorium.

(A) 사람들이 매표소 앞에 모여 있다.
(B) 음악가들이 무대로 걸어 올라가고 있다.
(C) 사람들이 공연을 보고 있다.
(D) 의자들이 강당에 설치되고 있다.

해설 (A) 모여 있는(gathered) 사람들은 보이나, 매표소(box office)는 보이지 않으므로 오답이다.
(B) 무대로 걸어 올라가고 있는(walking onto a stage) 모습은 아니므로 오답이다.
(C) 사람들이 공연을 관람하고 있는(watching a performance) 모습을 묘사한 정답이다.
(D) 의자가 설치되고 있는(are being set up) 모습은 아니므로 오답이다.

어휘 gather 모이다 box office 매표소 performance 공연 set up 설치하다 auditorium 강당, 객석

3.

(A) A flight attendant is assisting people.

(B) Passengers are waiting in the baggage claim area.

(C) Some people are using a ramp to board a plane.

(D) Luggage is being moved on the conveyor belt.

(A) 승무원이 사람들을 돕고 있다.
(B) 승객들이 수화물을 찾는 곳에서 기다리고 있다.
(C) 사람들이 비행기에 탑승하기 위해 경사로를 이용하고 있다.
(D) 짐이 컨베이어 벨트 위에서 옮겨지고 있다.

> **해설** (A) 승무원이 사람들을 돕는(assisting) 모습은 보이지 않으므로 오답이다.
> (B) 승객들은 보이나, 컨베이어 벨트는 보이지 않으므로 오답이다.
> (C) 사람들이 비행기를 타기 위해(to board a plane) 경사로(ramp)를 이용하는 모습을 묘사한 정답이다.
> (D) 짐이 컨베이어 벨트 위에서 옮겨지고 있는(is being moved on the conveyor belt) 모습이 아니므로 오답이다.

> **어휘** flight attendant 승무원 assist 돕다 passenger 승객 baggage claim area 짐 찾는 곳 ramp (항공기 탑승 등을 위한) 경사 계단 conveyor belt 컨베이어 벨트

4.

(A) A group of people are entering a building.

(B) Some diners are eating indoors.

(C) A brick street is being swept.

(D) An awning extends over a store entrance.

(A) 한 무리의 사람들이 건물로 들어가고 있다.
(B) 식당 손님들이 실내에서 식사하고 있다.
(C) 벽돌 길을 쓸고 있다.
(D) 차양이 가게 입구 위에 드리워져 있다.

> **해설** (A) 건물에 들어가는(entering a building) 사람들의 모습은 보이지 않으므로 오답이다.
> (B) 식당에 손님들(diners)은 보이지만, 실내에서 식사 중(are eating indoors)인 모습은 아니므로 오답이다.
> (C) 사물을 주어로 하는 수동태 진행형(is being swept)으로, 사진에서 길을 쓸고 있는 사람은 보이지 않으므로 오답이다.

(D) 차양(awning)이 가게 입구 위에 드리워져 있는(extends over a store entrance) 모습을 묘사한 정답이다.

> **어휘** a group of 한 무리의 diner 식사하는 사람, 손님 indoors 실내에서 brick 벽돌 sweep (빗자루로) 쓸다 awning (창이나 문 위의) 차양 extend 뻗다, 펼치다

5.

(A) Some chairs are unoccupied.

(B) The man is leaning on a counter.

(C) The cashier is bagging some items.

(D) Some beverages are being poured.

(A) 일부 좌석이 비어 있다.
(B) 남자가 카운터에 기대고 있다.
(C) 계산원이 물건들을 봉지에 넣고 있다.
(D) 음료수들이 따라지고 있다.

> **해설** (A) 일부 좌석이 비어 있는(are unoccupied) 모습을 묘사한 정답이다.
> (B) 카운터에 기대어 있는(leaning on a counter) 남자는 보이지 않으므로 오답이다.
> (C) 물건들을 포장하는(bagging some items) 계산원은 보이지 않으므로 오답이다.
> (D) 음료를 따르고 있는(are being poured) 사람은 보이지 않으므로 오답이다.

> **어휘** unoccupied 비어 있는 lean on ~에 기대다 cashier 출납원, 계산원 bag 봉지에 넣다 beverage 음료 pour 따르다

6.

(A) Some people are having a conversation.

(B) Some people are walking in the park.

(C) Some people are seated facing the same direction.

(D) Some people are waiting in a line.

(A) 몇몇 사람들이 대화하고 있다.
(B) 몇몇 사람들이 공원에서 산책하고 있다.
(C) 몇몇 사람들이 같은 방향을 향해 앉아 있다.
(D) 몇몇 사람들이 한 줄로 서서 기다리고 있다.

해설 (A) 사람들이 대화하고 있는(are having a conversation) 모습이 아니므로 오답이다.
(B) 사람들이 공원에서 산책하고 있는(are walking in the park) 모습을 묘사한 정답이다.
(C) 사람들이 같은 방향으로 앉아 있는(are seated facing the same direction) 모습이 아니므로 오답이다.
(D) 한 줄로 서서 기다리는 사람들은 보이지 않으므로 오답이다.

어휘 have a conversation 대화하다 direction 방향
in a line 한 줄로

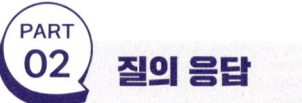

PART 02 질의 응답

UNIT 04 Who/When/Where 의문문

PRACTICE 본문 p.52

| 1. (A) | 2. (B) | 3. (A) | 4. (B) | 5. (A) |
| 6. (C) | 7. (B) | 8. (B) | 9. (C) | 10. (B) |

1. Who is the director's new secretary?
(A) It's Betty Rodman.
(B) Sending an e-mail.
(C) On the table.

이사님의 새 비서가 누구인가요?
(A) Betty Rodman이에요.
(B) 이메일을 보내는 거요.
(C) 탁자 위에요.

해설 (A) Who 의문문에 직접적으로 사람 이름을 언급한 정답, (B) What 의문문에 적합한 오답, (C) Where 의문문에 적합한 오답.

어휘 director 이사, 임원 secretary 비서

2. Who's coming to the staff meeting tomorrow?
(A) In the museum.
(B) The design team.
(C) Yes, 2 o'clock.

누가 오늘 직원 회의에 오나요?
(A) 박물관에서요.
(B) 디자인 팀이요.
(C) 네, 2시에요.

해설 (A) Where 의문문에 적합한 오답, (B) Who 의문문에서 '부서나 팀 이름'이 들리면 정답일 확률이 높다. (C) 의문사 의문문에 Yes로 응답 불가.

어휘 staff meeting 직원 회의 museum 박물관

3. Who decorated the restaurant?
(A) The supervisor.
(B) No, she didn't.
(C) In red.

누가 사무실을 장식했나요?
(A) 관리자가요.
(B) 아니요, 그녀는 안 했어요.
(C) 빨간색으로요.

해설 (A) Who 의문문에서 '직책 이름'이 들리면 정답일 확률이 높다. (B) 의문사 의문문에 Yes/No로 응답 불가, (C) Which color ~? 에 적합한 오답.

어휘 decorate 장식하다, 꾸미다 supervisor 상사, 관리자

4. Who should I call to reserve a meeting room?

(A) It's in the cinema.

(B) Ask Andy to do it.

(C) For dinner.

회의실을 예약하려면 누구에게 전화해야 하나요?
(A) 극장 안에 있어요.
(B) Andy에게 하라고 요청하세요.
(C) 저녁식사를 위해서요.

해설 (A) Where 의문문에 적합한 오답, (B) '다른 사람에게 시키라'는 의도의 회피성 유형의 정답, (C) Why 의문문에 적합한 오답.

어휘 reserve 예약하다 meeting room 회의실 cinema 극장

5. When will the office supplies be delivered?

(A) Within three days.

(B) The professor asked for them.

(C) To my home address.

사무용품이 언제 배송되나요?
(A) 3일 이내로 도착합니다.
(B) 교수님이 요청했습니다.
(C) 저희 집 주소로요.

해설 (A) 배송 시기를 묻는 질문에, 구체적인 시점을 언급한 정답, (B) Who 의문문에 적합한 오답, (C) Where 의문문에 적합한 오답.

어휘 deliver 배송하다, 배달하다 home address 자택 주소

6. When was Mr. Erickson supposed to arrive?

(A) Near the park.

(B) Yes, he drove.

(C) At one o'clock.

Erickson 씨는 언제 도착할 예정이었나요?
(A) 공원 근처에요.
(B) 네, 그가 운전했어요.
(C) 1시 정각에요.

해설 (A) Where 의문문에 적합한 오답, (B) 의문사 의문문에 Yes/No로 응답 불가, (C) '전치사+시점'을 이용해 도착 시간을 언급한 정답.

어휘 be supposed to ~하기로 되어 있다

7. When should I submit the travel expense report?

(A) Yes, be sure to do it as soon as possible.

(B) Before leaving the office today.

(C) I'm going on a business trip next Monday.

출장 경비 보고서는 언제 제출해야 하나요?
(A) 네, 되도록 빨리 해주세요.
(B) 오늘 퇴근하기 전에요.
(C) 저는 다음 주 월요일에 출장을 갑니다.

해설 (A) 의문사 의문문에서는 Yes/No로 응답 불가, (B) 보고서 제출 시기를 묻는 질문에, '오늘 퇴근 전까지'라는 구체적인 기한을 언급한 정답, (C) '다음 주 월요일'이라는 시점이 언급되긴 하지만 보고서 제출 시점이 아니라 출장을 가는 시점이므로 오답.

어휘 submit 제출하다 travel expense report 출장 경비 보고서 be sure to do 꼭 ~하세요 as soon as possible 되도록 빨리 leave the office 퇴근하다 go on a business trip 출장 가다

8. Where can I find our office supplies?

(A) We close at 6 o'clock.

(B) In that cabinet by the door.

(C) No, I haven't been there.

사무용품을 어디서 찾을 수 있나요?
(A) 저희는 6시에 문을 닫습니다.
(B) 문 옆에 있는 캐비닛에요.
(C) 아니요, 거기에 가보지 못했습니다.

해설 (A) When 의문문에 적합한 오답, (B) 'in + 장소'를 이용해 구체적인 장소를 언급한 정답, (C) 의문사 의문문에 Yes/No로 응답 불가.

어휘 office supply 사무용품 cabinet 보관함, 캐비닛

9. Where should I send this package?

(A) By international mail.

(B) After 5:00 P.M.

(C) To the new office.

이 소포를 어디로 보내야 하나요?
(A) 국제우편으로요.
(B) 오후 5시 이후에요.
(C) 새로운 사무실로요.

해설 (A) How 의문문에 적합한 오답, (B) When 의문문에 적합한 오답, (C) '전치사 + 장소'를 이용해 구체적인 장소를 언급한 정답.

어휘 package 소포 international mail 국제우편

10. Where should I file the report?

(A) Any time before you leave.

(B) On the second bookshelf.

(C) I heard from him.

어디에 이 보고서를 보관해야 하나요?
(A) 당신이 떠나기 전 아무 때나요.
(B) 두 번째 책꽂이에요.
(C) 그에게서 들었어요.

해설 (A) When 의문문에 적합한 오답, (B) '전치사+장소'를 이용해 구체적인 보관 장소를 언급한 정답, (C) 질문과 관련 없는 오답.

어휘 file (문서 등을 정리하여) 보관하다 bookshelf 책꽂이

1. (B) **2.** (A) **3.** (B) **4.** (B) **5.** (B)
6. (C) **7.** (B) **8.** (C) **9.** (A) **10.** (C)

1. When 의문문

When will the merger take place?

(A) Many companies.

(B) Sometime in November.

(C) No, not yet.

언제 합병할 건가요?
(A) 많은 회사들이요.
(B) 11월 중으로요.
(C) 아니요. 아직은 아니에요.

해설 (A) 연상 어휘(merger-companies)로 혼동을 준 오답, (B) 'in+날짜'를 이용해 합병 시기를 언급한 정답, (C) 의문사 의문문에 Yes/No로 응답 불가.

어휘 merger 합병 take place 개최되다, 일어나다 sometime 언젠가

2. Who 의문문

Who's designing the new office building?

(A) The Merch Architectural Firm.

(B) In the storage area.

(C) A new design.

누가 새 사무실 건물을 설계하나요?
(A) Merch 건축사에서요.
(B) 창고에서요.
(C) 새로운 디자인이요.

해설 (A) 구체적인 회사 이름을 언급한 정답, (B) Where 의문문에 적합한 오답, (C) 유사 어휘(designing-design)를 이용한 오답.

어휘 design 설계하다, 디자인하다 architectural firm 건축 회사 storage area 창고

3. Where 의문문

Where did Nelson leave the agenda?

(A) By two o'clock.

(B) On the desk.

(C) From Chicago.

Nelson 씨가 어디에 안건을 두었나요?
(A) 2시 정각까지요.
(B) 책상 위에요.
(C) Chicago로부터요.

해설 (A) When 의문문에 적합한 오답, (B) 안건의 위치를 묻는 질문에, 'on+장소'로 구체적인 위치를 언급한 정답, (C) 출처를 묻는 질문에 적합한 오답.

어휘 leave 남기다, 두다 agenda 안건

4. Who 의문문

Who will be giving the presentation?

(A) In the meeting room.

(B) Ms. Miranda.

(C) In December.

누가 프레젠테이션을 할 건가요?
(A) 회의실에서요.
(B) Miranda 씨요.
(C) 12월에요.

해설 (A) Where 의문문에 적합한 오답, (B) 프레젠테이션을 진행할 사람의 이름을 구체적으로 언급한 정답, (C) When 의문문에 적합한 오답.

어휘 give a presentation 발표하다

5. Where 의문문

Where did you put my key?

(A) A locker room.

(B) Isn't it on the chair?

(C) I will leave soon.

열쇠를 어디에 뒀어요?
(A) 라커룸요.
(B) 의자 위에 있지 않나요?
(C) 저는 곧 떠날 거에요.

해설 (A) 연관 어휘(key-locker room)로 혼동을 준 오답, (B) 열쇠를 둔 위치를 묻는 질문에, '~에 있지 않냐'고 반문하는 정답, (C) When 의문문에 적합한 오답.

어휘 put 두다, 놓다 locker room 라커룸 leave 떠나다

6. When 의문문

When do we get reimbursed for our travel expenses?

(A) One thousand dollars.

(B) The prices are fixed.

(C) After the form's been approved.

언제 출장비를 환급 받을 수 있나요?
(A) 1,000달러요.
(B) 정찰제입니다.
(C) 양식이 승인된 후에요.

해설 (A) How much 의문문에 적합한 오답, (B) 연상 어휘(expenses-prices)로 혼동을 유도한 오답, (C) '양식이 승인된 후'라는 의미로 'after+주어+동사'의 시간 부사절을 이용한 정답.

어휘 get reimbursed 환급 받다, 돌려받다 travel expense 출장비 approve 승인하다

7. Who 의문문

Who's in charge of the order?

(A) We only need an invoice.

(B) Mr. Park is.

(C) It's too expensive.

누가 주문을 담당하나요?
(A) 저희는 청구서만 필요합니다.
(B) Park 씨가요.
(C) 너무 비싸네요.

해설 (A) 연상 어휘(order-invoice)로 혼동을 유도한 오답, (B) 주문 담당자를 묻는 질문에, 담당자의 이름을 구체적으로 언급한 정답, (C) 연상 어휘(charge-expensive)로 혼동을 유도한 오답.

어휘 be in charge of ~을 맡다, 담당하다 order 주문; 주문하다 invoice 송장, 청구서

8. Where 의문문

Where should I put those bills?

(A) He isn't.

(B) Not until tomorrow.

(C) Ask the accountant.

영수증들은 어디에 둘까요?
(A) 그는 아니에요.
(B) 내일까지는 안 돼요.
(C) 회계사에게 물어보세요.

해설 (A) 3인칭 주어(He)를 이용한 인칭 오류 오답, (B) When 의문문에 적합한 오답, (C) '모른다, 다른 사람에게 물어보라'는 회피성 의미의 정답.

어휘 bill 계산서, 청구서 accountant 회계사

9. Who 의문문

Who's responsible for this department?

(A) Janet is.

(B) This apartment is too small.

(C) He responded to it.

누가 이 부서 담당인가요?
(A) Janet 씨요.
(B) 이 아파트는 너무 작아요.
(C) 그는 그것에 응답했어요.

해설 (A) 부서 담당자를 묻는 질문에, 구체적인 이름을 언급한 정답, (B) 유사 어휘(department-apartment)를 이용한 오답, (C) 유사 어휘(responsible-responded)를 이용한 오답.

어휘 responsible 책임이 있는 department 부서 respond 대답하다

10. When 의문문

When does the new manager begin the project?
(A) For a week.
(B) The conference room downstairs.
(C) On August 30.

언제 신임 매니저가 프로젝트를 시작하나요?
(A) 1주일 동안요.
(B) 아래층 회의실요.
(C) 8월 30일에요.

해설 (A) '기간'을 언급해, How long 의문문에 적합한 오답, (B) Where 의문문에 적합한 오답, (C) 프로젝트 시작 시기를 묻는 질문에, 'on+날짜'로 구체적인 시기를 언급한 정답.

어휘 begin 시작하다 meeting room 회의실

UNIT 05 What · Which/How/Why 의문문

PRACTICE 본문 p.61

1. (A)	2. (C)	3. (B)	4. (C)	5. (B)
6. (A)	7. (A)	8. (A)	9. (B)	10. (A)

1. What's the registration deadline?

(A) It's a week from today.

(B) One of the staff members finished it.

(C) On the corner of Bull Street.

등록 마감일이 언제죠?
(A) 오늘부터 일주일 후에요.
(B) 직원 중 한 명이 그것을 끝마쳤어요.
(C) Bull Street 모퉁이에요.

해설 (A) 마감일을 묻는 질문에, 구체적인 시점을 언급한 정답, (B) 연상 어휘(deadline-finished)로 혼동을 노린 오답, (C) Where 의문문에 적합한 오답.

어휘 registration 등록, 등록 서류 deadline 기한, 마감 시간 corner 모서리, 모퉁이

2. Which copier should I use?

(A) Only a hundred copies.

(B) The manager has arrived.

(C) The one next to the door.

어떤 복사기를 사용해야 하나요?
(A) 100부만요.
(B) 매니저가 도착했어요.
(C) 문 옆에 있는 거요.

해설 (A) 유사 어휘(copier-copies)를 이용한 오답, (B) 질문과 관계없는 오답, (C) 'Which + 명사' 의문문에 'the one ~'은 자주 등장하는 정답 패턴이다.

어휘 copier 복사기 copy 복사(본) next to ~ 옆에

3. What are the papers in the meeting room?

(A) In the first hall beside the stairs.

(B) A report I'm writing.

(C) I will bring it later.

회의실에 있는 서류들은 뭐죠?
(A) 계단 옆에 있는 첫 번째 복도요.
(B) 제가 쓰고 있는 보고서예요.
(C) 이따가 제가 가져올게요.

> **해설** (A) Where 의문문에 적합한 오답, (B) 회의실에 있는 서류가 뭔지를 묻는 질문에, 본인이 쓰고 있는 보고서라고 말한 정답, (C) When 의문문에 적합한 오답.

> **어휘** paper 종이, 서류 hall 현관 복도 stair 계단

4. How long will it take us to get downtown?
(A) I'm leaving town soon.
(B) It starts at 7:00 P.M.
(C) About an hour.

시내까지 가는 데 얼마나 걸리나요?
(A) 저는 곧 도시를 떠나요.
(B) 저녁 7시에 시작합니다.
(C) 한 시간쯤요.

> **해설** (A) 유사 어휘(downtown-town)를 이용한 오답 함정, (B) When 의문문에 적합한 오답, (C) 구체적인 소요 시간을 언급한 정답.

> **어휘** downtown 시내; 시내로 leave 떠나다

5. How can I make sure Bruce gets this form?
(A) I will pay for it.
(B) Put it in his mailbox.
(C) He is in New York now.

어떻게 Bruce가 이 양식을 받게 할 수 있을까요?
(A) 제가 계산하겠습니다.
(B) 그의 우편함에 넣어두세요.
(C) 그는 지금 New York에 있어요.

> **해설** (A) 질문과 관계없는 오답, (B) Bruce 씨가 양식을 받게 하려면 어떻게 해야 하는지 묻는 질문에, 우편함에 두라고 지침을 준 정답, (C) Where 의문문에 적합한 오답.

> **어휘** form 양식 pay 지불하다, 계산하다 mailbox 우편함

6. How long will it take to process my order?
(A) Only one day.
(B) No, it already arrived.
(C) Yes, more than I expected.

제 주문을 처리하는 데 얼마나 걸릴까요?
(A) 하루면 됩니다.
(B) 아니요. 이미 도착했습니다.
(C) 네, 예상했던 것보다 훨씬 더요.

> **해설** (A) 주문 처리 기간을 묻는 질문에, 하루면 된다며 구체적인 소요 시간을 언급한 정답, (B) 의문사 의문문에 No로 응답 불가, (C) 의문사 의문문에 Yes로 응답 불가.

> **어휘** process 처리하다 arrive 도착하다 expect 기대하다, 예상하다

7. Why did you leave the office early yesterday?
(A) I had another meeting.
(B) I lost it this morning.
(C) Just before the end.

어제 왜 일찍 퇴근했나요?
(A) 다른 회의가 있었어요.
(B) 오늘 아침에 잃어버렸어요.
(C) 끝나기 바로 전에요.

> **해설** (A) 일찍 퇴근한 이유를 묻는 질문에, 회의가 있었다며 직접적인 이유를 언급한 정답, (B) 연상 어휘(yesterday-this morning)를 이용한 오답, (C) When 의문문에 적합한 오답.

> **어휘** leave the office 퇴근하다

8. Why is there a billing delay?
(A) The computer system is down.
(B) I just saw it today.
(C) Yes, I guess so.

왜 계산서가 지연되고 있죠?
(A) 컴퓨터 시스템이 고장 났습니다.
(B) 오늘 봤어요.
(C) 네, 그렇게 생각해요.

> **해설** (A) 지연 이유를 묻는 질문에, 문제점을 언급한 정답(because 생략), (B) 연상 어휘(delay-today)를 이용한 오답, (C) 의문사 의문문에 Yes/No로 응답 불가.

> **어휘** billing 청구서 발부 delay 지연; 미루다 be down 고장 난

9. Why did you throw away that calendar?
(A) Yes, I'm planning to go to the meeting.
(B) It was outdated.
(C) Once a month, I think.

왜 그 달력을 버렸나요?
(A) 네, 회의에 갈 계획이에요.
(B) 오래된 거예요.
(C) 한 달에 한 번일 거예요.

> **해설** (A) 의문사 의문문에 Yes로 응답 불가, (B) 달력을 버린 이유를 직접적으로 언급한 정답, (C) How often ~?에 적합한 오답.

> **어휘** outdated 구식인

10. Why is the J&J office closing?
(A) Because the company is remodeling.
(B) The restaurant is open.
(C) The new staff.

J&J 사무실은 왜 문을 닫나요?
(A) 리모델링을 할 거라서요.
(B) 식당이 문을 열었어요.
(C) 새로운 직원이요.

해설 (A) 사무실이 문을 닫는 이유를 묻는 질문에, Because를 이용해 리모델링을 할 거라며 이유를 언급한 정답, (B) 연상 어휘(closing-open)를 이용한 오답, (C) Who 의문문에 적합한 오답.

어휘 close 문을 닫다 remodeling 개조, 리모델링

ACTUAL TEST 본문 p.63

1. (A)	2. (C)	3. (C)	4. (B)	5. (B)
6. (C)	7. (B)	8. (B)	9. (B)	10. (C)

1. What 의문문

What kind of experience do you have in sales?

(A) I sold furniture for five years.

(B) The sale will begin next weekend.

(C) It will be a good experience.

어떤 종류의 판매 경험이 있습니까?
(A) 5년 동안 가구를 판매했습니다.
(B) 할인은 다음 주말에 시작됩니다.
(C) 좋은 경험이 될 거예요.

해설 (A) 어떤 판매 경력이 있는지 묻는 질문에, 구체적인 경력과 기간을 언급한 정답, (B) 유사 어휘(sales-sale)로 혼동을 노린 오답, (C) 동일 어휘(experience)를 반복한 오답.

어휘 furniture 가구 begin 시작하다 experience 경험, 경력

2. Why 의문문

Why was the seminar rescheduled?

(A) On the top shelf.

(B) Whenever you like.

(C) Because the manager hasn't arrived yet.

세미나 일정이 왜 변경되었나요?
(A) 맨 위 선반에요.
(B) 원하실 때 언제든지요.
(C) 매니저가 아직 도착하지 않아서요.

해설 (A) Where 의문문에 적합한 오답, (B) When 의문문에 적합한 오답, (C) Because를 이용해 일정 변경 이유를 구체적으로 언급한 정답.

어휘 reschedule 일정을 변경하다 whenever ~할 때는 언제든지

3. What 의문문

What's your manager's name?

(A) For three years now.

(B) Yes, it was him.

(C) It's Monica Ben.

당신의 상사 이름이 뭐예요?
(A) 지금까지 3년 동안요.
(B) 네, 그였어요.
(C) Monica Ben입니다.

해설 (A) How long ~?에 적합한 오답, (B) 의문사 의문문에 Yes로 응답 불가, (C) 'What ~ name?'으로 이름을 묻는 질문에, 구체적인 이름을 밝힌 정답이다.

어휘 manager 경영자, 관리자

4. Which 의문문

Which café has the fastest service?

(A) From here to the bank.

(B) French Coffee House.

(C) A variety of cakes.

어떤 카페가 제일 빠른 서비스를 제공하나요?
(A) 여기서부터 은행까지요.
(B) French Coffee House요.
(C) 다양한 케이크요.

해설 (A) How far ~?에 적합한 오답, (B) 서비스가 빠른 카페를 묻는 질문에, 구체적인 이름을 언급한 정답, (C) 연상 어휘(café-cakes)를 이용한 오답.

어휘 fast 빠른 variety 여러 가지, 각양각색

5. How 의문문

How do I call the front desk?

(A) It's only for guests.

(B) Just dial 0.

(C) Yes, it's at the front desk.

프런트 데스크에 어떻게 연락하나요?
(A) 고객 전용입니다.
(B) 0번을 누르세요.
(C) 네, 프런트 데스크에 있습니다.

해설 (A) Who 의문문에 적합한 오답, (B) 프런트 데스크에 연락하는 방법을 묻는 질문에, 구체적으로 가이드를 준 정답, (C) 의문사 의문문에 Yes/No로 응답 불가.

어휘 front desk 프런트 데스크, 안내 데스크 guest 손님, 고객 dial 전화를 걸다, 다이얼을 돌리다

6. Why 의문문

Why don't you ask Mr. Roy if you can leave early tomorrow?

(A) A scheduled meeting.

(B) No, it isn't.

(C) Yes, I'd like that.

Roy 씨에게 내일 조퇴해도 되는지 물어보는 게 어때요?
(A) 회의 일정요.
(B) 아니요, 그건 아니에요.
(C) 네, 그게 좋겠네요.

해설 (A) What 의문문에 적합한 오답, (B) 일반 의문문에 적합한 오답, (C) 상대방의 제안에, 그게 좋겠다고 답변한 정답.

어휘 leave 떠나다 schedule 일정; 일정을 잡다

7. Which 의문문

Which switch turns off the heater?

(A) I sent him yesterday.

(B) The one on the right.

(C) No, I won't be there.

어떤 스위치로 난방기를 끄나요?
(A) 어제 그에게 보냈어요.
(B) 오른쪽에 있는 거요.
(C) 아니요, 저는 거기 없을 거예요.

해설 (A) When 의문문에 적합한 오답, (B) 'Which + 명사' 의문문에, 'the one ~'은 자주 등장하는 정답 패턴이다. (C) 의문사 의문문에 Yes/No로 응답 불가.

어휘 turn off ~을 끄다   heater 난방기

8. Why 의문문

Why did you decide to move to Moil Village?

(A) Yes, very decisive.

(B) It's closer to my office.

(C) Since last month.

왜 Moil 빌리지로 이사하기로 결정했나요?
(A) 네, 정말 결단력 있네요.
(B) 제 사무실과 가깝거든요.
(C) 지난달부터요.

해설 (A) 의문사 의문문에 Yes/No로 응답 불가, (B) 사무실과 가깝다며 이사 이유를 구체적으로 밝힌 정답(because 생략), (C) When 의문문에 적합한 오답.

어휘 move 움직이다, 옮기다   decisive 결단력 있는   since ~로부터, ~이후

9. What 의문문

What are the advantages of using a membership card?

(A) Yes, it's expired.

(B) You can receive special discounts.

(C) You have to pay here.

회원카드를 이용하는 것의 이점은 무엇인가요?
(A) 네, 만료되었습니다.
(B) 특별 할인을 받을 수 있습니다.
(C) 여기에서 지불하셔야 합니다.

해설 (A) 의문사 의문문에 Yes/No로 응답 불가, (B) 멤버십 카드의 장점을 묻는 질문에, 특별 할인을 받을 수 있다며 구체적으로 이점을 언급한 정답, (C) 연상 어휘(card-pay)로 혼동을 노린 오답.

어휘 advantage 유리한 점, 이점   membership 회원   expire 만료되다, 끝나다

10. How 의문문

How do I clean the computer screen?

(A) If you want to come.

(B) I like your keyboard.

(C) With a dry cloth.

컴퓨터 화면을 어떻게 청소하죠?
(A) 당신이 오고 싶다면요.
(B) 당신의 키보드가 마음에 드네요.
(C) 마른 천으로요.

해설 (A) 유사 어휘(computer-come)로 혼동을 노린 오답, (B) 연상 어휘(computer-keyboard)로 혼동을 노린 오답, (C) How ~?로 수단이나 방법을 묻는 질문은 by through, with 등의 전치사를 이용해 답변할 수 있다.

어휘 screen 화면   clean 청소하다   cloth 천

UNIT 06 일반/선택 의문문

PRACTICE   본문 p.68

1. (A)   **2.** (C)   **3.** (C)   **4.** (A)
5. (C)   **6.** (B)   **7.** (C)   **8.** (C)

1. Have you found an apartment to rent?

(A) Yes, I just signed the contract.

(B) It's in the Sales Department.

(C) He asked me yesterday.

임차할 아파트를 찾았나요?
(A) 네, 방금 계약했어요.
(B) 영업부에 있어요.
(C) 그가 어제 저한테 물어봤어요.

해설 (A) 임차할 아파트를 찾았는지 묻는 질문에, 방금 계약했다고 말한 정답, (B) 유사 어휘(apartment-department)를 이용한 오답, (C) 3인칭으로 답한 인칭 오류 오답.

어휘 rent 임대하다, 임차하다   sign a contract 계약서에 서명하다   Sales Department 영업부

2. Isn't Paul going to the train station?

(A) No, it's not raining.

(B) Attend the training session.

(C) He was planning to go.

Paul이 기차역에 가지 않나요?
(A) 아니요, 비가 오지 않아요.
(B) 교육에 참석하세요.
(C) 그는 갈 계획이었죠.

해설 (A) 유사 어휘(train-raining)를 이용해 혼동을 노린 오답, (B) 유사 어휘(train-training)를 이용한 오답, (C) 질문의 Paul을 He로 지칭해 적절히 응답한 정답.

어휘 train station 기차역   attend 참석하다   training session 교육

3. Didn't Mr. Smith send the papers to us yesterday?

(A) Anywhere around here.

(B) From a newspaper article.

(C) Yes, they're right here.

Smith 씨가 어제 우리에게 서류를 보내지 않았나요?
(A) 이 근처 아무 곳이나요.
(B) 신문 기사에서요.
(C) 네, 여기 있습니다.

해설 (A) Where 의문문에 적합한 오답, (B) 유사 어휘(papers-newspaper)를 이용한 오답, (C) 서류가 이미 도착해 여기 있다고 말하는 정답.

어휘 paper 종이, 서류 anywhere 어디든 article 기사

4. Will the weather be nice today?

(A) I hope so.

(B) Whenever you can.

(C) I'm sorry.

오늘 날씨가 좋을까요?
(A) 그러기를 바래요.
(B) 가능한 언제든지요.
(C) 죄송합니다.

해설 (A) 오늘 날씨가 좋을 것 같은지를 묻는 질문에, '그러기를 바란다'고 표현한 정답, (B) When 의문문에 적합한 오답, (C) 질문과 관련 없는 응답.

어휘 weather 날씨 whenever 언제든지

5. Do you want my home or work address?

(A) Yes, I will be there.

(B) He will leave the office soon.

(C) Could I have both?

저희 집 주소를 원하시나요, 아니면 직장 주소를 원하시나요?
(A) 네, 저는 거기로 갈 거예요.
(B) 그는 곧 퇴근할 거예요.
(C) 둘 다 알 수 있을까요?

해설 (A) 선택 의문문에 Yes/No로 응답 불가, (B) You로 물었는데 3인칭 He로 응답한 주어 지칭 오류, (C) 선택 의문문에서 both가 들리면 정답일 가능성이 높다.

어휘 address 주소 both 둘 다

6. Are you buying a house or renting?

(A) 110 Main Street.

(B) We're renting for two years.

(C) No, it isn't.

집을 구입하실 건가요, 아니면 임차하실 건가요?
(A) 110 Main 가요.
(B) 2년 동안 임차할 예정이에요.
(C) 아니요, 그렇지 않습니다.

해설 (A) Where 의문문에 적합한 오답, (B) A(buying)와 B(renting) 중 하나(renting)를 선택한 정답, (C) 선택 의문문에 No로 응답 불가.

어휘 buy 사다 rent 임대하다, 임차하다

7. Would you like dessert or coffee?

(A) He sent it yesterday.

(B) She will like it.

(C) I'll have coffee.

후식을 드시겠습니까, 아니면 커피를 드시겠습니까?
(A) 그가 그걸 어제 보냈어요.
(B) 그녀가 좋아할 거예요.
(C) 커피로 주세요.

해설 (A) You로 질문했는데 He(3인칭)로 응답한 주어 지칭 오류, (B) 역시 주어 지칭 오류, (C) A(dessert)와 B(coffee) 중 하나를 선택한 정답.

어휘 dessert 후식 send 보내다

8. Are the best seats in front or in the balcony?

(A) At the ticket counter.

(B) I'll send them back later.

(C) You can see better from the balcony.

앞 좌석과 발코니석 중 어떤 좌석이 가장 좋나요?
(A) 매표소에서요.
(B) 그것들을 돌려보내겠습니다.
(C) 발코니에서 더 잘 보이실 겁니다.

해설 (A) Where 의문문에 적합한 오답, (B) 연상 어휘(front-back)로 혼동을 노린 오답, (C) A(in front)와 B(in the balcony) 중 하나를 선택한 정답.

어휘 seat 좌석 ticket counter 매표소

ACTUAL TEST 본문 p.70

1. (A)	2. (A)	3. (B)	4. (B)	5. (A)
6. (A)	7. (B)	8. (A)	9. (B)	10. (B)

1. 일반 의문문

Have you hired a receptionist yet?

(A) Yes. He'll start next month.

(B) I will call you later.

(C) It is the newest one.

접수 담당자를 벌써 고용했나요?
(A) 네, 그는 다음 달부터 시작할 거예요.
(B) 나중에 전화 드리겠습니다.
(C) 가장 최신 거예요.

해설 (A) 고용 여부를 묻는 질문에, Yes로 긍정으로 답한 후 부가 설명

한 성납, (B) 연상 어휘(receptionist-call)로 혼동을 노린 오답, (C) 주어의 인칭이 맞지 않는 오답.

어휘 hire 고용하다 receptionist 접수 담당자

2. 일반 의문문

Does this building have more storage space?

(A) Yes, there's more on the top floor.

(B) I bought a new wardrobe.

(C) He will send an e-mail.

이 건물에 더 많은 저장 공간이 있나요?
(A) 네, 맨 위층에 더 있습니다.
(B) 새로운 옷장을 구입했습니다.
(C) 그가 이메일을 보낼 거예요.

해설 (A) 저장 공간이 더 있냐는 질문에, Yes로 긍정으로 답한 후 구체적인 위치를 언급한 정답, (B) 연상 어휘(storage-wardrobe)로 혼동을 노린 오답, (C) 주어의 인칭이 맞지 않는 오답.

어휘 storage 저장, 보관소 space 공간 top 맨 위, 꼭대기 wardrobe 옷장

3. 선택 의문문

Is this a full-time or part-time position?

(A) About three years ago.

(B) We're hoping to hire someone full time.

(C) James is the general manager.

이 자리는 정규직입니까, 아니면 시간제입니까?
(A) 3년 전쯤에요.
(B) 저희는 정규직을 고용하기를 원합니다.
(C) James는 총지배인이에요.

해설 (A) When 의문문에 적합한 오답, (B) A(full-time)와 B(part-time) 중 하나를 선택한 정답, (C) 연상 어휘(position-manager)를 이용해 혼동을 노린 오답.

어휘 full-time 정규직의 part-time 시간제의 position 위치, 자리 general manager 총지배인

4. 일반 의문문

Do we have an appointment tomorrow?

(A) Once a day.

(B) Sorry. I have to cancel.

(C) Mary was appointed president.

우리 내일 약속이 있죠?
(A) 하루에 한 번요.
(B) 죄송한데, 취소해야 할 것 같습니다.
(C) Mary는 사장으로 임명되었어요.

해설 (A) How often ~?에 적합한 오답, (B) 약속이 있냐는 질문에, 취소해야 할 것 같다고 한 정답, (C) 유사 어휘(appointment-appointed)로 혼동을 노린 오답.

어휘 appointment 약속 appoint 임명하다, 지명하다 president 사장

5. 일반 의문문

Did you pay for the order in advance?

(A) Yes, here's the receipt.

(B) No, there is no advantage.

(C) She didn't make an order.

앞서 주문한 것은 지불하셨나요?
(A) 네, 영수증 여기 있어요.
(B) 아니요, 이득이 없어요.
(C) 그녀는 주문하지 않았어요.

해설 지불했냐는 질문에, (A) Yes로 긍정으로 답한 후 영수증이 여기 있다고 덧붙이는 정답, (B) 유사 어휘(advance-advantage)를 이용한 오답 함정, (C) You로 물었는데 She로 응답한 인칭 오류 오답.

어휘 order 주문 in advance 앞서, 사전에 receipt 영수증 advantage 이점, 장점

6. 선택 의문문

Does he speak German or Spanish?

(A) I think he speaks both.

(B) It was a good speech.

(C) Yes, I've been to Germany before.

그는 독일어를 하나요, 아니면 스페인어를 하나요?
(A) 둘 다 하는 걸로 알아요.
(B) 좋은 연설이었어요.
(C) 네, 전에 독일에 가본 적 있어요.

해설 (A) 독일어와 스페인어 중 어떤 걸 구사하냐는 질문에, 둘 다(both) 하는 걸로 안다는 뜻의 정답, 'I think ~' 등 의견을 나타내는 표현은 정답 선택지에 자주 등장한다. (B) 유사 어휘(speak-speech)로 혼동을 노린 오답, (C) 연상 어휘(German-Gemany)로 혼동을 노린 오답으로, 선택 의문문은 Yes/No로 응답 불가.

어휘 German 독일어; 독일의 Spanish 스페인어; 스페인의 both 둘 다 speech 연설

7. 일반 의문문

Do you have the secretary's phone number?

(A) Ten copies of a document.

(B) Let me check the directory.

(C) Nobody is here.

비서의 연락처를 갖고 있나요?
(A) 서류 10부요.
(B) 책자를 확인해 볼게요.
(C) 여기에는 아무도 없습니다.

해설 (A) How many ~?에 적합한 오답, (B) '모른다, 다른 사람(출처)에 확인해 보겠다' 유형의 정답, (C) 질문과 관계없는 오답.

어휘 secretary 비서 document 서류 directory 안내 책자

8. 일반 의문문

Did you know that the concert will be outdoors?

(A) I hope it doesn't rain.

(B) No, I have never heard that song.

(C) I will leave for a business trip.

음악회가 야외에서 열린다는 거 알고 있었어요?
(A) 비가 안 오면 좋겠네요.
(B) 아니요, 그 음악은 들어본 적이 없어요.
(C) 출장을 떠날 예정이에요.

해설 (A) Yes를 생략하고 관련 부가 설명을 덧붙인 정답. 보통 I hope, I think 같이 바람이나 의견을 말하는 보기는 정답일 가능성이 높다. (B) 연상 어휘(concert-song)로 혼동을 노린 오답, (C) 질문과 관련 없는 오답.

어휘 outdoors 야외에서 business trip 출장

9. 일반 의문문

Have you already booked a room?

(A) There won't be enough time to review.

(B) No, not yet.

(C) I'll read it again.

객실을 이미 예약했나요?
(A) 검토할 시간이 없을 거예요.
(B) 아니요 아직요.
(C) 그것을 다시 읽을 거예요.

해설 (A) 연상 어휘(booked-review)를 이용한 오답 함정, (B) 방을 예약했냐는 질문에, 아직 하지 못했다고 답한 정답, (C) 연상 어휘(booked-read)로 혼동을 노린 오답.

어휘 book 예약하다 already 이미, 벌써

10. 선택 의문문

Is the chairperson arriving this week or next?

(A) Oh, the new staff member.

(B) He'll be here on the 25th.

(C) Yes, just a little.

의장은 이번 주에 도착하나요, 아니면 다음 주에 도착하나요?
(A) 아, 새로운 직원이요.
(B) 25일에 이곳에 올 거예요.
(C) 네, 아주 조금요.

해설 (A) Who 의문문에 적합한 오답, (B) A(this week), B(next week) 중 하나가 아닌 제3의 정보를 언급한 정답, (C) 선택의문문에 yes로 응답 불가.

어휘 chairperson 의장 staff member 직원 just a little 아주 조금

PRACTICE 본문 p.75

1. (C) **2.** (C) **3.** (B) **4.** (A)
5. (B) **6.** (C) **7.** (B) **8.** (C)

1. Would you like to see our latest catalog?

(A) I'll bring it.

(B) In five categories.

(C) Do you have a copy?

저희의 최신 목록을 보시겠어요?
(A) 제가 가져올게요.
(B) 다섯 가지 카테고리에요.
(C) 사본이 있나요?

해설 (A) 질문과 관계 없는 오답, (B) 유사 어휘(catalog-categories)로 혼동을 노린 오답, (C) 반문하는 유형으로, 사본이 있냐고 되묻는 정답.

어휘 catalog 목록 category 범주 copy 사본

2. May I suggest an idea for a new product?

(A) It's for you.

(B) I have an idea for you.

(C) I'd be glad to consider your idea.

신상품에 대해 아이디어를 하나 제안해도 될까요?
(A) 당신을 위한 거예요.
(B) 당신을 위한 안건이 하나 있어요.
(C) 기꺼이 고려해 보겠습니다.

해설 (A) Who 의문문에 적합한 오답, (B) 동일 어휘(idea) 반복으로 혼동을 노린 오답, (C) 'I'd be glad to ~'로 아이디어 제안을 수락하는 정답.

어휘 suggest 제안하다 consider 고려하다

3. Why don't we travel together?

(A) At the bus station.

(B) When are you leaving?

(C) I don't want to call him.

여행을 함께 가시겠어요?
(A) 버스 정류장에서요.
(B) 언제 떠나는데요?
(C) 그에게 전화하고 싶지 않아요.

해설 (A) Where 의문문에 적합한 오답, (B) '같이 여행 가자'는 제안에, 언제 갈 거냐고 되묻는 정답, (C) Why 의문문에 적합한 오답.

어휘 bus station 버스 정류장

4. Can you give me a hand with this project?

(A) Sure, I'll be right there.

(B) We handed him a document.

(C) I don't remember.

이 프로젝트를 좀 도와주시겠어요?
(A) 물론이죠. 바로 갈게요.
(B) 우리는 그에게 서류를 넘겼어요.
(C) 기억나지 않아요.

해설 도와달라는 요청에, (A) sure로 긍정으로 답한 후, 곧 가겠다고 덧붙인 정답, (B) 유사 어휘(hand-handed)로 혼동을 유도한 오답, (C) 질문과 관련 없는 응답.

어휘 give a hand 거들어주다 hand 건네주다

5. Today's meeting shouldn't take too long.

(A) I have some.

(B) What will we be talking about?

(C) This is the longest one.

오늘 회의는 오래 걸리지 않을 거예요.
(A) 조금 있습니다.
(B) 무엇에 관한 거죠?
(C) 이것이 가장 긴 거예요.

해설 (A) 질문과 관련 없는 오답, (B) 회의가 오래 걸리지 않을 거라는 말에, 무엇에 관한 회의인지 반문하는 정답, (C) 유사 어휘(long-longest)로 혼동을 유도한 오답.

어휘 meeting 회의 take (시간이) 걸리다

6. The copy machine is making loud noises.

(A) I waited for you.

(B) You have to come.

(C) I think it's broken.

복사기에서 큰 소음이 나네요.
(A) 기다렸습니다.
(B) 꼭 오셔야 합니다.
(C) 고장 난 것 같아요.

해설 (A) 질문과 관계없는 오답, (B) 질문과 관계없고 인칭이 맞지 않는 오답, (C) 고장 난 것 같다며 I think로 의견에 동조하는 정답.

어휘 copy machine 복사기 make noises 잡음을 내다

7. Maybe we should extend the deadline.

(A) It's in the office.

(B) Okay, let's do that.

(C) No, I don't want to attend.

우리 마감일을 연장해야 할 것 같아요.
(A) 그것은 사무실에 있어요.
(B) 좋아요, 그렇게 하죠.
(C) 아니요, 참석하고 싶지 않아요.

해설 (A) Where 의문문에 적합한 오답, (B) 마감일을 연장하자는 제안에, 그렇게 하자고 Okay로 동의하는 정답, (C) 유사 어휘(extend-attend)로 혼동을 유도한 오답.

어휘 extend 연장하다 deadline 기한, 마감 시간 attend 참석하다

8. I can't open this window latch.

(A) It closes around 7:00 P.M.

(B) I sent it with an attachment.

(C) Let me take a look.

이 창문의 걸쇠를 열 수가 없네요.
(A) 그곳은 저녁 7시쯤 문을 닫아요.
(B) 첨부 파일과 함께 보냈어요.
(C) 제가 한번 볼게요.

해설 (A) 연상 어휘(open-closes)로 혼동을 노린 오답, (B) 유사 어휘(latch-attachment)으로 혼동을 유도한 오답, (C) 창문 걸쇠를 열 수 없다는 말에, 본인이 한번 보겠다고 제안하는 정답.

어휘 latch 걸쇠, 자물쇠 attachment 첨부 파일

ACTUAL TEST 본문 p.77

| 1. (A) | 2. (B) | 3. (A) | 4. (B) | 5. (C) |
| 6. (B) | 7. (C) | 8. (C) | 9. (C) | 10. (B) |

1. 평서문

The directory is in the filing cabinet.

(A) In the top drawer?

(B) The files are missing.

(C) No, the director left the office.

안내 책자는 서류함 안에 있어요.
(A) 맨 위 서랍예요?
(B) 서류들이 없어졌어요.
(C) 아니요, 이사님은 퇴근하셨어요.

해설 (A) 책자가 서류함에 있다는 말에, 맨 위 서랍이냐고 반문하는 형태의 정답으로, 이렇게 반문형의 보기는 정답 가능성이 높다. (B) 유사 어휘(filing-files)를 이용한 오답, (C) 유사 어휘(directory-director)를 이용한 오답.

어휘 directory 안내책자 filing cabinet 서류함 top drawer 맨 위 서랍 director 임원, 이사

2. 제안·요청 의문문

Could you put together an inventory of our merchandise?

(A) I'll buy it for you.

(B) Sure, I have some time.

(C) The new inventory will arrive.

우리 제품의 재고를 모아 주실래요?
(A) 제가 사드릴게요.
(B) 물론입니다. 시간이 좀 있어요.
(C) 새로운 상품 재고가 도착할 거예요.

해설 (A) 연상 어휘(merchandise-buy)를 이용한 오답, (B) 상대방의 요청에, Sure로 긍정한 후 시간이 있다고 덧붙이는 정답, (C) 동일 어휘(inventory) 반복으로 혼동을 노린 오답.

어휘 inventory 물품 목록, 재고 merchandise 상품, 물품

3. 평서문

I need ten copies of this document by this afternoon.

(A) Where should I leave them for you?

(B) He is the leader of that club.

(C) No, I have it already.

오늘 오후까지 이 서류의 복사본이 10부 필요해요.
(A) 그것들을 어디에 두면 될까요?
(B) 그는 그 동호회의 대표예요.
(C) 아니요, 저는 이미 가지고 있습니다.

해설 (A) 복사본이 필요하다는 말에, 어디에 두면 되냐고 반문하는 정답, (B) Who 의문문에 적합한 오답, (C) 질문과 관련 없는 내용의 오답.

어휘 copy 복사본 document 서류 leader 대표, 지도자
club 동호회, 클럽

4. 제안·요청 의문문

Can I fax my job application to you?

(A) No, there is no tax on education.

(B) Yes, that would be fine.

(C) The interview will start soon.

제 구직 신청서를 팩스로 보내 드려도 될까요?
(A) 아니요, 교육에는 세금이 없습니다.
(B) 네, 좋습니다.
(C) 면접이 곧 시작됩니다.

해설 (A) 유사 어휘(fax-tax)로 혼동을 노린 오답, (B) 팩스로 지원서를 보내도 되는지 묻는 제안 의문문에, Yes로 수락하는 정답, (C) 연상 어휘(job-interview)로 혼동을 노린 오답.

어휘 job application 구직 신청서 tax 세금 education 교육
interview 면접

5. 평서문

I'll introduce you to the new cashier.

(A) No, we paid with cash.

(B) It's the old one I have.

(C) Thanks, but we've already met.

당신을 새 점원에게 소개시켜 드리겠습니다.
(A) 아니요, 저희는 현금으로 계산했습니다.
(B) 제가 가지고 있는 것은 오래된 거예요.
(C) 고맙지만, 우리는 이미 만난 적이 있습니다.

해설 (A) 유사 어휘(cashier-cash)로 혼동을 노린 오답, (B) 연상 어휘(new-old)로 혼동을 노린 오답, (C) 소개해 주겠다는 말에, 이미 만난 적이 있다며 우회적으로 거절하는 정답.

어휘 introduce 소개하다 cashier 출납원, 계산원

6. 제안·요청 의문문

Would you like a copy of our newsletter?

(A) I'm feeling better.

(B) That would be nice.

(C) In the newspaper.

뉴스레터를 한 부 보시겠습니까?
(A) 좀 좋아졌어요.
(B) 네, 좋습니다.
(C) 신문에서요.

해설 (A) How 의문문에 적합한 오답, (B) Would you like ~?로 제안하는 말에, 그게 좋겠다며 수락하는 정답, (C) Where 의문문에 적합한 오답으로, 유사 어휘(newsletter-newspaper)로 혼동을 주고 있다.

어휘 newsletter 소식지 newspaper 신문

7. 제안·요청 의문문

Could you give me the blueprints for the Lael Project?

(A) It is one of our branches.

(B) Those come from here.

(C) I think Bob has them.

Lael 프로젝트의 청사진을 주시겠어요?
(A) 우리 지사 중 하나예요.
(B) 그것들은 여기에서 나온 거예요.
(C) Bob이 가지고 있는 것 같아요.

해설 (A) What 의문문에 적합한 오답, (B) Where 의문문에 적합한 오답, (C) 본인한테는 없고 제3자가 가지고 있다고 말하는 정답.

어휘 blueprint 청사진, 계획 branch 지사

8. 평서문

I think we should hire Mr. Davidson.

(A) About 1 hour later.

(B) Our profits need to be higher.

(C) Unfortunately, he withdrew his application.

Davidson 씨를 고용해야 할 것 같습니다.
(A) 1시간쯤 뒤에요.
(B) 우리 수익이 더 올라야 합니다.
(C) 안타깝게도, 그는 지원을 취소했어요.

해설 (A) When 의문문에 적합한 오답, (B) 유사 어휘(hire-higher)로 혼동을 노린 오답, (C) Unfortunately로 부정한 후 지원을 취소했다며 부연 설명을 덧붙이는 정답.

어휘 hire 고용하다 withdraw 취소; 철회하다 application 지원(서)

9. 제안·요청 의문문

Could you make me a copy of this receipt?

(A) Yes, I received a good job offer.

(B) I have to take the bus.

(C) I'm afraid the copy machine is broken.

이 영수증을 복사해 주시겠어요?
(A) 네, 좋은 일자리 제의를 받았어요.
(B) 버스를 타야 해요.
(C) 복사기가 고장 난 것 같아요.

해설 (A) 유사 어휘(receipt-received)로 혼동을 노린 오답, (B) 유사 어휘(make-take)로 혼동을 노린 오답, (C) I'm afraid로 요청 사항을 거절하며 이유를 덧붙이는 정답.

어휘 receipt 영수증 copy machine 복사기

10. 평서문

I'd like to see last year's sales figures.

(A) I have to go attend a sales meeting.

(B) Would you like me to print you a copy?

(C) It's too expensive.

작년 판매 수치를 좀 보고 싶은데요.
(A) 영업 회의에 참석해야 해요.
(B) 사본을 출력해 드릴까요?
(C) 너무 비싸네요.

해설 (A) 동일 어휘(sales) 반복으로 혼동을 노린 오답, (B) 판매 수치를 보고 싶다는 말에, 사본을 출력해 주길 원하는지를 되묻는 정답, (C) 연상 어휘(sales-expensive)로 혼동을 노린 오답.

어휘 figure 수치, 숫자 print 인쇄하다, 출력하다

UNIT 08 부정/부가 의문문

PRACTICE 본문 p.82

| 1. (B) | 2. (A) | 3. (C) | 4. (C) |
| 5. (A) | 6. (B) | 7. (B) | 8. (C) |

1. Isn't Rosa Sanchez the most experienced candidate?

(A) A few more interviews.

(B) No, she just graduated from university.

(C) In the Finance Department.

Rosa Sanchez가 가장 경험 많은 후보 아니에요?
(A) 몇 번 더 인터뷰가 있어요.
(B) 아니요, 그녀는 막 대학을 졸업했어요.
(C) 재무부에서요.

해설 (A) 질문의 candidate에서 연상할 수 있는 interviews를 이용한 오답, (B) 부정의 No 뒤에 부연 설명을 덧붙이는 정답, (C) Where 의문문에 가능한 응답.

어휘 experienced 경험이 많은 candidate 후보자 graduate 졸업하다 Finance Department 경리부, 재무부

2. Doesn't Emma usually leave at 6:00?

(A) Yes, but she's working late tonight.

(B) Actually, I think she does have a few.

(C) It shouldn't take long.

Emma 씨는 보통 6시에 퇴근하지 않나요?
(A) 네, 그런데 오늘 밤은 늦게까지 일해요.

(B) 사실, 그녀가 몇 개 가지고 있는 것 같아요.
(C) 오래 걸리지는 않을 거예요.

해설 (A) Emma 씨가 6시에 퇴근하지 않냐는 질문에, Yes로 긍정한 후 오늘 야근한다고 부연 설명하는 정답, (B) 질문과는 관련 없는 내용의 오답, (C) 질문의 leave at 6:00에서 연상 가능한 take long을 이용한 오답.

어휘 leave 떠나다, 퇴근하다 take (시간이) 걸리다

3. Didn't our new copier become a bestseller?

(A) Just press the start button.

(B) Thanks for the recommendation.

(C) No, but it's gaining market share.

우리 새 복사기가 베스트셀러가 되지 않았나요?
(A) 시작 버튼만 누르면 됩니다.
(B) 추천해 주셔서 감사합니다.
(C) 아뇨, 하지만 시장 점유율이 높아지고 있어요.

해설 (A) 질문의 copier에서 연상 가능한 start button으로 혼동을 유도한 오답, (B) 질문과 어울리지 않는 내용의 오답, (C) No로 부정으로 답한 후, 시장 점유율이 오르고 있다고 부연 설명하는 정답.

어휘 press 누르다 recommendation 추천 gain 얻다 market share 시장 점유율

4. Isn't the budget report due tomorrow?

(A) You've been a big help.

(B) The budget committee has five members.

(C) I'm not sure about that.

예산 보고서 기한이 내일까지 아닌가요?
(A) 당신은 큰 도움이 됐습니다.
(B) 예산 위원회는 5명의 위원이 있어요.
(C) 그건 잘 모르겠어요.

해설 (A) 질문과 어울리지 않는 내용의 오답, (B) 동일 어휘(budget) 반복으로 혼동을 유도한 오답, (C) 보고서 기한이 내일 아니냐는 질문에, '모른다'는 의미의 정답.

어휘 budget report 예산 보고서 committee 위원회

5. The packaging machine was repaired yesterday, wasn't it?

(A) No, it'll be done tomorrow.

(B) Several large packages.

(C) Yes, I have one of those.

포장 기계가 어제 수리되었죠, 그렇죠?
(A) 아니요, 내일 완료될 예정입니다.
(B) 큰 패키지들 몇 개요.
(C) 네, 제가 그것 중 하나를 가지고 있어요.

해설 (A) 기계가 어제 수리됐냐는 질문에, No로 부정한 후 내일 수리될 거라고 부연 설명한 정답, (B) 유사 어휘(packaging-packages)를 이용한 오답, (C) 질문과 관련 없는 내용의 오답.

어휘 packaging machine 포장 기계 repair 수리하다 package 짐, 소포

6. I really liked the job candidate we <u>interviewed today</u>. Didn't you?

(A) <u>I'll do it</u> tomorrow.

(B) Yes, I think <u>we should offer</u> her the position.

(C) I <u>brought a copy</u> of my résumé.

오늘 면접 본 지원자가 정말 마음에 들었어요, 그렇지 않아요?
(A) 내일 할게요.
(B) 네, 그녀에게 그 자리를 제안하는 게 좋을 것 같아요.
(C) 제 이력서 사본을 가져왔어요.

해설 (A) 시제가 어색한 오답, (B) 지원자가 마음에 들지 않았냐는 질문에, Yes로 긍정으로 답한 후, 부연 설명을 한 정답, (C) 질문의 job candidate, interviewed 등에서 연상할 수 있는 résumé를 이용한 오답.

어휘 job candidate 지원자 interview 인터뷰하다 offer 제안하다 position 직책, 자리

7. The prototype will <u>be ready by</u> next Monday, right?

(A) Yes, I can type.

(B) No, we need <u>a little more time</u>.

(C) I read that book <u>last month</u>.

견본이 다음 주 월요일까지 준비되는 거죠?
(A) 네, 제가 타이핑할 수 있어요.
(B) 아니요, 우리는 시간이 조금 더 필요해요.
(C) 지난달에 그 책을 읽었어요.

해설 (A) 유사 어휘(prototype-type)를 이용한 오답, (B) 견본이 다음 주에 준비되는지를 묻는 질문에, No로 부정한 후 시간이 더 필요하다고 부연 설명하는 정답, (C) 연상 어휘(next Monday-last month)를 이용한 오답.

어휘 prototype 견본, 시제품 type 타이핑하다, 입력하다

8. You get your bank statements online, <u>don't you</u>?

(A) No, a <u>savings account</u>.

(B) It's a <u>temporary password</u>.

(C) I do, but they are <u>also mailed</u>.

은행 명세서를 온라인으로 받지 않나요?
(A) 아니요, 저축 계좌입니다.
(B) 그것은 임시 비밀번호입니다.
(C) 네, 하지만 우편으로도 받습니다.

해설 (A) 연상 어휘(bank statements-savings account)를 이용한 오답, (B) 질문과 관련 없는 내용의 오답, (C) 명세서를 온라인으로 받지 않냐는 질문에, 긍정으로 답한 후 우편으로도 받는다고 부연 설명한 정답.

어휘 bank statement 은행 명세서 online 온라인으로 savings account 저축 계좌 temporary 임시의 password 암호, 비밀번호

ACTUAL TEST   본문 p.84

| 1. (C) | 2. (B) | 3. (C) | 4. (A) | 5. (B) |
| 6. (B) | 7. (C) | 8. (B) | 9. (C) | 10. (B) |

1. 부정 의문문

Isn't the press conference supposed to be on June 7th?

(A) You should have received one last week.

(B) To discuss our newest product.

(C) No, it's been postponed.

기자 회견이 원래 6월 7일로 예정되어 있지 않나요?
(A) 지난주에 하나 받았어야 했어요.
(B) 우리의 최신 제품을 논의하기 위해서요.
(C) 아니요, 연기됐어요.

해설 (A) 질문의 June 7th에서 연상 가능한 last week로 혼동을 주는 오답, (B) 질문과 관련 없는 내용의 오답, (C) 기자 회견이 6월 7일 아니냐는 질문에, No로 부정한 후 연기됐다고 부연 설명한 정답.

어휘 press conference 기자 회견 discuss 논의하다 postpone 연기하다

2. 부가 의문문

Ella completed that project on her own, didn't she?

(A) The projector's all set up.

(B) Yes, I think she did.

(C) Okay. I'll take care of it.

Ella 씨가 혼자서 그 프로젝트를 완성했죠, 그렇죠?
(A) 프로젝터가 모두 설치됐어요.
(B) 네, 그런 것 같아요.
(C) 알겠어요. 제가 처리할게요.

해설 (A) 유사 발음(project-projector)을 이용한 오답, (B) Ella 씨 혼자 프로젝트를 완성했냐는 질문에, Yes로 긍정으로 답한 정답, (C) 질문과 관련 없는 내용의 오답.

어휘 complete 완성하다 on one's own 혼자서 set up 설치하다 take care of 처리하다

3. 부정 의문문

Didn't you say you wanted to buy a copier?

(A) No, it was on sale.

(B) In the file cabinet.

(C) Yes, I need one.

복사기 사고 싶다고 하지 않았어요?
(A) 아니요, 그것은 세일 중이었어요.
(B) 문서 보관함에요.
(C) 네, 하나 필요해요.

해설 (A) 질문의 buy a copier에서 연상할 수 있는 on sale을 이용한 오답, (B) Where 의문문에 어울리는 응답으로, 질문의 copier의

연상 어휘(tile cabinet)로 혼동을 노린 오답 함정, (C) Yes로 긍정으로 답한 후, 하나 필요하다고 부연 설명한 정답.

어휘 copier 복사기 **on sale** 세일 중인 **file cabinet** 문서 보관함

4. 부정 의문문

Shouldn't the crew members be wearing hard hats?

(A) You're right.

(B) I think they are going tomorrow.

(C) Please put it on my desk.

승무원들이 안전모를 써야 하지 않나요?
(A) 맞아요.
(B) 제 생각에 그들은 내일 갈 거예요.
(C) 제 책상 위에 두세요.

해설 (A) 안전모를 써야 하지 않냐는 말에, 맞다며 동의하는 정답, (B) 질문과 어울리지 않은 내용의 오답, (C) 연상 어휘(wearing-put)를 이용한 오답.

어휘 crew member 승무원 **hard hat** 안전모

5. 부가 의문문

Ellen will prepare the press release, won't she?

(A) I was relieved.

(B) No, but she will help with it.

(C) In next month's issue.

Ellen이 보도 자료를 준비할 거죠, 그렇죠?
(A) 안심이 되네요.
(B) 아니요, 하지만 그녀가 그것을 도울 거예요.
(C) 다음 달 호예요.

해설 (A) 인칭이 어색한 오답, (B) No로 부정한 후, 그녀가 준비하지는 않지만 도와줄 거라고 덧붙이는 정답, (C) When 의문문에 어울리는 오답.

어휘 prepare 준비하다 **press release** 보도 자료 **relieved** 안도하는 **issue** (잡지의) 호, 문제

6. 부정 의문문

Aren't you supposed to go to the head office?

(A) I suppose it should.

(B) Oh, thanks for reminding me.

(C) It's not that cold outside.

본사에 가기로 하지 않았어요?
(A) 그래야 한다고 생각합니다.
(B) 아, 상기시켜 줘서 고마워요.
(C) 밖은 그렇게 춥지 않아요.

해설 (A) 유사 발음(supposed-suppose)를 이용해 혼동을 유도한 오답, (B) 본사에 가기로 하지 않았냐는 질문에, 상기시켜 줘서 고맙다는 우회적인 표현의 정답, (C) 질문과 관련 없는 내용의 오답.

어휘 be supposed to V ~하기로 되어 있다 **remind** 상기시키다

7. 부가 의문문

You called the travel agency, right?

(A) In Europe this summer.

(B) I'll give you a ride there.

(C) I'm not sure I can go on a trip.

여행사에 전화했죠? 그렇죠?
(A) 이번 여름 유럽에서요.
(B) 제가 거기까지 태워다 드릴게요.
(C) 여행을 갈 수 있을지 확실치 않아요.

해설 (A) 질문의 travel agency에서 연상 가능한 Europe으로 혼동을 노린 오답, (B) 유사 발음(right-ride)을 이용한 오답, (C) 'I'm not sure ~'를 이용해 부정하고 있는 정답.

어휘 travel agency 여행사 **give a ride** 태워 주다 **go on a trip** 여행 가다

8. 부정 의문문

Didn't Mr. Johnson submit the expense report on Friday?

(A) No, it's Saturday today.

(B) I'll ask him at the meeting.

(C) The hotel rate was very expensive.

Johnson 씨가 금요일에 비용 보고서를 제출하지 않았나요?
(A) 아니요, 오늘은 토요일입니다.
(B) 제가 회의에서 물어볼게요.
(C) 호텔 비용이 너무 비쌌어요.

해설 (A) 연상 어휘(Friday-Saturday)로 혼동을 노린 오답, (B) '모른다, 물어보겠다'며 우회적으로 표현한 정답, (C) 유사 어휘(expense-expensive)를 이용한 오답.

어휘 submit 제출하다 **expense report** 비용 보고서

9. 부가 의문문

You brought the copies of the résumés, didn't you?

(A) About my work experience.

(B) He printed some documents.

(C) Didn't you receive my e-mail about them?

이력서 가지고 오셨죠, 그렇죠?
(A) 제 경력에 대해서요.
(B) 그가 서류를 인쇄했어요.
(C) 그것에 관한 제 이메일을 못 받으셨어요?

해설 (A) 연상 어휘(résumés-work experience)를 이용한 오답, (B) 인칭이 맞지 않는 오답, (C) 이력서를 가지고 왔냐는 물음에, 메일을 받지 못했냐고 반문하는 정답.

어휘 bring 가지고 오다 **résumé** 이력서 **work experience** 경력 **print** 출력하다

10. 부가 의문문

There are no more trains to Kingstown today, are there?

(A) Kingstown is twenty kilometers away.

(B) No, but you can take a bus instead.

(C) Two more stops before the city.

오늘은 Kingstown으로 가는 열차가 더 이상 없죠, 그렇죠?
(A) Kingstown은 20킬로미터 떨어져 있어요.
(B) 아니요, 대신 버스를 타시면 됩니다.
(C) 도시에 도착하기 전에 정거장이 두 개 더 있어요.

해설 (A) 동일 어휘(Kingstown) 반복을 이용한 오답, (B) No로 부정으로 답한 후, 부연 설명으로 다른 대안을 제시한 오답, (C) 질문의 trains에서 연상할 수 있는 stops를 이용한 오답.

어휘 instead 대신에 stop 정거장

PART 03 짧은 대화

UNIT 09 주제·목적/대화 장소 문제

PRACTICE 본문 p.96

1. (A)   **2.** (D)   **3.** (D)

Question 1 refers to the following conversation.

M How are you doing with the computer program <u>you use to enter</u> customer data?

W I'm quite <u>familiar with</u> it. I did the same kind of data entry <u>at my last job</u>.

M <u>That sounds</u> really great! If you have any problems, don't <u>hesitate to</u> call me.

남 고객 자료를 입력하기 위해 사용하는 컴퓨터 프로그램은 어떻게 잘돼 가나요?
여 네, 제가 그건 꽤 잘 알아서요. 전 직장에서 같은 종류의 데이터 입력을 했었거든요.
남 잘됐네요! 혹시 무슨 문제가 있으면 주저하지 말고 연락주세요.

어휘 enter 입력하다 be familiar with ~에 익숙하다 hesitate 주저하다

1. 대화는 무엇에 관한 것인가?

(A) 컴퓨터 프로그램 사용
(B) 새로운 컴퓨터 구입
(C) 고객 초대
(D) 고용 조건

해설 주제 문제이므로 대화 첫 부분을 잘 들어야 한다. 남자가 말하는 부분(How are you doing with the computer program you use to enter customer data?)을 통해 컴퓨터 프로그램 사용에 관한 대화임을 알 수 있으므로 (A)가 정답이다.

Question 2 refers to the following conversation.

W Hello. I bought a refrigerator <u>at your store</u> this morning, and I heard from the store that <u>you'll be delivering</u> my new refrigerator today.

M Yes, we will. You are Ms. Jackson, right?

W Yes, I am. Can you <u>take away</u> my old refrigerator as well?

M Sure. There will be <u>an additional cost</u> for that service though.

여 여보세요. 오늘 아침에 귀하의 매장에서 냉장고를 구입했는데, 냉장고를 오늘 배달해 주신다고 들었습니다.

남 네, 맞습니다. 잭슨 씨 맞으시죠?

여 네, 맞아요. 제 예전 냉장고도 가져가 주실 수 있나요?

남 물론입니다. 하지만 그에 대한 추가 비용이 있을 겁니다.

어휘 refrigerator 냉장고 delivery 배달 as well ~도 역시 additional 추가의, 부가의

2. 여자가 전화를 건 목적은 무엇인가?

(A) 주문하기 위해

(B) 수리를 요청하기 위해

(C) 새로운 냉장고를 구입하기 위해

(D) 배송을 확인하기 위해

해설 목적 문제이므로 대화 첫 부분을 잘 들어야 한다. 여자가 말하는 부분(I heard from the store that you'll be delivering my new refrigerator today.)을 통해 배송을 확인하기 위해 전화한 것을 알 수 있으므로 (D)가 정답이다.

Question 3 refers to the following conversation.

W I can't believe the trouble we had coming up with the design for our new logo. It seemed to have taken forever.

M Yes, but the results are worthwhile. It sums up exactly what our company stands for: It looks both sporty and dependable.

W Yes, and it comes out well both small on our letterhead and large on our products. Look at these badminton rackets and our new treadmills. They look fantastic!

여 우리 회사 새 로고 디자인이 이렇게 힘들 줄은 몰랐어요. 도대체 끝이 날 것 같지 않았어요.

남 그러게요. 그래도 결과는 좋잖아요. 우리 회사를 정확히 표현하고 있어요. 활동적이면서도 신뢰를 주는 것 같아요.

여 맞아요. 그리고 회사 편지지에 작게 나온 것과 제품에 크게 나온 것 둘 다 잘된 것 같아요. 배드민턴 라켓과 신형 러닝머신 좀 보세요. 진짜 멋진데요!

어휘 come up with ~을 고안하다 logo 로고, (회사/단체 등을 나타내는) 이미지 take forever 시간이 오래 걸리다 result 결과 worthwhile ~한 보람이 있는 sum up 요약하다 exactly 정확히 stand for ~을 나타내다 sporty 화려한, 민첩한 dependable 믿음직한 come out well (일 등이) 잘되다 letterhead 편지지 위쪽의 인쇄 문구 treadmill 러닝머신

3. 화자들은 어떤 회사에서 일하는 것 같은가?

(A) 광고 회사

(B) 사무용품 매장

(C) 인쇄소

(D) 스포츠용품 제조회사

해설 여자의 마지막 대사(Look at these badminton rackets and our new treadmills.)에서 단서를 찾을 수 있다. 배드민턴 라켓과 러닝머신을 만드는 회사는 스포츠용품 제조회사로 볼 수 있으므로 (D)가 정답이다.

ACTUAL TEST 본문 p.97

1. (A)	2. (B)	3. (A)	4. (A)	5. (B)	6. (A)
7. (A)	8. (C)	9. (B)	10. (B)	11. (D)	12. (D)

Questions 1-3 refer to the following conversation.

M Hello. I'm calling to book a ticket to go to Chicago on October 1.

W Okay, let me check to see if any seats are available. Sometimes the flight is full because of groups of tourists.

M Oh, and could you please check whether a window seat is available or not?

W Sure. But before I do that, could you please give me your full name, passport number, and phone number?

남 안녕하세요. 10월 1일 Chicago로 가는 티켓을 예약하려고 전화했습니다.

여 네, 좌석이 있는지 알아보겠습니다. 가끔 단체 관광객으로 인해 만석이거든요.

남 아, 그리고 창가 좌석이 아직 남아 있는지 확인해 주시겠습니까?

여 물론이죠. 그 전에 이름, 여권 번호, 그리고 전화번호를 알려주시겠습니까?

어휘 book a ticket 표를 예약하다 seat 좌석 available 구할 수 있는, 이용할 수 있는 passport number 여권 번호

1. 남자는 왜 전화하는가?

(A) 예약하기 위해

(B) 좌석을 변경하기 위해

(C) 예약을 확정하기 위해

(D) 지불하기 위해

해설 전화를 건 이유는 전화를 건 사람의 첫 번째 대사에서 주로 단서가 나온다. 특히 'I'm calling ~, I hope/wish ~'가 포함된 문장을 잘 듣는다. 남자가 말하는 부분 I'm calling to book a ticket to go to ~을 통해 (A)가 정답임을 알 수 있다.

2. 남자는 무엇을 요청하는가?

(A) 할인

(B) 창가 좌석

(C) 통로 쪽 좌석

(D) 채식주의 식사

해설 요청/제안 문제는 그 주체를 정확히 파악하는 것이 중요하다. 여기서는 남자가 요청하는 것을 묻고 있으므로 남자의 대사에 집중한다. 특히 'Could you ~?, Why don't you ~?'가 포함된 문장을 잘 듣는다. 남자가 could you please check whether a window seat is available or not?이라며 창가 쪽 좌석이 있는지 묻고 있으므로 (B)가 정답이다.

3. 대화에 따르면, 남자는 다음에 무엇을 할 것 같은가?

(A) 개인정보를 준다

(B) 비행기표 값을 지불한다

(C) 공항으로 간다

(D) 다른 항공사에 전화한다

해설 다음에 할 일 문제는 대화 후반부를 잘 들어야 한다. 여자가 인적 정보를 요청하고 있고 남자가 이에 응할 것임을 유추할 수 있으므로 (A)가 정답이다.

Questions 4-6 refer to the following conversation.

M Did you hear that Victor, the manager of the Sales Department, is retiring?

W Yes, he made a lot of contributions to our company. It is really sad news that he is leaving.

M Well, I came here to ask you to replace him. You have done quite a lot of things at our company as well. I believe you can do more than him.

남 영업부의 매니저인 빅터 씨가 은퇴한다는 소식 들으셨나요?

여 네, 그는 우리 회사에 많은 기여를 했어요. 그가 떠난다는 것은 정말 슬픈 소식이에요.

남 그래서 제가 당신에게 그의 자리를 대신할 것을 요청하러 온 겁니다. 당신도 우리 회사를 위해 많은 일을 해 왔어요. 나는 당신이 그보다 더 잘할 거라고 믿습니다.

어휘 retire 은퇴하다 contribution 기여, 공헌 replace 대체하다

4. 화자들은 무엇을 논의하고 있는가?

(A) 직원의 은퇴

(B) 신임 부장 고용

(C) 회사의 재정난

(D) 신임 사장의 취임식

해설 주제 문제이므로 대화 도입부를 잘 듣는다. 영업부의 매니저인 빅터 씨의 '은퇴'에 대해 화두를 꺼내고 있으므로 (A)가 정답이다.

5. 빅터 씨는 회사에서 무슨 자리를 맡고 있는가?

(A) 이사

(B) 부장

(C) 감독관

(D) 회장

해설 특정 인물의 이름을 언급하면서 그 사람의 직업이나 직책을 묻는 문제는 질문에 언급된 이름이 대화에서 나올 때 특히 집중한다. 보통 사람의 이름 바로 뒤에 동격의 형태로 직책이 언급된다. Victor, the manager of the Sales Department라고 언급된 부분을 통해 (B)가 정답임을 알 수 있다.

6. 남자는 여자에게 무엇을 하라고 요청하는가?

(A) 빅터 씨의 자리를 맡아달라고

(B) 새로운 직원을 찾으라고

(C) 새로운 직원을 교육시키라고

(D) 구직자를 면접하라고

해설 제안/요청 문제이므로 제안 관련 표현이 나오는 부분을 집중해서 듣는다. 'I came here to ask you to replace him(빅터 자리를 맡아 달라)'고 요청하고 있으므로 (A)가 정답이다.

Questions 7-9 refer to the following conversation with three speakers.

M1 Have you guys visited the new company fitness room on the 15th floor?

W I haven't been there yet, but I heard that it's much better than before.

M2 Yeah, it is. I started working out there this Monday, and I was really impressed by all the cutting-edge equipment.

M1 And don't forget the view. It's fantastic! You can see the entire city while you're on a bicycle.

M2 I know. It was a great idea to move the facility up from the first floor.

W Wow, it sounds amazing. I'm definitely stopping by there after work today.

남1 15층에 있는 새로운 회사 피트니스 룸 가봤어요?

여 전 아직 안 가봤는데, 이전보다 훨씬 좋다고 들었어요.

남2 맞아요. 이번 주 월요일부터 거기서 운동을 시작했는데, 최신 장비에 정말 감탄했어요.

남1 경치도 빼먹지 마요. 진짜 대단해요! 자전거 타면서 도시 전체를 볼 수 있어요.

남2 그러니까요. 그 시설을 1층에서 위로 옮긴 건 훌륭한 아이디어였던 것 같아요.

여 와, 대단할 것 같네요. 오늘 퇴근 후에 꼭 가봐야겠어요.

어휘 be impressed by ~에 감명받다 cutting-edge 최신식의
equipment 장비 facility 시설 definitely 반드시 stop by
들르다

7. 어디에서 이루어지는 대화인 것 같은가?

(A) 사무실에서

(B) 건강관리 세미나에서

(C) 피트니스 센터에서

(D) 스포츠용품 가게에서

해설 대화가 일어나는 장소를 묻는 문제로, 남자1이 회사에 새로 생긴
피트니스 센터에 가본 적 있냐고 묻는 걸로 대화가 시작되고 있다.
대화 전반적으로 세 사람이 직장 동료라는 것을 알 수 있으므로 정
답은 (A)이다.

8. 남자들이 새로운 시설에 대해 뭐라고 얘기하는가?

(A) 중고 스포츠 장비들이 있다.

(B) 1층에 있을 때 더 북적거렸다.

(C) 여러 면에서 업그레이드되었다.

(D) 이전보다 더 비싼 기계들이 있다.

해설 새로운 시설에 대한 남자들의 의견을 묻는 문제로, 두 번째 순서로
나왔으므로 대화 중반부에 힌트가 나올 확률이 높다. 질문의 대상
이 남자들(the men)이므로 두 남자 모두의 말에 주목해야 한다.
한 남자는 최신 장비에 감탄했다고 했고, 다른 남자는 높은 층으로
옮겨서 경치가 좋다고 했으므로, 두 내용을 종합해 보면 여러 가지
로 좋아졌음을 알 수 있다. 따라서 정답은 (C)이다.

9. 여자는 무엇을 하겠다고 말하는가?

(A) 1층을 방문한다

(B) 시설에 가본다

(C) 공원에서 운동한다

(D) 피트니스 센터에 전화한다

해설 세 번째 문제는 주로 후반부에 정답 단서가 나온다. 남자들의 얘
기를 쭉 듣고 나서 퇴근 후 피트니스 센터에 가볼 거라고 했으므로
(B)가 정답임을 알 수 있다.

Questions 10-12 refer to the following conversation.

M Here are some skirts you might be interested in,
Ms. Stephenson. They are made of silk.

W They're very nice, but I was hoping to get
something in red or wine. Do you have anything
else in those colors?

M Certainly. I'll be back in a second with some more
skirts for you to try on.

남 스티븐슨 씨, 당신이 마음에 들어 하실 만한 치마들이 여기 있습니다. 실
크로 만들어졌어요.

여 아주 좋네요, 하지만 저는 빨강이나 와인색을 찾고 있었어요. 그 색상으
로 다른 제품들이 있나요?

남 그럼요. 입어 보실 만한 치마들을 금방 가지고 오겠습니다.

어휘 be interested in ~에 관심이 있다, 흥미가 있다 be made of
~로 만들어지다 silk 실크 certainly 틀림없이, 그럼요 try on
입어 보다

10. 화자들은 어디에 있는 것 같은가?

(A) 은행에

(B) 옷가게에

(C) 식당에

(D) 신발가게에

해설 대화 장소를 묻고 있으므로 도입부를 잘 들어야 한다. 대화 장소
에 대한 단서로 언급된 'skirts, silk'를 통해 (B)가 정답임을 알 수
있다.

11. 여자는 무엇을 요청하는가?

(A) 다른 무늬

(B) 좀 더 긴 것

(C) 독특한 디자인

(D) 다른 색상

해설 요청 문제이므로 요청/제안 표현이 포함된 문장을 집중해서 듣는
다. 또한 여자가 요청하는 것을 묻고 있으므로 여자의 대사에서 정
답 단서가 등장할 확률이 높다. 여자가 red or wine을 언급한 후
Do you have anything else in those colors?라고 말하는 부
분에서 다른 색을 원하고 있음을 알 수 있으므로 (D)가 정답이다.

12. 남자는 다음에 무엇을 할 것인가?

(A) 할인 요금을 제시한다

(B) 다른 지점들에 연락한다

(C) 구매품을 환불해 준다

(D) 더 많은 물건을 가져온다

해설 다음에 할 일을 묻고 있으므로 대화 마지막 부분에 집중한다. I'll
be back in a second with some more skirts for you to try
on에서 입어볼 만한 치마를 금방 가지고 오겠다고 말하고 있으므
로 (D)가 정답이다.

PRACTICE 본문 p.103

1. (C) **2.** (C) **3.** (C)

Question 1 refers to the following conversation.

M Hello there. I moved in to the apartment complex last month. I'd like to register for the fitness center.

W No problem. I'll need a copy of your lease, a utility bill, or anything that proves you are currently living in your apartment.

M Unfortunately, I didn't bring anything with me. Can I come back after work?

W Of course. We close early on Wednesdays though, so try to make it by 7 o'clock. This information brochure lists our gym hours and the office hours.

남 안녕하세요. 지난달에 이 아파트 단지로 이사 왔습니다. 헬스클럽에 등록하고 싶은데요.

여 그러시죠. 현재 아파트에 거주 중임을 입증할 수 있는 임대 계약서나 공과금 고지서 사본이 필요합니다.

남 안타깝게도 아무것도 가지고 오질 않았네요. 퇴근 후에 다시 들러도 될까요?

여 물론입니다. 하지만 수요일에는 일찍 문을 닫기 때문에 7시까지는 오세요. 이 안내책자에 저희 체육관 운영 시간과 사무실 업무 시간이 나와 있습니다.

어휘 apartment complex 아파트 단지 register for ~에 등록하다 fitness center 헬스클럽 lease 임대 utility bill 공과금 고지서 prove ~을 증명하다, ~을 입증하다 currently 현재 information brochure 안내책자 gym 헬스클럽, 체육관 office hours 영업 시간, 업무 시간

1. 남자가 여자로부터 받은 것은 무엇인가?
(A) 서명한 임대 계약서
(B) 신청서
(C) 일정 정보
(D) 공과금 고지서

해설 남자가 여자에게서 받은 것을 묻는 세부사항 문제다. 여자가 남자에게 브로셔를 보여주며 헬스클럽의 운영 시간과 사무실 운영 시간이 나와 있다고 알려주고 있다. 대화의 gym hours and the office hours가 schedule information으로 패러프레이징된 (C)가 정답이다.

Question 2 refers to the following conversation.

W Hi, Mr. Anderson. I'm sorry I was late for the meeting this morning because of a traffic jam. What did I miss?

M Oh, on Thursday, we are going to install a new program on all of the computers in the Sales Department.

W So is there anything we have to do to prepare for it?

M No, but I suggest that you come early on that day. We will have a lot of work to do.

여 안녕하세요, 앤더슨 씨. 죄송합니다. 교통체증 때문에 오늘 아침 미팅에 늦었습니다. 제가 놓친 것이 있나요?

남 아, 목요일에 우리는 영업부의 모든 컴퓨터에 새로운 프로그램을 설치할 거예요.

여 그럼 준비해야 할 사항이 있나요?

남 아니요, 하지만 그날 할 일이 많으니 일찍 오는 것이 좋을 겁니다.

어휘 traffic jam 교통체증 install 설치하다 Sales Department 영업부

2. 여자는 왜 회의에 늦었는가?
(A) 대중교통을 이용했다.
(B) 휴가에서 방금 돌아왔다.
(C) 교통체증에 갇혀 있었다.
(D) 회사에서 먼 곳에 산다.

해설 여자가 대사 중 I was late for the meeting this morning because of a traffic jam.을 통해 회의에 늦은 이유를 알 수 있다. traffic jam을 stuck in traffic으로 바꿔 표현한 (C)가 정답이다.

Question 3 refers to the following conversation.

M Hi, Rhonda. I just heard from Jordan Mitts, one of the speakers. He said that he cannot make it to the training session for our new employees.

W Oh, that's really short notice. We only have ten days left before the training session. What should we do?

M Well, why don't we ask Andrew Ling in the Marketing Department? He gave a speech about time management last year. The audience response was very positive. I also thought it was a very good speech.

W That's a great idea. I'll give him a call right now.

정답과 해설

남 Rhonda 씨, 안녕하세요? 연설자 중에 한 분인 Jordan Mitts 씨께서 방금 연락하셨는데 신입사원 훈련 프로그램에 참석할 수 없다고 합니다.

여 아, 너무 임박해서 알려주셨네요. 신입사원 교육까지 열흘 밖에 남지 않았어요. 어떻게 해야 할까요?

남 글쎄요, 마케팅 부서에 Andrew Ling에게 부탁해보는 것은 어떨까요? 지난해에 그는 시간 관리에 대해 연설했었어요. 청중의 반응이 매우 호의적이었고요. 저 또한 매우 좋은 연설이었다고 생각했어요.

여 좋은 생각이에요. 지금 당장 그에게 연락할게요.

어휘 make it 약속을 지키다, 시간 내에 오다 notice 통지, 통보 give a speech 연설하다 management 관리 audience 청중 response 반응 positive 긍정적인

3. 여자는 다음에 무엇을 할 것 같은가?
(A) 매니저에게 보고한다
(B) 연설을 한다
(C) 전화 연락을 한다
(D) 회의를 한다

해설 다음에 할 일을 묻는 문제의 단서는 대화 후반부에 등장한다. 마지막 문장을 통해 여자는 Andrew Ling에게 전화할 것임을 알 수 있다. 따라서 (C)가 정답이다.

ACTUAL TEST 본문 p.104

| 1. (D) | 2. (C) | 3. (A) | 4. (D) | 5. (A) | 6. (D) |
| 7. (C) | 8. (D) | 9. (B) | 10. (B) | 11. (B) | 12. (A) |

Questions 1-3 refer to the following conversation.

W Our overseas clients will be here next week. I'd like to book some rooms for them at the Manchester Hotel. What do you think about that hotel?

M I like it, but I want to know about the facilities there.

W Let's check online to find out about them. We can use the computer in my office if you don't mind.

여 우리의 해외 고객들이 다음 주에 이곳에 옵니다. 저는 그들을 위해 맨체스터 호텔을 예약하고 싶어요. 그 호텔에 대해 어떻게 생각하세요?

남 저도 그곳을 좋아하지만 거기서 어떤 편의시설을 제공하는지 알고 싶어요.

여 인터넷으로 확인해 봅시다. 괜찮으시다면 제 사무실로 가서 컴퓨터를 사용하죠.

어휘 overseas 해외에; 해외의 client 고객 facility 편의시설

1. 여자는 누구를 맨체스터 호텔에 머물게 하고 싶어 하는가?
(A) 동료들
(B) 가족
(C) 친구들
(D) 고객들

해설 문제에 고유명사가 등장할 경우 대화에 해당 고유명사가 들리는 곳에 집중해서 듣는다. Our overseas clients will be here next week. I'd like to book some rooms for them at the Manchester Hotel에서 고객들을 맨체스터 호텔로 데려가고 싶다고 했으므로 (D)가 정답이다.

2. 남자는 호텔의 어떤 것에 대해 알고 싶어 하는가?
(A) 위치
(B) 수익
(C) 시설
(D) 가격

해설 남자가 알고 싶어 하는 것을 묻고 있으므로 남자의 대사에 집중해서 듣는다. 남자가 I want to know about the facilities there.에서 호텔의 편의시설에 대해 알고 싶다고 했으므로 (C)가 정답이다.

3. 여자는 왜 그녀의 사무실로 가자고 제안하는가?
(A) 홈페이지를 확인하기 위해
(B) 고객을 만나기 위해
(C) 예약을 하기 위해
(D) 회의를 준비하기 위해

해설 제안 문제는 제안 표현(Let's ~/We can ~)이 나오는 부분에 정답 단서가 나올 확률이 높다. Let's check online to find out about them.에서 여자는 사무실로 가서 컴퓨터로 확인해 보자고 제안하고 있으므로 (A)가 정답이다.

Questions 4-6 refer to the following conversation.

W Hi. Before we order our meal, could you please check this coupon that I printed from the Web site? It indicates that if we order at least two meals, we can get some free drinks.

M I'm so sorry, but that coupon is only good during lunch.

W Really? I thought I could use this coupon. That's a shame.

M But don't be disappointed. We are having a special offer today, so you can get 20% off any meal.

여 안녕하세요. 식사를 주문하기 전에, 제가 홈페이지에서 출력해 온 쿠폰을 확인해 주시겠어요? 쿠폰에 최소 2인분 식사를 주문하면 무료 음료를 받을 수 있다고 나와 있는데요.

남 죄송합니다만, 그 쿠폰은 점심식사에만 사용하실 수 있습니다.
여 정말요? 저는 이 쿠폰을 사용할 수 있을 줄 알았어요. 아쉽네요.
남 하지만 실망하지 마세요. 오늘 저희는 특별 할인이 있어서, 어떤 식사든 20퍼센트 할인을 받으실 수 있습니다.

어휘 meal 식사 print out 출력하다, 인쇄하다 indicate 나타내다 disappointed 실망한 special offer 특가 할인

4. 여자는 어디에서 쿠폰을 얻었는가?

(A) 책에서
(B) 잡지에서
(C) 신문에서
(D) 홈페이지에서

해설 출처와 연관된 세부사항 문제로, 첫 번째 문제로 나왔으므로 대화 초반부에 단서가 나올 확률이 높다. could you please check this coupon that I printed from the Web site?에서 웹사이트에서 쿠폰을 얻었음을 알 수 있으므로 (D)가 정답이다.

5. 남자가 쿠폰에 대해 언급한 문제는 무엇인가?

(A) 점심식사만 가능하다.
(B) 주말에만 가능하다.
(C) 이미 만료되었다.
(D) 다른 식당용이다.

해설 but 다음에는 중요한 정답 단서가 등장할 확률이 높으므로, 대화에 but이 나오면 집중해서 듣자. I'm so sorry, but that coupon is only good during lunch.에서 쿠폰은 점심에만 유효하다고 했으므로 (A)가 정답이다.

6. 남자는 지금 무엇이 일어나고 있다고 말하는가?

(A) 개업 기념 할인
(B) 재고정리 할인
(C) 특별 할인 시간대
(D) 특별가 제공

해설 남자가 말한 내용을 묻고 있으므로 남자의 대사에 집중한다. 남자가 We are having a special offer today, so you can get 20% off any meal.에서 special offer를 제공한다고 했으므로 (D)가 정답이다.

Questions 7-9 refer to the following conversation.

M Do you know when the mechanic will come to fix the air conditioner?

W Tomorrow afternoon, I guess. Is there a problem?

M I'm concerned about my meeting. If it isn't working by today, I'll have to reschedule my meeting. I'd rather postpone it.

W Don't worry about it. I can call someone else and check whether he can fix it by this afternoon or not.

남 정비사가 언제 에어컨을 수리하러 오는지 알아요?
여 제가 알기로는 내일 오후입니다. 무슨 문제가 있나요?
남 회의 때문에요. 오늘까지 작동되지 않는다면, 미팅 일정을 다시 잡아야 해요. 차라리 미뤄야겠네요.
여 걱정하지 마세요. 제가 다른 정비사에게 전화해서 오늘 오후까지 고칠 수 있는지 확인해 볼게요.

어휘 mechanic 정비공 fix 수리하다 be concerned about ~을 걱정하다 reschedule 일정을 다시 잡다 postpone 미루다, 연기하다

7. 남자는 무엇에 대해 묻는가?

(A) 직원 회의
(B) 새로운 비서
(C) 수리 문제
(D) 국제 회의

해설 남자가 묻고 있는 것에 대해 물었으므로 남자의 대화를 잘 듣는다. 남자가 Do you know when the mechanic will come to fix the air conditioner?에서 '에어컨 수리 문제 건'에 대해 말하고 있으므로 (C)가 정답이다.

8. 남자는 무엇을 미뤄야 한다고 말하는가?

(A) 예약
(B) 교육
(C) 출장
(D) 회의

해설 남자가 If it isn't working by today, I'll have to reschedule my meeting.에서 회의를 미뤄야겠다고 했으므로 (D)가 정답이다.

9. 여자는 다음에 무엇을 할 것 같은가?

(A) 보고서를 제출한다
(B) 정비사에게 전화한다
(C) 회의를 준비한다
(D) 창문을 연다

해설 다음에 할 일을 묻고 있으므로 대화 마지막 부분을 잘 들어야 한다. 여자가 I can call someone else and check whether he can fix it by this afternoon or not.에서 다른 사람에게 전화해서 확인해 보겠다고 했으므로 (B)가 정답이다.

Questions 10-12 refer to the following conversation.

M Tracy, I just heard that we have to reduce our expenses by 20 percent. How do you think we can do that?

W Really? I haven't heard that yet. How are we going to pay for the dinner for our department?

M Hmm. I think we need to reconsider the budget for it again. We have to look for another supplier.

W I should call the supplier as soon as possible to notify him that we have to break the contract.

남 트레이시, 방금 우리 경비를 20퍼센트까지 줄여야 한다는 소식을 들었어요. 우리가 할 수 있을 거라고 생각해요?

여 정말요? 전 아직 못 들었어요. 그럼 우리 부서 저녁 식사 비용을 어떻게 마련하죠?

남 흠, 제 생각에는 우리가 그 예산을 다시 짜야 할 것 같아요. 다른 공급처를 찾아봐야겠어요.

여 제가 그 공급업체에 최대한 빨리 전화해서 우리가 계약을 파기해야 할 것 같다고 알려야겠어요.

어휘 reduce 줄이다, 축소하다 expense 비용, 경비 reconsider 재고하다, 다시 생각하다 budget 예산 notify 알리다, 통보하다 break 깨다, 파기하다 contract 계약

10. 화자들은 무엇을 논의하는가?

(A) 저녁 식사 예약

(B) 저녁 식사 비용 절감

(C) 저녁 식사 시간 변경

(D) 식당 보수

해설 주제를 묻고 있으므로 대화 도입부에 집중한다. '~ reduce our expenses by 20 percent' 등 '경비 삭감'에 관해 언급하고 있으므로 (B)가 정답이다.

11. 남자는 무엇을 제안하는가?

(A) 다른 식당 예약하기

(B) 예산 다시 짜기

(C) 기부 요청하기

(D) 메뉴 변경하기

해설 제안 문제이므로 제안 표현(We need to ~)이 언급된 곳을 집중해서 들어야 한다. 남자가 'I think we need to reconsider the budget for it again.'에서 '예산을 다시 짜야 할 것 같다'고 했으므로 (B)가 답이다.

12. 여자는 다음에 무엇을 할 것 같은가?

(A) 식당에 연락한다

(B) 모든 직원들에게 알린다

(C) 다른 부서를 방문한다

(D) 예약을 취소한다

해설 다음에 할 일을 묻는 문제이므로 대화 마지막 부분에 집중한다. I should call the supplier as soon as possible to notify him that we have to break the contract.에서 '공급업체에 전화하겠다'고 했으므로 (A)가 정답이다.

UNIT 11 **요청·제안 / 화자 문제**

PRACTICE 본문 p.109

1. (D) **2.** (C) **3.** (B)

Question 1 refers to the following conversation.

W David, I've been trying to access my e-mail, but when I enter my password, I get a message that it's invalid.

M Did you ask the technician about that?

W I already tried calling technical support, but it appears that no one is working there now.

M There is a 24-hour technical service line you can call. I can look up the phone number for you.

여 데이비드 씨, 제가 이메일에 접속하려고 비밀번호를 입력하면 틀린 번호라고 메시지가 뜹니다.

남 그것에 대해 기술자에게 물어봤어요?

여 기술지원팀에 이미 전화해 봤지만, 이미 업무 시간이 지난 것 같아요.

남 아마도 24시간 운영하는 곳의 전화번호가 있을 겁니다. 제가 찾아드릴게요.

어휘 access 접속, 접근 password 비밀번호 invalid 효력 없는, 무효한 technical support 기술지원팀 appear ~인 것처럼 보이다 look up 찾아보다

1. 남자는 무엇을 하겠다고 하는가?

(A) 다음 날 여자를 도와준다

(B) 다른 지원팀에게 전화한다

(C) 비밀번호를 찾아 준다

(D) 전화번호를 찾아본다

해설 제안 표현에 정답 단서가 제시될 확률이 높다. 남자의 두 번째 대사에서 'There is a 24-hour technical service line you can call. I can look up the phone number for you(24시간 운영하는 곳의 전화번호가 있을 테니 찾아주겠다)'고 했으므로 (D)가 답이다.

Question 2 refers to the following conversation.

W I was <u>almost late again</u> this morning. I <u>got stuck in</u> a terrible traffic jam.

M Really? Driving is <u>even worse than</u> taking the subway.

W <u>I wish I could</u> take the subway, too, but my house is quite far from the subway station.

M Maybe <u>someone who lives</u> near you would like to carpool to the station. <u>Why don't you</u> talk with some of our colleagues?

여 오늘 아침에 또 지각할 뻔했어요. 끔찍한 교통체증에 갇혀 있었어요.
남 정말요? 운전하는 건 지하철 타는 것보다 더 고역이죠.
여 저도 지하철을 탈 수 있다면 좋을 텐데, 지하철역이 집에서 너무 멀어요.
남 근처에 사는 사람 중에 역까지 차로 데려다 줄 사람이 있을지도 몰라요. 동료들하고 얘기해 보는 게 어때요?

<u>어휘</u> get stuck 갇히다, 막히다 traffic jam 교통체증 quite 꽤, 상당히 carpool 카풀(승용차 함께 타기)을 하다, 합승하다 colleague 동료

2. 남자는 여자에게 무엇을 하라고 제안하는가?
   (A) 차를 구입하라고
   (B) 지하철을 타라고
   (C) 동료들과 얘기하라고
   (D) 걸어서 통근하라고

<u>해설</u> 제안하는 표현(Why don't ~?)이 포함된 문장을 잘 들어야 한다. Why don't you talk with some of our colleagues?라며 '역까지 차로 데려다 줄 사람이 있을지도 모르니 동료들과 얘기해 보는 게 어때요?'라고 제안하고 있으므로 (C)가 정답이다.

Question 3 refers to the following conversation.

W Hi, Tom. How's the design work for our <u>new brochure going</u>?

M I've completed most of it. I can e-mail you the final design <u>within a couple of hours</u>.

W Sounds good. Then we can send it to the printing office tomorrow <u>at the latest</u>. Come to think of it, we should put some <u>customer reviews</u> on the last page.

M <u>That makes sense.</u> I'll add some testimonials from our satisfied customers on the back page.

W Great. And please contact B&M Printers and <u>find out how long</u> the printing will take and how much <u>it will cost</u>. I have always been happy with its high-quality work.

M Okay, I'll call the store <u>right away</u>.

여 Tom, 안녕하세요? 우리 회사의 새 책자 디자인 작업은 어떻게 진행되고 있어요?
남 거의 다 끝나갑니다. 한 두 시간 내에 최종 디자인을 이메일로 보내 드릴 수 있어요.
여 잘됐군요. 그러면 늦어도 내일은 인쇄소에 보낼 수 있겠네요. 생각해 보니 고객 후기를 마지막 장에 추가해야 할 것 같아요.
남 맞는 말씀인 것 같아요. 만족도가 높은 고객 후기를 마지막 장에 추가할게요.
여 좋아요. 그리고 B&M 인쇄소에 연락해서 인쇄가 얼마나 걸릴지 그리고 비용이 얼마나 들지 알아봐 주실래요? 그 인쇄소의 품질 높은 서비스는 항상 만족스러워요.
남 네, 지금 바로 인쇄소에 연락하겠습니다.

<u>어휘</u> brochure 소책자, 브로셔 complete 끝마치다 most 대부분 final 최종적인 within ~이내에 printing office 인쇄소 at the latest 늦어도 come to think of it 생각해 보니 review 후기 make sense 이치에 맞다 add 추가하다 testimonial 후기 satisfied 만족한 contact 연락하다 find out 알아내다 cost 비용이 들다 high-quality 고급의, 고품질의 right away 즉시, 당장

3. 화자들이 진행하고 있는 업무는 무엇인가?
   (A) 의류 디자인
   (B) 브로셔 제작
   (C) 광고 예산
   (D) 안전 설명서

<u>해설</u> 대화 도입부에서 여자가 How's the design work for our new brochure going?라며 브로셔 작업 진행 상태에 대해 물었고, 이어서 we should put some customer reviews on the last page라며 브로셔에 고객 후기를 추가할 것을 제안하고 있으므로 (B)가 정답이다.

ACTUAL TEST 본문 p.110

| 1. (C) | 2. (D) | 3. (A) | 4. (A) | 5. (C) | 6. (B) |
| 7. (A) | 8. (A) | 9. (B) | 10. (D) | 11. (B) | 12. (D) |

Questions 1-3 refer to the following conversation.

W Hi. I need to get a new laptop for my daughter, and my friend recommended your store.

M You are lucky because a special promotion just started yesterday. You can get 30% off everything.

W Wow, that sounds great! So could you recommend the newest product?

M Sure. Let me show you the laptop that just arrived. I'm sure you'll love it.

어 안녕하세요. 세 딸을 위해 새로운 노트북이 필요한데, 제 친구가 당신의 가게를 추천해 줬어요.
남 운이 좋으시네요. 저희 특별행사가 어제 막 시작됐거든요. 모든 제품에 30퍼센트 할인을 받으실 수 있습니다.
여 와, 잘됐네요! 그럼 최신 상품으로 추천해 주시겠어요?
남 물론이죠. 막 입고된 노트북들을 보여드리겠습니다. 분명 좋아하실 겁니다.

어휘 laptop 노트북 컴퓨터 recommend 추천하다 special promotion 특별행사 newest 최신의

1. 대화가 어디에서 일어나고 있는 것 같은가?
(A) 슈퍼마켓에서
(B) 가구점에서
(C) 전자제품 매장에서
(D) 옷가게에서

해설 대화 전반부에 특정 장소 관련 어휘가 제시된다. I need to get a new laptop for my daughter, and my friend recommended your store를 통해 (C)가 정답임을 알 수 있다.

2. 남자는 매장에서 무엇이 진행되고 있다고 하는가?
(A) 보수공사
(B) 개업 기념 세일
(C) 재고 정리 세일
(D) 특별 행사

해설 남자가 언급한 부분을 묻고 있으므로 남자의 대사에 집중해서 들어야 한다. You are lucky because a special promotion just started yesterday.에서 어제부터 특별 행사가 진행되고 있다고 했으므로 (D)가 정답이다.

3. 여자는 무엇을 요청하는가?
(A) 최신 제품
(B) 가장 저렴한 제품
(C) 가장 가벼운 제품
(D) 가장 작은 사이즈의 제품

해설 요청/제안 사항 문제는 주로 후반부에 등장하는 제안 관련 표현을 들어야 한다. 여자가 could you recommend the newest product?라고 말하는 부분에서 여자가 최신 상품을 요구하고 있음을 알 수 있으므로 (A)가 정답이다.

Questions 4-6 refer to the following conversation.

W Did you already sign the contract with the agent for your new restaurant?
M Well, I sent an e-mail to the agent to get some information about the renovations yesterday. But I still haven't got a response.

W I think you should give her a call. Anyway, I'm worried that buying it is going to be complicated.

여 그 중개인이랑 새로운 식당을 계약했어요?
남 수리와 관련해 정보를 얻으려 어제 중개인에게 이메일을 보냈는데 아직 연락을 못 받았어요.
여 그녀에게 전화해야 할 것 같네요. 그건 그렇고, 식당을 매입하는 게 복잡해질 것 같아 걱정되네요.

어휘 sign the contract 계약서에 서명하다 renovation 개조, 보수 still 아직 response 대답 complicated 복잡한

4. 남자는 무엇을 요청했다고 말하는가?
(A) 보수 정보
(B) 소유주의 연락처
(C) 식당의 위치
(D) 건물의 가격

해설 남자가 요청한 것을 묻고 있으므로 남자의 대사에 집중한다. I sent an e-mail to the agent to get some information about the renovations yesterday.에서 남자는 보수에 대한 정보를 얻고자 이메일을 발송했음을 알 수 있으므로 (A)가 정답이다.

5. 여자는 남자에게 무엇을 하라고 제안하는가?
(A) 영업시간을 바꾸라고
(B) 초대장을 만들라고
(C) 부동산에 연락하라고
(D) 내일까지 중개인을 방문하라고

해설 제안/요청 문제이므로 제안(you should ~) 표현이 나오는 문장에서 단서를 찾는다. I think you should give her a call.에서 전화를 걸 것을 제안하고 있으므로 (C)가 정답이다.

6. 여자는 무엇을 걱정하는가?
(A) 실내 장식가를 찾는 것
(B) 식당을 매입하는 것
(C) 오래된 가구를 버리는 것
(D) 새로운 직원을 고용하는 것

해설 여자가 걱정하고 있는 것을 묻고 있으므로 여자의 대사 중 부정적인 뉘앙스의 표현으로 단서가 나올 확률이 높다. I'm worried that buying it is going to be complicated.에서 여자는 '식당을 사는 게 복잡해질 것 같아 걱정된다'고 말하고 있으므로 (B)가 정답이다.

Questions 7-9 refer to the following conversation.

W Hi. I'm calling from the SMC Company. I am calling because we just received a bill, and it is far more than what we had expected.

M Oh, I remember that you ordered 10 photocopiers for your new office, right? The bill includes the service charge as well.

W Service charge? I didn't know anything about that.

M The fee was included in the contract that Ms. Park signed with our company.

여 안녕하세요. SMC 회사입니다. 방금 청구서를 받았는데 예상했던 것보다 비용이 훨씬 많이 나와서 연락드렸습니다.

남 아, 새로운 사무실에 둘 복사기 10대를 주문하셨죠? 그 청구서는 봉사료도 포함된 것입니다.

여 봉사료요? 전 그런 것에 대해 들은 적이 없는데요.

남 Park 씨가 저희 회사와 서명한 계약서에 그 비용이 있습니다.

어휘 bill 청구서 expect 예상하다 photocopier 복사기 service charge 봉사료 contract 계약서

7. 여자는 무슨 종류의 사업체에 전화했는가?

(A) 사무기기 판매점

(B) 서점

(C) 식당

(D) 인쇄소

해설 업종 및 업체를 묻는 문제는 대화 초반부에 단서가 나온다. 여자가 전화한 업체의 종류를 묻고 있으므로 남자의 대사에서 정답 단서가 등장할 것이다. 남자가 말하는 부분 중 I remember that you ordered 10 photocopiers for your new office, right?에서 남자가 일하는 업체는 사무기기 관련 업종임을 알 수 있으므로 (A)가 정답이다.

8. 여자는 무슨 문제를 언급하는가?

(A) 청구서에 예상하지 않은 요금이 포함되어 있다.

(B) 복사기가 잘못 배송되었다.

(C) 일부 복사기가 늦게 배송되었다.

(D) 파손된 부품이 있다.

해설 문제점을 묻는 문제는 부정적인 뉘앙스의 표현에 집중한다. 여자가 언급한 문제점을 물었으므로 여자의 대사에 집중한다. 여자가 I am calling because we just received a bill, and it is far more than what we had expected.에서 '예상했던 것 이상으로 비용이 청구된 것'을 문제 삼고 있으므로 (A)가 정답이다.

9. 남자는 Park 씨에 대해 뭐하고 말하는가?

(A) 그녀가 주문했다.

(B) 그녀가 계약서에 서명했다.

(C) 그녀가 새로운 청구서를 보낼 것이다.

(D) 그녀가 계약서를 복사할 것이다

해설 제3자에 대해 묻고 있으므로 해당 이름(Ms. Park)이 언급된 부분에 집중해서 듣는다. The fee was included in the contract that Ms. Park signed with our company.에서 Park 씨가 회사와 서명한 계약서에 요금이 포함되어 있다고 말하고 있으므로 (B)가 정답이다.

Questions 10-12 refer to the following conversation.

M Hi. This is Martin from the technical support team. I got a call from someone on your staff that a computer isn't working.

W Thanks for coming. Suddenly, the computer shut down when I was about to complete my project. After that, I couldn't turn it back on.

M I think I should bring your computer to my office for me to check it out.

W Okay. But can you fix it by tomorrow? I have to finish my work before this weekend.

남 안녕하세요. 저는 기술지원팀의 Martin입니다. 컴퓨터가 작동하지 않는다고 직원에게 연락을 받았습니다.

여 와 주셔서 감사합니다. 제가 프로젝트를 완성할 때쯤 갑자기 꺼졌습니다. 그 뒤로는 컴퓨터를 켤 수 없었어요.

남 제 생각에는 컴퓨터를 제 사무실로 가져가서 확인해야 할 것 같네요.

여 알겠습니다. 하지만 내일까지 고쳐 주실 수 있나요? 이번 주말까지 작업을 끝내야 하거든요.

어휘 technical support team 기술지원팀 suddenly 갑자기 shut down (기계가) 멈추다 complete 완성하다, 끝마치다 fix 고치다, 수리하다

10. 남자는 누구인 것 같은가?

(A) 회계사

(B) 건축가

(C) 은행원

(D) 기술자

해설 직업, 회사, 부서 등의 단서는 초반부에 등장한다. 남자가 Hi. This is Martin from the technical support team.라며 기술 지원팀이라고 소속을 밝혔으므로 (D)가 정답이다.

11. 여자의 문제는 무엇인가?

(A) 그녀는 프로그램을 설치할 수 없다.

(B) 그녀의 컴퓨터가 고장이 났다.

(C) 그녀는 시간에 맞춰 프로젝트를 끝낼 수 없다.

(D) 그녀는 서류를 잃어버렸다.

해설 문제점, 불평 사항 등은 초반부에 단서가 등장한다. 남자가 말하는 부분 중 I got a call from someone on your staff that a computer isn't working.과 여자가 말하는 부분 중 Suddenly, the computer shut down when I was about to complete my project.을 통해 컴퓨터가 고장 난 것을 알 수 있으므로 (B)가 정답이다.

12. 여자는 남자에게 무엇을 하라고 요청하는가?

(A) 보고서의 마감 기한을 연장해 달라고
(B) 국제 세미나에 그녀를 초대해 달라고
(C) 회의에 그녀 대신 참석해 달라고
(D) 내일까지 컴퓨터를 수리해 달라고

해설 요구나 제안은 해당 표현(Can you ~?, Could you ~?, Why don't you ~?)이 나오는 문장을 잘 들어야 한다. 대화 후반부에 But can you fix it by tomorrow?라고 요청하는 부분을 통해 (D)가 정답임을 알 수 있다.

UNIT 12 의도 파악/시각 자료 문제

1. (C) **2.** (A) **3.** (C)

PRACTICE
본문 p.116

Question 1 refers to the following conversation.

M Did you hear the radio announcement about the blue jazz concert yesterday?
W Yes, I did. I thought the show would definitely sell out. **How shocking!**
M I know. Everyone was so excited about the concert. Who would've imagined that so few people would attend?
W What do you think the reason was?
M Well, critics are saying that the tickets were way overpriced. The venue, the Golden Lion Theater, does have high prices.

남 블루 재즈 콘서트에 대해서 어제 라디오 들었어요?
여 네, 들었어요. 공연이 당연히 매진될 줄 알았어요. **정말 충격적이에요!**
남 그러니까요. 모두들 콘서트를 정말 기대하고 있었는데, 그렇게 적은 사람들이 갈 거라고 누가 상상이나 했겠어요.
여 이유가 뭐였던 것 같아요?
남 글쎄요, 비평가들의 말에 의하면 티켓 가격이 지나치게 높대요. 공연장인 골든 라이언 극장이 가격이 높긴 하죠.

어휘 sell out 매진되다 critic 비평가 overpriced 너무 비싼 venue (콘서트, 스포츠 등의) 장소 overbook 예약을 한도 이상으로 받다 turnout 참가자의 수

---

1. 여자가 "정말 충격적이에요!"라고 말한 이유는 무엇인가?

(A) 공연이 별로였다고 생각한다.
(B) 공연이 초과 예약되었다고 들었다.
(C) 낮은 참석률에 대해 알게 되었다.
(D) 콘서트가 취소되었다고 들었다.

해설 화자 의도 문제는 제시 문장 외에, 앞뒤 내용과의 문맥을 따져서 풀어야 한다. 여자가 공연이 매진될 줄 알았다며 "How shocking"이라 말했다. 이에 남자가 여자 말에 동의하며 이렇게 적은 인원이 올 줄 상상도 못했다고 이야기했으므로 결국 공연의 저조한 참석률을 듣고 여자가 놀란 것임을 알 수 있다. 저조한 참석률을 a low turnout이라 표현한 (C)가 정답이다.

Question 2 refers to the following conversation.

W Hello. I'd like to discuss a mortgage application. Could I speak to Marianne Lemoute, please?
M I'm sorry, but Ms. Lemoute no longer works here.
W Really? I can't believe it! I have always gotten excellent advice and service from her as my financial advisor.
M She doesn't work in the banking industry anymore from what I understand.
W Oh, that's too bad. Well, then who can I talk to about my mortgage?
M It's best if you consult with Mr. Flooder. He is the new regional manager.

여 안녕하세요. 대출 신청에 대해 얘기하고 싶어서요. 마리안느 르모테와 얘기 나눌 수 있을까요?
남 죄송하지만, 르모테 씨는 더 이상 이곳에서 일하지 않아요.
여 정말요? 믿을 수 없군요! 저는 항상 그녀에게 제 재정자문가로서 훌륭한 조언과 서비스를 받았거든요.
남 제가 알기론 그분은 더 이상 금융계에서 일하지 않아요.
여 안타깝군요. 그럼, 제 대출에 대해서는 누구랑 얘기하면 될까요?
남 플루더 씨와 말씀 나누시는 게 가장 좋습니다. 그분은 새로 오신 지역 매니저입니다.

어휘 mortgage 대출, 융자 application 신청, 적용 no longer 더 이상 ~가 아니다 consult with ~와 상의하다

---

2. 여자는 왜 "믿을 수 없군요"라고 말하는가?

(A) 직원이 회사를 떠났다는 사실에 놀랐다.
(B) 남자를 신뢰하지 않는다.
(C) 거짓 정보를 받았다.
(D) 어떤 소식을 듣게 되어 기쁘다.

해설 남자가 앞 문장에서 르모테 씨는 더 이상 이곳에서 일하지 않는다고 알려주자 여자가 "믿을 수 없다"고 말하며 그녀에게 뛰어난 조언과 서비스를 받았던 사실을 말하는 것으로 보아, 르모테 씨가 회

사를 떠난 사실을 알고서 안타까움과 놀라움을 표시한 것을 알 수 있다. 따라서 정답은 (A)이다.

Question 3 refers to the following conversation and map.

M Excuse me, Amanda. I <u>have a problem with</u> my ID. It doesn't open the doors to the building, so I have to get someone on the <u>front desk staff</u> to let me in. Could you add my information to the <u>security system</u>?

W Well, the staff in Human Resources is only <u>in charge of</u> IDs for our building. Why don't you go to the <u>personnel office</u>? Someone there should be able to put you <u>in the database</u>.

M Okay. I'll try. Thanks.

남 실례합니다. Amanda. 제 신분증에 문제가 있는데요. 신분증으로 건물의 문을 열지 못해서 프런트 데스크 직원에게 들어가게 해달라고 해야 합니다. 보안 시스템에 제 정보를 추가해 줄 수 있나요?

여 음, 인사과 직원들만 건물 신분증을 담당하고 있어요. 인사과에 가보는 게 어때요? 그곳의 누군가가 데이터베이스에 당신을 저장해줄 수 있을 거예요.

남 알겠습니다. 그렇게 해볼게요. 감사합니다.

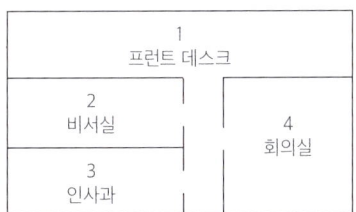

어휘 security system 보안 시스템 Human Resources 인사과 in charge of ~을 맡아서, 담당하는 personnel office 인사과 사무실

3. 도표를 보시오. 남자는 어떤 장소로 갈 것을 지시받는가?

  (A) 방 1
  (B) 방 2
  (C) 방 3
  (D) 방 4

해설 남자가 지시받는 내용을 묻고 있으므로 여자의 대사에 집중해서 들어야 한다. 여자가 Why don't you go to the personnel office?라며 인사과로 가보라고 권유하고 있고 도표에서 인사과는 3번 방이므로 정답은 (C)이다.

ACTUAL TEST 본문 p.117

1. (A) **2.** (B) **3.** (D) **4.** (B) **5.** (A)
6. (C) **7.** (C) **8.** (B) **9.** (D)

Questions 1-3 refer to the following conversation.

M Welcome back to *Music Hour*. Let's continue the interview with our special guest, Michelle O'Conner. Michelle, can you tell us more about your newly released album?

W Sure! It's a contemporary crossover album of pop and jazz, and I think the best part is that you can all enjoy the songs no matter how old you are.

M That sounds great. Now, I heard that you're planning to hold a nationwide tour concert. Which states will you be visiting?

W <u>Thanks for asking</u>. Right now, we're still deciding which cities to visit. The details will be announced next week.

남 <Music Hour>와 함께하고 계십니다. 우리 특별 게스트 미셸 오코너 씨와의 인터뷰를 계속해 봅시다. 미셸, 당신의 새로 출시된 앨범에 대해 더 설명해 주실래요?

여 물론이죠! 팝과 재즈의 현대적인 크로스오버 앨범이고요. 가장 훌륭한 부분은 나이에 상관없이 모두 즐길 수 있는 노래들이라는 점입니다.

남 그거 좋네요. 자, 전국 투어 콘서트를 계획 중이라고 들었어요. 어느 주를 방문하실 건가요?

여 물어봐 주셔서 감사합니다. 지금은 아직 어느 도시들을 방문할지 결정하는 중이고, 자세한 사항은 다음 주중에 발표될 거예요.

어휘 release 출시하다, 개봉하다 contemporary 현대적인 no matter how ~에 상관없이 be planning to ~할 계획이다 nationwide 전국적인

1. 여자는 자신의 앨범에 대해 어떤 부분을 좋아하는가?

  (A) 모든 연령대의 관심을 끌 수 있다.
  (B) 역대 가장 많이 팔린 앨범이다.
  (C) 고전 음악을 특징으로 한다.
  (D) 그녀의 첫 번째 앨범이다.

해설 여자가 I think the best part is that you can all enjoy the songs no matter how old you are.이라며 자신의 앨범에 대해 설명하면서 나이에 상관없이 모두 즐길 수 있는 노래라고 했으므로 정답은 (A)이다.

2. 여사는 무엇을 할 계획인가?

    (A) 다음 앨범 출시한다

    (B) 공연을 한다

    (C) 고향에 방문한다

    (D) 음악을 쉰다

해설 여자가 앞으로 할 일을 묻는 문제로, 대화 중반부에 남자가 여자에게 I heard that you're planning to hold a nationwide tour concert. Which states will you be visiting?(콘서트를 계획 중이라고 알고 있다, 어디를 갈 예정이냐?)이라고 묻고 있다. 콘서트를 give a performance로 표현한 (B)가 정답이다.

3. 여자가 "물어봐 주셔서 감사합니다"라고 말한 의도는 무엇인가?

    (A) 그녀는 같은 질문을 다시 물어보고 싶다.

    (B) 그녀는 새로운 주제에 대해 얘기하고 싶다.

    (C) 그녀는 질문을 여러 번 들었다.

    (D) 그녀는 지금 질문에 답할 수가 없다.

해설 화자 의도 파악 문제로, 대화의 흐름과 앞뒤 문맥을 파악해야 한다. 앞에서 남자가 어디에서 전국 투어 콘서트를 하냐고 묻자, 여자가 물어봐 줘서 고맙다면서 아직 어느 도시를 방문할지 고민 중이라고 말하고 있다. 따라서 여자의 의도는 아직 정해지지 않아 바로 답할 수 없다는 것이다. 따라서 정답은 (D)이다.

Questions 4-6 refer to the following conversation.

M Hello. The fridge in my room is making strange noises. I can't put up with it. I think it's broken.

W I'm very sorry about inconvenience. I'll send one of our maintenance workers to check it out. Is there anything else I can do for you?

M Can you bring me a bottle of ice water? All the water in the fridge is getting warm.

W Of course. I'll get that for you right away.

남 안녕하세요. 제가 묵고 있는 방의 냉장고에서 이상한 소리가 들려요. 도저히 참을 수가 없어요. 냉장고가 고장 난 것 같아요.

여 불편을 드려 정말 죄송합니다. 확인차 관리직원을 보내드리겠습니다. 그 외 더 필요한 것이 있으신가요?

남 차가운 물 한 병을 좀 갖다 주시겠어요? 냉장고 안에 있는 모든 물이 미지근해지고 있어서요.

여 물론입니다. 바로 가져다 드릴게요.

어휘 fridge 냉장고 make noise 소음을 내다 put up with 참다, 인내하다 broken 고장 난 inconvenience 불편 maintenance 유지, 보수, 관리 check out 확인하다 bring 가져다 주다, 가지고 오다 right away 바로, 즉시 electronics 전자제품 fix 고치다 immediately 바로, 즉시 for long 오랫동안 be satisfied with ~에 만족하다 reservation 예약

4. 화자들이 있는 장소는 어디인가?

    (A) 식당에

    (B) 호텔에

    (C) 사무실에

    (D) 전자제품 매장에

해설 대화 장소의 근거는 주로 도입부에 나온다. 남자의 대사 중 The fridge in my room is making strange noises.에서 'in my room'을 통해 호텔에서 일어나는 대화임을 알 수 있다. 따라서 정답은 (B)이다.

5. 남자가 "도저히 참을 수가 없어요"라고 말한 의도는 무엇인가?

    (A) 냉장고가 바로 수리되기를 바란다.

    (B) 여성과 오랫동안 대화할 수 없다.

    (C) 룸서비스에 만족하지 못한다.

    (D) 호텔 예약을 취소할 것이다.

해설 대화 초반부의 The fridge in my room is making strange noises. I can't put up with it.을 통해 남자가 냉장고에서 발생하는 소음 때문에 힘들어한다는 것을 알 수 있으므로 해당 문장은 냉장고가 신속하게 수리되기를 바라는 의도로 한 말임을 알 수 있다. 따라서 (A)가 정답이다.

6. 여자는 다음에 무엇을 할 것 같은가?

    (A) 디저트를 제공한다

    (B) 환불 처리한다

    (C) 물을 가져다준다

    (D) 일정을 확인한다

해설 다음에 할 일을 묻는 문제의 단서는 대화 후반부에 주로 등장한다. 남자가 Can you bring me a bottle of ice water?하고 하자, 여자가 Of course. I'll get that for you right away.라고 말하는 부분에서, 차가운 물을 가져다 달라는 남자의 요청에 여자가 바로 가져다주겠다고 했으므로 (C)가 정답임을 알 수 있다.

Questions 7-9 refer to the following conversation and chart.

W Hi, Steve. Sorry to interrupt. I just got out of a budget meeting. I heard that we are going to scale down our corporate fitness programs due to the recent budget cuts.

M I also heard that Mr. Olson said we are going to cut the most expensive class to operate.

W That doesn't make sense. According to the survey we took last month, that is the most popular class with employees.

M I know what you're saying. Many employees will be disappointed to learn that we are not going to offer the program anymore.

여 Steve 씨, 안녕하세요? 잠깐 실례할게요. 방금 예산회의에 다녀왔는데요. 최근 예산삭감으로 인해 사내 운동 프로그램 규모를 축소할 예정이라고 들었어요.

남 저도 들었어요. Olson 씨가 그러는데 운영비가 가장 많이 드는 수업을 중단할 거라고 하더군요.

여 말도 안 돼요. 지난달 실시했던 조사에 따르면 그 수업이 직원들에게 가장 인기 있는 수업이었어요.

남 그러게 말이에요. 회사에서 그 프로그램을 더 이상 제공하지 않을 거라는 걸 알면 많은 직원들이 실망할 거예요.

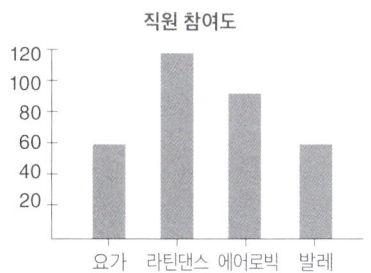

직원 참여도

어휘 interrupt 방해하다 budget 예산 scale down 축소하다
corporate 기업의 fitness 신체 단련, 건강 due to ~때문에
recent 최근의 budget cut 예산 삭감 operate 운영하다,
작동하다 make sense 이치에 맞다, 일리가 있다
according to ~에 따르면 survey 조사 be disappointed
실망하다 trade fair 무역 박람회 awards ceremony 시상식
be concerned 걱정하다 behind schedule 일정에 뒤처진
upcoming 곧 있을 be ready for ~를 위한 준비를 하다
let down 실망시키다

7. 여자는 방금 어떤 행사에 참석했는가?

(A) 세미나

(B) 무역 박람회

(C) 회의

(D) 시상식

해설 행사의 종류와 주제는 대화 초반부에 힌트가 나온다. 여자가 대화 도입부에서 I just got out of a budget meeting.라며 방금 예산 회의에 다녀왔다고 했으므로 (C)가 정답이다.

8. 도표를 보시오. 어떤 수업이 중단될 예정인가?

(A) 요가

(B) 라틴댄스

(C) 에어로빅

(D) 발레

해설 남자가 Mr. Olson said we are going to cut the most expensive class to operate.에서 운영비가 가장 많이 드는 수업을 중단할 거라는 말을 전해 들었다고 하자 여자가 According to the survey we took last month, that is the most popular class with employees.라며 조사 결과를 보면 그 수업이 직원들 사이에서 가장 인기가 많다고 하고 있다. 도표를 통해 직원들 사이에서 가장 인기가 많은 프로그램은 라틴댄스임을 알 수 있으므로 (B)가 정답이다.

9. 남자는 왜 걱정하는가?

(A) 조사가 많이 지연되었다.

(B) 그는 곧 있을 회의에 늦을 것이다.

(C) 그는 발표 준비가 되어 있지 않다.

(D) 최근의 결정이 직원들을 실망시킬 것이다.

해설 남자가 걱정하는 이유를 묻고 있으므로 남자의 대사에서 단서가 나올 확률이 높다. 또한 마지막 문제이므로 대화 후반부에서 단서가 나올 것이다. 남자가 Many employees will be disappointed to learn that we are not going to offer the program anymore.라며 회사 측에서 라틴댄스를 제공하지 않으면 많은 직원들이 실망할 것을 걱정하고 있으므로 (D)가 정답이다.

UNIT 13 공지&소개

PRACTICE   본문 p.126

1. (A)   2. (C)   3. (B)   4. (C)   5. (D)   6. (B)

Questions 1-3 refer to the following announcement.

Attention, all employees. <u>I'd like to remind</u> you that some of the printers in our department <u>will be replaced with</u> new ones this afternoon. A maintenance man will come <u>to replace them</u> this afternoon. All employees should <u>step out of</u> the office while the replacement work <u>is going on</u>. If you have any further questions, please call the <u>Maintenance Department</u>.

직원 여러분께 알려드립니다. 우리 부서의 일부 프린터가 오늘 오후에 최신 제품으로 교체될 예정입니다. 기술자가 오늘 오후에 프린터 교체를 위해 올 것입니다. 모든 직원들은 오후에 작업이 진행될 동안 잠시 사무실을 비워 주셔야 합니다. 질문이 있으시면 관리팀으로 연락바랍니다.

어휘 **attention** 주의, 주목 **remind** 상기시키다 **replace** 교체하다 **step out** (잠깐) 나가다 **Maintenance Department** (유지, 보수) 관리부

1. 청자들은 어디에 있는가?
   (A) 사무실에
   (B) 공항에
   (C) 슈퍼마켓에
   (D) 박물관에

해설 장소는 초반부에 단서가 등장한다. 따라서 인사말(Attention, all employees.) 다음을 집중해서 듣는다. '부서 내 프린터가 새 것으로 교체될 예정'임을 공지하고 있으므로(I'd like to remind you that some of the printers in our department will be replaced with new ones this afternoon.) 청자들이 있는 장소는 사무실임을 알 수 있다. 따라서 (A)가 정답이다.

2. 누구를 대상으로 하는 공지인가?
   (A) 기술자들
   (B) 고객들
   (C) 사무실 직원들
   (D) 상점 매니저들

해설 담화 초반에 Attention, all employees.라고 하는 부분을 통해 공지 대상은 직원들임을 알 수 있다. 따라서 (C)가 정답이다.

3. 공지에 따르면, 오늘 오후에 무엇이 시작되는가?
   (A) 사무실 개조
   (B) 기기 교체
   (C) 작업 현장 점검
   (D) 이사회 회의

해설 시점(this afternoon) 관련 정보를 묻는 문제는 시점이 언급된 곳을 잘 들어야 한다. 오후에는 프린터 교체가 있다고 공지하고 있으므로(A maintenance man will come to replace them this afternoon.) (B)가 정답이다.

Questions 4-6 refer to the following introduction.

Thank you for coming to our annual <u>awards ceremony</u>. I'm pleased to announce this year's <u>best salesperson</u> is Jinny. She joined the Sales Department nearly three years ago. She <u>has worked on</u> many projects, and they were all very successful. Our sales have also <u>increased dramatically</u>. And now I would like to invite Jinny to <u>come up to the stage</u> to receive her award. Let's <u>give a big hand</u> for Jinny, who has worked tirelessly to <u>contribute to</u> our company.

연례 시상식에 참석해 주셔서 감사드립니다. 올해의 최우수 판매직원인 Jinny를 소개하게 되어 기쁩니다. 그녀는 거의 3년 전에 판매부에 합류했습니다. 그녀는 많은 프로젝트를 해왔고, 그 프로젝트들은 매우 성공적이었으며, 우리의 매출이 급격히 증가했습니다. 자, 이제 저는 시상을 위해 Jinny를 무대 위로 초대하고자 합니다. 지칠 줄 모르고 우리 회사에 공헌한 Jinny에게 큰 박수를 보내주시기 바랍니다.

어휘 **awards ceremony** 시상식 **announce** 발표하다 **dramatically** 극적으로, 급격히 **invite** 초대하다 **stage** 무대 **give a big hand** 큰 박수를 보내다 **tirelessly** 지칠 줄 모르고, 끊임없이 **contribute to** ~에 기여하다

4. 연설의 주된 목적은 무엇인가?
   (A) 프로젝트를 제안하기 위해
   (B) 직원 회의를 공지하기 위해
   (C) 직원의 성과를 인정하기 위해
   (D) 보너스를 지급하기 위해

해설 담화의 목적은 초반부에 인사말, 자기소개와 함께 등장한다. I'm pleased to announce this year's best salesperson is Jinny.에서 최우수 판매직원을 소개하고 있으므로 (C)가 정답이다.

5. Jinny 씨는 영업부에서 얼마 동안 일해 왔는가?
   (A) 반년
   (B) 1년

(C) 2년

(D) 3년

해설 질문에 언급된 이름(Jinny)이 나오는 부분에 집중해서 들어야 한다. 해당 직원 이름을 언급한 후 She joined the Sales Department nearly three years ago.라면서 판매부서에서 3년간 일해 왔다고 했으므로 (D)가 정답이다.

6. 화자에 따르면, Jinny 씨는 무엇을 했는가?

(A) 많은 나라를 방문했다.

(B) 많은 프로젝트를 끝냈다.

(C) 많은 제품을 개발했다.

(D) 계약을 성사시켰다.

해설 소개 대상의 업적은 담화 중후반부에 등장한다. She has worked on many projects, and they were all very successful. Our sales have also increased dramatically.에서 많은 프로젝트를 수행했다고 했으므로 (B)가 정답이다.

ACTUAL TEST 본문 p.127

1. (B)	2. (A)	3. (C)	4. (D)	5. (A)	6. (B)
7. (A)	8. (C)	9. (C)	10. (D)	11. (D)	12. (B)

Questions 1-3 refer to the following announcement.

Good morning, employees. I'd like to announce that we're going to move to our company's new building next Monday. I'm sure that everyone is excited about having a pleasant environment to work in. The movers will be transporting everything this Friday. It's a good opportunity for us to throw away unnecessary office supplies. Please make sure you do this by Thursday.

직원 여러분, 안녕하십니까? 다음 주 월요일 우리 회사가 새 건물로 이전하는 것에 대해 알려드리고자 합니다. 모든 분들이 사무실의 쾌적한 분위기에 대해 기대하고 계실 겁니다. 이삿짐 센터 직원들이 이번 주 금요일에 모든 짐을 옮길 예정입니다. 불필요한 사무용품을 버리기에 좋은 기회입니다. 목요일까지 치워 주시기 바랍니다.

어휘 be excited about ~에 대해 들뜨다 pleasant 쾌적한 environment 환경 transport 이동시키다 opportunity 기회 throw away 치우다, 버리다 unnecessary 불필요한

1. 화자에 따르면, 새 사무실은 어떤가?

(A) 완벽히 갖춰진 회의 공간이 있다.

(B) 쾌적한 환경을 갖췄다.

(C) 전망이 아름답다.

(D) 넓은 주차장을 갖췄다.

해설 담화 초반에 I'm sure that everyone is excited about having a pleasant environment to work in.라고 언급한 부분에서 '쾌적한 환경'이라고 했으므로 (B)가 정답이다.

2. 회사는 언제 새 건물로 이사하는가?

(A) 월요일에

(B) 목요일에

(C) 금요일에

(D) 토요일에

해설 일정 변경 및 공지 사항에 대한 문제는 초/중반부를 잘 듣는다. I'd like to announce that we're going to move to our company's new building next Monday.에서 이전 날짜는 월요일이라고 언급되었으므로 (A)가 정답이다.

3. 청자들은 무엇을 하도록 요청 받는가?

(A) 사무용품을 주문한다

(B) 오래된 가구를 버린다

(C) 본인의 사무용품을 정리한다

(D) 본인의 서류를 옮긴다

해설 요청 사항을 묻는 문제는 후반부에 단서가 등장하며, 관련 표현(Please ~)을 잘 들어야 한다. It's a good opportunity for us to throw away unnecessary office supplies. Please make sure you do this by Thursday.에서 불필요한 물건을 치우라고 하고 있으므로 (C)가 정답이다.

Questions 4-6 refer to the following announcement.

Attention, all passengers on Sky Airlines' Flight 302 to Paris. Due to unexpected bad weather conditions, all flights have been delayed. This flight was originally scheduled to depart at 7:00 A.M., but it has been rescheduled and will now leave at 11:00 A.M., so it will be delayed by four hours. Thank you for your understanding. We sincerely apologize for this inconvenience. Instead, we will provide all passengers with meal coupons which you can use at any of the restaurants at the airport.

파리행 Sky 에어라인 302편 승객 여러분들께 알립니다! 예상치 못한 악천후로 인하여 모든 항공편이 지연되었습니다. 이 항공편은 원래 아침 7시에 출발 예정이었지만 일정이 조정되어 4시간 후인 오전 11시에 이륙할 예정입니다. 양해해 주셔서 감사드리며, 불편을 드려 진심으로 사과 드립니다. 대신 저희는 공항 내 모든 식당에서 사용할 수 있는 식사 쿠폰을 제공할 것입니다.

어휘 passenger 승객 unexpected 예상치 못한 weather conditions 기상 조건 originally 원래 depart 출발하다 delay 지연시키다; 지연 inconvenience 불편 meal coupon 식권

4. 이 안내는 어디에서 이루어지고 있는 것 같은가?

    (A) 비행기에서

    (B) 버스 정류장에서

    (C) 유람선에서

    (D) 공항에서

해설 장소는 초반부에 단서가 등장한다. all passengers on Sky Airlines' Flight 302 to Paris.라고 했고 이어서 비행기 출발 지연, 변경된 이륙 시간 등을 안내하고 있으므로 (D)가 정답임을 알 수 있다. 아직 출발한 상태가 아니기 때문에 (A)는 답이 될 수 없다.

5. 문제의 원인은 무엇인가?

    (A) 악천후

    (B) 기계 결함

    (C) 이전 항공기의 지연

    (D) 활주로 보수

해설 담화 초반에 Due to unexpected bad weather conditions, all flights have been delayed.에서 악천후로 비행기가 지연되었다고 했으므로 (A)가 정답이다.

6. 안내 방송에 따르면, 무엇이 바뀌었는가?

    (A) 출발일

    (B) 출발 시간

    (C) 여행 일정

    (D) 식사 시간

해설 공지 목적이 나온 후 안내 사항이 등장한다. This flight was originally scheduled to depart at 7:00 A.M., but it has been rescheduled and will now leave at 11:00 A.M., so it will be delayed by four hours.에서 비행기 출발 시간이 뒤로 밀렸다고 언급되어 있으므로 (B)가 정답이다.

Questions 7-9 refer to the following introduction.

Ladies and gentlemen, welcome to the Hospitality Management Conference. I'd like to introduce our special guest, the general manager of the Brighton Hotel, Michael Rupin. I'm sure all of you know his recent book on hospitality management, which has sold more than two million copies. Many people are eager to hear about his experiences in the hospitality industry because of his good reputation. Now, everyone, please welcome Mr. Rupin.

신사 숙녀 여러분, 저희 호텔 경영 회의에 오신 것을 환영합니다. 저희 특별 손님이자, Brighton 호텔의 총지배인이신 Michael Rupin을 소개합니다. 여러분은 호텔 경영에 관한 그의 최근 책이 2백만 부 이상 팔렸다는 것을 아실 것이라 생각합니다. 그의 명성에 따라 서비스업에서의 그의 경험에 대해 듣고 싶어 하는 사람들이 많습니다. 자 여러분, Rupin 씨를 환영해 주

시기 바랍니다.

어휘 hospitality management 호텔 경영 conference 회의 general manager 총지배인 reputation 명성, 평판 hospitality industry 서비스업

7. 담화는 어디에서 이루어지고 있는가?

    (A) 회의에서

    (B) 시상식에서

    (C) 직원 교육에서

    (D) 지역 방송국에서

해설 소개가 이루어지는 장소에 대한 단서는 담화 초반에 등장한다. welcome to the Hospitality Management Conference.를 통해 (A)가 정답임을 알 수 있다.

8. 담화의 목적은 무엇인가?

    (A) 직원들에게 회의에 대해 알리기 위해

    (B) 새로운 책을 광고하기 위해

    (C) 초청 연사를 소개하기 위해

    (D) 새로운 매니저를 선발하기 위해

해설 담화 초반에 인사말과 목적이 나온다. I'd like to introduce our special guest, the general manager of the Brighton Hotel, Michael Rupin.에서 특별 게스트이자 새로운 호텔 총지배인 Michael Rupin을 소개한다고 했으므로 (C)가 정답이다.

9. Michael Rupin은 누구인가?

    (A) 판매원

    (B) 회의 기획자

    (C) 호텔 총지배인

    (D) 회계사

해설 담화 초반에 인사말과 목적이 나온 후 소개 대상의 이름과 신분/직책 등이 함께 언급된다. I'd like to introduce our special guest, the general manager of the Brighton Hotel, Michael Rupin.에서 호텔 지배인이라고 소개하고 있으므로 (C)가 정답이다.

Questions 10-12 refer to the following announcement.

Good morning. I'll be your guide today. First, we will start our tour by looking at some mosques. Please look to the right. You can see a mosque that looks quite different than other mosques. It is called the B.P. Mosque. It was built by famous architect Bryan Peter. He always sought to make a unique design for each of his structures. If anyone wants to know more about this mosque, we will come back here and look around tomorrow. After that, our next stop on the tour will be another one of Mr. Peter's unique designs.

안녕하세요. 저는 오늘 여러분의 가이드 역할을 하게 될 겁니다. 먼저, 사원을 둘러보면서 우리의 여행을 시작하겠습니다. 오른쪽을 보시면 다른 사원들과는 상당히 달라 보이는 사원이 하나 있습니다. 이것은 B.P. 사원으로 불립니다. 이것은 유명한 건축가 Bryan Peter가 지은 것입니다. 그는 항상 그의 모든 건축물에 독특한 디자인을 추구해 왔습니다. 누구든 이 사원에 대해 더 알고 싶으시다면, 우리는 내일 다시 이곳으로 와서 둘러볼 것입니다. 이제 이 관광의 다음 목적지는 Peter 씨의 독특한 디자인이 반영된 또 다른 건물입니다.

어휘 mosque (이슬람) 사원 architect 건축가 structure 구조물, 건축물 unique 독특한

10. 화자는 누구인 것 같은가?
　(A) 사진작가
　(B) 기술자
　(C) 건축가
　(D) 관광 가이드

해설 화자의 신분/직업은 담화 초반부에 등장한다. I'll be your guide today. First, we will start our tour by looking at some mosques.에서 본인을 가이드라고 밝히고 있으므로 (D)가 정답이다.

11. 담화에 따르면, BP 사원은 다른 사원들과 어떻게 다른가?
　(A) 다른 사원과는 다른 색상이다.
　(B) 다른 사원들보다 오래돼 보인다.
　(C) 다른 사원들보다 크다.
　(D) 다른 사원들과 디자인이 다르다.

해설 질문에 나온 B.P. 사원이 키워드로, He always sought to make a unique design for each of his structures.에서 B.P. 사원의 독특한 디자인에 대해 언급했으므로 (D)가 정답이다.

12. 청자들은 다음에 무엇을 할 것인가?
　(A) 작품의 사진을 찍는다
　(B) Peter 씨의 다른 건축물을 둘러본다
　(C) 사원에서 짧은 휴식을 취한다
　(D) 관광버스를 타고 호텔로 돌아간다

해설 다음에 할 일을 묻는 문제는 담화 후반부에 단서가 등장한다. After that, our next stop on the tour will be another one of Mr. Peter's unique designs.에서 (B)가 정답임을 알 수 있다.

UNIT **14** 　전화 메시지

PRACTICE　　　　　　본문 p.132

1. (C)　**2.** (D)　**3.** (C)　**4.** (B)　**5.** (A)　**6.** (C)

Questions 1-3 refer to the following telephone message.

Hello, Sam Taylor. This is Emily from the Meadowlands Medical Center. Thank you so much for showing interest in helping out at our medical center's fundraising banquet next week. **We already have many volunteers signed up for this event**, but I'd love to add you to our list for future volunteer opportunities. Could you please visit our Web site and complete a short volunteer application form? This way, we'll have your information on file, and we'll notify you as soon as there's a chance to get involved in the future. Thanks again and have a fantastic day!

안녕하세요, Sam Taylor 씨. 저는 Meadowlands 의료센터의 Emily입니다. 다음 주에 있을 저희 의료 센터의 기금 모금 행사에 도움을 주시겠다는 관심을 보여주셔서 정말 감사드립니다. 이번 행사에는 이미 많은 자원봉사자가 등록되어 있지만, 향후에 있을 자원봉사 기회에도 참여해 주셨으면 합니다. 저희 웹사이트에 방문하셔서 간단한 자원봉사 신청서 양식을 작성해 주실 수 있을까요? 이렇게 하면 귀하의 정보를 파일에 저장해 두고, 추후 자원봉사 기회가 생길 때 바로 연락드릴 수 있습니다. 다시 한번 감사드리며, 좋은 하루 보내세요!

어휘 show interest 관심을 표하다 help out 돕다, 지원하다 fundraising banquet 기금 모금 행사 volunteer 자원 봉사자 sign up for ~을 신청하다 opportunity 기회 application form 신청서 on file 기록으로 남아 있는 notify 알리다, 통지하다 get involved 참여하다, 관여하다

1. 화자는 어디에서 일하는가?
　(A) 채용 대행사에서
　(B) 종이 공급 회사에서
　(C) 병원에서
　(D) 대학교에서

해설 지문 초반에 "This is Emily from the Meadowlands Medical Center."를 통해 화자는 병원에서 일한다는 것을 알 수 있다. 따라서 (C)가 정답이다.

2. 화자가 "이번 행사에 이미 많은 자원봉사자가 등록했습니다"라고 말하는 이유는 무엇인가?

(A) 요청하기 위해

(B) 초대하기 위해

(C) 행사 기획자를 안심시키기 위해

(D) 제안을 거절하기 위해

해설 화자는 자원봉사자가 이미 충분히 등록되었음을 언급하며 뒤에 이어 "but I'd love to add you to our list for future volunteer opportunities."를 통해 이번 행사에는 참여할 수 없지만, 미래의 자원봉사 기회에 참여할 수 있도록 명단에 포함하고 싶다고 말하고 있다. 따라서 이는 제안을 정중히 거절하는 의미를 담고 있으므로 (D)가 정답이다.

3. 화자는 청자에게 무엇을 하라고 요청하고 있는가?

(A) 등록비를 지불한다

(B) 회의에 참석한다

(C) 온라인 양식을 작성한다

(D) 날짜와 시간을 선택한다

해설 지문 마지막에 부분에 "Could you please visit our Web site and complete a short volunteer application form?"를 통해 화자는 청자에게 병원 웹사이트에 방문하여 간단한 자원봉사 신청서를 작성해 달라고 요청하고 있다. 따라서 (C)가 정답이다.

Questions 4-6 refer to the following recorded message.

Thank you for calling the Victory Zoo. Our zoo is internationally famous for our wide variety of animals. We're open every day from 10:00 A.M. to 5:00 P.M. Entrance tickets can only be booked by phone. If you want to make a reservation now, press 1. Cash and credit cards are accepted, and you can pay at the ticket booth near the entrance. For more information, please call one of our customer service representatives at 999-6738.

Victory 동물원에 전화 주셔서 감사합니다. 저희 동물원은 다양한 동물들로 세계적으로 유명합니다. 저희는 오전 10시부터 오후 5시까지 매일 문을 엽니다. 입장권은 전화로만 예매하실 수 있습니다. 지금 예매를 원하시면 1번을 눌러주십시오. 현금과 신용카드로 결제가 가능하며, 입구 근처에 있는 티켓 창구에서 지불할 수 있습니다. 자세한 사항은 999-6738번으로 전화해 고객서비스 직원에 문의 바랍니다.

어휘 internationally 국제적으로, 세계적으로 famous 유명한 a variety of 다양한 book 예약하다 make a reservation 예약하다 credit card 신용카드 accept 받다 entrance 입구 representative 직원

4. 메시지에 의하면, Victory 동물원은 무엇으로 유명한가?

(A) 맛있는 음식

(B) 다양한 동물

(C) 다양한 곤충

(D) 희귀식물

해설 회사 소개 내용은 담화 초반에 주로 언급된다. Our zoo is internationally famous for our wide variety of animals.에서 다양한 동물을 보유하고 있다고 했으므로 (B)가 정답이다.

5. 청자들은 왜 1번을 눌러야 하는가?

(A) 티켓 예매를 위해

(B) 상담원과 통화하기 위해

(C) 예약을 취소하기 위해

(D) 정보를 물어보기 위해

해설 서비스 번호 안내는 'press + 번호'로 제시된다. If you want to make a reservation now, press 1.에서 예매를 원하면 1번을 누르라고 했으므로 (A)가 정답이다.

6. 청자들은 어떻게 더 많은 정보를 얻을 수 있는가?

(A) 1번을 눌러서

(B) 홈페이지를 방문해서

(C) 주어진 번호로 전화해서

(D) 안내 책자를 읽어서

해설 요청 및 당부 사항은 후반부에 주로 제시된다. For more information, please call one of our customer service representatives at 999-6738.에서 추가 정보를 원하면 전화해 달라고 했으므로 (C)가 정답이다.

ACTUAL TEST 본문 p.133

1. (C)	2. (B)	3. (C)	4. (D)	5. (B)
6. (C)	7. (C)	8. (B)	9. (C)	

Questions 1-3 refer to the following telephone message.

Good morning. This is Liam Rey from Star Realty. I'm calling to let you know that an office which you might be interested in has become available. It's near the bus station, the bank, and the post office. The rent is $1,000 per month. I'm sure you will be interested in seeing the office. Please get in touch with me as soon as possible, and I'll ask the owner of the building whether you can have a look at it tomorrow or not. You can call me on my mobile phone. Thanks, Mr. Anderson. I hope to hear from you soon.

안녕하세요. 저는 스타 부동산의 Linda Rey입니다. 당신이 관심 가질만한 사무실이 나왔다는 것을 알려드리기 위해 전화 드립니다. 그곳은 버스 정류장, 은행, 그리고 우체국에 가깝습니다. 임대료는 한 달에 1,000달러입니다. 분명 당신이 보고 싶을 거라고 생각합니다. 가능한 한 빨리 알려주시면, 내일 보고 싶을 없을지 건물 주인에게 물어보겠습니다. 제 휴대전화로 연락 주십시오. 감사합니다, Anderson 씨. 연락 기다리겠습니다.

어휘 realty 부동산 available 구할 수 있는, 이용할 수 있는 get in touch with ~와 연락하다 owner 주인, 소유주 whether ~인지 mobile phone 휴대전화

1. 전화를 건 사람은 누구인 것 같은가?
(A) 아파트 세입자
(B) 정비사
(C) 부동산 중개인
(D) 집주인

해설 발신자 및 수신자의 직업, 업종, 회사 정보에 대한 단서는 담화 초반에 나온다. This is Linda Rey from Star Realty.에서 (C)가 정답임을 알 수 있다.

2. 메시지의 목적은 무엇인가?
(A) 사무실의 위치를 제공하기 위해
(B) 남자에게 사무실이 임대 가능하다는 것을 알려주기 위해
(C) 건설 공사를 알리기 위해
(D) 새로운 건물을 광고하기 위해

해설 목적을 묻는 문제는 'I'm calling ~.'으로 시작되는 문장을 잘 들어야 한다. I'm calling to let you know that an office which you might be interested in has become available.에서 관심 있어 할 만한 사무실이 나왔다고 했으므로 (B)가 정답이다.

3. 청자는 다음에 무엇을 할 것인가?
(A) 계약서에 서명한다
(B) 새 사무실로 옮긴다
(C) Linda Rey에게 연락한다
(D) 건물주에게 전화한다

해설 다음에 할 일을 묻는 문제는 후반부에 단서가 등장한다. Please get in touch with me as soon as possible, You can call me on my mobile phone. 등에서 전화 달라고 했으므로 청자가 곧 전화할 것으로 추측할 수 있다. 따라서 (C)가 정답이다. Linda Rey는 부동산 중개인이지 건물주가 아니므로 (D)는 오답이다.

Questions 4-6 refer to the following telephone message.

Hi, Jamie. It's Alex. I'm still waiting for the airline to locate my luggage and the prototype of our new coffee maker. Given the service I've experienced so far, I don't expect them to find either before my presentation on Friday, and the presentation won't make much of an impression without a working model. So at this point, I think the best option is for you to fly out here yourself with the backup model. I know it's a long trip, but I don't think we have any other choice.

Jamie님, 안녕하세요. Alex입니다. 항공사가 제 짐과 새로운 커피 메이커 시제품을 찾는 데 여전히 어려움을 겪고 있습니다. 지금까지 겪어 본 서비스를 고려할 때, 금요일 프레젠테이션 전에 둘 다 찾을 가능성은 낮아 보입니다. 시연 모델 없이 프레젠테이션을 진행하면 큰 인상을 주기 어려울 것 같아요. 그래서 현재로서는 당신이 예비 모델을 가지고 직접 여기로 오시는 것이 최선의 선택이라고 생각합니다. 긴 여정이라는 건 알지만, 다른 선택지가 없을 것 같아요.

어휘 locate 찾다, 위치를 파악하다 luggage 짐, 수하물 prototype 원형, 시제품 coffee maker 커피 메이커 presentation 발표, 프레젠테이션 impression 인상 option 선택 fly out 비행기로 이동하다 backup model 예비 모델 long trip 긴 여정

4. 남자는 무엇을 기다리고 있는가?
(A) 그의 탑승권이 출력되는 것
(B) 그의 호텔 객실이 청소되는 것
(C) 그의 고객들이 도착하는 것
(D) 그의 짐을 되찾는 것

해설 지문 초반부에 "I'm still waiting for the airline to locate my luggage and the prototype of our new coffee maker."를 통해 남자는 항공사가 그의 짐을 찾기를 기다리고 있음을 알 수 있으므로 (D)가 정답이다.

5. 금요일에 예정된 것은 무엇인가?
(A) 취업 면접
(B) 제품 프레젠테이션
(C) 공장 점검
(D) 언론 발표

해설 지문 초중반에 "Given the service I've experienced so far, I don't expect them to find either before my presentation on Friday, and the presentation won't make much of an impression without a working model."에서 금요일에 프레젠테이션이 있다고 언급하며, 그 프레젠테이션을 위해 시연 모델이 필요하다고 했다. 따라서 금요일에 예정된 것은 (B)이다.

6. 남자가 "긴 여정이라는 건 알지만"이라고 말한 이유는 무엇인가?

(A) 청자에게 휴식을 취하라고 조언하기 위해

(B) 여행이 불필요하다고 제안하기 위해

(C) 불편에 대해 사과하기 위해

(D) 청자에게 신중히 계획할 것을 상기시키기 위해

해설 앞서 그는 상대방에게 백업 모델을 가지고 직접 오라고 요청하며, 긴 여정이 될 것을 알고 있다고 언급했으므로 이는 상대방에게 불편을 끼친 것에 대한 사과의 의미를 담고 있는 것으로 유추할 수 있다. 따라서 (C)가 정답이다.

Questions 7-9 refer to the following telephone message and schedule.

Hi, Charlotte. It's Isabella. I've just forwarded the company's promotional video link to you. I'd like to discuss the possibility of adding French subtitles so that we can share it with our North American partners. I'm conducting an advertising workshop tomorrow morning, but my afternoon appointment with the board of directors has been canceled. Therefore, I have an hour free in the afternoon, and we could meet then. Please let me know if that works for you.

안녕하세요, Charlotte. 저는 Isabella입니다. 방금 회사 홍보 영상 링크를 보내드렸습니다. 북미 파트너들에게 공유하기 위해 프랑스어 자막을 추가하는 것에 대해 논의하고 싶습니다. 내일 아침에 광고 워크숍을 진행할 예정이지만, 오후에 이사진들과의 일정이 취소되어 오후에 한 시간이 빕니다. 그때 만날 수도 있습니다. 괜찮으신지 알려주시면 감사하겠습니다.

Isabella의 오후 일정	
1시	고객과의 점심
2시	이사회 회의
3시	개인 상담
4시	이사회 회의
5시	성과 평가

어휘 forward 전달하다, 보내다 promotional video 홍보 영상 discuss 논의하다, 의논하다 possibility 가능성 subtitle 자막 share 공유하다, 보내다 conduct 진행하다, 수행하다 advertising workshop 광고 워크숍 appointment 약속, 일정

7. 화자는 청자와 무엇에 대해 논의하고 싶어 하는가?

(A) 북미 출장

(B) 고객 설문 조사 수정

(C) 비디오에 자막 추가

(D) 부서 비용 절감

해설 지문 초반 "I'd like to discuss the possibility of adding French subtitles so that we can share it with our North American partners."를 통해 화자는 회사 홍보 영상에 프랑스어 자막을 추가하는 것에 대해 논의하기 위해 만남을 요청하고 있으므로 (C)가 정답이다.

8. 화자는 내일 무엇을 진행할 거라고 말하는가?

(A) 국제 회의

(B) 광고 워크숍

(C) 최종 면접

(D) 분기별 리뷰

해설 지문 중반에 "I'm conducting an advertising workshop tomorrow morning, ~"를 통해 화자는 내일 아침에 광고 워크숍을 진행할 것임을 알 수 있으므로 (B)가 정답이다.

9. 도표를 보시오. 화자와 청자는 언제 만날 것 같은가?

(A) 오전 10시에

(B) 오전 11시에

(C) 오후 4시에

(D) 오후 5시에

해설 지문 후반에 "my afternoon appointment with the vice president has been canceled. Therefore, I have an hour free in the afternoon, and we could meet then."에서 화자가 오후에 이사진들과의 일정이 취소되어 한 시간이 빈다며, 이 시간에 만날 것을 요청하고 있다. 도표에서 오후 4시 이사진 회의가 취소되어 이 시간에 만날 것으로 유추할 수 있으므로 (C)가 정답이다.

UNIT 15 **방송&광고**

PRACTICE 본문 p.140

1. (C) **2.** (B) **3.** (C) **4.** (C) **5.** (A) **6.** (D)

Questions 1-3 refer to the following radio broadcast.

Good morning. There will be no rain for a few days. Through the morning, the temperature will increase rapidly, and there will be scorching hot weather along with humid air. However, I have some good news for you. The wind will blow on Saturday, and it will be a perfect day for surfing. But it looks like a big typhoon is coming our way on Sunday. We'll keep you posted. Now, let's go to Jane Watson for an update on today's sports news.

좋은 아침입니다. 앞으로 며칠 동안은 비가 오지 않을 것입니다. 오전 내내 온도가 급격히 올라가서 찜통더위와 함께 공기가 습할 것입니다. 하지만 여러분들에게 좋은 소식이 있습니다. 토요일에 바람이 불어 서핑을 하기에 좋을 것입니다. 하지만 일요일에는 큰 태풍이 다가올 것 같습니다. 계속해서 여러분께 알려 드리겠습니다. 다음은 Jane Watson의 오늘의 스포츠 뉴스가 있겠습니다.

어휘 temperature 온도 rapidly 급격히 scorching 맹렬한, 태워버릴 듯이 더운 humid 습한 typhoon 태풍 keep ~ posted ~에게 최신 정보를 전하다

1. 오늘 날씨는 어떻게 될 것인가?
   (A) 눈이 내릴 것이다.
   (B) 추워질 것이다.
   (C) 더워질 것이다.
   (D) 안개가 낄 것이다.

해설 현재 날씨는 인사 및 프로그램 소개 후 등장한다. the temperature will increase rapidly, and there will be scorching hot weather along with humid air.에서 오전 내내 찜통 더위가 있을 거라고 예보하고 있으므로 (C)가 정답이다.

2. 일요일에는 무슨 일이 일어날 것인가?
   (A) 기온이 올라갈 것이다.
   (B) 거센 바람이 불 것이다.
   (C) 눈이 올 것으로 예상된다.
   (D) 현재 기온을 유지할 것이다.

해설 향후 날씨는 But, However 뒤에 주로 언급된다. But it looks like a big typhoon is coming our way on Sunday.에서 태풍이 올 거라고 예보하고 있으므로 (B)가 정답이다.

3. 청자들은 다음에 무엇을 들을 것 같은가?
   (A) 교통 소식
   (B) 광고
   (C) 스포츠 보도
   (D) 경제 뉴스

해설 next 문제는 후반부를 잘 들어야 한다. Now, let's go to Jane Watson for an update on today's sports news.에서 스포츠 뉴스가 진행될 예정이라고 했으므로 (C)가 정답이다.

Questions 4-6 refer to the following advertisement.

The UCA Company's new digital camera looks very cute, and it has many functions. First, it's easy to use. It has an auto-system, so you only have to set up the camera the way you like it once. It uses Wi-Fi as well, and it can be connected to a personal computer without any wires. This adorable camera is easy for anyone to use. For more information, visit our Web site at www.ucaelectronics.com.

우리 UCA 회사의 새로운 디지털 카메라는 귀엽게 보이지만, 많은 기능이 있습니다. 첫째, 사용하기 쉽습니다. 자동 시스템이 있어, 사람들은 처음에만 필요한 설정을 하면 매번 다시 하지 않아도 됩니다. 무선 인터넷 기능도 갖고 있어, 개인용 컴퓨터에 케이블 없이 연결할 수 있습니다. 이 사랑스러운 카메라는 누구든 쉽게 사용할 수 있습니다. 추가 정보는 저희 홈페이지 www.ucaelectronics.com를 방문하세요.

어휘 function 기능 set up 설정하다 connect 연결하다, 잇다 personal computer 개인용 컴퓨터 without ~없이 wire 전선 adorable 사랑스러운

4. 무엇을 위한 광고인가?
   (A) 네트워크 시스템
   (B) 사무용 가구
   (C) 전자기기
   (D) 주방용품

해설 광고하는 제품이나 서비스 관련 내용은 담화 초반부에 등장한다. The UCA Company's new digital camera looks very cute, and it has many functions.에서 카메라가 언급되었으므로 (C)가 정답이다.

5. 물품의 장점으로 언급된 것은 무엇인가?
   (A) 사용하기 매우 쉽다.
   (B) 작년 모델보다 더 저렴하다.
   (C) 세계에서 가장 작다.
   (D) 색상이 다양하다.

해설 초반부에 광고 대상 및 광고 제품이 나온 후 제품의 특장점이 등장한다. First, it's easy to use. 에서 사용하기 쉽다고 했으므로 (A)가 정답이다.

6. 화자들은 어떻게 더 많은 정보를 얻을 수 있는가?
   (A) 매장을 방문해서
   (B) 이메일을 보내서
   (C) 특정 번호로 전화해서
   (D) 홈페이지를 방문해서

해설 추가 정보에 관한 문제는 마지막 문장을 잘 들어야 한다. For more information, visit our Web site at www.ucaelectronics.com에서 홈페이지를 방문해 정보를 얻으라고 했으므로 (D)가 정답이다.

정답과 해설

1. (C)	2. (D)	3. (C)	4. (A)	5. (A)
6. (B)	7. (C)	8. (D)	9. (C)	

Questions 1-3 refer to the following broadcast.

Good morning. This is Caroline Mack at WABC. Starting next Monday, Highway 10 will be closed due to road repairs. Traffic jams around the airport area will become unavoidable when the roadwork starts. It is recommended that drivers take Route 27 until the roadwork is completed next month. Please visit our Web site at www.wabcstation.com to check out news about the construction.

안녕하세요. 저는 WABC 방송국의 Caroline Mack입니다. 다음 주 월요일을 시작으로, 10번 고속도로는 도로공사로 인해 폐쇄될 것입니다. 도로공사가 시작되면, 공항 지역은 교통체증을 피할 수 없을 것 같습니다. 다음 달 공사가 마무리될 때까지 운전자들은 27번 도로를 이용하시기를 권장합니다. 저희 웹사이트 www.wabcstation.com으로 방문하여 공사에 대한 소식을 확인하시기 바랍니다.

어휘 road repair 도로공사 (= roadwork) traffic jam 교통체증 unavoidable 불가피한, 어쩔 수 없는 roadwork 도로 보수 작업

1. 보도의 주요 목적은 무엇인가?
(A) 날씨 정보를 제공하기 위해
(B) 시 축제에 대해 알리기 위해
(C) 공사 관련 정보를 제공하기 위해
(D) 새로운 자동차를 광고하기 위해

해설 교통방송은 초반부에 교통 상황과 정체 이유가 등장한다. Starting next Monday, Highway 10 will be closed due to road repairs.를 통해 (C)가 답임을 알 수 있다.

2. 화자는 무엇을 권장하는가?
(A) 뉴스 속보를 듣는 것
(B) 주의하여 운전하는 것
(C) 대중교통을 이용하는 것
(D) 다른 도로를 이용하는 것

해설 권장 사항은 recommend 등 요청, 추천 등의 표현이 들어간 문장을 잘 들어야 한다. It is recommended that drivers take Route 27 until the roadwork is completed next month.에서 우회로로 갈 것을 권유하고 있으므로 (D)가 정답이다.

3. 청자들은 어떻게 최신 정보를 얻을 수 있는가?
(A) 라디오 청취를 통해서
(B) TV 시청을 통해서
(C) 홈페이지를 방문함으로써
(D) 특정 번호로 전화함으로써

해설 대안 및 다음 방송 안내는 후반부에 등장한다. Please visit our Web site at www.wabcstation에 check out news about the construction.에서 홈페이지에서 추가로 공사 상황을 확인하라고 했으므로 (C)가 정답이다.

Questions 4-6 refer to the following advertisement.

LX Apartments will be available to rent next month. This is an eco-friendly apartment complex. The property is located in the city center, and there are several restaurants nearby. All residents of LX Apartments will be able to enjoy free facilities such as a gym, a swimming pool, and a tennis court 24 hours a day. To look around LX Apartments, please call 3451-1156.

LX 아파트가 다음 달부터 임대가 가능해졌습니다. 이곳은 친환경 아파트 단지입니다. 이 아파트 단지는 시내 중심가에 위치해 있으며, 주변에는 식당들도 있습니다. LX 아파트의 모든 입주자들은 체육관, 수영장, 테니스 코트와 같은 무료 시설을 24시간 즐기실 수 있습니다. LX 아파트를 둘러보기를 원하시면, 3451-1156으로 전화 주세요.

어휘 eco-friendly 친환경적인 property 재산, 토지 be located 위치해 있다 nearby 인근에 resident 거주자, 입주자 facility 시설 such as ~와 같은 gym 체육관 look around ~을 둘러보다

4. 무엇이 광고되고 있는가?
(A) 부동산
(B) 스포츠용품점
(C) 가구 공장
(D) 페인트 가게

해설 광고하는 제품은 담화 초반에 등장한다. LX Apartments will be available to rent next month.에서 Apartment가 언급되었으므로 (A) 부동산 광고임을 알 수 있다.

5. 아파트는 언제 임대가 가능한가?
(A) 다음 달
(B) 내년
(C) 다음 주 금요일
(D) 연말에

해설 LX Apartments will be available to rent next month.에서 다음 달부터 임대가 가능하다고 했으므로 (A)가 정답이다.

6. LX 아파트의 입주자 전원에게 무료인 것은 무엇인가?

(A) 슈퍼마켓

(B) 헬스 시설

(C) 놀이터

(D) 주차장

해설 제품의 특장점은 담화 중후반에 등장한다. All residents of LX Apartments will be able to enjoy free facilities such as a gym, a swimming pool, and a tennis court 24 hours a day.에서 체육관, 수영장, 테니스장이 무료라고 했으므로 (B)가 정답이다.

Questions 7-9 refer to the following advertisement and price table.

It's the most special peak season here at the Raymond Hotel London! To celebrate our renovation, we are providing our guests with all-time special deals. Spend your holidays in one of our newly remodeled suites at a discounted price. This month only, our executive suite will be available for the price of the executive standard room, and the luxury suite will be available for the price of our executive suite. Hurry up and make your booking to take advantage of these special rates!

여기 레이몬드 호텔 런던의 가장 특별한 성수기 시즌입니다! 저희의 개조를 기념하기 위해, 역대 특별 할인을 투숙객분들께 제공하려고 합니다. 할인된 가격으로, 새롭게 리모델링된 저희 스위트룸에서 휴가를 보내십시오. 이번 달만, 저희의 이그제큐티브 특실은 이그제큐티브 일반실 가격으로, 그리고 럭셔리 특실은 이그제큐티브 특실 가격으로 이용 가능합니다. 이 특별 가격 혜택을 보시려면 서둘러 예약하십시오!

룸 타입	가격
슈페리어 객실	190유로
이그제큐티브 일반실	215유로
이그제큐티브 특실	245유로
럭셔리 특실	270유로

어휘 peak season 성수기 renovation 개조 special deal 특별한 혜택 discounted price 할인된 가격 suite 스위트룸 standard room 일반실 available 이용 가능한 take advantage of ~을 이용하다

7. 이 광고는 누구를 대상으로 하는 것 같은가?

(A) 회사 임원들

(B) 수리업체 직원들

(C) 여행객들

(D) 호텔 직원들

해설 광고 대상을 묻는 문제로, 담화 초반에서 단서를 찾을 수 있다. It's the most special peak season here at the Raymond Hotel London!에서 호텔의 성수기 시즌임을 알리고 있다. 뒤이어 할인된 호텔 객실 가격을 홍보하는 것으로 보아, 광고 대상은 호텔에서 묵을 투숙객들임을 알 수 있다. 따라서 (C)가 정답이다.

8. 왜 이 사업체는 특별 가격을 제공하는가?

(A) 기념일을 축하하기 위해

(B) 개업을 홍보하기 위해

(C) 개조를 위한 기금을 모으기 위해

(D) 리모델링을 기념하기 위해

해설 특별 가격을 제공하는 이유를 묻는 세부사항 문제로, To celebrate our renovation, we are providing our guests with all-time special deals.에서 renovation(개조, 수리)을 기념하기 위해서 역대 특가 상품을 제공한다고 했으므로 정답은 (D)이다.

9. 도표를 보시오. 럭셔리 특실은 이번 달에 얼마에 제공되는가?

(A) 190유로

(B) 215유로

(C) 245유로

(D) 270유로

해설 문제의 'luxury suite'이 키워드로, the luxury suite will be available for the price of our executive suite.에서 럭셔리 특실이 이그제큐티브 특실 가격으로 제공된다고 했고, 도표에서 이그제큐티브 특실 가격은 (C) 245유로이다.

정답과 해설

PART 05 단문 빈칸 채우기

UNIT 01 명사

CHECK-UP 본문 p.148

1. (B)	2. (B)	3. (B)	4. (B)	5. (B)	6. (B)
7. (A)	8. (B)	9. (B)	10. (B)	11. (B)	12. (B)

1. Blackwell 씨는 이전 고용주로부터 인상적인 추천장을 받았다.

해설 빈칸은 전치사의 목적어 자리이자 소유격 her 뒤에서 형용사 previous의 수식을 받는 명사 자리이므로 (B) employer가 정답이다.

어휘 impressive 인상적인 recommendation 추천장 previous 이전의 employ 고용하다 employer 고용주

2. 우리 팀은 현재 새로운 마케팅 전략의 개발을 진행 중이다.

해설 빈칸은 전치사의 목적어 자리이자 정관사 the 뒤의 명사 자리이므로 보기 중 명사 (B) development가 정답이다.

어휘 currently 현재 marketing strategy 마케팅 전략 develop 개발하다 development 개발

3. G-Motors는 전기 자동차의 디자인에 있어 남다른 창의성을 보여주었다.

해설 빈칸은 타동사 demonstrate의 목적어 자리이자 형용사 extraordinary의 수식을 받는 명사 자리이므로 보기 중 명사 (B) creativity가 정답이다.

어휘 demonstrate 보여주다, 설명하다 extraordinary 보기 드문, 대단한 creative 창조적인, 창의적인 creativity 창의성

4. Elite Decor 사는 3일간의 협의 끝에 Max Marketing 사와 계약을 맺었다.

해설 빈칸은 타동사 sign의 목적어 자리이자 관사(a) 뒤의 단수 가산 명사 자리이다. 보기 중 문맥상 '계약서에 서명하다'라는 의미가 적절하므로 (B) contract이 정답이다. 참고로 (A) construction은 불가산 명사이다.

어휘 talk 협상, 회담 sign a contract 계약서에 서명하다 construction 공사

5. 직원들은 회사 자원을 사용하기 전에 허가를 요청해야 합니다.

해설 빈칸은 전치사 for의 목적어 자리이다. 빈칸 앞에 a(n)이 없는 것으로 보아 불가산 명사 자리이므로 (B) permission이 정답이다. (A) permit은 형태의 변화 없이 동사와 명사가 둘 다 가능한데, 명사로 쓰일 때 '허가증'이라는 의미로 가산 명사이다.

어휘 ask for ~요청하다 resource 자원, 물자

6. 계약서의 마지막 장에 서명하기 전에 각 페이지를 주의 깊게 검토하세요.

해설 빈칸은 타동사 Review의 목적어인 page를 수식하는 수량 형용사 자리로, 단수 가산 명사인 page 앞에 올 수 있는 (B) each가 정답이다. (A) little은 불가산 명사 앞에 쓰인다.

어휘 review 검토하다 carefully 주의 깊게

7. Blue Café는 지역 주민들에게 해산물 요리가 맛있다는 평을 받고 있다.

해설 전치사의 by의 목적어 자리이자 빈칸 앞 area와 복합 명사를 이루는 명사 자리이다. 문맥상 '지역 주민들'이라는 의미가 적절하므로 (A) residents가 정답이다.

어휘 be highly regarded for ~에 대해 높이 평가되다 resident 거주자 residence 거주지 dish 요리

8. 주차증이 파손된 경우에는 출입구로 가지고 오셔서 교환해 주세요.

해설 전치사 for의 목적어 자리로, 명사 자리이다. 문맥상 '파손된 주차증의 교체'의 의미가 적절하므로 (B) replacement가 정답이다.

어휘 parking permit 주차증 entrance station 출입구 recipient 받는 사람, 수령[수취]인 replacement 교체, 후임

9. 자격증은 지원서와 함께 제출되어야 한다.

해설 전치사 with의 목적어 자리이자 소유격 대명사 your 다음 명사 자리이다. 문맥상 '지원서와 함께 자격증을 제출하라'는 의미가 적절하므로 (B) applications가 정답이다.

어휘 certificate 자격증 submit 제출하다 along with ~와 함께, ~에 덧붙여

10. 저희 고객 서비스 부서는 모든 고객 문의를 24시간 이내에 처리합니다.

해설 빈칸 앞의 customer와 함께 복합 명사를 이루어 '고객 문의를 처리하다'라는 의미가 적절하므로 명사 inquiry의 복수형인 (B) inquiries가 정답이다.

어휘 address 다루다, 처리하다 within ~이내에 inquire 문의하다 inquiry 문의

11. 우리 분기별 판매 실적은 수익의 꾸준한 증가를 보여준다.

해설 빈칸 뒤의 figures와 함께 복합 명사를 이루어 '판매 실적'이라는 의미를 완성하는 명사 (B) sales가 정답이다.

어휘 quarterly 분기별의 indicate 나타내다, 보여주다 steady 꾸준한 increase in ~에서의 증가 revenue 수익

12. 다가오는 회의에 참석할 대표자를 지정해 주시기 바랍니다.

해설 빈칸은 타동사 designate의 목적어 자리이자 관사 a 다음 명사 자리이므로 명사인 (B) representative가 정답이다. representative는 형태의 변화 없이 형용사와 명사로 둘 다 쓰인다.

어휘 designate 지정하다 attend 참석하다 upcoming 곧 다가올 represent 대표하다 representative 대표하는; 대표

PRACTICE
본문 p.152

1. (B) **2.** (C) **3.** (D) **4.** (D) **5.** (C) **6.** (C)
7. (B) **8.** (C)

1. 다행히도, 건설 프로젝트의 비용은 귀하의 후한 기부금으로 충당되었습니다.

해설 빈칸은 전치사 by의 목적어 역할을 하는 명사 자리이자 형용사 generous의 수식을 받는 명사 자리이다. 따라서 보기 중 유일한 명사인 (B) donation이 정답이다.

어휘 fortunately 다행히 cost 비용 be covered 충당되다 generous 관대한, 아낌없는 donate 기부하다 donation 기부(금)

2. 영업부장은 판매 촉진을 위한 효과적인 방법에 대한 제안을 그의 팀으로부터 받고 있다.

해설 빈칸은 타동사 seek의 목적어 자리이다. 따라서 보기 중 유일한 명사인 (C) suggestions가 정답이다.

어휘 seek 구하다, 찾다 effective 효과적인 boost 부양책; 신장시키다 suggest 제안하다 suggestion 제안, 제의, 의견

3. 직원 교육 사무소의 관리자들은 모든 신입 사원의 성과를 검토했다.

해설 빈칸 앞에 관사 the가 있으므로 동사 reviewed의 목적어로 쓰일 수 있는 명사가 필요하다. 따라서 보기 중 유일한 명사인 (D) performance가 정답이다. [the ---- of]의 형태는 명사가 정답이 되는 토익 빈출 유형이다.

어휘 review 검토하다 employee 직원 perform 수행하다, 이행하다 performance 수행, 성과, 실적

4. 지정 주차 공간을 이용하고자 하는 직원은 허가증을 받아야 합니다.

해설 빈칸은 타동사 obtain의 목적어 자리이므로 명사가 들어가야 한다. 빈칸 앞에 부정관사 a가 있으므로 복수형인 (B) permits는 쓸 수 없다. (A) permission은 '허락, 승인'의 의미의 불가산 명사이므로 부정관사 a와 함께 쓸 수 없다. 따라서 (D) permit이 정답이다. 참고로 permit은 형태의 변화 없이 명사와 동사로 둘 다 쓰인다.

어휘 designated 지정된 parking space 주차 공간 obtain 얻다, 구하다 permit 허락하다; 허가증 permission 허락, 승인

5. 회사의 영업 담당자는 이번 주말 워크숍에서 고객들을 만날 것이다.

해설 명사 앞이나 뒤에 빈칸이 있을 때에는 복합명사로 쓰인 것인지 확인해야 한다. 여기서는 sales representatives '영업 사원, 영업 담당자'로 쓰이는 복합명사로 (C) representatives가 정답이 된다. 참고로 representative는 형태의 변화 없이 명사와 형용사가 둘 다 가능한데, 형용사로는 be representative of '~을 대표하다'라는 의미로 토익에 출제된 바 있다.

어휘 client 고객 workshop 워크숍 represent 대표하다, 대신하다 representative 대표, (판매) 외판원; 대표하는

6. H&K 사는 생산 시설의 보수 공사가 완료될 때까지는 국내 매출이 일시적으로 악화할 것으로 예상한다.

해설 명사 앞에 빈칸이 오면 형용사와 명사가 모두 정답이 될 수 있으므로 해석이 필요하다. '생산적인 시설이 완료될 때까지'는 어색하고 '생산 시설이 완료될 때까지'가 문맥상 적절하다. 따라서 (C) production이 정답이다.

어휘 renovation 보수 공사 complete 완전한 domestic 국내의 worsen 악화되다 temporarily 일시적으로 produce 생산하다 productive 생산적인 production 생산

7. Ryan 씨는 내일 오전 10시부터 오후 12시까지 간단한 상담이 가능하다.

해설 빈칸은 형용사 brief의 수식을 받는 명사 자리로, 사람 명사와 사물 명사를 구분하는 문제이다. 문맥상 '간단한 상담'을 완성하는 (B) consultations가 정답이 된다. (A) consultant는 사람 명사로 한정사 없이 단수 형태로 쓸 수 없다.

어휘 available 이용 가능한 brief (시간이) 짧은, 잠시 동안의 consultant 상담가 consultation 상담 consult 상담하다

8. TX Chemicals 사의 방문객들은 정문에서 안내원으로부터 보안 출입증을 받아야 합니다.

해설 빈칸은 문장의 주어 자리로, 보기가 모두 명사이므로 문맥상 적절한 것을 골라야 한다. 문장의 동사와 목적어를 해석해 보면 주어가 출입증을 받는 '사람'이 되어야 하므로 (C) Visitors가 정답이다. 참고로 visit은 형태의 변화 없이 동사와 명사가 둘 다 가능하다.

어휘 security pass 보안 출입증 receptionist 접수원 main entrance 정문 visit 방문하다; 방문 visitation 방문 visitor 방문객

UNIT 02 대명사

CHECK-UP 본문 p.153

1. (A)	2. (B)	3. (A)	4. (B)	5. (B)	6. (B)
7. (A)	8. (A)	9. (B)	10. (A)	11. (A)	12. (B)

1. 관리자들은 연락처 정보를 업데이트하라는 요청을 받았다.

해설 대명사의 격을 묻는 문제이다. 명사 앞에 올 수 있는 것은 소유격이므로 (A) their가 정답이다.

어휘 update 업데이트하다, 새로운 정보를 주다 contact information 연락처

2. Shaw 씨는 직원 피트니스 프로그램을 도와줄 자원봉사자를 요청했다.

해설 help의 목적어로 쓰일 목적격 대명사가 필요한 자리이므로 (B) her가 정답이다. 소유대명사인 (A) hers도 목적어 역할은 가능하지만, 그녀를(her) 돕는 것이지, 그녀의 것(hers)을 돕는 것은 아니므로 오답이다.

어휘 ask for 요청하다 volunteer 자원봉사자

3. Dian 씨는 휴가 신청서를 제출했지만, Boden 씨는 아직 제출하지 않았다.

해설 빈칸은 submit의 목적어 자리이며, 문맥상 'Boden 씨의 휴가 신청서'가 적절하다. 따라서 <소유격+명사>를 대신하는 소유대명사 (A) his가 정답이다. 참고로 his는 소유격 인칭대명사와 소유대명사의 형태가 같다.

어휘 turn in 제출하다 request form 신청서 have yet to 아직 ~하지 못하다 submit 제출하다

4. Kim 씨가 혼자서 프로젝트를 시작했지만 나중에 동료 두 명의 도움을 받았다.

해설 by oneself는 '혼자서'라는 뜻의 재귀대명사 관용 표현으로, 프로젝트를 시작하는 주체는 Mr. Kim이므로 (B) himself가 정답이다.

어휘 assist 돕다, 도움이 되다 colleague 동료

5. Mary는 그녀가 직접 작성한 메모를 보면서 연설 준비를 했다.

해설 빈칸이 없어도 완전한 문장이므로 빈칸에는 생략이 가능한 강조 용법의 재귀대명사가 적절하다. 의미상 주어인 Mary를 강조하는 재귀대명사 (B) herself가 정답이다.

어휘 prepare for ~을 준비하다, 대비하다

6. V-Lands 사는 농업 분야의 선도적인 회사로 자리매김했다.

해설 빈칸은 타동사의 목적어 자리로, V-Lands 사가 스스로 자리를 잡았다는 의미로 쓰여 주어와 목적어가 같다. 따라서 재귀대명사 (B) itself가 정답이다.

어휘 establish oneself as ~로서 자리를 잡다 agriculture 농업

7. 등산 여행이 취소되면 등록비를 선납한 사람은 전액 환불 받는다.

해설 주격 관계대명사 who가 이끄는 형용사절의 수식을 받으면서 '~하는 사람들'의 의미를 나타내는 지시대명사 (A) those가 정답이다.

어휘 prepay 선불하다 registration fee 등록비 full refund 전액 환불

8. 이 물건들은 깨지기 쉬우므로, 매우 조심해서 포장해야 한다.

해설 빈칸은 복수 명사 items를 수식할 수 있는 지시형용사 자리로, (A) these가 정답이다.

어휘 fragile 깨지기 쉬운 pack (짐을) 싸다 with care 주의 깊게, 신중히

9. 보고서는 올해 간접비가 작년과 비슷하다고 분명하게 보여준다.

해설 빈칸 앞에 나온 overhead expenses라는 복수 명사를 대신할 수 있는 지시대명사 (B) those가 정답이다.

어휘 overhead expense 간접비 comparable to ~에 비길 만한 the preceding year 지난해

10. 저희 제품에 문제가 있다면 다른 것으로 교체해 드립니다.

해설 빈칸은 전치사의 목적어 자리로, 이미 언급된 것(one) 외에 '또 다른 것'을 의미하는 부정대명사 (A) another가 정답이다. (B) other은 '다른 몇몇'이라는 의미로, 형용사로만 쓰이기 때문에 오답이다.

어휘 replace A with B A를 B로 교체하다

11. 대다수 사람들은 그 결정이 도시에 도움이 될 것으로 생각하지 않는다.

해설 빈칸은 명사 people을 수식하며 '대다수 사람'이라는 의미를 완성하는 부정형용사 (A) most가 정답이다. 부정대명사로도 쓰일 수 있는 most는 [most of + the/소유격 + 명사] 형태로만 가능하다.

어휘 benefit 유익[유용]하다

12. 그 지역 모든 농부는 Borough Greenmarket에서 그들의 농산물을 판다.

해설 빈칸은 부정대명사 자리로 All of the local farmers에서 of가 생략된 형태이다. 따라서 (B) All이 정답이다. (A) Most도 부정대명사이지만, of를 생략해서 쓸 수 없다.

어휘 local 지역의, 현지의 produce 농산물

PRACTICE
본문 p.157

1. (C) **2.** (A) **3.** (D) **4.** (B) **5.** (C) **6.** (B)
7. (D) **8.** (C)

1. 우리 호텔에 머무는 동안 무료 아침 식사를 즐기세요.

해설 전치사 during의 목적어로 쓰인 명사 stay 앞에는 명사를 수식하는 소유격을 써야 하므로 빈칸에는 소유격 대명사인 (C) your가 정답이다.

어휘 complimentary breakfast 무료 아침 식사 during ~동안[내내] stay 머무름, 방문

2. Green 씨는 수요일에 지원자들을 만나기 전에 그들의 이력서를 검토할 것입니다.

해설 빈칸은 접속사 before가 이끄는 부사절의 주어 자리로, 주격과 소유격 대명사 둘 다 주어 자리에 올 수 있으므로 문맥을 살펴봐야 한다. 문맥상 '그녀가 그들을 만나기 전에'가 적절하며 '그녀의 것이 그들을 만나기 전에'는 어색하다. 따라서 Ms. Green을 가리키는 주격 (A) she가 정답이다. 참고로 재귀대명사는 주어 자리에 올 수 없다.

어휘 review 검토하다 applicant 지원자 résumé 이력서

3. Parisse 씨가 직접 Schindler Electronics 사의 대표들에게 발표할 것이다.

해설 [주어 + 동사 + 목적어]의 완전한 문장 형태이므로 빈칸에는 주어 Ms. Parisse를 강조하는 재귀대명사가 오는 것이 적절하다. 따라서 (D) herself가 정답이 된다.

어휘 give a presentation 발표하다 representative 대표(자), (판매) 대리인, 외판원

4. 그 회사는 자사의 상품을 구매하는 사람들을 대상으로 설문 조사를 할 것이다.

해설 빈칸은 전치사 of의 목적어 자리로, 주격 관계대명사 who 앞에서 '사람들'이라는 뜻으로 쓰일 수 있는 대명사는 (B) those이다. those who는 '~하는 사람들'이라는 뜻을 가진 빈출 관용 표현이므로 외워두자.

어휘 conduct a survey 설문조사를 하다 purchase 구매하다

5. 우리 신제품에 관심이 있는 사람들을 위해, 많은 정보가 세미나에서 제공될 겁니다.

해설 빈칸은 전치사 for의 목적어 자리이며, 문맥상 '우리 신제품에 관심이 있는 사람들'이라는 의미가 되어야 하므로 (C) those가 정답이다.

어휘 interested 관심 있는 information 정보 provide 제공하다

6. 그 책들 중 일부는 절판되었지만, 다른 것들은 서점을 통해 이용할 수 있다.

해설 빈칸 뒤 동사 are에 어울리는 복수 명사 주어를 선택하는 문제로, (B) others가 정답이다. the other와 another는 각각 '나머지 하나', '또 다른 하나'라는 의미로, 단수 동사와 함께 써야 하며, 단수 취급하고, other는 형용사로만 쓰인다.

어휘 out of print 절판된 through ~을 통해서

7. 귀하가 주차 카드를 분실하면 주차 관리자가 카드를 정지시키고 다른 카드를 발급해 드릴 것입니다.

해설 빈칸은 타동사 issue의 목적어 자리로, '주차 카드를 정지시키고 다른 하나를 발급해 준다'는 의미가 문맥상 적절하다. (D) another가 '다른 하나'라는 의미로, 단수 취급하는 명사이므로 정답이다.

어휘 lose 분실하다 deactivate 정지시키다 issue 발급해 주다

8. 직원 중 몇몇은 다음 주 회의에 참석할 예정이다.

해설 Every는 대명사로 쓰일 수 없으며 Much는 [much of the +불가산 명사] 형태로 쓰고, [some of the + 복수 명사 + 복수 동사], [each of the + 복수 명사 + 단수 동사]로 쓰이므로 (C) Some이 정답이다.

어휘 employee 직원 participate in ~에 참석하다

UNIT 03 형용사

CHECK-UP
본문 p.158

1. (A) **2.** (B) **3.** (A) **4.** (B) **5.** (A) **6.** (B)
7. (A) **8.** (B) **9.** (B) **10.** (B) **11.** (B) **12.** (A)

1. Miller 박사는 환자에게 합리적인 가격에 뛰어난 치과 진료를 제공한다.

해설 빈칸은 전치사 at의 목적어인 명사 앞에서 명사를 수식하는 형용사 자리이므로 (A) affordable이 정답이다.

어휘 provide A with B A에게 B를 제공하다 exceptional 뛰어난 affordable 합리적인

2. 네트워크는 2시간 이상 사용할 수 없을 것으로 예상된다.

해설 빈칸은 to부정사 to 다음 be동사의 보어 자리로, 명사와 형용사가 모두 나올 수 있으나 명사는 주어와 동격일 경우일 때만 사용하므로 형용사인 (B) unavailable이 정답이다.

어휘 unavailable 손에 넣을[획득할] 수 없는

3. 대다수 주민은 새로운 재활용 프로그램이 편리하다고 생각했다.

해설 빈칸은 동사 have found의 목적격 보어 자리로, 목적어인 the new recycling program을 수식할 수 있는 형용사 (A) convenient가 정답이다.

어휘 resident 거주민　recycling program 재활용 프로그램　convenient 편리한　conveniently 편리하게

4. 첨부된 문서에는 너무 많은 기밀 정보를 담고 있다.

해설 (A) many 뒤에는 복수 가산 명사가 와야 하므로 오답이다. 반면 much는 불가산 명사(information)가 올 수 있으므로 (B)가 정답이다.

어휘 attached 첨부된　contain 포함하다　confidential 비밀의, 기밀상의

5. 편집자들은 금요일까지 책의 모든 수정사항을 저자들에게 제출해야 한다.

해설 (B) every 뒤에는 단수 가산 명사가 와야 하므로 오답이다. 반면 all 뒤에는 복수 가산 명사나 불가산 명사가 올 수 있으므로 (A)가 정답이다.

어휘 editor 편집자　submit 제출하다　revision 수정 (사항)

6. 이 제품은 여기에는 재고가 없지만 다른 곳에서 이용 가능할 수 있습니다.

해설 (A) other 뒤에는 복수 명사 또는 불가산 명사가 와야 하므로 오답이다. 반면 another 뒤에는 가산 명사의 단수 가산 명사가 올 수 있으므로 (B)가 정답이다.

어휘 in stock 재고가 있는　available 이용 가능한

7. 그 소설은 1910년대에 제작된 기록물에 기반을 두고 있다.

해설 문맥상 '기록물에 기반을 두다'가 적합하므로 (A) based가 정답이다.

어휘 be based on ~에 기초하다, 근거하다　produce 제작하다

8. 세미나에 참가하는 사람들은 여행 경비 영수증을 제출하지 않아도 된다.

해설 문맥상 '여행 경비 영수증을 제출하지 않아도 된다'가 적합하므로 (B) exempt가 정답이다. (A) obliged는 <be obliged to+동사원형>으로 '하는 수 없이 ~하다'라는 의미로 쓰인다.

어휘 turn in 제출하다　travel expense 여행 경비 영수증　be exempt from ~에서 면제되다

9. 그 업무는 복잡하고 다양한 기술이 요구되는데, Lee 씨는 그런 조건에 적임자입니다.

해설 '~에 적합하다'의 의미를 가진 be suitable for을 알고 있으면 (B) for가 정답임을 알 수 있다.

어휘 complex 복잡한　require 요구하다

10. 손님들은 회사 연회를 위한 테이블 장식에 감명을 받았다.

해설 impressed는 감정 동사에서 온 형용사로, 주어가 감정을 느끼는 사람일 때 '~에 감명을 받다'라는 의미로 쓰인다. 따라서 (B)가 정답이다.

어휘 decoration 장식　banquet 연회　impressive 인상적인

11. 우리는 모든 서신에 적시에 응답하는 것을 목표로 한다는 유념하세요.

해설 빈칸은 명사 manner를 수식하는 형용사 자리로, -ly 형태의 형용사인 (B) timely가 정답이다. (A) timing은 '적당한 시기'라는 뜻의 명사이다.

어휘 please note that ~ ~에 유념하세요　aim to V ~하는 것을 목표로 하다　respond to N ~에 대응하다　correspondence 서신

12. 효과적인 계획은 프로젝트의 성공적인 완료에 필수다.

해설 빈칸은 명사 completion을 수식하는 형용사 자리로, '성공적인 완료'의 의미를 완성하는 (A) successful이 정답이다.

어휘 effective 효과적인　planning 계획　essential 필수적인　completion 완료, 완성　successive 연속적인

PRACTICE　본문 p.162

1. (B)　**2.** (A)　**3.** (C)　**4.** (A)　**5.** (B)　**6.** (D)
7. (C)

1. 지금에 와서 마케팅 회의에 적합한 장소를 찾는 것은 어려울 것이다.

해설 빈칸은 명사 venue를 수식하는 형용사 자리이다. 따라서 (B) suitable이 정답이다. (D) suiting은 동사 suit(적합하다)의 현재분사로, 형용사로 쓰이지 않는다.

어휘 venue (콘서트·스포츠 경기·회담 등의) 장소　at this late date 지금에 와서　suitable 적합한, 적절한, 알맞은

2. 신임 사장은 시장 점유율 증가의 필요성에 대해 상당히 강조한다.

해설 빈칸 앞 부사 very의 수식을 받으면서 is의 보어가 될 수 있는 형용사 자리이다. 따라서 (A) emphatic이 정답이다. [be emphatic about N] '~에 대해서 강조하다'를 기억해두자.

어휘 necessity 필요(성)　market share 시장 점유율　emphatic (분명히) 강조하는　emphasize(= stress) (중요성을) 강조하다

3. 시장에는 당신이 사업을 시작하는 데 도움이 되는 몇몇 참고 도서들이 많이 있다.

해설 수량 형용사는 종류에 따라 뒤에 오는 명사의 성격이 다르다는 점에 주의해야 한다. 빈칸 뒤 복수 명사 reference books가 있으므로 복수 가산 명사와 어울리는 (C) a few가 정답이다. a little/much는 뒤에 불가산 명사, each 뒤에는 단수 가산 명사가 온다.

어휘 reference book 참고 도서　on the market 시장에 나와 있는

4. 몇몇 행정 정책들이 시대에 뒤떨어져서 임원들이 검토하고 있습니다.

해설 much 뒤에는 불가산 명사가, every/another 뒤에는 단수 가산 명사가 온다. 빈칸 뒤에 복수 가산 명사 administrative policies 가 왔으므로 복수 가산 명사를 수식하는 (A) Several이 정답이다.

어휘 administrative 관리[행정]상의 outdated(= out of date) (더는 쓸모가 없게) 구식인 executive officer (단체의) 임원

5. 프로그램에 신청할 수 있는 자격을 갖추려면 마감일까지 신청서를 제출해야 한다.

해설 빈칸은 be 동사의 보어 역할을 하는 형용사 자리이다. [be eligible to V]는 '~할 자격이 되다'라는 의미로, (B)가 정답이다.

어휘 apply for ~에 지원[신청]하다 submit 제출하다 application 신청[지원]서 deadline 마감일

6. 회사는 인프라 업그레이드에 상당한 금액을 투자했다.

해설 같은 어근에서 온 형용사들이나 철자가 비슷해서 헷갈리기 쉬운 형용사들은 주의해야 한다. 빈칸은 명사 sum(액수)을 수식하는 형용사 자리로, '상당한 금액을 투자하다'가 문맥상 적합하므로 (D) considerable이 정답이 된다. 형용사 (A) considerate(사려 깊은)은 보통 사람 명사를 수식할 때 쓴다.

어휘 invest 투자하다 considerably 상당히 consideration 고려, 숙고

7. A.T. Analysis Group 사는 연간 예산의 균형을 유지하기 위한 성공적인 방법을 추천했다.

해설 빈칸은 명사 way를 수식하는 형용사 자리이다. (C) successful 은 '성공적인', (D) successive는 '연속적인'이라는 의미로 둘 다 형용사이다. '성공적인 방법을 추천하다'가 문맥상 적절하므로 (C) 가 정답이다.

어휘 recommend 추천하다 balance 균형을 유지하다[잡다] annual budget 연간 예산 succeed 성공하다 success 성공

UNIT 04   부사

CHECK-UP   본문 p.163

1. (B)	2. (A)	3. (B)	4. (B)	5. (B)	6. (B)
7. (A)	8. (B)	9. (A)	10. (B)	11. (B)	12. (B)

1. 고객 서비스 직원은 나의 문의에 즉각 응답했다.

해설 빈칸은 동사를 뒤에서 수식하는 부사 자리로, (B) promptly가 정답이다.

어휘 representative (판매) 대리인 respond 응답하다 inquiry 문의 promptly 즉각

2. Nellie's 사의 저렴한 클리닝 제품들은 믿을 수 없을 정도로 강력하다.

해설 빈칸은 형용사를 앞에서 수식하는 부사 자리로, (A) unbelievably 가 정답이다.

어휘 inexpensive 저렴한 unbelievably 믿을 수 없을 정도로

3. 우리 호텔 청소 매니저들은 목욕 수건을 꽃 모양으로 창의적으로 접는다.

해설 빈칸은 주어와 동사 사이에서 동사를 수식하는 부사 자리이므로 (B) creatively가 정답이다.

어휘 housekeeper 호텔 객실 청소 매니저 fold 접다 bath towel 목욕 타월 creative 독창적인 creatively 독창적으로

4. Aston 대학을 졸업한 직후 Paul Rudd 씨는 컨설팅 회사를 설립했다.

해설 빈칸 뒤의 구 after graduating을 수식하여 '대학을 졸업한 직후' 라는 의미를 나타내는 부사 (B) Shortly가 정답이다.

어휘 graduate 졸업하다 found 설립하다 shortly 곧, 즉시

5. Tom Seaver 씨는 회사 내 난방 시스템을 정기적으로 점검하는 일을 담당하고 있다.

해설 빈칸은 전치사 for의 목적어로 쓰인 동명사(준동사) checking를 수식하는 부사 자리이므로 (B) regularly가 정답이다.

어휘 heating system 난방 장치 regularly 정기적으로

6. 안타깝게도 이 회사는 인력의 3분의 1을 해고하기로 결정했다.

해설 콤마 뒤의 문장 전체를 수식하는 부사 (B) Unfortunately가 정답이다.

어휘 lay off 해고하다 workforce 인력 unfortunately 안타깝게도

7. Lynskey 씨는 불과 3개월 만에 거의 12차례에 가까운 발표를 했다.

해설 빈칸 뒤에 수량을 나타내는 a dozen이 있으므로 '거의'라는 뜻의 부사인 (A) nearly가 정답이다.

어휘 dozen 12개의; 12개, 1다스 presentation 발표

8. 지난 두 달 동안 Fine 극장의 관객 수가 급격히 증가했다.

해설 빈칸 앞에 has increased라는 동사가 있으므로 '급격히'라는 뜻의 증가나 감소의 의미가 있는 동사를 수식하는 부사 (B) dramatically가 정답이다.

어휘 attendance 참석자 수, 참석률 dramatic 극적인

9. 새로운 제품 라인을 출시한 이후 이익이 크게 증가했다.

해설 빈칸은 조동사 have와 과거분사 increased 사이에서 동사를 수식하는 부사 자리로, '매우'라는 뜻의 (A) greatly가 정답이다.

어휘 profit 수익 launch 출시하다 proudly 자랑스럽게

10. 우리 직원들은 모두 정기적으로 전문성 개발 세미나에 참석한다.

해설 빈칸은 동사 participate를 수식하는 부사 자리로, 현재 시제와 어울리는 (B) regularly가 정답이다. 반면 (A) soon은 미래 시제와 어울리므로 오답이다.

어휘 soon 곧 regularly 정기적으로 participate in ~에 참석하다

11. CEO는 최근에 분기별 이익에 대해 우려를 표현했다.

해설 빈칸은 동사 has expressed를 수식하는 부사 자리로, 현재완료 시제와 어울리는 (B) recently가 정답이다. 반면 (A) previously는 과거 시제와 어울리므로 오답이다.

어휘 express 의사[감정]를 표현하다 concern 우려, 걱정

12. 매우 기대되는 새 연극 <Homecoming>이 어젯밤 Louis 강당에서 개막했다.

해설 빈칸은 과거분사 anticipated를 수식하는 부사 자리로, high/highly 둘 다 부사라서 가능하나 문맥상 '매우 기대되는 새 연극'이라는 의미가 되어야 어울리므로 (B) highly가 정답이다.

어휘 high 높은; 높게 anticipated 기대되는 play 연극

PRACTICE
본문 p.167

1. (C) 2. (A) 3. (D) 4. (C) 5. (C) 6. (A)
7. (A) 8. (C)

1. 수년간의 휴학 끝에, Baker 씨는 마침내 생물학 학위를 받았다.

해설 주어진 문장은 [주어 + ---- + 동사]의 형태로, 빈칸은 문장의 주어와 동사 사이에 있다. 따라서 동사 earned를 앞에서 수식하는 부사 (C) eventually가 정답이다.

어휘 postpone one's studies 학업을 미루다 earn a degree 학위를 받다 biology 생물학

2. 마케팅 부장인 Jo Maer가 현재의 영업 전략을 보다 면밀히 살펴볼 것이다.

해설 주어진 문장은 [동사 + 목적어 + ----]의 형태이다. 부사가 동사를 수식할 때는 동사 앞이나 목적어 뒤에서 수식할 수도 있다. 따라서 빈칸은 동사 examine를 수식하는 부사 (A) closely가 정답이다.

어휘 examine 검사하다, 조사하다 current 현재의 sales strategy 영업 전략 closely 면밀히 close 가까운; 가까이

3. E-bay 지역의 다른 호텔들과는 달리, Waverly Inn는 해안가와 비교적 가깝다.

해설 주어진 문장은 [be + ---- + 형용사]의 형태로, 형용사 close를 수식하는 부사인 (D) relatively가 정답이다.

어휘 unlike ~와 달리 be close to ~에 가깝다 waterfront 해안가 relative 상대적인; 친척 related 관련된 relatively 비교적

4. 온라인 판매가 늘어남에 따라, 소비자들은 쇼핑하기 위해 집을 나서는 것이 훨씬 덜하다.

해설 빈칸은 to부정사 to shop을 수식하는 부사 자리로, 보기 중 유일한 부사인 (C) frequently가 정답이다.

어휘 with the rise of ~의 증가[성장]와 더불어 online sales 온라인 판매 frequency 빈도 frequent 빈번한 frequently 자주

5. Kern 씨는 마감 직전에 Dulwich School에 재정 지원 신청서를 제출했다.

해설 빈칸은 빈칸 뒤 전치사구 before the deadline을 수식하는 부사 자리이다. 따라서 (C) immediately가 정답이다.

어휘 financial aid 학자금 지원[융자] immediate 즉각적인 immediately(= at once) 즉시, 즉각

6. 고객들은 훌륭한 고객서비스 때문에 Garret Savings 사를 자주 다시 찾는다.

해설 빈칸은 동사 return 앞에서 동사를 수식하는 부사 자리로, 현재 시제와 어울려 '자주 찾는다'는 의미를 완성하는 (A) frequently가 정답이다.

어휘 because of ~때문에 excellent 우수한, 훌륭한

7. Smith 씨가 거래 기록을 조작해서 우리는 그를 해고하기로 결정했다.

해설 앞뒤 문장의 문맥을 파악하면 '기록을 조작해서 그를 해고하기로 결정했다'는 인과 관계이다. 따라서 '그러므로'의 의미를 가지고 있는 접속부사 (A) therefore가 정답이다.

어휘 manipulate 조작하여 속이다 transaction 거래, 매매 make a decision 결정하다 fire 해고하다 therefore 그러므로 however 그러나 otherwise (…와는) 다르게, 달리 meanwhile 그 동안에

8. McCallan 씨의 비행기가 너무 늦게 도착해서 그는 특별 환영회에 참석하지 못했다.

해설 빈칸은 부사 too의 수식을 받는 부사 자리로, 문맥상 '너무 늦게 도착하다'라는 의미의 (A) late가 정답이다. late는 형태의 변화 없이 형용사(늦은)와 부사(늦게)가 모두 가능하다. (C) lately는 '최근에'라는 의미의 부사다.

어휘 attend 참석하다 welcoming reception 환영회

UNIT 05 전치사

CHECK-UP 본문 p.168

1. (B) **2.** (B) **3.** (A) **4.** (A) **5.** (B) **6.** (B)
7. (A) **8.** (B) **9.** (B) **10.** (B) **11.** (A) **12.** (B)

1. 5월 6일에 Aron 사는 새로운 사장을 임명한다고 발표했다.

해설 빈칸 뒤에 특정 날짜 5월 6일이 있고 문맥상 '~에'라는 의미를 가지는 전치사 (B) on이 정답이다. 참고로 (A) in은 특정 날짜가 아닌 년/월 앞에서 '~에'라는 의미로 쓰인다.

어휘 announce 발표하다 appointment 임명

2. 새로운 소프트웨어에 대한 발표는 다음 월요일로 연기될 것이다.

해설 (A) by와 (B) until 모두 '~까지'라는 의미의 전치사로, 동사의 의미로 by와 until을 구분할 수 있다. 동사가 일회성 동작 또는 완료를 의미하면 by를, 동사가 상태 또는 지속을 의미하면 until을 쓴다. will be postponed(연기될 것이다)는 지속, 계속의 의미를 나타내므로 (B) until이 정답이다.

어휘 presentation 발표 postpone 연기하다

3. 프로젝트 마감일을 지키기 위해 2주 내에 마케팅 전략을 확정해야 한다.

해설 within은 특정 기간이나 제한된 시간 '내에' 어떤 일이 발생한다는 것을 나타내므로 문맥상 (A) within이 정답이다. (B) during은 특정 기간 또는 시간 '동안' 어떤 일이 발생하거나 지속적인 상태를 나타낼 때 쓴다.

어휘 finalize 마무리하다 marketing strategy 마케팅 전략

4. 회의장 옆에 위치한 Croy 역은 최근에 보수공사를 했다.

해설 빈칸 뒤의 the conference center와 결합하여 '회의장 옆에 위치한 Croy 역'이라는 의미를 완성하는 전치사 (A) next to가 정답이다.

어휘 located ~에 위치한 recently 최근에 renovate 보수하다

5. 임박한 눈보라로 인해 내일은 모든 시 관공서가 문을 닫을 것이다.

해설 빈칸 뒤의 the impending snowstorm과 결합하여 '눈보라가 임박해서'라는 이유의 의미를 완성하는 전치사 (B) Due to가 정답이다.

어휘 despite ~에도 불구하고 impending 임박한 snowstorm 눈보라

6. 대부분의 직원이 적절한 보상 없이 초과근무하는 것을 거부했다.

해설 빈칸 뒤의 proper compensation과 결합하여 '적절한 보상 없이'라는 의미를 완성하는 전치사 (B) without이 정답이다.

without은 어떤 것이 결여된 상태(없는 상태)를 나타낼 때 사용한다.

어휘 refuse 거절하다 work overtime 초과근무를 하다 proper compensation 적절한 보상

7. 건설업자에 따르면, 사무실 개조 비용은 10,000달러가 조금 안 될 것이라고 한다.

해설 빈칸 뒤의 the building contractor와 결합하여 '건설업자에 따르면'이라는 의미를 완성하는 전치사 (A) According to가 정답이다.

어휘 instead of ~대신에 building contractor 건설업자 cost 비용이 들다

8. 구내 주차권은 차고 내 주차 가능 여부에 따라 발행된다.

해설 빈칸 뒤의 the availability of spaces in the garage와 결합하여 '차고 내 주차 가능 여부에 따라'라는 의미를 완성하는 전치사 (B) depending on이 정답이다.

어휘 parking pass 주차권 availability 유용성, 이용도 garage 차고 such as ~와 같은

9. 팀 회의 후에, 우리는 회의록을 모든 참가자들에게 배포할 것이다.

해설 빈칸 뒤의 the team meeting와 결합하여 '팀 회의 후에'라는 의미를 완성하는 전치사 (B) Following이 정답이다.

어휘 distribute 배포하다 meeting minutes 회의록 participant 참가자

10. 우리는 신축성이 뛰어난 신소재 개발에 주력할 계획이다.

해설 빈칸은 to부정사의 동사 focus와 어울려 '~에 주력하다'의 의미를 완성하는 전치사 (B) on이 정답이다.

어휘 intend to ~할 작정이다, ~하려고 생각하다 flexibility 탄력성

11. 당신의 요청에 따라, 우리는 당신의 계정 비밀번호를 이메일로 보냈습니다.

해설 빈칸 앞뒤의 전치사와 어울려 '~에 응하여'라는 의미의 어구 in response to를 완성하는 (A) response가 정답이다.

어휘 request 요청 by e-mail 이메일로

12. 회사는 올해 안에 귀하의 출장 경비를 상환해 줄 것입니다.

해설 빈칸 앞 동사 reimburse와 어울려 reimburse A for B 'A에게 B에 대해 상환[보상]하다'를 완성하는 전치사 (B) for가 정답이다.

어휘 travel expense 출장 경비

PRACTICE

본문 p.172

1. (A) **2.** (C) **3.** (D) **4.** (D) **5.** (D) **6.** (C)
7. (C)

1. 현재 시스템에 있는 모든 회사 파일은 9월 1일에 새로운 시스템으로 전송됩니다.

[해설] 빈칸 뒤 September 1(9월 1일)은 특정 날짜를 나타낸다. 특정 날짜와 함께 쓰여 '~에'를 뜻하는 (A) on이 정답이다.

[어휘] transfer 보내다, 전송하다

2. Chappelle 씨는 규정에 관한 많은 정보를 내게 제공했다.

[해설] [provide A(사람) with B(사물)] 'A에게 B를 제공하다'의 숙어를 알고 있으면 쉽게 해결할 수 있는 문제로, (C)가 정답이다. 참고로 [provide A(사물) for B(사람)] 'A를 B를 위해 제공하다'와 구별해서 알아두자.

[어휘] a great deal of 다량의, 많은 regarding ~에 관하여[대하여] regulation 규정, 규제

3. 모든 메뉴의 신선도를 보장하기 위해 저희는 현지 농장의 재료만 사용합니다.

[해설] 보기의 전치사와 연결되는 숙어 표현이 없을 경우 해석해 본다. '현지 농장에서 나오는 재료'가 문맥상 적절하므로 '~로 부터'의 의미인 (D) from이 정답이다.

[어휘] ensure 보장하다 freshness 신선도 ingredient (특히 요리 등의) 재료[성분]

4. 목요일에 CEO는 Adecco Financials 사와의 합병 계획에 관한 기자 회견을 가졌다.

[해설] 'Adecco Financials 사와의 합병에 관한 기자 회견'이 문맥상 적절하므로 '~관한'이라는 의미의 분사형 전치사인 (D) concerning이 정답이다.

[어휘] press conference 기자 회견 merge with ~와 통합, 합병되다 except ~을 제외하고는 versus ~에 비해 along ~을 따라 concerning ~에 관한[관련된]

5. 신청서가 승인되면 일주일 이내에 우편으로 새 신용 카드를 받게 됩니다.

[해설] during은 '~동안에'라는 의미로 뒤에 숫자 기간이 아닌 명사 기간이 와야 한다. before는 시점 표현과 함께 쓰이고, while은 접속사로 뒤에 문장이 와야 한다. 따라서 '~이내에'라는 의미로 기간을 나타내는 명사와 어울리는 전치사 (D) within이 정답이다.

[어휘] approve 승인[찬성]하다 by mail 우편으로

6. 요리사인 Peter Carr는 식당을 성공한 후 베스트셀러 요리책을 집필했다.

[해설] 빈칸 뒤에 명사구 the success of his restaurant이 왔으므로 보기 중 유일한 전치사인 (C) Following이 정답이다.

[어휘] bestselling 베스트셀러의 already 이미, 벌써

7. 계약서에 서명하기 전에 우리는 모든 조항을 주의 깊게 검토해야 한다.

[해설] 명사구 signing the contract가 왔으므로 '계약서에 서명하기 전에'라는 의미를 완성하는 전치사 (C) Before가 정답이다. 참고로 before는 접속사로도 쓰인다.

[어휘] sign 서명하다 contract 계약서 terms and conditions (계약이나 지불 등의) 조건

UNIT 06 동사의 형태와 종류

CHECK-UP

본문 p.173

1. (B) **2.** (B) **3.** (A) **4.** (B) **5.** (B) **6.** (A)
7. (B) **8.** (B) **9.** (A) **10.** (B) **11.** (A) **12.** (A)

1. 퇴사하는 직원은 사원증을 인사과에 반납해야 한다.

[해설] 조동사 must 뒤에는 동사원형이 오므로 (B) return이 정답이다.

[어휘] depart (직장을) 떠나다 return 돌려주다, 반납하다

2. 몇 장의 티켓을 추가로 구매하고 싶은지 알려주세요.

[해설] [would like to + 동사원형]의 형태로 '~하고 싶다'를 완성하는 (B) purchase가 정답이다.

[어휘] additional 추가적인 would like to ~하고 싶다 purchase 구매하다

3. 제가 없는 사이에 중요한 이메일은 제 동료인 Jane에게 전달해 주세요.

[해설] 명령문 [please + 동사원형]의 형태로 '~해 주세요'를 완성하는 (A) forward가 정답이다.

[어휘] forward 전송하다 absence 부재, 결석, 자리 비움 colleague (직장) 동료

4. 공장장은 장비 오작동으로 인한 지연에 차분히 대응해야 한다.

[해설] 빈칸 뒤의 to과 결합하여 '~에 대응하다'라는 뜻을 갖는 자동사 (B) react가 정답이다.

[어휘] plant manager 공장장 calmly 차분하게 delay 지연, 지체 malfunction 고장, 오작동

5. 100명이 넘는 사람들이 우리의 연례 회의에 참석할 예정이다.

해설 빈칸 뒤의 in과 결합하여 '~에 참석하다'라는 뜻을 갖는 자동사 (B) participate이 정답이다. (A) attend 뒤에는 전치사 없이 바로 목적어가 와야 하므로 오답이다.

어휘 expect 예상하다, 기대하다 annual 연례의 conference 회의

6. 지역 사회의 많은 주민들이 새 고속도로 건설에 반대한다.

해설 빈칸 뒤의 to과 결합하여 '~에 반대하다'라는 뜻을 갖는 자동사 (A) object가 정답이다. (B) oppose 뒤에는 전치사 없이 바로 목적어가 와야 하므로 오답이다.

어휘 resident 주민 community 지역 사회 highway 고속도로

7. Martin 씨의 지원서는 11월 15일까지 완전히 검토되지 않았다.

해설 보기 중 be동사 뒤에 나올 수 있는 것은 분사로, 주어인 Ms. Martin's application(Martin 씨의 지원서)은 검토되는 대상이므로 수동적 의미를 나타내는 과거분사 (B) reviewed가 정답이다.

어휘 application 지원[신청]서 completely 완전히

8. 꾸준히 성장하는 경제는 실업률의 감소로 이어졌다.

해설 빈칸 앞의 has 뒤에는 동사원형이 올 수 없고, 과거분사(p.p.)가 오면 완료 시제를 만든다. 과거부터 이어져 현재에도 영향을 주는 사건을 나타내는 완료 시제가 문맥상 적절하므로 과거분사 (B) led가 정답이다.

어휘 steadily 꾸준하게 decline 감소 unemployment 실업[률]

9. Sam Derek 씨는 다음 주에 출장으로 뉴욕에 갈 예정이다.

해설 빈칸 앞에 온 be동사 뒤에는 현재분사(-ing)가 와서 진행 시제를 만든다. [be동사 + ing] 형태는 문맥에 따라 미래 시제를 의미하기도 한다. 따라서 현재분사 (A) flying이 정답이다. fly 동사의 과거형인 (B) flew는 be동사와 함께 쓸 수 없다.

어휘 fly (비행기를) 타다[타고 가다] business trip 출장

10. 도로 위 결빙 때문에 시 터미널을 떠나는 버스들이 지연되었다.

해설 Buses가 문장의 주어이고, leaving the city terminal는 주어를 꾸미는 수식어구이다. 빈칸은 문장의 동사 자리로, 주어가 복수이므로 복수 동사인 (B) were이 정답이다.

어휘 delay 지연시키다 due to ~때문에

11. Berkshire 사의 모든 직원은 일주일에 36.5시간을 일한다.

해설 All of the employees가 문장의 주어이고, 빈칸은 문장의 동사 자리이다. All of와 같은 부분이나 전체를 나타내는 표현은 of 뒤의 명사에 수를 일치한다. 여기서는 복수 명사인 the employees가 왔으므로 복수 동사인 (A) work가 정답이다.

어휘 employee 직원 work 근무하다, 일하다

12. 저희 마케팅 매니저 직책 지원자의 수가 증가하고 있습니다.

해설 The number가 문장의 주어이고, 빈칸은 문장의 동사 자리이다. 따라서 단수 동사인 (A) is increasing이 정답이다. 참고로 [a number of 복수 명사 + 복수 동사]의 수 일치와 혼동하지 않도록 주의한다.

어휘 the number of ~의 수 applicant 지원자 position 직책

PRACTICE 본문 p.177

1. (C) **2.** (A) **3.** (C) **4.** (B) **5.** (B) **6.** (C)
7. (D) **8.** (A)

1. 작업자들이 건물 전면에 표지판을 설치하는 동안 후문을 이용해 주시기 바랍니다.

해설 빈칸에는 please와 함께 명령문을 이루는 동사원형이 와야 하므로 (C) use가 정답이다.

어휘 rear entrance 후문 install 설치하다 sign 표지판, 간판 in front of ~앞에

2. 주민들은 개발자들이 역사적인 유적지를 보존할 것인지를 묻기 위해 시청을 방문했다.

해설 빈칸 앞에 조동사 will이 있으므로 주어와 수 일치의 영향을 받지 않는 동사원형 (A) preserve가 정답이다.

어휘 resident 거주자[주민] whether ~인지 (아닌지) developer 개발자 historic 역사적인 property 부동산, 소유지, 토지 preserve 보존[관리]하다 preservation 보존[관리]

3. 호텔 운영진은 모든 고객의 문의 및 불만 사항에 즉시 응답한다.

해설 빈칸은 동사 자리이다. 보기 중 respond 이외에는 모두 타동사로 쓰이므로 빈칸 뒤 전치사 to와 연결되는 (C) responds가 정답이다. respond to는 '~에 응답하다'라는 의미로, 이와 같이 일부 자동사는 특정 전치사와 함께 암기하는 것이 좋다.

어휘 promptly 즉시, 지체 없이 inquiry 질문, 문의 complaint 불평 address 다루다 suggest 제안하다

4. 현재의 금융 위기를 다루기 위하여, TD Bank는 다른 금융기관과 협력해야 한다.

해설 빈칸은 전치사 with와 어울리는 자동사 자리로, 보기 중 자동사인 collaborate와 comply가 정답이 될 수 있다. comply with는 '~을 준수하다', collaborate with는 '~와 협력하다'라는 의미로, '다른 금융기관과 협력해야 한다'라는 뜻이 문맥상 적절하므로 (B) collaborate가 정답이다.

어휘 deal with ~을 다루다 current 현재의, 지금의 financial crisis 금융 위기 financial institution 금융기관 recall 기억해 내다, 상기하다 employ 쓰다[이용하다]

5. 매니저들은 근무시간 동안에 직원이 사적인 전화를 하는 것을 제한한다.

해설 빈칸은 동사 자리로, 복수 주어인 the managers와 수 일치가 맞는 복수 동사 (B) restrict가 정답이 된다.

어휘 working hours 근무시간 restrict A from V-ing A가 ~하는 것을 제한[통제]하다 make a phone call 전화하다

6. 직원들에게 더욱 효율적으로 일할 수 있도록 동기를 부여하는 것은 유능한 관리자가 되기 위한 중요한 요소이다.

해설 빈칸은 동사 자리로, 단수 주어인 동명사 Motivating employees와 수 일치가 맞는 (C) is가 정답이다. to부정사/동명사/명사절이 문장의 주어가 되는 경우에는 단수 취급한다. 주어와 동사 사이에 있는 수식어 to work more efficiently는 동사의 형태에 영향을 주지 않는다.

어휘 motivate A[사람] to V A가 ~하도록 동기를 부여하다 efficiently 효율적으로 crucial 중대한, 결정적인 effective 유능한

7. 계약서의 모든 수정안은 이사회에 의해서 철저하게 점검받고 검토되었다.

해설 빈칸은 동사 자리로, 문장의 주어는 All of the agreements이므로 동사는 All of 뒤의 명사에 수 일치를 시킨 (D) have been이 정답이다. 참고로 [all of the + 명사] 형태의 명사 자리에 복수 가산 명사/불가산 명사가 올 수 있고, 명사에 수 일치한다.

어휘 agreement 협정, 협약 contract 계약[약정](서) thoroughly 철저히, 철두철미하게 the board 이사회

8. 설문 조사에 따르면 직원의 거의 절반이 1년 전보다 직장에서 스트레스를 더 많이 느끼는 것으로 나타났다.

해설 빈칸은 that이 이끄는 명사절의 동사 자리이다. [half of + 복수 가산 명사/불가산 명사]는 수와 양의 표현에 모두 쓸 수 있다. 동사는 of 뒤에 나오는 명사와 수 일치시키므로 복수 명사인 employees와 수 일치를 맞춘 (A) feel이 정답이다.

어휘 survey 설문 조사 almost 거의 stressed 스트레스를 받는 [느끼는] at work 일터에서

UNIT 07 태와 시제

CHECK-UP 본문 p.178

1. (A)	2. (A)	3. (B)	4. (B)	5. (B)	6. (A)
7. (B)	8. (B)	9. (B)	10. (B)	11. (B)	12. (A)
13. (A)	14. (B)	15. (B)	16. (A)	17. (B)	18. (B)
19. (B)	20. (A)	21. (B)	22. (B)	23. (A)	24. (B)

1. 회사는 내년에 본사를 더 큰 도시로 이전할 예정이다.

해설 빈칸은 조동사 will 뒤의 동사원형 자리로, 주어 The company가 목적어 its headquarters를 이전시키는 주체이므로 능동태인 (A) relocate가 정답이다.

어휘 relocate A to B A를 B로 이전하다 headquarters 본사

2. Cafferky 씨는 복사기가 손상되어 전액 환불을 요청했다.

해설 빈칸은 접속사 because가 이끄는 부사절의 동사 자리로, 주어 the photocopier가 손상되는 대상이므로 수동태인 (A) was damaged가 정답이다.

어휘 request 요청하다 full refund 전액 환불 photocopier 복사기 damage 손상시키다

3. 수년간의 노력 끝에 그는 마침내 선임 분석가로 승진되었다.

해설 빈칸은 be동사 was와 연결되어 현재분사와 과거분사가 올 수 있는 자리로, 문맥상 주어 he는 승진되는 대상이므로 수동태를 이루는 과거분사 (B) promoted가 정답이다.

어휘 hard work 노고 finally 마침내 promote 승진시키다 senior 선임의, 상급의 analyst 분석가

4. Page 씨는 새로운 급여 정책에 대한 모든 문의를 회사 이메일로 답변했다.

해설 빈칸은 문장의 동사 자리로, 주어 Mr. Page가 목적어 all questions를 답하는 주체이므로 능동태인 (B) answered가 정답이다.

어휘 payroll policy 급여 정책

5. 장비 사용 지침은 회사 내부 웹 사이트에서 확인할 수 있다.

해설 빈칸은 조동사 can 뒤의 동사원형 자리로, 주어 The equipment-use guidelines는 확인되는 대상이므로 수동태인 (B) be found가 정답이다.

어휘 guideline 지침 internal 내부의

6. 모든 공장 방문객은 생산 구역으로 들어가기 전 반드시 안내 데스크에 도착해야 한다.

해설 빈칸은 조동사 must 뒤의 동사원형 자리이고 동사 arrive는 수동태가 될 수 없는 자동사이므로 (A) arrive가 정답이다.

어휘 register 등록하다 before ~ 전에

7. 직원들은 회사 내에서 다른 직무로 전환하기 위한 교육을 받았다.

해설 빈칸은 문장의 동사 자리로, 문맥상 '직원들이 교육을 받는다'는 의미가 적절하므로 4형식 동사의 수동태인 (B) were offered가 정답이다.

어휘 training 교육 transition 전환 role 역할

8. Griffin 씨는 마케팅 분야에서 가장 전문적인 사람으로 여겨진다.

해설 빈칸은 문장의 동사 자리이다. consider는 5형식 동사로, 수동태로 쓰일 때 '주어가 ~라고 여겨진다'의 의미로 쓰인다. 따라서 (B) is considered가 정답이다.

어휘 consider 간주하다, 여기다 professional 전문적인

9. Allergan 사는 최근 설문 조사에서 최고의 신흥 기업으로 선정되었다.

해설 빈칸은 문장의 동사 자리이다. name은 5형식 동사로, 수동태로 쓰일 때 '주어가 ~로 선정되다'라는 의미로 쓰인다. 따라서 (B) was named가 정답이다.

어휘 survey 설문 조사

10. 관객들은 공연 시작 10분 전에 착석해야 합니다.

해설 빈칸 뒤 to be seated와 결합하여 '착석하도록 요청 받는다'라는 수동적 의미를 나타내므로 수동태를 완성하는 (B) asked가 정답이다. ask는 to부정사를 목적격 보어로 취하는 5형식 동사로, 수동태 구문은 <be asked to부정사>의 형태가 된다.

어휘 audience 관객 be seated 앉다 performance 공연

11. Scott 씨는 패브릭 샘플에 만족하여 다양한 스타일을 주문했다.

해설 주어인 Mr. Scott은 감정을 느끼는 대상이고, 빈칸 뒤 with the fabric samples와 결합하여 '패브릭 샘플에 만족하다'라는 수동적 의미를 나타내므로 수동태인 (B) was pleased가 정답이다. <be pleased with + 명사>의 형태로 기억하자.

어휘 fabric 직물 as a result 그 결과 place an order 주문하다 a variety of 다양한

12. 직원들은 퇴근 전에 컴퓨터를 끄라는 알림을 받는다.

해설 빈칸 뒤 to shut과 결합하여 '컴퓨터를 끄도록 직원들에게 상기되다'라는 수동적 의미를 나타내므로 수동태 (A) are reminded가 정답이다. remind는 to부정사를 목적격 보어로 취하는 5형식 동사로, 수동태 구문은 <be reminded to부정사>의 형태가 된다.

어휘 leave for the day 퇴근하다

13. 우리 경영진은 직원 생산성을 높이기 위해 정기적으로 인센티브를 제공한다.

해설 빈칸은 문장의 동사 자리로, 현재 시제와 자주 쓰이는 부사 periodically와 어울려 회사의 현재 상황을 나타내므로 현재 시제인 (A) offers가 정답이다. (B) are offering은 복수이므로 주어와 수 일치가 되지 않아 오답이다.

어휘 management 경영진 periodically 정기적으로 incentive 장려금 stimulate 자극하다, 활발하게 하다 productivity 생산성

14. 작년에 시는 소상공인에게 건축 허가 500건을 발급했다.

해설 빈칸은 문장의 동사 자리로, 과거를 나타내는 시간 표현 Last year가 있으므로 과거 시제인 (B) issued가 정답이다.

어휘 issue 발급하다 permit 허가[증]

15. 앞으로 몇 달 동안 Alfa Vehicles 사는 세단에 더 많은 기능을 추가할 것이다.

해설 빈칸은 문장의 동사 자리로, 미래를 나타내는 시간 표현 Over the next few months가 있으므로 미래 시제인 (B) will add가 정답이다.

어휘 feature 특징, 기능

16. Kelly 씨는 수년 동안 얻어온 지식을 새로운 동료들과 공유하는 것을 즐긴다.

해설 빈칸은 문장의 목적어 the knowledge를 수식하는 절의 동사 자리로, 과거부터 현재까지의 기간을 나타내는 over the years가 있으므로 현재완료 시제인 (A) has gained가 정답이다.

어휘 share 공유하다 colleague 동료 knowledge 지식 over the years 수년 동안

17. 우리가 제품을 출시할 때쯤 경쟁사는 이미 그들의 제품을 출시했을 것이다.

해설 빈칸은 주절의 동사 자리로, 부사절 By the time we launch는 현재 시제를 쓰고 있지만 실제로 미래를 의미하며, 이와 어울리는 미래완료 시제 (B) will have released가 정답이다.

어휘 launch 출시하다 competitor 경쟁사 release 출시하다

18. 매니저는 팀이 마감일 전에 작업을 완료한 것을 알고 기뻐했다.

해설 매니저가 that 이하의 사실을 알고 기뻐한 시점이 과거이고, 팀이 마감일 전에 작업을 완료한 시점은 매니저가 기뻐한 시점보다 더 앞선 시점이므로 과거완료 시제인 (B) had completed가 정답이다.

어휘 be pleased to ~해서 기쁘다 task 임무 deadline 마감일

19. 매주 목요일에 우리 팀원들은 지역 작가들이 쓴 소설에 관해 토론하기 위해 만난다.

해설 빈칸은 문장의 동사 자리로, 주어가 복수이고 반복되는 일을 나타내는 Every Thursday가 있으므로 현재 시제인 (B) meet이 정답이다.

어휘 discuss 토론하다 novel 소설 author 작가

20. Portney 사는 매년 지역 자선 단체에 지속해서 기부해 왔다.

해설 빈칸은 has와 donated 사이의 부사 자리로, 현재완료 시제와 어울리는 (A) consistently가 정답이다. 참고로 (B) shortly는 미래 시제와 어울리는 부사이다.

어휘 consistently 꾸준히, 지속적으로 donate 기부하다 charity 자선[구호] 단체

21. CEO는 최근에 분기별 이익에 대해 우려를 표했다.

해설 빈칸은 has와 expressed 사이의 부사 자리로, 현재완료 시제와 어울리는 (B) recently가 정답이다. 참고로 (A) soon은 미래 시제와 어울리는 부사이다.

어휘 express 표현하다 concern 우려, 걱정 quarterly profit 분기별 수익

22. Jones 씨가 월요일에 사무실로 돌아오면 음성 메시지를 받을 것이다.

해설 빈칸은 when이 이끄는 부사절의 동사 자리이다. 시간/조건 부사절에서는 미래의 일을 나타낼 때 현재 시제를 사용하므로 (B) returns가 정답이다.

어휘 voice message 음성 메시지

23. Pot Bistro는 월요일까지 저녁 식사 손님 수를 명시해 달라고 요청했다.

해설 that이 이끄는 절 앞에 has requested라는 요구, 요청의 동사가 있으므로 that절의 동사는 <(should)+동사원형>이 되어야 한다. 따라서 (A) specify가 정답이다.

어휘 specify 명시하다 the number of ~의 수

24. 작업 현장에서는 모든 안전 예방조치를 취하는 것이 필수다.

해설 that이 이끄는 절 앞에 imperative(필수적인)라는 '필수, 의무'의 의미를 나타내는 형용사가 있으므로, that절의 동사는 <(should)+동사원형>이 되어야 한다. 따라서 (B) be taken이 정답이다.

어휘 safety precaution 안전 예방조치 factory floor 작업 현장

PRACTICE
본문 p.186

1. (B)	**2.** (C)	**3.** (D)	**4.** (D)	**5.** (D)	**6.** (B)
7. (C)	**8.** (B)	**9.** (B)	**10.** (D)	**11.** (C)	**12.** (C)
13. (B)	**14.** (B)	**15.** (D)	**16.** (C)		

1. 고객의 욕구를 충족시키기 위한 노력으로 저희는 신제품을 위한 웹사이트를 개설할 것입니다.

해설 조동사 다음에 오는 동사원형을 묻는 문제로, 능동태인 launch와 수동태인 be launched 중, 빈칸 다음에 목적어 a Web site가 있으므로 능동태인 (B) launch가 정답이다.

어휘 in an effort to ~하기 위한 노력으로 meet the needs 요구를 충족시키다 launch 시작[개시/착수]하다

---

2. 저자의 최종 승인을 받으면 원고는 인쇄소로 보내진다.

해설 빈칸 뒤에 목적어가 없으며 주어인 원고는 인쇄소로 '보내지는 대상'이므로 수동태를 완성하는 (C) be sent가 정답이다.

어휘 author 작가, 저자 final approval 최종 승인 manuscript 원고 printer 인쇄소

---

3. 판매 기록이 가장 좋은 영업 사원은 해변 호텔에서 1주일의 휴가를 부여받게 된다.

해설 빈칸은 조동사 뒤의 동사원형 자리로, award는 능동태, be awarded는 수동태이다. 빈칸 뒤에 목적어만 보고 능동태를 정답으로 고르기 쉽지만, 보기에 주어진 동사가 4형식 동사이므로 해석을 통해 풀어야 한다. 주어 salesperson이 1주일의 휴가를 '받는' 대상이므로 수동태인 (D)가 정답이다.

어휘 salesperson 판매원[외판원] sales record 판매 기록 seaside 해변[바닷가] award 주다, 수여하다

---

4. Luton 지역의 최초의 학교였던 Milton House는 역사적인 랜드마크로 지정되었다.

해설 빈칸 뒤 명사구 a historical landmark만 보고 능동태를 정답으로 고르기 쉽지만, 보기에 주어진 동사가 5형식 동사이므로 해석을 통해 풀어야 한다. 주어 Milton House가 '역사적인 랜드마크로 지정되었다'가 문맥상 적절하므로 (D) designated가 정답이다.

어휘 serve as ~의[으로] 역할을 하다 schoolhouse 학교 건물 historical 역사적, 역사상의 landmark 주요 지형지물, 랜드마크 designate 지정하다

---

5. Elliott 박사는 그녀가 은퇴할 때쯤이면 BPA Volks 제약 회사에서 30년간 근무하게 될 것이다.

해설 빈칸은 동사 자리로, 동사 serve가 '일하다'라는 의미로 쓰일 때는 자동사이므로 수동태가 될 수 없다. 수 일치가 맞지 않는 (A) serve를 제외하면 (D) will have served가 정답이다.

어휘 by the time ~할 무렵에, ~할 때쯤에는(이미) retire 은퇴[퇴직]하다 serve as ~의[으로] 역할 하다[일하다]

---

6. 도로 공사가 끝나지 않았기 때문에 기조 연설자는 제때에 도착할 수 없었다.

해설 빈칸은 to부정사의 수동과 능동을 묻는 문제로, 빈칸 뒤에 목적어가 없다고 수동태인 be arrived를 선택하는 실수를 범하지 말아야 한다. 자동사 arrive는 수동태로 쓸 수 없으므로 (B) arrive가 정답이다.

어휘 keynote speaker 기조 연설자 in time (~에) 시간 맞춰[늦지 않게] complete 완료하다, 끝마치다

388 | 잉글리쉬앤 토익 600+

7. 만약 저희 신제품 식기 세척기가 마음에 들지 않으면 전액 환불받으실 수 있습니다.

해설 '~에 만족하다'라는 의미의 숙어 표현 be satisfied with를 알면 쉽게 풀 수 있다. 따라서 (C)가 정답이다.

어휘 dishwasher 식기 세척기 full refund 전액 환불 satisfaction 만족(감) satisfy 만족시키다

8. 도시 주민들은 자금난으로 인한 Vic 극장 폐쇄에 대해 우려하고 있다.

해설 '~에 대해서 걱정하다'라는 의미의 숙어 표현 be concerned about을 알면 쉽게 풀 수 있다. 따라서 (B)가 정답이다.

어휘 resident 거주자[주민] extremely 매우, 몹시 closing (공장·학교·병원 등의 영구적인) 폐쇄 financial difficulty 재정적 어려움

9. 어제 회의에서 Franco 씨는 성수기에 충분한 인력을 고용할 필요성을 강조했다.

해설 단순 시제를 묻는 문제는 시간을 나타내는 부사(구)가 단서가 된다. 과거 시점을 나타내는 시간 부사구 At yesterday's meeting을 통해 시제가 과거임을 알 수 있다. 따라서 (B) emphasized가 정답이다.

어휘 enough(= sufficient) 필요한 만큼의[충분한] peak season 성수기 emphasize(= stress) (중요성을) 강조하다

10. 다음 달에 AT Motors 사는 본사의 직원들을 이란의 새로운 지사에서 근무하도록 전근 보낼 것이다.

해설 빈칸은 동사 자리로, 미래 시점을 나타내는 부사 Next month(다음 달)가 있으므로 (D) will send가 정답이다.

어휘 head office 본점 branch 지점

11. Bush 씨는 지난주 이후로 제안서 마감 기한을 지키기 위해 연장 근무를 하고 있다.

해설 과거의 어느 시점부터 현재까지 계속되는 일을 나타내는 현재완료 시제와 어울리는 <since + 과거 시점> 표현이 있으므로 (C) has been working이 정답이다.

어휘 work overtime 시간 외로 일하다 meet the deadline 마감에 맞추다 proposal 제안[서] submission (서류·제안서 등의) 제출

12. Redgrave 씨는 이달의 총매출 실적이 이번 달 말까지 제출되어야 한다고 요청한다.

해설 주절과 종속절로 이루어진 문장에서 주절의 시제와 종속절의 시제가 일치해야 하지만 주절의 동사가 주장, 명령, 제안, 요구 등의 의미일 경우 종속절(that) 이하의 동사는 주절의 시제와 상관없이 동사원형을 쓴다. 따라서 요구 동사 requests로 인해 정답은 (C) be submitted이다.

어휘 request 요청하다 submit (서류·제안서 등을) 제출하다

13. 관리자가 작업장에서 일어날 수 있는 문제들을 어떻게 예방하는지 익혀두는 것은 매우 중요하다.

해설 적절한 동사의 형태를 묻는 문제이다. 주어 a manager와의 수 일치만 고려하여 (C) is learned를 선택하는 실수를 범하지 말아야 한다. 문장의 important와 같이 필요성을 나타내는 형용사 뒤 that 절의 동사는 조동사 should가 생략된 동사원형으로 사용한다. 따라서 (B) learn이 정답이다.

어휘 prevent 막다[예방/방지하다] potential 가능성이 있는, 잠재적인 occur 일어나다, 발생하다 workplace 직장, 업무 현장 learn 배우다, 학습하다

14. 계약의 모든 측면을 상세히 검사하는 것은 매우 중요하다.

해설 that절의 동사 자리에 should가 생략된 동사원형(be examined)이 왔으므로 의무 표현 형용사인 (B) important가 정답이다.

어휘 aspect 측면 contract 계약[약정](서) as much detail as possible 가능한 한 상세하게 useful 유용한, 도움이 되는 sensitive 세심한, 예민한

15. Highmore 씨는 내년 12월에 새로운 공장이 개장할 때 공장 건설을 감독할 것이다.

해설 주절의 동사가 will supervise(미래 시제)이므로 종속절의 시제도 미래를 표현해야 한다. 하지만 when은 시간을 나타내는 부사절 접속사로, 시간 부사절에서는 미래 대신 현재 시제를 써야 하므로 (D) opens가 정답이다.

어휘 supervise 감독[지휘/지도]하다 construction 건설, 공사 factory 공장 open 문을 열다, 개업하다

16. Cimic 사는 최근에 자사의 경영팀에 합류할 자격을 갖춘 후보자를 찾기 위해 컨설턴트를 고용했다.

해설 현재완료 시제 동사 has hired를 수식할 수 있는 부사 (C) recently가 정답이다. (A) currently(현재)는 의미상 현재 시제와 어울린다. 나머지 보기도 의미상 어울리지 않는다.

어휘 consultant 상담가 search for ~를 찾다 qualified 자격을 갖춘 candidate 후보자 currently 현재 regularly 정기적으로 recently 최근에 highly 매우

UNIT 08 — to부정사와 동명사

CHECK-UP 본문 p.188

1. (A)	2. (A)	3. (B)	4. (A)	5. (B)	6. (B)
7. (A)	8. (A)	9. (A)	10. (B)	11. (B)	12. (B)
13. (B)	14. (A)	15. (B)	16. (B)	17. (B)	18. (B)
19. (A)	20. (B)	21. (B)	22. (B)	23. (A)	24. (B)

1. 우리 회사의 정책은 작업 환경을 항상 깨끗하게 유지하는 것이다.

해설 Our company policy가 문장의 주어이고, is가 동사이며, 빈칸은 is의 보어 자리이다. 따라서 '~하는 것'의 의미로 is의 보어 역할을 할 수 있는 to부정사 (A) to keep이 정답이다. to부정사 뒤에는 동사원형만 올 수 있으므로 (B) to keeping의 to는 전치사이다.

어휘 policy 정책 workplace environment 직장 환경 at all time 항상

2. 새로운 컴퓨터 기술은 사람들이 직장에서 더 효율적으로 일할 수 있게 할 것이다.

해설 빈칸은 타동사 enable의 목적어인 people의 동작을 보충 설명하는 목적격 보어 자리이다. enable은 to부정사를 목적격 보어로 취하므로 (A) to be가 정답이다.

어휘 technology 기술 efficient 효율적인 at work 직장에서

3. 회사는 직원들의 노고를 치하하기 위해 연회를 열었다.

해설 in order to(~하기 위하여)는 '목적'을 나타내는 to부정사 표현이므로 동사원형 (B) honor가 정답이다.

어휘 honor 예우하다, 존중하다 hard work 노고 hold a banquet 연회를 열다

4. 경영진은 새로운 성과 평가 시스템을 도입하기로 했다.

해설 빈칸은 동사 decided의 목적어 자리로, a new performance evaluation system을 목적어로 취하면서 명사 역할을 할 수 있는 to부정사 (A) to implement가 정답이다. decide는 to부정사를 목적어로 취하는 동사이다.

어휘 management 경영진 implement 실행하다, 이행하다 performance evaluation 성과 평가

5. 다른 사람들과 일을 원만하게 잘하는 Foley 씨의 능력은 그의 가장 훌륭한 자질이다.

해설 문장의 주어는 Mr. Foley's ability이고, 동사는 is이다. 빈칸부터 동사 is 앞까지 주어를 수식하므로 형용사 역할을 할 수 있는 to부정사 (B) to work가 정답이다.

어휘 ability 능력 admirable 훌륭한, 우수한

6. 직원들의 기술을 향상시키기 위한 일련의 워크숍이 예정되어 있습니다.

해설 to부정사 숙어 표현 'be scheduled to'를 알면 쉽게 풀 수 있는 문제로, (B) to enhance가 정답이다.

어휘 a series of 일련의 be scheduled to ~할 예정이다 enhance 향상시키다

7. Sarah의 끈기 덕분에 그녀는 많은 어려움을 극복하고 영업 목표를 달성할 수 있었다.

해설 빈칸은 문장의 동사 allowed의 목적어인 her의 동작을 보충 설명하는 목적격 보어 자리이다. allow는 to부정사를 목적격 보어로 취하므로 (A) to overcome이 정답이다.

어휘 persistence 고집, 끈기 overcome 극복하다 numerous 수많은 challenge 난제 achieve 달성하다

8. 우리의 새로운 시스템을 통해 관리자는 실시간으로 기술자와 의사소통을 할 수 있다.

해설 빈칸은 사역동사 let의 목적어인 managers의 동작을 보충 설명하는 목적격 보어 자리이다. 사역동사는 동사원형을 목적격 보어로 취하므로 동사원형 (A) communicate가 정답이다.

어휘 technician 기술자 in real time 실시간으로 communicate 의사소통하다

9. 귀하의 의견은 저희 제품과 서비스를 향상하는 데 도움이 될 것입니다.

해설 준사역동사인 help 뒤에는 원형 부정사 또는 to부정사를 쓸 수 있다. 따라서 (A) improve가 정답이다.

어휘 feedback 의견 improve 향상시키다

10. 이번 합병 프로젝트를 위해 지속적으로 노력해준 Detroit 지사 팀의 노고에 감사합시다.

해설 빈칸은 전치사 for의 목적어 자리로, 뒤의 to this merger project와 결합하여 '합병 프로젝트에 대한 지속적인 기여'라는 의미가 어울리므로 (B) contributions가 정답이다. 참고로 명사 contribution은 주로 전치사 to와 함께 쓰인다.

어휘 thank 감사하다 merger 합병 authority 권리, 권한 contribution 기여

11. 조기 퇴실은 취소로 간주되며 취소 수수료가 부과됩니다.

해설 '~의 대상이다'라는 의미를 나타내는 [be subject to N]에서 to는 전치사이므로 뒤에 명사나 동명사를 써야 한다. 따라서 (B) cancelation이 정답이다.

어휘 early departure 조기 퇴실 cancelation 취소 cancelation fees 취소 수수료, 해약금

12. 연구팀은 다가오는 분기에 대한 시장 분석을 아직 수행하지 않았다.

해설 '아직 ~하지 않았다'라는 의미를 나타내는 [have yet to V]를 완성하는 (B) yet이 정답이다.

어휘 research team 연구팀 conduct 수행하다 analysis 분석 upcoming 다가오는

13. 새로운 전략을 시행하는 것에는 신중한 계획과 실행이 필요하다.

해설 빈칸은 문장의 주어 자리로, new strategies를 목적어로 취하면서 명사 역할을 할 수 있는 동명사 (B) Implementing이 정답이다.

어휘 implement 실행[이행]하다 strategy 전략 planning 계획 execution 실행

14. 재사용 가능한 물병을 사용하는 것은 플라스틱 쓰레기를 줄이는 데 도움이 된다.

해설 빈칸은 문장의 동사 자리로, 동명사구 Using a reusable water bottle이 주어로 쓰였으므로 동사는 단수 취급한다. 따라서 단수 동사인 (A) helps가 정답이다. 동명사 (B) helping은 동사의 성질을 가지고 있으나 동사가 될 수 없으므로 오답이다.

어휘 reusable 재사용 가능한 reduce 줄이다

15. Hardy 씨는 회사 전체의 사무용품 주문을 담당하고 있다.

해설 빈칸은 전치사 of의 목적어 자리로, office supplies를 목적어로 취하면서 명사 역할을 할 수 있는 동명사 (B) ordering이 정답이다.

어휘 be in charge of ~을 담당하다 office supplies 사무용품

16. 우리 회사의 고문들은 불필요한 비용을 줄일 것을 제안했다.

해설 빈칸은 동사의 목적어 자리로, suggest는 동명사를 목적어로 취한다. unnecessary expenses를 목적어로 취하면서 명사 역할을 할 수 있는 동명사 (B) reducing이 정답이다.

어휘 consultant 컨설턴트 unnecessary expenses 불필요한 비용

17. 연체료를 지급하지 않으려면 기한 일자까지 도서를 반납해야 한다.

해설 빈칸은 to부정사의 목적어 자리로, avoid는 동명사를 목적어로 취하므로 (B) paying이 정답이다.

어휘 avoid 피하다 a late fee 연체료 due date 마감일, 기일

18. 귀하의 입사 원서가 통과되지 못했음을 알리게 되어 유감입니다.

해설 동사 regret은 to부정사와 동명사를 둘 다 목적어로 취할 수 있으면서, 목적어의 형태에 따라 의미가 달라진다. 문맥상 '입사 원서가 통과되지 못했음을 알리게 되어 유감이다'라는 의미가 적합하므로 (B) to inform이 정답이다. 참고로 동명사가 오면 '한 것을 후회하다'라는 의미이다.

어휘 job application 입사 지원서 successful 성공적인, 합격한

19. Kaplan 씨는 열심히 노력하여 결국 자신의 사업을 성공적으로 시작하게 됐다.

해설 빈칸은 전치사 in의 목적어 자리로, her own business를 목적어로 취하면서 명사 역할을 할 수 있는 동명사 (A) launching이 정답이다. succeeded in V-ing 형태는 시험에 자주 나오는 동명사

숙어 표현이다.

어휘 eventually 결국 launch (사업 따위에) 손을 대다, 착수하다 succeed in V-ing ~하는 데 성공하다

20. Obget 회사의 로고를 사용하기 전에 서면 허가를 받아야 한다.

해설 빈칸은 전치사 before의 목적어 자리로, Obget Company's logo를 목적어로 취하면서 명사 역할을 할 수 있는 동명사 (B) using이 정답이다. 전치사 다음에는 to부정사가 올 수 없다.

어휘 written permission 서면 허가

21. 최종 채용 결정을 내리시면 연락 주실 것을 기다리겠습니다.

해설 빈칸은 전치사 to의 목적어 자리로, 동명사 (B) hearing이 정답이다. to부정사의 to와 전치사 to는 형태가 같아서 주의해야 하는데, 여기서 look forward(~을 기대하다)와 결합하는 to는 전치사이다. look forward to V-ing 형태는 시험에 자주 나오는 동명사 숙어 표현이다.

어휘 look forward to V-ing ~를 기대하다, 고대하다 final decision 최종 결정

22. Redmayne 씨는 회사에서 웹사이트 개발을 담당하고 있다.

해설 빈칸은 전치사 for의 목적어 자리로, 빈칸 뒤 the company's Web sites를 목적어로 취하면서 명사 역할을 할 수 있는 동명사 (B) developing이 정답이다. 동명사 뒤에는 목적어가 올 수 있지만, 명사 뒤에는 목적어가 올 수 없으므로 (A) development는 오답이다.

어휘 be responsible for ~을 담당하다 development 개발

23. 회사는 이번 분기 우수한 팀 성과에 대한 감사의 뜻으로 보너스를 수여했다.

해설 빈칸은 전치사 in의 목적어 자리로, 빈칸 뒤 전치사 of가 이끄는 구가 있으므로 명사 (A) appreciation이 정답이다. 동명사 뒤에는 목적어가 올 수 있지만, 명사 뒤에는 목적어가 올 수 없다.

어휘 award 수여하다 exceptional 뛰어난, 우수한 performance 성과, 실적

24. 프로젝트는 신중한 기획 덕분에 성공적으로 완료되었다.

해설 빈칸은 형용사 careful의 수식을 받는 명사 자리이다. (A) plan은 가산 명사로, 정답이 되려면 careful 앞에 관사가 있거나 복수형 plans가 되어야 하므로 오답이다. 불가산 명사이자 ing형 명사인 (B) planning이 정답이다.

어휘 successfully 성공적으로 careful 신중한

PRACTICE

본문 p.196

1. (D)	**2.** (C)	**3.** (A)	**4.** (B)	**5.** (C)	**6.** (A)
7. (C)	**8.** (C)	**9.** (C)	**10.** (B)	**11.** (B)	**12.** (B)
13. (C)	**14.** (C)	**15.** (A)			

1. 회사는 인건비를 줄이기 위해 직원 수를 줄이기로 했다.

해설 빈칸은 목적어 자리로, 동사 decide는 to부정사를 목적어로 취하며 '~하기로 결정하다'라는 의미로 쓰인다. 따라서 (D) to reduce가 정답이다.

어휘 decide 결심하다 save 절약하다, 아끼다 labor cost 인건비 reduce 줄이다, 감축하다

2. CB & I 사는 향후 2년 이내에 스페인 동부에 3개의 센터를 추가로 건설할 계획이다.

해설 빈칸은 동사 자리로, 빈칸 뒤 목적어를 to부정사로 취하는 동사 (C) intends가 정답이다. [intend to V]는 '~할 작정이다'라는 의미로 쓰인다.

어휘 build (건물을) 짓다, 건설[건축]하다 eastern 동쪽의 refer 참고[참조]하다 deliver 배달하다 intend 의도[작정]하다 indicate 나타내다[보여주다]

3. Larsen & Toubro 사 직원들은 유효한 신분증이 있어야 건물에 들어갈 수 있다.

해설 빈칸 앞은 주어, 동사, 목적어를 갖춘 완전한 문장이므로, 빈칸 뒤 동사원형을 연결할 수 있는 부사구를 이끄는 전치사 (A) in order to가 정답이다.

어휘 valid (법적·공식적으로) 유효한 in order to ~하기 위하여 as long as ~하는 한 regarding ~에 관하여

4. 우리는 이달 말까지 운영 경비를 줄일 방법을 논의해야 한다.

해설 빈칸은 앞에 나온 명사 ways를 수식하고, 뒤의 목적어를 취하는 to부정사가 들어갈 자리이다. 따라서 (B) to reduce가 정답이다.

어휘 discuss 상의하다 operating cost 운영비, 영업 경비 reduce 줄이다, 낮추다

5. 그 회사는 행사 기획자에게 직원 만찬을 준비해 달라고 요청했다.

해설 빈칸은 동사 ask의 목적격 보어 자리로, ask는 to부정사를 목적격 보어로 취하여 'ask + 목적어 + to부정사'의 형태로 쓴다. 따라서 (C) to organize가 정답이다.

어휘 organize (어떤 일을) 준비[조직]하다

6. GK Motors 사는 유럽 시장으로의 사업 확장을 열망하고 있다.

해설 빈칸 앞 is eager가 문제 해결의 단서로, '~하는 것을 열망하다'라는 의미의 표현인 'be eager to V'를 완성하는 (A) to expand가 정답이다.

어휘 be eager to ~을 간절히 원하다 expand A into B A를 B로 확장하다, 넓히다

7. The Butcher's Tale은 지난달에 그만둔 주방장을 대신할 사람을 아직 찾지 못했다.

해설 빈칸 앞에 온 has와 뒤의 to부정사가 문제 해결의 단서로, '아직 ~하지 않다'라는 의미의 'have(has) + yet + to V'를 완성하는 (C) yet이 정답이다.

어휘 replacement 후임, 대체자 chef 주방장

8. 매출이 늘지 않는다면, 고객의 관심을 증가시키기 위한 다른 전략들을 써보는 것이 현명하다.

해설 빈칸 앞에 온 consider가 문제 해결의 단서로, consider는 동명사를 목적어로 취하는 동사이다. 따라서 (C) using이 정답이다.

어휘 sales 매출 improve 개선하다 consider 고려하다, 숙고하다 strategy 계획[전략] interest 관심, 흥미

9. GE Power 사는 기기 손상을 막기 위해 정품을 사용할 것을 추천한다.

해설 빈칸은 동사 자리로, 빈칸 뒤 목적어를 동명사로 취하는 (C) recommends가 정답이다. [recommend V-ing]는 '~할 것을 권하다, 추천하다'라는 의미이다. 나머지 보기는 모두 to부정사를 목적어로 취하는 동사들이다.

어휘 authentic 진본[진품]인 avoid 방지하다, 막다 strive 노력하다, 힘쓰다

10. 귀하의 주문품 배달이 지연된 점에 대해서 깊이 사과드립니다.

해설 빈칸 앞 전치사 in의 목적어 자리로, 동명사 또는 명사가 올 수 있다. 빈칸 뒤 명사구 your order를 목적어로 취하면서 전치사의 목적어 자리에 올 수 있는 동명사 (B) delivering이 정답이다.

어휘 sincerely 진심으로 apologize for ~에 대해 사과하다 delay 지연, 지체 deliver 배달하다 delivery 배달

11. Fluor Corp 사는 출장을 제한하고 인터넷 회의 사용을 장려함으로써 비용을 줄였다.

해설 by는 전치사로, 뒤에 명사나 동명사가 모두 가능하므로 문맥에 적절한 것을 선택해야 한다. '출장을 제한함으로써 비용을 줄였다'가 문맥상 적절하므로 동명사 (B) limiting이 정답이다.

어휘 reduce expense 비용을 절감시키다 encourage 권장[장려]하다 conferencing 인터넷 회의 by ~ing ~함으로써 limitation 제약[규제], 제한 limit 한정[제한]하다

12. Gates 씨는 여러 자선 단체에 후하게 기부하는 것으로 잘 알려져 있다.

해설 빈칸은 전치사 for 뒤에서 동명사 donating을 수식할 수 있는 부사가 와야 하므로, (B) generously가 정답이다.

어휘 be well known for ~로 잘 알려져 있다 donate 기부하다 charity 자선[구호] 단체 generous 후한 generously 후하게

13. 저희는 제품의 품질을 철저히 검사한 후 제품 판매를 시작합니다.

해설 빈칸은 전치사 After 뒤에서 동명사 inspecting을 수식할 수 있는 부사가 와야 하므로, (C) thoroughly가 정답이다.

어휘 inspect 점검[검사]하다 quality 품질 thorough 철저한 thoroughly 철저히, 철두철미하게

14. Calaca Global Industries 사는 고객들이 그들의 재정 목표를 달성하는 것을 지원하기 위해 최선을 다하고 있다.

해설 [be committed to V-ing] '~하는 데 헌신하다'와 같은 동명사 관용 표현으로, 문장에 사용된 to는 전치사이다. 따라서 전치사 뒤에 올 수 있는 동명사 형태의 (C) helping이 정답이다.

어휘 achieve 달성하다 financial 재무의

15. 귀하의 소포 위치를 추적하기 위하여, 운송 부서로 주문 번호를 알려 주세요.

해설 [be sure to 부정사]는 '반드시 ~하다'라는 의미로, 이를 완성하는 동사원형 (A) provide가 정답이다.

어휘 track 추적하다 location 위치 package 소포 order number 주문 번호 Shipping Department 발송부

UNIT 09 분사

CHECK-UP
본문 p.198

| 1. (B) | 2. (B) | 3. (B) | 4. (B) | 5. (A) | 6. (B) |
| 7. (A) | 8. (B) | 9. (B) | 10. (B) | 11. (B) | 12. (A) |

1. Bob 씨가 프로그램을 설치하는 도중에 예상치 못한 문제가 발생했다.

해설 빈칸은 명사 problem을 수식하는 자리로 형용사 역할을 할 수 있는 과거분사 (B) unexpected가 정답이다. 부사는 명사를 수식할 수 없으므로 (A) unexpectedly는 오답이다.

어휘 occur 발생하다 install 설치하다 unexpected 예기치 않은, 예상 밖의

2. 유감스럽게도 올해 2분기 실적은 아주 실망스러웠다.

해설 빈칸은 주어 the second quarter performance(2분기 실적)을 보충 설명하는 주격 보어 자리이다. 주어가 '실망감을 주는' 대상이

므로 능동의 의미를 나타내면서 형용사 역할을 할 수 있는 현재분사 (B) disappointing이 정답이다. disappointing은 '실망스러운'이라는 의미의 형용사로 관용적으로 쓰인다.

어휘 unfortunately(= regrettably) 불행하게도, 유감스럽게도 performance 실적, 성과 disappointing 실망스러운, 기대에 못 미치는

3. Tom은 자신의 고용 계약서에 서명하기 전에 조건들을 수정하길 희망한다.

해설 빈칸은 소유격 대명사와 명사 contract 사이의 자리로, 과거분사와 명사 둘 다 모두 올 수 있다. 문맥상 '고용 계약서에 서명하다'가 적절하므로 복합 명사를 완성하는 (B) employment가 정답이다.

어휘 modify 수정[변경]하다 terms (합의·계약 등의) 조건 employment contract 고용 계약[서] sign 서명하다

4. 시장 조사를 실시한 후, 회사는 새로운 제품 라인을 출시하기로 결정했다.

해설 분사 구문의 생략된 주어 the company가 동사 conduct의 주체로서 '시장 조사를 실시하다'라는 능동적 의미가 적절하므로 현재분사 (B) Conducting이 정답이다. 빈칸 앞에는 '~이후에'라는 의미의 부사절 접속사가 생략되어 있다.

어휘 conduct 실시하다 market research 시장 조사 launch 출시하다 product line 제품 라인

5. 최근에 업그레이드되어서 사무실 컴퓨터들이 훨씬 빨라졌다.

해설 분사 구문의 생략된 주어 the office computers가 '업그레이드되었다'는 수동적 의미가 적절하므로 과거분사 (A) Upgraded가 정답이다. 빈칸 앞에는 '~때문에'라는 의미의 부사절 접속사가 생략되어 있다. 동사원형 (B) Upgrade가 빈칸에 들어가면 콤마 앞이 명령문이 되는데, 이 경우 뒷문장과 이어지기 위해 접속사가 필요하므로 답이 될 수 없다.

어휘 recently 최근에 much 훨씬

6. 출장비의 예산을 편성할 때, 관리자들은 회사 정책을 검토해야 한다.

해설 분사 구문에서 주어만 생략된 경우이다. 생략된 주어는 주절의 주어와 같다. 주절의 주어 managers가 budget의 주체로서 '출장비의 예산을 편성하다'라는 능동적 의미를 나타내고 있으므로 현재분사 (B) budgeting이 정답이다.

어휘 budget 예산을 세우다 travel cost 출장비 policy 정책

7. 예정된 고객과의 회의가 다음 주로 연기되었다.

해설 빈칸은 명사 meeting을 수식하는 자리로, '예정된 회의'라는 수동적 의미의 형용사 역할을 할 수 있는 과거분사 (A) scheduled가 정답이다.

어휘 postpone 연기하다, 미루다

8. 유리창 수리에 대한 청구금액의 오류에 대해 사과드립니다.

해설 빈칸은 명사 the amount를 수식하는 자리로, '청구된 금액'이라는 수동적 의미의 형용사 역할을 할 수 있는 과거분사 (B) charged가 정답이다. 분사가 명사를 뒤에서 수식하는 경우 분사 뒤에 목적어가 있으면 현재분사를, 목적어가 없으면 과거분사를 주로 쓴다.

어휘 apologize for ~에 대해 사과하다 charge 청구하다

9. 이력서에 업적들을 기재할 때, 반드시 구체적인 날짜를 포함하세요.

해설 분사 구문에서 주어만 생략된 경우이다. 생략된 주어 you가 목적어 accomplishments를 '기재한다'는 능동적 의미가 적절하므로 현재분사 (B) listing이 정답이다. 참고로 주절인 명령문의 주어는 you로, 주로 생략된다.

어휘 list 기록하다, 기재하다 accomplishment 업적, 성취 specific 구체적인

10. 업데이트된 안전 수칙은 공장 전체에 대한 지침을 포함한다.

해설 빈칸은 복합명사 safety manual을 수식하는 자리로 '업데이트된[최신의] 안전 수칙'이라는 수동적 의미의 형용사 역할을 할 수 있는 과거분사 (B) updated가 정답이다.

어휘 safety manual 안전 수칙 guidelines 지침 entire 전체의 updated 최신의

11. 새로운 Galaxy 매장은 우리의 기존 상업 공간보다 훨씬 더 커질 것이다.

해설 빈칸은 명사 commercial space를 수식하는 자리로, '기존의 상업 공간'이라는 의미를 완성하는 현재분사 (B) existing이 정답이다. 참고로 exist는 자동사로, 명사를 수식하는 분사로 쓰일 때 수동의 형태인 p.p.가 될 수 없다.

어휘 commercial 상업의

12. 요청하신 대로, 일정을 잡기 위해 저희 팀원이 연락을 드릴 것입니다.

해설 부사절 접속사 as가 과거분사와 결합하면 '~된 대로'라는 의미의 관용표현으로 쓰인다. 따라서 '요청하신 대로'라는 의미를 완성하는 과거분사 (A) requested가 정답이다.

어휘 contact 연락하다 arrange 준비하다, 계획을 짜다

PRACTICE
본문 p.202

1. (B) **2.** (C) **3.** (D) **4.** (B) **5.** (B) **6.** (D)
7. (C) **8.** (C)

1. 첨부된 워크숍 일정을 열 수 없다면 우리 사무실로 알려 주십시오.

해설 수식어나 보어 자리에 분사를 넣을 때 명사와의 관계에서 수동인 경우에는 과거분사를, 능동인 경우에는 현재분사를 선택해야 한다. workshop schedule(워크숍 일정)은 첨부되는 대상이므로 (B) attached가 정답이다.

어휘 notify(= inform) (공식적으로) 알리다 attach 첨부하다 attached 첨부된 attachment 부착[부가]물

2. 밤 9시 이후에 사무실에 남아 있는 직원들은 나가실 때 불을 꺼 주십시오.

해설 문장의 주어는 Employees이고, 동사는 are asked이므로 빈칸은 동사 자리가 아니다. 따라서 '남아 있는 직원들'이라는 의미로 앞의 Employees를 수식하는 (C) remaining이 정답이다. 참고로 remain은 자동사로, 과거분사 형태로 명사를 수식할 수 없다.

어휘 employee 직원 turn off (전기·가스·수도 등을) 끄다

3. 피트니스 프로그램에 참가할 주민들은 등록 양식서를 작성해야 합니다.

해설 빈칸은 사람 명사 Residents(주민들)를 수식하는 형용사 자리이다. 감정 동사인 interest는 사람 명사를 과거분사 형태로만 수식하므로 (D) interested가 정답이다.

어휘 complete a form 서식을 작성하다 interest ~의 관심[흥미]을 끌다 interesting 흥미로운 interested 관심[흥미] 있어 하는

4. 프로젝트 지연에 대한 실망스러운 소식은 모두를 좌절하게 만들었다.

해설 빈칸 뒤에 사물 명사인 news를 수식하는 자리로, 형용사 역할을 할 수 있는 분사가 빈칸에 들어가야 한다. '실망스러운 소식'이라는 의미가 적절하며, news가 감정을 유발하는 대상이므로 현재분사인 (B) disappointing이 정답이다.

어휘 news 소식 delay 지연, 지체 feel frustrated 좌절을 느끼다

5. 뉴욕에 본사를 둔 Chevron Motors 사는 차량 렌탈 사업을 선도하는 기업 중 하나이다.

해설 보기 중 '선도하는 기업 중 하나'라는 의미를 만들어 주는 형용사인 (B) leading이 정답이다. 본래 leading은 lead(~을 이끌다)의 현재분사로 사용되었지만 '선도하는'이라는 의미로 형용사화된 어휘이다.

어휘 based in ~에 기반을 둔 rental 임대, 대여 expected 예상되는 leading 선두의 dependent 의존[의지]하는 complicated 복잡한

6. 손상된 부품은 구매 후 1년 이내에는 무료로 교환될 것이다.

해설 빈칸은 뒤의 명사를 수식하는 형용사 자리로, 보기 중 형용사인 damaging(손상시키는)과 damaged(손상된) 중 '손상된 부품'이 적합하므로 (D) damaged가 정답이다.

어휘 replace 교체하다 free of charge 무료로

7. 새로운 정책이 이사회에서 승인되는 대로 다음 달부터 시행될 예정이다.

해설 분사 구문의 형태는 목적어의 유무를 통해 결정할 수 있다. 빈칸 뒤에 목적어 없이 전치사구가 나오므로 목적어를 필요로 하지 않는 수동의 의미인 (C) Approved가 정답이다. 빈칸 앞에는 '~하자마자'라는 의미의 부사절 접속사가 생략되어 있다.

어휘 policy 정책 implement 실행[이행]하다 approve 승인하다 approval 승인

8. 분기 보고서를 발표할 때, 그는 회사의 성과를 강조했다.

해설 분사 구문의 주어가 주절의 주어와 같아서 생략되었다. 주절의 주어 he가 동사 present의 주체로서 '보고서를 발표하다'라는 능동적 의미를 나타내고 있으므로 현재분사 (C) presenting이 정답이다.

어휘 quarterly report 분기 보고서 highlight 강조하다 achievement 성과 present 발표하다

UNIT 10 · 등위/상관/형용사절 접속사

CHECK-UP 본문 p.203

1. (B) **2.** (B) **3.** (A) **4.** (A) **5.** (A) **6.** (B)
7. (B) **8.** (B) **9.** (B) **10.** (B) **11.** (A) **12.** (A)

1. 사무실에 새 컴퓨터 서버가 설치되었지만 아직 작동하지 않는다.

해설 빈칸은 앞뒤에 있는 대등한 절과 절을 연결하는 등위 접속사 자리로, 문맥상 앞뒤가 대조적 의미를 나타내고 있으므로 (B) but이 정답이다.

어휘 install 설치하다 operational 가동[운영]상의

2. 직원들은 교육 과정에 참가하거나 온라인 개별 학습을 이수하는 것 중에서 선택할 수 있다.

해설 선택 대상을 등위 접속사 or로 연결하고 있으므로 빈칸은 빈칸 앞 전치사 of의 목적어인 attending a training class와 동일한 동명사 형태로 연결해야 한다. 따라서 (B) completing이 정답이다.

어휘 option 선택 사항 complete 완료하다 tutorial 개별 지도

3. 새롭게 출시된 제품은 가볍고 휴대 가능하며 내구성이 좋다.

해설 빈칸 앞 등위 접속사 and로 연결되었으므로, 앞뒤가 대조적 관계가 아닌 순접 관계가 되어야 한다. 따라서 제품의 장점인 가볍고 휴대 가능하다는 말에 이어서 나올 내용으로 내구성이 좋다는 의미가 적절하다. 따라서 (A) durable이 정답이다.

어휘 released 출시된 lightweight 가벼운 portable 휴대 가능한 durable 내구성이 좋은 breakable 깨지기 쉬운

4. 마케팅팀과 영업팀 모두 제품 출시의 성공에 기여했다.

해설 빈칸 뒤의 and와 함께 짝을 이루어 'A와 B 둘 다'의 의미를 나타내는 (A) Both가 정답이다.

어휘 contribute to ~에 기여[공헌]하다 successful 성공적인

5. 매니저는 Harris 씨나 Haynes 씨 중 한 사람이 다음 달에 열릴 회의에 참석해야 한다고 제안했다.

해설 빈칸 뒤의 or와 함께 짝을 이루어 'A나 B 둘 중 하나'의 의미를 나타내는 (A) either가 정답이다.

어휘 attend 참석하다 conference 회의, 회담

6. Davis 씨는 오늘까지 보고서를 끝내야 할 뿐만 아니라 내일 회의도 취소해야 한다.

해설 빈칸 앞뒤로 두 동사구 finish the report today와 cancel tomorrow's meeting이 나열되었으므로, '~뿐만 아니라 ~도'라는 의미의 상관 접속사 (B) as well as가 정답이다. (A) not only는 but (also)와 짝을 이루어 쓴다.

어휘 finish 끝내다, 마치다 cancel 취소하다

7. 휴가를 사용하지 않은 직원은 연말까지 사용해야 합니다.

해설 빈칸 뒤에 있는 동사 have not used의 주어 역할을 하면서 앞의 사람 명사 Employees를 수식하는 관계대명사 자리로, 주격 관계대명사 (B) who가 정답이다. (A) whom은 목적격 관계대명사이다.

어휘 vacation time 휴가 [시간]

8. 메릴랜드에 위치한 Media World 사는 직원이 100명이 넘는다.

해설 빈칸 뒤에 있는 동사 is located의 주어 역할을 하면서 앞의 사물 명사 Media World를 수식하는 관계대명사 자리로, 주격 관계대명사 (B) which가 정답이다. 관계대명사 that은 콤마 뒤에 쓸 수 없다.

어휘 be located in ~에 위치하다 over ~이상

9. 쇼윈도에 진열된 신상품은 할인가로 판매된다.

해설 빈칸은 주어인 New products를 수식하는 자리로, '~에 위치한 회사'라는 수동적 의미를 나타내면서 형용사 역할을 할 수 있는 (B) displayed가 정답이다. 빈칸과 주어 사이에는 <관계대명사 + be동사>가 생략됐다.

어휘 at discounted prices 할인된 가격으로

10. Tommy's 사의 주방 도구는 3년 동안 유효한 보증서가 제공된다.

해설 빈칸은 관계사절의 동사 is valid의 주어 역할을 하면서 앞의 사물 명사 a warranty를 수식하는 관계대명사 자리로, 주격 관계대명사 (B) that (= which)이 정답이다. 대명사 (A) it은 절을 연결할 수 없다.

어휘 kitchen tool 주방 도구 warranty 보증[서] valid 유효한

11. 배송 중 주문품이 파손된 모든 고객은 환불받을 것이다.

해설 빈칸은 관계사절의 주어인 orders와 동사 are damaged를 이끌면서 사람 명사 all customers를 수식하는 관계대명사 자리로, 소유격 관계대명사 (A) whose가 정답이다. 여기서 all customers와 orders는 '모든 고객의 주문'이라는 소유 관계를 나타낸다. (B) that은 주격/목적격 관계대명사 또는 명사절 접속사로 쓰인다.

어휘 refund 환불 in shipping 배송 중

12. 실험실에 설치된 각 보안 카메라는 24시간 작동한다.

해설 빈칸은 관계사절의 동사 was installed의 주어 역할을 하면서 앞의 사물 명사 Each security camera를 수식하는 관계대명사 자리로, 주격 관계대명사 (A) which가 정답이다. (B) because는 부사절 접속사이다.

어휘 security camera 보안 카메라 laboratory 실험실

PRACTICE
본문 p.207

1. (B) **2.** (D) **3.** (C) **4.** (D) **5.** (A) **6.** (B)
7. (D) **8.** (C)

1. 저희는 모든 직원에게 노고와 뛰어난 헌신에 대해 감사를 표하고자 합니다.

해설 등위 접속사를 고를 때에는 의미를 자연스럽게 연결해주는 것으로 선택해야 한다. 여기서는 '노고와 헌신에 감사드리고 싶다'를 완성하는 '그리고'라는 의미의 (B) and가 정답이다. 등위 접속사 (A) so(그래서)는 완전한 문장과 완전한 문장만을 연결한다는 것을 기억하자.

어휘 hard work 노고 commitment to ~에의 헌신 excellence 뛰어남, 탁월함

2. 현재 Angie's Online에서는 익일 배송 서비스를 제공하지만, 이 옵션에는 추가 요금이 부과됩니다.

해설 빈칸 앞 문장은 '익일 배송 서비스를 제공한다'이고 뒤 문장은 '이 옵션은 추가 요금이 부과된다'이므로 역접의 등위 접속사 (D) but이 정답이다.

어휘 overnight shipping 익일 배송 involve 수반[포함]하다 additional charge 추가 요금

3. Graham 씨와 Krause 씨 중 한 명이 전화응대를 하기 위해 사무실에 있을 것이다.

해설 상관 접속사는 짝을 지어 쓰이며 여기서는 Either A or B가 'A나 B 둘 중 하나'의 의미로 쓰였다. 따라서 (C) Either가 정답이다.

어휘 answer the phone 전화를 받다

4. Bruno 씨의 가게는 훌륭한 제품뿐만 아니라 친근하고 박식한 직원들로도 유명하다.

해설 빈칸 앞에 not only가 있으므로 not only A but (also) B 형태임을 알 수 있다. 따라서 (D) but이 정답이다.

어휘 be known for ~로 알려져 있다 friendly (행동이) 친절한 knowledgeable 지식 있는, 아는 것이 많은

5. 그 회사는 기밀 정보를 처리할 책임이 있는 모든 직원을 교육한다.

해설 주격 관계대명사 뒤에는 동사가 온다. 선행사가 사람일 때와 사물일 때 쓰이는 관계대명사가 각각 다르므로 주의해야 한다. 빈칸 앞 선행사는 사람이고 빈칸 뒤에 동사가 왔으므로 주격 관계대명사인 (A) who가 정답이다.

어휘 train 교육시키다 be responsible for ~에 책임이 있다 handle 다루다, 처리하다 confidential information 기밀 정보

6. 저희는 고객들에게 할인 쿠폰과 무료 영화 티켓을 포함하는 혜택을 제공합니다.

해설 문장의 주어는 We, 동사는 provide이며 빈칸부터 movie tickets까지는 빈칸 앞의 benefits를 수식하므로 빈칸은 관계대명사 자리이다. 선행사 benefits(혜택들)는 사물이며 빈칸 뒤에 주어가 없으므로 주격 관계대명사 (B) that (= which)이 정답이다.

어휘 provide A with B A에게 B를 제공하다 benefit 혜택 include 포함하다

7. 우리는 해당 분야에서 실적이 뛰어난 유통업체를 찾고 있습니다.

해설 빈칸 뒤의 명사 track record와 앞의 distributor가 '유통업체의 실적'이라는 소유 관계를 나타내고, 빈칸 뒤에 완전한 문장이 왔으므로 소유격 관계대명사 (D) whose가 정답이다.

어휘 currently 현재 seek 구하다, 찾다 distributor 유통업자[체] track record 실적 in the field 전문 분야에서

8. Lou Dorfman's Houses 사는 독창적인 디자인을 하는 건축가들로 평판이 높다.

해설 빈칸 뒤의 architects와 designs는 '건축가들의 디자인'이라는 소유 관계를 나타내고, 빈칸 뒤에 완전한 문장이 왔으므로 소유격 관계대명사 (C) whose가 정답이다.

어휘 have a good reputation ~라는 평을 얻다, ~로 유명하다 architect 건축가 original 독창적인

부사절/명사절 접속사

CHECK-UP 본문 p.208

1. (A)	**2.** (B)	**3.** (A)	**4.** (A)	**5.** (B)	**6.** (A)
7. (A)	**8.** (B)	**9.** (B)	**10.** (A)	**11.** (A)	**12.** (A)
13. (B)	**14.** (B)	**15.** (B)	**16.** (B)	**17.** (A)	**18.** (A)
19. (A)	**20.** (A)	**21.** (A)	**22.** (A)	**23.** (A)	**24.** (B)

1. Barry 씨가 부서를 인수했기 때문에 매출이 증가할 것으로 예상된다.

해설 빈칸은 앞뒤로 완전한 절이 왔으므로 부사절 접속사 자리이다. '인수했기 때문에'라는 의미를 나타내는 이유의 부사절 접속사 (A) because가 정답이다. 참고로 despite은 전치사로 뒤에 절이 나올 수 없다.

어휘 increase 증가하다 take over 인수하다

2. 온라인 뱅킹을 등록하는 것이 필수 사항은 아니지만, 적극적으로 추천한다.

해설 빈칸 뒤에 있는 완전한 절을 이끌면서 콤마 뒤의 완전한 문장 전체를 수식하는 부사절 접속사 자리로, '비록 필수 사항은 아니지만'이라는 양보의 의미를 나타내는 (B) Although가 정답이다.

어휘 register for ~을 등록하다 strongly 강력히 recommend 추천하다

3. Elgar 씨는 제품이 매우 비싸서 구매하지 않았다.

해설 빈칸은 앞뒤로 완전한 절이 왔으므로 부사절 접속사 자리이다. '매우 비싸서'의 의미를 나타내는 이유의 부사절 접속사 (A) since가 정답이다. (B) due to는 전치사이다.

어휘 purchase 구매하다 extremely 매우

4. 날씨가 안 좋아서 축구 경기가 취소되면 모든 티켓이 환불될 것이다.

해설 빈칸은 앞뒤로 완전한 절이 왔으므로 부사절 접속사 자리이다. '축구 경기가 취소되면'이라는 의미를 나타내는 조건 부사절 접속사 (A) if가 정답이다.

어휘 refund 환불하다 cancel 취소하다 because of ~때문에

5. 환기 시스템을 수리하는 동안 3번 회의실에 접근할 수 없다.

해설 빈칸은 뒤에 있는 완전한 절을 이끌면서 콤마 뒤의 완전한 문장을 수식하는 부사절 접속사 자리로, '환기 시스템을 수리하는 동안'이라는 의미를 나타내는 시간 부사절 접속사 (B) While이 정답이다.

어휘 ventilation 환기 repair 수리하다 inaccessible 접근할 수 없는

6. 비록 프로젝트가 어려웠지만, 우리는 제시간에 완료했다.

해설 빈칸은 뒤에 있는 완전한 절을 이끌면서 콤마 뒤의 완전한 문장을 수식하는 부사절 접속사 자리로, '비록 프로젝트가 어려웠지만'이라는 의미를 나타내는 양보 부사절 접속사 (A) Although가 정답이다.

어휘 challenging 힘든, 도전하는 on time 정시에

7. 그 제품은 너무 비싸서 쇼핑객들 대부분이 구입하기를 주저한다.

해설 빈칸은 be동사 is의 주격 보어인 형용사 expensive를 수식하는 부사 자리로, 접속사 that과 결합하여 '너무 ~해서 ~하다'라는 의미를 나타내는 부사 (A) so가 정답이다. 참고로 '너무 ~해서 …하다'는 <so+형용사/부사+that 완전한 절>이나 <such+(형용사)+명사+that 완전한 절>의 형태로 쓰인다.

어휘 expensive 비싼 be reluctant to do ~하는 것을 꺼리다

8. Ritzy Boutique는 경쟁력을 유지하기 위해 매장 영업시간을 연장했다.

해설 빈칸은 앞뒤로 완전한 절이 나왔으므로 부사절 접속사 자리이다. '경쟁력을 유지하기 위해'라는 의미로 연결해 주는 부사절 접속사 (B) so that이 정답이다.

어휘 store hours 가게 영업시간 remain competitive 경쟁력을 유지하다

9. 경쟁사들은 가격을 내린 반면, 우리는 요금을 유지했다.

해설 빈칸은 앞뒤로 완전한 절이 왔으므로 부사절 접속사 자리이다. 대조되는 앞뒤 내용을 연결해주는 부사절 접속사 (B) whereas가 정답이다. 양보 사절 접속사인 (A) although는 '비록 ~일지라도'라는 의미로, 대조의 의미로 사용되면서 동시에 종속절과 주절에 제한적인 영향을 미치는 경우에 사용한다.

어휘 competitor 경쟁사[자] lower ~을 내리다 maintain 지속하다, 유지하다 rate 요금, 사용료

10. Hart 씨는 목표를 달성했지만 상사는 여전히 만족하지 않았다.

해설 빈칸은 뒤에 있는 완전한 절을 이끌면서 콤마 뒤의 완전한 문장을 연결하는 부사절 접속사 자리로, (A) Although가 정답이다. (B) Despite는 전치사이므로 <주어+동사> 앞에 올 수 없다.

어휘 meet 충족시키다 satisfy 만족시키다

11. Garden Bridge는 역사적 의미 때문에 보존되어 왔다.

해설 빈칸 앞뒤로 완전한 절이 왔으므로 부사절 접속사 (A) because가 정답이다. (B) because of는 전치사이므로 <주어+동사> 앞에 올 수 없고, 명사(구)와 함께 쓴다.

어휘 preserve 보존하다 historical 역사적인 significance 의미, 중요성

12. 글로벌 시장 동향을 분석하자마자 우리는 새로운 광고 캠페인을 시작하기로 결정했다.

해설 빈칸 뒤로 동명사구가 나오므로 접속사 (B) as soon as가 아닌 전치사 (A) Upon이 정답이다. 전치사 upon은 <upon -ng> '~하자마자'라는 뜻으로 쓰인다.

어휘 analyze 분석하다 market trend 시장 동향 launch 시작하다, 개시하다 advertising 광고

13. 출장 중에 발생한 비용은 상환될 거라는 점을 알아두세요.

해설 빈칸은 동사 note의 목적어 역할을 하는 명사절 접속사 자리로, '상환될 거라는 점'의 의미를 나타내는 (B) that이 정답이다. 관계대명사인 (A) which는 뒤에 완전한 절이 올 수 없고 선행사를 필요로 하므로 오답이다.

어휘 please note that ~을 알아두세요 incurred 발생한 reimburse 변제하다, 상환하다

14. 현재 로고의 문제점은 색깔이 너무 많다는 것이다.

해설 빈칸은 be동사 is의 보어 역할을 하는 명사절 접속사 자리로, '색깔이 너무 많다는 것'이라는 의미를 나타내는 명사절 접속사 (A) that이 정답이다. 전치사 (B) about 뒤에는 문장이 올 수 없고 명사(구)가 온다.

어휘 current 현재의

15. 영업사원들은 그들의 분기 매출 목표치를 달성해야 한다는 것을 알고 있다.

해설 빈칸은 뒤에 있는 완전한 절을 이끌면서 앞의 동사 know의 목적어 역할을 할 수 있는 명사절 접속사 자리로, '매출 목표치를 달성해야 한다는 것'의 의미를 나타내는 명사절 접속사 (B) that이 정답이다. 관계대명사 (A) what도 '~것'이라는 의미지만, 뒤에 불완전한 절이 나온다.

어휘 sales representative 영업사원, 판매 직원 quarterly 분기별, 분기의

16. 프로젝트 기한이 1주일 연장되었음을 팀에 알려주세요.

해설 빈칸은 notify의 직접 목적어 자리로, 프로젝트 기한이 1주일 연장됐다는 것'이라는 의미를 완성하는 명사절 접속사 (B) that이 정답이다. notify는 직접 목적어 자리에 that 절을 취할 수 있는 4형식 동사이다. (A) because는 부사절 접속사이다.

어휘 deadline 기한, 마감 시간[일자] extend 연장하다

17. 점검 결과, 건물의 안전 기능이 부족한 것으로 나타났다.

해설 빈칸은 뒤에 있는 완전한 절을 이끌면서 동사 revealed의 목적어 역할을 할 수 있는 명사절 접속사 자리로, '건물의 안전 기능이 부족하다는 것'이 자연스러우므로 (A) that이 정답이다. (B) unless는 부사절 접속사이다.

어휘 inspection 점검 deficient (필수적인 것이) 부족한[결핍된] safety feature 안전 사양/장치 unless ~하지 않는다면

18. Andrews 씨는 새로운 마케팅 광고가 큰 성공을 거둘 것이라고 확신한다.

해설 빈칸 앞에 온 is confident가 문제 해결의 단서로, 완전한 절을 이끌면서 be confident와 결합하여 '~에 대해 확신하다'라는 의미를 나타내는 명사절 접속사 (A) that이 정답이다.

어휘 be confident that ~을 확신하다 success 성공

19. Taylor 씨는 고객들에게 이메일을 보내 사무실 근처에 기차역이 있는지 물어보았다.

해설 빈칸 이하는 to ask의 목적어 자리로, 빈칸 뒤의 완전한 절을 이끌면서 '기차역이 있는지를'이라는 의미를 나타내는 명사절 접속사 (A) if가 정답이다. (B) though는 부사절 접속사로, 목적어 역할을 할 수 없다.

어휘 client 고객

20. Berks 사의 사장은 Xenon 사와의 계약을 연장할지 말지를 놓고 숙고하고 있다.

해설 빈칸은 동사 is considering의 목적어 자리이다. (A) whether는 '~인지 아닌지'를 의미하면서 'whether+주어+동사' 또는 'whether + to V'의 구조를 취할 수 있으므로 (A) whether가 정답이다. 참고로 명사절 if는 to부정사구와 연결할 수 없다.

어휘 consider 고려하다, 숙고하다 renew (계약 등을) 갱신하다, 연장하다

21. 추가 자금을 받든 받지 않든 우리는 이 프로젝트를 진행할 것이다.

해설 빈칸은 완전한 절을 이끄는 부사절 접속사 자리로, 해당 절은 콤마 뒤 주절을 수식한다. 빈칸 뒤 or not이 단서가 되어 (A) Whether가 정답이다. whether가 부사절 접속사로 쓰일 때는 반드시 or ~ 또는 or not이 와야 한다는 점을 알아 두자.

어휘 additional 추가적인 funding 자금 proceed with ~을 진행하다

22. 회의 참석자 대부분이 지금 발표자가 하는 말을 이해하지 못하고 있다.

해설 빈칸은 동사 do not understand의 목적어 자리이다. 뒤에 불완전한 문장이 왔으므로 명사절을 이끄는 관계대명사 (A) what이 정답이다. (B) since는 접속사와 전치사가 모두 가능하며, 접속사로 쓰일 때는 부사절 접속사로 완전한 절과 완전한 문장을 이끈다.

어휘 attendee 참석자 presenter 발표자

23. 경영진은 신제품을 언제 출시할지 아직 결정하지 않았다.

해설 빈칸은 뒤에 있는 완전한 절을 이끌면서 문장의 동사인 have not yet decided의 목적어 역할을 할 수 있는 명사절 접속사 자리로, '언제'라는 의미를 나타내는 의문부사 (A) when이 정답이다. (B) who는 불완전한 절을 이끌고 문맥상으로도 적절하지 않다.

어휘 management 경영진 launch 출시하다

24. 어떤 팀이 새 프로젝트를 담당할지 매니저가 결정할 것이다.

해설 빈칸은 뒤에 있는 절을 이끌면서 문장의 동사인 decide의 목적어 역할을 할 수 있는 명사절 접속사 자리이다. [which + A(명사) + B(동사)] 패턴으로 '어느 A가 B 할지'라는 의미를 완성하는 (B) which가 정답이다. 의문부사 (A) where은 문맥상 적절하지 않다.

어휘 handle 다루다, 논하다

PRACTICE
본문 p.216

1. (C)	2. (C)	3. (A)	4. (D)	5. (A)	6. (C)
7. (C)	8. (C)	9. (A)	10. (C)	11. (A)	12. (D)
13. (B)	14. (D)	15. (A)	16. (C)	17. (D)	

1. Kravitz 씨가 베네수엘라 출장 기간에 Casey 씨를 도울 것이다.

해설 빈칸 뒤에 [주어+동사]가 왔으므로 보기 중 유일한 접속사인 (C) while이 정답이다. (A) during과 (B) for도 '~동안'이라는 의미가 있지만 전치사이므로 절을 이끌 수 없어 오답이다. 전치사 뒤에는 명사(구)나 대명사가 오며, 접속사 뒤에는 [주어+동사]가 온다.

어휘 assist 돕다 on a business trip 출장 중인 meanwhile 그동안에

2. 매니저는 일정이 겹쳐서 회의를 연기했다.

해설 빈칸 뒤에 명사구 a scheduling conflict가 왔기 때문에 전치사 자리이다. 문맥상 이유를 나타내고 있으므로 (C) because of가 정답이다. (A) otherwise는 접속부사이므로 오답, (D) In case (that)은 접속사이므로 오답이다. (B) since는 접속사와 전치사가 모두 가능하나 전치사로 쓰일 때는 [since+시점] 형태로 쓰여 '~이후로'라는 의미이므로 오답이다.

어휘 postpone 연기하다, 미루다 scheduling conflict 일정 충돌 otherwise 그렇지 않으면 In case (that) ~할 경우에는

3. Glam Uniforms의 월 매출은 Luxe Medical Center가 인근에 개업하자마자 두 배로 증가했다.

해설 빈칸 앞뒤로 주어와 동사를 갖춘 완전한 절이 왔으므로 빈칸은 접속사 자리이다. 따라서 '개업하자마자'라는 의미를 완성하는 부사절 접속사인 (A) as soon as가 정답이다. (B) due to와 (D) during은 전치사로, 문장과 문장을 연결하지 못하므로 오답이며, (C) even though는 '비록 ~일지라도'라는 의미의 접속사로, 문맥상 적절하지 않다.

어휘 monthly sales 월 매출 double 두 배로 되다 nearby 인근에, 가까운 곳에

4. 공간이 제한되어 있으므로 충분한 좌석을 예약하기 위해 빠른 회신이 필요하다.

해설 빈칸은 앞뒤 두 개의 절을 연결하는 접속사 자리로, '공간이 제한되어서'라는 의미가 자연스러우므로 '~ 때문에'라는 뜻의 접속사

인 (D) Because가 정답이다. (B) Meanwhile은 접속부사, (C) Instead는 부사이므로 오답이다. (A) In order that은 '~하기 위해'라는 뜻의 접속사로, 문맥상 적절하지 않다.

어휘 space (비어 있는) 공간 quick response 신속한 답변 reserve 예약하다 in order that ~하기 위해 instead 대신에

5. 세미나는 무료이지만 참석자는 최소 2주 전에 전화로 등록해야 합니다.

해설 빈칸은 앞뒤 두 개의 절을 연결하는 접속사 자리로, '세미나는 무료이지만'이라는 의미가 적절하므로 '(비록) ~이긴 하지만'이라는 뜻의 양보 부사절을 이끄는 접속사 (A) Although가 정답이다. (C) Nonetheless는 부사이므로 오답이다. (B) Before과 (D) Until은 각각 '~전에', '~까지'라는 의미의 접속사로, 문맥상 적절하지 않다.

어휘 attendee 참석자 register 등록하다 by phone 전화로 at least 최소한 in advance 미리 nonetheless 그럼에도 불구하고

6. 담당 의사의 서면 허가가 없다면 누구도 진료 기록을 볼 권한이 없다.

해설 빈칸은 앞뒤 두 개의 절을 연결하는 접속사 자리이다. 보기 중에서 (A) though(비록 ~이지만)와 (C) unless(만약 ~이 아니라면)가 접속사로, '담당 의사의 서면 허가가 없으면'이라는 내용이 되어야 자연스러우므로 (C)가 정답이다.

어휘 have the right to ~할 권리를 가지다 medical record 진료 기록 written authorization 서면 결재 appropriate doctor 담당 의사

7. 영업 담당자는 파일에 원격으로 접속할 수 있도록 온라인 데이터 저장소를 이용할 것을 요청받는다.

해설 빈칸 앞뒤 두 개의 절을 연결하는 접속사로, 보기 중에서 (B) whereas(그런데)와 (C) so that(~하기 위해서)가 접속사이다. '그들이 파일에 원격으로 접속할 수 있도록'이라는 의미가 자연스러우므로 (C)가 정답이다. (A) due to(~때문에)와 (D) despite (~에도 불구하고)는 전치사이다.

어휘 sales representative 영업 담당자 make use of ~을 이용하다 storage 저장 access 이용하다, 접속하다 remotely 원격으로

8. 사립대학의 등록율은 감소하고 있는 반면, 공립대학은 꾸준한 성장세를 보이고 있다.

해설 빈칸 앞뒤 두 개의 절을 연결하는 접속사 자리이다. decline(감소)과 growth(성장)를 대조하는 내용이므로 (C) whereas(~인 반면에)가 정답이다.

어휘 enrollment 등록, 등록자 수 private university 사립대학 public university 국립대학 steady growth 꾸준한 성장

9. 풍부한 경험을 가지고 있다는 점을 고려하면, Edward Smith가 그 일에 가장 적합한 후보이다.

해설 빈칸 앞뒤 두 개의 절을 연결하는 접속사 자리이다. '그가 풍부한 경험을 가지고 있다는 점을 고려하면'이라는 의미가 자연스러우므로 접속사 (A) Given that(~을 고려하면)이 정답이다. (B) Whereas는 두 가지 사실을 비교/대조할 때 쓰는 접속사이므로 의미가 적절하지 않다. (C) Currently(현재)는 부사, (D) According to(~에 따라서)는 전치사이므로 오답이다.

어휘 extensive 광범위한 candidate 후보자

10. 전 직원은 반드시 매일 오전 8시 정각까지 출근해야 한다.

해설 it은 가주어이며 빈칸부터 끝까지는 진주어이다. 빈칸은 문장을 명사로 만드는 명사절 접속사 자리이므로 (C) that이 정답이다.

어휘 imperative 반드시 해야 하는 precisely at 정각 ~시에

11. 사무실 관리자는 Ryman Supply나 WHSmith에서 새 서류 캐비닛을 구매할지를 결정할 것이다.

해설 빈칸은 동사 decide의 목적어 자리이다. [명사절 접속사 + to V] 형태는 명사 역할을 하므로 whether to V와 what to V는 둘 다 decide의 목적어가 될 수 있다. whether to V는 뒤에 주어만 생략된 완전한 문장이 오고, what to V에서 의문사 what이 문장 성분 역할도 하므로 뒤에 불완전한 문장이 온다. 따라서 (A) whether가 정답이다.

어휘 purchase 구입[구매/매입]하다 filing cabinet 서류 캐비닛

12. 새 공사 프로젝트에 투자할지 여부는 불확실하다.

해설 빈칸부터 project까지가 문장의 주어로 빈칸은 명사절을 이끄는 접속사 자리이다. '~인지 아닌지'라는 의미의 접속사 (D) Whether가 정답이다. 명사절 접속사 (A) If는 타동사의 목적어 자리에서만 명사절로 쓸 수 있다.

어휘 invest in ~에 투자하다 uncertain 불확실한

13. 경쟁사와 합병할지에 관한 결정은 시장에서 우리의 위치에 영향을 미칠 것이다.

해설 빈칸은 바로 뒤의 to부정사구와 결합하여 전치사 on의 목적어 역할을 할 수 있어야 한다. '경쟁사와 합병할지'라는 의미가 자연스러우므로 (B) whether가 정답이다. 명사절 접속사 (A) that과 (C) if는 전치사의 목적어 자리에 올 수 없다.

어휘 merge 합병하다 competitor 경쟁자 impact 영향을 주다 market position (기업이나 제품이) 시장에서 차지하고 있는 유명도나 비중

14. 직무 기술서를 보면 현재의 직원들에게 기대되는 행동이 무엇인지 알 수 있다.

해설 빈칸은 to부정사의 목적어 자리로, 빈칸 뒤의 주어가 없는 불완전한 문장을 이끌면서 명사 역할을 할 수 있는 (D) what이 정답이다. 나머지 보기는 모두 완전한 문장과 결합하는 접속사이다.

어휘 job description 직무 기술서 enable A to V A가 ~할 수 있게 하다

15. Keough 씨는 그녀가 고객들에게 광고 캠페인을 소개할 것이라고 확정했다.

해설 빈칸은 타동사 has conformed의 목적어 자리로, 빈칸 뒤 완전한 문장을 이끌면서 명사 역할을 할 수 있는 (A) that이 정답이다. (B) what은 불완전한 문장을 이끌기 때문에 오답이다. (C) though와 (D) unless는 부사절 접속사이다.

어휘 confirm 사실임을 보여주다[확인해 주다] present 소개하다, 제안하다

16. 당사의 고객 설문 조사 결과는 고객 지원 서비스를 강화해야 한다는 것을 보여준다.

해설 빈칸은 동사 indicate의 목적어 자리로, 명사절을 이끌면서 '~라는 것을 나타내다'라는 의미를 완성하는 (C) that이 정답이다. 동사 indicate는 명사절 접속사 that을 자주 취하는 타동사 중 하나다.

어휘 indicate 나타내다[보여 주다] enhance 높이다[향상시키다]

17. 의사들은 Ibrahim 씨가 한 달 이내에 업무에 복귀하게 될 것을 확신했다.

해설 빈칸은 be동사 were의 보어 자리로, 빈칸 뒤에 온 that절과 함께 쓸 수 있는 형용사가 와야 한다. 따라서 정답은 '~을 확신하다'라는 뜻을 나타내는 (D) confident가 정답이다.

어휘 be ready to ~할 준비가 되다 confidential 비밀[기밀]의 responsible 책임이 있는 strict 엄격한[엄한] confident 확신하는

UNIT 12 비교/도치

CHECK-UP 본문 p.218

| 1. (A) | 2. (A) | 3. (B) | 4. (B) | 5. (B) | 6. (A) |
| 7. (B) | 8. (A) | 9. (A) | 10. (B) | 11. (A) | 12. (A) |

1. Natale Group 사는 현재 경쟁업체인 Super Supreme Protection 사만큼 유명하다.

해설 빈칸은 형용사 famous를 수식하는 부사 자리로, 뒤에 있는 as와 결합하여 '~만큼 유명한'의 원급 비교 의미를 나타내는 (A) as가 정답이다.

어휘 famous 유명한 competitor 경쟁자

2. 개조한 휴게실은 7층에 있는 구내식당만큼 넓다.

해설 빈칸은 be동사 is의 주어인 The renovated breakroom을 보충 설명하는 주격 보어 자리이다. 따라서 앞뒤에 있는 as 원급 비교 사이의 품사는 형용사인 (A) spacious가 적절하다.

어휘 breakroom 휴게실 spacious 넓은 spaciously 넓게, 거대하게

3. 우리는 마감일을 맞추기 위해 가능한 한 효율적으로 일해야 한다.

해설 빈칸은 동사 work를 수식하는 부사 자리이면서, 'as ~ as' 원급 비교 구문에 올 수 있는 원급 부사 (B) efficiently가 정답이다. as ~ as possible은 '가능하면 ~하게'라는 의미로 자주 쓰인다.

어휘 meet 충족시키다 deadline 마감일 efficiently 효율적으로

4. 프로젝트는 우리가 처음에 기대한 것보다 덜 원활하게 진행되었다.

해설 빈칸 앞의 비교급 부사 less smoothly와 결합하여 '~보다 덜 원활하게'의 의미를 나타내는 비교급 표현 (B) than이 정답이다.

어휘 progress 진행하다 smoothly 순조롭게 initially 처음에

5. 투자자들은 BMC 그룹의 성장세가 예상보다 훨씬 강할 것으로 보고 있다.

해설 빈칸은 비교급 형용사 stronger를 강조하는 부사 자리로, 비교급 강조 부사 (B) much가 정답이다. 비교급 앞에서 '훨씬'이라는 의미로 비교급을 강조하는 부사에는 much, even, still, far, a lot 등이 있다.

어휘 investor 투자가[자] growth 성장 expect 기대하다

6. 시장 상황에 대한 Perri 씨의 가장 최근 분석은 이전보다 훨씬 더 긍정적이었다.

해설 빈칸은 was 뒤의 보어 자리로, 빈칸 뒤 than과 결합하여 '보다 더 긍적적인'이라는 의미를 나타내는 비교급 형용사 (A) more positive가 정답이다. significantly는 비교급 앞에서 비교급을 강조하는 부사로, 동의어인 considerably와 함께 알아두자.

어휘 analysis 분석 market condition 시장 상황 significantly (= considerably) 훨씬

7. 자동차 산업에서 사용된 모든 재료 중에서 강철이 가장 강하다.

해설 빈칸 앞의 정관사 the와 결합하여 '가장 강력한'이라는 의미를 나타내는 최상급 형용사 (B) strongest가 정답이다.

어휘 material 재료, 원료 available 구할[이용할] 수 있는 auto industry 자동차 산업

8. 모든 영업직원 중에서 Hill 씨가 가장 뛰어난 직원으로 여겨진다.

해설 빈칸은 전치사 as의 목적어 자리로, 빈칸 뒤의 형용사 outstanding과 결합하여 '가장 뛰어난 직원'이라는 최상급 의미를 완성하는 (A) the most가 정답이다. <the + 최상급>은 최상급 자체가 명사 역할을 하여, 특정 사람이나 사물을 지칭하는 의미로도 자주 쓰인다.

어휘 regard 여기다, 간주하다 outstanding 뛰어난 sales personnel 영업직원

9. 회사는 지금까지의 우리 역사상 가장 큰 거래를 막 성사시켰다.

해설 빈칸은 최상급 표현 뒤에서 최상급을 강조하는 부사 자리로, '이제껏 중에서'라는 의미의 (A) ever가 정답이다.

어휘 close a deal 거래를 체결하다

10. Overton 씨는 특히 회의 중에 공개적으로 거의 말하지 않았다.

해설 부정어가 도치되어 문장 앞에 쓰이는 경우에는 [부정어 + 조동사 + 주어 + 동사]의 어순이 된다. 빈칸 뒤에 [조동사(did) + 주어(Mr. Overton) + 동사(speak)]의 어순이므로, 부정어 (B) Seldom이 정답이다.

어휘 moreover 더욱이

11. 귀하의 뉴욕 여행에 대한 임시 여행 일정이 동봉되어 있습니다.

해설 (A) Enclosed는 '동봉된'이라는 의미의 형용사이고, (B) Enclosure는 '동봉된 물건'을 의미하는 명사이다. 빈칸에 명사와 형용사 둘 다 올 수 있지만 의미상 '임시 여행 일정을 동봉한다'가 적절하므로 (A)가 정답이다. 주어가 길 때 [보어 + 동사 + 주어] 형태로 문장이 도치된다.

어휘 enclose 동봉하다 tentative 임시의 itinerary 여행 일정 계획(서)

12. 이번 캠페인이 더 효과적이었다면 회사가 더 큰 시장 점유율을 차지했을지도 모른다.

해설 빈칸을 포함한 절에서 the campaign이 주어이며 동사의 일부인 been이 있으므로 도치가 이루어졌음을 알 수 있다. 그리고 주절의 동사가 'would have p.p.'이므로 if가 생략된 문장 맨 앞에 가정법 과거완료의 조동사가 와야 한다. 따라서 (A) Had가 정답이다.

어휘 effective 효과적인 market share 시장 점유율

PRACTICE 본문 p.222

1. (B)   **2.** (C)   **3.** (C)   **4.** (D)   **5.** (B)
6. (D)   **7.** (A)   **8.** (D)

1. Eric 사는 올해 새롭게 출시된 복사기가 예전의 제품만큼이나 믿을 만하다고 확신한다.

해설 원급 비교 as ~ as 사이에는 형용사/부사의 원급이 들어가므로 (B) reliable와 (D) reliably 중 하나가 정답이다. 빈칸 앞의 as를 지우면 be동사 다음 보어 자리이므로 (B) reliable이 정답이다.

어휘 confident 확신하는 photocopier 복사기 rely 의지하다 reliable(= dependable) 믿을[신뢰할] 수 있는 reliably 믿을 수 있게, 확실히

2. 모든 교육 참석자들은 가능한 한 완벽하게 평가서를 작성하도록 요청받았다.

해설 원급 비교 as ~ as 사이에는 형용사/부사의 원급이 들어가므로 (B) competitive와 (C) completely 중 하나가 정답이다. 빈칸 앞의 as를 생략해도 문장이 완전하므로 부사인 (C)가 정답이다.

어휘 fill out 작성하다 evaluation form 평가지, 설문지 compete 경쟁하다 competitive 경쟁력 있는 completely 완전히, 전적으로 competitiveness 경쟁력

3. 새로운 도구는 과학자들이 전보다 더 정확한 측정을 할 수 있도록 해준다.

해설 빈칸 뒤의 than은 비교급과 함께 쓰이는 표현이므로 보기 중 유일한 비교급인 (C) more precise가 정답이다.

어휘 tool 도구, 수단 measurement 측정, 측량 precise 정확한, 정밀한 precisely (틀리지 않고) 정확하게

4. 생물학자로서의 나의 경력은 예상했던 것보다 훨씬 보람이 있었다.

해설 비교급 표현 more 앞에서 비교급을 강조하는 부사인 (D) even이 정답이다. 부사 (A) soon(곧), (B) alone(혼자), (C) about(대략)은 비교급을 강조하며 수식할 수 없다.

어휘 career 경력 biologist 생물학자 rewarding 보람 있는 expect 예상[기대]하다

5. 소매업 부문의 소비자 지출 증가는 일반적으로 가을에 가장 크다.

해설 빈칸은 be동사 is의 보어 자리이다. 정관사 the와 함께 쓰고, 형용사의 최상급 표현인 (B) greatest가 '가장 큰 것'이라는 의미를 완성하므로 정답이다. 명사 (A) greatness(큼, 위 대함)도 보어 자리에 올 수 있지만 문맥상 어색하므로 오답이다.

어휘 increase in ~의 증가 spending (정부·조직체의) 지출 retail sector 소매업 부문 typically 보통, 일반적으로 autumn 가을 greatly 대단히, 크게

6. Tewkesbury 근처에 이제껏 지어진 건물 중에서 가장 큰 건물의 공사가 현재 마지막 단계이다.

해설 빈칸에는 형용사와 형용사의 최상급 모두 올 수 있다. 문맥상 빈칸 뒤 ever(이제껏)와 어울리는 최상급 (D) biggest가 정답이다.

어휘 construction (특히 도로·빌딩·교량 등의) 건설, 공사 ever [비교급·최상급 뒤에서 그 말을 강조하여] 이제까지, 지금까지

7. 회사가 자금 부족 때문에 어려움을 겪고 있다는 것을 알았다면, 우리는 계약을 하지 않았을 것이다.

해설 문장 맨 앞에 조동사 Had가 도치되어 있다. 가정법 과거완료의 도치 구문의 종속절은 [Had + 주어 + 과거분사]의 형태이므로 과거완료 (A) known이 정답이다.

어휘 suffer from ~로 고통받다 shortage 부족 contract 계약[서]

8. 귀하의 향후 요구사항을 충족시키는 것을 도와줄 고객 설문지를 첨부 드립니다.

해설 문장의 주어는 be동사 뒤의 a customer survey(고객 설문지)이다. 보어를 강조하기 위해 주어와 동사가 된 구문으로 빈칸은 주격 보어 자리이다. 따라서 형용사 (D) Attached가 정답이다.

어휘 attach 첨부하다 attached 첨부된 attachment 첨부 파일, 부가물 meet the needs 요구를 충족시키다

UNIT 13 　문법/어휘

PRACTICE 1　　본문 p.231

1. (C)　**2.** (D)　**3.** (C)

1.

직원 여러분께 알립니다.

다음 주에 새로운 전자 근무시간 기록 시스템을 도입할 예정입니다. 교체 사원증은 이번 주 금요일까지 여러분께 배부할 것입니다. 또한, 이 사원증은 근무시간 기록표의 기능을 하게 될 것입니다. 근무시간 기록 기계는 여러분의 사무실에 가장 가까운 출입구에 설치될 예정입니다.

어휘 introduce 도입하다, 소개하다　electronic 전자의　timecard 근무시간 기록(표)　replacement 교체　distribute 배부하다　function 기능; 기능하다　entrance 입구

해설 빈칸이 있는 바로 앞 문장 "We are going to introduce a new electronic timecard system next week."에서 다음 주에 새로운 전자 근무시간 기록표 시스템을 도입할 예정이라고 했으므로 사원증을 배부하는 시점도 문맥상 미래 시제가 적절하다. 따라서 사원증이 '나누어질 것이다'라는 의미의 (C) will be distributed 가 정답이다.

2.

eMachines 매장 관리자에게::

6월 1일부터 새로운 환불 규정이 모든 eMachines 매장에서 시행될 것을 안내드립니다. 이날부터 eMachines 사는 특정한 조건에서 고객들이 환불을 받을 수 있도록 보장하는 정책을 시행할 것입니다. 이 정책에 의하면 지난 3개월 안에 구매된 모든 상품은 상태가 양호하고 크게 마모되지 않았을 경우 전액 환불될 수 있습니다.

어휘 inform 알리다　starting ~부터　refund 환불　go into effect 발효되다　policy 정책　guarantee 보장하다　purchase 구입하다　condition 상태　extensive 광범위한, 넓은　wear 마모

해설 빈칸이 포함된 문장 안에는 시제를 알 수 있는 단서가 없으므로 전체 문맥을 고려해서 정답을 찾아야 한다. 지문의 첫 문장 "starting on June 1, new refund rules will go into effect at all eMachines stores"에서 6월 1일부터 새로운 환불 규정이 적용될 것이라고 했다. 문맥상 from this date가 가리키는 날짜는 바로 6월 1일이기 때문에, '정책을 시행할 것이다'라는 의미를 완성하는 (D) will implement가 정답이다.

3.

저희 경영진에서는 Rina Boutique 사에서 7년간 근무하고 있는 Neeta Joshi 씨가 올해의 직원으로 선정되었음을 알리게 되어 기쁩니다. Joshi 씨는 대학교 2학년 때 시간제 비서로 우리 회사에서 일했습니다. 그 후 그녀는 Drexel 대학교의 명성 있는 패션 스쿨을 졸업한 후 이곳에서 신입 패션 디자이너로 일하게 되었습니다.

어휘 management 경영진　assistant 비서　on a part-time basis 시간제로　sophomore (대학의) 2학년　prestigious 일류의, 명성 있는　junior 신입의

해설 빈칸 뒤에 이어지는 문장 "Then, after graduating from the prestigious Fashion School of Drexel University, she was employed as a junior fashion designer here."에서 대학 졸업 후 디자이너로 고용된 사실을 알 수 있다. 따라서 대학교 2학년 때 시간제 근무를 한 것은 과거의 일이므로 과거 시제 (C) served가 정답이다.

PRACTICE 2　　본문 p.233

1. (D)　**2.** (C)　**3.** (B)

1.

Houston 씨께,

12월 3일자 메시지에 감사드립니다. 당사의 기록에 따르면 고객님은 지난 11월 28일 당사 웹사이트를 통해 4개의 Chemex 스노타이어(모델 DW04 145R13)를 주문하셨으며, 해당 제품은 12월 2일에 도착 예정이었습니다. 고객님께서 아직 그것들을 받지 못하셨다니 죄송합니다. 배송은 보통 2~3일밖에 걸리지 않습니다.

어휘 indicate 나타내다, 표시하다　order 주문하다　be scheduled to ~할 예정이다　delivery 배송, 배달　no more than 고작

해설 빈칸 앞 "Our records indicate that you ordered four Chemex snow tires"에서 고객이 주문한 타이어 4개를 언급했으므로 해당 주문품을 지칭하는 복수명사 (D) them이 정답이다.

2.

수신: Martin Branson
발신: Ella Moore
날짜: 3월 9일
제목: 답장: 구직 공고

안녕하세요, Branson 씨,

전화받지 못해서 미안합니다. 마이애미 지역의 새 지사 건설과 관련한 그룹 토론을 진행하느라 매우 바빴습니다.
어쨌든, 제가 며칠 전에 얘기했듯이, 이전의 회계 부장인 Jerry Page 씨가 갑자기 회사를 그만두게 되어서, 적합한 후임자를 찾는 것이 매우 어려운 상

정답과 해설

황입니다. 우리 회사 웹사이트에 구직 공고를 게재해 주셨으면 합니다. Page 씨의 업무를 할 수 있는 사람이 필요하며, 현재 홍콩 지사에도 몇몇 자리가 비어 있습니다.

어휘 be busy -ing ~하느라 바쁘다 branch 지사 unexpectedly 예상치 못하게, 갑자기 replacement 후임자 job posting 구직 공고

해설 빈칸은 명사 company's Web site(회사의 웹사이트)를 앞에서 수식하는 형용사 자리로, 이어지는 문장 "We need a manager who can perform Mr. Page's duties"에서 이메일의 발신자인 Moore 씨가 회사에 사람이 필요하다고 했으므로 우리 회사 웹사이트에 공고를 올려달라는 것이 의미상 적절하다. 따라서 빈칸에는 we의 소유격인 (C) our가 정답이다.

3.

Ellison 씨께,

선도적인 온라인 커리어 매칭 서비스인 Workipedia 네트워크에 오신 것을 환영합니다. 귀하의 주소, 경력, 선호 사항이 저희 데이터베이스에 등록되었습니다. 이 정보는 귀하와 같은 구직자를 찾고 있는 고용주를 식별하는 데 사용됩니다. 귀하는 앞으로 해당 지역 일자리에 관한 알림을 정기적으로 받게 됩니다.

어휘 leading 선도적인 preference 선호 identify 식별하다, 찾다 job candidate 구직자 periodic 정기적인 notification 알림, 통지

해설 빈칸은 전치사 like의 목적어 자리로, 빈칸을 포함한 전치사구가 명사 job candidates를 수식하고 있다. 빈칸 뒤 문장 "In the future, you will receive periodic notifications about open positions in your area."에서 '귀하는 일자리에 관한 알림을 정기적으로 받게 된다'고 했으므로, 이메일의 수신자인 Ellison 씨는 구직자임을 알 수 있다. 따라서 '귀하와 같은 구직자들'이라는 내용이 되어야 자연스러우므로 목적격 대명사 (B) you가 정답이다.

PRACTICE 3   본문 p.235

1. (D)   **2.** (B)   **3.** (A)

1.

Keller 씨께,

저희 보안 카메라 설치 서비스에 관한 문의 사항에 답변드립니다. 귀하의 불편을 최소화하기 위해 정규 업무시간을 피해서 작업할 수 있습니다. 아울러 보안 카메라에 대한 전문 지식을 갖춘 직원이 SimpliCam 및 Wyze Cam과 같은 저렴하고 간단한 다양한 옵션들을 보여줄 수 있습니다.

어휘 respond to ~에 응답하다, 대응하다 installation 설치 definitely 분명히, 틀림없이 work around ~를 피해서 일하다

regular 정기적인 minimize 최소화하다 inconvenience 불편 expertise 전문 지식 affordable (값이) 알맞은 a wide variety of 다양한 in addition 게다가 in fact 사실은

해설 빈칸 앞 "We are definitely able to work around your regular business hours~"에서 불편을 최소화하기 위해 정규 업무시간을 피해서 작업할 수 있다고 하고, 빈칸 뒤 "members of our staff with expertise in security cameras can show you a wide variety of affordable and simple options~"에서 보안 카메라에 대한 전문 지식을 갖춘 직원이 다양한 옵션들을 보여줄 수 있다고 했다. 따라서 빈칸 앞뒤로 Keller 씨에게 제공할 수 있는 회사의 혜택들을 나열하고 있으므로 추가적인 내용을 연결해주는 접속부사 (D) in addition이 정답이다.

2.

안녕하세요, Goldberg 씨,

오늘 아침 회의에서 저희가 동부 해안에 새로운 물류센터를 지을 여력이 안 된다는 결정이 났습니다. 하지만 늘어나는 제품의 수요를 맞추고자 한다면 더 큰 물류시설로 이전을 해야 합니다. 그래서 지역 내 다음의 조건을 만족하는 몇몇 기존 물류시설의 위치를 파악해 주시기 바랍니다.

어휘 cannot afford to ~할 여유가 없다 logistics 물류 facility 시설 demand 수요 locate 정확한 위치를 알아내다 existing 기존의 specification 사양, (명세)사항, 조건

해설 빈칸 앞 "it was decided that we cannot afford to build a new logistics center"에서 새로운 물류센터를 지을 여력이 안 된다는 제한적인 상황을 설명하고 있고, 빈칸 뒤 "we must move into a larger facility"에서 더 큰 물류 시설로 이전을 해야 한다고 했으므로 대조되는 내용을 연결해주는 접속부사 (B) However (하지만)이 정답이다.

3.

전직원 여러분께,

다음 달에 도입될 변경사항을 사전에 공지하고자 이 메모를 씁니다. 이는 직원들의 연간 급여 인상을 처리하기 위해 개선된 새 시스템입니다. 직원들이 이 시스템을 이해하고 문의할 기회를 갖는 것이 중요합니다. 이런 이유로, 다음 주에 이 주제에 관해 저와 다른 인사부서 관리자들이 주최하는 일련의 회의가 있을 것입니다.

어휘 advance 사전의 introduce 도입하다 refined 개선된, 정제된 raise 임금 인상 have a chance to ~할 기회가 있다 a series of 일련의 in short 요컨대 for instance 예를 들어

해설 빈칸 앞 "It is important that employees understand this system and have a chance to ask questions about it"에서는 직원들이 새롭게 도입된 시스템을 이해하고 문의할 기회를 갖는 것이 중요하다고 했고, 빈칸 뒤 "there will be a series of meetings on the topic next week ~"에서 이 주제에 관해 인사부서 관리자들이 주최하는 일련의 회의가 있을 것이라고 했으므로 빈칸 앞의 내용이 회의를 여는 것의 이유가 된다. 따라서 접속부사 (A) For this reason(이런 이유로)이 정답이다.

PRACTICE 4
본문 p.237

1. (D) **2.** (A) **3.** (D)

1.

안녕하세요, Taylor 씨.

저는 Magnolia Journal의 Stephen Miller입니다. 이 이메일은 당신의 잡지 구독이 11월에 만료됨을 알려 드리기 위한 것입니다. 이번 달에 구독을 갱신하시면, 20% 할인을 해드리겠습니다. 이 특가는 저희 업체를 지난 5년간 애용해 주신 고객님을 위한 감사 표시입니다.

어휘 subscription 구독 renew 갱신하다 special offer 특가, 특별 할인 express 표현하다 loyal 충성스러운 patronage 단골, 애호 dedication 헌신 sympathy 동정 enthusiasm 열정 gratitude 감사

해설 빈칸 앞 "If you renew your subscription this month, we will give you a 20% discount"에서 구독을 갱신할 경우 20%의 할인 혜택을 제공한다고 했다. 따라서 빈칸이 포함된 문장에서 주어인 This special offer는 앞서 언급한 20% 할인 금액을 나타내며 이는 5년간 업체를 애용해 준 단골 고객에 대한 '감사' 표시가 적절하므로 (D) gratitude가 정답이다.

2.

Reyes 씨께,

앞으로 열리게 될 연례 Sales Success 학회 모임의 초청 연사 자리를 제안해 주셔서 감사드립니다. 그 자리에 저를 고려해 주셔서 정말로 영광입니다. 유감스럽게도, 저는 지금 곧 출판하게 될 제 최신 책의 마지막 원고 작업을 하느라 시간을 낼 수가 없습니다.

어휘 upcoming 다가오는 honor 명예, 영광 be engaged in ~하느라 바쁘다 draft 초안, 원고 proposal 제안 temptation 유혹 acceptance 수락 approval 승인

해설 빈칸 뒤에 이어지는 내용 "Unfortunately, I am currently engaged in writing the final draft of my latest book and simply cannot take any time away from that"에서 글쓴이가 원고 작업 때문에 시간이 없어서 초청 연사 자리를 정중히 거절하고 있다. 그러므로 빈칸에는 '제안'해 주셔서 감사드린다는 의미로 (A) proposal이 적절하다.

3.

Nick Frost와 Halle Parker 주연의 고전 미스터리 영화 <Perfect Blue>가 다음 주에 극장가로 다시 돌아올 것입니다. 작년에 개봉했던 그 영화의 리부트의 대성공 때문에, 많은 팬이 원작을 극장에서 다시 한번 보고자 하는 희망을 나타냈습니다. 너무 어려서 극장에서 원작을 볼 수 없었던 많은 팬들 또한 큰 화면에서 그것을 볼 기회를 얻기를 간절히 바라고 있습니다.

어휘 star 주연을 맡다 huge success 대성공 reboot 리부트(이미 만들어진 영화의 컨셉과 캐릭터만을 가져와 새로운 이야기로 다시 만든 작품) express 표하다, 나타내다 desire 바람, 희망, 욕구 original 원작 get a chance to ~할 기회를 얻다 decisive 결단력 있는 fearful 두려워하는 hesitant 주저하는 eager 간절히 바라는

해설 be동사 are의 보어 자리에 들어갈 형용사를 고르는 어휘 문제이다. 앞 문장 "many fans have expressed a desire to see ~)"에서 많은 팬이 다시 영화를 보고자 하는 희망을 나타냈다는 것과 빈칸 앞의 also가 단서로, 너무 어려서 원작을 극장에서 못 본 팬들 역시 원작을 볼 기회를 얻기를 '간절히 바란다'는 내용으로 전개되는 것이 적절하므로 (D) eager가 정답이다.

UNIT 14 문장 삽입

PRACTICE 1
본문 p.239

1. (C) **2.** (B) **3.** (C)

1.

2월 8일—오늘 아침, 소프트웨어 기술자 Lucas Ellison은 새로운 회사를 창업했습니다. 새로운 회사 L-Ellison Tech는 온라인 상점의 스타일과 기능 향상을 전문으로 할 것입니다. Ellison의 기술팀은 고객의 사이트에서 자료를 수집하고 사용자들의 선호도에 따라 사이트를 개편하는 작업에 참여하고 있습니다. 이것은 방문자들의 행동을 분석하는 새로운 소프트웨어의 도움으로 가능합니다. Ellison은 회사의 서비스가 수요가 있을 것으로 기대하면서 "휴대폰에서 태블릿에 이르기까지 모든 화면 크기에서 향상된 사용자 경험을 위해 고객의 웹 인터페이스를 업그레이드할 것입니다."라고 말했습니다.

어휘 enhance 향상시키다 functionality 기능성 technician 기술자 be engaged in ~으로 바쁘다 gather 모으다 based on ~에 근거하여 preference 선호도 wider audience 폭넓은 고객층 examine 조사[검토]하다 behavior 행동 prefer 선호하다

(A) 한편, 그것은 대부분의 온라인 상점들이 더 폭넓은 고객층에 도달하는 것을 도울 것입니다.
(B) 시장 조사에 따르면 가정용품을 판매하는 온라인 상점이 증가한 것으로 나타났습니다.
(C) 이것은 방문자들의 행동을 분석하는 새로운 소프트웨어의 도움으로 가능합니다.
(D) 고객들은 종종 매장을 방문하기보다는 온라인 쇼핑을 선호합니다.

해설 지시어와 대명사가 있는 보기들은 빈칸 앞 문장과의 연관성을 고려해야 한다. 앞 문장 "Mr. Ellison's team of technicians is engaged in gathering data from clients' sites and reorganizing the sites based on users' preferences"에서 방문자의 특성을 분석하여 사이트를 개편한다고 했고, 앞 문장 전체를 This로 가리키며 사이트 개편 작업에 대한 설명을 덧붙이는 내용의 (C)가 가장 자연스럽다. (A)는 it과 앞 문장의 내용과 연결되지만, 접속 부사 Meanwhile(한편)은 두 문장의 관계가 역접일 때 사용하므로 오답이다.

2.

Green 씨에게,

저희 기록에 따르면 귀하의 지난 치과 검진이 12월 8일이었습니다. 곧 추가 예약을 잡으실 것을 제안 드립니다. 이는 연구에서 3개월마다 검진을 받는 것이 귀하의 치아와 잇몸을 건강하게 유지하는 데 도움이 될 것임을 보여줬기 때문입니다. 시간대를 예약하시려면, 주중 오전 9시와 오후 6시 사이에 언제든 7928 4474로 저희에게 연락하세요.

> **어휘** record 기록 show 보여주다, 나타내다 dental checkup 치과 검진 research 연구 get a checkup 검진을 받다 teeth 치아 gum 잇몸 healthy 건강한 book 예약하다 time slot 시간대 take a moment 잠깐 시간을 내다 appointment 약속, 예약 outstanding 미지불된 charge 요금

(A) 잠시 시간을 내어 귀하의 경험에 관한 피드백을 저희에게 주시기 바랍니다.
(B) 곧 추가 예약을 잡으실 것을 제안 드립니다.
(C) 이 서비스는 아직 39.99달러의 미지불된 요금이 있습니다.
(D) 저희 병원이 7번가로 이전했다는 것을 아셔야 합니다.

> **해설** 빈칸 앞에서 지난 치과 검진(your dental checkup)이 언급되고, 빈칸 뒤에서 이것에 대한 이유(The reason for this)로 3개월마다 검진받는 것의 효과에 대해 설명하고 있다. 따라서 지시어 This는 빈칸 문장 전체를 가리키고, 빈칸에 추가 검진을 곧 받으라는 내용의 (B)가 적절하다.

3.

다음 주 금요일 12월 23일에 사무실 크리스마스 파티가 열릴 예정입니다. 많은 직원들이 매년 이 행사를 기대하고 있고, 올해도 다르지 않습니다. 행사 날짜가 다가옴에 따라, 사무실 주변이 장식될 것입니다. 여러 가지 활동이 그 날 내내 열릴 것으로 계획되어 있습니다. 일부 또는 모든 활동에 참여하려면, 인사부에 놓여 있는 적절한 참가 신청서에 이름을 작성하세요.

> **어휘** approach 다가오다 put up decorations 장식을 하다 appropriate 적절한 sign-up sheet 참가 신청서 currently 현재 recruit 모집하다 celebration 축하 행사 kick off 시작하다 throughout ~내내 exchange 교환하다 present 선물

(A) 파티 위원회가 현재 새 회원들을 모집하고 있습니다.
(B) 이 축하 행사는 연휴 주말을 시작할 훌륭한 방법일 것입니다.
(C) 여러 가지 활동이 그날 내내 열릴 것으로 계획되어 있습니다.
(D) 선물을 교환하는 것에 관심이 있는 직원들은 선물을 가져올 수 있습니다.

> **해설** 빈칸 뒤 문장의 대명사 them과 연결되는 명사를 찾아야 한다. 빈칸 뒤 "To join in any or all of them, just put your name on the appropriate sign-up sheets located in HR"에서 무언가의 참여 방법을 설명하고 있으므로 '파티가 열리는 날 있을 여러 가지 행사'에 대해 언급한 (C)가 정답이다. 대명사 them은 명사 activities를 가리킨다.

PRACTICE 2 본문 p.241

1. (B) **2.** (D) **3.** (A)

1.

예기치 못한 문제로 인해 Starfall의 중앙 로비 보수 공사 완료일은 이제 5월 6일이 아닌 5월 13일입니다. 이번 지연은 여러분이 계속해서 남문을 통해서 건물 안으로 들어오셔야 한다는 의미입니다. 게다가, 로비에 인접한 사무실들은 다음 주 내내 가끔 소음 방해를 경험하게 될 것입니다. 보수 공사의 지연에 따른 불편함을 끼쳐 죄송합니다. 하지만 결과적으로 고객들에게 더욱 매력적이고 현대적인 분위기를 제공할 수 있을 것입니다. 일단 작업이 마무리되면 여러분 모두가 이해하실 것으로 확신합니다.

> **어휘** due to ~ 때문에 unforeseen(= unexpected) 예측하지 못한, 뜻밖의 completion date 완공일 renovation 수리, 보수 instead of ~ 대신에 delay 지연, 지체 in addition 게다가 occasional 가끔의, 때때로의 noise 소음 disruption 방해 inconvenience 불편 attractive 매력적인 modern 현대의 impress 감명을 주다 once 일단 ~하면

(A) 우리는 지장을 겪어 왔습니다.
(B) 일단 작업이 마무리되면 여러분 모두가 이해하실 것으로 확신합니다.
(C) 주된 문제는 바닥에 있습니다.
(D) 남문은 24시간 열려 있습니다.

> **해설** 보수 공사에 대한 양해를 구하는 공지이다. 마지막 문장 "We apologize for the inconvenience, but the end result will be an attractive, modern space that impresses customers"에서 현재는 다소 불편하더라도 결과는 좋을 것이라는 말했으므로 문맥상 공사가 끝난 후, 자신의 의견에 동의할 것이라는 내용의 (B)가 정답이다. 그리고 (B) 문장에 포함된 the work는 빈칸 앞에서 언급된 중앙 로비 보수 공사(the renovation of Starfall's main lobby)를 의미한다.

2.

여러분, 좋은 오후입니다.

당사의 연례 직무 만족도 설문조사(JSS)는 Bridgerock에서의 근무에 대한 의견을 공유할 수 있는 기회입니다. 귀하의 의견은 우리 회사의 미래를 설계하는 데 도움이 될 겁니다. 늦어도 11월 30일까지 온라인 설문조사에 참여해 주시기 바랍니다. 앞으로 며칠 내에 설문조사 링크가 포함된 이메일을 받게 될 것입니다. 시간을 좀 내셔서 여러분의 피드백을 주세요. 이러한 여러분의 기여는 회사를 성장하게 합니다.

> **어휘** annual 매년의 opportunity 기회 share 나누다, 공유하다 opinion 의견 shape 만들다, 구체화하다 fill out 작성하다 no later than 늦어도 ~까지 response 응답 contribute 기여하다 reply 응답하다 promptly 즉시 deadline 마감 시간, 최종 기한 take the time to ~ ~할 시간을 내다 provide 제공하다

(A) 모든 직원은 메시지에 즉시 응답했습니다.
(B) 프로젝트의 마감 기한은 이번 달 30일입니다.
(C) 그 작업의 최종 마감일은 내일 오후 6시입니다.
(D) 시간을 좀 내셔서 여러분의 피드백을 주세요.

해설 지문의 도입부 "Our annual job satisfaction survey"에서 만족도 설문 조사에 관한 내용임을 알 수 있다. 빈칸 앞 "you will receive an e-mail containing a link to the survey"에서 설문조사를 할 수 있는 링크를 포함한 이메일을 보낸다고 했으므로 피드백을 요청하는 (D)가 정답이다. 보기에 정관사 the가 있는 경우 단서로 활용할 수 있다. 참고로 (B)의 'the project'와 (C)의 'the work'에 해당하는 내용이 본문에 언급이 없으며 설문조사와 의미상 관계가 없으므로 오답이다.

3.

Newfoundland (4월 3일)—새로운 수력 발전소의 건설이 다음 달에 시작하기로 예정되어 있다. Churchill Falls Generating Station (CFGS)는 그 발전소가 Newfoundland 전력망 전체를 감당하기에 충분한 전력을 만들어 낼 것으로 추정한다. 그 발전소의 비용에 투입되는 초기 견적액은 거의 5천만 달러이다. 이러한 초기 비용을 부담하기 위해, Newfoundland의 주민들은 공공요금이 약 15% 인상이 예상된다고 들었다.

어휘 hydroelectric power plant 수력 발전소 estimate 추정하다, 추산하다, 견적액, 예상액 generate 생산하다 handle 감당하다 entire 전체의 power grid 전력망 cover 부담하다 initial cost 초기 비용 resident 주민 increase 인상 utility 공공 요금 nearly 거의 grant 보조금 environmental protection group 환경 보호 단체

(A) 그 발전소의 비용에 투입되는 초기 견적액은 거의 5천만 달러이다.
(B) 신규 발전소 건설은 수년이 걸릴 것으로 보인다.
(C) 초기 비용을 지불하기 위해 정부가 보조금을 지급할 것으로 예상된다.
(D) 환경 보호 단체들은 재생 가능한 에너지원을 지지한다.

해설 빈칸 뒤 "To cover the initial costs, ~"에서 정관사 the를 사용해 초기 비용(initial costs)을 언급했으므로 빈칸에는 초기 비용에 관한 구체적인 내용이 들어가야 한다. 따라서 비용(the cost)의 금액(nearly 50 million dollars)을 구체적으로 제시한 (A)가 정답이다.

PRACTICE 3　　본문 p.243

1. (D)　　**2.** (A)　　**3.** (D)

1.

런던에서의 Eton 마라톤을 위한 중요한 날이 다가오고 있습니다. 저희 육상 그룹에서 14명의 사람들이 참석하기로 했고, 여러분은 이미 제가 예약한 호텔에 관한 정보를 받으셨어야 합니다. 그렇지 않을 경우, 저에게 알려주시면 다시 보내드릴 수 있습니다. 저희는 두 사람씩 더블 룸을 함께 쓸 것입니다.

어휘 receive 받다 book 예약하다 share 공유하다 wear 입다 require 필요하다 entrance fee 입장료, 참가비 send 보내다

(A) 경기 동안에 저희 단체 티셔츠를 입어 주시기 바랍니다.
(B) 우리는 토요일 아침에 함께 카풀을 할 것입니다.
(C) 경주에는 30달러의 참가비가 필요합니다.
(D) 그렇지 않을 경우, 저에게 알려주시면 다시 보내드릴 수 있습니다.

해설 빈칸 앞 문장 "you should have already received the information about the hotel I've booked"에서 예약한 호텔에 관한 정보를 이미 받았어야 한다고 했으므로 빈칸에는 이미 받았어야 할 정보를 받지 못했을 경우에 관해 언급하는 (D)가 들어가는 것이 가장 자연스럽다. 보기 중 접속부사 if not(= unless)는 정답을 고르는 데 결정적인 단서가 된다. 또한 send it에서 it이 지칭하는 것은 앞 문장의 information about the hotel이다.

2.

우리 지역의 기상 전문가들이 내일 심한 폭설을 예상하고 있으니, 우리 시 밴드 연습을 취소하는 것이 좋을 것 같습니다. 그렇게 하면, 춥고 쌀쌀한 환경에서 이동할 필요가 없으니까요. 우리는 연습 일정이 뒤처지는 것은 원치 않습니다. 그러니, 이번 주에 시간을 내서 각자 음악을 연습해 주세요. 시의 창립일을 기념하기 위한 우리 콘서트가 빠르게 다가오고 있으니 모두 준비하시기를 바랍니다.

어휘 weather expert 기상 전문가 severe 심한 snowstorm 눈보라 cancel 취소하다 practice 연습 travel 이동하다 work on 작업하다, 연습하다 on one's own 혼자, 스스로 commemorate 기념하다 founding day 창립일 approaching 다가오는 prepared 준비된 get behind 뒤지다, 뒤처지다 recruit 모집하다 indoors 실내에서

(A) 우리는 연습 일정이 뒤처지는 것을 원치 않습니다.
(B) 모두들 지난주 연습에서 환상적인 소리를 냈습니다.
(C) 우리 밴드에 회원들을 더 모집하는 것이 최선일 겁니다.
(D) 다행히도, 우리 리허설은 모두 실내에서 열립니다.

해설 빈칸 뒤에 접속부사 Therefore(그러므로)를 쓰며 "please take some time this week to work on the music on your own"이라고 혼자 집에서 연습할 것을 당부하는 내용이 이어지므로 빈칸에는 연습이 필요한 이유에 해당되는 일정에 관한 내용의 (A)가 들어가는 것이 가장 자연스럽다.

3.

보수 공사는 5월 7일에 완료될 예정이며, 일시적으로 사무실 문을 닫기로 결정했습니다. 사무실은 이번 주 금요일과 토요일 그리고 다음 주 월요일 아침까지 닫을 계획입니다. 따라서 직원들은 월요일 오후 12시까지 다시 사무실로 출근해야 합니다. 전 직원이 새로운 사무실이 일하기에 더욱 편안한 장소라고 느끼길 바랍니다.

어휘 complete 완성하다, 완료하다 shut down 문을 닫다, 폐쇄하다
comfortable 편안한 e-mail 이메일; 이메일을 보내다
questionnaire 설문조사지 relocation 이전 cause ~의
원인이 되다 inconvenience 불편

(A) 우리는 여러분에게 사무실 이전에 관한 설문 조사지를 이메일로
보낼 것입니다.
(B) 그리고 최근 보수 공사로 인해 여러분이 불편을 겪었을 수도
있을 것입니다.
(C) 보수 공사가 이루어지는 동안 B동 건물에서 근무하는 직원들은
A동 건물에서 일했습니다.
(D) 따라서 직원들은 월요일 오후 12시까지 다시 사무실로 출근해야
합니다.

해설 빈칸 앞 "The office will be closed this Friday and Saturday
and on Monday morning"에서 사무실이 일시적으로 금요일,
토요일, 월요일 오전에 닫는다고 했으므로, 폐쇄가 끝난 시점인 월
요일 오후 12시에 출근하라는 내용의 (D)가 적절하다. 빈칸 앞 문
장과 해당 문장을 접속부사 therefore이 인과 관계로 연결해준다.

ACTUAL TEST 1 본문 p.244

1. (B)	2. (C)	3. (B)	4. (D)	5. (D)	6. (C)
7. (A)	8. (B)	9. (B)	10. (C)	11. (B)	12. (C)
13. (D)	14. (C)	15. (C)	16. (C)	17. (B)	18. (A)

1. 귀하의 급여에 대한 문의는 경리부의 Turner 씨 쪽으로 보내주
세요.

해설 빈칸은 주어 없이 please로 시작하는 명령문이므로 동사원형 (B)
direct가 정답이다.

어휘 inquiry 문의 accounting office 회계 사무실, 경리부 direct
~(에게)로 보내다 directly 바로, 곧장

2. 반환된 상품을 저희가 받은 후 귀하의 돈이 입금될 것입니다.

해설 빈칸은 명사 account를 수식하는 형용사 자리로, 형용사 역할을
하는 소유격 대명사 (C) Your가 정답이다.

어휘 account 예금(액) credit 입금하다 merchandise (매매한)
물품, (상점에서 파는) 상품

3. Cameron 씨는 어린 시절부터 피아노에 대한 놀라운 재능을 보
여주었다.

해설 빈칸은 동사 displayed의 목적어인 명사 talent를 수식하는 형용
사 자리로, 보기 중 유일한 형용사 (B) remarkable이 정답이다.

어휘 display 보이다, 드러내다 talent 재능, 재주 childhood 어린
시절, 유년 시절 remark 언급[말/논평/발언]하다 remarkable
주목할 만한, 남다른

4. Home Grown 사는 상품이 창고에서 출고된 경우에만 고객의
신용카드에 요금을 청구한다.

해설 빈칸은 앞뒤로 완전한 절이 나오므로 부사절 접속사 자리이다.
'상품이 창고에서 출고된 때'라는 의미를 나타내는 시간 부사절
접속사 (D) when이 정답이다. (A) from, (C) up은 전치사, (B)
should는 조동사이므로 오답이다.

어휘 credit card 신용카드 warehouse 창고

5. Elemental Ads 사에서는 고객의 요구를 직관적으로 이해하는
관리자를 찾고 있다.

해설 빈칸은 조동사 can과 동사원형 understand 사이에서 동사를 수
식하는 부사 자리로, (D) intuitively가 정답이다.

어휘 intuit 직관으로 알다[이해하다] intuitive 직관적인 intuitively
직관적으로

6. Emma Decor 사는 가정용 가구 취향이 단순하면서도 세련된
고객들에게 어필한다.

해설 문장의 주어는 Emma Decor, 동사는 appeals이며 빈칸부터
sophisticated까지는 앞의 customers를 수식하므로 빈칸은 관
계대명사 자리이다. 빈칸 뒤의 문장은 완전한 문장이며, '고객들의
취향'이라는 뜻의 소유 관계가 문맥상 자연스러우므로 소유격 관
계대명사 (C) whose가 정답이다.

어휘 appeal 마음에 들다 taste 기호, 취향 home furnishing
가정용 가구 sophisticated 세련된

7. 안전 기준을 충족시키는 것은 모든 건설 프로젝트에 대한 필수조
건이다.

해설 빈칸은 문장의 주어 자리로, the safety standards를 목적어로
취하면서 명사 역할을 할 수 있는 동명사 (A) Meeting이 정답이다.

어휘 safety standard 안전 기준 requirement 요구사항

8. 2개월간 문을 닫았던 Preston에 있는 Darnell 식료품점은 토요
일에 마침내 다시 문을 엽니다.

해설 빈칸은 (B) having been과 (D) having 모두 들어갈 수 있는 분
사 자리로, 능동/수동을 확인해야 한다. 빈칸 뒤에는 목적어가 없
으므로 수동형인 (B) having been이 정답이다.

어휘 finally(= eventually) 마침내 reopen 다시 문을 열다, 시작하다

9. Watt 씨는 Kempten Tech 사에서 기계 엔지니어로 10년 넘게
근무하고 있다.

해설 빈칸은 has와 함께 동사를 완성하는 과거분사 자리로, '엔지니
어로 10년 넘게 근무하고 있다'가 자연스러우므로 자동사 (B)
served가 정답이다. 참고로 <serve as + 명사>는 '~로서 일하
다'라는 뜻의 빈출 표현이니 외워두자.

어휘 mechanical engineer 기계 기사 hire 고용하다 provide
제공하다

10. 회사 정책에 따르면 모든 직원은 분기별 회의에 참석해야 한다.

해설 빈칸은 동사 require의 목적어 자리로, 완전한 문장을 이끌며 목적어 역할을 하는 (C) that이 정답이다. 보기 중 또 다른 명사절 접속사인 (A) what은 뒤에 불완전한 문장이 온다.

11. 회사는 배우고 성장하기를 간절히 바라는 유망한 지원자들을 찾고 있다.

해설 빈칸은 일부 형용사와 어울리는 to부정사 자리로, <be동사 + 형용사 + to부정사>의 관용 표현을 알면 쉽게 풀 수 있다. 형용사 eager는 to부정사와 함께 쓰여 '간절히 ~하고 싶어하다'를 의미하므로 (B) to learn이 정답이다.

어휘 prospective 유망한, 장래의

12. 백화점의 프로모션을 통해 쇼핑객들은 10% 할인을 받거나 상품권을 받을 수 있다.

해설 <either A or B>의 형태로, 'A 또는 B'라는 뜻의 상관접속사 (C) either가 정답이다. (A) unless는 접속사이므로 뒤에 주어와 동사를 갖춘 완전한 절이 필요하고, (B) both은 <both A and B>의 형태로, (D) neither는 <neither A nor B>의 형태로 쓰인다.

어휘 promotion 판촉활동, 홍보 obtain 얻다, 획득하다 voucher 상품권, 할인권

13. 올해의 연례 회의는 2,000명이 넘는 참석자가 함께해 지금까지 가장 큰 규모였다.

해설 빈칸 앞에 정관사 the가 있고, 문맥상 '지금까지(여태껏) 가장 큰'이라는 의미가 되어야 한다. 따라서 형용사의 최상급 표현인 (D) largest가 정답이다.

어휘 attendee 출석자, 참석자

14. 내일 세미나를 위해 수정된 의제의 사본 한 부가 메모에 첨부되었다.

해설 보어가 도치되어 문장 앞에 쓰이면 <보어 + 동사 + 주어>의 어순이 된다. 따라서 보어 역할을 할 수 있는 형용사 (C) Attached가 정답이다.

어휘 revised 수정된, 개정된 agenda 의제, 안건 attach 첨부하다

[15-18] 공지

Belgrave Road 건설 공사에 대한 소식

Belgrave Road의 공사는 10월 31일까지 완료될 예정이었습니다. 그러나 지난 금요일부터 일요일까지 열린 연례 Notting Hill 축제로 인해 공사 일정에 있어서 불가피하게 3일간의 지연을 초래하였습니다. 결과적으로, Belgrave Road는 공사가 완료되는 11월 3일에 개통될 예정입니다. 공사 기간 동안 상가나 주거지로의 진입은 허용됩니다. 다만, Kensington Park Road는 계속해서 Westbourne Grove로 연결될 것이며, Stanley Avenue의 동쪽 방향 차선은 5번가와 6번가 사이에서 모든 통행이 영구적으로 폐쇄될 것입니다.

프로젝트 일정에 대한 다른 소식들은 시의 웹사이트 www.cityinfo.org에서 확인 가능하고, 최신 상태로 유지됩니다.

공사 기간 동안 양해해 주셔서 감사합니다.

어휘 construction 공사 annual 매년의, 연례의 inevitably 불가피하게 cause 야기하다 access 진입 residence 주거지 permit 허가하다 meanwhile 한편 regrettably 유감스럽게도 at last 마침내[드디어] alternatively 그 대신에 revision 개정, 수정 advance 진보, 전진 permanently 영구적으로 patience 인내

15.

해설 빈칸은 동사 자리로, 주어 The construction이 단수이므로 복수 동사인 (D) are being scheduled는 오답이다. be scheduled to(~할 예정이다)의 형태가 의미상 적절하므로 능동태 (B) had scheduled도 오답이다. 이어지는 문장 "the annual Notting Hill Carnival, which was held from last Friday to Sunday, inevitably caused a 3-day"에서 기존의 일정에 변경이 생긴 시점을 과거로 표현하고 있으므로 빈칸은 문맥상 10월 31일에 공사가 완료되기로 일정이 '잡혀 있었다'를 나타내는 과거 시제 (C) was scheduled가 정답이다.

16.

해설 명사 어휘 문제로, 빈칸 앞에서 원래 공사 완료 일정이 10월 31일이었다고 했으므로 지난 금요일부터 일요일까지 개최된 행사로 인해 공사 일정이 3일의 '지연'을 초래했다고 하는 것이 문맥상 자연스럽다. 따라서 (C) delay가 정답이다.

17.
(A) 따라서 Belgrave Road는 이 시점부터 영구적으로 폐쇄됩니다.
(B) 결과적으로, Belgrave Road는 공사가 완료되는 11월 3일에 개통될 예정입니다.
(C) 지역 주민은 추후 공지가 있을 때까지 축제에 참석할 수 없습니다.
(D) 공사 현장을 지날 때는 천천히 운전해 주십시오.

해설 지문 초반부에서, 10월 31일에 예정되었던 도로 공사의 완료가 Notting Hill 축제로 인해 3일 지연되었다고 했으므로, 예정된 일정보다 3일 후인 11월 3일에 공사가 끝난다고 하는 (B)가 들어가는 것이 가장 자연스럽다.

18.

해설 빈칸 앞뒤로 공사 연장 기간 동안에 지역 상가나 주거지로의 통행 상황을 설명한 후, 도로 이용 상황에 대한 내용이 이어지고 있으므로 화제를 전환하는 의미를 가지는 접속부사 (A) Meanwhile(한편, 다만)이 정답이다.

1. (D)	2. (C)	3. (B)	4. (C)	5. (B)	6. (D)
7. (A)	8. (C)	9. (D)	10. (C)	11. (A)	12. (D)
13. (D)	14. (A)	15. (A)	16. (A)	17. (D)	18. (A)

1. 새로운 마케팅 캠페인은 브랜드 인지도를 높이는 데 성공적이었다.

해설 빈칸은 be동사 뒤 보어 자리로, 명사나 형용사가 올 수 있다. 문맥상 마케팅 캠페인의 상태를 나타내는 형용사 (D) successful이 정답이다.

어휘 brand awareness 브랜드 인지도 success 성공 succeed 성공하다 successfully 성공적으로

2. Lopez 씨는 기획부터 실행까지 회사 행사를 혼자서 준비했다.

해설 by와 결합하여 '혼자서, 스스로'라는 의미를 나타내는 재귀대명사 (C) herself가 정답이다.

어휘 organize 준비[조직]하다 from A to B A부터 B까지 planning 계획 execution 실행, 실시

3. 몇몇 팀원들이 마케팅 캠페인을 위한 새로운 전략을 제안했다.

해설 빈칸은 동사 have suggested의 주어 자리로, 동사에 복수형 have가 쓰였으므로 복수 취급하는 부정대명사 (B) Some이 정답이다. (C) Each는 대명사로 쓰일 때 〈each of the + 복수 명사 + 단수 동사〉 형태로 쓰이고, (D) Much는 대명사로 쓰일 때 〈much of the + 불가산 명사 + 단수 동사〉 형태로 쓰인다. (A) Every는 한정사로, 명사를 수식한다.

어휘 suggest 제안하다 strategy 전략

4. 2021년에 우리는 유럽으로 사업을 확장하여 파리와 마드리드에 사무소를 열었다.

해설 빈칸은 동사 자리로, 동사가 될 수 없는 명사 (B) expansion은 오답이다. (A) expands는 단수 동사로 주어 we와 수 일치되지 않으므로 오답이다. 특정한 시점을 나타내는 in + 2025(연도)가 있으므로, 과거에서 현재까지 일어난 상황을 나타낼 때 사용하는 현재완료 시제 (D) have expanded도 오답이다. 따라서 과거 시제 (C) expanded가 정답이다.

어휘 expand 확장하다 operation 회사, 기업

5. 새로운 마케팅 전략이 시행된 이후 매출이 급격히 증가했다.

해설 빈칸 앞의 be동사가 문제 해결의 단서로, was와 함께 능동적 의미인 현재분사(-ing)나 수동적 의미인 과거분사(p.p.)가 쓰여 since가 이끄는 시간 부사절의 동사 역할을 한다. 따라서 부사절의 marketing strategy가 주어이며, 문맥상 '마케팅 전략이 시행되다'라는 수동적 의미가 적절하므로 과거분사 (B) implemented가 정답이다.

어휘 sales 매출 dramatically 급격히 marketing strategy 마케팅 전략

6. 새로운 서비스의 출시 이후 구독자 수가 상당히 증가했다.

해설 빈칸은 동사 has risen를 수식하는 부사 자리로, '상당히'라는 뜻의 (D) considerably가 정답이다.

어휘 the number of ~의 수 subscriber 구독자 launch 출시 considerable 상당한 considerably 상당히

7. 예산 삭감으로 인해 부서의 지출이 10% 감소할 것이다.

해설 빈칸은 전치사 자리로, 복합 명사 budget cuts와 결합하여 '예산 삭감 때문에'라는 의미를 나타내는 전치사 (A) Due to가 정답이다. 참고로 (B) Because, (C) Since, (D) Unless는 접속사이다.

어휘 budget cut 예산 삭감 expense 비용

8. 2분기 실적이 발표되면 우리는 기자 회견을 열 것이다.

해설 빈칸은 접속사 When이 이끄는 부사절의 동사 자리로, 시간/조건 부사절에서는 현재 시제가 미래를 대신하므로 '2분기 실적이 발표되면'이라는 의미를 완성하는 동사 (C) is announced가 정답이다.

어휘 performance 실적 press conference 기자 회견

9. 주민들은 소음 공해를 줄이기 위한 회사의 노력에 만족을 표했다.

해설 빈칸은 문장의 주어 자리로, 보기 중 주어 자리에 올 수 있는 명사인 (B) Residences(주택, 거주지)와 (D) Residents(거주민, 거주자) 중 문맥상 '주민들이 만족을 표했다'가 어울리므로 (D)가 정답이다.

어휘 express (감정·의견 등을) 나타내다, 표현하다 satisfaction 만족[감] noise pollution 소음 공해

10. 우리는 품질 높은 서비스를 통해 고객 만족도 향상에 전념하고 있습니다.

해설 빈칸은 전치사 to의 목적어 자리로, customer satisfaction을 목적어로 취하면서 명사 역할을 할 수 있는 동명사 (C) improving이 정답이다.

어휘 be dedicated to V-ing ~하는 것에 전념하다 customer satisfaction 고객 만족

11. 영업팀은 새로운 마케팅 전략을 시행했기 때문에 목표를 초과 달성했다.

해설 빈칸은 앞뒤로 완전한 절이 나오므로 부사절 접속사 자리이다. '새로운 마케팅 전략을 시행했기 때문에'라는 의미를 나타내는 이유 부사절 접속사 (A) since가 정답이다. 접속사 (B) provided와 (D) whereas는 문맥상 적절하지 않고, (C) in case of는 절과 절을 연결할 수 없는 전치사이므로 오답이다.

어휘 exceed 초과하다 implement 이행[실행]하다 provided(= if) 만약 ~라면, ~하는 경우에 whereas(= while) ~에 반해서 in case of ~의 경우에

12. 주제의 민감성 때문에, 그것에 주의 깊게 접근하는 것이 중요하다.

해설 빈칸은 전치사 due to의 목적어인 명사 nature(특징, 성격)를 수식하는 형용사 자리로, 문맥상 '주제의 민감성' 때문에 주의 깊은 접근이 필요하다는 것이 적절하므로 (D) sensitive(민감한)가 정답이다.

어휘 nature 특질, 특징 approach 접근하다 with care 주의 깊게, 신중히 appropriate 적절한 effective 효과적인 careful 주의 깊은

13. <모닝 저널>의 연간 구독료는 다음 달에 5달러 인상됩니다.

해설 빈칸은 $5.00를 목적어로 취하는 전치사 자리로, '다음 달에 5달러 증가하다'가 문맥상 적절하므로 전치사 (D) by가 정답이다.

어휘 yearly subscription 연간 구독 except ~을 제외하고

14. 프로젝트 매니저는 리더십과 조직 능력으로 널리 칭찬받고 있다.

해설 빈칸은 be동사 is와 과거분사 praised 사이에서 동사를 수식하는 부사 자리로, '널리 칭찬받고 있다'가 문맥상 적절하므로 (A) widely가 정답이다.

어휘 praise 칭찬하다 organizational skills 조직 기술 closely 자세히 separately 따로따로, 각기

[15-18] 이메일

수신: Donovan Blake <d.blake@quickmail.net>
발신: 고객 서비스부
제목: 회신: 문의에 대한 답변
날짜: 2월 4일

Blake 씨께,

저희 프로그램에 관심을 가져주셔서 감사합니다. Kurtosys Systems는 항상 고객에게 최고의 프로그램을 제공하기 위해 열심히 노력합니다. 귀하는 예산에 맞는 새로운 절약 프로그램에 가입하고 싶다고 말씀하셨습니다. 그러나 더 이상 프로그램을 사용할 수 없음을 알려드리게 되어 유감입니다. 100명의 고객들께서 이미 그 프로그램에 신청하셨습니다. 그리고 저희는 100명 이상의 고객들에게는 그 프로그램을 제공할 수 없습니다.

대신 50달러 이상의 모든 주문에 대해 10% 할인을 받을 수 있는 또 다른 프로그램이 있습니다. 관심이 있으시면 저희에게 알려주시기 바랍니다. 그러면, 이 프로그램의 세부 사항을 보내드리겠습니다.

곧 귀하로부터 소식을 듣기를 고대하고 있겠습니다.
감사합니다.

어휘 mention 언급하다, 말하다 sign up for ~을 신청하다, 가입하다 budget 예산, 비용 attend 참석하다 interest 관심, 흥미 interestingly 흥미롭게도 savings 절약, 저금, 예금 supply 공급 emergency 비상 상황 alternative 대안 resolve 해결하다

15.

해설 빈칸은 소유격(your) 뒤 명사 자리로, 보기 중 유일한 명사인 (A) interest가 정답이다.

16.

해설 빈칸은 명사 program을 수식하는 형용사 어휘 문제로, 어떤 프로그램인지는 빈칸이 포함된 문장만으로는 알 수 없다. 다음 단락의 "we have another program in which ~ over $50"에서 50달러 이상의 주문에 대해 10퍼센트 할인을 받을 수 있는 또 다른 프로그램이 있다고 한 것으로 보아 '절약 프로그램'이라는 말이 자연스럽다. 따라서 (A) saving이 정답이다.

17.
(A) 가족의 긴급 상황으로 인해 프로그램에 참석할 수 없었습니다.
(B) 그러므로 당신에게 그것을 만회할 어떤 대안도 없습니다.
(C) 우리가 이 문제를 해결하기 위해 최선을 다했다는 것을 당신도 알고 있습니다.
(D) 100명의 고객들께서 이미 그 프로그램에 신청하셨습니다.

해설 빈칸 앞 "we are sorry to let you know that program is not available anymore"에서 Blake 씨가 신청한 프로그램을 이용할 수 없고, 빈칸 뒤 "we cannot offer the program to more than 100 customers"에서는 100명 이상의 고객에게 그 프로그램을 제공할 수 없다고 했다. 따라서 프로그램을 이용할 수 없는 이유로 앞뒤 문장을 자연스럽게 연결하는 (D)가 정답이다.

18.

해설 빈칸은 in which가 이끄는 절의 주어 자리로, 보기의 인칭대명사 중 50달러 이상 사면 10% 할인을 받을 수 있는 대상을 골라야 한다. 이메일의 수신자는 Blake 씨이며, Blake 씨에게 신청할 수 있는 프로그램에 대해 설명하고 있으므로, (A) you가 정답이다.

ACTUAL TEST 3 본문 p.248

1. (B)	2. (B)	3. (A)	4. (B)	5. (B)	6. (C)
7. (D)	8. (B)	9. (D)	10. (C)	11. (C)	12. (C)
13. (D)	14. (A)	15. (C)	16. (B)	17. (D)	18. (B)

1. 오찬에 참석할 계획이라면 동봉된 카드에 선호하는 식사를 표시하십시오.

해설 빈칸은 타동사 indicate의 목적어 자리로, 앞에서 소유격 your의 수식을 받고 명사 meal과 결합할 수 있는 명사 (B) preference(선호도)가 정답이다. 참고로 meal preference는 '선호하는 식사'라는 의미의 복합 명사로 자주 쓰인다.

어휘 luncheon 오찬 indicate 나타내다, 보여 주다 enclosed 동봉된 prefer ~을 선호하다 preferred 우선의

2. 지난달 화창한 날씨로 인해 Cheshire 시골 지역의 농부들은 옥수수 재배를 완료할 수 있었다.

해설 동사 complete의 목적어인 명사 corn planting을 앞에서 수식할 수 있는 소유격 인칭대명사 (B) their가 정답이다.

어휘 enable A to V A가 ~할 수 있도록 하다 rural 시골의; 시골 complete 끝마치다 corn planting 옥수수 재배

3. 계약 조건은 매년 변경될 수 있음을 인지해 주세요.

해설 계약 조건이 변경될 수 있음을 인지해 달라는 의미가 적합하므로 형용사 (A) aware가 정답이다. 참고로 aware는 be aware of[that]의 형태로 자주 쓰이므로 외워 두자.

어휘 terms and conditions 계약 조건 be subject to ~의 대상이다 annually 매년 be aware of ~를 알고 있다

4. 고객들은 탁월한 고객 서비스 때문에 Middleton Market을 자주 다시 방문한다.

해설 빈칸은 주어인 Customers와 동사 return 사이에서 동사를 수식하는 부사 자리로, 보기 중 유일한 부사 (B) frequently가 정답이다.

어휘 return to ~로 돌아가다 excellent 우수한, 훌륭한 frequently 자주, 흔히 frequent 잦은, 빈번한 frequency 빈도

5. EMI Group은 안전 규칙을 엄격히 준수하기 위해 항상 주의를 기울이고 있다.

해설 빈칸 뒤의 전치사 to와 함께 '~을 준수하다, 따르다'의 의미를 가지고 있는 자동사 (B) conform이 정답이다. 나머지 어휘들도 같은 의미로 쓰이지만 (A) observe와 (D) follow는 타동사이며, 자동사인 (C) comply는 전치사 with와 어울리므로 오답이다.

어휘 strictly 엄격히 safety rules 안전 규칙

6. 시는 두 개의 국제 무역 박람회를 준비하기 위해 대중교통 시스템을 개선하고 있다.

해설 빈칸은 be동사 is와 결합하여 동사 역할을 하는 분사 자리로, its public transportation system을 목적어로 취하며 '대중교통 시스템을 개선하다'는 능동적 의미를 나타내는 현재분사 (C) improving이 정답이다.

어휘 public transportation 대중교통 improve 향상시키다 improvement 향상

7. Excel Softworks 사는 내년 초에 다른 소프트웨어 회사와 합병할 것이다.

해설 빈칸은 동사 자리로, 동사가 될 수 없는 (B) merging과 (C) to merge는 오답이다. 문장 끝에 미래를 나타내는 표현 early next year가 있으므로 미래 시제인 (D) will merge가 정답이다.

어휘 another 다른 하나의 merge 합병하다

8. 귀하의 주문을 완료할 수 없음을 알려드리게 되어 유감입니다.

해설 빈칸 앞의 are not able이 문제 해결의 단서로, '~할 수 있다'라는 의미의 to부정사 관용 표현인 <be able + to부정사>를 완성하는 (B) to complete가 정답이다.

어휘 order 주문 complete 완료하다

9. 프로젝트가 완료되는 대로, 우리는 팀 회의 일정을 잡을 것이다.

해설 빈칸은 뒤에 있는 완전한 절을 이끄는 부사절 접속사 자리이다. 문맥상 '프로젝트가 완료되는 대로'라는 의미를 나타내는 시간 부사절 접속사 (D) As soon as가 정답이다. 부사절 접속사 (A) Unless(만약 ~하지 않으면)는 문맥상 어울리지 않는다. (B) In case of, (C) On account of는 전치사로, 뒤에 문장이 올 수 없다.

어휘 schedule 일정을 잡다 in case of ~인 경우에 on account of ~ 때문에

10. 귀하가 지원한 관리직은 경력이 있는 영업 직원만 참여할 수 있습니다.

해설 빈칸은 명사 sales worker를 수식하는 자리로, '경력이 있는 영업 직원'이라는 의미를 나타내는 과거분사 (C) experienced가 정답이다. experienced는 '능숙한, 숙련된, 경험이 많은'이라는 뜻으로 자주 사용되는 형용사이다.

어휘 managerial position 관리직 apply for ~을 지원[신청]하다 sales worker 영업 직원

11. Blue National Park는 인기 있는 관광지이며 그곳의 온화한 기후를 일 년 내내 즐길 수 있다.

해설 빈칸은 대등한 절과 절을 연결하는 접속사 자리이다. 콤마 뒤로 Blue National Park에 대한 추가 정보가 이어지므로 문맥상 등위 접속사 (C) and(그리고)가 정답이다.

어휘 year round 1년 내내 due to ~ 때문에 as if 마치 ~인 것처럼

12. 기차가 제시간에 도착했다면 우리는 회의에 참석할 수 있었을 것이다.

해설 주절의 동사가 'would have p.p.'이므로 콤마 앞의 if절에는 과거완료 시제가 와야 한다. 빈칸 뒤에 the train이 주어이며 동사의 일부인 arrived와 도치되었으므로, 과거완료 시제를 완성하는 (C) Had가 정답이다. 원래 문장은 'If the train had arrived on time, ~'으로, if가 생략된 가정법 과거완료 도치 구문이다.

어휘 on time 시간을 어기지 않고, 정각에 participate in ~에 참석하다

13. 모든 창고 작업자들은 깨지기 쉬운 물건들은 선적을 위해 조심해서 포장해야 한다고 권고받는다.

해설 빈칸은 동사 be packed를 수식하는 부사 자리로, 문맥상 '깨지기 쉬운 물건들을 조심해서 포장하다'라는 의미를 완성하는 (D) carefully가 정답이다.

어휘 warehouse 창고 fragile 깨지기 쉬운 pack 포장하다
shipment 선적 slightly 약간, 조금 relatively 상대적으로
powerlessly 무력하게, 효과 없이

14. 우리는 지역 병원을 위한 기금 마련을 위해 자선 행사에 협력할 것이다.

해설 빈칸은 전치사 on과 어울리는 자동사 자리이다. 문맥상 '기금 마련을 위해 자선 행사에 협력할 것이다'는 의미가 가장 적절하므로 (A) collaborate(협력하다)가 정답이다.

어휘 charity event 자선 행사 raise (자금을) 모으다 compete 경쟁하다 ignore 무시하다 oppose 반대하다

[15-18] 공지

모든 고객분들은 주목해 주세요.

최근 저희 온라인 스토어 웹사이트에서 몇 가지 기술적인 문제가 발견되었습니다.

일부 고객들은 저희 웹사이트에 접속할 수 없는 것에 대해 불만을 표시했고, 문제를 분석한 결과, 웹사이트가 자동으로 일부 방문자들을 차단하고 있다는 것을 확인했습니다. 이 문제로 인해 불편을 끼쳐 드려 죄송합니다.

저희는 현재 문제의 원인을 찾기 위해 최선을 다하고 있습니다. 따라서, Wavebox 브라우저를 사용하면 모든 방문자가 웹사이트에 접근할 수 있습니다. 그래서 웹사이트에 접근하는 데 문제가 있으시면 Wavebox 기반 브라우저를 사용해 주세요.

협조 부탁드립니다.

어휘 recently 최근에 discover 발견하다 access 접속하다, 접근하다 analyze 분석하다 determine 알아내다, 밝히다 automatically 자동적으로 block 막다, 차단하다 currently 현재, 지금 find out 발견하다 have a hard time -ing ~하는 데 어려움을 겪다 multiple 많은, 다수의 social 사회적인 in advance 사전에 accordingly 따라서 nevertheless 그럼에도 불구하고

15.

해설 형용사 어휘 문제로, 뒤에 이어지는 내용 "after analyzing the problem, we determined that the Web site was automatically blocking some access by visitors"에서 웹사이트 내 접속이 차단되는 문제를 언급했으므로 기술적인 문제가 있음을 알 수 있다. 따라서 (C) technical이 정답이다.

16.

해설 빈칸은 동사 was blocking의 목적어인 불가산 명사 access를 수식하는 형용사 자리이다. 빈칸 앞 문장 "Some customers complained about not being able to access our Web site"에서 일부 고객이 불만을 제기했다고 했고, 지문 후반 "So, if you are having trouble accessing our Web site, please use a Wavebox-based browser"에서 Wavebox 브라우저로

는 접속이 가능하다고 했으므로 문맥상 모두를 뜻하는 (A) any나 (D) all은 정답이 될 수 없고, '다른 (종류의)'라는 뜻의 (C) other 도 문맥상 적절하지 않다. '약간, 몇몇'을 뜻하며, 불가산 명사를 수식할 수 있는 (B) some이 정답이다.

17. 빈칸 앞에서 문제를 설명한 후, 빈칸 뒤에서는 그 문제를 해결하는 방법을 제시하고 있다. 따라서 앞서 말한 문제와 해결책 사이의 논리적 연결을 만들어 주는 (B) Accordingly(따라서)가 적절하다.

(A) 방문자 중 누구도 온라인 상점에 접속하는 데 어려움을 겪지 않았습니다.
(B) 저희는 당사 웹사이트에 새로운 광고를 게재했습니다.
(C) 귀하의 지역에서는 온라인 구매가 불가능합니다.
(D) 이 문제로 인해 불편을 끼쳐 드려 죄송합니다.

해설 빈칸 앞에서 웹사이트 몇몇 접속을 자동으로 차단하는 문제를 알아냈다고 했으므로 이어질 내용으로 고객들에게 문제에 대해 사과의 말을 전하는 (D)가 적합하다.

18.

해설 빈칸 앞에서 문제를 설명한 후, 빈칸 뒤에서는 그 문제를 해결하는 방법을 제시하고 있다. 따라서 앞서 말한 문제와 해결책 사이의 논리적 연결을 만들어 주는 (B) Accordingly(따라서)가 적절하다.

ACTUAL TEST 4 본문 p.250

1. (D)	2. (D)	3. (A)	4. (C)	5. (C)	6. (A)
7. (C)	8. (C)	9. (D)	10. (A)	11. (B)	12. (B)
13. (B)	14. (A)	15. (C)	16. (B)	17. (A)	18. (D)

1. 이사는 팀 회의를 위해 회의실을 예약해 달라고 그녀의 비서에게 요청했다.

해설 빈칸은 동사 asked의 목적어 자리로, 명사 assistant를 앞에서 수식할 수 있는 소유격 인칭대명사인 (D) her가 정답이다.

어휘 director (회사의) 중역, 이사 assistant 비서, 조수 book 예약하다

2. 재활용 쓰레기통은 편의를 위해 전자레인지 옆에 놓여 있다.

해설 동사 is located와 어울려 '전자레인지 옆에 위치해 있다'라는 의미를 완성하는 전치사 (D) beside가 정답이다.

어휘 recycling bin 재활용 쓰레기통 convenience 편의, 편리 beside ~옆에

3. 체육관은 장비 업그레이드를 위해 이번 주말에 잠시 문을 닫는다.

해설 빈칸은 be동사와 과거분사 closed 사이에서 동사를 수식하는 부사 자리로, 보기 중 유일한 부사 (A) briefly가 정답이다.

어휘 gym 체육관 equipment 장비, 설비 briefly 잠시 brief 짧은, 단시간의

4. 다음 달에, 더 많은 고객을 유치하기 위해 새로운 마케팅 캠페인이 시작될 것이다.

해설 빈칸은 문장의 동사 자리로, 미래를 나타내는 표현 next month가 있으므로 미래 시제 (C) will start가 정답이다.

어휘 attract (주의·흥미 등을) 끌다

5. 자격이 되는 직원들은 내부 승진 기회에 지원하도록 권장된다.

해설 빈칸은 명사 employees를 수식하는 형용사 자리로, '자격이 되는'이라는 의미의 형용사 (C) Qualified가 정답이다.

어휘 apply for ~에 지원하다, 신청하다 internal 내부의 promotion 승진 opportunity 기회 qualification 자격, 능력 qualify 자격을 갖추다

6. 우리는 만족한 고객들의 지속적인 지원에 보답하기 위해 고객 보상 프로그램을 제공한다.

해설 빈칸은 명사 customers를 수식하는 형용사 자리로, 감정을 느끼는 대상인 customers가 '만족한다'는 의미를 나타내면서 형용사 역할을 할 수 있는 과거분사 (A) satisfied가 정답이다. 감정을 유발하는 주체인 사물은 현재분사와, 감정을 느끼는 대상인 사람은 과거분사와 결합하여 주로 쓰인다.

어휘 reward ~에게 보답[보상]하다 continued support 지속적인 지원[후원] satisfaction 만족

7. 마케팅팀은 새로운 라인의 제품 출시를 다음 분기까지 연기하기로 결정했다.

해설 빈칸은 to부정사인 to delay의 목적어 자리이며, 명사 product와 결합하여 '제품 출시'라는 의미의 복합 명사를 완성하는 명사 (C) launch가 정답이다.

어휘 delay 미루다, 연기하다 launch 출시

8. CEO는 최고의 거래를 성사시키기 위해 직접 협상을 처리하기로 결정했다.

해설 빈칸이 없어도 완전한 문장이므로, 문장 맨 뒤에서 주어인 CEO를 강조하는 재귀대명사 강조 용법으로 쓰인 (C) herself가 정답이다.

어휘 handle 다루다, 처리하다 negotiation 협상 secure (특히 힘들게) 얻어 내다, 획득하다 deal 거래

9. 회사는 연중무휴의 지원 서비스를 제공함으로써 고객 만족도를 향상시켰다.

해설 빈칸은 동명사구 providing 24/7 support services를 목적어로 취하는 전치사 자리로, '24시간 지원 서비스를 제공함으로써'라는 의미를 완성하는 전치사 (D) by가 정답이다. by ~ing(~함으로써)는 시험에 자주 출제되는 빈출 구문으로 외워두자.

어휘 improve 향상시키다 customer satisfaction 고객 만족 24/7 연중 무휴의

10. 건설적인 피드백을 제공하는 것은 보다 나은 성과와 사기를 이끌어낼 수 있다.

해설 빈칸은 동명사의 목적어인 명사 feedback을 수식하는 형용사 자리로, 보기 중 유일한 형용사 (A) constructive가 정답이다.

어휘 lead to 이끌다, 초래하다 performance 성과, 실적 morale 사기, 의욕 constructive 건설적인 constructor (특히 자동차나 항공기) 제작자[제작 회사] construction 건설, 공사 construct 건설하다

11. 예상치 못한 기술적 문제가 있었지만, 회의는 오전 10시 정시에 시작되었다.

해설 빈칸은 뒤에 있는 완전한 절을 이끌면서, 콤마 뒤의 완전한 문장 전체를 수식하는 부사절 접속사 자리로, '예상치 못한 기술적 문제가 있었지만'이라는 의미를 나타내는 양보 부사절 접속사 (B) Even though가 정답이다. 나머지 보기도 모두 부사절 접속사지만, 문맥상 적절하지 않다.

어휘 unexpected 예상치 못한 on time 시간을 어기지 않고, 정각에 unless 만약 ~하지 않으면 untill ~할 때까지

12. 프로젝트 종료를 기념하기 위해 팀은 모든 구성원을 위한 활기찬 게임의 밤을 열었다.

해설 빈칸은 관사 a와 복합 명사 game night 사이에서 명사를 수식하는 형용사 자리이다. 의미상 '활기찬 게임의 밤'이라는 의미를 완성하는 (B) lively가 정답이다.

어휘 celebrate 기념하다, 축하하다 lively 활기 넘치는, 활발한 current 현재의 erasable 지울 수 있는

13. 새로 업데이트된 소프트웨어는 이전 버전보다 훨씬 더 사용자 친화적이다.

해설 빈칸은 형용사 비교급 more user-friendly를 강조하는 부사 자리로, 비교급 강조 부사 (B) much가 정답이다. (A) highly, (C) very, (D) overly는 원급만 수식할 수 있다.

어휘 user-friendly 소비자가 사용하기 쉬운, 소비자 친화적인 previous 이전의

14. W-Labs가 실시한 음식 선호도 조사는 우리가 예상한 것과 반대되는 결과를 보여줬다.

해설 문장의 주어는 The study이고 동사는 yields로, 빈칸부터 expected까지는 불완전한 문장의 형태로 빈칸 앞의 명사 results를 수식하고 있다. 따라서 빈칸은 관계대명사 자리로, 선행사 results는 사물이며 빈칸 뒤에 주어가 없으므로 주격 관계대명사 (A) that (= which)이 정답이다.

어휘 preference 선호(도) conduct 수행[이행]하다 yield (결과 등을) 초래하다, 야기하다 be contrary to ~와 상반되다

[15-18] 이메일

수신: 모든 의회 구성원
발신: Maurice Richard, 부장
날짜: 11월 18일
제목: 연례 세계 투자 학회

이번 주 금요일에 지난번 학회가 개최되었던 곳과 같은 장소인 South Wharf의 Sibelius Center 3층에서 연례 세계 투자 학회가 열릴 예정입니다. 하지만, 올해는 정오부터 오후 4시까지 꼬박 4시간 동안 진행될 예정이므로 휴식 시간에 모든 참석자들에게 무료 점심이 제공될 것입니다. 따라서 모든 의원들은 늦어도 이번 주 수요일까지 학회에 참여할 것인지에 대한 여부를 이 이메일의 답장으로 보내주시기 바랍니다. 그래야 참석자 수에 맞게 식사를 사전에 준비할 수 있습니다. <u>채식 식사가 필요한 경우라면 답장에서 말씀해 주십시오.</u>

귀하의 신속한 회신에 미리 감사드리며, 금요일에 귀하를 뵙기를 고대하고 있겠습니다.

어휘 annual 매년의, 연례의 hold 개최하다 attendee 참석자 council 의회 indicate 나타내다, 암시하다 accordingly 따라서 otherwise 달리, 그렇지 않으면 no later than 늦어도 ~까지 beforehand 사전에, 미리 prompt 신속한 ultimately 궁극적으로 nonetheless 그럼에도 불구하고

15.

해설 빈칸은 문장의 동사 자리로, 준동사인 (D) being held는 정답이 될 수 없다. 빈칸 뒤의 this Friday는 시간 부사로 목적어가 없으므로 능동태인 (B) has held도 정답이 될 수 없다. 빈칸 뒤 바로 이어지는 다음 문장 "the forum will be held for a full four hours from noon to 4:00 P.M."에서 학회가 꼬박 4시간 동안 계속될 거라고 했으므로, 학회는 앞으로 일어날 일임을 알 수 있다. 따라서 미래 시제인 (C) will be held가 정답이다.

16.

해설 앞에서 지난해와 올해 학회 장소가 같다고 했으므로 이어지는 내용으로 '올해' 다른 점이 나오는 것이 적절하다. 따라서 (B) This가 정답이다. (C) First는 항상 앞에 the를 동반하고, (D) Each는 반복이나 습관적인 사실을 나타낼 때 쓴다.

17.

해설 빈칸 앞 "a free lunch will be provided to every attendee during a short break."에서 무료 점심 식사가 제공된다고 하고 빈칸 뒤 "we ask all council members to reply to this e-mail indicating whether you will attend the forum or not ~"에서 참석 여부를 이메일로 알려달라는 내용이 나온다. 따라서 두 문장을 원인과 결과의 관계로 연결해주는 (A) Accordingly(그런 이유로, 그래서)가 정답이다.

18.

(A) 또한 모든 회원들이 새로운 요리를 저희 레스토랑에서 맛보시기를 추천합니다.
(B) 따라서 회신하지 않을 경우를 대비하여 여분의 식사를 준비할 것입니다.
(C) 작년 회의는 점심시간도 없이 3시간 동안 진행되었습니다.
(D) 채식 식사가 필요한 경우라면 답장에서 말씀해 주십시오.

해설 식사 사전 준비를 위해 학회 참석 여부를 이메일 회신으로 알려 달라는 빈칸 앞의 내용에 이어서 채식 식사가 필요한 경우에도 답장에서 알려 달라고 하는 내용의 (D)가 들어가는 것이 문맥상 가장 적합하다. (B)는 접속부사 Therefore이 앞의 내용과 연결되지 않으므로 오답이다.

ACTUAL TEST 5   본문 p.252

1. (D)	2. (D)	3. (A)	4. (A)	5. (B)	6. (C)
7. (C)	8. (D)	9. (A)	10. (D)	11. (B)	12. (B)
13. (B)	14. (C)	15. (D)	16. (A)	17. (C)	18. (C)

1. Cowall 개발 사업의 자금 할당이 지난주 회의에서 시 의회에 의해 승인되었다.

해설 빈칸은 관사 the의 수식을 받는 명사 자리로, (D) allocation이 정답이다.

어휘 city council 시 의회 allocate (특정 목적을 위해 공식적으로) 할당하다 allocation 할당, 할당량[액]

2. Luxe Interior 사의 수수료는 창작팀이 고객에게 제공하는 가치를 반영한다.

해설 빈칸은 소유격 our 뒤에서 명사 team을 수식하는 형용사 자리로, (D) creative가 정답이다.

어휘 fee 수수료 reflect 나타내다, 반영하다 value 가치

3. 경제학자들은 향후 6개월 동안 소비자 지출이 5~10% 사이로 증가할 것이라고 예측한다.

해설 빈칸 뒤 and와 함께 짝을 이루어 'A와 B 사이에'의 의미를 나타내는 (A) between이 정답이다.

어휘 economist 경제학자 predict(= forecast) 예측[예견]하다 spending 지출

4. 안타깝게도, Hopper 씨의 컴퓨터에 있는 데이터는 복구할 수 없다.

해설 빈칸은 could not be와 결합하는 분사 자리이다. 빈칸 뒤에 목적어가 없고, 주어 the data가 '복구되는' 대상이므로 과거분사 (A) retrieved가 정답이다. be동사 뒤에 동사원형이나 단수형은 오지 못하므로 동사원형 (B) retrieve와 3인칭 단수형 (D) retrieves는 적합하지 않다.

어휘 unfortunately(= regrettably) 불행하게도, 유감스럽게도
retrieve 되찾아오다, 복구하다

5. 필라델피아에 있는 Tribute Museum에 매달 평균 대략 약 3,000명의 방문객이 방문한다.

해설 숫자 앞에 올 수 있는 부사로 (B) nearly가 정답이다. nearly는 '거의, 대략'이라는 의미로 숫자나 정도를 표현할 때 자주 사용된다. 다른 예시로는 approximately(대략), almost(거의), about (대략) 등이 있다.

어휘 average 평균 ~이 되다 visitor 방문객

6. 여름 카탈로그에서 주문하셨던 품목은 더는 구매할 수 없는 점을 안내드립니다.

해설 빈칸은 명사절의 주어인 the item을 수식하는 형용사절의 주어 자리로, 주격 인칭대명사인 (C) you가 정답이다. 빈칸과 ordered 사이에 목적격 관계대명사 which(= that)가 생략되었다.

어휘 note that ~을 유념하다 order 주문하다 no longer 더 이상 ~않다 available 이용 가능한

7. 귀하는 소중한 회원이시기에 저희의 특별 보상 프로그램에 참여할 수 있는 초대장을 보내드립니다.

해설 빈칸은 be동사 are과 결합하는 분사 자리이다. 빈칸 뒤에 목적어가 있으므로 '초대장을 보내다'라는 능동적 의미를 나타내는 현재분사 (C) extending이 정답이다.

어휘 valued 소중한 extend an invitation 초대장을 보내다, 초대하다 reward 보상, 사례

8. BizAid는 비영리 단체와 협력하여 지역 사회를 지원하는 것이 임무인 단체이다.

해설 빈칸은 문장의 주격 보어 organization을 수식하는 관계사절을 이끈다. 빈칸 뒤에 완전한 문장이 오고, organization과 mission은 '조직의 임무'라는 소유 관계이므로, 소유격 관계대명사 (D) whose가 정답이다.

어휘 mission 임무, 사명 partner 제휴[협력]하다 non-profit organization 비영리 단체

9. 건축업자에 따르면 사무실 개조 비용은 10,000달러 미만이 될 것이라고 한다.

해설 빈칸은 명사를 목적어로 취하는 전치사 자리로, the building contractor와 함께 '건축업자에 따르면'이라는 의미가 자연스러우므로 전치사 (A) According to가 정답이다.

어휘 building contractor 건축업자 cost (값·비용이) ~이다[들다] instead of ~ 대신에 out of ~ 중에서

10. 다음 전략 회의에서는 유럽 시장으로의 확장을 통해 얻을 수 있는 잠재적 이점을 검토할 것이다.

해설 빈칸은 정관사 the 뒤에서 명사 benefits를 수식하는 형용사 자리이다. 문맥상 '잠재적 이점을 검토할 것이다'라는 의미가 자연스러우므로 (D) potential이 정답이다.

어휘 strategy 전략 examine 검사[검토]하다 benefit 혜택 capable (능력·특질상) ~을 할 수 있는, 유능한 motivated 의욕을 가진, 동기가 부여된 dependent 의존[의지]하는, 의존적인

11. 날씨 상황이 예측 불가능하여, 사전 통보 없이 항공편이 취소될 수 있다.

해설 빈칸은 명사구를 목적어로 취하는 전치사 자리로, 항공편 취소 원인으로 '날씨 상황이 예측 불가능하기 때문에'라는 의미를 나타내는 전치사 (B) Due to가 정답이다. 전치사 (A) as for(~에 관해서)와 (D) Despite(~에도 불구하고)는 문맥상 적합하지 않고, 부사절 접속사 (C) Now that(~ 때문에)는 뒤에 완전한 절이 온다.

어휘 unpredictable 예측할 수 없는 flight 항공편 without prior notice 사전 통보 없이

12. Keller 씨는 회사의 합병이 도움이 될 것이라고 직원들에게 확신시켰다.

해설 빈칸은 동사 자리로, 문맥상 '직원들에게 확신시켰다'라는 의미가 자연스러우므로 (B) assured가 정답이다. assure는 [assure + 사람 + that ~] '~(사람)에게 ~를 확신시키다'의 뜻으로, 목적어를 두 개를 취하는 4형식 패턴으로 자주 쓰인다.

어휘 merger 합병 benefit 유익하다, 득을 보다 observe 지키다, 준수하다 deny 부인[부정]하다 inspire 영감을 주다

13. 예산안이 승인되면 내년에 사무실이 개조될 예정이다.

해설 빈칸은 뒤에 있는 완전한 절을 이끌면서 콤마 뒤에 완전한 문장 전체를 수식하는 부사절 접속사 자리로, '만약 ~라면'이라는 의미의 부사절 접속사 (B) Provided that이 정답이다. 나머지 보기들은 모두 전치사로, 뒤에 절이 이어질 수 없다.

어휘 budget proposal 예산안 approve 승인하다 alongside of ~와 함께 in addition to ~에 덧붙여 as a result of ~의 결과로서

14. 50년 전에 설립된 Apsley House는 Barnet에서 지속적으로 운영되고 있는 가장 오래된 박물관이다.

해설 빈칸은 접속사와 주어가 생략된 분사구의 분사 자리로, 의미상 '50년 전에 설립된 ~'라는 의미가 자연스러우므로 과거분사 (C) Established가 정답이다.

어휘 continuously 계속해서, 연속적으로, 끊임없이 appear 나타나다 settle 정착하다 originate 유래하다, 발명하다

[15-18] 공지

전 직원들은 주목해 주세요.

저희는 일부 직원들이 다시 발급된 사원증을 아직 수령하지 않았다는 것을 알게 되었습니다. 만약 여러분이 아직 사원증을 찾아가지 않았지만 다음 주 전에 필요하다면, 근무 시간 내에 인사부에 방문하셔서 찾아가시길 바랍니다. 그렇지 않으면, 모든 남은 카드들은 각 부서로 다음 주 월요일에 보내질 것입니다. 그때 여러분은 사원증을 받을 수 있습니다.

또한 사원증 재발급은 첫 발급 시에는 무료로 제공되고 다음에 발급을 요청할 시에는 10달러의 발급 비용이 든다는 것을 유념해 주십시오. 사원증을 재발급 받기 전에는 또한 간단한 발급 요청서를 작성해야 합니다. 따라서 사원증을 분실하지 않도록 항상 주의하는 것이 좋습니다.

어휘 attention 주의, 주목 extra 여분의 reissue 재발급하다 remaining 남아 있는 note ~을 유의하다 consequently 결과적으로 otherwise 그렇지 않으면 in addition 게다가 missing 없어진 advisable 권할 만한, 바람직한 respective 각각의

15.

해설 빈칸은 명사구 employee ID cards를 수식하는 형용사 자리로, 빈칸이 포함된 문장만으로는 정답을 선택할 수 없다. 공지문 후반부 "Please also note that the reissuance of an ID card is provided for free upon first request only, and it will cost $10 the next time you request one"에서 사원증의 재발급이 처음에는 무료지만 다음부터 10달러의 비용이 발생한다고 한 것으로 보아, (D) reissued(재발급된)가 정답이다.

16.

해설 빈칸은 명사구를 연결하는 전치사 자리로, 접속사인 (D) while은 제외한다. 이어지는 다음 문장 "all the remaining cards will be sent to each department next Monday ~"에서 찾아 가지 않은 사원증은 다음 주 월요일에 각 부서로 보내진다고 했으므로 먼저 필요한 사람들은 '다음주 전에' 인사팀을 방문해 찾아가면 된다는 의미가 적절하다. 따라서 전치사인 (A) before가 정답이다.

17.

해설 접속부사[연결어] 문제로, 빈칸 앞뒤 문장의 관계를 확인해야 한다. 빈칸 앞 "If you have not picked yours up yet but need to it before next week, please visit the Human Resources ~"에서는 다음 주 전에 사원증이 필요한 사람은 인사부를 방문해 찾아가라고 했고, 빈칸 뒤에서는 남아 있는 사원증은 각 부서로 보내질 것이라는 대안을 설명하고 있다. 따라서 빈칸에는 (C) Otherwise(그렇지 않으면)가 정답이다.

18.

(A) 다시 말씀드리지만, 다음 주 말이 사원증을 받을 수 있는 가장 빠른 시간입니다.
(B) 분실한 신분증을 찾는 데 도움이 되기를 바랍니다.
(C) 따라서 신분증을 분실하지 않도록 항상 주의하는 것이 좋습니다.
(D) 신분증을 주인에게 돌려주는 데 협조해 주셔서 감사합니다.

해설 빈칸 앞에서 사원증 재발급 비용과 관련 서류(a brief request form)를 언급하며 주의사항에 대해 설명하고 있으므로 카드를 분실하지 말라고 권하는 내용의 (C)가 들어가는 것이 가장 적합하다.

ACTUAL TEST 6 본문 p.254

1. (B)	2. (B)	3. (A)	4. (C)	5. (C)	6. (D)
7. (C)	8. (C)	9. (C)	10. (A)	11. (C)	12. (A)
13. (A)	14. (B)	15. (C)	16. (B)	17. (C)	18. (B)

1. Christie 씨와 상담하기 전에 전체 계약서를 읽어보세요.

해설 주어 없이 please로 시작하는 명령문이므로 동사원형 (B) read 가 정답이다.

어휘 read through ~을 쭉 읽다 entire 전체의 consult 상담하다

2. Nice Service의 CEO는 직원들을 위해 설정한 엄격한 기준에 대해 종합적으로 설명했다.

해설 빈칸은 주어와 동사 사이에서 동사 explained를 수식하는 부사 자리로, 보기 중 유일한 부사 (B) comprehensively가 정답이다.

어휘 strict 엄격한 standard 기준 comprehend 이해하다 comprehensively 포괄적으로 comprehensive 포괄적인, 종합적인 comprehension 이해력

3. 뛰어난 리더십 능력을 보여주는 사람들은 승진 대상으로 고려될 것이다.

해설 빈칸은 who가 이끄는 관계절의 수식을 받는 대명사 자리로, '~하는 사람들'이라는 의미로 사용되는 지시대명사 (A) those가 정답이다.

어휘 demonstrate 증명하다, 보여주다 exceptional 뛰어난 consider 고려하다 promotion 승진

4. Electro 사는 모든 고객 불만 사항을 접수한 후 24시간 이내에 응답할 것을 약속합니다.

해설 빈칸은 동명사 receiving의 목적어 자리로, customer complaints를 대신하는 목적격 대명사 (C) them이 정답이다.

어휘 respond to ~에 답하다 customer complaint 고객 불만

5. Gurus 씨와는 달리 Cook 씨는 이사회가 제안한 확장 전략에 반대표를 던졌다.

해설 빈칸은 Mr. Gurus를 목적어로 취하는 전치사 자리이다. 보기 중 유일한 전치사로, '~와 달리'라는 의미의 (C) Unlike가 정답이다. (A) Unless(만약 ~하지 않으면)는 접속사, (B) Moreover(게다가)는 부사, (D) opposed(반대하는)는 형용사이다.

어휘 vote against ~에 반대 투표를 하다 expansion strategy 확장 전략

정답과 해설

6. Smith 박사는 연구 자금 부족으로 프로젝트를 계속할 수 없었다.

해설 빈칸은 전치사 because of의 목적어 자리이다. 의미상 프로젝트를 지속하지 못한 이유로 '연구 자금 부족'이 자연스러우므로 (D) shortage(부족, 결핍)가 정답이다.

어휘 research fund 연구 자금 supply 공급 direction 감독, 관리

7. River Road의 포장 작업이 완료될 때까지 운전자들은 Mary Street를 이용하여 시내로 이동하도록 안내된다.

해설 빈칸은 주절의 동사 자리로, 주어 drivers와 수 일치가 맞지 않는 (B) directs는 오답이다. direct는 '(길을) 안내하다'라는 뜻으로, '운전자들은 Mary Street를 이용하도록 안내받다'라는 수동의 의미가 적절하다. 따라서 수동태인 (C) are directed가 정답이다.

어휘 paving work 포장 공사 downtown 시내로 direct (길을) 안내하다[알려 주다]

8. 건축과 경치가 아름다운 이 지역은 연간 50만 명 이상의 방문객을 끌어들인다.

해설 빈칸은 동사 자리로, 주어는 the region이다. 동사가 될 수 없는 현재분사 (B) attracting과 복수 동사 (A) attract는 오답이다. annually(매년)는 반복적인 사실을 나타내므로 현재 시제인 (C) attracts와 어울린다.

어휘 architectural 건축상의 scenic 경치의, 경치가 좋은

9. 금융 컨설팅 회사를 설립하기 전에 Moore 씨는 은행 업계에서 10년 이상 근무했다.

해설 빈칸은 전치사 Prior to의 목적어 자리로, her financial consulting company를 목적어로 취하면서 명사 역할을 할 수 있는 동명사 (C) launching이 정답이다.

어휘 prior to ~이전에 banking industry 은행 업계 launch 시작[개시/착수]하다

10. 수정된 예산이 승인될 때까지 구인 공고 게재하는 것을 기다려 주세요.

해설 빈칸은 명사 budget을 수식하는 형용사 자리로, '수정된 예산'이라는 수동적 의미를 나타내는 과거분사 (A) revised가 정답이다.

어휘 post 게시하다 budget 예산 approve 승인하다

11. Kelly 씨는 올해 의료 기술 컨퍼런스에서 발표하게 되어 기쁘다고 말했다.

해설 빈칸은 be동사 뒤의 주격 보어 자리이다. 주어인 사람 명사 he는 감정을 느끼는 대상이므로 과거분사 (C) delighted가 정답이다. 형용사 (B) delightful은 사람의 감정이 아니라 사물이나 상황을 묘사할 때 쓴다.

어휘 give a presentation 발표하다 be delighted to ~해서 기쁘다

12. 이 레스토랑은 해변이 보이는 멋진 전망은 아니었지만 훌륭한 음식은 방문할 만한 가치가 충분했다.

해설 빈칸은 뒤에 있는 완전한 절을 이끌면서 콤마 뒤의 완전한 문장 전체를 수식하는 부사절 접속사 자리이다. 멋진 해변의 전망은 아니지만 음식이 훌륭했다는 대조적인 상황을 연결해주는 양보 부사절 접속사 (A) Although(비록 ~일지라도)가 정답이다. (B) Within (~이내에)는 전치사, (C) Therefore(그러므로)와 (D) However (그러나)는 접속부사이다.

어휘 spectacular 화려한, 장관인 well worth 가치가 충분한

13. 기술 지원 직원들은 귀하의 컴퓨터에 문제가 있는 경우 도움을 주기 위해 24시간 대기하고 있습니다.

해설 빈칸 앞 to부정사의 동사 어휘 문제로, 의미상 문제가 생겼을 경우 '기술 지원 담당자들이 도움을 주기 위해' 대기하고 있다는 내용이 자연스러우므로 (A) assist가 정답이다.

어휘 personnel (전)직원 assist 돕다 lend 빌리다

14. Fab Café는 평일 야간 근무조를 감독할 보조 관리자를 찾고 있다.

해설 빈칸은 to부정사 to oversee의 목적어 자리이다. 명사 evening과 결합하여 '저녁 근무조'라는 뜻의 복합 명사를 이루는 (B) shift가 정답이다.

어휘 look for ~를 찾다 oversee 감독하다, 관리하다 on weekdays 주중에

[15-18] 회람

발신: Howard Lee, Production Supervisor
수신: 모든 공장 직원들
날짜: 3월 25일
제목: 임원 방문 알림

이미 아시다시피 Rian Automotive 사의 임원인 Barrett 씨가 다음 주 금요일에 우리의 사기를 북돋우기 위해 제조 공장을 연례 방문할 예정입니다.

이에 따라, 모든 직원은 금요일 오후 6시까지 세미나실에 모일 것을 권고합니다. 야간 근무를 배정받은 사람도 참여해야 합니다.

임원의 간단한 격려사 후 식당에서 연회가 열릴 것입니다. 또한 올해 방문은 5일 연기된 것이며, 다음 방문은 내년 3월 20일로 예정되어 있음을 안내드립니다.

다음 주 금요일 세미나실에서 뵙겠습니다.

어휘 executive 간부 임원 boost 북돋우다 morale 사기, 의욕 accordingly 따라서 brief 간단한 banquet 연회 informal 비공식적인 annual 연례의, 매년의 abrupt 갑작스러운 accommodate 수용하다 participant 참가자 be supposed to V ~하기로 되어 있다 assign 맡기다, 배정하다 self-development 자기 개발 farewell 작별 encouragement 격려 gratitude 고마움

15.

해설 형용사 어휘 문제로, 회람의 끝 부분 "Please also note that this year's visit has been delayed by 5 days, and the next visit is scheduled for March 20 next year"에서 임원의 방문이 매년 있는 계획된 방문임을 추론할 수 있으므로 (C) annual이 정답이다.

16.

해설 빈칸은 동사 자리로, 주어인 all employees는 복수이므로 보기 중 주어와 수 일치가 맞는 복수 동사 (B) are advised가 정답이다.

17.

(A) 회의실은 모든 참가자를 수용할 수 없습니다.
(B) 당신은 세미나실에서 문제를 논의해야 합니다.
(C) 야간 근무를 배정받은 사람도 참여해야 합니다.
(D) 자기 개발에 관한 강의가 진행될 것입니다.

해설 빈칸 앞 문장 "all employees are advised to gather in the seminar room by 6:00 P.M. on Friday"에서 모든 직원들에게 금요일 오후 6시까지 세미나실에 모이라고 했으므로, 덧붙여 야간 근무하는 직원들도 참여해야 한다는 내용의 (C)가 적합하다. (A)와 (B)는 세미나실을 언급했으나, 글의 전체 흐름에서 보면 적합하지 않은 내용이다.

18.

해설 명사 어휘 문제로, 첫 번째 문장 "Mr. Barrett, an executive at Rian Automotive, will make his ~ visit to the manufacturing plant to boost our morale ~"에서 임원이 직원의 사기를 올리기 위해 공장을 방문한다고 언급했다. 따라서 '임원의 간략한 격려사'가 있을 것이라는 내용을 완성하는 (B) encouragement(격려, 고무)가 정답이다.

ACTUAL TEST 7 본문 p.256

1. (D)	**2.** (B)	**3.** (C)	**4.** (B)	**5.** (D)	**6.** (C)
7. (C)	**8.** (B)	**9.** (C)	**10.** (D)	**11.** (D)	**12.** (A)
13. (B)	**14.** (B)	**15.** (D)	**16.** (D)	**17.** (C)	**18.** (D)

1. 많은 분석가들이 우리의 신제품들이 시장에서 성공할 것이라고 확신한다.

해설 빈칸은 조동사 다음 동사원형 자리이므로 (D) succeed가 정답이다.

어휘 analyst 분석가 success 성공 successor 계승자, 후계자 successive 연속적인 succeed (in) 성공하다

2. 전국에 있는 저희 창고는 다양한 신제품들로 채워져 있습니다.

해설 빈칸은 전치사의 목적어 자리이자 관사 a 다음 명사 자리로, 보기 중 유일한 명사인 (B) variety가 정답이다.

어휘 warehouse 창고 be stocked 채워져 있다 vary 변하다, 달라지다 variety 다양성 various 다양한

3. 구매일로부터 7일 이내에는 전액 환불을 받으실 수 있습니다.

해설 빈칸은 전치사 of의 목적어인 명사 purchase를 수식하는 형용사 자리로, 소유격 대명사 (C) your가 정답이다.

어휘 entitle 권리[자격]을 주다 full refund 전액 환불 purchase 구매

4. 100달러 이상 구매하는 모든 고객들은 사은품을 받은 자격이 있다.

해설 빈칸은 명사 customer를 수식하는 형용사 자리로, 단수 가산 명사와 어울려 함께 쓰이는 (B) Every가 정답이다. (A) All은 가산 명사의 복수형 또는 불가산 명사와 함께 쓰이고 (C) A few는 가산 명사의 복수형과 쓰인다. (D) Little은 불가산 명사와 함께 쓰인다.

어휘 be eligible to ~할 자격이 있다

5. Social Media 33은 마케팅 업계에서 전도유망한 회사로 잘 알려져 있다.

해설 빈칸은 관사 a 뒤에서 명사 firm(회사)를 수식하는 형용사 자리로, (D) promising(유망한, 촉망되는)이 정답이다.

어휘 be well known as ~로 잘 알려져 있다

6. 다른 의견이 있으시면, 주저하지 말고 의견을 남겨주세요.

해설 빈칸은 조동사 do 다음 동사원형 자리로, (C) hesitate가 정답이다. 시험에 자주 출제되는 'do not hesitate to(주저하지 말고 ~하다)'를 묶어서 외워두자.

어휘 leave 남기다 comment 의견 hesitant 주저하는, 자신 없는 hesitate 망설이다, 주저하다

7. Mary Somerville 씨는 2020년에 Smart Media 사의 신임 사장으로 임명되었다.

해설 빈칸은 동사 자리로, '신임 사장으로 임명되다'라는 의미를 나타내는 수동태 표현이 필요하다. 보기 중 수동태 표현인 (C) was appointed와 (D) will be appointing 중에 문장 끝에 과거 시점 표현 in 2020이 있으므로 과거 시제인 (C) was appointed가 정답이다.

어휘 be appointed ~로 임명되다

8. 저희는 마케팅 전략에 대한 광범위한 지식을 지닌 분을 찾고 있습니다.

해설 빈칸은 관계사절의 주어 역할을 하면서 선행사 someone을 수식하는 관계대명사 자리로, 주격 관계대명사 (B) who가 정답이다.

어휘 look for ~을 찾다 extensive 광범위한 marketing strategy 마케팅 전략

9. 예측할 수 없는 날씨 때문에, 사전 공지 없이 비행편이 취소될 수 있다.

해설 빈칸은 명사 prior notice를 목적어로 취하는 전치사 자리로, 문맥상 (C) without이 정답이다.

어휘 unpredictable 예측할 수 없는, 예측이 불가능한 prior notice 사전 통보 besides ~ 외에

10. 전 직원은 교육 프로그램 중 적어도 한 개는 등록하도록 요구된다.

해설 빈칸은 to부정사의 동사원형 자리로, 빈칸 뒤 전치사 in과 어울려 '등록하다'의 의미를 완성하는 자동사 (D) enroll이 정답이다. (B) register도 같은 의미의 자동사이긴 하지만 전치사 for와 어울리며, (A) attend과 (C) sign은 타동사이다.

어휘 at least 최소한, 적어도 register for ~에 등록하다 sign 서명하다

11. 우리는 고객들이 적절한 아파트를 선택하는 동안 그들이 예산 범위를 유지할 수 있도록 도와준다.

해설 빈칸 이하는 접속사 while이 생략되지 않은 분사 구문이다. 분사구문의 생략된 주어 clients(they)가 목적어 the right apartment를 '선택하다'라는 능동적 의미를 나타내고 있으므로 현재분사 (D) choosing이 정답이다.

어휘 remain within a budget 예산의 범위를 유지하다 right 알맞은 choose 선택하다 choice 선택

12. Giant Food Stores의 이사는 회사 로고의 약간의 변경이라도 반대한다.

해설 빈칸은 2형식 동사(remain)의 보어 자리로, 뒤에 온 명사구(any changes)와 어울려 의미상 '약간의 변경이라도 반대한다'가 적절하다. 따라서 (A) opposed가 정답이다. (B) anxious와 (C) eager는 뒤에 오는 전치사로 각각 about과 for를 쓴다.

어휘 managing director 관리 이사 opposed to ~에 반대하는 anxious 불안해하는, 염려하는 eager 열렬한, 간절히 바라는 interfere 간섭하다

13. Global Partners는 입사 지원서를 1년 동안 보관합니다.

해설 빈칸은 전치사의 목적어 자리로, '입사 지원서는 1년 동안 보관됩니다'라는 문맥이 자연스러우므로 명사 (B) period(기간, 시기)가 정답이다.

어휘 application 신청[서], 지원[서] on file 정리[기록] 보관되어 calendar 달력 capacity 수용력, 역량 section 부분, 구획

14. 수화물에 3일 이상 분실 상태인 경우 저희 웹사이트를 방문하셔서 자세한 지침을 확인하시기 바랍니다.

해설 빈칸 뒤 주어 your luggage와 동사 remain이 도치되었고, 주절이 명령문이므로 가정법 미래가 사용된 문장이다. 따라서 조동사 (B) Should가 정답이다.

어휘 luggage 짐 instructions 지침

[15-18] 이메일

날짜: 12월 3일
제목: 객실 무료 업그레이드

Wilson 씨에게,

Bell Savage Inn의 단골손님이 돼 주셔서 감사합니다. 이 편지는 귀하가 다음 방문 시에 무료로 객실 업그레이드를 받을 자격이 있다는 것을 알리기 위한 것입니다. 아래의 상세 정보를 확인하여 이 절호의 기회를 놓치지 마세요.

무료 객실 업그레이드는 디럭스 룸 또는 더 큰 객실일 때 가능합니다. 디럭스 룸을 예약하시면 객실이 스위트 룸 또는 비즈니스 룸으로 업그레이드됩니다.

이 제안에 관심이 있으시면 첨부된 양식을 작성하여 월말까지 보내주십시오.

저희는 곧 귀하를 뵐 수 있기를 고대하고 있으며, 귀하가 업그레이드된 객실에서 좋은 시간을 가지기를 바랍니다.

어휘 regular customer 단골손님 inform 알리다 deluxe 고급의, 호화스러운 fill out 작성하다 attach 붙이다, 첨부하다 be eligible to ~할 자격이 있다 acceptable 받아들일 수 있는 suitable 적합한 rate 요금 renovate 개보수하다 spectacular 장관을 이루는 miss out on ~을 놓치다 reserve 예약하다 browse 둘러보다

15.

해설 형용사 어휘 문제로, 빈칸 앞 문장 "Thank you for being a regular guest ~"에서 단골 고객이 된 것에 대해 감사의 뜻을 전하고 있으므로 문맥상 '다음에 방문할 때 추가 비용 없이 방을 업그레이드할 자격이 있다'고 혜택을 설명하는 것이 적절하다. 따라서 (D) eligible이 정답이다.

16.

(A) 다음 달부터 요금이 인상될 것임을 유념하세요.
(B) 식사 공간이 개조되어 곧 재개장할 예정입니다.
(C) 저희 호텔은 East Lyn River의 멋진 전망으로 유명합니다.
(D) 아래의 상세 정보를 확인하여 이 절호의 기회를 놓치지 마세요.

해설 빈칸 앞 "This letter is to inform you that you are eligible to get a room upgrade at no cost on your next visit"에서 편지를 쓴 목적이 객실 무료 업그레이드에 대해 알리기 위한 것이라고 했고, 빈칸 뒤에서 무료 업그레이드를 받는 방법을 설명하고 있다. 따라서 아래의 정보를 언급하며 무료 혜택 이용을 권장하는 내용의 (D)가 적절하다.

17.

해설 빈칸 앞 "The free room upgrade is available if you get a deluxe room or something bigger"에서 무료 업그레이드는 디럭스 룸부터 가능하다고 했다. 따라서 '디럭스 룸을 예약하면 스위트 룸이나 비즈니스 룸으로 업그레이드 가능하다'는 의미를 완성하는 (C)가 정답이다.

18.

해설 빈칸은 부사절 접속사 if가 이끄는 조건 부사절의 동사 자리로, 주어인 you와 수 일치가 맞지 않는 단수형 (C) interest는 오답이다. 동사 interest는 '~에게 흥미를 일으키게 하다, 관심을 갖게 하다'라는 의미로, 능동태로 쓰이면 뒤에 목적어(사람)가 와야 한다. 그러나 빈칸 뒤에 사람 목적어가 없으므로 수동태 표현 중에 답을 골라야 한다. 주절(please ~)이 미래 시제나 명령문일 때 조건 부사절에서는 현재 시제가 미래 시제를 대신하므로 (D) are interested가 정답이다.

ACTUAL TEST 8 본문 p.258

1. (D)	2. (C)	3. (B)	4. (D)	5. (C)	6. (B)
7. (D)	8. (B)	9. (A)	10. (D)	11. (D)	12. (A)
13. (A)	14. (B)	15. (C)	16. (D)	17. (D)	18. (A)

1. 웹 사이트에서 등록 양식을 작성하거나 고객 서비스 전화 708-555-0115에 전화하여 도움을 받으십시오.

해설 빈칸은 전치사(for)의 목적어 자리로, 보기 중 명사인 (A) assistants(조수)와 (D) assistance(도움) 중 의미상 어울리는 명사를 선택한다. '도움을 위해 전화하라'가 어울리므로 추상 명사 (D)가 정답이다.

어휘 simply 간단히 enrollment form 등록 양식 assistant 조수, 보조원 assist 돕다, 보조하다 assistance 보조, 도움

2. 시판 중인 몇몇의 경쟁력 있는 제품을 살펴본 후, Crates 씨는 우리 제품 중 하나를 사기로 결정했다.

해설 빈칸은 전치사(of)의 목적어 자리로, 형용사 역할을 하는 소유격 대명사 (B) our는 오답이다. 목적격 대명사 (A) us, 소유대명사 (C) ours, 재귀대명사 (D) ourselves 중 문맥상 '우리의 제품들(our products) 중 하나를 구매하다'가 적합하므로 our products를 대신하는 소유대명사 (C) ours가 정답이다.

어휘 examine ~을 점검하다 competitive 경쟁력 있는 on the market 시중에 나와 있는

3. Sarek 공원의 산책로 유지 보수는 여러 단체로부터의 상당한 기부금 덕분에 가능하게 되었다.

해설 산책로 유지 보수가 기부금 덕분에 '가능해졌다'는 의미가 어울리므로 (B) possible가 정답이다.

어휘 maintenance 유지 보수 walk 산책로 thanks to ~덕분에 substantial 상당한 clear 알아듣기[보기] 쉬운, 분명한 possible 가능한 generous 후한, 관대한 honorary (학위·지위 등이) 명예의

4. PCL Electronics 사의 정책에 따르면, 직원들은 최소 한 달 전에 휴가를 정식으로 신청해야 한다.

해설 조동사와 동사원형 사이에 위치하여 동사를 수식하는 부사 자리로, 보기 중 유일한 부사 (D) formally(공식적으로)가 정답이다.

어휘 according to ~에 따르면 policy 정책 vacation time 휴가 at least 최소한 in advance 미리 formal 공식적인 formality 형식상의 절차 formalize 공식화하다

5. 20개국 이상에서 온 500명이 넘는 사람들이 제3회 국제 환경 포럼에 참석했다.

해설 보기가 모두 전치사이므로 해석이 필요하다. '20개국 이상에서 온 500명 이상의 사람들'이 문맥상 적절하므로 '~로부터'라는 의미의 (C) from이 정답이다.

어휘 more than ~이상 over ~이상 participate in ~에 참석하다

6. 아리조나 관광청은 컨벤션 센터 개장이 도시에서 수백 개의 일자리를 창출할 것이라고 보고했다.

해설 빈칸은 조동사 will 뒤의 동사원형 자리로, 문맥상 컨벤션 센터가 열리면 '일자리가 창출되는' 것이 적절하므로 (B) create가 적절하다.

어휘 Tourism Authority 관광청 agree 동의하다 create 만들다, 창출하다 refer 언급하다, 참조하다

7. The National Olive 극장은 Redwood에서 가장 소중한 역사적인 명소 중 하나이며 보존되어야 한다.

해설 빈칸은 to부정사를 목적어로 취하는 타동사 need의 목적어 자리로, (B) to preserve와 (D) to be preserved 중에서 답을 골라야 한다. 빈칸 뒤에 목적어가 없으며, 극장은 '보존되는 것'이므로 수동형인 (D)가 정답이다.

어휘 treasure 대단히 귀하게 여기다 historic 역사적인 landmark 주요 지형지물, 랜드마크 preserve 보존하다

8. 영업 부서가 승인을 받자마자 영업 사원을 추가 모집하기 시작했다.

해설 빈칸은 주절의 동사 자리로, 부사절에서 과거 시제 received를 사용했으므로 문맥상 과거 시제 동사인 (B) began이 정답이다. 현재완료 시제 (A) has begun은 '승인을 받자마자'라는 특정 시점과 어울려 쓸 수 없고, (C) were beginning과 (D) begin은 주어 the team과 수 일치하지 않으므로 오답이다.

어휘 as soon as ~하자마자 approval 승인 recruit 뽑다, 선출하다 additional 추가의 sales clerk 영업 사원

9. 인상적인 공연 후, 관객들은 간단한 설문 조사를 위해 머물러 달라는 요청을 받았다.

해설 빈칸 앞에는 be동사가, 빈칸 뒤에는 to부정사가 있으므로 연결되는 숙어 표현이 있는지 보기를 먼저 살펴본다. be asked to V가 '~하도록 요청받다'라는 뜻의 숙어 표현으로, 문맥상 '간단한 설문

조사를 위해 머물러 달라고 요청받았다'가 되어 적절하다. 따라서 (A)가 정답이 된다.

어휘 impressive 인상적인 performance 공연 continue 계속되다 depend 의존하다 accomplish 성취하다

10. 정부는 계속되는 실업 문제를 해결할 방법을 찾기 위해 보다 지속적인 노력을 기울여왔다.

해설 빈칸 앞에는 관사 a, 뒤에는 명사 effort가 있으므로 빈칸은 명사를 수식하는 형용사 자리이다. 문맥상 '지속적인 노력을 기울이다'가 어울리므로 (D) lasting가 정답이 된다. 동사 last는 자동사이므로 명사를 수식하는 과거분사 (C) lasted는 답이 될 수 없다.

어휘 last 지난, 지속하다 lastly 마지막으로 lasting 지속적인 effort 노력 continuing 계속되는 unemployment 실업

11. 문제가 있는 제품은 교환하거나, 구매 가격의 전액을 환불받을 수 있다.

해설 빈칸은 문장과 문장을 연결하는 접속사 자리이다. (A) nor는 앞 문장이 부정문이 되어야 하므로 오답이며, (C) instead of는 전치사이므로 오답이다. 접속사인 (B) but과 (D) or 중 문맥상 '문제가 있는 제품은 교환하거나 환불받을 수 있다'가 적절하므로 등위 접속사 (D)가 정답이다.

어휘 replace 교체하다 fully 완전히 refund 환불하다 original 원래의, 처음의 purchase 구매

12. Wang 씨가 파리 본사로 전근을 가서 새로운 매니저가 홍콩 사무실을 책임지고 있다.

해설 빈칸은 두 문장을 연결하는 접속사 자리이다. (B) In case of (~인 경우에)는 전치사, (D) Furthermore(더욱이)는 접속부사이므로 오답이다. 따라서 보기 중 접속사인 (A) Now that(~ 때문에)과 (C) Considering that(~라는 점을 고려해 보면) 중 'Wang 씨가 파리 본사로 전근을 가서 새로운 매니저가 홍콩 사무실을 맡고 있다'는 인과 관계가 문맥상 적합하므로 (A)가 정답이다.

어휘 transfer 이동하다, 전근 가다 headquarters 본사 be responsible for ~을 책임지다

13. CEO는 고객의 문제를 지속적으로 해결하는 것이 회사의 성공을 위한 중요한 요소 중 하나라고 말했다.

해설 동사 stated의 목적어가 완전한 형태이므로 빈칸은 명사절 접속사 자리이다. 따라서 (A) that이 정답이다. 불완전 문장과 결합하는 (B) what과 (C) who는 오답이고, (D) which는 선행사가 필요하므로 오답이다.

어휘 state 말하다 address 처리하다 consistently 일관되게 crucial 결정적인, 중대한 element 요소

14. 실험실 매뉴얼은 가능한 한 안전하게 재료를 다루기 위한 절차를 자세히 설명한다.

해설 as ~ as 사이에는 형용사/부사의 원급이 들어가므로 (B) safely

와 (C) safe 중 하나를 골라야 한다. as ~ as를 뺀 문장 구조가 완전하므로 부사인 (B) safely가 정답이다.

어휘 detail 상세히 알리다(열거하다) handle 다루다 safety 안전 safely 안전하게 safe 안전한 safest 가장 안전한

[15-18] 회람

수신: 전 직원
발신: Tom Clift, 경영진
날짜: 8월 7일
제목: 퇴직 파티에 대한 의견

직원들에게,

Catalyst Pharmaceuticals 사에서의 마지막 날인 Garcia 씨를 위한 지난 은퇴 파티를 멋지게 준비해 주신 모든 분들께 감사드립니다. 그는 진심으로 파티를 즐겼으며 잊지 못할 순간들로 가득 찬 하루를 만들어준 여러분 모두에게 고마워했습니다.

Garcia 씨는 매우 열정적이고 부지런한 사람이었습니다. 그의 헌신이 없었다면 회사는 지금의 위치에 도달할 수 없었을 것입니다. 그는 30년 동안 영업부장으로 회사에 성실히 봉사했습니다. Catalyst Pharmaceuticals 사는 그의 봉사와 공헌을 항상 기억할 것입니다.

Garcia 씨는 회사를 떠났지만, 그의 정신은 여기에 남아 있을 것입니다. 우리가 우수성을 위해 노력하는 동안 그가 Catalyst Pharmaceuticals 사를 지속적으로 지원하도록 성원합시다.

어휘 retirement party 은퇴식 unforgettable 잊을 수 없는 passionate 열정적인 dedication 헌신 contribution 기여 remain 남다 strive to ~을 얻으려고 노력하다 upcoming 다가오는 ultimate 궁극적인, 최후의 preferably 오히려, 가급적 gradually 서서히 truly 정말로, 진심으로 farewell 작별 resume 다시 시작하다

15.

해설 빈칸 다음 문장에서 Garcia 씨가 은퇴 파티를 즐겼고, 고마움을 전했다고 했으므로 은퇴 파티는 이미 과거의 사실이라는 것을 알 수 있다. 따라서 (C) past가 정답이다.

16.

해설 빈칸 뒤에서 Garcia 씨가 잊을 수 없는 순간으로 가득한 날(the day filled with unforgettable moments)이었다고 말한 것으로 보아, 그가 진심으로 파티를 즐겼음을 알 수 있다. 따라서 (D) truly가 정답이다.

17.

(A) 그의 협조 덕분에 우리의 협력 관계를 연장할 수 있을 것 같습니다.

(B) 그러므로 모두가 은퇴 파티에 참석하여 작별 인사를 하시기를 바랍니다.

(C) 그는 여기서 일을 재개할 때까지 오랜 기간 동안 일을 쉴 것입니다.

(D) 그는 30년 동안 영업부장으로 회사에 성실히 봉사했습니다.

해설 빈칸 앞 "Mr. Garcia was a very passionate and diligent man, and without his dedication, the company would not have been able to get to where it is now"에서 Garcia 씨의 헌신 없이 회사가 지금의 위치에 있지 못했을 것이라는 내용과 빈칸 뒤 그의 봉사와 공헌(his service and contributions)을 언급한 것으로 보아, 그가 오랜 기간 회사를 위해서 성실히 일했다는 (D)가 가장 적절하다.

18.

해설 은퇴 파티가 열린 것은 과거의 일이므로 Garcia 씨는 이미 회사를 떠났고 현재 회사에 없는 상태를 나타내는 현재완료 시제 (A) has left가 정답이다.

ACTUAL TEST 9   본문 p.260

1. (C)	2. (B)	3. (C)	4. (A)	5. (C)	6. (B)
7. (C)	8. (C)	9. (C)	10. (A)	11. (B)	12. (C)
13. (D)	14. (B)	15. (A)	16. (D)	17. (B)	18. (A)

1. KG Electronics는 생산 비용을 절감하기 위해 인력 수요를 줄여줄 최신식 조립 기계 설비를 구입했다.

해설 빈칸은 to부정사의 목적어 자리이다. 인력 수요를 줄여줄 최신 설비를 구매한 이유로, '생산 비용' 절감이 자연스러우므로 복합 명사 production costs를 완성하는 (C)가 정답이다.

어휘 state-of-the-art 최신식의 assembly 조립 reduce 줄이다 human labor 노동력 value 가치 profit 이익 cost 비용 outcome 성과

2. Oak Office Furniture의 사장은 다른 사람들의 사무실 디자인 요구를 돕는 일을 즐기는 영업 사원을 고용한다.

해설 빈칸은 동명사 helping의 목적어 자리로, 문맥상 정해진 수나 범위가 아닌 막연하게 다른 사람들을 의미하므로 (B) others가 정답이다.

어휘 hire 고용하다 salespeople 영업 사원 needs 필요성, 수요

3. 제조팀이 제품을 만들기 전에 우리는 고객이 받아들일 수 있는 견본인지 확실히 해야 한다.

해설 빈칸 앞에 is, 빈칸 뒤에 전치사 to가 있으므로 빈칸은 형용사 보어 자리이다. 따라서 형용사 (C) acceptable이 정답이 된다. 과거분사 (B) accepting은 is와 결합하여 능동태가 되고, 빈칸 뒤에 목적어가 없으므로 오답이다.

어휘 manufacturing 제조 be certain ~를 확신하다 prototype 견본 accept 받아들이다 acceptable 용인되는, 받아들여지는 acceptance 받아들임(수락)

4. Better Furniture의 연례 회의가 여러 관련 부서의 협력 덕분에 순조롭게 진행됐다.

해설 빈칸은 동사 went를 수식하는 부사 자리이다. went는 go의 과거형으로, '(일의 진행이 어떻게) 되다'라는 의미이다. 따라서 문맥상 관련 부서의 협력 덕분에 '행사가 순조롭게 진행됐다'가 적절하므로 (A) smoothly가 정답이다.

어휘 annual meeting 연례 회의 thanks to ~ 덕분에 various 다양한 involved 관련된 entirely 전적으로 justly 정당하게 tightly 단단히, 꽉

5. 최근 설문에 따르면, 그 지역의 부동산 가격이 작년에 15%까지 올랐다.

해설 빈칸은 명사구 the recent survey를 목적어로 취하는 전치사 자리이다. (B) Whether(~인지 아닌지)는 접속사이므로 오답이다. 나머지 보기 (A) Instead of(~대신에), (C) According to(~에 따르면), (D) Upon(~하자마자) 모두 전치사로 쓰일 수 있으니 해석이 필요하다. 문맥상 '최근 조사에 따르면'이라는 의미가 가장 적합하므로 (C)가 정답이다.

어휘 recent 최근의 property 부동산 rise 오르다

6. 제조 과정 중 원자재의 과도한 낭비는 Pepsico Industries 사의 이윤을 하락하게 만들었다.

해설 문장에 동사가 없으므로 빈칸은 동사 자리이다. 따라서 동사가 아닌 (D) to have caused는 오답이다. 문장의 주어 Excessive waste는 단수이므로 주어와 수 일치가 되는 단수형인 (B) has caused가 정답이다.

어휘 excessive 과도한, 지나친 waste 낭비, 허비 raw material 원자재 cause ~을 야기하다, 초래하다 decline 하락하다

7. 저희 여름 카탈로그에서 주문하신 책이 절판되었음을 알려드립니다.

해설 주어가 생략된 명령문의 형태로, 빈칸은 be동사와 결합하여 동사 역할을 할 수 있는 형용사나 분사 자리이다. 동사 advise는 <Please be advised that ~>의 형태로 '~을 알려드립니다'라는 뜻으로 자주 쓰인다. 따라서 과거분사 (C)가 정답이다.

어휘 catalog 목록, 카탈로그 no longer 더 이상 ~아니다 in print 아직도 출간되는, 인쇄된

8. 사장은 Gruber 씨에게 사무실 운영비를 줄일 수 있는 가능한 모든 방법들을 조사하라고 요청했다.

해설 빈칸은 문장의 목적어인 that절의 동사 자리이다. 주절의 동사가 요청의 의미인 request이므로 that절의 동사는 주어의 수와 관계없이 <(should) + 동사원형>의 형태가 와야 한다. 따라서 동사원형 (C) investigate가 정답이다.

어휘 request 요청하다 reduce 줄이다 operating cost 운영비 investigate 조사하다

9. Haselton 씨는 매우 적합해서 그녀를 DHL Chemicals 사의 그 자리에 추천하는 데 문제가 없다.

해설 문장이 <have no problem V-ing>의 형태로, 빈칸은 동명사 자리이므로 (C) recommending이 정답이다.

어휘 highly 매우 qualified 자격을 갖춘 recommend 추천하다 have no problem -ing ~하는 데 문제가 없다

10. 제안된 발의안은 외곽의 교외에 거주하는 통근자들을 위한 대중 교통을 제공하는 것을 목표로 한다.

해설 빈칸 앞에는 관사 The, 뒤에는 명사 initiative가 있으므로 빈 칸은 명사를 수식하는 형용사 자리이다. 보기 중 형용사는 (A) proposed(제안된)과 (B) proposing(제안하는)이며, 문맥 상 initiative(발의안)은 '제안되는' 대상이므로 과거분사 (A) proposed가 정답이다.

어휘 initiative 국민[주민] 발의 aim to ~를 목표로 하다 commuter 통근자 suburbs 교외

11. Toray Group Holdings는 남미 지역으로 확장할 계획이라고 보도 자료에서 발표했다.

해설 빈칸은 타동사 announced의 목적어 역할을 하면서 빈칸 뒤의 완전한 문장을 이끄는 명사절 접속사 자리이다. 따라서 (B) that 이 정답이다.

어휘 announce 발표하다 press release 공식 발표[성명] be planning to V ~할 계획이다 expand into ~로 확장하다

12. 1,000달러 이상의 구매는 배송료가 면제되지만, 부가 가치세는 여전히 적용된다.

해설 빈칸은 문장과 문장을 연결하는 접속사 자리이다. (A) However 와 (D) Nonetheless는 부사이므로 오답이다. 앞 문장은 '1,000 달러 이상 구매 시 배송료가 면제된다'는 내용이고, 뒤의 문장 은 '여전히 부가가치세는 적용된다'는 내용이므로 접속사 (B) Because(~때문에)와 (C) Although(~에도 불구하고) 중 문맥 상 (C)가 적절하다.

어휘 exempt 면제되는 shipping charge 배송료 value added taxes(= VAT) 부가 가치세 apply 적용하다

13. 두 회사가 가장 큰 식품 제조업체가 되기 위해 합병을 할 건지는 여전히 두고 볼 문제다.

해설 빈칸부터 or not까지가 문장의 주어이고, remains가 문장의 동사이므로 빈칸은 명사절 접속사 자리이다. 명사절 접속사인 whether가 or not과 함께 '~인지 아닌지'라는 의미로 쓰이므로 (D)가 정답이다.

어휘 merge 합병하다 manufacturer 제조업체 remain to be seen 두고 볼 일이다

14. Gottlieb Steen Industries는 새로운 시설을 구매하기보다는 생산 현장을 확장할 것이다.

해설 빈칸은 접속사 자리로, 보기 중 유일하게 접속사 역할을 할 수 있는 (B) rather than(~보다는)이 정답이다. 참고로 would rather A than B = A rather than B 'B할 바에 차라리 A하다'의 비교급 형 태의 표현을 암기해 두자. (A) at first와 (D) for instance는 부사 이고, (C) with reference to는 전치사이다.

어휘 production floor 생산 작업장 facility 시설 at first 처음에 rather than ~라기보다는 오히려 with reference to ~에 관하여 for instance 예를 들면

[15-18] 공지

Technova Solutions에서는 직원의 안전을 중요하게 생각합니다. 악천후가 예상되는 경우에는 그 상황을 면밀히 감시합니다. 상황이 잠재적으로 위험 이 예상되는 상황일 경우 사무실이 폐쇄될 수 있습니다.

교대근무 감독자는 팀 구성원에게 폐쇄를 전달할 책임이 있습니다. <u>모든 직 원이 메시지를 받을 수 있도록 총력을 기울일 것입니다.</u> 직원은 폐쇄 기간 동 안 근무하기로 예정된 모든 시간에 대해 기본 급여를 받게 됩니다. 회사가 다 시 문을 열면 그들은 예정된 다음 교대 근무를 위해 직장으로 복귀해야 합니 다. 회사 폐쇄에 관해 질문이 있는 경우 감독자에게 문의하십시오.

어휘 seriously 심각하게, 진지하게 severe 험한, 극심한 potentially 잠재적으로 hazardous 위험한 closure 폐쇄 shift 교대 근무(시간) be responsible for ~을 책임지다 regular pay 기본급, 정규 임금 satisfaction 만족 compensation 보상 predict 예상하다 under review 검토 중인 ensure 반드시 ~하게 하다, 보장하다

15.

해설 빈칸 앞 employee와 문맥상 어울리는 명사를 선택하는 어휘 문 제이다. 빈칸 뒤 "When severe weather is expected, we monitor the event closely. If conditions are expected to become potentially hazardous, an office closure may be necessary"에서 날씨가 안 좋은 경우 상황을 면밀히 감시하고, 위험성이 있는 경우 사무실 폐쇄한다고 하는 것으로 보아 회사 가 '직원 안전'을 중요하게 생각한다는 것이 적합하다. 따라서 (A) safety가 정답이다.

16.

(A) 악천후를 항상 예측할 수는 없습니다.
(B) 다행히도 작년에는 폐쇄를 전혀 하지 않았습니다.
(C) 이 정책은 검토 중이며 변경될 수 있습니다.
(D) 모든 직원이 메시지를 받을 수 있도록 총력을 기울일 것입니다.

해설 빈칸 앞 "Shift supervisors are responsible for ~ team members"에서 교대근무 감독자가 팀 구성원에게 폐쇄를 전달할 책임이 있다고 했으므로 문맥상 빈칸에 모든 직원이 메시지를 받 을 수 있도록 노력할 것이라는 내용의 (D)가 오는 것이 적절하다. (D)에서 언급한 the message는 빈칸 앞에서 언급된 '사무실 폐 쇄'를 가리킨다.

17.

해설 빈칸은 동사 자리로, 문맥상 폐쇄는 아직 일어난 일이 아니며, 이와 같은 일이 발생할 경우, 근무하기로 예정된 시간에 대해 기본 급여를 받게 될 것이라고 하는 것이 자연스러우므로 미래 시제 (B) will receive가 정답이다.

18.

해설 return은 자동사로, 전치사 to와 함께 '~로 돌아오다[가다]'라는 뜻으로 쓰인다. 따라서 '직장으로 돌아오다'라는 의미를 완성하는 (A)가 정답이다.

ACTUAL TEST 10   본문 p.262

1. (B)	2. (B)	3. (B)	4. (D)	5. (B)	6. (D)
7. (B)	8. (C)	9. (C)	10. (A)	11. (C)	12. (C)
13. (D)	14. (C)	15. (A)	16. (C)	17. (D)	18. (B)

1. 금융 컨설턴트의 조언에 따라 회계 시스템을 개편했다.

해설 빈칸은 전치사 on의 목적어 자리이자 관사 the의 수식을 받는 명사 자리이다. 문맥상 '금융 컨설턴트의 조언에 따라'가 적합하므로 사람 명사 (A) adviser(조언자)가 아닌 (B) advice(충고, 조언)가 정답이다.

어휘 financial consultant 재무상담사 reorganize 재조직하다 accounting 회계 advisory 자문의 advise 조언하다, 충고하다

2. Curtis 씨는 새로운 정책 조치를 어떻게 시행할 것인지에 대한 구체적인 지침을 제공했다.

해설 빈칸은 문장의 동사 has provided의 목적어 guidelines를 수식하는 형용사 자리로, 보기 중 유일한 형용사 (B) specific이 정답이다.

어휘 guideline 가이드라인, 지침 implement(= carry out) 시행하다 policy measure 정책 방안[대안] specify (구체적으로) 명시하다 specific 구체적인 specifics 세부사항 specifically 분명히, 특별히

3. 모든 신규 채용자는 오리엔테이션 교육에서 직원 안내서 사본을 받을 것이다.

해설 빈칸은 동사 will receive의 목적어 자리로, 명사 employee와 결합하여 '직원 안내서'라는 의미의 복합 명사를 완성하는 명사 (B) handbook이 정답이다.

어휘 new hire 신입 직원 copy 사본 identification 신원 확인 locker (자물쇠가 달린) 개인 물품 보관함 lunchroom (학교·회사 등의) 구내식당

4. Greenbrier 호텔 메인 로비의 개조 공사는 이달 말부터 시작될 예정이다.

해설 빈칸은 문장의 동사 자리로, 빈칸 뒤 to부정사와 연결하여 '~할

예정이다'를 완성하는 (D) is scheduled가 정답이다. 타동사 schedule은 'be scheduled to V'의 형태로 자주 나온다.

어휘 renovation 개조, 보수 later this month 이달 말에

5. 우리 사무실에 새로운 소프트웨어가 설치되었지만, 아직 작동하지 않는다.

해설 빈칸은 앞뒤의 대등한 절과 절을 연결하는 등위 접속사 자리로, 문맥상 앞뒤가 대조적 의미를 나타내고 있으므로 등위 접속사 (B) but이 정답이다.

어휘 install 설치하다 not yet 아직 ~않다 operational (기계 따위가) 가동할 준비가 갖춰진, 운행 가능한

6. 직원들이 회사에 있는 동안 사원증을 착용하는 것은 회사의 요구 사항이다.

해설 빈칸은 진주어인 to부정사구를 수식하는 주격 보어 자리이다. 문맥상 빈칸 앞에 온 company와 함께 복합 명사 '회사 요구사항'을 의미하는 (D) requirement가 적절하다.

어휘 require 필요하다, 요구하다 requirement 필요조건, 요구사항

7. 직원들은 복사기가 수리될 때까지 2층에 있는 복사기를 사용하도록 지시받는다.

해설 빈칸 앞 be동사 are과 결합하여 수동태 표현을 만드는 과거분사 어휘 문제로, 문맥상 '2층에 있는 복사기를 사용하도록 지시받는다'는 의미가 적합하므로 (B) instructed가 정답이다.

어휘 copier 복사기 repair 수리하다 adjust 조정하다 instruct 지시하다 respond 대답하다 respect 존경하다

8. 첨부된 책자에는 회사가 보안을 강화하기 위해 추진하고 있는 진행 상황이 자세히 나와 있다.

해설 빈칸은 전치사 in의 목적어로 쓰인 동명사 boosting의 목적어 자리로, 명사인 (C) security가 정답이다.

어휘 enclosed 동봉된 detail 상세히 알리다, 열거하다 progress 진척, 진행 boost 증진시키다 secure 안전한 security 보안, 경비 securely 단단히

9. 서명이 필요한 모든 수신 소포들은 Ritz Tower의 프런트로 배달되어야 한다.

해설 빈칸 앞 be동사와 결합하여 수동태 표현을 만드는 과거분사 어휘 문제로, 문맥상 '모든 수신 소포는 프런트로 배달되어야 한다'는 의미가 적합하므로 (C) delivered가 정답이다.

어휘 incoming 들어오는 package (포장용) 상자, 포장물 signature 서명

10. Fairfield Clinic은 환자 치료를 개선하는 동시에 수용 능력을 극대화하기 위해 재설계되고 있다.

해설 빈칸은 to부정사의 동사 어휘 문제로, 문맥상 '환자 수용 능력을 극대화하기 위해 재설계되다'가 적합하므로 (A) maximize가 정답이다.

어휘 redesign 재설계하다 capacity 용량, 수용력 patient 환자 care 치료 specialize (~을) 전문적으로 다루다 summarize 요약하다 visualize 시각화하다

11. 운영비를 줄이는 것은 CFO인 Jamie Brooks 씨의 최우선 과제이다.

해설 문맥상 빈칸 앞에 온 top과 함께 쓰여 복합 명사 '최우선 과제'를 의미하는 (C) priority가 정답이다.

어휘 reduce 줄이다 operating expense 운영비 incident 사건 excellence 우수, 장점 priority 우선 사항 imagination 상상(력)

12. TVC 뉴스 채널은 Mayfair의 새로운 주차 표지판이 이미 설치되었다고 잘못 보도했다.

해설 빈칸은 과거완료 시제인 had와 been installed 사이에서 동사를 수식하는 부사 어휘 자리로, 문맥상 '새로운 주차 표지판이 이미 설치되었다고 잘못 보도했다'라는 의미가 자연스러우므로 (C) already가 정답이다.

어휘 report 보도하다, 보고하다 incorrectly 부정확하게 highly 대단히 hourly 매시간의 already 이미, 벌써 every 모든, 매~

13. Atlantic Electrics 사의 고효율 냉장고는 기존 냉장고보다 에너지 사용량이 25% 적다.

해설 비교급 than 뒤에서 명사 refrigerators를 수식하는 형용사 어휘 문제로, '기존 냉장고보다 에너지 사용량이 25% 적다'가 문맥상 어울리므로 '기존의, 종래의'의 의미를 가진 (D) conventional이 정답이다.

어휘 high-efficiency 고효율 fridge(= refrigerator) 냉장고 reasonable 타당한, 적당한 individual 개개의, 개인의 responsible 책임 있는, 책임을 져야 할

14. 이사회는 다른 어떤 제안보다 Webb 씨의 제안에 더 긍정적으로 반응했다.

해설 빈칸은 동사를 수식하는 부사 자리로, 빈칸 뒤에 비교급 표현인 than이 있으므로 이와 짝을 이루는 (C) more positively가 정답이다.

어휘 executive board 이사회 proposal 제안(서) positively 긍정적으로

[15-18] 정보

East Camphill 시민 회관은 East Camphill의 역사적인 도심지에서 걸어갈 수 있는 거리의 편리한 위치에 있습니다. East Camphill 주민들은 시민 회관에서 제공하는 여러 자원봉사 프로그램을 통해 지역 사회에 있는 모든 사람의 삶의 질을 유지하는 데 적극적인 역할을 합니다. 자원봉사자들은 예술, 교육, 시 정부와 같은 지역 생활의 모든 면에서 찾아볼 수 있습니다. East Camphill은 기꺼이 시간과 재능을 나누는 사람들의 관대함으로부터 혜택을 받고 있습니다. 저희 자원봉사 프로그램에 참여하는 것을 고려해 주세요. 자원봉사를 희망하신다면 7739-8066으로 전화 주십시오.

어휘 be located 위치하다 within ~이내에 distance 거리 district 구역 resident 주민 volunteer 자원봉사자 aspect 측면 including ~을 포함하여 benefit from ~로부터 혜택을 받다 be willing to 기꺼이 ~하다 talent 재능 exactly 정확히 approximately 대략 almost 거의 privilege 특전 responsibility 책임 obligation 의무 generosity 너그러움, 아량, 관대 various 다양한 previously 이전에 entertainment 오락, 연예 currently 현재 vacancy 공석

15.

해설 빈칸 뒤 "within easy walking distance of"에서 시민 회관이 '걸어갈 수 있는 거리 내'에 위치한다고 했으므로 문맥상 '편리하게 위치하다'라는 의미를 완성하는 (A) conveniently가 정답이다.

16.

해설 빈칸은 전치사 in의 목적어 역할을 하면서 동시에 빈칸 뒤의 명사 the quality를 목적어로 취할 수 있는 동명사 자리로, (C) maintaining이 정답이다.

17.

해설 '시간과 재능을 기꺼이 나누는 자원봉사자들의 ~로부터 혜택을 받다'에서 빈칸에 들어갈 수 있는 가장 적절한 명사를 골라야 한다. 문맥상 '아량, 너그러움'의 의미를 가지고 있는 (D) generosity가 적절하다.

18.

(A) 다양한 수업과 프로그램이 과거에 제공되었습니다.
(B) 저희 자원봉사 프로그램에 참여하는 것을 고려해 주세요.
(C) 저희는 현재 영업부에 공석이 있습니다.
(D) 달력에 기록할 많은 오락 행사가 마련되어 있습니다.

해설 빈칸 앞에서 자원봉사자에 관한 내용이 제시되었고, 빈칸 다음 문장 "If you would like to become a volunteer, please call us at 7739-8066"에서 자원봉사 지원 방법을 설명하고 있다. 따라서 자원봉사 프로그램 참여를 독려하는 내용의 (B)가 가장 적절하다.

PRACTICE 본문 p.271

1. (B) **2.** (B) **3.** (C) **4.** (A)

[1-2] 이메일

1. 이메일의 주된 목적은 무엇인가?

(A) 무료 식사를 제공하기 위해

(B) 고객에게 사과하기 위해

(C) 식당의 최근 사업을 설명하기 위해

(D) 고객의 의견에 감사하기 위해

해설 글의 목적이 무엇인지를 묻는 문제이며, 주제와 목적은 지문의 첫 부분에 나와 있는 경우가 많으므로 우선 지문의 첫 단락을 읽고 정답을 찾는다. 제목(Apology)과 첫 단락 두 번째 문장 "I would like to apologize for the horrible experience you had"를 보아, 주된 목적은 고객에게 사과하기 위함이고, 무료 식사는 사과에 대한 보상으로 언급한 내용이므로 (B)가 정답이다.

2. Peaty 씨는 무엇을 하겠다고 말하는가?

(A) Shelton 씨에게 무료 선물을 받을 수 있는 상품권을 제공한다.

(B) Shelton 씨의 가족에게 무료 식사를 제공한다.

(C) 직원들에게 충분한 훈련을 제공한다.

(D) Shelton 씨가 주문하는 음식에 대해 할인을 제공한다.

해설 글쓴이 Peaty 씨가 무언가를 하겠다고 언급한 문장을 찾으면 된다. "I can offer you a free meal for three when you come again"에서 사과의 표시로 다시 한번 방문하면 무료 식사를 제공해 주겠다고 했으므로 (B)가 정답이다.

[3-4] 공지

3. 회의에 초대되지 않은 사람은 누구인가?

(A) 이사회 임원

(B) 대량의 주식을 보유한 사람들

(C) Starlight Metal Industrials 사의 사업 파트너

(D) 영업 팀원들

해설 NOT TRUE 유형은 소거법으로 오답을 제거해 가면서 푼다. 지문 첫 번째 문장에서 연례 영업 회의(annual sales meeting)가 열리는 것을 알 수 있고, 바로 이어지는 다음 문장 "All major shareholders and company representatives are invited to attend"에서 주주와 임원들 모두 초대한다고 언급되어 있다. 따라서 지문에서 언급되지 않은 (C)가 정답이다. 지문 중후반 "We

will be celebrating the achievements of the sales team"에서 (D)도 언급되었다.

어휘 board (of directors) 이사회 own 소유하다 a lot of 많은 shares 주식

4. 회의에 참석하지 못하는 사람이 참여할 수 있는 방법은?

(A) 인터넷을 통해 본다.

(B) 회의 담당자에게 전화한다.

(C) 예약을 취소한다.

(D) Richmond로 간다.

해설 의문사와 키워드를 확인하고 지문에 해당 정보가 있는 부분을 찾는다. 두번째 단락 "Those who cannot attend can participate by video conferencing, ~"에서 참석할 수 없는 사람들은 회사 웹사이트를 통해 비디오 화상 회의로 참석할 수 있다고 했으므로 인터넷을 통해 본다고 한 (A)가 정답이다.

어휘 through the Internet 인터넷을 통해 organizer 담당, 조직자 cancel 취소하다

ACTUAL TEST 본문 p.276

1. (D)	**2.** (B)	**3.** (C)	**4.** (A)	**5.** (B)	**6.** (A)
7. (D)	**8.** (B)	**9.** (A)	**10.** (D)	**11.** (B)	**12.** (C)
13. (B)	**14.** (C)	**15.** (D)	**16.** (D)	**17.** (A)	**18.** (B)
19. (B)					

[1-2] 이메일

발신: customersupport@gridelectric.com
수신: Mlawley@gmail.com
제목: 최근 연락 건
날짜: 6월 5일

Lawley 씨에게,

저희 기록에 따르면 귀하는 최근 청구서 발송부로 연락하셨습니다. 이 기회를 통해 귀하의 문의 건에 대한 저희 담당자의 처리 방식에 만족하시는지 알고 싶습니다. 문의에 대한 답변은 받으셨나요? 전기 요금 액수에 대한 추가 정보가 필요하신가요? 잠시 시간을 내어 www.gridelectric.com/billing에서 간단한 설문지를 작성해 주세요.

감사합니다.

고객 서비스 부서
Grid Electric Ltd.

어휘 billing office 청구서 발송부 opportunity 기회 find out ~을 알아내다 whether ~인지 아닌지 be satisfied with ~에 만족하다 representative 대표, 대리인 handle 다루다, 처리하다 additional 추가적인 electricity bill 전기 요금 take a moment (to V) (~할) 시간을 갖다 fill out 작성하다 brief 간략한 questionnaire 설문지 advertise 광고하다 confirm 확인하다

employment 고용, 취업 payment 지불, 납입 cause 원인
power failure 정전 directions 길 안내

1. 이메일의 목적은 무엇인가?
(A) 비용을 절약하는 방법을 제안하기 위해
(B) 새로운 서비스를 광고하기 위해
(C) 수리 날짜를 확인하기 위해
(D) 의견 요청하기 위해

해설 이메일 도입부 "Our records show that you recently contacted our billing office"에서 이메일을 받는 Lawley 씨가 청구서 발송부로 연락한 사실을 언급하며, 담당자의 일 처리에 대한 만족도를 묻고 있다. 마지막 문장 "Please take a moment to fill out a brief questionnaire at ~"에서 설문 조사를 해달라는 요청을 하고 있으므로 고객에게 의견을 요청하기 위한 이메일로 볼 수 있다. 따라서 (D)가 정답이다.

2. Lawley 씨는 무엇에 대해 문의했을 것 같은가?
(A) 취업 기회
(B) 전기 요금 결제
(C) 최근 정전의 원인
(D) Grid Electric 회사로 가는 길

해설 이메일 중반 "Do you need additional information about the amount of your electricity bill?"에서 전기 요금에 대한 추가 정보가 필요한지 묻는 것을 보아, Lawley 씨가 전기 요금 지불에 관해 문의했다는 것을 유추할 수 있다. 따라서 (B)가 정답이다.

[3-4] 편지

Metro National 은행
12 Queens St, 글래스고
1-322-221-2860

Charline Turner
17 Oxford Road
GLA city

10월 15일

Turner 씨께,

Metro National 은행 신용카드를 활성화해 주셔서 감사합니다. Metro National 은행의 고객들이 즐기는 가장 인기 있는 혜택 중 하나는 온라인 계좌 관리 시스템입니다. 이 시스템은 계좌 소유자에게 컴퓨터, 태블릿 또는 스마트폰에서 하루 24시간 최신 계좌 정보를 제공합니다. 아직 가입하지 않았다면, 오늘 바로 www.metronationalbank.ca에서 가입하세요.

가입에 도움이 되는 편리한 약식 안내서를 동봉했습니다.

안녕히 계세요,

Jessica Bailey
고객 서비스 담당자

동봉

어휘 activate 활성화하다 credit card 신용카드 management 관리 access 접근, 이용 up-to-date 최신의 enclose 동봉하다 guide 안내(서) get started (어떤 일을 하기) 시작하다 customer service representative 고객 서비스 상담원 explain 설명하다 gather 모으다 announce 발표하다 instruction 설명(서) fill out 작성하다 billing statement 대금 청구서

3. 편지가 발송된 이유는 무엇인가?
(A) 계좌 활성화 방법을 설명하기 위해
(B) 고객의 의견을 수렴하기 위해
(C) 이용 가능한 서비스를 홍보하기 위해
(D) 새로운 웹사이트를 발표하기 위해

해설 지문 초반부 "Thank you for activating your Metro National Bank credit card"에서 은행이 고객에게 신용카드를 활성화한 것에 대한 감사를 전하며 고객이 누릴 수 있는 여러 혜택 중 하나인 특정 시스템(online account management system)에 대한 안내를 하고 있으므로 (C)가 정답이다.

4. 편지와 함께 무엇이 보내졌는가?
(A) 지침서
(B) 작성해야 할 양식
(C) 신용카드
(D) 청구 명세서

해설 지문 마지막에 "We've enclosed a convenient summary guide to help you get started"에서 약식 안내서를 편지에 동봉한 것을 알 수 있다. 따라서 지문의 summary guide를 Instructions(지침, 사용법)으로 패러프레이징한 (A)가 정답이다.

[5-6] 이메일

수신: gorwell@uhemail.net
발신: salesteam@citylitbooks.com
제목: Joseph의 신간
날짜: 1월 28일

Orwell 씨에게,

Joseph Hall의 베스트셀러 책을 구매하신 고객으로서 같은 작가의 <The Realm Beyond>가 곧 출간될 예정이라는 소식을 관심 있으실 겁니다.
지금 사전 주문을 하시면 4월 12일에 배송되며, 초판 인쇄본을 받으실 수 있습니다. 사전 주문을 원하시면 www.citylitbooks.com/coming_soon을 방문해 주세요.

감사합니다.
Citylitbooks.com 영업팀

어휘 best-selling book 베스트셀러 책 author 작가 publish 출간하다 preorder 선주문하다 guarantee 약속하다, 보장하다 copy (책·신문 등의) 한 부 first edition 초판

5. 이메일은 왜 발송되었는가?

(A) 구매를 확인하기 위해

(B) 제품을 광고하기 위해

(C) 북 투어를 알리기 위해

(D) 고객 리뷰를 요청하기 위해

해설 지문 첫 문장 "As a customer who purchased a best-selling book by Joseph Hall"에서 Joseph Hall의 책을 구입했던 이력이 있는 Orwell 씨에게 신간 소식을 알리고 있고, 두번째 문단에서 신간의 사전 주문과 관련된 내용이 이어지므로 (B)가 정답이다.

6. <The Realm Beyond>에 대해 언급된 것은?

(A) 아직 출시되지 않았다.

(B) 이미 매진되었다.

(C) 베스트셀러 책의 제목이다.

(D) 웹사이트에서 논평되었다.

해설 지문 첫 문장 "~ The Realm Beyond by the same author will be published soon)에서 곧 출시될 책이라고 했으므로 아직 출시되지 않았다는 (A)가 정답이다.

[7-8] 공지

제6회 연례 Dinos 책 박람회
메인 플라자

9월 23-24일, 오전 9시부터 오후 5시까지

여러분 모두를 Dinos 공립 도서관이 후원하는 제6회 연례 Dinos 도서 박람회에 초대합니다. 모든 연령의 책 애호가들이 이 행사에 참여하여 가족이나 친구들과 즐거운 시간을 보낼 수 있습니다. 시 낭독, 작가 인터뷰, 책 소개, 사인회 등과 같은 다양한 행사가 진행될 예정입니다. 올해는 다음과 같은 게스트분들을 초청하였습니다:

- Elena Hutts, 『엄마가 들려주는 최고의 동화』의 작가
- James Castellano, 『르네상스 시대의 위대함』의 작가
- Cindy Houston, 『시간이 다 되었다』의 극작가이자 작가
- Elise Pierna, 『내 안에, 너 밖에』의 음악 감독

Dinos 도서 박람회는 누구나 무료로 참여할 수 있는 행사입니다. 올해의 행사에 대한 더 많은 정보는 www.dinosconvention.com/eventlist를 방문해 주세요.

어휘 welcome 환영하다 sponsor 후원하다 all age 남녀노소 poetry 시 author 작가 musical director 음악 감독 available 이용 가능한 be intended for ~을 위한 것이다

7. 도서 박람회에 대해 언급된 것은?

(A) 일 년에 여섯 번 열린다.

(B) Dinos 공립 도서관에서 열린다.

(C) 초대된 사람만 참석할 수 있다.

(D) 어린이와 성인을 대상으로 한다.

해설 첫 번째 문단 "Booklovers of all ages may join this event and spend a good time with family or friends"에서 모든 연령의 책 애호가들이 참여할 수 있다고 했으므로 성인과 유아 대상의 행사임을 유추할 수 있다. 따라서 (D)가 정답이다.

8. 누가 역사적 주제에 대해 논의할 것 같은가?

(A) Elena Hutts

(B) James Castellano

(C) Cindy Houston

(D) Elise Pierna

해설 초청받은 게스트들 중에서 르네상스 시대(The Greatness of the Renaissance Era)에 대한 책을 쓴 (B) James Castellano로 유추할 수 있다.

[9-11] 회람

회람

발신자: Cole McQueen, 회장
수신자: Allbirds Holdings 직원들
날짜: 9월 27일
제목: 11월 회의

우리 회사 5층의 새로운 공간에 대한 계획을 논의하기 위해 여러분을 탐색 회의에 초대합니다. 기존에 5층에 있던 Micro Research는 다른 곳으로 이전하였고, 우리는 이 새롭게 생긴 공간을 임대하기로 결정했습니다.

이 공간에 새로운 멀티미디어 회의실과 직원들을 위한 피트니스 센터를 포함할 계획입니다. 업체를 선정하기 전에 여러분이 피트니스 센터에서 원하는 것이 무엇인지 의견을 듣고 싶습니다.

예를 들어, 최첨단 운동기구를 선호하는지, 아니면 더 넓은 개방 공간을 원하는지를 말씀해 주세요.
프로젝트에 대한 아이디어를 제시하고 싶다면, 11월 7일 오후 2시에 구내식당에서 열리는 회의에 참석해 주세요.
참석할 수 없는 경우, 인사부의 Simon에게 내일까지 이메일로 제안사항을 보내주시기 바랍니다.

어휘 invite 요청하다 exploratory 탐사의 formerly 이전에 relocate 이전하다 lease 임대하다 include 포함시키다 contractor 시공사, 도급업자 prefer 선호하다 state-of-the-art 최신의 contribute 제공하다, 기고하다 cafeteria 구내식당 suggestion 제안, 제의 attendance 출석 recruit 모집하다

9. 회람의 목적은 무엇인가?

(A) 직원들로부터 제안을 받기 위해

(B) 새로운 출석 정책을 검토하기 위해

(C) 다가오는 행사의 자원봉사자를 모집하기 위해

(D) 건물 보수 작업을 위한 시공사를 선정하기 위해

해설 초반부 "You are invited to attend an exploratory meeting to discuss plans for our company's new space on the fifth floor"에서 새로운 공간에 대한 계획을 논의하기 위해 회의 참석을 요청했고, 중반부 "~ we would like to hear from you about what you would like to see in the fitness center"에서 새로운 공간에 들어설 피트니스 센터에 대한 의견을 구하고 있으므로 (A)가 정답이다.

10. Allbirds Holdings가 계획하고 있는 일은 무엇인가?

(A) 이름을 변경한다
(B) 새로운 도시로 이전한다
(C) 여러 직원을 고용한다
(D) 더 많은 사무 공간을 임대한다

해설 초반부 "Micro Research, which was formerly on the fifth floor, has relocated, and our company has decided to lease the newly available space"에서 Micro Research 사가 5층에서 다른 곳으로 이전함에 따라 그 공간을 우리 회사 (Allbirds Holdings)가 임대할 계획이라고 했으므로 (D)가 정답이다.

11. 회의는 어디에서 열릴 예정인가?

(A) 회의실에서
(B) 구내식당에서
(C) 인사부 사무실에서
(D) 피트니스 센터에서

해설 마지막 부분 "To contribute your ideas to the project, join us in the cafeteria on November 7 at 2:00 P.M."에서 회의는 11월 7일 오후 2시에 구내식당에서 열릴 예정이라고 했으므로 (B)가 정답이다.

[12-13] 공지

MidFirst 은행 근처의 도로 개선 작업

Scottsdale Street의 도로 개선 작업이 다음 주 화요일에 시작될 예정입니다. 보수 작업에는 신호등 설치, 하수관 교체, 계단 수리, 연석 및 보도 콘크리트 공사가 포함될 것입니다.

안전에 대한 우려 때문에 5월 23일부터 이틀간 MidFirst 은행 정문 출입이 제한될 것입니다. MidFirst 은행의 직원들과 고객들은 Van Buren Street에 있는 후문을 이용하실 것을 권해 드립니다.

덧붙여, 보수 작업이 소음과 먼지를 유발하여 여러분께 불편을 드릴지도 모릅니다. 양해를 부탁드립니다.

어휘 enhancement 향상, 개선 include 포함하다 traffic signal 신호등 installation 설치 sewer 하수관 replacement 교체 stairway 계단 curb 연석 sidewalk 보도 concern 염려, 걱정 main entrance 정문 accessible 접근할 수 있는, 이용할 수 있는 suggest 제안하다 back entrance 후문 in addition 덧붙여 renovation 보수 cause ~를 발생시키다 dust 먼지 bother 괴롭히다 appreciate 고마워하다

policy 정책 temporary 일시적인 closure 폐쇄 update 최신 정보를 알려주다 relocate 이전하다 retain 보유하다

12. 공지가 작성된 이유는 무엇인가?

(A) 오래된 문을 교체하는 것을 보고하기 위해
(B) 회사 정책의 변화에 대해 설명하기 위해
(C) 일시적으로 문을 폐쇄하는 것을 알리기 위해
(D) 직원들에게 새로운 사업 프로젝트에 대한 소식을 알리기 위해

해설 지문의 시작 "Road enhancements on Scottsdale Street are scheduled to begin next Tuesday"에서 다음 주 화요일에 도로 개선 작업이 진행될 것이라고 언급하고, 이어지는 내용 "the main entrance to MidFirst Bank will not be accessible"에서 공사로 인해 정문 이용이 불가능할 것이라고 했으므로 (C)가 정답이다.

13. MidFirst 은행에 대해 추론할 수 있는 것은 무엇인가?

(A) 화요일에 이전할 것이다.
(B) 정문이 Scottsdale Street에 있다.
(C) 많은 고객들을 보유하고 있다.
(D) 보수 작업이 1주일 이상 걸릴 것이다.

해설 지문의 첫 문장 "Road enhancements on Scottsdale Street are scheduled to begin next Tuesday"를 통해 Scottsdale Street에서 보수 공사가 예정되어 있음을 알 수 있고, 그로 인해 회사의 정문을 이용할 수 없을 거라는 내용을 근거로 MidFirst Bank의 정문이 Scottsdale Street에 있다고 추론할 수 있다. 따라서 (B)가 정답이다. 지문에서 선택지 (A)와 (C)에 대한 근거는 찾을 수 없고, 지문에서 정문 이용이 금지되는 기간이 "for two days from May 23"라고 명시되어 있으므로 (D)는 오답이다.

[14-16] 공지

Havertys Furniture 교환 정책

구매하신 제품에 대해 완전히 만족하지 못하신다면, 해당 제품을 30일 이내에 교환하실 수 있습니다. 하지만 교환 시 영수증 원본을 지참하셔야 한다는 점을 잊지 마십시오. 영수증과 함께 구매하신 물건을 반환해 주시고 새로운 가구를 선택하십시오. 또한, 사진이 부착된 유효한 신분증을 제시해 주셔야 합니다. 고객님의 개인 정보는 교환을 승인하기 위한 목적으로만 이용되며 사내 데이터베이스에 보관될 것입니다. 구매하신 물건이 더럽혀져 있거나, 얼룩이 졌거나, 훼손되어 있다면 교환할 수 없습니다.

구매하신 제품에 대해 픽업 서비스를 원하신다면, Havertys Furniture 고객 서비스 센터, 888-428-3789로 연락 주십시오. 매장 운영 시간은 오전 8시부터 오후 7시까지입니다. 모든 경우에, 교환 배송료가 적용됩니다.

어휘 totally 완전히 satisfy 만족시키다 purchase 구매, 구매한 제품 exchange 교환하다 accompany 동반하다 original 원래의, 원본의 receipt 영수증 return 반품하다 merchandise 상품

require 요구하다 present 제시하다, 보여주다 valid 유효한
retain 보유하다 company-wide 회사 전반의 authorize 승인
하다 pick up ~을 가지러 가다 operating hours 운영 시간
fee 수수료 apply 적용되다 exchange 교환하다 ineligible
자격이 없는 sold-out 매진된 proof 증거 branch 지점
stained 얼룩진 damaged 파손된

14. 교환 정책에 대해 사실인 것은?

(A) 온라인으로 구매된 물건은 교환이 불가능하다.

(B) 매진된 상품에 대해서는 적용되지 않는다.

(C) 고객은 교환을 위해 구매 증거가 필요하다.

(D) 고객은 어떤 지점에서든 물건을 반품할 수 있다.

> **해설** 첫 문단 두 번째 문장 "But don't forget that exchanges must
> be accompanied by the original receipt"에서 교환 시 영수
> 증 원본을 지참하라는 내용이 있으므로 (C)가 정답이다. (A), (B),
> (D)는 언급되지 않았다.

15. 교환 절차로 언급되지 않은 것은?

(A) 픽업 트럭 요청하기

(B) 배송료 지불하기

(C) 사진이 부착된 신분증 제시하기

(D) 파손된 제품의 사진 보내기

> **해설** 지문의 후반 "If you would like to have your merchandise
> picked up, ~"에서 픽업 서비스가 언급되었으므로 (A)는 오답이
> 고, 마지막 문장 "exchange delivery fees will apply"에서 배
> 송료가 적용된다고 했으므로 (B)도 오답이다. 지문의 중반 "You
> will also be required to present a valid photo ID"에서 물건
> 을 교환하려면 사진이 부착된 유효한 신분증이 필요하다고 했으므
> 로 (C)도 오답이다. 파손된 제품의 사진을 보내라는 내용은 본문에
> 언급되지 않았으므로 (D)가 정답이다.

16. [1], [2], [3], [4]로 표시된 곳 중 다음 문장이 들어가기에 가장 적
절한 곳은?

"구매하신 물건이 더럽혀져 있거나, 얼룩이 졌거나, 훼손되어 있다
면 교환할 수 없습니다."

(A) [1]

(B) [2]

(C) [3]

(D) [4]

> **해설** 제시된 문장은 교환할 수 없는 경우를 나열하고 있다. 지문에서 교
> 환 절차와 교환 시 필요한 영수증, 신분증에 대해 안내하고 있으므
> 로 주어진 문장은 부연 설명 부분으로 들어가야 한다. 따라서 문
> 장의 처음인 [1]에 제시된 문장이 들어가기에는 부적절하다. [2]는
> 뒤 문장의 but과 연결이 자연스럽지 않고, [3]은 앞뒤에 신분증에
> 관한 내용이므로 적절하지 않다. 따라서 교환이 불가한 경우를 부
> 연 설명하는 이 문장의 위치로 (D) [4]가 가장 적절하다.

Bround Coffee Machines 사

577 파머 가

루벅, 텍사스

10월 3일

Jim Freeman

449 오렌지 그로브

댈러스, 텍사스

Freeman 씨께,

에스프레소 기계의 고장과 관련해 저희에게 연락 주셔서 감사합니다.

저희 Bround Coffee Machines는 모든 고객님께 만족을 드리고자 합니다.
저희는 Freeman 씨께서 구입하신 에스프레소 기계에 대해 많은 편지를 받
아왔습니다. 따라서 저희는 이 기계에 문제가 있는 것으로 보고 리콜을 실
시할 것입니다.

고객님들께 비용을 청구하지 않고 저희가 기계를 모두 수거해서 수리할 것입
니다. 또한 배송비와 취급비도 저희가 부담할 것입니다. 또는, 더 편하시다면,
가까운 매장으로 기계를 가지고 가시면 저희가 수리를 위해 특별히 대기 중
인 기술자가 있을 겁니다. 귀하께서 계신 곳 근처에서 기술자가 상주하고 있
는 매장을 알아보시려면 1800-888-7000으로 전화 주십시오.

안녕히 계세요,

Jerry Spangler

고객 서비스부

> **어휘** appreciate 감사하다 regarding ~에 관한 defect 결함
> ensure 보장하다 satisfaction 만족 repair 수리하다
> at no cost 무료로 shipping 배송(료) handling 취급(료)
> technician 기술자 on hand 대기 중인, 준비된 specifically
> 특히 respond to ~에 응답하다 parts 부품 confirm 확인하다
> outlet 매장 appear ~인 것 같다

17. Spangler 씨는 왜 편지를 썼는가?

(A) 고객의 편지에 답장하기 위해

(B) 교체 부품을 요청하기 위해

(C) 최신 커피메이커를 광고하기 위해

(D) 구매 주문을 확정하기 위해

> **해설** 첫 문장 "We appreciate your contacting us regarding the
> defect in your espresso machine"에서 에스프레소 기계의
> 고장과 관련해 저희에게 연락 주셔서 감사하다는 인사말로 편지를
> 시작하고 있다. 따라서 (A)가 정답이다.

18. Freeman 씨는 무엇을 하도록 권고받는가?

(A) 에스프레소 기계를 새로 구입한다.

(B) 수리를 위해 매장에 간다.

(C) 에스프레소 기계에서 빠진 부품을 추가한다.

(D) Spangler 씨에게 빨리 연락한다.

해설 마지막 문단 "just take it into any of our nearest outlets, where we will have a technician on hand specifically to repair these machines"에서 가까운 곳에 있는 매장으로 기계를 가지고 가서 기술자에게 맡기라고 했으므로 (B)가 정답이다.

19. [1], [2], [3], [4]로 표시된 곳 중 다음 문장이 들어가기에 가장 적절한 곳은?

"따라서 저희는 이 기계에 문제가 있는 것으로 보고 리콜을 실시할 것입니다."

(A) [1]
(B) [2]
(C) [3]
(D) [4]

해설 주어진 문장에서 인과 관계를 나타내는 접속부사 therefore가 단서가 된다. [2]의 앞 문장 "We have received a number of letters about the espresso machine that you bought"에서 Spangler 씨가 고장과 관련해 여러 차례 편지를 받았다는 것이 원인이 되고, 그로 인해 리콜을 실시하는 것이 결과이므로 (B) [2]가 가장 적절하다.

UNIT 16 기사/안내문/광고

PRACTICE 본문 p.287

1. (A) **2.** (C) **3.** (B) **4.** (A) **5.** (B)

[1-3] 기사

1. 기사의 목적은 무엇인가?

(A) 호텔 체인의 새로운 지점이 개장한 것을 알리기 위해
(B) 괌의 새로운 호텔의 투자자를 유치하기 위해
(C) 직원들에게 호텔 보수에 대해 알리기 위해
(D) 호텔 위치에 대한 정보를 주기 위해

해설 기사의 목적을 묻고 있으므로 제목을 포함한 첫 단락을 잘 읽는다. 도입부 "The Lewis Grand Hotel opens its third overseas hotel in Guam on July 10"에서 7월 10일 괌에서 호텔을 개장한다고 했으므로 (A)가 정답이다.

2. 두 번째 단락, 첫 번째 줄의 "overlooks"와 의미가 가장 가까운 것은?

(A) 무시하다
(B) 용서하다
(C) 내려다보다
(D) 감시하다

해설 동의어 찾기 문제는 한 단어이 여러 가지 의미 중에서 문맥상 의미와 뜻이 가장 비슷한 단어를 답으로 골라야 한다. overlook은 '간과하다, 눈감아 주다, 내려다 보다, 감시하다'의 의미를 가지고 있다. 문맥상 'Tumon 만이 내려다보이는 호텔'이 적절하므로 (C) looks down이 정답이다.

3. 기사에서 Lewis Grand 호텔에 대해 무엇이 암시되는가?

(A) Guam 국제공항 옆에 위치한다.
(B) 다른 나라에도 지점이 있다.
(C) 200개 이상의 객실이 있다.
(D) Rockwood 리조트라고도 불린다.

해설 첫 단락 도입부 "The Lewis Grand Hotel opens its third overseas hotel"에서 괌에서 개장하는 호텔이 해외에서의 세 번째 호텔이라고 언급되었다. 따라서 다른 나라에 호텔 지사를 보유하고 있다는 (B)가 정답이다. (A)는 호텔의 위치가 괌 국제공항에서 차로 10분 거리라고 했으므로 오답이고, (C)는 객실 수가 200개라고 명시되었으므로 오답이다. 그리고 기존의 Rockwood 리조트를 리모델링한 사실만으로 그 이름으로 불린다고 추론할 수 없으므로 (D)도 오답이다.

[4-5] 광고

4. 무엇이 광고되고 있는가?

(A) 차량 렌트 회사
(B) 픽업서비스
(C) 여행 상품
(D) 신차

해설 광고되고 있는 것을 묻고 있으므로 제목을 포함한 첫 단락을 잘 읽는다. 지문 도입부 "Premium self-drive cars are available at reasonable rates at Budget Motors"에서 프리미엄 렌터카 차량을 합리적인 가격으로 제공한다고 했고, 전체적으로 렌탈 서비스와 관련된 내용이 이어지고 있으므로 (A)가 정답이다.

어휘 rental 임대, 임차 public transportation 대중교통 travel 여행

5. 광고에서 언급된 것은?

(A) 복잡한 예약 시스템
(B) 훌륭한 자동차 품질
(C) 일일 할인
(D) 전 고객을 위한 무료 선물

해설 지문에서 언급된 내용을 묻는 문제는 보기를 읽어 키워드를 확인한다. 첫 번째 단락 "Whether your rental needs are for leisure, business, or special events, we provide the best vehicles available"에서 최고의 품질을 가진 차량을 제공한다고 했으므로 (B)가 정답이다.

ACTUAL TEST 본문 p.292

1. (B) **2.** (C) **3.** (B) **4.** (D) **5.** (B) **6.** (D)
7. (A) **8.** (D) **9.** (D) **10.** (C) **11.** (C) **12.** (C)
13. (B) **14.** (A) **15.** (B) **16.** (D) **17.** (C) **18.** (B)
19. (C) **20.** (D) **21.** (A)

[1-3] 기사

Flexport Automotive 임금 식감

시카고, 10월 3일—최근의 경제적 불황을 고려하여 Flexport Automotive 사는 직원들을 해고하지 않으면서도 비용을 절감하고 이익 마진을 유지하기 위해 할 수 있는 모든 것을 다하고 있다고 발표했다. 회사 임원들 모두가 주말 동안 아이디어를 모으고 문제 해결 방법을 찾기 위해 노력했다. 월요일 아침, 최고경영자 Henry Petersen은 목표를 이루기 위해서는 직원들이 15%의 임금 삭감을 받아들여야 하며 경기가 다시 살아날 때까지 계획된 급여 및 상여금 인상을 동결한다고 발표했다. Flexport Automotive 사의 직원들은 이와 같은 경영상의 결정에 실망하기는 했지만, 현재와 같은 어려운 시장 속에서 직장이 없는 것보다는 급여 일부가 삭감되는 것이 낫다고 말했다. 따라서 오는 11월 1일부터 임원을 포함한 모든 직원의 실소득액이 삭감될 것이다.

어휘 pay cut 임금 삭감 in light of ~에 비추어, ~을 고려하여 economic downturn 경기 침체 announce 발표하다 lay off 해고하다 profit margin 이윤, 이익 company executive 회사 임원 solution 해결책 chief executive officer 최고경영자 in order to ~하기 위하여 meet 충족시키다 goal 목표 pick back up 회복하다, 다시 시작하다 would rather ~하는 것이 낫다 reduction 감소, 절감 take-home pay (세금 등을 공제한) 실소득 management 경영진 model 모범으로 삼다

1. 기사는 어떤 종류의 회사 정책에 대해 다루고 있는가?
(A) 광고
(B) 예산
(C) 교육
(D) 채용

해설 기사 제목 "Flexport Automotive Pay Cut"에서 임금 삭감이 언급되었고, 임금 삭감이 결정된 배경과 정책의 세부적인 내용 및 그에 대한 임직원들의 반응 등 관련 내용이 이어지고 있다. 임금은 예산 정책과 관련이 있으므로 (B)가 정답이다.

2. Flexport Automotive 사는 언제부터 새로운 정책을 실행할 것인가?
(A) 1월
(B) 10월
(C) 11월
(D) 12월

해설 기사에서 최고경영자 Henry Petersen이 임금 삭감 정책을 발표했다고 했고, 마지막 문장 "So beginning on November 1, all staff, including executives, will see a reduction in their take-home pay"에서 임금 삭감은 11월 1일부터 시행될 것이라고 했으므로 (C)가 정답이다.

3. 회사의 새로운 정책에 대해 무엇이 언급되었는가?
(A) 국제적인 전문가들이 고안했다.
(B) 일자리와 자금을 확보하는 데 도움이 될 것으로 기대된다.
(C) 직원들과 경영진에 의해 결정되었다.
(D) 다른 회사의 정책을 모범으로 삼았다.

해설 기사의 첫 번째 문장 " Flexport Automotive has announced that it is doing all that it can not to lay off any of its workers yet save money and maintain a profit margin."에서 Flexport Automotive가 직원 해고 없이 비용을 절감하고 이익 마진을 유지하기 위한 새로운 정책을 발표했다고 했으므로 (B)가 정답이다. 지문 중반부 "On Monday morning, Chief Executive Officer Henry Petersen, announced that in order to meet their goals they would have to ask their workers to accept a 15-percent pay cut ~"에서 회사 임원들이 문제 해결 방법을 고안했고 최고경영자가 새 정책을 발표했다고 했으므로 (A)와 (C)는 오답이다. (D)는 지문에서 확인할 수 없다.

[4-5] 정보

신규 할인!

Z-Mobile은 현재 Dole Electronics 사의 모든 직원에게 휴대폰 및 데이터 요금을 30% 할인을 제공하고 있습니다. 이 멋진 거래를 놓치지 않으려면 인사부로 가서 Z-Mobile 할인 쿠폰을 가져가세요. 이 쿠폰은 모든 공인 판매점에서 12개월 데이터 요금제와 함께 새 Z-Mobile 휴대폰을 구매할 때 사용할 수 있습니다.

구매할 때 사원증을 제시해야 합니다. 질문이 있으시면 Z-Mobile 고객 서비스 부서 917-488-4884로 전화하여 담당자에게 문의하세요.

어휘 currently 현재 offer 제공하다 discount 할인 miss out on ~을 놓치다 deal 거래 head over to ~로 출발하다 authorized retailer 공인 소매점 present 제시하다 consult with ~와 상담하다 representative 직원

4. 이 정보는 어디에서 찾을 수 있을 것 같은가?
(A) 지역 신문
(B) 휴대 전화 카탈로그
(C) 기술 잡지
(D) 사보

해설 초반부에서 Dole Electronics 직원들에게 30% 할인을 제공한다(Z-mobile is offering a 30% discount)는 것과 인사부로 가서 할인 쿠폰을 받으라(head over to the Human Resources Department and pick up a Z-Mobile discount coupon there)는 내용을 통해 직원들을 대상으로 하는 사보에서 볼 수 있는 정보로 유추할 수 있다. 따라서 (D)가 정답이다.

5. 할인 쿠폰을 어떻게 사용할 수 있는가?

    (A) 고객 서비스 담당자와 상담한다

    (B) 사원증을 제시한다.

    (C) 인사과 사무실을 방문한다

    (D) 공인 판매점에 전화한다

해설 두 번째 단락 "You are expected to present your employee identification card upon purchase"에서 쿠폰을 사용해서 구매할 때 사원증이 필요함을 알 수 있다. 따라서 (B)가 정답이다.

[6-7] 광고

이번 주의 제품: Kirk's 코코넛 비누

Kirk's 코코넛 비누는 메이플턴 주민인 Kirk Walmsley가 손수 만든 제품입니다. Walmsley 씨는 Bubble & Body Works와 계약을 통해 현지에서 그 비누를 판매하고 있습니다. 유기농 코코넛 오일로 만든 손 비누는 오래 쓸 수 있으며, 시원하고 건조한 곳에 잘 보관하면 유통 기한이 1년입니다. 1월부터 판매됐으며, Bubble & Body Works 고객들 사이에서 인기 있는 품목으로 자리 잡고 있습니다. 현재 두 개 묶음에 6.50달러에 판매되고 있으며, 사용자에게 많은 장점을 자랑합니다.

    - 손을 깨끗이 닦아줍니다.
    - 손을 부드럽게 유지해줍니다.
    - 은은한 향이 특징입니다.
    - 순수 유기농 재료로 구성되어 있습니다.
    - 인공 화학물질이 포함되어 있지 않습니다.

Kirk's 코코넛 비누를 15% 할인 받고 구매하시려면, 런던의 New Oxford Street에 있는 Bubble & Body Works 매장에서 계산원에게 할인 코드 KCS466을 말씀해 주세요.

어휘 handmade 수제의, 손으로 만든 resident 거주자 contract 계약 organic 유기농의, 자연적인 store 저장하다, 보관하다 long lasting 오래 지속되는 shelf life 유통 기한, 저장 수명 properly 적절하게 boast 뽐내다, ~을 갖고 있다 benefit 혜택, 장점 delicate scent 은은한 향 purely 순수하게, 완전히 artificial chemicals 인공 화학물질 discount code 할인 코드 cashier 계산원

6. 광고의 목적은 무엇인가?

    (A) 세정 절차 설명하기

    (B) 비누 제조 과정 시연하기

    (C) 새로운 매장의 개점 광고하기

    (D) 지역 주민의 상품 홍보하기

해설 첫 문장 "Kirk's Coconut Soap is handmade by Mapleton resident, Kirk Walmsley"에서 메이플턴 주민이 만든 코코넛 비누를 언급했고, 이어지는 내용에서 비누의 장점(The organic coconut oil hand soap is long lasting ~)과 할인 코드(simply mention discount code KCS466 to a cashier ~)를 광고하고 있다. 따라서 (D)가 정답이다.

7. 비누에 대해 언급된 내용은 무엇인가?

    (A) 자연 재료로 만들어졌다.

    (B) 주요 백화점에서 판매된다.

    (C) 1개 패키지로만 구매할 수 있다.

    (D) 여러 장소에서 제조될 예정이다.

해설 비누의 장점에 대한 내용 중 "Consists of purely organic materials"와 "Contains no artificial chemicals"에서 비누가 자연 재료로 만들어졌고, 인공적인 물질이 들어있지 않다고 했다. 따라서 (A)가 정답이다.

[8-10] 기사

로스엔젤레스 (6월 15일)—일본에 기반을 두고 있는 Fujio Games 사의 인기 있는 컴퓨터 게임의 새 버전인 Party Fight 3가 어제 출시되었다. 업데이트된 게임을 구입하는 첫 고객이 되기 위해 전 지역에서 수백 명의 사람들이 매장 밖에서 수시간을 기다렸다.

Fujio 사가 계획한 마케팅 전략은 가장 인기 있는 액션 게임 출시 소식을 퍼뜨리면서 성공적으로 진행되었다. 게임 비평가들은 Party Fight 3이 이전 시리즈보다 덜 주목을 받을 거라 생각했다. 그 이유는 Fujio 사가 어떤 마케팅 회사에도 의존하지 않았기 때문이다. 대신 Fujio 사는 자체 마케팅 부서에 투자했으며 그들의 전략은 게임 팬들의 의견을 반영하는 것이었다. 또한, 프로 격투기 선수들의 싸우는 동작을 모션 캡처해 이 게임이 더욱 높은 수준의 강렬한 게임 경험을 제공할 수 있도록 했다. 게임을 더 알리기 위해 일부 유명한 격투기 선수들을 매장에 초청해서, 생방송 인터뷰를 진행하고 팬들과 사진을 찍도록 했다.

어휘 release 출시하다 hundreds of 수백 명의 retail store 소매점 eager 간절히 바라는 strategy 전략 turn out 모습을 드러내다 spread 퍼트리다 critic 비평가 spotlight 주시, 관심 previous 이전의 rely on ~에 의존하다 instead 대신 invest in ~에 투자하다 reflect 반영하다 in addition 또한, 게다가 fighter 격투기 선수 intense 강렬한 popularize 대중화하다 high-profile 세간의 이목을 끄는

8. 기사에 따르면, 왜 사람들은 몇 시간 동안 기다렸는가?

    (A) 새 컴퓨터 모델을 주문하기 위해

    (B) 유명인사를 만나기 위해

    (C) 큰 행사 후 파티 참석하기 위해

    (D) 컴퓨터 게임을 사기 위해

해설 첫 번째 단락 "Hundreds of people eager to be among the first to purchase the updated game waited for hours outside retail stores across the region"에서 수백 명의 사람들이 게임을 구매하기 위해 매장 밖에서 수시간을 기다렸다는 것을 알 수 있다. 따라서 (D)가 정답이다.

9. Fujio Games 사에 대해 암시하는 것은?

    (A) 본사는 Los Angeles에 있다.

    (B) 최근에 다른 회사와 합병했다.

    (C) 제품이 경쟁사보다 비싸다.

    (D) 고객의 의견에 주의를 기울인다.

해설 본문 중반부 "Instead, Fujio invested in its own marketing divisions, and their strategy was to reflect suggestions from gaming fans"에서 회사가 고객의 의견을 마케팅 전략에 반영했다는 것을 알 수 있다. 따라서 (D)가 정답이다.

10. [1], [2], [3], [4]로 표시된 곳 중에서 다음 문장이 들어가기에 가장 적합한 곳은?

"그 이유는 Fujio 사가 어떤 마케팅 회사에도 의존하지 않았기 때문이다."

(A) [1]

(B) [2]

(C) [3]

(D) [4]

해설 [3]의 앞 문장 "Game critics believed that Party Fight 3 would receive less of a spotlight than its previous series"에서 게임 비평가들은 Party Fight 3이 이전 시리즈보다 덜 주목을 받을 거라 생각한다고 했고, 그 뒤에 그렇게 생각한 이유에 대한 내용으로 이어지는 것이 문맥상 적절하다. 그리고 [3]의 뒤에서 연결어 Instead를 통해 화제가 전환되며 Fujio 사의 자체 마케팅과 관련된 내용이 이어진다. 따라서 (C)가 정답이다.

[11-12] 광고

구인 공고

Michael's 의류 매장이 현재 Newbury Street와 Sunset Boulevard 지점에서 상근직 매니저를 모집하고 있습니다. 이상적인 후보자는 적어도 1년의 관리직 경험과 최소 5년의 소매업 분야 경력이 있어야 합니다. 관심 있는 분들은 희망 연봉을 포함한 자기소개서와 이력서, 이전 고용주의 추천서와 함께 Rebecca Clarke씨에게 rclarke@michaels.com으로 보내주시기 바랍니다.

어휘 clothing store 의류점 currently 현재 look for ~을 찾다 full-time 상근의, 전임의 branch 지점 ideal candidate 이상적인 후보자 at least 최소한 managerial 관리의 retail 소매업 party 사람 cover letter 자기소개서 salary requirement 희망 연봉 reference 추천서 previous employer 이전 고용주 sales associate 판매원 assistant 보조 supervisor 관리자 willingness 기꺼이 하는 마음 travel 출장

11. 어떤 자리가 광고되고 있는가?

(A) 소매점 판매원

(B) 행정 보조

(C) 매장 관리자

(D) 커뮤니티 센터 관리자

해설 첫 번째 문장 "Michael's Clothing Store is currently looking for a full time manager ~"에서 상근직 매니저를 구한다고 했으므로 (C)가 정답이다.

12. 자리에 대한 자격 요건으로 언급된 것은?

(A) 대학 학위

(B) 출장에 대한 의향

(C) 관리자 경력

(D) 조직 기술

해설 두 번째 문장 "The ideal candidate should have at least one year of managerial experience and at least five years in retail"에서 관리 경력이 요구 조건으로 언급되었다. 따라서 (C)가 정답이다.

[13-14] 광고

Archer Travel Services

환상적인 휴가를 준비하고 계신가요? Archer Travel Services가 도와드립니다!

6월 1일부터 8월 31일까지 동반자 항공 요금을 최대 100유로까지 절약하세요.

- 유럽 대륙 내 항공편에만 적용됩니다
- 동반자 항공 요금 한 명에게만 해당됩니다
- 5월 15일까지 예약해야 유효합니다

호텔과 렌터카 예약도 www.atservices.com에서 하세요. 그리고 추후 할인과 막바지 세일 정보를 받으시려면 저희 로열티 클럽에 가입하세요.

어휘 save 절약하다 up to ~까지 companion fare 동반자 요금 (항공사에서 한 사람이 표를 구매할 때, 동반자에게 할인을 적용해주는 요금제) apply to ~에 적용되다 continental Europe 유럽 대륙 good 유효한 book 예약하다 as well 또한, 역시 stay informed 계속 정보를 얻다 last-minute sales 막바지 세일

13. 무엇이 할인 중인가?

(A) 자동차 렌탈

(B) 항공권

(C) 크루즈 패키지

(D) 호텔 숙박

해설 초반부 "Save up to €100 on companion fares from June 1 to August 31"에서 동반자 항공 요금에 최대 100유로 할인을 받을 수 있다고 했고, "Applies only to flights within continental Europe"에서 할인이 유럽 내 항공편에만 적용된다고 했으므로 (B)가 정답이다.

14. 할인에 대해 명시된 것은 무엇인가?

(A) 제한된 시간 동안에만 제공된다.

(B) 온라인 구매에만 한정된다.

(C) 어디로 여행을 가든 유효하다.

(D) Archer Travel Services의 로열티 클럽 회원에게만 제공된다.

해설 할인 조건이 언급된 부분 "Offer valid when you book by May 15"에서 5월 15일까지의 예약에만 적용된다고 했으므로 할인이 제한된 시간 동안만 제공된다는 (A)가 정답이다.

[15-17] 정보

시드니 Shangri-La 호텔에 오신 것을 환영합니다!

시드니에 업무 목적이든 여가를 위해 방문하시든, 시간을 내시어 세계 최고 수준의 편의시설을 즐기시기 바랍니다. 귀하의 숙박을 향상시키기 위해 최고 품질의 서비스를 제공하게 되어 기쁘게 생각합니다.

문서 작업이나 인터넷 검색이 필요하신가요? 1층에 있는 비즈니스 센터인 Enterprise Hub는 24시간 운영되며 팩스, 컴퓨터, 프린터 등 최첨단 장비를 갖추고 있습니다. Enterprise Hub 옆에는 합리적인 가격의 다양한 음료와 스낵을 제공하는 Horizon 라운지가 있습니다.

출장이나 휴가 중에도 건강을 유지하고 싶으신가요? 그러면 2층에 위치한 새로 단장한 피트니스 센터 the F-zone을 방문하세요. 최신 운동기구가 있습니다.

배가 고프신가요? 호텔의 룸서비스 메뉴는 안내 책자 37페이지부터 시작하는 다이닝 섹션을 참조하세요. 또는 수상 경력이 있는 저희 식당에서 식사하세요. 현대적이고 전통적인 프랑스 요리를 제공하며 아침, 점심, 저녁 식사가 가능합니다.

시드니 방문 기간 동안 Shangri-La 호텔을 선택해 주셔서 감사합니다.

머무시는 동안 즐거운 시간 되십시오.

어휘 amenity 편의시설 enhance 높이다, 향상시키다 state-of-the-art 최첨단의, 최신식의 equipment 장비 including ~을 포함하여 a variety of 다양한 reasonably priced 합리적인 가격의 stay in shape 건강을 유지하다 directory 안내 책자 dine (잘 차린) 식사를 하다 award-winning 상을 받은 bistro (편안한 분위기의) 작은 식당 contemporary 현대적인 traditional 전통적인 cuisine 요리

15. 호텔에 대해 언급된 것은?

(A) 관광지 근처에 위치해 있다.
(B) 투숙객을 위한 다양한 서비스를 제공한다.
(C) 비즈니스 전문가들에게 인기가 높다.
(D) 단골손님에게 할인 혜택을 제공한다.

해설 전체적으로 호텔을 안내하는 글로, 문단마다 호텔의 각 층에서 누릴 수 있는 서비스 혜택들을 안내하고 있다. 지문에 호텔의 위치를 언급한 내용은 없으며, 특정 고객에게 인기가 높다는 내용과 고객에게 제공하는 할인 혜택은 언급되지 않았다. 따라서 투숙객들에게 다양한 서비스를 제공하고 있다는 (B)가 정답이다.

16. Horizon Lounge에 관해 언급된 것은?

(A) 예약이 필요하다.
(B) 최근에 재단장되었다.
(C) 차와 커피를 무료로 제공한다.
(D) 1층에 위치해 있다.

해설 두 번째 문단 두번째 문장 "Our business center on the first floor, the Enterprise Hub ~"를 통해 비즈니스 센터가 1층에 있다는 것을 알 수 있고, 두 번째 문단 마지막 문장 "Located next to the Enterprise Hub is the Horizon Lounge, ~"에서 Horizon Lounge는 비즈니스 센터 옆, 즉 1층에 있다는 것을 알 수 있으므로 (D)가 정답이다.

17. 호텔의 특징으로 언급되지 않은 것은?

(A) 운동 센터
(B) 레스토랑
(C) 수영장
(D) 비즈니스 센터

해설 각 문단마다 편의 시설을 안내하고 있다. 비즈니스 센터(business center), 운동 센터(fitness center), 식당(bistro)을 언급했으나 수영장에 대한 내용은 없으므로 (C)가 정답이다.

[18-21] 기사

자동차 제조업체 Bruen 사와 Headley 사의 합병

북미 자동차 시장의 선두를 달리며, 세계적으로 알려진 자동차 브랜드인 Bruen 사는 어제 기자회견을 열고 영국의 Headley 자동차 회사와 마침내 합병을 성사시켰다고 발표했다. 양측은 이번 합병이 서로에게 이로울 것이라는 데 동의했다. 최근 Bruen은 경기 침체로 인해 자금적으로 많은 어려움에 직면했다.

영국에서 가장 큰 자동차 제조업체인 Headley 사는 합병 결과에 매우 만족한다고 했다. Headley 사의 CEO인 Jonathon Green이 새로운 회사를 이끌어갈 것이다. 그는 Bruen의 이미지를 쇄신할 계획이라고 밝혔다. 그는 앞으로 추세인 전기 자동차 생산에 매진할 것이라고 했다.

이번 합병으로 많은 미국인이 실망했는데, 그들은 Bruen 사가 국경 내에 있는 국내 업체와 합병할 것을 원했기 때문이다.

Bruen 사의 많은 이들은 일자리를 잃을까 우려하고 있지만 Headley 사는 인력 감축은 없을 것이라고 약속했다. 그렇지만 Bruen 사에서 판매량이 저조한 스포츠카 부문은 생산을 중단할 계획이다.

어휘 foremost 선두의 manufacturer 제조업체 renowned 유명한, 잘 알려진 hold a press conference 기자 회견을 열다 indeed 사실상 merge 합병하다 face 직면하다 financial difficulties 재정적인 어려움 slowdown 둔화, 경기 침체 head ~을 이끌다 plan on ~할 예정이다 wave 추세 upset 속상하게 하다 border 국경 be concerned about ~에 대해서 걱정하다 discontinue 중단하다 electric car 전기차 by half 절반으로 beneficial 도움이 되는

18. 기사에 따르면, Bruen 사의 합병은 왜 일부 사람들을 실망시켰는가?

(A) 많은 사람들은 일자리를 잃을 것이다.

(B) 외국 회사와 합병했다.

(C) 미국인들이 영국으로 이사를 해야 할 것이다.

(D) 전기차에 대한 관심이 적다.

해설 기사 첫 문장에서 미국의 Bruen 사와 영국의 Headley 사가 합병한다고 했고, 기사 세 번째 문단 "a number of Americans, who were hoping that Bruen would merge with a national company within its borders"에서 국내에 있는 회사와 합병하기를 바란 미국 사람들이 두 회사의 합병에 대해 실망했다고 했으므로 (B)가 정답이다.

19. Bruen 사에 대한 Headley 사의 계획은 무엇인가?

(A) 직원 수를 절반으로 줄인다.

(B) 스포츠카 모델을 개선한다.

(C) 더 많은 전기차를 생산한다.

(D) Bruen의 본사를 영국으로 옮긴다.

해설 두 번째 문단 "He said that he will go ahead and produce more electric cars, as this is the wave of the future"에서 새로운 회사를 이끌어갈 CEO인 Jonathon Green이 앞으로의 추세인 전기 자동차 생산에 매진할 것이라고 했으므로 (C)가 정답이다.

20. 합병의 결과로 언급된 것이 아닌 것은 무엇인가?

(A) 전기차 생산 증대

(B) 브루엔 사의 이미지 쇄신

(C) 일부 모델 생산 중단

(D) 인력 감축

해설 마지막 문단 "~ but Headley has promised that no jobs will be cut"에서 합병으로 인한 인원 감축은 없을 것이라고 했으므로 (D)가 정답이다.

21. [1], [2], [3], [4]로 표시된 곳 중에서 다음 문장이 들어가기에 가장 적합한 위치는?

"양측은 이번 합병이 서로에게 이로울 것이라는 데 동의했다."

(A) [1]

(B) [2]

(C) [3]

(D) [4]

해설 주어진 문장의 both parties가 단서가 된다. 주어진 문장 앞에서 Bruen 사와 Headley 사가 둘 다 언급되고, 합병을 발표하면서 합병 이유와 배경을 설명하는 흐름이 자연스러우므로 (A)가 정답이다.

UNIT 17 기타 지문

PRACTICE
본문 p.303

1. (D)   **2.** (A)   **3.** (D)   **4.** (C)

[1-2] 문자 메시지

1. Garcia 씨는 Perry 씨가 무엇을 하길 원하는가?

(A) 일부 주문을 처리하기

(B) 채용 여부 결정하기

(C) 회의 일정을 변경하기

(D) 지원자와 이야기하기

해설 10시 30분에 "The job applicants are here"에서 Perry 씨가 Garcia 씨에게 지원자들이 도착했다고 하자, 10시 31분에 "I should be there in about an hour. Please start without me"에서 Garcia 씨가 1시간 정도 늦는다고 먼저 시작하라고 했으므로 지원자와 이야기해 달라는 (D)가 정답이다.

2. 10시 37분에, Garcia 씨가 "그러게요"라고 썼을 때, 그가 의도한 것은 무엇인가?

(A) 그 또한 회사의 성장에 놀랐다.

(B) 그는 봉급이 더 높아야 한다고 생각한다.

(C) 그는 Fleer 씨와 만난 적이 있다.

(D) 그는 버스가 1시간 내로 도착할 거라고 확신한다.

해설 10시 36분 Perry 씨의 메시지 "Can you believe our company has grown so much that we need to hire someone just to process orders?"에서 회사가 꽤 성장해서 주문을 처리할 인원을 고용하게 된 것이 믿어지지 않는다고 하는 말에 Garcia 씨가 I know(그러게요)라고 응답했으므로, 회사의 성장에 본인도 놀랐다는 의도의 (A)가 정답이다.

[3-4] 초대장

3. 누구에게 초대장이 보내진 것 같은가?

(A) 연회 기획자들

(B) 호텔 관리자들

(C) 행사 준비자들

(D) 협회 회원들

해설 첫 문장 "All of the members of the International Working Men's Association (IWMA) are cordially invited to its 10th annual banquet"에서 협회의 회원들이 초대받았음을 알 수 있다. 따라서 정답은 (D)가 된다.

4. 수신자들은 무엇을 하도록 요청을 받는가?

(A) 오찬에 참석하는 것

(B) 초대장을 가져오는 것

(C) 행사 참석 여부를 알려주는 것

정답과 해설

(D) 행사 준비자에게 이메일을 보내는 것

해설 지문 마지막 "Please reply to James McGough, the event coordinator, to indicate whether you will participate in the dinner"에서 행사 참여 여부를 알려 달라고 요청했으므로 정답은 (C)이다.

ACTUAL TEST
본문 p.308

1. (D)	2. (C)	3. (C)	4. (B)	5. (B)	6. (D)
7. (B)	8. (C)	9. (D)	10. (D)	11. (B)	12. (B)
13. (A)	14. (A)	15. (B)	16. (C)	17. (B)	

[1-2] 문자 메시지

Eleanor Jones (오전 10시 22분)
안녕하세요, Anastasia. 계약서를 저에게 보내셨나요?

Anastasia Phillips (오전 10시 30분)
아니요, 그럴 여유가 없었어요. 긴 휴가에서 복귀한 후 밀린 일을 하느라 너무 바빴어요.

Eleanor Jones (오전 10시 32분)
무슨 말씀인지 알겠어요! 여기 법무부는 모든 직원이 오늘 밤 늦게까지 일할 거예요.

Anastasia Phillips (오전 10시 33분)
점심 식사 후에 사람을 시켜서 시내 사무실로 계약서를 보낼 수 있어요. 괜찮을까요?

Eleanor Jones (오전 10시 35분)
알겠습니다, 계약서들이 모두 서명이 된 상태로 준비된다면 괜찮을 것 같아요.

Anastasia Phillips (오전 10시 36분)
그럴 겁니다. 대략 오후 1시에는 도착할 거예요.

어휘 contract 계약서 extremely 매우 catch up 따라잡다
messenger 전달자, 배달원 downtown 시내 as long as
~하는 한 about 대략 fix 수정하다

1. 오전 10시 32분에, Jones 씨가 "무슨 말씀인지 알겠어요"라고 쓴 의도는?
(A) 그녀는 계약서를 깜박했다.
(B) 그녀는 계약서상의 오류를 수정할 것이다.
(C) 그녀도 휴가를 즐겼다.
(D) 그녀도 할 일이 많다.

해설 10시 30분에 Phillips 씨가 "We've been extremely busy trying to catch up after the long holiday weekend"에서 휴가 복귀 후 밀린 일을 하느라 너무 바빴다고 말했다. 이에 대해 10시 32분에 Jones 씨가 "I know what you mean! Everyone here in the Legal Affairs department Department is going to work late this evening"에서 무슨 말인지 알겠다며

법무부 모든 직원이 오늘 밤 늦게까지 일할 거라고 했으므로 해당 표현은 공감의 표시로 한 말임을 알 수 있다. 따라서 (D)가 정답이다.

2. 글쓴이들에 대해 암시하는 것은 무엇인가?
(A) 그들은 점심 식사를 위해 만날 것이다.
(B) 그들은 자주 늦게 일한다.
(C) 그들은 다른 건물에서 일한다.
(D) 그들은 우체부이다.

해설 10시 33분 Phillips 씨의 메시지 "I can have a messenger bring them to the downtown office after lunch. Would that work?"에서 사람을 시켜서 시내에 있는 사무실로 계약서를 가져다 준다고 했으므로 서로 다른 사무실에서 일한다는 것을 유추할 수 있다. 따라서 (C)가 정답이다.

[3-4] 문자 메시지

Alice Eve [오전 8시 45분]
안녕하세요, Cory. 인사부가 저희에게 당신의 연례 평가 일정을 잡아달라고 요청하고 있어요. 어떤 날이 편하세요?

Cory Glover [오전 8시 50분]
제가 다음 주에 회의가 있어서 Interlaken으로 출장을 가는데, 12월 19일 수요일은 어떨까요?

Alice Eve [오전 8시 52분]
안 될 것 같아요. 서류 작업을 처리하려면 모든 연례 평가가 그 전에 마무리가 되어야 해요. 월요일 또는 화요일에 시간을 내주실 수 없나요?

Cory Glover [오전 9시 10분]
방금 제가 18일에 있는 오전 회의의 일정을 조정했어요. 오전 9시에 사무실에 갈 수 있을 것 같아요. 괜찮죠?

Alice Eve [오전 9시 12분]
좋아요. 다음 주에 당신에게 알림 이메일을 보낼게요. 회의 잘 다녀오시고 안전한 출장 되세요.

어휘 Human Resources 인사부 ask 요청하다 schedule 일정을 잡다 annual review 연간 평가, 연간 보고서 work 가능하다 travel 이동하다, 출장가다 complete 끝마치다 process 처리하다 paperwork 서류 작업, 문서 업무 reschedule 일정을 변경하다 clear 비우다

3. 왜 Stone 씨는 Glover 씨에게 연락을 했나?
(A) 회의안을 검토하기 위해
(B) Glover 씨에게 지연된 보고서가 있다는 것을 알리기 위해
(C) Glover 씨에게 회의를 요청하기 위해
(D) 비행 일정을 잡는 것을 돕기 위해

해설 8시 52분 Stone 씨의 메시지 "All of the annual reviews need to be completed before then so that we can process the paperwork. Can you clear a couple hours on that

Monday or Tuesday?"에서 연례 평가를 하기 위해 일정을 비워달라고 요청하자 Glover 씨가 일정을 조정해서 사무실로 가겠다고 했다. 따라서 Stone 씨는 연례 평가를 위한 미팅을 요청하기 위해 연락한 것이므로 (C)가 정답이다.

4. 오전 8시 52분에, Stone 씨가 "안 될 것 같아요"라고 쓴 의도는?

(A) 그녀는 Interlaken으로 출장을 갈 수 없을 것이다.

(B) Glover 씨는 다른 시간을 선택해야 한다.

(C) Glover 씨가 서류에서 몇 가지 실수를 했다.

(D) 그녀는 프로젝트를 도울 수 없을 것이다.

> **해설** 8시 50분에 Glover 씨가 다음 주에 회의 때문에 Interlaken으로 출장을 가서 12월 19일 수요일로 연례 평가 일정을 잡겠다는 제안(I'll be traveling to Interlaken for the conference next week. How about Wednesday, December 19?)에 대한 대답이므로, Glover 씨는 다른 시간을 선택해야 한다는 (B)가 정답이다.

[5-7] 송장

Abraxas Cookshop

주문 송장

소중한 고객님께 10년 이상 서비스를 제공해 왔습니다.
42 St Giles Street
Northampton, NN1 1JW, England

고객명: Melinda Paraie
청구 주소: 44 St James Mill Road, Northampton, NN5 5RA, England
배송 주소: 268 Wellingborough Road, Northampton, NN1 4EJ, England
배송 날짜: 2월 8일

제품 코드	내역	수량
34GU	계량컵	1
* 657UH	로스팅 팬	2
* 466GT	장식용 냅킨	20
54RD	전문 식칼 세트	1

* 466GT와 657UH 제품은 현재 품절 상태이므로 추후 배송될 예정입니다.

> **어휘** invoice 송장 valued 소중한 billing address 청구 주소 shipping address 발송 주소 description 묘사, 설명 quantity 수량 deliver 배달하다 currently 현재 out of stock 재고가 없는 pharmacy 약국 grocery store 식료품점 payment 지불 return 반품하다 shipment 수송, 수송품 decade 10년 warehouse 창고 import 수입하다; 수입

5. Paraie 씨가 어떤 종류의 사업체를 소유하고 있을 것 같은가?

(A) 세탁소

(B) 레스토랑

(C) 약국

(D) 식료품점

> **해설** Paraie 씨가 주문한 송장의 구매 항목을 보면 계량컵, 로스팅 팬, 장식용 냅킨, 식칼을 구입했음을 알 수 있다. 이를 통해 Paraie 씨의 사업체는 (B) 레스토랑임을 짐작할 수 있다.

6. 송장에 따르면, 2월 8일에 무슨 일이 일어나는가?

(A) 추가 주문이 있을 것이다.

(B) 결제가 완료될 것이다.

(C) 제품 하나가 반품될 것이다.

(D) 물건이 발송될 것이다.

> **해설** 질문에 2월 8일이라는 특정 날짜가 언급되었으므로 지문에 날짜 정보가 명시된 부분을 찾는다. 중반부에 "Shipping date: February 8"라고 명시되어 있으므로 2월 8일에 물품이 발송될 것임을 알 수 있다. 따라서 (D)가 정답이다.

7. Abraxas Cookshop에 대해 명시된 것은 무언인가?

(A) 20년 이상 운영되어 왔다.

(B) 현재 일부 제품이 창고에 없다.

(C) 다른 나라에서 제품을 수입한다.

(D) 전 세계에 많은 지점을 보유하고 있다.

> **해설** 지문의 하단 "Items 466GT and 657UH will be delivered on a later date because they are currently out of stock"에서 현재 일부 제품이 품절 상태임을 알 수 있다. 따라서 (B)가 정답이다.

[8-9] 영수증

Metro Outfitters

1520 N Milwaukee Ave
Chicago, IL 60622
(215) 454-5500

계산원: Frank Conforti
계산대: 3번
날짜/시각: 12월 19일 / 오후 6시 15분

상품번호	구매내역	수량	가격
854387	특대 Vintage Tommy 패딩 (검은색)	1	125.00달러
543978	특대 스웨터 (빨간색)	2	120.00달러

소계: 245.00달러
Metro Outfitters 회원 할인:- 49.00달러
세금: 19.60달러

합계: 215.60달러
지불 방법: 현금 216.00달러
거스름돈: 0.40달러

Metro Outfitters 회원 개인 정보:
이름: Kate Spencer   전화번호: (215) 457-7685
오늘 적립된 포인트: 216   남은 포인트: 3,233

3,000달러 상당의 상품권을 포함한 환상적인 상품 추첨에 참여하기 위해 12월 31일 이전에 저희 웹사이트 www.metrooutfitters.com/event 를 방문하세요.
다음의 홍보 코드를 입력하세요: FLASH504395800

어휘 cashier 계산원 cash register 계산대 quantity 수량 amount 가격, 액수 puffer jacket 패딩 subtotal 소계 tax 세금 total 합계 cash 현금 change 거스름돈 personal information 개인 정보 remaining 남은 drawing 추첨 prize 상(품) gift certificate 상품권 following 다음의 promotion code 홍보 코드 in person 직접 waive 적용하지 않다 raffle 추첨, 판매

8. Spencer 씨에 관해 암시되는 것은 무엇인가?

(A) Metro Outfitters에서 일한다.
(B) 새 바지를 구매했다.
(C) 12월 19일에 Conforti 씨를 직접 만났다.
(D) 그녀의 신용카드로 계산했다.

해설 지문은 Kate Spencer가 12월 19일에 Metro Outfitters에서 패딩과 스웨터를 현금으로 사고 받은 영수증이다. 영수증의 Cashier에서 계산원 Frank Conforti의 이름을 확인할 수 있고, 회원 개인 정보에서 Kate Spencer의 이름을 확인할 수 있다. 따라서 구매일인 12월 19일에 계산원인 Conforti 씨와 Spencer씨가 계산대에서 직접 만났을 것이므로 (C)가 정답이다.

9. Spencer 씨는 홍보 코드로 무엇을 할 것 같은가?

(A) 추가 할인 받기
(B) 소식지 구독하기
(C) 배송비 면제받기
(D) 추첨에 참여하기

해설 지문 아래 "Visit our Web site ~ to participate in a drawing for fantastic prizes, including a $3,000 gift certificate! Enter the following promotion code ~"에서 경품 추첨에 참여하기 위해 웹사이트를 방문하여 홍보 코드를 입력하라고 했으므로 (D)가 정답이다. 지문 속의 participate in a drawing을 Enter a raffle로 패러프레이징했다.

[10-11] 초대장

수신: Pablo McHenry

MedStar 의료 센터는 Summer Dreamland Dinner에 정중히 귀하를 초대합니다.
Plaza 호텔의 Venetian Room에서 8월 15일 토요일, 오후 7시에 열립니다.

이 행사는 기부자들의 후한 재정적 지원에 감사하기 위해 일 년에 한 번 개최됩니다. 저녁은 다섯 가지 코스로 나오는 식사와 Philharmonic Symphony의 엄선된 단원들이 제공하는 즐길거리가 포함될 것입니다.

Ashley Hinson에게 a.hinson@medstarmc.com으로 이메일을 보냄으로써 늦어도 8월 1일까지는 답장해 주시기 바랍니다. 귀하와 함께 손님을 2명까지 데리고 오실 수 있습니다. 입장을 위해 이 초대장을 입구에서 제시해 주세요. 저희와 함께하실 수 있기를 바랍니다!

어휘 cordially 진심으로 host 주최하다 annually 일년에 한 번 donor 기부자 generous 후한, 너그러운 financial support 재정적 지원 select 엄선된 no later than 늦어도 ~까지는 entry 입장, 출입 be nominated for ~의 후보로 지명되다 monetary 금전적인 invitee 초청객

10. McHenry 씨는 왜 행사에 초대되었을 것 같은가?

(A) 수상 후보자로 지명되었다.
(B) 자원봉사자로 일했다.
(C) 직원 중 한 명이다.
(D) 금전적 기부를 했다.

해설 두 번째 단락에 행사의 목적이 제시되어 있다. "This event is hosted annually to thank our donors for their generous financial support"에서 기부자들의 재정적 지원에 감사하기 위한 행사임을 밝힌 것으로 보아 이 초대장의 수신자인 McHenry 씨 역시 돈을 기부했기 때문에 이 행사에 초대되었음을 알 수 있다. 따라서 (D)가 정답이다.

11. 행사에 관해 사실이 아닌 것은 무엇인가?

(A) 주말에 열릴 것이다.
(B) Ashley Hinson이 하는 연설이 포함될 것이다.
(C) 초청객들은 손님들을 데리고 올 수 있다.
(D) 음악 공연이 포함될 것이다.

해설 (A)는 행사 날짜가 on Saturday, August 15(8월 15일 토요일) 이라고 했고, (C)는 마지막 단락 "You are welcome to bring up to two guests with you(손님 2명까지 동반할 수 있다)"에서, (D)는 두 번째 단락 "entertainment provided by select members of the Philharmonic Symphony(단원들이 제공하는 즐길거리)"에서 확인할 수 있다. Ashley Hinson에게 참석 여부에 대한 답장을 보내라고 했고 연설에 관한 내용은 언급된 바 없으므로 (B)가 정답이다.

[12-13] 문자 메시지

Landon Hemsworth [오전 9시 12분]
사무실에 있으세요?

Dakota Malone [오전 9시 12분]
네, 9시부터 여기에 있었어요.

Landon Hemsworth [오전 9시 13분]
제 프린터가 고장 났어요. 수리 서비스 센터에 전화했는데 오늘 오후까지는 기술자가 올 수 없대요. 10시에 고객과의 미팅 전에 설문지를 인쇄해야 해요.

Dakota Malone [오전 9시 14분]
제가 인쇄해 드릴게요. 설문지는 어디 있어요?

Landon Hemsworth [오전 9시 15분]
내부 웹사이트에 올려놓았어요. Client Survey 폴더에서 찾을 수 있어요.

Dakota Malone [오전 9시 16분]
알겠어요. 제가 바로 할게요.

Landon Hemsworth [오전 9시 17분]
정말 감사해요! 제가 5분 후에 사무실로 가지러 갈게요.

> **어휘** broken 고장난 technician 기술자 questionnaire 설문지 print 인쇄하다 upload 업로드하다 right away 당장, 바로 stop by 잠깐 들르다

12. Hemsworth 씨가 언급한 문제는 무엇인가?

    (A) 그의 비서가 늦는다.

    (B) 기술자가 바로 올 수 없다.

    (C) 회의가 예상보다 일찍 시작될 것이다.

    (D) 일부 설문지가 승인되지 않았다.

> **해설** Hemsworth 씨의 9시 13분 메시지 "My printer is broken. I called the repair service center, but a technician cannot come until this afternoon"에서 프린터가 고장나서 수리 서비스 센터에 전화했는데 오늘 오후까지는 기술자가 올 수 없다고 했으므로 (B)가 정답이다.

13. 오전 9시 16분에, Malone 씨가 "제가 바로 할게요"라고 쓴 의도는?

    (A) 문서를 인쇄할 것이다.

    (B) 설문지를 복사할 것이다.

    (C) 수리 서비스에 전화할 것이다.

    (D) Client Survey 폴더를 삭제할 것이다.

> **해설** 9시 14분에 Malone 씨가 인쇄해 준다고 했고 설문지를 어디서 찾을 수 있는지를 묻자, 9시 15분에 Hemsworth 씨가 내부 웹 사이트의 Client Survey 폴더에서 찾을 수 있다고 했다. 따라서 "제가 바로 할게요"라는 말은 바로 문서를 인쇄하겠다는 의도로 한 것이다. 따라서 (A)가 정답이다.

[14-17] 온라인 채팅

Mia Thompson [오후 2시 15분]
안녕하세요, Ellie, Fatima. 제가 시작하라고 한 웹로그 작업은 어떻게 진행되고 있나요?

Fatima Rashad [오후 2시 17분]
우리 투자 자문팀의 프로필을 작성하는 것을 생각하고 있어요.

Mia Thompson [오후 2시 19분]
좀 더 자세히 설명해 줄 수 있나요?

Fatima Rashad [오후 2시 21분]
네, 매달 다른 팀원을 인터뷰해서 특집으로 다루고 싶어요. 개인적이고 직업적인 배경 정보를 좀 얻을 수 있고, 그들의 투자 전략에 대한 견해 같은 것들을 물어볼 수 있을 것 같아요.

Mia Thompson [오후 2시 22분]
좋네요. 우리 고객들이 정말 좋아할 것 같아요. Ellie 씨는 어때요?

Ellie Friedman [오후 2시 24분]
저는 최신 주식 시장 동향에 대해 알리는 것을 생각하고 있습니다. 이 주제에 대한 자료를 벌써 많이 수집했어요.

Mia Thompson [오후 2시 25분]
흥미롭네요. 작업하시는 데 도움이 필요한가요?

Ellie Friedman [오후 2시 26분]
고마워요, 하지만 제가 처리할 수 있을 것 같아요.

Mia Thompson [오후 2시 27분]
좋아요. 월요일까지 여러분의 이 아이디어들의 진행 상황을 알려주세요.

> **어휘** come along 되어 가다 profile 인물을 소개하다 investment advisor 투자 고문 details 세부사항 feature 특집으로 다루다 professional 전문적인 inquire about ~에 관해 문의하다 that sort of thing 그런 종류의 것 emerging 신생의 collect 수집하다, 모으다 assistance 도움, 보조 cover 다루다, 처리하다 progress 과정 supervise 감독하다 subject matter 주제, 소재

14. 대화 참석자들은 어떤 분야에서 일하는 것 같은가?

    (A) 금융

    (B) 건강관리

    (C) 기술

    (D) 부동산

> **해설** Rashad 씨와 Friedman 씨의 메시지에서 언급된 investment advisors, investment strategies, emerging stock market trends 등의 표현을 통해 금융 관련 분야에서 일한다는 것을 유추해 볼 수 있다. 따라서 (A)가 정답이다.

15. Thompson 씨에 대해서 암시되는 것은 무엇인가?

    (A) 그녀는 Friedman 씨의 자료 조사를 도울 것이다.

    (B) 그녀는 Rashad 씨의 일을 감독한다.

    (C) 그녀는 월요일에 사무실에 없을 것이다.

    (D) 그녀는 취업 지원자에 대한 정보가 필요하다.

> **해설** Thompson 씨의 2시 15분 메시지 "How are things coming along with those weblogs I asked you to start?"에서 지시한 업무의 진행 상황을 묻고 있고, 2시 27분 메시지 "I'd like both of you to get back to me about your progress on these ideas by Monday"에서 진행 상황을 월요일까지 보고하라고 했으므로 Thompson 씨가 Rashad 씨의 일을 관리 감독하는 사람이라고 유추할 수 있다. 따라서 (B)가 정답이다.

16. Rashad 씨의 웹로그에 관해 명시된 것은 무엇인가?

(A) 오늘 안에 준비가 될 것이다.

(B) 여러 팀 구성원들이 쓸 것이다.

(C) 한 달에 한 번 게재될 것이다.

(D) 회사 내부용으로 기획될 것이다.

해설 2시 21분에 Rashad 씨의 메시지 "Well, I want to feature an interview with a different team member every month"에서 매달 다른 팀원을 인터뷰하고 싶다고 했다. 따라서 (C)가 정답이다.

17. 오후 2시 25분에, Thompson 씨가 "흥미롭네요"라고 쓴 의도는?

(A) 그녀는 Rashad 씨의 팀원들에 대해 더 알고 싶어 한다.

(B) 그녀는 Friedman 씨의 웹로그 주제가 마음에 든다.

(C) 그녀는 최근의 주식 시장 동향에 만족한다.

(D) 그녀는 긍정적인 고객 피드백을 받기를 좋아한다.

해설 Friedman 씨의 2시 24분 메시지 "I'm thinking of reporting on emerging stock market trends"에서 웹로그 주제로 신흥 주식 시장 동향에 대해 알리는 것을 생각하고 있다고 하자, 그에 대한 대답으로 흥미롭다고 했으므로 (B)가 정답이다.

UNIT 18 복수 지문

PRACTICE 본문 p.319

1. (B)

1. Shaw 씨에 따르면, Graizer 씨는 온라인 계정 시스템에 언제 다시 접속할 수 있는가?

(A) 월요일 아침 6시까지

(B) 월요일 저녁 5시 전

(C) 금요일 오전까지

(D) 주말 동안

해설 질문을 읽고 질문의 키워드인 Shaw, Graizer, access the online account system, again을 확인한다. 첫 번째 지문과 두 번째 지문이 시간의 흐름에 따라 내용이 전개되고 있으므로 시점을 키워드로 내용을 파악해야 한다. 첫 번째 이메일의 발신자인 Graizer 씨가 월요일 오전에 시스템에 로그인 오류 문제를 보고하면서 "it's imperative that I enter account information for six new loan applicants by 5:00 P.M. today"에서 당일 오후 5시까지 처리해야할 업무를 언급했다. 두 번째 이메일의 발신자인 기술지원팀 Shaw 씨는 "~ expect to have the system fully operational within the next couple of hours, which will be in time for you to submit your clients' loan applications"에서 몇 시간 내에 오류가 처리될 것이고, Graizer 씨가 하려던 업무를 제시간에 할 수 있다고 했으므로 계정 시스템에 접속이 가능한 시간은 월요일 저녁 5시 전이라고 추측할 수 있다. 따라서 정답은 (B)이다.

1. (C)	**2.** (A)	**3.** (D)	**4.** (D)	**5.** (C)	**6.** (A)
7. (B)	**8.** (C)	**9.** (C)	**10.** (D)	**11.** (C)	**12.** (A)
13. (A)	**14.** (D)	**15.** (B)	**16.** (B)	**17.** (C)	**18.** (B)
19. (D)	**20.** (A)				

[1-5] 광고 & 이메일

Equinox 헬스 클럽

Dakota에 있는 저희의 새로운 클럽에 방문하세요. Equinox 헬스 클럽의 고객이라면 곧 Fargo와 Williston에 있는 이 놀라운 시설을 회원 혜택의 일부로 이용할 수 있게 됩니다. 독점적인 무료 사전 방문 행사를 통해 누구보다 먼저 체험할 수 있습니다.

날짜: 9월 15일 토요일
시간: 오후 1시부터 오후 5시까지
활동 사항: 시설 둘러보기, 카페 메뉴 체험하기, 전문 강사 만나기

왜 Dakota 클럽을 가입해야 하는가?

- Clean Eats 카페에서는 영양가 있는 샌드위치, 샐러드, 과일 주스를 제공합니다.
- 실내 수영장에는 운동과 휴식을 위한 다양한 공간이 마련되어 있습니다.
- Gold's 체육관에서는 5세에서 12세 사이의 어린이를 위한 활동들을 제공합니다.
- Spinning Hub Room에서는 고급 모니터와 제어 장치가 장착된 최첨단 운동용 자전거가 있는데, 이는 이 지역에서 최초 도입된 것입니다.

일반 대중을 대상으로 한 개장 행사는 9월 22일 토요일에 진행될 예정입니다.
체험 수업과 더 많은 추가 무료 간식을 위해서 다시 방문해 주세요. 일부 손님은 Equinox 티셔츠와 모자를 받으실 수 있습니다.

수신: ajames@equinox.com
발신: jhernandez@freemayle.net
날짜: 9월 23일
제목: 취업 기회

친애하는 James 씨,

어제 오후에 당신과의 대화는 너무 좋았습니다. 헬스 클럽을 둘러보게 해주셔서 감사합니다. 직원들이 많은 열정을 보였고, 많은 분들이 Equinox에 가입하고 싶어 한다는 것을 알게 되어 좋았습니다. 저는 Dakota에 있는 Equinox 헬스 클럽에서 당신 팀의 일원이 되는 것에 대한 논의를 계속하고 싶습니다. 우리가 이야기한 대로 이력서를 첨부했습니다.

제 경력에서 확인할 수 있듯이, 저는 건강을 촉진하는 환경에서 뛰어난 성과를 냅니다. 가장 중요한 것은, 저는 청소년들과 함께 일하는 것을 즐기며, 항상 아이들을 위한 지도 및 상담 기회를 찾아왔습니다. 저는 청소년들에게 매일 신체 활동을 장려하는 것이 중요하다고 생각합니다. 가능한 직책에 대해 논의하고 싶으니 (607) 555-0118로 전화해 주세요.

안녕히 계세요,
Jennifer Hernandez

어휘 brand-new 아주 새로운 patron 고객 have access to ~을 이용하다 take tours 둘러보다, 견학하다 skilled 숙련된 nutritious 영양가가 높은 indoor pool 실내 수영장 state-of-the-art 최신식의 grand opening 개장, 개점 treat 대접 enthusiasm 열정, 열의 discussion 토론, 논의 attach 첨부하다 consideration 고려, 숙려 as per ~에 따라 thrive 성공하다, 번창하다 counsel 상담하다, 조언하다 youth 젊음 commercial real estate 상업용 부동산

1. 누구를 대상으로 한 광고 같은가?
(A) Dakota 지역의 신규 주민
(B) 운동 강사가 되기 위해 훈련 중인 사람들
(C) Equinox 헬스 클럽의 현재 회원들
(D) 상업용 부동산 투자자들

해설 광고 도입부 “Come and visit our brand-new club in Dakota. As patrons of the Equinox Health Club, you will soon have access to this amazing facility in Fargo and Williston as a part of your membership”에서 기존 Equinox 헬스 클럽 회원들이 다른 지역의 새로운 클럽도 이용할 수 있다고 했고, 이어서 사전 방문 행사에 대해 안내하고 있으므로 (C)가 정답이다.

2. 참석자들은 9월 15일에 무료로 무엇을 받을 것인가?
(A) 음식과 음료
(B) 개인 지도
(C) 1주일 무료 이용권
(D) 의류 한 벌

해설 광고의 사전 방문 이벤트 날짜인 9월 15일에 있는 활동 사항(Activities)에서 확인할 수 있다. 활동 사항의 “try samples of our café items”에서 카페에서 파는 제품을 체험해보라고 했으므로 음식과 음료 샘플을 무료로 제공한다는 것으로 볼 수 있다. 따라서 (A)가 정답이다. 광고에서 티셔츠와 모자가 언급되었으나 사전 체험 이벤트 이후 클럽이 개장한 뒤에 재방문시 제공되는 상품이므로 (D)는 오답이다.

3. 광고에 따르면, Dakota 클럽에서만 이용 가능한 것은 무엇인가?
(A) 수영 레슨
(B) 영양 상담
(C) 할인된 회원 가격
(D) 특수 운동용 자전거

해설 광고의 Why Try The Dakota Club? 아래로 언급된 내용에서 Spinning Hub Room을 소개하면서 Dakota 지점의 운동용 자전거가 지역 내 처음 도입된 것(the first of their kind in the area)이라고 했으므로 (D)가 정답이다.

4. Hernandez 씨가 James 씨를 언제 만났을 것 같은가?
(A) 예정된 직무 인터뷰 중에
(B) 채용 콘퍼런스 중에
(C) 클럽의 사전 체험 행사 중에
(D) 클럽의 개장 행사 중에

해설 이메일을 보낸 날짜는 9월 23일로 확인되고 이메일 도입부 “I enjoyed talking with you yesterday afternoon”에서 Hernandez 씨는 어제 오후에 James 씨를 만났다고 했다. 광고 마지막 단락 “Our grand opening to the general public will be held on Saturday, September 22”에서 9월 22일은 개장 행사가 있는 날임을 알 수 있으므로 (D)가 정답이다.

5. Hernandez 씨가 클럽 내에서 일하고자 하는 곳은 어디일 것 같은가?
(A) Clean Eats 카페
(B) 수영장 구역
(C) Gold's 체육관
(D) Spinning Hub Room

해설 이메일 두 번째 단락 중 “I enjoy working with young people and have always sought out opportunities for coaching and counseling children”에서 Hernandez 씨가 아이들을 지도하고 상담하는 일을 하고 싶다고 했고, 광고의 Why Try The Dakota Club?의 내용 중 Gold's 체육관에서 어린이를 위한 활동이 있다고 했으므로 (C)가 정답이다.

[6-10] 구인 광고 & 편지

직위: 관리자, Hip Kitchen 사 소매점

상점 위치 (6월 중순 개장): 4528 Hornet Avenue, 멤피스

업무: 영업 직원을 관리하고 모든 고객이 높은 수준의 서비스를 받도록 보장하며 월간 매출 목표를 달성하는 일을 포함합니다. 매월 최소 6회의 마감 근무를 할 수 있어야 합니다.

자격 조건: 소매업에 관한 기본 지식과 우수한 조직력. 직원들을 교육하고 지도할 수 있는 능력이 있어야 합니다. 요리 장비와 요리 업계에 익숙한 사람이 추천됩니다. 마케팅 분야의 학사 학위와 적어도 4년간의 매니저 경험이 필수 요건입니다. 합격자는 6월 5일에 교육에 참여할 수 있어야 합니다.

회사 소개: Hip Kitchen 사는 요리 장비에서의 선도적인 소매업체입니다. 중남부 지역에서 최고의 공급업체로부터 주방 도구를 제공하는 30개의 매장을 운영하고 있습니다.

지원 방법: 이력서, 자기소개서 및 작성을 완료한 입사 지원서 사본을 다음 주소로 보내십시오.

Gina Webb, 인사부장
Hip Kitchen, Inc., 595 Arby Road, 내슈빌 테네시 주, 37458
또는 3월 3일까지 ginawebb@hipkitchen.com으로 보내십시오.

www.hipkitchen.com/jobs에서 입사 지원서를 다운로드 할 수 있습니다.

Brian Somerset · 1870 Trump Street · 테네시주 멤피스 37514

2월 21일

Gina Webb
인사부장
Hip Kitchen 사
595 Arby Road
테네시주 내슈빌 37458

친애하는 Webb 씨께,

Tennessee Job Search에 광고된 관리자 직책에 지원하고 싶습니다. 제 이력서에서 볼 수 있듯이 저는 Crown 대학에서 마케팅 학위를 취득했습니다. 저는 County Attire 사의 영업 매니저로 5년간 근무했고, 올해 멤피스 지점은 폐업 예정입니다. County Attire에 있는 동안 15명의 신규 직원을 교육했으며 영업 사원들이 추천하는 모범적인 고객 서비스 상도 여러 번 수상했습니다.

Hip Kitchen 사에서 취급하는 제품에 대한 경험이 부족하지만 3년 동안 매니저로 Savory Caterers에서 일했기 때문에 특정 산업에 대한 기본적인 지식을 가지고 있습니다. 또한, County Attire에서의 고용 계약이 Hornet Avenue에서 귀하의 새 매장이 오픈하기 약 1개월 전에 종료됩니다. 따라서 귀하의 광고에 언급된 6월 5일 교육에 참여하는 데 문제가 없습니다. 검토해 주셔서 감사합니다.

안녕히 계세요,
Brian Somerset

어휘 retail store 소매점 task 임무, 업무 manage 관리하다 meet 충족 시키다 qualification 자격요건 organization skill 조직 기술 ability 능력 train 훈련시키다 at least 최소한 culinary 요리의 apply for 지원하다 be awarded 상을 받다 exemplary 본보기의, 모범적인 lack 부족; 부족하다 handle 다루다, 처리하다 participate in ~에 참석하다 employer 고용주

6. 광고된 직책에 명시된 업무가 아닌 것은?
  (A) 판매 상품의 새로운 공급자 찾기
  (B) 높은 수준의 고객 서비스 유지하기
  (C) 판매 목표에 도달하기
  (D) 마감 근무조로 일하기

해설 지문의 tasks를 질문의 duty와 연결해서 단서를 찾아야 한다. 첫 번째 지문 구인광고에서 tasks(임무) 부분을 살펴보면 새로운 공급자를 찾는 업무에 관한 언급은 없으므로 (A)가 정답이다.

7. 신청서를 언제까지 제출해야 하는가?
  (A) 2월 21일
  (B) 3월 3일
  (C) 5월 31일
  (D) 6월 5일

해설 보통 서류를 제출하는 방법에 관한 내용은 지문의 중반부에서 찾을 수 있다. 구인 광고의 마지막 How to apply(지원 방법) 부분에 신청서를 보낼 주소와 이메일 주소가 나오고 3월 3일까지(by March 3) 제출하라고 언급되어 있으므로 (B)가 정답이다.

8. Somerset 씨는 현재 어디에서 근무 중인가?
  (A) Hip Kitchen 사
  (B) Crown 대학교
  (C) County Attire
  (D) Savory Caterers

해설 두 번째 지문 중 "I have worked for five years as a sales manager for County Attire"에서 현재 Somerset 씨가 County Attire에서 5년간 근무 중인 것을 알 수 있다. 따라서 (C)가 정답이다.

9. 왜 Webb 씨는 Somerset 씨를 그 직책에 적합한 후보자라고 생각하지 않을 수 있는가?
  (A) 그는 요구되는 학위를 아직 받지 못했다.
  (B) 그는 관리 경험이 너무 적다.
  (C) 요리 장비에 익숙하지 않다.
  (D) 그는 직원들을 훈련시키는 일을 해본 적이 없다.

해설 구인 광고의 자격요건(Qualifications) 부분 중 "Recommend an individual who is familiar with cooking equipment and the culinary industry"에서 요리 장비에 익숙한 사람을 선호한다고 했다. 그러나 Somerset 씨의 편지 두 번째 문단 "Despite my lack of experience with the type of merchandise Hip Kitchen, Inc. handles, I have some basic knowledge of this particular industry as I spent three years as a manager at Savory Caterers"에서 Hip Kitchen 사에서 취급하는 제품에 대한 경험이 부족하지만, 이 산업에 대한 기본적인 지식을 가지고 있다고 했으므로 (C)가 정답이다. 나머지 보기는 모두 Somerset 씨가 충족하는 조건이다.

10. Somerset 씨는 5월에 무슨 일이 있을 거라고 예상하는가?
  (A) 그의 영업 직원이 15명으로 늘어날 것이다.
  (B) 그는 내슈빌로 이주할 것이다.
  (C) 그는 고객 서비스 상을 받을 것이다.
  (D) 현재 고용주와 그의 계약이 만료될 것이다.

해설 구인광고의 상점 위치(Store Location) 부분 "opening mid-June"에서 6월 중순에 Hip Kitchen의 상점이 오픈한다고 했다. 그리고 Somerset 씨가 Hip Kitchen의 인사부장에게 쓴 편지 중 "In addition, my employment with County Attire ends roughly a month before the opening of your new store on Hornet Avenue"에서 상점이 오픈하기 약 1개월 전에 계약이 만료된다고 했으므로 5월에 직장을 그만두게 된다는 것을 알 수 있다. 따라서 (D)가 정답이다.

[11-15] 회람 & 웹페이지 & 문자 메시지

수신: Fortress Holdings 직원들
발신: Daniel Bass, 인사부장

10월 16일

Andrew McKnight이 Marana 지점의 지점장 직책으로 승진되었음을 알리게 되어 기쁩니다. 그는 이곳 Phoenix 지점에서 부점장으로서 대단한 일을 했고, 그의 리더십 능력이 새로운 팀에 훌륭한 자산이 될 것이라고 확신합니다.

10월 31일 수요일 오후 4시에 회의실에서 McKnight 씨를 위한 파티를 열 것입니다. Fortress Holdings의 부사장님이 연설을 하신 후, 다과가 제공될 것입니다. 회사에서 McKnight 씨를 위한 선물을 준비할 것입니다. 그에게 카드도 줄 것입니다. Julia Hartz의 사무실에 잠시 들러 카드에 서명하고 개인적인 메시지를 남겨 주세요.

이곳에서 McKnight 씨의 업무 마지막 날은 11월 2일 금요일이 될 것이고, 11월 5일 월요일에 새로운 곳에서 일을 시작할 것입니다. McKnight 씨와 긴밀히 협력해 일해 왔던 분들에게는 그가 새로운 역할에 뛰어들기 전에 휴식기를 전혀 갖지 않는다는 것이 분명 놀랍지 않을 것입니다. 우리 모두 그의 행운을 빕니다.

---

https://www.fortresshols.com/staffforum

메시지를 게시하려면, Fortress Holdings 직원 계정으로 로그인해야 합니다..

최신 소식! / 10월 23일 Daniel Bass에 의해 게시됨

McKnight 씨를 위한 파티가 10월 26일 금요일로 옮겨졌습니다. 유감스럽게도, 그가 예정보다 일주일 일찍 Marana 지점에 출근해야 한다고 합니다. 한 주요 고객이 싱가포르에서 그 지점을 방문할 것인데, McKnight 씨가 이를 준비할 시간이 더 필요합니다. 다행히, 그가 순조롭게 인수인계할 수 있도록 자신의 업무들을 다른 이들에게 이미 잘 넘겨줬습니다. 변경에도 불구하고 여러분 모두 송별 파티에 오실 수 있기를 바랍니다.

수신: Andrew McKnight (602) 555-0295
발신: Vera Simmons (602) 555-3081

10월 26일 17:33:37

당신의 사무실 번호로 연락했는데, 전화를 받지 않으시더라고요. 오늘 당신의 송별 파티에 참석할 수 없었던 것 죄송합니다. 좋은 시간 보냈기를 바랍니다! Cole 씨의 연설이 아주 감동적이었다고 들었어요.
떠나기 전에 시간이 있으시다면, 제가 점심을 대접하고 싶어요. 시간이 되시면 저에게 알려주세요.

어휘 be promoted to ~로 승진되다 branch manager 지점장
asset 자산 hold a party 파티를 열다 give a speech 연설하다 refreshment(s) 다과 be served 제공되다 stop by 잠깐 들르다 work closely with ~와 긴밀히 협력하다 take time off

휴식 시간을 가지다 jump into ~로 뛰어들다 wish A all the best A에게 행운을 빌다 earlier than expected 예상보다 일찍 major 주된, 주요한 hand off ~을 넘겨주다 responsibility 책임, 책무 make a smooth transition 인수인계하다 make it to ~에 가다, 이르다 farewell party 송별 파티 reach 연락하다 moving 감동적인 take A to lunch A에게 점심을 대접하다 food preference 음식 선호도 reject 거절하다, 거부하다 unavailable 구할 수 없는

11. 사람들은 왜 Hartz 씨의 사무실로 가도록 요청받는가?
(A) 선물을 위한 돈을 기부하기 위해
(B) 음식 선호도를 전하기 위해
(C) 카드에 짧은 편지를 쓰기 위해
(D) 행사 참석을 확정하기 위해

해설 첫 번째 지문 "We will also have a card for him. Please stop by Julia Hartz's office to sign it and to write a personal message"에서 Julia Hartz의 사무실에 들러 Andrew McKnight에게 줄 카드에 메시지를 남겨줄 것을 요청했으므로 (C)가 정답이다. 지문의 a personal message를 a note로 패러프레이징했다.

12. McKnight 씨가 Marana 지점에서 근무하는 첫날은 언제일 것인가?
(A) 10월 29일
(B) 10월 16일
(C) 11월 2일
(D) 11월 5일

해설 첫 번째 지문 "he will start work at his new place on Monday, November 5"에서 Marana 지점에서의 근무 시작일이 11월 5일이라고 했고, 두 번째 지문 "he is needed at the Marana branch one week earlier than expected"에서 예정보다 일주일 일찍 일을 시작해야 한다고 했으므로 10월 29일에 시작할 것으로 추론할 수 있다. 따라서 (A)가 정답이다.

13. 웹페이지에 따르면, 변경의 이유는 무엇인가?
(A) 방문객이 올 것이다.
(B) 대량 주문이 들어왔다.
(C) 일자리 제안이 거절되었다.
(D) 여행 티켓을 구할 수 없었다.

해설 두 번째 지문 "A major client from Singapore will come to the branch"에서 McKnight 씨가 예정보다 일주일 먼저 일을 시작해야 하는 이유로 싱가포르에서 온 방문객이 싱가포르에서 온 방문객이 언급되었으므로 (A)가 정답이다. 지문의 A major client from Singapore가 A visitor로 패러프레이징되었다.

14. 문자 메시지에서, 첫 번째 단락, 첫 번째 줄의 "reach"와 그 의미가 가장 유사한 단어는?

(A) 성취하다
(B) 파악하다
(C) 연장하다
(D) 연락하다

해설 문자 메시지의 "I tried to reach you on your office line ~"에서 '당신의 사무실 번호로 연락했다'라고 했고 여기서 reach는 '연락하다'라는 의미로 쓰인 것임을 알 수 있다. 따라서 (D) contact가 정답이다.

15. Cole 씨는 누구일 것 같은가?

(A) 인사부장
(B) 부사장
(C) 부점장
(D) 지점장

해설 세 번째 지문 "I heard that Mr. Cole's speech was quite moving"에서 Cole 씨가 연설했음을 알 수 있다. 그리고 첫 번째 지문 "Fortress Holdings' vice president will give a speech"에서 부사장이 연설을 할 것이라고 제시되어 있으므로, 이를 종합해 볼 때 감동적인 연설할 Cole 씨는 Fortress Holdings의 부사장임을 유추할 수 있다. 따라서 (B)가 정답이다.

[16-20] 이메일 & 보고서 & 이메일

수신: Cox Network <inquiries@coxnetwork.ca>
발신: Eddie Garcia <egarcia@garcediting.ca>
날짜: 8월 3일
제목: 계정 번호 120805

Cox Network 직원 귀하,

저는 지난 몇 달간 Cox Network의 고객이었는데, 제 7월 청구서의 요금에 놀랐습니다. 저는 있을 수 있는 연체료를 피하려고 오늘 아침에 완납을 했는데, 해결될 필요가 있는 사안이 하나 있습니다.
7월에 연결에 있어 일부 중단된 시간이 있었음에도, 7월 전체에 해당하는 49.95달러가 청구되었습니다. 귀사의 시스템이 업그레이드되고 있어 중단되는 상황이 발생할 수 있다는 것을 이해하기는 하지만, 제가 사용하지 않았던 날의 서비스에 대해 지불해야 한다고 생각하지는 않습니다. 그래서 그날에 대해 환불해 주실 것을 요청합니다. 가능하다면, 제가 청구액을 지불하는 데 사용했던 신용카드로 환불받고 싶습니다. 아니면 수표를 제 거주지로 보내주시면 좋겠습니다. 제 Cox 계정으로 입금되지는 않았으면 합니다.

안녕히 계세요,

Eddie Garcia

Cox Network

7월 중단 시간 보고서
Matthew Haymond 제출

서비스 지역	평가	총 중단 시간	메모
오로라	양호	하루	손상된 케이블
네이퍼빌	양호	이틀	손상된 케이블
블루밍턴	좋음	12시간	없음
스프링필드	등급 미지정	해당 없음	7월 20일에 개시

수신: Eddie Garcia <egarcia@garcediting.ca>
발신: Cox Network <inquiries@coxnetwork.ca>
날짜: 8월 4일
제목: 회신: 계정 #120805

Garcia 씨에게,

최근에 Cox Network 때문에 실망스러운 경험을 하신 것에 사과드립니다. 저희는 서비스가 끊임없이 가동되도록 최선을 다하고 있지만, 항상 가능한 것은 아닙니다. 보통, 중단 시간에 대해 환불을 해 드리지 않지만, 귀하의 상황은 합당한 듯 보입니다.
따라서 귀하가 중단 시간을 겪은 며칠에 기반해서 환불해 드릴 것입니다. 저희가 환불 수표를 발행할 수는 없지만, 환불 지급에 대해 귀하가 요청한 다른 방법은 수용할 수 있습니다. 이는 처리하는 데 며칠이 걸리며, 모든 것이 완료되면 제가 다시 이메일을 드리겠습니다.

안녕히 계세요,

Katherine Lee
Cox Network, 고객 서비스 센터

어휘 charge 요금 payment in full 전액 지불 so as to ~하기 위해 avoid 피하다 late fee 연체료 resolve 해결하다 entire 전체의 despite ~에도 불구하고 downtime 중단 시간, 고장 시간 refund 환불 prefer 선호하다 residence 거주지, 거처 credit 입금하다 submit 제출하다 unrated 등급 미지정의 N/A(= not applicable) 해당 없음 launch 개시하다, 착수하다 recently 최근에 do one's best 최선을 다하다 continuously 끊임없이, 계속하여 reasonable 합당한 based on ~에 기반하여 accommodate 수용하다 dispute 이의를 제기하다, 반박하다 bank transfer 은행 계좌 이체 get in touch 연락을 취하다 supervisor 상사

16. 첫 번째 이메일의 목적은 무엇인가?

(A) 인터넷 선을 추가하기 위해
(B) 청구서에 이의를 제기하기 위해
(C) 지불하기 위해
(D) 서비스를 업그레이드하기 위해

해설 첫 번째 이메일 "I made the payment in full this morning so as to avoid any possible late fees, but there is an issue that needs to be resolved"에서 청구서 요금을 완납했지만 해결되어야 하는 문제가 있다고 했으므로 청구서에 대한 이의를 제기하고자 보낸 이메일임을 알 수 있다. 따라서 (B)가 정답이다.

17. Garcia 씨는 어떻게 환불을 받을 것인가?

(A) 수표로

(B) 은행 계좌 이체로

(C) 신용카드로

(D) Cox 계정 계좌로

해설 첫 번째 이메일의 "I would like it returned to the credit card I used to pay the bill. if not, I would prefer a check sent to my residence"에서 Garcia 씨가 신용카드 환불이나 거주지로 수표를 보내 달라고 요청했고, 두 번째 이메일의 "We cannot issue refund checks, but we can accommodate your other requested method ~"에서 업체 측은 수표로 환불은 불가하지만, 요청한 다른 방법은 수용할 수 있다고 했다. 따라서 Garcia 씨가 요청했던 두 가지 방법 중 신용카드로 환급될 것이므로 정답은 (C)이다.

18. Garcia 씨는 어느 지역에 사는 것 같은가?

(A) 오로라

(B) 네이퍼빌

(C) 블루밍턴

(D) 스프링필드

해설 두 번째 이메일 중반부의 "You will receive a refund based on the days of downtime you experienced"에서 Garcia 씨가 서비스가 중단을 겪은 기간이 며칠(the days)임을 알 수 있고, 보고서의 표에서 서비스 중단이 하루 이상이었던 지역은 Naperville(2 days)이다. 따라서 Garcia 씨의 거주 지역은 (B) 네이퍼빌임을 유추할 수 있다.

19. 두 번째 이메일에서, 첫 번째 단락, 세 번째 줄의 "case"와 의미가 가장 가까운 것은?

(A) 업무

(B) 용기, 그릇

(C) 논쟁

(D) 상황

해설 두 번째 이메일의 "~ but in your case, it seems reasonable to do so"에서 case는 '상황, 경우'라는 뜻으로 쓰여 '당신의 상황에는 그것이 합당한 것으로 보인다'라는 의미가 된다. 따라서 '상황, 처지'라는 뜻을 가진 (D) situation이 정답이다.

20. Lee 씨는 무엇을 할 것이라고 말하는가?

(A) 작업이 완료되면 연락한다

(B) 정책에 관한 정보를 이메일로 보낸다

(C) 그녀의 상사에게 문제를 보고한다

(D) Garcia 씨의 집에 기술자를 보낸다

해설 Lee 씨는 두 번째 이메일의 발신자로, Cox Network의 고객 서비스 담당자이다. 두 번째 이메일 마지막 부분 "I will e-mail you again when everything is done"에서 모든 것이 완료되면 다시 이메일을 보내겠다고 했으므로 (A)가 정답이다.

books.english.co.kr